(Continued on back endsheets)

Dictionary of Literary Biography® • Volume One Hundred Sixty

British Children's Writers, 1914–1960

British Children's Writers, 1914–1960

Edited by
Donald R. Hettinga
Calvin College
and
Gary D. Schmidt
Calvin College

A Bruccoli Clark Layman Book
Gale Research Inc.
Detroit, Washington, D.C., London

The paper used in this publication meets the minimum requirements
of American National Standard for Information Sciences–Permanence
Paper for Printed Library Materials, ANSI Z39.48-1984. ∞ ™

Library of Congress Cataloging-in-Publication Data

British children's writers, 1914–1960 / edited by Donald Hettinga and Gary D. Schmidt.
   p. cm. – (Dictionary of literary biography; v. 160)
"A Bruccoli Clark Layman book."
Includes bibliographical references and index.
ISBN 0-8103-9355-7 (alk. paper)
1. Children's literature, English – Dictionaries. 2. Authors, English – 20th century – Biography – Dictionaries. 3. Authors, English – 19th century – Biography – Dictionaries. 4. English literature – 20th century – Bio-bibliography. 5. English literature – 19th century – Bio-bibliography. 6. English literature – 20th century – Dictionaries. 7. Children's literature, English – Bio-bibliography.
I. Hettinga, Donald R., 1953– . II. Schmidt, Gary D. III. Series.
PR990.B75 1995
820.9'9282 – dc20
                                                95–41045
                                                 CIP

[B]

10 9 8 7 6 5 4 3 2 1

For Roy Hettinga, with thanks for all you taught me

D.R.H.

For Martha Edith Stickney

Recalling, in her fittest phrase,
        So rich and picturesque and free. . .
The story of her early days, —
She makes us welcome to her home;
Old hearths grow wide to give us room.

G.D.S.

Contents

Plan of the Series

. . . Almost the most prodigious asset of a country, and perhaps its most precious possession, is its native literary product — when that product is fine and noble and enduring.

Mark Twain*

The advisory board, the editors, and the publisher of the *Dictionary of Literary Biography* are joined in endorsing Mark Twain's declaration. The literature of a nation provides an inexhaustible resource of permanent worth. We intend to make literature and its creators better understood and more accessible to students and the reading public, while satisfying the standards of teachers and scholars.

To meet these requirements, *literary biography* has been construed in terms of the author's achievement. The most important thing about a writer is his writing. Accordingly, the entries in *DLB* are career biographies, tracing the development of the author's canon and the evolution of his reputation.

The purpose of *DLB* is not only to provide reliable information in a convenient format but also to place the figures in the larger perspective of literary history and to offer appraisals of their accomplishments by qualified scholars.

The publication plan for *DLB* resulted from two years of preparation. The project was proposed to Bruccoli Clark by Frederick C. Ruffner, president of the Gale Research Company, in November 1975. After specimen entries were prepared and typeset, an advisory board was formed to refine the entry format and develop the series rationale. In meetings held during 1976, the publisher, series editors, and advisory board approved the scheme for a comprehensive biographical dictionary of persons who contributed to North American literature. Editorial work on the first volume began in January 1977, and it was published in 1978. In order to make *DLB* more than a reference tool and to compile volumes that individually have claim to status as literary history, it was decided to organize volumes by topic, period, or genre. Each of these freestanding volumes provides a biographical-bibliographical guide and overview for a particular area of literature. We are convinced that this organization — as opposed to a single alphabet method — constitutes a valuable innovation in the presentation of reference material. The volume plan necessarily requires many decisions for the placement and treatment of authors who might properly be included in two or three volumes. In some instances a major figure will be included in separate volumes, but with different entries emphasizing the aspect of his career appropriate to each volume. Ernest Hemingway, for example, is represented in *American Writers in Paris, 1920–1939* by an entry focusing on his expatriate apprenticeship; he is also in *American Novelists, 1910–1945* with an entry surveying his entire career. Each volume includes a cumulative index of the subject authors and articles. Comprehensive indexes to the entire series are planned.

With volume ten in 1982 it was decided to enlarge the scope of *DLB*. By the end of 1986 twenty-one volumes treating British literature had been published, and volumes for Commonwealth and Modern European literature were in progress. The series has been further augmented by the *DLB Yearbooks* (since 1981) which update published entries and add new entries to keep the *DLB* current with contemporary activity. There have also been *DLB Documentary Series* volumes which provide biographical and critical source materials for figures whose work is judged to have particular interest for students. One of these companion volumes is entirely devoted to Tennessee Williams.

We define literature as the *intellectual commerce of a nation:* not merely as belles lettres but as that ample and complex process by which ideas are generated, shaped, and transmitted. *DLB* entries are not limited to "creative writers" but extend to other figures who in their time and in their way influenced the mind of a people. Thus the series encompasses historians, journalists, publishers, and screenwriters. By this means readers of *DLB* may be aided to perceive literature not as cult scripture in the keeping of intellectual high

*From an unpublished section of Mark Twain's autobiography, copyright by the Mark Twain Company

priests but firmly positioned at the center of a nation's life.

DLB includes the major writers appropriate to each volume and those standing in the ranks immediately behind them. Scholarly and critical counsel has been sought in deciding which minor figures to include and how full their entries should be. Wherever possible, useful references are made to figures who do not warrant separate entries.

Each *DLB* volume has a volume editor responsible for planning the volume, selecting the figures for inclusion, and assigning the entries. Volume editors are also responsible for preparing, where appropriate, appendices surveying the major periodicals and literary and intellectual movements for their volumes, as well as lists of further readings. Work on the series as a whole is coordinated at the Bruccoli Clark Layman editorial center in Columbia, South Carolina, where the editorial staff is responsible for accuracy of the published volumes.

One feature that distinguishes *DLB* is the illustration policy – its concern with the iconography of literature. Just as an author is influenced by his surroundings, so is the reader's understanding of the author enhanced by a knowledge of his environment. Therefore *DLB* volumes include not only drawings, paintings, and photographs of authors, often depicting them at various stages in their careers, but also illustrations of their families and places where they lived. Title pages are regularly reproduced in facsimile along with dust jackets for modern authors. The dust jackets are a special feature of *DLB* because they often document better than anything else the way in which an author's work was perceived in its own time. Specimens of the writers' manuscripts are included when feasible.

Samuel Johnson rightly decreed that "The chief glory of every people arises from its authors." The purpose of the *Dictionary of Literary Biography* is to compile literary history in the surest way available to us – by accurate and comprehensive treatment of the lives and work of those who contributed to it.

The *DLB* Advisory Board

Introduction

The authors and poets represented in the following pages have among them some of the best-known writers of children's literature of the twentieth century. C. S. Lewis and J. R. R. Tolkien established fantasies whose mythic worlds have become part of our culture. A. A. Milne, P. L. Travers, and Hugh Lofting each created characters almost universally recognizable in Winnie the Pooh, Mary Poppins, and Dr. Dolittle, respectively. Enid Blyton's sheer productivity is still today remarkable and daunting. And Eleanor Farjeon's elegant and simple language has contributed enormously to the shape of English prose narrative for children.

In *Secret Gardens* (1985) Humphrey Carpenter places the end of the golden age of British children's literature with A. A. Milne's closing passage in *The House at Pooh Corner* (1928), as Christopher Robin and Pooh skip merrily away from the reader, forever in 100-Akre Wood. But the works of Lewis and Tolkien and Travers and Farjeon suggest that at least vestiges of that golden age have endured. Such works suggest that the creative impulses that led to late-Victorian and early-Edwardian works such as Kenneth Grahame's *The Wind in the Willows* (1908) and George MacDonald's *At the Back of the North Wind* (1871) have endured as well, generating similar kinds of strong narrative stances, intriguing secondary worlds, and imaginative interactions between extraordinary settings and apparently ordinary children.

If the gold of this later age does not gleam as brightly for Carpenter as that of the Victorian period, perhaps it may be because it came in a disturbed and unquiet time, trying to hold on with easy assurance to the assumptions that undergirded children's literature of the Victorian period: that the world is a secure place, that society is capable of both technological and moral progress, that happiness is accessible, that homes can be established or reestablished, that secret gardens do not always have to remain secret but can gladly yield their healing fruit. For writers working after World War I, these same assumptions were not always easy to keep. There was the disturbing and distorting presence of war. Lewis's four Pevensie children first enter Narnia because they have been evacuated out of London during the Blitz. For many, the

blighted landscape of The Shire in Tolkien's work resembles the blighted landscape of England during World War II. And though the world of Dr. Dolittle is distanced to the safe days of Victoria's early years, its writing comes out of the despair of the trenches of World War I. It was hard for Lofting to believe the Victorian assumptions, and though he tried almost desperately to maintain these in the early Dolittle books, he was unable to sustain the illusion by the end of the series. If the period from 1914 to 1960 has vestiges of the golden era, they are vestiges that have the scrapes and dull gleams of survival marked upon them.

In this post–golden era Enid Blyton looms large; her sheer presence is almost overwhelming. Never before in children's literature – certainly not in Carpenter's golden era – had one writer produced so many novels. And this is not a case of Samuel Johnson's dog perched on two legs; Blyton was able to produce satisfying novels at a rate so astonishing that even today it is difficult to formulate a complete bibliography. And, perhaps even more astonishing, the majority of her work is still in print.

Blyton's work cannot be called golden in any real sense – popular, but not golden. It is formulaic, with predictable situations and resolutions. The staunchly British middle-class characters are, for the most part, interchangeable. The narrative voice is consistent from one novel to the next; Blyton was not one for innovation and experimentation. And perhaps in all of this lies another reason that this era cannot be considered a golden one, despite its luminaries: It is a period marked by the enormous popularity of mediocre novelists who could write dozens of books with apparent ease.

Never was this more obvious than in the school stories and pony stories. Few today would remember such authors as A, Stephen Tring, Mabel Esther Allan, Dorita Fairlie Bruce, or Hylton Cleaver, yet each of these wrote literally scores of books, sometimes at the rate of three or four a year, matching Enid Blyton's annual output, though not for such a prolonged period of time. The titles of school and pony books suggested their essentially repetitive nature, as in Elsie Oxenham's *The Abbey Girls* (1920), *The*

Girls of the Abbey School (1921), *The Abbey Girls Go Back to School* (1922), *The New Abbey Girls* (1923), *The Abbey Girls Again* (1924), and so on through *Strangers at the Abbey* in 1963. These are not books known for their originality and innovation or for their fine writing and their contribution to the field. They were not meant to be known in this way.

Yet the enormous number of school and pony stories, mediocre as they were in terms of their writing, does suggest something about popular children's literature of the period – and, in fact, about that of our own period: such books convey the pleasure of the familiar. Readers see the same group of girls or boys living at school, or learning to manage a horse, or, more fantastically, having exotic adventures that are, the reader knows, safe; after all, the characters must survive because the series must go on. The authors may as well be anonymous, for the reader is looking for the continuation of an old series, for his or her friends of their next set of adventures, not for an individual author's style or poetics.

Thus, if there is J. R. R. Tolkien, there is also Malcolm Saville, who, measured in terms of productivity, puts Tolkien and his few children's novels to shame. If there is Walter de la Mare, there is Rose Fyleman. If there is Arthur Ransome, there is W. E. Johns. In each case the first has survived while the second has not, despite a prodigious output. If some of the names represented in these pages are instantly recognizable, many more are today forgotten and ignored except by the most avid of book collectors. It may be the case that books in Kathleen Hale's Orlando series can command fantastic sums on the rare-book market, but they can also be found on the discard piles of library sales. Few children would recognize the marmalade cat. And even the formidable Mary Poppins is remembered popularly today more because of Walt Disney than because of P. L. Travers.

Hale's Orlando is typical of the characters of the minor novelists represented here in his ties to war. Like the Pevensies, Orlando and many of the characters discussed in the following pages enter into situations affected or established by World War I or World War II. W. E. Johns used Biggles and Worrals through scores of novels to fight off nasty Germans. Kitty Barne's characters, when they are not being musical, are escaping Nazi U-boats. While some novels transcend their war experience, so that the war becomes a context in which human situations are worked out, the war in these novels often becomes more than a context; it becomes a raison d'être, thus instantly and inevitably dating these novels, confining them to a period and making them seem anachronistic today.

This is not to say that the age following World War I is to be considered leaden, however. If there is mediocrity and formulaic writing with occasional flashes of brilliance during this time, the same may be said about most literary periods. Aside from its use of world wars, there are, however, certain distinguishing characteristics that mark this era and that make it distinctive.

First, this is a period dominated by stories of groups of children bonded together who set out on some more or less extraordinary adventure that strains, but then reaffirms, these bonds. Certainly the Pevensies in *The Lion, the Witch, and the Wardrobe* (1950) are an example of this pattern of camaraderie, being at first unified, then divided, then gloriously reunited. The master of these fantasies, of course, was Arthur Ransome, who, beginning with *Swallows and Amazons* (1930), sent his children off to explore exotic places. But the same formula is used by Enid Blyton, Elfrida Vipont, Eve Garnett, Edward Ardizzone, Malcolm Saville, Geoffrey Trease in his Bannerdale series, and the writers of the school stories in which groups are forced together through school contexts, though they frequently seem to be on holiday. A variant of the form appears in the works of writers such as Bessie Marchant and W. E. Johns: here a group of older characters – older than adolescents but younger than adults and certainly too young or too busy to be married just yet – form a bond of like-minded comrades who engage in adventures, often against sinister and usually foreign adversaries.

The formula establishes a pleasingly complex use of relationships that, at the same time, aids in the unfolding of the narrative. The plot can develop through dialogue rather than exposition or through the constant presence of the author within the character's mind. It also allows for a series of several seemingly disparate adventures to occur simultaneously, leading to resolution as the adventures come together to a climax. The life of these novels – or lack of life – lies with the reality of the characters and their relationships.

Secondly, the period following World War I marked the emergence of strong female protagonists, like the children of Frances Hodgson Burnett but grown up to be more plucky, resourceful, and adventurous than any little princess. Sarah Crewe would have been astonished at W. E. John's Worrals, flying about to save the world – but less astonished at Kitty Barne's characters, who dominate their groups and give order to their imaginative gaming – and perhaps even less astonished at C. S. Lewis's Lucy, the most perceptive of all the Narnian children.

The significance of the emergence of such female protagonists can hardly be overestimated; it paved the way for American books such as Louise Fitzhugh's *Harriet the Spy* (1964) and Maurice Sendak's *The Sign on Rosie's Door* (1960). While female characters had previously been firmly ensconced in society codes – sometimes pushing against these codes, but ensconced nonetheless – here were characters who were redefining those codes in the context of a changing world. It is hard to imagine Worrals during the height of Victoria's reign; she needed the war to establish the arena within which she could flourish.

The emergence of the female protagonist is also linked to the school and holiday adventures. Though at times these groups were all boy or all girl, more often the group was mixed. The interaction of the group was almost always on a preromantic level that often had a leveling effect, where male and female characters all were able to engage equally in an adventure, despite the frequent character of the older brother (like Peter Pevensie) who could take on leadership roles.

The growth of the female protagonist is not unrelated to the development of what Roger Lancelyn Green calls in his *Tellers of Tales* (1947) "the career book," in which a child begins to move toward a career that is indicated by his or her own peculiar gifts. Kitty Barne wrote several novels in this vein, all showing the musical propensities of children who became prodigies. Richard Armstrong placed his characters on the high seas. But the great practitioner of this genre was Noel Streatfeild, and the titles of her novels are indicative of the chosen careers of her characters: *Ballet Shoes* (1936), *Tennis Shoes* (1937), *The Circus is Coming* (1938), and *Curtain Up* (1944). There are generally few surprises in these novels; young girls move toward safe, culturally acceptable careers, while young boys move toward their expected lives. But what has changed here from the earlier golden age is that these young girls do have careers of some sort, and they are allowed to pursue them aggressively.

If there is little unexpected in the career stories, it may be because the children's books of this period rigorously upheld British culture. That culture is, for the most part, completely unchallenged. In fact, especially before World War II, few foreign books for children were translated and published in Britain other than books like Jean de Brunhoff's *Babar* (translated into English in 1934) and Carlo Collodi's *Pinnochio* (first translated in 1892). Perhaps this focus is to be expected in a period during which Britain's culture was challenged by two world wars.

Certainly one function of the novels, especially those set in a war context, was to reassure children, to make them feel secure in a world at war, to remind them that Britannia rules and that the British never, never shall be slaves. The German spies are always caught, foiled by clever children. Home is always reestablished. The soldier (almost) always comes home from the war. The British individual will stand unabashed, courageous in the face of the most dire circumstances.

The unfortunate outcome of this stance is a cast of villains who are frequently foreign. They wear dark clothes, speak with thick accents, and hide in the darkness. They are swarthy or disfigured or practice ancient and evil arts in smoky rooms. They are the antithesis of the English children, who are innocent, outside, abiding by the rules of duty and fair play.

Though a late-twentieth-century sensibility might deplore this dichotomy, it is still important to remember the context of it. In a world at war, children read stories that established and affirmed the very attributes that Winston Churchill would call for in his British speeches. Duty, honor, self-sacrifice – all unfashionable now – were extolled. Hard work, courage, and pluck were celebrated. Whether these qualities were evidenced in the resourcefulness of Mary Norton's Borrowers, in the courage of T. H. White's Mistress Markham, or in Hugh Lofting's Dr. Dolittle and Tommy Stubbins, they always point to the essential – perhaps mythic – character of the British under duress.

The use of fantasy to exhibit those qualities suggests one area of continuity with the Victorian golden age: writers of literature of the imaginative world produced the most creative and aesthetically appealing work for children. The Victorian period had been marked by such literature, evidenced by the work of Lewis Carroll, Andrew Lang, Robert Louis Stevenson, H. Rider Haggard, J. M. Barrie, Beatrix Potter, Arthur Rackham, and Kenneth Grahame. Even purportedly realistic works from this period were enhanced by fantasy elements, as in works by Anna Sewall, Thomas Hughes, and Frances Hodgson Burnett. The same would be true for the period following World War I; of the major figures from the time, most would be known for their work in fantasy: C. S. Lewis, A. A. Milne, J. R. R. Tolkien, Eleanor Farjeon, Hugh Lofting, Mary Norton, P. L. Travers, Marjorie Williams, John Masefield, and Alison Uttley.

John Rowe Townsend, in his *Written for Children,* has suggested that "realism of the rougher kind was not common in children's books of the interwar years. There was a prevailing feeling that this was something that ought not to be inflicted on children." Certainly Hugh Lofting, and perhaps also writers like John Masefield, A. A. Milne, Walter de la Mare, and Arthur Ransome, all of whom fought and lived through World War I, believed that realism was not de rigueur. This may explain in part the prevalence of fantasy, as difficulties are safely distanced by writers who had had difficulties that were not distanced at all. In his *The Nesbit Tradition* Marcus Crouch argues that writers after World War I deplored the "grimness and false gaiety of post-war England" and so "preferred to interpret timeless themes, like the necessity of courage and the truth of life, without relating them directly to the ills of contemporary society." But perhaps both are too easy an explanation for the prevalence of fantasy during this period; C. S. Lewis claimed, after all, that he chose the form simply because it was appropriate to the story – nothing more.

One final element of the work in children's literature during this period is a negative one: the taboos now discarded in our time were still squarely in place; they changed little from the beginning to the ending of the period. Certainly these included the kinds of references to drugs, sexuality, and societal ills such as homelessness (handled realistically rather than romantically) that so easily sprinkle the pages of contemporary children's literature. But the novels of this period also show a consciously subdued presence of pain and suffering for children in the world. It is hard to imagine Michelle Magorian's *Good Night, Mr. Tom* (1981) written during the first half of the century, with its graphic portrayal of terrible abuse and its effects. And it is difficult to imagine Susan Cooper's Dark is Rising series (1965–1977) being written during such a period, with the books' dreadful suggestion that the good may at times resort to evil for the greater good.

Despite the looming presence of two world wars in this period, the world of the British children's novel was essentially a safe one, where children could go through wardrobes and off to islands and out to the country and through pluck and ingenuity, defeat the nasties and come into their own – a folktale world played out against the backdrop of twentieth-century England. It is a world of hope and security and the assurance that everything will be all right.

Many of the works represented in this collection have long been out of print – perhaps in part because few of them see the world as a place of hope and security and few are assured that everything does turn out all right. Many of the writers are vir-

tually unrecognized today. Though there were once literally hundreds of Biggles books, none are published now. Writers like Elfrida Vipont are difficult to find except in special collections. In part their decline came about with changing tastes and fashions in children's literature. In part it came about as many of the novels inextricably tied to a period or event became dated. And in part it came about as the culture that produced the novels lost its perception that these characters have anything to say to it. Children who occupy islands while on holiday have given way to other mythic incarnations.

The result is that many of these works hold value today not so much for their aesthetic merit but for the window they provide upon a culture now gone. At times the society depicted in these works may be so different from contemporary society that it seems as alien as Narnia. And yet, like Narnia, it is attractive in its security and integrated wholeness. We may not want the four Pevensie children up on thrones, but we do want the ordered ease of Narnia's golden age. The novels do present violence and squalor and hatred and evil, but the children, having defeated it all, seem blithely untouched, ready to go into the next adventure as if it were a game, free from the stain of a desperate world, free to play out their lives as children.

There are, of course, those authors like Tolkien and Lewis and de la Mare who stand above most of the writers collected here. These speak within and outside of their period, addressing large issues of the human experience without being bound to a certain time. But perhaps the Bessie Marchants and Elfrida Viponts and Malcolm Savilles are equally representative of the period, speaking to the needs of a culture in a given time. If such novelists sought to convey reassurance to children during a time when the whole world was at war, it is not for us to condemn them for deception and naiveté and a simplistic vision. In their own ways they do what writers for children have done in many different ways over many different years: they hold out hope amid terrible despair.

– Donald R. Hettinga and Gary D. Schmidt

Acknowledgments

This book was produced by Bruccoli Clark Layman, Inc. Karen L. Rood is senior editor for the *Dictionary of Literary Biography* series. James W. Hipp was the in-house editor.

Production coordinator is James W. Hipp. Photography editor is Bruce Andrew Bowlin. Photographic copy work was performed by Joseph M. Bruccoli. Layout and graphics supervisor is Penney L. Haughton. Copyediting supervisor is Laurel M. Gladden. Typesetting supervisor is Kathleen M. Flanagan. Systems manager is George F. Dodge. Julie E. Frick is editorial associate. The production staff includes Phyllis A. Avant, Ann M. Cheschi, Melody W. Clegg, Patricia Coate, Denise W. Edwards, Joyce Fowler, Stephanie C. Hatchell, Rebecca Mayo, Margaret Meriwether, Kathy Lawler Merlette, Jeff Miller, Pamela D. Norton, Delores Plastow, Laura Pleicones, Emily R. Sharpe, William L. Thomas Jr., Allison Trussell, and Jonathan B. Watterson.

Walter W. Ross and Robert S. McConnell did library research. They were assisted by the following librarians at the Thomas Cooper Library of the University of South Carolina: Linda Holderfield and the interlibrary-loan staff; reference-department head Virginia Weathers; reference librarians Marilee Birchfield, Stefanie Buck, Cathy Eckman, Rebecca Feind, Jill Holman, Karen Joseph, Jean Rhyne, Kwamine Washington, and Connie Widney; circulation-department head Caroline Taylor; and acquisitions-searching supervisor David Haggard.

Dictionary of Literary Biography® • Volume One Hundred Sixty

British Children's Writers, 1914–1960

Dictionary of Literary Biography

Edward Ardizzone

(16 October 1900 – 8 November 1979)

Joanne Lewis Sears
California State University, Fullerton

BOOKS: *Little Tim and the Brave Sea Captain* (London & New York: Oxford University Press, 1936; redrawn edition, London: Oxford University Press, 1953; New York: Walck, 1955);

Lucy Brown and Mr. Grimes (London & New York: Oxford University Press, 1937; revised edition, New York: Walck, 1971);

Tim and Lucy Go to Sea (London & New York: Oxford University Press, 1938; redrawn edition, London: Oxford University Press, 1958; New York: Walck, 1958);

Baggage to the Enemy (London: John Murray, 1941);

Nicholas and the Fast-Moving Diesel (London: Eyre/Spottiswoode Penguin, 1947; redrawn edition, New York: Walck, 1959);

Paul, the Hero of the Fire (London: Penguin, 1948; revised edition, New York: Houghton Mifflin, 1949);

Tim to the Rescue (London & New York: Oxford University Press, 1949);

Tim and Charlotte (London & New York: Oxford University Press, 1951);

Tim in Danger (London: Oxford University Press, 1953; New York: Walck, 1953);

Tim All Alone (London & New York: Oxford University Press, 1956);

Johnny the Clockmaker (London & New York: Oxford University Press, 1960);

Tim's Friend Towser (London: Oxford University Press / New York: Walck, 1962);

Peter the Wanderer (London: Oxford University Press, 1963; New York: Walck, 1964);

Diana and Her Rhinoceros (London: Bodley Head, 1964; New York: Walck, 1964);

Sarah and Simon and No Red Paint (London: Constable, 1965; New York: Delacorte, 1966);

Tim and Ginger (London: Oxford University Press, 1965; New York: Walck, 1965);

The Little Girl and the Tiny Doll, by Ardizzone and Aingelda Ardizzone (London: Constable, 1966; New York: Delacorte, 1967);

Tim to the Lighthouse (London: Oxford University Press, 1968; New York: Walck, 1968);

The Wrong Side of the Bed (Garden City, N.Y.: Doubleday, 1970); republished as *Johnny's Bad Day* (London: Bodley Head, 1970);

Young Ardizzone, an Autobiographical Fragment (London: Studio Vista, 1970; New York: Macmillan, 1970);

Tim's Last Voyage (London: Bodley Head, 1972; New York: Walck, 1973);

Diary of a War Artist (London: Bodley Head, 1974);

Ship's Cook Ginger (London: Bodley Head, 1977);

On the Illustrating of Books (Fallbrook, Cal.: Weatherbird Press, 1986).

OTHER: Sheridan Le Fanu, *In a Glass Darkly,* illustrated by Ardizzone (London: Davies, 1929);

George Crabbe, *The Library,* illustrated by Ardizzone (London: De La More Press, 1930);

Eleanor Farjeon, *The Old Nurse's Stocking Basket,* illustrated by Ardizzone (London: Stokes, 1931; New York: Walck, 1965);

Paul Bloomfield, comp. *The Mediterranean,* illustrated by Ardizzone (London: Cassell, 1935);

Neil Lyons, *Tom, Dick, and Harriet,* illustrated by Ardizzone (London: Cresset, 1937);

Edward Ardizzone

Maurice Gorham, *The Local,* illustrated by Ardizzone (London: Cassell, 1939);

Charles Dickens, *Great Expectations,* illustrated by Ardizzone (New York: Heritage, 1939);

H. E. Bates, *My Uncle Silas,* illustrated by Ardizzone (London: Cape, 1939);

H. J. Kaeser, *Mimff,* illustrated by Ardizzone (London: Oxford University Press, 1939);

André Maurois, *The Battle of France,* illustrated by Ardizzone (London: Bodley Head, 1940);

Dennis Freeman and Douglas Cooper, *The Road to Bordeaux,* illustrated by Ardizzone (London: Cresset, 1941);

François Villon, *The Poems of François Villon,* translated by W. B. McCaskie, illustrated by Ardizzone (London: Cresset, 1946);

Walter de la Mare, *Peacock Pie,* illustrated by Ardizzone (London: Faber & Faber, 1946);

Margaret Black, *Three Brothers and a Lady,* illustrated by Ardizzone (London: Acorn Press, 1947);

Noel Langley, *The True and Pathetic History of Desbarollda, the Waltzing Mouse,* illustrated by Ardizzone (London: Lindsay Drummond, 1947);

John Bunyan, *The Pilgrim's Progress,* illustrated by Ardizzone (London: Faber & Faber, 1947);

Anonymous, *Hey Nonny Yes,* illustrated by Ardizzone (London: Saturn, 1947);

Dickens, *Charles Dickens' Birthday Book,* illustrated by Ardizzone (London: Faber & Faber, 1948);

Leonard Daniels, *Camberwell School of Arts and Crafts: 1989 Jubilee,* illustrated by Ardizzone (London: London County Council, 1948);

Cecil Day-Lewis, *The Otterbury Incident,* illustrated by Ardizzone (London: Putnam, 1948; Cleveland: World, 1948);

Kaesar, *Mimff in Charge,* illustrated by Ardizzone (London: Oxford University Press, 1949);

Noel Langley and Hazel Pynegar, *Somebody's Rocking My Dreamboat,* illustrated by Ardizzone (London: Arthur Barker, 1949);

Anonymous, *Ali Baba,* illustrated by Ardizzone (Cambridge: Limited Editions, 1949);

Gorham, *Back to the Local,* illustrated by Ardizzone (London: Percival Marshall, 1949);

William Shakespeare, *The Comedies,* illustrated by Ardizzone (New York: Heritage, 1951; London: Heritage, 1957);

Gorham, *Showmen and Suckers,* illustrated by Ardizzone (London: Percival Marshall, 1951);

Gorham, *Londoners,* illustrated by Ardizzone (London: Percival Marshall, 1951);

Zareh Nubar, *The Modern Prometheus,* illustrated by Ardizzone (London: Forge Press, 1952);

Anthony Trollope, *The Warden,* illustrated by Ardizzone (London & New York: Oxford University Press, 1952);

James Reeves, *The Blackbird in the Lilac,* illustrated by Ardizzone (London & New York: Oxford University Press, 1952);

Trollope, *Barchester Towers,* illustrated by Ardizzone (London & New York: Oxford University Press, 1953);

Stephen Corrin, *The Fantastic Tale of the Plucky Sailor and the Postage Stamp,* illustrated by Ardizzone (London: Faber & Faber, 1954);

Kaesar, *Mimff Takes Over,* illustrated by Ardizzone (London: Oxford University Press, 1954);

William M. Thackeray, *The Newcomes,* illustrated by Ardizzone (Cambridge: Limited Editions, 1954);

Dickens, *David Copperfield,* illustrated by Ardizzone (London: Oxford University Press, 1954);

Dickens, *Bleak House,* illustrated by Ardizzone (London: Oxford University Press, 1954);

James Kenward, *The Suburban Child,* illustrated by Ardizzone (Cambridge: Cambridge University Press, 1955);

G. W. Stonier, *Pictures on the Pavement,* illustrated by Ardizzone (London: M. Joseph, 1955);

Ann Philippa Pearce, *The Minnow on the Say,* illustrated by Ardizzone (London: Oxford University Press, 1955); republished as *The Minnow Leads to Treasure,* illustrated by Ardizzone (Cleveland: World, 1958);

Farjeon, *The Little Bookroom,* illustrated by Ardizzone (London: Oxford University Press, 1955; New York: Walck, 1956);

Miriol Trevor, *Sun Slower, Sun Faster,* illustrated by Ardizzone (London: Collins, 1955; New York: Sheed, 1957);

R. S. Surtees, *Hunting with Mr. Jorrocks,* illustrated by Ardizzone (London & New York: Oxford University Press, 1956);

Reeves, *Pigeons and Princesses,* illustrated by Ardizzone (London: Heinemann, 1956);

Thackeray, *The History of Henry Esmond,* illustrated by Ardizzone (New York: Limited Editions, 1956);

George Scurfield, *A Stickful of Nonpareil,* illustrated by Ardizzone (Cambridge: Privately printed at the University Press, 1956);

St. Luke's Life of Christ, illustrated by Ardizzone (London: Collins, 1956);

Bates, *Sugar for the Horse,* illustrated by Ardizzone (London: M. Joseph, 1957);

John Symonds, *Lottie,* illustrated by Ardizzone (London: Bodley Head, 1957);

Joan M. Goldman, *The School in Our Village,* illustrated by Ardizzone (London: B. T. Batsford, 1957);

Ding Dong Bell: A First Book of Nursery Rhymes, illustrated by Ardizzone (London: Dobson, 1957; New York: Dover, 1957);

Reeves, *Prefabulous Animiles,* illustrated by Ardizzone (London: Heinemann, 1957);

Reeves, *The Wandering Moon,* illustrated by Ardizzone (London: Heinemann, 1957);

Eleanor Estes, *Pinky Pye,* illustrated by Ardizzone (New York: Harcourt, Brace, 1958; London: Constable, 1959);

Farjeon, *Jim at the Corner,* illustrated by Ardizzone (London: Oxford University Press, 1958; New York: Walck, 1958);

de la Mare, *The Story of Joseph,* illustrated by Ardizzone (London: Faber & Faber, 1958);

Kaesar, *Mimff-Robinson,* illustrated by Ardizzone (London: Oxford University Press, 1958);

Henry Cecil, *Brief to Counsel,* illustrated by Ardizzone (London: M. Joseph, 1958);

G. K. Chesterton, *Father Brown Stories,* illustrated by Ardizzone (London: Folio, 1959);

Reeves, *Titus in Trouble,* illustrated by Ardizzone (London: Bodley Head, 1959; New York: Walck, 1960);

Exploits of Don Quixote, illustrated by Ardizzone (London: Blackie, 1959; New York: Walck, 1960);

Joan Ballantyne, *Holiday Trench,* illustrated by Ardizzone (Edinburgh: Nelson, 1959);

John A. Symonds, *Elfrida and the Pig,* illustrated by Ardizzone (London: Harrap, 1959);

Ursula Moray-Williams, *The Nine Lives of Island MacKenzie,* illustrated by Ardizzone (London: Chatto & Windus, 1959; New York: Morrow, 1960);

de la Mare, *The Story of Moses,* illustrated by Ardizzone (London: Faber & Faber, 1959);

T. H. White, *The Godstone and the Blackymore,* illustrated by Ardizzone (London: Cape, 1959; New York: Putnam, 1959);

Cyril Ray, *Merry England,* illustrated by Ardizzone (London: Vista Books, 1960);

Naomi Mitchison, *The Rib of the Green Umbrella,* illustrated by Ardizzone (London: Collins, 1960);

Catherine Gough, *Boyhoods of the Great Composers I,* illustrated by Ardizzone (London: Oxford University Press, 1960; New York: Walck, 1960);

Estes, *The Witch Family,* illustrated by Ardizzone (New York: Harcourt, Brace & World, 1960; London: Constable, 1962);

de la Mare, *The Story of Samuel,* illustrated by Ardizzone (London: Faber & Faber, 1960; New York: Knopf, 1961);

Ballantyne, *Kidnappers of Coombe,* illustrated by Ardizzone (Edinburgh: Nelson, 1960);

Farjeon, *Eleanor Farjeon's Book,* illustrated by Ardizzone (London: Penguin, 1960);

Farjeon, *Italian Peepshow,* illustrated by Ardizzone (London: Oxford University Press, 1960; New York: Walck, 1960);

Robert Graves, *The Penny Fiddle,* illustrated by Ardizzone (London: Cassell, 1960; Garden City, N.Y.: Doubleday, 1961);

de la Mare, *Stories from the Bible,* illustrated by Ardizzone (London: Faber & Faber, 1961; New York: Knopf, 1961);

Folk Songs of England, Ireland, Scotland and Wales, illustrated by Ardizzone (Garden City, N.Y.: Doubleday, 1961);

Mark Twain, *Tom Sawyer,* illustrated by Ardizzone (London: Heinemann, 1961);

Nicholas Stuart Gray, *Down in the Cellar,* illustrated by Ardizzone (London: Dobson, 1961);

Reeves, *Sailor Rumbelow and Brittania,* illustrated by Ardizzone (London: Heinemann / New York: Dutton, 1962);

J. M. Barrie, *J. M. Barrie's Peter Pan,* illustrated by Ardizzone (Leicester: Brockhampton, 1962; New York: Scribners, 1962);

John Hayes, *London Since 1912,* illustrated by Ardizzone (London: H. M. S. O., 1962);

Farjeon, *Mrs. Malone,* illustrated by Ardizzone (London: Oxford University Press, 1962; New York: Walck, 1962);

Eric Crozier, *The Story of Let's Make an Opera,* illustrated by Ardizzone (London: Oxford University Press, 1962);

Eva-Lis Wuorio, *The Island of Fish in the Trees,* illustrated by Ardizzone (Cleveland: World, 1962);

Dana Faralla, *The Singing Cupboard,* illustrated by Ardizzone (London: Blackie, 1962; Philadelphia: Lippincott, 1963);

John Betjeman, *A Ring of Bells,* illustrated by Ardizzone (London: J. Murray, 1962; Boston: Houghton Mifflin, 1963);

Clive King, *Stig of the Dump,* illustrated by Ardizzone (London: Penguin, 1962);

Christianna Brand, comp., *Naughty Children,* illustrated by Ardizzone (London: Gollancz / New York: Dutton, 1963);

Gough, *Boyhoods of the Great Composers II,* illustrated by Ardizzone (London: Oxford University Press, 1963);

Reeves, *Hurdy Gurdy,* illustrated by Ardizzone (London: Heinemann, 1963);

Farjeon, *Kaleidoscope,* illustrated by Ardizzone (New York: Walck, 1963; London: Oxford University Press, 1964);

Reeves, *The Story of Jackie Thimble,* illustrated by Ardizzone (London: Chatto & Windus, 1964; New York: Dutton, 1964);

Jan Wahl, *Hello Elephant,* illustrated by Ardizzone (New York: Rinehart, 1964);

Brand, *Nurse Matilda,* illustrated by Ardizzone (Bath: Brockhampton Press, 1964; New York: Dutton, 1964);

Faralla, *Swanhilda-of-the-Swans,* illustrated by Ardizzone (London: Blackie, 1964; Philadelphia: Lippincott, 1964);

Wuorio, *The Land of Right Up and Down,* illustrated by Ardizzone (Cleveland: World, 1964; London: Dobson, 1968);

Reeves, *Three Tall Tales,* illustrated by Ardizzone (London: Abelard-Schuman, 1964; New York: Abelard, 1964);

Graves, *Ann at Highwood Hall: Poems for Children,* illustrated by Ardizzone (London: Cassell, 1964; Garden City, N.Y.: Doubleday, 1966);

John Buchan, *The Thirty-Nine Steps,* illustrated by Ardizzone (London: Dent, 1964; New York: Dutton, 1964);

Diana Ross, *Old Perisher,* illustrated by Ardizzone (London: Faber & Faber, 1965);

William J. Lederer, *Timothy's Song,* illustrated by Ardizzone (London: Dutton, 1965; New York: Norton, 1965);

John Walsh, *The Truants,* illustrated by Ardizzone (London: Heinemann, 1965);

Leonard Clark, *The Year Round,* illustrated by Ardizzone (London: Hart-Davis, 1965);

Cecil, *Know About English Law,* illustrated by Ardizzone (London: Blackie, 1965); republished as *Learn About English Law,* illustrated by Ardizzone (London: William Luscombe, 1974);

Freda Nichols, *The Milldale Riot,* illustrated by Ardizzone (London: Ginn, 1965);

Jean Webster, *Daddy Long-Legs,* illustrated by Ardizzone (Leicester: Brockhampton Press, 1966; New York: Meredith, 1967);

Ardizzone's illustration "Mr. Grimes convalescing with Lucy Brown and Mrs. Smawley" from Lucy Brown
and Mr. Grimes *(1937)*

Archibald Marshall, *The Dragon,* illustrated by Ardizzone (London: Hamish Hamilton, 1966; New York: Dutton, 1966);

The Book for Eleanor Farjeon, illustrated by Ardizzone (London: Hamish Hamilton, 1966); republished as *A Book for Eleanor Farjeon,* illustrated by Ardizzone (New York: Dutton, 1966);

Noel Streatfeild, *The Growing Summer,* illustrated by Ardizzone (London: Collins, 1966); republished as *The Magic Summer,* illustrated by Ardizzone (New York: Random House, 1967);

Reeves, *The Secret Shoemakers,* illustrated by Ardizzone (London: Abelard-Schuman, 1966; New York: Abelard, 1967);

Paula Fox, *A Likely Place,* illustrated by Ardizzone (New York: Macmillan, 1966; London: Macmillan, 1968);

Symonds, *The Stuffed Dog,* illustrated by Ardizzone (London: Dent, 1967);

Wuorio, *Kali and Her Golden Mirror,* illustrated by Ardizzone (Cleveland: World, 1967);

Brand, *Nurse Matilda Goes to Town,* illustrated by Ardizzone (Leicester: Brockhampton Press, 1967; New York: Dutton, 1968);

Estes, *Miranda the Great,* illustrated by Ardizzone (New York: Harcourt, Brace & World, 1967);

Reeves, *Rhyming Will,* illustrated by Ardizzone (London: Hamish Hamilton, 1967; New York: McGraw-Hill, 1968);

R. L. Stevenson, *Travels with a Donkey,* illustrated by Ardizzone (London: Folio, 1967);

Dorothy Clewes, *Upsidedown Willie,* illustrated by Ardizzone (London: Hamish Hamilton, 1967);

Clewes, *Special Branch Willie,* illustrated by Ardizzone (London: Hamish Hamilton, 1968);

Daniel Defoe, *Robinson Crusoe,* illustrated by Ardizzone (London: Nonesuch, 1968; New York: Franklin Watts, 1968);

Reeves, *The Angel and the Donkey,* illustrated by Ardizzone (London: Hamish Hamilton, 1969; New York: McGraw-Hill, 1970);

Jean Chapman, *Do You Remember What Happened?,* illustrated by Ardizzone (London: Angus & Robertson, 1969);

Virginia Sicotte, *A Riot of Quiet,* illustrated by Ardizzone (New York: Holt & Rinehart, 1970);

Stevenson, *Home from the Sea,* illustrated by Ardizzone (London: Bodley Head, 1970);

Kathleen Lines, *Dick Whittington,* illustrated by Ardizzone (London: Bodley Head, 1970; New York: Walck, 1970);

Clewes, *Firebrigade Willie,* illustrated by Ardizzone (London: Hamish Hamilton, 1970);

Dickens, *The Short Stories of Charles Dickens,* illustrated by Ardizzone (New York: Limited Editions, 1971);

Estes, *The Tunnel of Hugsy Goode,* illustrated by Ardizzone (New York: Harcourt Brace Jovanovich, 1971);

Shirley Morgan, *Rain, Rain, Don't Go Away,* illustrated by Ardizzone (New York: Dutton, 1972);

Mary Lavin, *The Second Best Children in the World,* illustrated by Ardizzone (New York: Houghton Mifflin, 1972);

The Old Ballad of the Babes in the Wood, illustrated by Ardizzone (London: Bodley Head / New York: Walck, 1972);

Graham Greene, *The Little Fire Engine,* illustrated by Ardizzone (London: Bodley Head, 1973; Garden City, N.Y.: Doubleday, 1973);

Greene, *The Little Train,* illustrated by Ardizzone (London: Bodley Head, 1973; Garden City, N.Y.: Doubleday, 1974);

Aingelda Ardizzone, *The Night Ride,* illustrated by Ardizzone (London: Longman, 1973; New York: Windmill Books, 1975);

Reeves, *Complete Poems for Children,* illustrated by Ardizzone (London: Heinemann, 1974);

Greene, *The Little Horse Bus,* illustrated by Ardizzone (London: Bodley Head, 1974; Garden City, N.Y.: Doubleday, 1974);

Greene, *The Little Steamroller,* illustrated by Ardizzone (London: Bodley Head, 1974; Garden City, N.Y.: Doubleday, 1974);

Reeves, *The Lion That Flew,* illustrated by Ardizzone (London: Chatto & Windus, 1974);

Reeves, *More Prefabulous Animiles,* illustrated by Ardizzone (London: Heinemann, 1975);

Ardizzone's Kilvert: Selections from the Diary of the Reverend Francis Kilvert, illustrated by Ardizzone (London: Cape, 1976);

Ardizzone's Hans Andersen: Fourteen Classic Tales, illustrated by Ardizzone (London: Deutsch, 1978; New York: Atheneum, 1979);

Reeves, *The James Reeves Story Book,* illustrated by Ardizzone (London: Heinemann, 1978).

SELECTED PERIODICAL PUBLICATIONS – UNCOLLECTED: "About Tim and Lucy," *Horn Book,* 14 (March 1938): 88–90;

"The Born Illustrator," *Signal,* 3 (September 1970): 73–80.

Best known in children's literature for writing and illustrating the Little Tim books, Edward Ardizzone had a long and distinguished career as an illustrator of works for both children and adults. Ardizzone, who described himself as a born illustrator, provided artwork for almost two hundred books, including books for children by Eleanor Farjeon, James Reeves, Grahame Greene, and Eleanor Estes. Eighteen children's books of his own, including nine in the Little Tim series, secured his place as a writer. In his art rounded shapes and simple forms belie the occasional sharp irony of his compositions. In his prose clear vocabulary and straightforward expression screen a complex awareness of human nature. His confident ink drawings and watercolors demonstrate a keen awareness of the conjunction of words and pictures. Self-taught in art and nurtured on good literature, Ardizzone worked in the tradition of Randolph Caldecott and Beatrix Potter, extending textual meaning and creating visual worlds for verbal creatures to inhabit.

Edward Ardizzone was born in Haiphong, Vietnam, in 1900, the first of five children; his middle-class childhood was marked by a series of moves, resettlements, and adjustments. His father, Auguste Ardizzone, an Italian-born naturalized French citizen, worked in French Indochina for the Far East Extension Telegraph Company. Auguste had married Margaret Irving, who was half English and half Scotch and whose grandfather had been a sea captain in the China trade. She was an independent spirit who studied art on her own in Paris at a time when few young Englishwomen did so.

Although all the Ardizzone children were born in the Orient, Margaret preferred that they be raised in England. Consequently, in 1905 five-year-old Edward and his two younger sisters sailed "home" with their mother and lived in a succession of rented houses in East Anglia. Margaret Ardizzone cultivated her children's literary tastes by reading aloud frequently, especially from William Shakespeare and Charles Dickens. When Mrs. Ardizzone rejoined her husband in the Orient the following year, Edward and his sister Betty remained with their maternal grandmother in East Bergholt, near the waterfront town of Ipswich.

Grandmother Irving experienced periodic rages, which Ardizzone later claimed had little effect on the children. He seems to have been more fascinated with than frightened by her anger. Equally fascinating to young Edward was his great-grandfather Kirby's logbook, which he had kept while serving as the second officer aboard the *Owen Glendower,* illustrating it profusely with ink drawings. Young Ardizzone also cherished a family copy of Dante's *Inferno,* illustrated by Gustave Doré. During this period Edward, playing on the waterfront and in the shipyards at Ipswich, stored up visual memories of ships, boats, and waterfront life that he later reproduced in the Little Tim books.

Ardizzone described his education as typically middle-class: a succession of nannies, private grammar schools, and public school for the boys. Edward was sent to Clayesmore, a public school with a reputation for progressive education. Ardizzone was neither a particularly good student nor a proficient athlete. He thought of himself as too fat, too clumsy, and too shy. His solace lay in filling the margins of his workbooks with sketches of classmates and masters. His first formal instruction in art – perspective, proportion, and form – was provided by a Miss Hazeldene, who soon regarded Ardizzone as her favorite pupil.

Ardizzone's formal schooling ended in 1918. He accepted a job in London as clerk with a telegraph company. The post was tedious but undemanding. When he finished his work each day, Ardizzone would spend hours making drawings of his fellow workers and London street scenes. In 1926 he began to take night courses in life drawing at the Westminster School of Art. There he profited from the instruction of Bernard Meninsky and from stimulating contact with his fellow students, many of whom remained his friends throughout his life. The praise and encouragement Ardizzone received at Westminster supported his 1927 decision to give up his office job and become a full-time artist.

A gift of £500 from his father financed a sketching and painting trip to the Continent and his entry into a career in art. In 1929 he got his first commission for book illustration and married Catherine Anderson. Their early years of marriage produced two children but little income. Commissioned illustrations for books of London scenes characterize what he later called his "pubs and tarts" years. The two children, Philip and Christianna, inspired the two books that brought Ardizzone his first recognition as a children's book author and commercial success. Neither *Little Tim and the Brave Sea Captain* (1936) nor *Lucy Brown and*

Mr. Grimes (1937) was planned with publication in mind. They originated as oral tales Ardizzone created to entertain his children.

After many retellings of Tim's and Lucy Brown's adventures, with much revision by his audience, Ardizzone took up a drawing pad and put together the picture book with text called *Lucy Brown and Mr. Grimes.* Philip's outrage at Tim's being left out inspired Ardizzone to do the same for *Little Tim and the Brave Sea Captain.* These dummy manuscripts were submitted to several publishers and subsequently turned down, until at last *Little Tim and the Brave Sea Captain* was seen by a New York representative of Oxford University Press, which was interested enough to assign Grace Hogarth, the children's book editor for Oxford University Press in the United States, to prepare it for publication. She persuaded Ardizzone to change the cursive script of his original text, beautiful as it was, to hand-lettering to help the book pass New York editorial review. Thus began a long connection with Oxford University Press, which published all the Little Tim books except the last.

Little Tim and the Brave Sea Captain establishes not only Tim's forthright yet modest character but the tone and structure of all subsequent Tim stories. The format of these earliest books established a pattern: double-page spreads balance blocks of text with colored pen-and-ink drawings. Text and pictures are perfectly integrated. Ardizzone was well aware of the specific challenges of the children's picture book. As he wrote in a 1959 essay, the text must be easy to read aloud, must be short, must "only give bones to the story." The pictures must extend the text: "Characters have to be created pictorially because there is no space to do so verbally in the text. Besides the settings and characters, the subtleties of mood and moment have to be suggested." Shortly after Tim and Lucy saw print, Ardizzone testified in *Horn Book* to the reality of the places in his books, identifying Lucy's park as the Paddington Recreation Ground and Tim's house by the sea as his brother's house near Deal. "I attempted to make the pictures in both stories as real as possible." He prefers to suggest character by gesture and body posture than to offer detailed portraits. His favorite view of the hero, he once wrote, was a back view, which allows room for individual imagination.

Ardizzone's plots and characters are deceptively simple. In *Tim and the Brave Sea Captain* the protagonist, a boy of seven or eight, wants to go to sea, stows away, cries when he has to work hard, is inured by degrees to life at sea, gets seasick, is ship-

Ardizzone's illustration "The Children came to see Diana and play with her Rhinoceros" from Diana and Her
Rhinoceros *(1964)*

wrecked, and stands firmly with brave Captain McFee, who fully expects to go down with his ship. Tim's parents remain far in the background. They are suitably astonished at Tim's knowledge of the sea when he says things like, "Look at that barkentine on the port bow." But they laugh at his desire to be a sailor. As is typical of Ardizzone's childlike combination of realism and improbability in plot and character, Tim's parents agree readily to his request to return to sea after his life-threatening adventure.

Lucy Brown and Mr. Grimes shares with *Tim and the Brave Sea Captain* Ardizzone's confident mix of reality with improbability. In both books his lonely, often misunderstood protagonist fulfills him- or herself through contact with a kindly older person. Orphaned Lucy lives with an old aunt who neglects her. Lucy's sympathetic nature prompts her friendship with lonely old Mr. Grimes, who adopts her and shares with her his considerable fortune. According to Gabriel White, the book's early history was a near disaster. It drew sharp criticism from adult reviewers, particularly in the United States. Lucy's lonely but friendly old man was a complete stranger, and the book's message was consequently considered dangerous to young girls. Unlike the Little Tim books, *Lucy Brown and Mr. Grimes* was not reprinted until it had been radically revised, with Mr. Grimes turned safely into an old family friend.

A third book, *Tim and Lucy Go to Sea* (1938), brings the two children together. Lucy, still with Mr. Grimes, is rich but lonely. Tim's enthusiasm for the sea infects Lucy and Mr. Grimes, who buys them a yacht. Tim is given more action and is bolder and more aggressive than Lucy, whose strengths are sturdy moral fiber and compassion. Poor Mrs. Smawley, the housekeeper, suffers the fate of most of Ardizzone's older women characters. Seasickness prevents her participation in most of the action. She would prefer to stay home, though in the end she is shown to be a good sport.

These three early books were produced in the large format of Ardizzone's original sketchbooks, although later editions, continuing to the present day, have appeared in a smaller format, begun in the interest of economy and a wider audience. His art exhibited his mastery of the technique of cross-hatching, producing amazing depth of mood and character through variations of light and shade. In these works he combines masterful pen-and-ink technique with luminous washes of watercolor. Another characteristic technique of Ardizzone's early books is the dialogue balloon. From eighteenth-century political cartoonists Ardizzone adapted the trick of placing colloquial comments in the mouths of figures, further developing the characters and extending the story's narrative. Sales of the first three books, unimpressive at first, steadily grew strong. By the outbreak of World War II in 1939, Ardizzone's reputation was firmly established, and income produced from the Little Tim books gave the Ardizzones a measure of economic stability.

Ardizzone's war paintings share with his children's books his unpretentious, uncompromising clear-sightedness. In 1939 Ardizzone joined an anti-aircraft unit of the territorial army. In 1940, to his delighted surprise, he was one of a group of painters appointed as official war artists. In this capacity he recorded World War II in France, North Africa, Italy, Belgium, and Germany, always just behind the front. His war journals and sketches published as *Diary of a War Artist* (1974) record the ironies of war – boredom coexisting with havoc and carnage – the same way his children's books dramatize the tedium of shipboard life in the midst of storm and shipwreck. The commissioned task of illustrating Walter de la Mare's *Peacock Pie* (1946) gave Ardizzone welome relief from life at the front.

Back home in London after the war, Ardizzone plunged into a long period of steady production and growing recognition. During the 1940s and 1950s he took on a succession of illustration projects and taught part-time at the Camberwell School of Arts and Crafts. His illustrations grace many editions of classic works as well as sociological studies of London life. In 1931 he illustrated one of Farjeon's early works, *The Old Nurse's Stocking Basket*. In the 1950s his illustrations for other Farjeon volumes and works by Reeves were among his most successful long-term collaborations with writers for children. Farjeon's depiction of rural Edwardian England was a world he understood, and he represents it honestly, even through the screen of nostalgia.

Two Ardizzone books of the late 1940s, *Nicholas and the Fast-Moving Diesel* (1947) and *Paul, the Hero of the Fire* (1948), employ the basic formula of the Little Tim books but with less success. The plots in which Nicholas and Paul figure force the mood toward melodrama. The formula is familiar: staunch but modest hero saves family and averts disaster through steadfastness and courage in the face of outrageous and improbable danger. The improbabilities of the Tim stories are more acceptable because their departures from reality are much more daring. Adventure is gratuitous: Tim is never forced to go to sea through disaster or orphanhood or economic necessity; he simply wants to. His life at sea reflects what happens at sea: work must be done; storms must be ridden out; discomforts must

be endured. In *Nicholas and the Fast-Moving Diesel* and *Paul, the Hero of the Fire,* though Ardizzone's drawings are as evocative and dynamic as ever, the protagonists face disasters of melodramatic proportions, and their heroic mettle is tested to an incredible degree through pressure on the young heroes to save their families from economic ruin. The illustrations are active and colorful, but neither of these books evokes a complete world with as much certainty as any of the Little Tim books.

Four more Tim books followed from 1949 at roughly two-year intervals, culminating with *Tim All Alone* (1956), for which Ardizzone won the newly established Kate Greenaway Medal in 1956. In *Tim to the Rescue* (1949) Tim is once more "bored with sums" and longs for the sea. Tim's parents remain unruffled as Tim ships out again with Captain McFee. Tim meets carrot top, working-class Ginger, who says things like "Blimey" and threatens to "bash" a much smaller Tim who stands up to him, winning Ginger's respect and friendship. The plot presents satisfying hints at anarchy: Ginger "borrows" the bosun's hair restorer and his red hair runs riot, and Tim disobeys the mate's orders to save Ginger, who has hidden from the storm.

In *Tim and Charlotte* (1951) Tim and Ginger rescue an amnesiac girl from a shipwreck. The scene in which Charlotte is named by decree of a family council demonstrates Ardizzone's humor and his peculiar brand of fantastic realism. The bare narrative asserts that Ginger's suggestions for her name were silly because he was "rather jealous." The asides provided by the balloon dialogue dramatize a child's view of parliamentary procedure:

> Tim: " 'I vote we call her Charlotte.' "
> Mother: " 'I like that.' "
> Father: " 'Hear, hear.' "
> Ginger, with an expression of disgust: " 'Fishy would be better.' "

The effect is neither realism, satire, nor fantasy. Anchored in psychological truth, Ardizzone's children's tales engage in the exaggerated play good parents, grandparents, and caretakers employ with children.

With the publication of *Tim in Danger* (1953), the Tim books adopted the smaller format that gave the group of books the look of a series. *Tim in Danger* employs Tim, Charlotte, and Ginger (Lucy has conveniently disappeared) and assumes that the three characters need no introduction. Bored with middle-class comfort, Ginger again runs off to sea. Tim and Charlotte pursue him, watch him sail away on a strange ship, find themselves penniless, and ship aboard a departing freighter to earn their passage home. As usual Ardizzone offers these improbabilities unblushingly, while his illustrations adhere to accuracy of detail. His narratives also insist that runaways work: Charlotte must cook and sew while Tim swabs decks. They both get tired, sad, and homesick. A telegram to Tim's parents satisfies minimal conditions of credibility. A subplot of friendship with a fat, unhappy second mate returns to the note of poignancy introduced in *Lucy Brown and Mr. Grimes.*

The poignant mood deepens in *Tim All Alone.* Tim returns home after "a long vacation" to find his house boarded up and his parents gone. The bulk of the narrative deals with the young hero making his way in the world, working first on a farm for his lodging, then on a small freighter as cabin boy. Tim seeks his parents in every port and is picked up by a social worker who would take him to a "home for lost children." He slips her grasp (around the corner a working-class character chortles into his balloon, "Ha ha! Baby's lost is he?") but misses his ship, stows away on another, becomes ill, is put ashore, and then is nursed to health by Miss Hetty, a lonely old lady who would like to adopt him. Instead he rejoins his first ship and saves the ship's cat from drowning, but the two of them are washed ashore alone. Coincidence resolves the plot when sad Tim sees his mother through a tea-shop window. Wild improbability and cozy reality are perfectly captured in a recognition scene. Ardizzone lovingly sketches and paints details of the shop window: "Morning coffee, Teas, Ices. . . . Baker's and Confectioners" read the signs on the Sunshine Cafe with its gothic-style windows. Tiered cakes, trays of sweets, aproned waitresses, and hatted ladies taking tea surround the figure of a weeping woman Tim recognizes as his mother. The pithy reconciliation scene itself avoids sentimentality. His mother explains that he had mistakenly been reported drowned, Tim relates his adventures, and they return to their old home, which has happily remained "un-Let." The final page shows Tim at an artist's drawing board writing Miss Hetty to invite her to visit. Tim's wildest adventures are punctuated by simple moral imperatives, a balanced formula tested and refined by Ardizzone over the years.

Johnny the Clockmaker (1960) and *Peter the Wanderer* (1963) repeat the successful pattern of *Tim All Alone.* The heroes of these tales are, in fact, versions of Tim, and an early manuscript of *Peter the Wanderer* in UCLA's Special Collections is called *Tim the Wanderer.* In order to function, Ardizzone's young boy heroes have to oppose dull or stubborn male

adults. They find their way alone in a world that, although harsh, is fair as long as one works hard and plays by the rules, the kind of world young children need, whether it exists or not. The best of Ardizzone's books are to English culture what the original Babar books were to French culture. Neither Ardizzone nor Jean de Brunhoff satirizes his native culture. Each renders that world lovingly, and yet in each of these writer's works the child's viewpoint provides an inadvertently critical vision of adult culture. Acceptance of class structures is a given in this world, but from it the child anarchist lives apart.

Ardizzone wrote four more Tim books: *Tim's Friend Towser* (1962), *Tim and Ginger* (1965), *Tim to the Lighthouse* (1968), and *Tim's Last Voyage* (1972). Themes and patterns remain the same. Each is illustrated with the familiar washes of color over pen-and-ink drawings, shaped and shaded by crosshatching. Each was welcomed critically, sold well, and is still in print, despite changing tastes in publishing for children in which simple moral structures and satisfying conclusions are out of favor.

Two departures from the Tim formula are worth noting. The first is an adventure into fantasy, *Diana and Her Rhinocerous* (1964), written for Ardizzone's grandchildren "who live at 43 Queen's Road, Richmond, Surrey." This is also the fictional address of Mr. Effingham-Jones and his daughter Diana. Diana is making buttered toast at the fireside when a sick rhinoceros appears at the door. In contrast to the panicked adults, Diana keeps her cool, cures the rhinoceros's cold, defies zookeepers, and settles her rhinoceros in for perpetuity. Diana and her exotic pet grow old together, still roaming the Ardizzone grandchildren's neighborhood as benign ghosts.

The other departure from the Ardizzone formula is a picture book without words, published in Britain as *Johnny's Bad Day* (1970) and in the United States as *The Wrong Side of the Bed* (1970). The book never attained the popularity of the Little Tim books, but it demonstrates Ardizzone's art of visual narrative. When Johnny gets up on the wrong side of the bed, the visual world is awry. A picture on the wall hangs crooked, Johnny's face is crumpled in a frown, and his shoulders are drawn with a downward sweep. His mother's and his own eyebrows repeat the downward line as he comes into the morning kitchen. While Mother washes his face and brushes his hair, Johnny is a Z-shaped figure of fury. The cat's tail swells as he streaks across the kitchen. The plot is simple, the moral satisfying. The visual text is detailed enough for many "readings."

Ardizzone will always be associated chiefly with his Little Tim books, which feature an uncomplicated hero who never flinches in the face of the most improbable dangers. Though Ardizzone's life and work span a dark and troubled century, first impressions of both suggest a simplicity and openness of character. Conventional though the sketched facts of his life may seem, he did not have a middle-class childhood of flawless happiness. Though his ink drawings and watercolors show almost none of the revolutionary impact of modern art, his illustrations of London, scenes of war, storms at sea, interiors of cozy British homes, the London Underground during the Battle of Britain, and children's playgrounds are all composed of solid forms massed and lighted by skillful cross-hatching suggesting far more depth and irony than other techniques would warrant. The tone of his children's stories is clear and light, but his characters' words in balloons almost always comment ironically or astringently on the narrative. The deceptive simplicity of the comfortable round shapes of his most familiar drawings and watercolors may delay recognition of Ardizzone's broad and deep command of the art of the picture book.

Interview:

Justin Wintle and Emma Fisher, *Pied Pipers* (New York: Paddington Press, 1975), pp. 35–48.

Bibliography:

Brian Alderson, *Edward Ardizzone: A Preliminary Hand-List of His Illustrated Books, 1929–1970* (Pinner: Private Library Association, 1972).

Biography:

Gabriel White, *Edward Ardizzone* (New York: Schocken, 1980).

References:

Quentin Bell, "Edward Ardizzone," *Studio,* 149 (May 1955): 144–147;

Grace Allen Hogarth, "Edward Ardizzone, 1900–1979: An Editor's View," *Horn Book,* 56 (December 1980): 680–686;

Helen Stone, "Artist's Choice," *Horn Book,* 26 (May 1950): 210–211;

Nicholas Tucker, "Edward Ardizzone," *CLE,* 3 (November 1970): 21–29.

Papers:

Edward Ardizzone's papers and original drawings are scattered. Many are still held by the Ardizzone family. Original drawings and manuscripts can be found in the Kerlan Collection (Minneapolis), the Lilian H. Smith Collection (Toronto), the British Library, and the Special Collections Room, University of California, Los Angeles. The Imperial War Museum in London holds papers and drawings from the war years.

Richard Armstrong

(18 June 1903 –)

Lisa A. Wroble

BOOKS: *The Mystery of Obadiah,* illustrated by Marjorie Sankey (London: Dent, 1943);

Sabotage at the Forge, illustrated by L. P. Lupton (London: Dent, 1946);

The Northern Maid (London: Dent, 1947);

Sea Change, illustrated by M. Leszczynski (London: Dent, 1948);

The Whinstone Drift, illustrated by Michael A. Charlton (London: Dent, 1951);

Wanderlust: Voyage of a Little White Monkey, illustrated by Frederick K. Crooke (London: Faber & Faber, 1952);

Passage Home (London: Dent, 1952);

Danger Rock, illustrated by Leszczynski (London: Dent, 1955); republished as *Cold Hazard* (Boston: Houghton Mifflin, 1956);

The Lost Ship: A Caribbean Adventure, illustrated by Edward Osmond (London: Dent, 1956; New York: Day, 1958);

No Time for Tankers, illustrated by Reg Gray (London: Dent, 1958; New York: Day, 1959);

Another Six (Oxford: Blackwell, 1959);

The Lame Duck, illustrated by D. G. Valentine (London: Dent, 1959); republished as *Ship Afire! A Story of Adventure at Sea* (New York: Day, 1961);

Before the Wind (Oxford: Blackwell, 1959);

Sailor's Luck (London: Dent, 1959);

Horseshoe Reef, illustrated by Valentine (London: Dent, 1960; New York: Duell, Sloan & Pearce, 1961);

Out of the Shallows, illustrated by Valentine (London: Dent, 1961);

Trial Trip, illustrated by Valentine (London: Dent, 1962; New York: Criterion Books, 1963);

The Ship Stealers, as Cam Renton, illustrated by Val Biro (Penshurst, Kent: Friday Press, 1963);

Island Odyssey, illustrated by Andrew Dodds (London: Dent, 1963); republished as *Fight for Freedom: An Adventure of World War II* (New York: McKay, 1966);

Big-Head, as Renton, illustrated by Biro (Penshurst, Kent: Friday Press, 1964);

The Big Sea, illustrated by Dodds (London: Dent, 1964; New York: McKay, 1965);

Storm Path (London: Dent, 1964);

The Greenhorn, illustrated by Roger Payne (London: Nelson, 1965);

The Secret Sea, illustrated by Payne (London: Dent, 1965; New York: McKay, 1965);

Grace Darling, Maid and Myth (London: Dent, 1965);

A History of Seafaring: The Early Mariners (London: Benn, 1967; New York: Praeger, 1968);

The Mutineers, illustrated by Gareth Floyd (London: Dent, 1968; New York: McKay, 1968);

A History of Seafaring: The Discoverers (London: Benn, 1968; New York: Praeger, 1969);

A History of Seafaring: The Merchantmen (London: Benn, 1969; New York: Praeger, 1969);

The Albatross, illustrated by Graham Humphreys (London: Dent, 1970; New York: McKay, 1970);

Themselves Alone: The Story of Men in Empty Places (London: Benn, 1972; Boston: Houghton Mifflin, 1972);

Powered Ships: The Beginnings (London: Benn, 1975).

OTHER: *Treasure and Treasure Hunters,* edited by Armstrong (London: Hamish Hamilton, 1969; New York: David White, 1969).

Richard Armstrong took adventure novels for boys, notably those taking place on the high seas, to new heights with his vivid details, captivating plots, and believable characters. Instructions and facts on navigation and life at sea, accentuated with the elements of his own positive life philosophy, reveal the dream that poverty and World War I took from him: to become a schoolteacher. Armstrong claimed his intention was to teach young readers "what the real world looks like to me and perhaps a little something of what life is all about." The result is not simply didactic; in fact, it serves to draw the

Richard Armstrong

reader into the story, for together the main character and the reader learn something about discipline, maturity, and making decisions, as well as the forging of steel and the sailing of ships.

Born 18 June 1903 near Northumberland in a village on Hadrian's Wall, located between the River Tyne and the Northumbrian moors, Armstrong is the son of a blacksmith and a miner's daughter. He grew up among miners and steelworkers and was educated with their children at the Walbottle Primary School. At the age of thirteen he went to work at the steel plant in Tyneside. After spending four years as errand boy, laborer, greaser, and crane driver in the steel mill, Armstrong joined the merchant navy, working as a sailor and radio operator while seeing the world. During his time at sea he learned to write, but he never submitted a manuscript to a publisher.

Settling in London in 1936, he worked at various jobs, including one at a small newspaper. In 1941 he submitted his first manuscript, a story drawing on his childhood experiences for its setting. *The Mystery of Obadiah* was published in 1943. It involves three boys who have become amateur detectives and who patiently pursue and catch a mysteri-

ous burglar in an abandoned mine. This book was followed in 1946 by a sequel, *Sabotage at the Forge*.

The best known of Armstrong's adventure novels is set at sea. *Sea Change* (1948) tells the story of Cam Renton, an apprentice seaman aching to be given "real and important responsibilities." Having gotten off to a bad start with Andy, the first mate, Renton is determined to prove he is capable of responsibility. His journey from adolescence to adulthood is not a smooth one, however: he regresses by playing pranks on Andy and his fellow seamen. But he moves forward again, realizing he must first take responsibility for himself and his future if Andy is to see him as a seaman rather than an apprentice. He finally emerges victorious, serving as Andy's temporary first mate to navigate a wounded ship to safe port.

The story is full of details of navigation and the running of a ship, including how stowage is marked and stored. As Cam learns from his shipmates, so learns the reader. The action, too, progresses as in daily life. Surprises occur, as when Cam is nearly washed overboard while the crew is frantically trying to repair a hatch broken open by waves in a storm, and the emotion and imagery is

Illustration by C. Walter Hodges from Cold Hazard *(1956)*

intense: "But Cam, looking up to see a great wall of water smashing down on him, lost his head for the first and last time in all his seafaring days, and turned to run." After this ordeal Cam realizes how little he knows about the sea and vows to watch closely and learn from his shipmates. But life on a ship is tedious and at times boring, and resolutions made in the face of danger are easily discarded.

It is at these slower moments in the story line that Armstrong slips in his own wisdom concerning life at sea. When Cam complains that chipping rust and painting are boring, a wise old seaman shares the secret of allowing his mind to roam back to the moors of his homeland in order to make such tedious tasks sufferable: "It is not a thing that comes to you itself. You must reach out for it, but when you have found the knack of it the nasty jobs that must be done don't matter any more!" Armstrong subtly weaves such lessons throughout the story. *Sea Change* received the Carnegie Medal in 1949.

Armstrong continued to write in his spare time and in 1956 won another honor. *Cold Hazard* (1956), originally published in Great Britain as *Dan-*

ger Rock (1955), won first prize in the *New York Herald Tribune* Festival of Books. The novel's protagonist is again a seaman apprentice, in this case named Jim Naylor. Jim is in his last year of apprenticeship and is acting third mate. With this responsibility also comes the night watch, which is how Jim manages, in the fog, to run the ship aground a growler, an iceberg that has melted down so that it is barely visible. The vessel must be quickly abandoned, and in the commotion Jim, three fellow apprentices, and a seasoned sailor are left behind. Escaping in a jolly boat, a craft much less seaworthy than a lifeboat, the survivors come upon an island. Through their own devices they manage to make a temporary home on the island until the sea is stable enough to allow them to escape and find the mainland. The plot develops through situation and character. Jim, elected as leader, feels guilty about the wreck and the predicament of his "crew." Pibworthy, equal to Jim in rank as an apprentice, is jealous and causes dissention. The island they first thought a haven is in reality a trap, because of the rocky terrain and the threatening sea; any chance at casting off would result in being washed back upon the rocks.

Despite a lack of formal education, Armstrong displays a wealth of knowledge and sensitivity as a writer. His scenes and settings are not painted backdrops but credible and concrete. The dialogue is vivid and descriptive, carrying the story along. The novel's conflict is clear, but the sea teaches the characters determination. A sailor learns to accept the hardships of the sea and to work with them. Once the characters also learn to work with one another, sharing their ingenuity, the solution to their predicament follows. Pieces begin to fit together, and soon Jim, with the help of a seasoned sailor named Shelty, convinces the others they must create an opportunity to leave the island rather than wait for help to arrive. The marooned sailors devise a pulley system to clear away rocks and transport the jolly boat to the other side of the island, where the harbor holds calmer water.

It is easy to assume that an author of so many sea-adventure novels would fall into a formula, but such is not the case with Armstrong. His novels include standard elements – the sea, apprentice, an older seaman who wins respect, a wreck of some type, and rescue – yet no two plots are the same. The characters and events of the various books are as noticeably different as well. Several themes, however, are repeated. A few of Armstrong's novels, such as *Sea Change,* deal with a youth maturing through the events of human conflict and natural disaster. Others, as in *Cold Hazard,* involve the relationships of several people trapped in a tense situation. Still other adventures, such as *The Lost Ship: A Caribbean Adventure* (1956), involve two apprentices of differing disposition linked by friendship, who find themselves in the midst of a mystery.

In 1954 Armstrong and his wife of thirty years, Edith, decided to move to the country. They settled on a three-hundred-year-old cottage in the Quantock hills of Somerset, England. It took two years for Armstrong to shed his London obligations, but in 1956 he began to work full-time as a writer, at a place where the sight of both sea and ships inspired him.

In 1958 Armstrong added a new twist to the story line of survivors led by apprentice seaman: war. *The Lame Duck* (1959), published in the United States as *Ship Afire! A Story of Adventure at Sea* (1961), takes place during World War II. A British oil tanker in a convoy en route from Halifax to England is torpedoed, and the surviving crew members abandon ship. The captain dies, leaving full responsibility for the safety of the others to an apprentice seaman. His competence and clear judgment, along with developing courage, bring his crew through nerve-wracking events in another of Armstrong's exciting stories.

Strong, realistic heroes fashion Armstrong's success as a novelist. His intended readers would be both alike and different from his fictional protagonists. Both are young, struggling to find their true selves on the journey through adolescence. Both have faults and sometimes make mistakes. Yet the characters in Armstrong's novels lead exciting lives at sea, away from the confines of home, and are able to visit faraway and exotic places. The similarities are meant to draw the reader in, the differences to keep him reading. Ideally, at the conclusion both reader and main character have learned and grown through the experiences. These heros, whom the reader can both relate to and admire, are the source of the continuing popularity of Armstrong's books.

Armstrong is ever sensitive to relationships, sharing his perceptions with the reader. Many of his novels deal with the hero learning to coexist in a confined space, such as a ship or a deserted island, with his shipmates. Often the hero learns to respect an older seaman or first mate and adopts him as a mentor. Through this man's advice and sometimes less than gentle guidance, the boy learns what courage is and to have faith in his own decisions.

In *Horseshoe Reef* (1960) the heroes, two apprentices, must learn to coexist with the peculiar inhabitants of a desolate island, while trying to solve the mystery behind their wrecked ship. When their ship, the *Melissa,* strikes a reef in a bad storm, third-year apprentices Curly and Peter are thrown overboard. Peter's "instinctive understanding of the sea, which made him respect it without fearing it" enables him to save himself and the unconscious Curly. They wash ashore Trull Island, a cliff-laden, desolate locale containing a crumbling mansion and a freakish family named Maddock. Curly remarks of the head of the family and the island: "You'd think to hear him it was the Garden of Eden instead of a dreary lump of rock you've got to hang on to by your eyebrows in case the perishing wind flicks you off it."

The boys have opposite personalities: Peter is thoughtful and logical; Curly is gregarious and quick to make decisions. They must learn to work together among the suspicious and queer family who hold them on Trull Island "only till the weather clears." Peter's intuition and persistence links the wreck of the *Melissa* with the Maddock's excuses for detaining the boys on the island. The adventure turns into a mystery of how and why the light the ship's crew mistook for a lighthouse was generated from Trull Island. The story is vivid and exciting. The growth of the heroes' and the reader's understanding revolves around learning to break a problem into pieces small enough to evaluate properly.

In these later decades Armstrong's novels reveal new emphases. The reader comes away from a story knowing less of the details of navigation and seafaring, but knowing more about interpersonal relationships and about himself. In books Armstrong wrote after 1960, the characters reflect the tumultuous times. These heroes are less naive than their earlier counterparts, and their impetuous behavior causes much of the conflict. To learn how the changing times were changing his readers, Armstrong spent considerable time with delinquent boys at a camp in Exmoor, England. Still writing about sea voyages and apprentice seaman, Armstrong draws on this Exmoor experience to bring authenticity to *The Mutineers* (1968) and *The Albatross* (1970).

Armstrong will continue to be known for his vivid and sensitive adventure stories of the sea. Whether the main character is seasoned or naive, whether the conflict is an external or internal force, or whatever theme or plot Armstrong uses, his reader will be entertained by an adventurous story and will perhaps realize he has gained knowledge of the sea and of himself. Armstrong's life taught him determination, gentle understanding of adolescence, and the inner workings of his fellow man.

Wilbert Vere Awdry

(15 June 1911 –)

M. Margaret Dahlberg
University of North Dakota

BOOKS: *The Three Railway Engines* (Leicester: Ward, 1945);

Thomas, The Tank Engine (Leicester: Ward, 1946);

James, The Red Engine (Leicester: Ward, 1948);

Tank Engine Thomas Again (Leicester: Ward, 1949);

Troublesome Engines (Leicester: Ward, 1950);

Henry, The Green Engine (Leicester: Ward, 1951);

Our Child Begins to Pray (Leicester: Ward, 1951);

Toby, The Tram Engine (Leicester: Ward, 1952);

Gordon, The Big Engine (Leicester: Ward, 1953);

Edward, The Blue Engine (Leicester: Ward, 1954);

Four Little Engines (London: Ward, 1955);

Percy, The Small Engine (London: Ward, 1956);

Eight Famous Engines (London: Ward, 1957);

Duck and the Diesel Engine (London: Ward, 1958);

Belinda the Beetle (Leicester: Brockhampton Press, 1958);

Railway Map of the Island of Sodor (London: Ward, 1958; revised edition, London: Kaye & Ward, 1971);

The Little Old Engine (London: Ward, 1959);

The Twin Engines (London: Ward, 1960);

Branch Line Engines (London: Ward, 1961);

Belinda Beats the Band (Leicester: Brockhampton Press, 1961);

Gallant Old Engine (London: Ward, 1962);

Stepney, the Bluebell Engine (London: Ward, 1963);

Mountain Engines (London: Ward, 1964);

Very Old Engines (London: Ward, 1965);

Main Line Engines (London: Ward, 1965);

Small Railway Engines (London: Kaye & Ward, 1967);

Enterprising Engines (London: Kaye & Ward, 1968);

Oliver, The Western Engine (London: Kaye & Ward, 1969);

Duke, The Lost Engine (London: Kaye & Ward, 1970);

Thomas the Tank Engine's Surprise Packet (London: Kaye & Ward, 1972);

Tramway Engines (London: Kaye & Ward, 1972);

Thomas's Christmas Party (London: Kaye & Ward, 1984);

Thomas Comes to Breakfast (London: Kaye & Ward, 1985);

The Birmingham and Gloucester Railway, with Peter Long (Gloucester: Sutton, 1987);

Thomas's A.B.C., 2 volumes (London: Heinemann, 1987).

OTHER: *Industrial Archaeology in Gloucestershire,* edited by Awdry (Cheltenham: Gloucestershire Community Council, 1973; revised edition, Cheltenham: Gloucestershire Society for Industrial Archaeology, 1975);

A Guide to the Steam Railways of Great Britain, edited by Awdry and Chris Cook (London: Pelham, 1979; revised edition, 1984).

For almost half a century Thomas the Tank Engine and his fellow engines from Rev. Wilbert Vere Awdry's Railway series have delighted children. World sales of more than 9 million copies, with 750,000 titles sold per year, attest to their continued popularity. The stories themselves, featuring talking steam engines with human emotions and behavior, present gentle lessons in life, conduct, and morality.

Wilbert Vere Awdry was born in Ampfield, Hampshire, on 15 June 1911 to Vere and Lucy Awdry. His love of trains began in early childhood, when his father, a clergyman and railway enthusiast, took him for walks along the embankment of the London and South Western Railway. His older brother had laid out a model train in the garden, complete with a working, two-and-a-half-inch steam engine; Awdry was sometimes allowed to push a carriage along the track.

When the family moved to Box, in Wiltshire, their house stood close to the Great Western's London-to-Bristol main line. Awdry recalls lying in bed at night, listening to the freight trains struggle up the grade: "It needed little imagination to hear, in the sounds they made, the engines talking to each other," he explains. "From that time there devel-

Wilbert Vere Awdry

oped in my mind the idea that steam engines all have personality."

When Awdry won a foundation scholarship to Dauntsey's in West Lavington, Wiltshire, his family moved to nearby Great Cheverell. During holidays he and his brother George built a new model railway: "In our imagination, the railway was on an island off the coast of Wales, connecting with the Great Western at Lampeter," Awdry recalled for Alan Hamilton in 1991. Soon he went to Oxford, leaving behind these childhood enthusiasms. He received his B.A. in 1932 and M.A. in 1936 from Saint Peter's College, Oxford, and his diploma in theology in 1933 from Wycliffe Hall, Oxford; he was ordained a priest of the Church of England in 1937.

After his marriage to Margaret Emily Wale in August 1938, Awdry served as curate in West Lavington from 1939 to 1940 and then at Saint Nicholas Church, King's Norton, in South Birmingham from 1940 to 1946. In 1943 his three-year-old son, Christopher, came down with the measles, and Awdry had to invent some amusements for him.

Together they recited, "Early in the morning, down by the station, See the little engines, all in a row." Then, as Christopher relates in a 1992 essay published in *Model Railroader,* "My father drew a picture to illustrate the rhyme – a row of six engines lined up in an engine shed, each with a face in the round space at the front, and each having a different expression." The story Awdry told about the picture became "Edward's Day Out," the first story in *The Three Railway Engines* (1945).

Two more stories soon followed; Awdry wrote them down because Christopher complained if the stories changed. That would have been the end of it if Mrs. Awdry had not encouraged her husband to send the stories to a publisher. Edmund Ward agreed to publish the stories if Reverend Awdry would write a fourth, resolving a situation introduced in the third story. *The Three Railway Engines,* published in May 1945, introduces three anthropomorphized steam engines, Edward, Gordon, and Henry. Like the twenty-five books that follow, the four-inch by six-inch book of approximately sixty pages presents four related stories, with a full-color illustration facing each page of text. Aside from the Fat Director (later the Fat Controller, along with the Thin and Small Controllers), the protagonists of the series are all engines, with a supporting cast of coaches, recalcitrant *trucks* (the British term for freight cars), drivers and other railway workers, and passengers.

In *The Three Railway Engines* Edward, smaller than the others, tries hard to be useful; boastful Gordon is shamed because he must take a freight train instead of the express; while Henry hides in a tunnel to keep the rain from ruining his paint, finally coming out only when Gordon bursts a safety valve and Edward needs help pulling the express. Two themes found throughout the series are already clear: boasting may make you look foolish; and being "useful" makes life rewarding, bringing (at least to engines on the Fat Controller's railway) the accolade "You are a Really Useful Engine" and often a new coat of paint.

After Christopher recovered from the measles in 1943, his father built him a small, wooden tank engine, painted blue. Christopher named the engine Thomas and asked for more stories. The four stories that resulted were published as *Thomas, The Tank Engine* in 1946. The text is prefaced by an author's note to Christopher, which asserts, "you helped me make them." The stories introduce Thomas, a cheeky little engine who teases Gordon, learns to manage the trucks, and proves he is "really useful" when James has an accident. He is rewarded with his own branchline.

Meanwhile, Awdry became rector of Elsworth and Knapwell in April 1946, much too busy with the demands of his first parish to write more picture books. But when Edmund Ward called to request another book, Awdry complied, and *James, The Red Engine* was published in September 1948. The new book reflects the 1947 Transportation Act, which nationalized the private railways in Britain: "We are nationalized now," Awdry explains in an introductory note, "but the same engines still work the region." The Fat Director of the earlier books has become the Fat Controller; the setting and characters are otherwise unchanged. James, repaired and painted red after his accident in "Thomas and the Breakdown Train" from *Thomas, The Tank Engine,* returns to the line. He damages a coach by pulling roughly (it must be mended with a bootlace) but then proves his worth by making a troublesome group of trucks behave and by pulling the express to give Gordon a rest.

Tank Engine Thomas Again (1949), the second book featuring Thomas, describes his branchline

Awdry with a model of Thomas the Tank Engine

experiences. Thomas goes fishing, meets Terence the tractor, and races Bertie the Bus. In *Troublesome Engines* (1950) Henry, James, and Gordon refuse to shunt their cars and are confined to the shed while Edward, Thomas, and a new green tank engine, Percy, run the line. Each of the next four books, published annually, features one of the engines: *Henry, The Green Engine* (1951); *Toby, The Tram Engine* (1952), whom the Fat Controller rescues from his retirement shed; *Gordon, The Big Engine* (1953), who is visited by the newly crowned queen; and *Edward, The Blue Engine* (1954), who races after runaway, driverless James and, as a reward for his rescue work, is rebuilt and painted.

Illustration by C. Reginald Dalby from Thomas, The Tank Engine *(1946)*

John Churcher suggests in *20th Century Children's Writers* that the characters of these early works seem like "pupils in a public school for trains." The trucks, wild, rude, boys, are "licked into shape by their natural leaders," while the coaches (always female in Awdry's series) are sisters "being shown the school." The texts amply illustrate how one should behave in difficult circumstances, especially when one has acted foolishly. James is rude to Edward in *Edward, The Blue Engine*, but later Edward comes to his rescue, and James meekly apologizes. The engines always reconcile their differences and close each book with a sense of growth after a lesson well learned.

What sets Awdry's stories apart from the usual train picture book is his attention to detail. Professional railway men have expressed their admiration of Awdry's books for children because the events accurately reflect railway conditions (with the fanciful addition of intelligent engines). In addition, the engines are all based on real prototypes; Gordon, for example, was inspired by the Gresley A3. The illustrations, first by C. Reginald Dalby, then by John Kenny, and finally by Gunvor and Peter Edwards, maintain the same careful representation (except, of course, for the faces drawn on the engines, trucks, and coaches).

In 1953 Awdry became vicar of Emneth in Norfolk. The mid 1950s also brought changes to the Railway series. To solve logistical problems created by the range of stories and a change in illustrators, Awdry mapped out his railway line, creating the mythical island of Sodor, which lies in the Irish Sea between the Isle of Man and Barrow-in-Furness on the Lancashire coast. Several books from this period show Awdry shaping details of his imaginary world. *Four Little Engines* (1955) introduces a new railway line on Sodor, run by the Thin Controller. In *Percy, The Small Engine* (1956) the Fat Controller uses Percy to build a new harbor at Thomas's Junction. With complementary main lines, active branches, and developing commercial interests, the railway business is clearly flourishing on Sodor in these stories.

During the 1950s the British Railway distressed many steam enthusiasts by gradually reducing its use of steam traction. In 1956, for the first time, more diesels than steam locomotives were made for the British Railway. Awdry's books begin to reflect the tension caused by the rising importance of diesel power. *Duck and the Diesel Engine* (1958), for example, celebrates a famous steam engine, City of Truro, in contrast with the newest engine, Diesel, who tells lies, stirs up trouble, and gets sent away. *The Little Old Engine* (1959), a sequel to *Four Little Engines,* emphasizes Awdry's interest in railway preservation. The author's note identifies the "real" Skarloey (the engine of the title) as

Talyllyn, and in the final story readers are encouraged to go visit him at Towyn in Wales.

Because no more steam engines were made in Britain by 1960 and steam traction was phased out by 1963, Sodor becomes a haven for engines escaping the cruelties of "The Other Railway." Donald and Douglas, for example, arrive from Scotland in *The Twin Engines* (1960). To the dismay of reviewers and probably of many parents reading the books aloud, as well, these engines speak in a phonetic Scots dialect.

Some of the later titles in the Railway series expose the readers to various steam railway preservation societies: *Stepney, the Bluebell Engine* (1963) introduces the first engine preserved on the Bluebell Railway at Sheffield Park in Sussex, for example, while *Small Railway Engines* (1967) acknowledges the Ravenglass and Eskadale Railway Preservation Society. *Oliver, The Western Engine* (1969) indicates that "Olivers" and "Ducks" (types of Great Western engines, and also the names of two engines in the Railway series) still work on the Dart Valley Railway in Devonshire. Though still quite inventive, the stories are often emphatically didactic and occasionally clear advertisements for steam preservation.

When Awdry retired in 1965, he had completed twenty books in the series (his son Christopher has written additional titles). *Tramway Engines* was published in 1972. Awdry explained to Russell Davies in 1983: "I discovered that the plots were becoming harder to find and I was losing the simplicity." He has, however, continued his interest both in steam railways and in Sodor. He edited *A Guide to the Steam Railways of Great Britain* in 1979.

Thomas the Tank Engine first appeared in his own BBC television series in 1984. The resulting videotapes, toys, and clothing spin-offs have boosted the sales of Awdry's books. But the television scripts are close to Awdry's original texts, and the continued popularity of the series demonstrates the power of Awdry's work. Although recently a few critics have pointed out the sexism inherent in making engines male and coaches female, the human emotions and behavior of the engines, the gentle lessons of the stories, and Awdry's attention to detail continue to delight children and form the basis of the success of the Railway series.

References:

Christopher Awdry, "Not Such an Ill Wind," *Model Railroader,* 59 (February 1992): 94–95;

Russell Davies, "Son of Steam," *Times Literary Supplement,* 30 December 1983, p. C1452;

Alan Hamilton, "A Childhood: The Rev. W. Awdry," *Times Saturday Review,* 14 September 1991, p. 42;

Katie Lynch, "All Aboard for a Magical Mystery Ride," *New York Times,* 14 August 1988, II: 29.

Enid Bagnold

(27 October 1889 – 31 March 1981)

Rosanne Donahue
University of Massachusetts – Boston

See also the Bagnold entry in *DLB 13: British Dramatists Since World War II.*

BOOKS: *The Sailing Ships and Other Poems* (London: Heinemann, 1917);

A Diary Without Dates (London: Heinemann, 1918; Boston: Luce, 1918);

The Happy Foreigner (London: Heinemann, 1920; New York: Century, 1920);

Serena Blandish; or The Difficulty of Getting Married, (London: Heinemann, 1924; New York: Doran, 1925);

Alice and Thomas and Jane, illustrated by Laurian Jones (London: Heinemann, 1930; New York: Knopf, 1931);

National Velvet, illustrated by Jones (London: Heinemann, 1935; New York: Morrow, 1935);

The Squire (London: Heinemann, 1938); republished as *The Door of Life* (New York: Morrow, 1938);

Lottie Dundass (London: Heinemann, 1941);

The Loved and Envied (London: Heinemann, 1951; Garden City, N.Y.: Doubleday, 1951);

Two Plays (London: Heinemann, 1951); republished as *Theatre* (Garden City, N.Y.: Doubleday, 1951)–includes *Lottie Dundass* and *Poor Judas*;

The Girl's Journey (London: Heinemann, 1954; Garden City, N.Y.: Doubleday, 1954)–includes *The Happy Foreigner* and *The Squire*;

The Chalk Garden (London: Heinemann, 1956; New York: Random House, 1956);

The Chinese Prime Minister (London: French, 1964; New York: Random House, 1964);

Autobiography: From 1889 (London: Heinemann, 1969); republished as *Enid Bagnold's Autobiography* (Boston: Little, Brown, 1970);

Four Plays (London: Heinemann, 1970; Boston: Little, Brown, 1971)–includes *The Chalk Garden, The Last Joke, The Chinese Prime Minister,* and *Call Me Jacky*;

A Matter of Gravity (London: Heinemann, 1978; New York: French, 1978).

Enid Bagnold

PLAY PRODUCTIONS: *Lottie Dundass,* London, Vaudeville Theatre, 21 July 1943;

National Velvet, London, Embassy Theatre, 23 April 1946;

Poor Judas, London, Arts Theatre, 18 July 1951;

Gertie, New York, Plymouth Theatre, 30 January 1952; produced again as *Little Idiot,* London, Q Theatre, 10 November 1953;

The Chalk Garden, New York, Ethel Barrymore Theatre, 26 October 1955; London, Haymarket Theatre, 11 April 1956;

The Last Joke, London, Phoenix Theatre, 28 September 1960;

The Chinese Prime Minister, New York, Royale The-
     atre, 2 January 1964; London, Globe Theatre,
     20 May 1965;
Call Me Jacky, Oxford, Oxford Playhouse, 27 Febru-
     ary 1968; revised as *A Matter of Gravity,* New
     York, Broadhurst Theatre, 3 February 1976.

Enid Bagnold was the only daughter – and for
the first six years of her life the only child – of Arthur Henry Bagnold and Ethel Alger Bagnold.
Bagnold admits that her parents doted on her as a
child: "You'd have thought I was the Infant Jesus,"
she wrote in her *Autobiography: From 1889* (1969).
When Bagnold was nine years old, her father, a
major in the Royal Engineers, received a command
in Jamaica, and the family left England. "The tropic
leapt into the spangled night," she recalled. "This
was the first page of my life as someone who can
see. It was like a man idly staring at a field suddenly
finding he had Picasso's eyes." Her three years in
Jamaica, although surrounded by beauty, were
lonely; she had no friends. The army doctor's
daughter, Mary Adams, studied with her, but she
had to go home promptly, because Mary's father
thought Enid was a hysterical child.

When the Bagnolds returned from Jamaica,
Enid, age twelve, was sent to Prior's Field Boarding
School, not only to get a good education but also for
refinement and discipline. The headmistress, the
mother of Aldous Huxley, was a kind woman who
amazed Bagnold because she appeared to think before she spoke, a habit Bagnold had never practiced. Her years with Mrs. Huxley were five of her
happiest. Mrs. Huxley left the school when Bagnold,
still outspoken and spontaneous for a young
woman, was seventeen. Bagnold spent the next year
or so traveling to finishing schools in Germany,
Switzerland, and France. At eighteen she returned
home to Woolwich and attended a coming-out at
the Royal Military Academy. It was during this
time that she decided she wanted to become a
writer. Major Bagnold provided her a private room
to develop her talents. In her autobiography she admits that "bit by bit I became the disciplined writer,
in that Tower Room." In 1920 she married Sir Roderick Jones, the owner and director of Reuters News
Agency; the couple had four children.

Bagnold was a dedicated writer for more than
sixty years of her life. Writing mainly for adults,
she has to her credit a book of poems, a nonfiction
book, novels, plays, and a screen adaptation of one
of her novels. Each of Bagnold's books appears to
be heavily influenced by events that occurred in her
life; she appears to have been, lived with, or met

each of her characters. Her female protagonists are
strong women who are independent and intelligent,
and the plots and themes of her stories are reflective
and thoughtful.

A Diary Without Dates (1918) and *The Happy
Foreigner* (1920) reflect Bagnold's war experiences. *A
Diary Without Dates* is about her experiences as a
member of the Volunteer Aid Detachment (VAD)
during World War I. She was immediately dismissed from the Royal Herbert Hospital, Woolwich, for a breech of military discipline when the
book appeared. Bagnold could never become accustomed to the pain or the callous way of the sisters in
the hospital, who made no effort to present the
news of death in a humane way. Edith Walton,
looking back on *A Diary Without Dates* for the 24 November 1935 *New York Times Book Review,* admits
that Bagnold "shows a certain hostility to the sisters
who were [her] superiors" but asserts that the book
"could only have been offensive in that it was too
clearheaded and realistic to please contemporary
patriots." In the book Bagnold moves from being
excited about being a VAD to becoming lonely and
insecure. She goes from admiring the nurses' uni-
forms to becoming critical about their insensitivity.
A Diary Without Dates is a personal account of
Bagnold's growing experience within the hospital.
The more experience she gains, the more disillusioned she becomes with the hospital and the lack of
relationships she is able to witness or establish.
Bagnold is young and looking for excitement and
romance. She does not find them as a volunteer. In
the third section of *A Diary Without Dates,* titled
"The Boys," Bagnold allows the reader to see the
impact of the war by showing the pain and suffering
of the nameless men who lie in bed. By stepping
closer to the action – the guns exploding in the distance – Bagnold pulls the reader in and makes *A
Diary Without Dates* a lasting novel.

The Happy Foreigner is Bagnold's fictional account of joining the First Air Nursing Yeomanry
(FANY) and becoming a driver for the French
army. She was the first woman to be sent as a driver
to Verdun, where she spent two nights in one of the
army's subterranean passages. Bagnold's protagonist, Fanny, who tells of her adventures, is a strong
woman much like herself. Writing in the 16 July
1920 *Athenaeum* Katherine Mansfield said of the
young narrator, "Praise be to Miss Bagnold for giving us a new heroine, a pioneer, who sees, feels,
thinks, hears, and yet is herself full of the sap of
life." The reviewer in the 28 August 1920 *Spectator*
said that Bagnold "has the courage to affirm what
we are all more or less aware of – i.e., the bad feel-

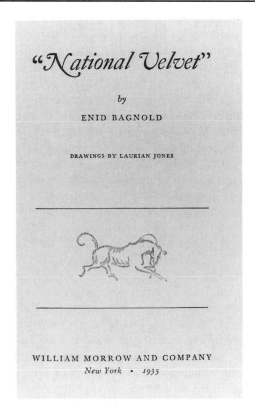

Title page for the American edition of Bagnold's novel about a girl disguising herself as a boy and riding her horse in the Grand National

ing which existed between them [French and American armies] – and she has insight enough to sympathize with both sides."

Serena Blandish; or The Difficulty of Getting Married (1924) was based on a character Bagnold met. In her autobiography she remembers this girl, who was an almost childlike girl, younger looking than her seventeen years, seeking money to get an abortion; she did not know who the father was. In talking with the girl, Bagnold finds out that "the girl did not get pleasure from men . . . saying yes [was] the pleasure [she got]." Even though this girl hardly spoke, her smile stayed in Bagnold's mind and became Serena's naive smile.

Most of the book focuses on Serena's search for a husband. Like the character on which she is based, her biggest weakness is saying yes to men. But Serena has wise friends. Martin, the butler, tells Serena that "a lady who stays to tea when she has been asked to luncheon . . . is never engaged to be married." Serena is also warned by the Countess, "you must keep your kisses till after you are married." Young Serena appears to have more guidance than did the young girl who requested abortion money from Bagnold.

Serena does marry at the end of the novel, but one is not sure that it will be a happy marriage. Much of the plot centers on things not being as they seem. Manila the model, who admits that none of the beautiful clothes she wears actually belong to her, has borrowed them so that she can get a husband. Serena's beloved Count is not actually a count; he is the illegitimate son of an Indian woman. Serena begs Martin to marry her so that she will not have to marry the count, but in the end she marries Montague.

Bagnold wrote *Alice and Thomas and Jane* (1930) for her four children. It is a simple collection of tales illustrated by her nine-year-old daughter, Laurian Jones. In the first chapter, for example, Alice, Thomas, and Jane have an adventure to raise money. They make themselves look dirty and poor, and then they take the bus into the village, where they draw chalk pictures on the pavement. Seven-year-old Jane and five-year-old Alice do the drawing, while eight-year-old Thomas holds out his cap for passersby to drop in money. The parents learn of this adventure and subsequent ones, but they never mention them to the children. Each episodic chapter contains a different adventure for children to enjoy.

National Velvet (1935) is perhaps Enid Bagnold's most famous book, a work that has captivated both young and old readers. Not only was it turned into a radio play for Theatre Guild, but in 1944 it was also made into a Metro-Goldwyn-Mayer film starring Elizabeth Taylor and Mickey Rooney. Sixty years after it was written it is still one of the most realistic girls' sports books available. The novel presents a fully developed plot and a three-dimensional protagonist in Velvet Brown, who recalls Bagnold herself, for in her admissions interview at Prior's Field Bagnold had also remarked that she wanted to be best at a sport. In *National Velvet* Bagnold created a character who embodied her youthful desire. The images of Velvet, a skinny fourteen-year-old girl, riding a massive horse's back toward victory in the Grand National are both realistic and exciting. But a strength of the book is the sense of immediacy and excitement Bagnold created.

The importance of personal achievement is a significant theme in *National Velvet*. Velvet's motive for disguising herself as a boy and riding the piebald, whom she calls "the Pie," in the Grand National is not glory or money: Velvet wants everyone to see how special her horse is. No boy jockey will ride the Pie because he lacks the needed credentials and is distrustful of people in general. If the Pie is going to get the recognition he deserves, then Velvet has to ride him. Long before the Grand National, the reader sees the special relationship developing between Velvet and her horse. The first race Velvet and the Pie enter is the gymkhana. She does not push or try to make him jump hurdles that are difficult; she wants to keep him thinking he is a winner. Velvet's values emerge slowly as she becomes involved with her horse; she is selfless when it comes to the Pie's needs.

Velvet's mother, Mrs. Brown, is one of the strongest mother characters in an adolescent book. Mr. Brown is the head of the family, but Mrs. Brown is the standard of the family. Mrs. Brown swam the English Channel when she was nineteen years old, and clearly she brings the same strength and determination to the rearing of her children. Like Velvet, she did not achieve this great task for the fame or fortune but for something deep within herself. Both she and Velvet have an inner compulsion to do one thing better than anyone else in the world; insofar as they are proving anything, they are proving it to themselves. Because Mrs. Brown is such a strong character, there is no problem in believing that Velvet could strive for a goal that seems unreachable. The strength of women is shown throughout, and the sensitivity that is associated with women is very much a part of their strength. Mrs. Brown is presented as a quiet woman, but her actions speak loudly. She has kept the gold sovereigns that she won for swimming the English Channel, and when Velvet needs an entrance fee to the Grand National, she hands over the box and says, "It's to bring you luck."

After Velvet wins the Grand National and becomes a public figure, it is still clear that the fame is not what she wanted. " 'Me! That's nothing. I'm nothing. If you could see what he did for me. He burst himself for me. N' when I asked him he burst himself more. N' when I asked him again he – he – doubled it. He tried near to death he did. I'd sooner have that horse happy than go to heaven!' " When she gets a movie offer for the Pie she refuses it because that is not the dignity he deserves. She wants him written about in books that people value, not magazines that people use to start fires. "He'll be in every book. He'll be the horse of his year, that won it this year. Though they disqualify us they'll never dare to drop him out altogether." Mrs. Brown tries to keep the Brown family from being seduced by the attention they are receiving. She knows that the news will become old quickly and that Velvet will stop receiving flowers, candy, and letters; the crowds will leave their backyard; the newspaper re-

porters will find other people to interview; nothing lasts forever. The reader already knows that Mrs. Brown did not like the attention she received when she swam the English Channel, and Velvet, after the Grand National, behaved humbly. Neither of them was motivated by self-aggrandizement.

Writing in the 4 May 1935 *Saturday Review of Literature*, Christopher Morley summed up the enduring attraction of *National Velvet:* "In its own vein, and for those who can ride the flying trapeze of fancy, this is a masterpiece. . . . you can learn more about the mind of childhood from this book than from many volumes of pedology. The mind of childhood, zigzag, indolent, unblemished by the subjunctive mood, is the mind of any great artist. Disregard the dull dutiful attempt of any critic to praise this lovely escapade. Read it for its humble magic. Read it to be one of the Browns."

The Squire (1938) presents another strong woman protagonist called only "the squire." The squire is a pregnant woman ready to deliver at any time; she is also acting as head of the house during her husband's three-month absence. She has four other children, and this is the first birth her husband has missed. The daily household problems that arise during the six-week period are handled adeptly by the squire. She can hire and fire the servants; she can change the fuses; and she can make sure that the house and the children are well taken care of. But the focus of the novel is the squire's reflection upon her own life. She thinks about the fifth of her children as well as her own death. This is not one of Bagnold's most popular novels, because of its subtlety, but it has drawn admiring comments from critics. Rosemary Benet said in a 2 October 1938 review in the *New York Herald Tribune Books* that *The Door of Life* "is feminism at its best. It combines vitality with sensitivity, an excellent combination."

Bagnold's last novel was *The Loved and Envied* (1951). The strong personality of her protagonist, Lady Ruby Maclean, was based on her friend Lady Diana Cooper. For the first twenty-five years of her life, Lady Ruby Maclean was more fun than anyone else. But now she is passing into what she calls "old age." Anthony West in a 27 January 1951 *New Yorker* review said that "The main business of the book is the discovery of the emotional poverty of a woman in her fifties who has lived so entirely to herself that love has died around her without touching her, and its contrast to the emotional wealth that love of one kind or another has brought to the people in her circle of acquaintance." While it is true that Ruby, in reflecting upon her life, is saddened by the death of her husband and some of her friends

Bagnold at about age twenty

found out between acts 2 and 3, Lottie begs to finish the play. She has a heart attack at the end of the play, and her mother withholds medicine so that she will die rather than stand trial.

In *Poor Judas* there is a similar theme. Edward Walker is a sneak who will do whatever is necessary to achieve his own goal. He is collaborating on a scholarly project with Jules Calas; they have spent the previous eleven years researching and writing "The History of Herd Treachery." When they are close to the completion of the work, Walker takes all the notes on his section and returns to England to finish the project. Four years later the men come together, and Calas realizes that Walker has done nothing further. It is not clear whether Walker had the creativity or the talent to finish, but clearly he lacked the conscience to care.

Bagnold turned her undivided attention to playwriting in the early 1950s and wrote her most successful play, *The Chalk Garden* (1956), which was first produced in 1955. The grandmother, Mrs. St. Maugham, in *The Chalk Garden* was portrayed in the London production by Dame Edith Evans. It is yet another character who could have been Bagnold herself. The play received rave reviews; Kenneth Tynan's review in the London *Observer* noted that "in *The Chalk Garden,* something is being said about the necessity of rescuing young people from the aridity of a rich, irresponsible life, but it is being said wittily, obliquely, in a manner that one would call civilized if one thought civilization was worthy of the tribute."

The plot of the play centers on Miss Madrigal, who is hired as a companion for Mrs. St. Maugham's granddaughter, Laurel. Even though all of the characters seem a little strange or eccentric, only Miss Madrigal seems to have a reason. This is her first interaction with people outside of prison, where she spent fifteen years for murder. Miss Madrigal convinces Laurel to go live with her mother, Mrs. St. Maugham's daughter. This will be best for Laurel and her mother. Miss Madrigal stays with the grandmother and presumably helps her live a better life.

In the 1960s Bagnold wrote her final plays, *The Last Joke* (1970), *The Chinese Prime Minister* (1964), and *Call Me Jacky* (1970). All three of these plays have autobiographical bases. The plots feature eccentric characters and are difficult to plod through. Produced in 1960, *The Last Joke* is about Bagnold's good friend Prince Antoine Bibesco. Bagnold had a special friendship with Bibesco, one which probably could have led to marriage if it were not for his relationship with his brother Em-

and may, in fact, live the rest of her life with part of this sadness hanging over her, it is not accurate to say that she was not touched by love. Bagnold meant for Ruby to be the friend that Diana was, of whom Bagnold asserted, "she puts friendship above everything, that is her gift of gifts. . . . When you are her friend you are socially made, but no one would be her friend who thought it." Lady Ruby was loved or envied by all who came in contact with her, and her character, like her beauty, was often misjudged.

Bagnold published two plays, *Lottie Dundass* (1941) and *Poor Judas* (1951), before she finished with her novel writing. Lottie Dundass wants to be an actress more than anything else in her life, but despite being only twenty years old she has been told that she must avoid strenuous work because of a heart condition. Lottie stops at nothing to appear on the stage: she even murders the actress to whom she is understudy so she can perform. When she is manuel, a suicide. Bagnold quoted many of Bibesco's sayings, mostly through the character of the butler in *Serena Blandish*. In the play Hugo and his brother Ferdinand have a turbulent relationship. After his stroke Ferdinand, a gifted mathematician who is always threatening suicide, lives secretly with Hugo. The play centers on the brothers' retrieval of a stolen painting of their mother in a garden, which is accomplished by means of disguises and suicidal diversions.

The Chinese Prime Minister, which premiered in 1964, is about accepting old age with grace. The play was almost finished when Bagnold's husband, Roderick, passed away; her loneliness and her determination to become a woman of leisure are incorporated into the play. The protagonist is an actress about to celebrate her seventieth birthday, retire from the theater, and enjoy a fulfilled life. Her two sons and their on-again, off-again relationships with their wives present a contrast to their mother's self-knowledge. Bagnold, nearly seventy-five at this time, was almost ready to forsake responsibility and bask in her life's accomplishments.

Call Me Jacky, which was first produced in 1968 and was later revised as *A Matter of Gravity* (1978), also presents an older woman, Mrs. Basil, who lives her life without responsibility. It, too, is a play filled with eccentric characters. Mrs. Basil's grandson Niggie, who is studying at Oxford University, brings four guests for the weekend because he believes his grandmother might be lonesome. The characters are all arrogant intellectuals who lack manners and courtesy. Niggie falls in love with one of the young women, Elizabeth, and after convincing her that he will inherit Mrs. Basil's country home, they marry. By the end of the play Mrs. Basil has given the house to Niggie and Elizabeth, and she is preparing to leave her home and go live at the asylum, in the wing designed for the sane elderly. Mrs. Basil recognizes that she could never live with her grandson and his wife because there is too much difference between the generations.

Call Me Jacky does not end on a happy note; it is Bagnold's last play and does not reflect the same toughness of mind as did her earlier works. Mrs. Basil is a wonderful character – again, similar to Bagnold herself. As in most of Bagnold's works, there is an eccentric domestic: the lesbian cook Jacky DuBois, who has been in and out of asylums for helping the elderly kill themselves. Rather than let Elizabeth have the house, it would have been better if Mrs. Basil had sent her off with DuBois. Instead, although Mrs. Basil does not accept DuBois's help with killing herself, she and DuBois do leave together.

In her autobiography Bagnold writes about why she became a writer: "Because it's the answer to everything. To Why am I here? To uselessness. It's the streaming reason for living. To note, to pin down, to build up, to create, to be astonished at nothing, to cherish the oddities, to let nothing go down the drain, to make something, to make a great flower out of life, even if it's a cactus." In her long career Bagnold provided many answers and planted many seeds. But to her credit she raised the consciousness of her readers so that they will have to continue plowing the fields. She left no easy solutions.

Biography:

Anne Sebba, *Enid Bagnold: The Authorized Biography* (New York: Taplinger, 1986).

Reference:

Lenemaja Friedman, *Enid Bagnold* (Boston: Twayne, 1986).

Kitty Barne
(Marion Catherine Barne)

(1883? – 1957?)

Gary D. Schmidt
Calvin College

BOOKS: *Tomorrow,* by Barne and D. W. Wheeler (London: Curwen, 1910);

Tomorrow, illustrated by Ethel King-Martyn (London: Hodder & Stoughton, 1912);

Winds, by Barne and Wheeler, illustrated by Lucy Barne (London: Curwen, 1912);

Timothy's Garden, by Barne and Wheeler, illustrated by Lucy Barne (London: Curwen, 1912);

Celadine's Secret, by Barne and Wheeler, illustrated by J. M. Saunders (London: Curwen, 1914);

Peter and the Clock (London: Curwen, 1919); reprinted in *Six Modern Plays,* edited by John Hampden (London & New York: Nelson & Nashville, 1931);

Susie Pays a Visit (London: Curwen, 1921);

The Amber Gate: A Pageant Play (London: Curwen, 1925);

Philemon and Baucis (London: Gowans & Gray, 1926; Boston: Baker, 1926);

Madge: A Camp-Fire Play (London: Novello, 1928);

Adventurers: A Pageant Play (London: Deane, 1931; Boston: Baker, 1936);

The Amber Gate, illustrated by Ruth Gervis (London & New York: Nelson, 1933);

The Easter Holidays, illustrated by Joan Kiddell-Monroe (London: Heinemann, 1935); republished as *Secret of the Sandhills* (New York: Dodd, Mead, 1949);

Young Adventures, illustrated by Gervis (London: Nelson, 1936);

Two More Mimes from Folk Songs: The Wraggle, Taggle Gipsies, O! Robin-Thrush (London: Curwen, 1936);

Two Mimes from Folk Songs: The Frog and the Mouse; The Flowers in the Valley (London: Curwen, 1937);

They Made the Royal Arms (London: Deane / Boston: Baker, 1937);

Mother at Large (London: Chapman & Hall, 1938);

She Shall Have Music, illustrated by Gervis (London: Dent, 1938; New York: Dodd, Mead, 1939);

Shilling Teas: A Comedy for Women in One Act (London: Deane, 1938; Boston: Baker International Play Bureau, 1938);

Songs and Stories for Acting, illustrated by Gervis (Glasgow: Brown & Ferguson, 1939);

Family Footlights, illustrated by Gervis (London: Dent, 1939; New York: Dodd, Mead, 1939);

Visitors from London, illustrated by Gervis (London: Dent, 1940; New York: Dodd, Mead, 1940);

May I Keep Dogs?, illustrated by Arnrid Johnston (London: Hamish Hamilton, 1941; New York: Dodd, Mead, 1942);

Listening to the Orchestra (London: Dent, 1941; revised edition, London: Dent, 1946; Indianapolis: Bobbs-Merrill, 1946);

We'll Meet in England, illustrated by Steven Spurrier (London: Hamish Hamilton, 1942; New York: Dodd, Mead, 1943);

While the Music Lasted (London: Chapman & Hall, 1943);

Enter Two Musicians (London: Chapman & Hall, 1944);

Three and a Pigeon, illustrated by Spurrier (London: Hamish Hamilton, 1944; New York: Dodd, Mead, 1944);

In the Same Boat, illustrated by Gervis (London: Dent, 1945; New York: Dodd, Mead, 1945);

Days of Glory: A Pageant Play (London: Deane, 1946);

The "Local Ass": A Documentary Play for Girl Guides (London: Girl Guides' Association, 1947);

The Lost Birthday (London: Curwen, n.d.);

Musical Honours, illustrated by Gervis (London: Dent, 1947; New York: Dodd, Mead, 1947);

Here Come the Girl Guides (London: Girl Guides' Association, 1947);

Duet for Sisters (London: Chapman & Hall, 1947);

Dusty's Windmill, illustrated by Marcia Lane Foster (London: Dent, 1949); republished as *The*

Kitty Barne

Windmill Mystery (New York: Dodd, Mead, 1950);

Roly's Dogs, illustrated by Alice Molony (London: Dent, 1950); published as *Dog Stars* (New York: Dodd, Mead, 1951);

Elizabeth Fry: A Story Biography (London: Methuen, 1950);

Vespa (London: Chapman & Hall, 1950);

Barbie, illustrated by Foster (London: Dent, 1952; Boston: Little, Brown, 1969);

Admiral's Walk, illustrated by Mary Gurnat (London: Dent, 1953);

Music Perhaps (London: Chapman & Hall, 1953);

Rosina Copper, the Mystery Mare, illustrated by Alfons Purtscher (London: Evans, 1954; New York: Dutton, 1956);

Cousin Beattie Learns the Fiddle (Oxford: Blackwell, 1955);

Tann's Boarders, illustrated by Jill Crockford (London: Dent, 1955);

Introducing Handel, illustrated by Crockford (London: Dent, 1955; New York: Roy, 1957);

Introducing Mozart, illustrated by Crockford (London: Dent, 1955; New York: Roy, 1957);

Rosina and Son, illustrated by Foster (London: Evans, 1956);

Introducing Schubert, illustrated by Crockford (London: Dent, 1957; New York: Roy, 1957).

OTHER: *The Grand Party,* adaptation of the novel *Holiday House,* by Catherine Sinclair, in *The Theatre Window: Plays for Schools,* edited by W. T. Cunningham (London: Arnold, 1933).

The childhood interests of Kitty Barne seemed as though they might well set her future career. From an early age she was interested in music, and by age eleven she was playing in an orchestra. At the same time, she was keen on writing dramas, producing one on Guy Fawkes in her elementary school and eventually starting a junior dramatic society. As a young adult she combined these interests while working at a hostel, as she studied music and started another dramatic society. But her real career began with the advent of World War I: she began to write children's books. It is no accident that many of her books focus on children of musical talent or on the production of plays by children. But it is her novels, and not her plays or musical abilities, that rank her among the significant artists of her time.

Though most of her work has faded from view, Barne is still remembered for two things.

First, she was the recipient of the Library Association Carnegie Medal in 1941 for *Visitors from London* (1940), a story of a group of children moved out of London to Sussex to escape the bombing by the Germans. Second, she is remembered as something of a pioneer in children's literature in dealing with difficult problems realistically, thereby moving away from literature that is patently escapist. Though the first accolade is merited, the second is perhaps less so.

Visitors from London is the second book in a series about the Farrar children, first introduced in *Family Footlights* (1939). Set at Steadings, a rambling farm, the novel deals with a set of families evacuated from London at the outbreak of World War II. The Farrar family is both caring and resourceful, opening up their home and lives to the families. But what is most remarkable about the novel is the portraits of the families. They display a wide variety of reactions to the war and the bombing of London. Mrs. Thompson is almost paralyzed by fear, and Mrs. Fell and some (not all) of her children are angry and resentful. But others, particularly Lily, are resolute and strong, anxious to prove their abilities to endure and even thrive under adversity.

This novel represents Kitty Barne at her best. Her characters are vividly drawn and realistic to the experiences of any child living in Britain during the war. The situations encountered – evacuations, blackouts, air raids – are also familiar to the time, but they are pushed behind the strong portraits of the Farrar children. The book is a celebration of British life, particularly country life, and several of the evacuated children find new lives in the country.

World War II provided Barne with settings for several of her novels, but while the settings are not incidental, the novels are not simply war stories. Barne has a specific message to send with her use of the war material: even as Britain is beset, British life in all of its regularity and predictability is still going on. The war rages and the shores are threatened, but there is still school to attend, and sibling relationships, and tea, and breakfast, and all of the comings and goings of domestic life. The war exists, but it is no more real or important than the normal life around the children.

It is this approach that dominates *In the Same Boat* (1945), a title with both literal and metaphoric implications. The novel opens with Bridgit traveling from India to England so that she can live with her grandmother and attend Ramparts, the traditional school for her family. On board the ship she meets Tossie, a young Polish refugee who becomes her close friend. When their ship is hit by a torpedo – a strong reminder of the presence of the war – they survive together for nineteen days in a lifeboat, telling stories and singing songs.

Once they reach Britain, both girls are caught up into traditional British life. Bridgit lives with her grandmother at Green Hedges and Tossie eventually comes to live with her. They attend the same school, and Bridgit conducts her into British life, picking out clothes, fixing hot chocolate, and mediating between Tossie and the system of English scholarship. Most of the book is thus concerned with the world of English private schools, which is symbolized by a wheel or solar system, where everything goes round and round, and everyone has her or his proper place in the order of things. There is no talk of bombing or raids, and only passing mention of rationing. Only at the end of the novel, when Tossie's father comes to bring her back to her native Poland to work with the underground, does the war reenter the world of Green Hedges. Only then does Bridgit understand why Tossie had been working so hard for so long to overcome fears and to become physically strong. The novel ends with their parting, but also with the suggestion that they are indeed in the same boat, that Britain will have need of similar courage.

We'll Meet in England (1942) also uses World War II in its principal plot conflict, but the approach here is quite different from that of *In the Same Boat* and *Visitors from London*. It is much more of an adventure novel and features an escape from occupied Norway. Since Hertha Larsen and her brother will soon be expected to join one of the Nazi youth camps, she is eager to escape. They find a boat and a sailor, Wapping Bill, but their actions are watched closely by Mr. Pieters, the nasty Nazi spy. Under cover of darkness they outfit the boat, but when Mr. Pieters becomes suspicious, the two children have to leave ahead of their plans, abandoning their mother and young siblings. During the journey to England they survive a storm and a leaky boat and rescue a downed English airman. Having arrived, they hear news of another daring escape from Norway: the rest of the family has made it as well.

For Barne, the primary focus is on the sheer adventure, on the ability of the children to outwit the spy. England is envisioned as the bastion of freedom, the goal of the refugees. If the ending is too perfect, certainly the vision of brave children battling extraordinary odds against an extraordinary enemy was enough to make this an appealing novel in 1942.

Three and a Pigeon (1944) is similarly set during the war, but here the actual fighting seems rather distant. Instead, Barne focuses on the immediate effects of the war that children would have been feeling when the book was published. The children in the story abide by the schedule of blackouts; there is rationing; and there are the urgencies of limited food and supplies. The children befriend a refugee, Emile, who raises carrier pigeons and eventually returns to the Belgian army. When the children in the novel move to the country, they do so because their house has been bombed. There they battle against a farmer smuggling eggs for the black market. Despite the bombed-out house, the children experience relatively normal lives, affected, though not devastated, by the war.

Barne saw her writing, despite her use of coincidences, as being realistic. She was determined not to write escapist literature that, she felt, had too long been the fare of child readers, and thus set out to write books about real and complex problems. "I knew they [children] were sensible, critical, and not at all romantic about their own affairs," Barne wrote in an autobiographical entry for the *The Junior Book of Authors*. "Whether the heroes and heroines of my books are running a dogs' motel, escaping from the Gestapo in Norway, getting up a play, helping a Polish girl find her feet in an English school, or persuading a returned POW father to change his mind about their future careers, they are all independent, energetic people, making up their minds about what they want to do with their lives and going all out to do it." Despite her intention, Barne is not entirely successful in getting this energy across; neither is she able to capture the realism she desires.

Barne's reputation as a pioneer in realistic fiction for children — insofar as such a reputation exists — rests on such a novel as *Musical Honours* (1947), which does tackle a difficult but all-too-common problem stemming from World War II. While sitting comfortably around the breakfast table the Redland family receives a letter from Charley, who is coming home after being held prisoner in Asia for years. Their mother having died, the four Redland children are living with their grandparents, who are overjoyed at the promised arrival of their son. But the children have mixed emotions, especially the older two who barely remember Father. The younger two, particularly Scrap, do not know their father at all, but have instead imagined their father. The adjustment of Father from a visitor to a participant in family life is not an easy one.

The central conflict of the novel revolves around music, as indeed is the case in several of Barne's works. Both Jimmy and Becky are fine musicians, as their father had been. Jinks, the younger brother, is also a gifted singer, though he is more interested in collecting bugs and reptiles. But when Father returns, he brings with him the news that he is giving up music, and that the children will have occupations as accountants or secretaries. Music, he reasons, is just too precarious an occupation. The conundrum of the novel is how to get Father to change his mind; Becky and Jimmy engage in all sorts of schemes — one involving the virtual abduction of the church organist so that Father can hear Jimmy play.

All of this is realistic: the uneasy return of the father into the family and the frustration of being told what one is to become when one is already embarked on a vocation. But Barne, to be a pioneer in realism, must deal with the problems realistically. And here she falls short. All of the strategies, no matter how outlandish, are successful: Becky wins a piano competition; Jinks wins a scholarship to study singing in London; and Jimmy seems likely to win a scholarship to study organ. But Father is still against all of this until — all on the same day — they receive a notice that a concerto by Father that Jimmy and Becky submitted without his knowledge has won a major prize; a telegram from a publisher offering to take the concerto and any other songs he might have as well; and a call from the vicar whose organ Father played, offering a renewal of his old position. They also receive telegrams from old friends urging Charley to come back to London. He gives in, and they all move to London to study music.

In his essay "Three Ways of Writing for Children" C. S. Lewis complains about the school stories that purport to be realistic but are in fact golden fantasies of the loner taken into the group, of the odd one out suddenly becoming the school hero. Barne's novel may certainly be faulted on such grounds. The ending is too expected, too happy to consider this as a pioneering work of realism. The fantasy comes true for the children and the reader; what they had hoped for all along, and what seemed so unattainable, is attained through an astonishing series of coincidences.

This is not to say that the child reader is necessarily annoyed by the ending. The reader identifying principally with the protagonist Becky has hoped all along for the fulfillment of the dreams. The city of Preston, the alternative to London and the place of secretaries and accountants, always remains invisible and menacing; it is a place to which Father disappears and that makes him tired. The reader is pleased that they are all happily heading to London. But a happy ending is not necessarily a realistic ending.

Perhaps most masterful in this novel is Barne's deft handling of character, done principally through dialogue. Each of the four children, though tied together by their love of music, is individualized. Scrap is the headstrong show-off likely to break down into tears when she finds that she is not what she had hoped. Jinks is the silent boy who loves all things slimy and reptilian, but who also loves song (this not to be admitted, though). Jimmy is the older child burning with a sense of the music in him, while Becky, from whose perspective the narrative most often proceeds, is awakening to her own potential.

A similar characterization lies at the heart of *She Shall Have Music* (1938), a title whose assertiveness suggests the plot situation of the novel: young Karen is musical but must find some means to train and fulfill her talent. Like *In the Same Boat,* this story covers a long period of time in a child's life – seven years. And like *Musical Honours* this novel depicts the tyranny of musical talent: it must come out. But the weakness in this novel is, once again, its failure to resolve problems realistically. This is a poor family, strapped for cash, and so they cannot hope to find a piano for Karen. But pianos seem to pop up all over in her small town, so that no matter where she goes – even on summer holidays – there is a piano to play. The family is always receiving mysterious gifts – pocket money for school, trips to India – from unlikely sources such as forgotten godparents. Karen receives free lessons, the money for professional lessons, and even a piano. In the end she wins – inevitably, it seems – a musical scholarship in London. The problem of fulfilling a musical talent is certainly a realistic one, but Barne's resolutions are as fanciful as Aladdin's carpet.

Yet once again there is indeed the satisfaction of a completeness to the novel. Barne is not Robert Cormier or Katherine Paterson; she will leave nothing incomplete or ambiguous. Hers is a world in which endings are secure and satisfying. Her characters know where they are headed, what their professions will be, how they will put the next meal on the table, and what they will wear to tea. Given the insecure world in which these books were written, perhaps it is not hard to understand the appeal of Barne's conclusions.

Where Barne is able to develop a strong plot situation, she is more successful; where she is dependent upon character alone, she is often forgettable. *Family Footlights,* for example, depends upon the weak plot line of a family putting on a play. The characters do not evolve and depend upon others to make their play successful. The slim plot line without dynamic characters makes for a long and uninteresting novel. But when Barne takes similar children and puts them in the middle of a mystery, she can generate some suspense. *Dusty's Windmill* (1949), for example, places two of the Farrar children (actually relatives of the children in *Family Footlights*) in the middle of a smuggling operation and a threat to a miller's windmill that they are eager to preserve. Here the characters are no sharper than those of *Family Footlights,* but the plot is compelling. While they are figuring out the machinations of the art smugglers, they are also figuring out how to prevent the sale of the windmill. Both plot situations come together when the smugglers turn out to be the ones trying to buy the windmill. The reward the children get for their detective work funds the repairs to the mill and ensures that it will stay in the family. The lack of a strong plot is again evident in *Roly's Dogs* (1950), the sequel to *Dusty's Windmill,* in which the same cast of characters trains sets of dogs and cats for stage and screen.

Barne's nonfiction works for children focus on music, as do so many of her novels. Her three introductory books on George Frideric Handel, Wolfgang Amadeus Mozart, and Franz Schubert are marked by a fine sense of detail meshed into an apparent overall pattern. Beginning with early family life, Barne proceeds to an examination of the composers' lives by centering them principally in a geographic setting more than in their music. In *Introducing Handel* (1955), for example, Barne pictures a man driven to succeed commercially, writing opera after opera and being thwarted by persons and natural calamities and turns of societal taste. Barne centers the book in London, which becomes a way of organizing his interests and activities.

If these works can be faulted, it is in an astonishing lack: though Barne mentions many musical titles, she seems unable to suggest textually the qualities of musical pieces. She can claim that Handel's "Harmonious Blacksmith" is one of the "world's best-loved classics," but she seems unable to suggest what there is in the music itself that leads to that. She can call Mozart's "Cosi fan tutte" "gay, absurd, amusing," but again seems unable to say what there is in the music itself to suggest these qualities.

Her most successful biography is *Elizabeth Fry: A Story Biography* (1950), written in a series titled Story Biographies, published by Methuen. (It is a series with an imposing list of authors, including

Geoffrey Trease and Roger Lancelyn Green.) Though parts of the biography develop through fictionalized dialogue and invention, most comes through the words of Elizabeth and her sisters, recorded in diaries and letters. Focusing on the activities of the prison reformer allows Barne to depict the world of London in all its filth, as well as to describe the unwarranted prejudice against the Quakers. What is most masterful in the biography is the balancing of Napoleon's international adventures, where death and conquest are all-important, with those domestic adventures of Elizabeth, whose healing hand brings reason and peace.

Well before the three musical biographies, Barne wrote a more general introduction for the young reader, *Listening to the Orchestra* (1941). This work, she writes in her preface, "is an offering to the more humble music lover; to the infrequent concert goer who knows nothing of music except his joy in it." Barnes suggests her strong belief in the power of music, which can produce undiluted joy, even without intellectual understanding on the part of the listener. (This belief is in fact the genesis of such characters as Karen in *She Shall Have Music* and Becky in *Musical Honours*.) She goes on to suggest, however, that greater enjoyment comes with greater understanding. And so she moves through the in-struments of the orchestra, and then into a general history of music and composers, including Handel, Mozart, and Schubert.

In the same way that her novels set during the war celebrate the normalcy of British life, so does *Listening to the Orchestra* suggest Barne's affirmation of the importance of continuing the arts even under the most difficult of circumstances. This book was published in 1941, one of the darkest years of World War II for Britain, but it seems to echo the brave speeches Winston Churchill was making in that same year, proclaiming the indomitable spirit of an embattled people. "It is to the symphony, great music without the encumbrance of words or the distraction of the human voice," writes Barne, "that the music-lover looks for the expression of the eternal truths above the din and smoke of the martyred earth."

It may well be that Barne's greatest contribution to children's literature is not her Carnegie Medal–winning novel or her attention to realistic conflicts. It may be her ability to take the most dreadful, calamitous atmospheres and pit against them the secure, safe worlds of loving families and music and tea by the fire in cozy chairs. In Barne's fictional world, the safe and comfortable world comes out on top.

Pauline Baynes

(9 September 1922 –   )

Wayne G. Hammond
Chapin Library, Williams College

BOOKS: *Victoria and the Golden Bird* (London: Blackie, 1948);

How Dog Began (London: Methuen, 1985; New York: Holt, 1987);

The Song of the Three Holy Children (London: Methuen, 1986; New York: Holt, 1986);

Good King Wenceslas (Cambridge: Lutterworth, 1987);

Noah and the Ark (London: Methuen, 1988; New York: Holt, 1988);

In the Beginning (London: Dent, 1990); republished as *Let There Be Light* (New York: Macmillan, 1991);

Thanks Be to God: Prayers from around the World (Cambridge: Lutterworth, 1990; New York: Macmillan, 1990).

SELECTED BOOKS ILLUSTRATED: Princess de Beaumont, *Beauty and the Beast* (London: Perry, circa 1942);

Hans Christian Andersen, *The Emperor's Nightingale* (London: Perry, circa 1942);

The Magic Flute (London: Perry, circa 1942);

Mythical Monsters (London: Perry, circa 1942);

Wild Flower Rhymes (London: Perry, circa 1942);

Oscar Wilde, *The Remarkable Rocket* (London: Perry, circa 1942);

Victoria Stevenson, *Clover Magic* (London: Country Life, 1944);

Stevenson, *Magic Footstool* (London: Country Life, 1946);

J. R. R. Tolkien, *Farmer Giles of Ham* (London: Allen & Unwin, 1949; Boston: Houghton Mifflin, 1950);

C. S. Lewis, *The Lion, the Witch and the Wardrobe* (London: Bles, 1950; New York: Macmillan,

1950); republished with new color illustrations (London: HarperCollins, 1991);

Stevenson, *The Magic Broom* (London: Country Life, 1950);

W. G. Bebbington, *And It Came to Pass: Stories from the Bible Selected and Arranged to be Read as Literature* (London: Allen & Unwin, 1951);

Lewis, *Prince Caspian* (London: Bles, 1951; New York: Macmillan, 1951);

E. G. Hume, *Days before History* (London: Blackie, 1952);

Lewis, *The Voyage of the "Dawn Treader"* (London: Bles, 1952; New York: Macmillan, 1952);

Hume, *Children through the Ages* (London: Blackie, 1953);

Lewis, *The Silver Chair* (London: Bles, 1953; New York: Macmillan, 1953);

Marjorie Phillips, *Annabel and Bryony* (Oxford: Oxford University Press, 1953);

Henri Pourrat, *A Treasury of French Tales,* translated by Mary Mian (London: Allen & Unwin, 1953; Boston: Houghton Mifflin, 1954);

Albert Hitchcock and Louisa J. Hitchcock, *Great People through the Ages* (London: Blackie, 1954);

Lewis, *The Horse and His Boy* (London: Bles, 1954; New York: Macmillan, 1954);

The Arabian Nights: Aladdin, Sindbad, Ali Baba (London: Blackie, circa 1955);

Hitchcock and Hitchcock, *The British People* (London: Blackie, 1955);

Lewis, *The Magician's Nephew* (London: Bodley Head, 1955; New York: Macmillan, 1955);

Emmeline Garnett, *The Civil War, 1640–1660* (London: Black, 1956);

Garnett, *Queen Anne and Her Times, 1700–1730* (London: Black, 1956);

Pauline Baynes

Garnett, *The Tudors, 1540–1560* (London: Black, 1956);

David Harvey, *Dragon Smoke and Magic Song* (London: Allen & Unwin, 1956);

Lewis, *The Last Battle* (London: Bodley Head, 1956; New York: Macmillan, 1956);

Rhoda D. Power, *From the Fury of the Northmen* (Boston: Houghton Mifflin, 1957);

Amabel Williams-Ellis, *The Arabian Nights* (London: Blackie, 1957; New York: Criterion, 1958); republished in 2 volumes as *The Story of Ali Baba and the Forty Thieves and More Tales from the Arabian Nights* and *The Story of Sindbad, Aladdin, and Other Tales from the Arabian Nights* (New York: Bedrick/Blackie, 1986);

Monica Backway, *Hassan of Basorah* (London: Blackie, 1958);

Joan Mary Bate, *The Curious Tale of Cloud City* (London: Blackie, 1958);

Enid Margaret Denton, *Stars and Candles: A Book about Prayer for Children* (London: Benn, 1958);

Roger Lancelyn Green, *The Tale of Troy* (Harmondsworth: Puffin, 1958);

Robert H. Hawkins, *Primary English Practice* (London: Longmans, Green, 1958);

Anne Malcolmson, *Miracle Plays: Seven Medieval Plays for Modern Players* (Boston: Houghton Mifflin, 1959);

Kenneth Nuttall, *Let's Act* (London: Longmans, Green, 1959–1960);

Loretta Burrough, *Sister Clare* (Boston: Houghton Mifflin, 1960);

Lewis Carroll, *Alice in Wonderland and Through the Looking-glass* (London: Blackie, circa 1960);

Miguel de Cervantes, *Don Quixote: Some of His Adventures,* adapted by Mary Cathcart Borer (London: Longmans, Green, 1960);

Dorothy Ensor, *The Adventures of Hatim Tai* (London: Harrop, 1960; New York: Walck, 1962);

A. G. Hughes, *Ali Baba and Aladdin* (London: Longmans, Green, 1960);

Williams-Ellis, *Fairy Tales from the British Isles* (London: Blackie, 1960; New York: Warne, 1964); republished in 2 volumes as *British Fairy Tales* and *More Fairy Tales from the British Isles* (Glasgow: Blackie, 1976);

G. M. Hickman and R. Elizabeth Mayo, *Adventure Begins at Home* (London: Blackie, 1961);

James Morris, *The Upstairs Donkey and Other Stolen Stories* (New York: Pantheon, 1961; London: Faber & Faber, 1962);

Lynette R. Muir, *The Unicorn Window* (London: Schuman, 1961);

Tolkien, *The Adventures of Tom Bombadil and Other Verses from the Red Book* (London: Allen & Unwin, 1962; Boston: Houghton Mifflin, 1962);

Alison Uttley, *The Little Knife Who Did All the Work* (London: Faber & Faber, 1962);

Hickman and Mayo, *Adventuring Abroad* (London: Blackie, 1963);

The Puffin Book of Nursery Rhymes, edited by Iona and Peter Opie (Harmondsworth: Puffin, 1963); republished as *A Family Book of Nursery Rhymes* (New York: Oxford University Press, 1964);

Sandol Stoddard Warburg, *Saint George and the Dragon* (Boston: Houghton Mifflin, 1963);

Robin Allan, *Come into My Castle* (London: Macmillan, 1964; New York: St. Martin's Press, 1964);

K. G. Lethbridge, *The Rout of the Ollafubs* (London: Faber & Faber, 1964);

Borer, *Boadicea* (London: Longmans, Green, 1965);

Borer, *Christopher Columbus* (London: Longmans, Green, 1965);

Borer, *Joan of Arc* (London: Longmans, Green, 1965);

Borer, *King Alfred the Great* (London: Longmans, Green, 1965);

Abigail Homans, *Education by Uncles* (Boston: Houghton Mifflin, 1965);

Radost Pridham, *A Gift from the Heart: Folk Tales from Bulgaria* (London: Methuen, 1965; Cleveland: World, 1967);

Tolkien, *Smith of Wootton Major* (London: Allen & Unwin, 1967; Boston: Houghton Mifflin, 1967);

Grant Uden, *A Dictionary of Chivalry* (London: Longmans, Young, 1968; New York: Crowell, 1968);

Jennifer Westwood, *Medieval Tales* (London: Hart-Davis, 1968; New York: Coward-McCann, 1968);

Joseph Wood Krutch, *The Most Wonderful Animals That Never Were* (Boston: Houghton Mifflin, 1969);

R. D. Blackmore, *Lorna Doone,* abridged by Olive Jones (London: Collins, 1970; Middletown, Conn.: American Education Publications, 1970);

Naomi Mitchison, *Graeme and the Dragon* (London: Combridge, 1970);

Westwood, *The Isle of Grammarye: An Anthology of the Poetry of Magic* (London: Hart-Davis, 1970);

Leonard Clark, *All Along Down Along: A Book of Stories in Verse* (London: Longman, Young, 1971);

Constance B. Hieatt, *The Joy of the Court* (New York: Crowell, 1971);

Westwood, *Tales and Legends* (London: Hart-Davis, 1971; New York: Coward, McCann & Geoghegan, 1971);

Andersen, *Stories from Hans Christian Andersen,* selected by Philippa Pearce (London: Collins, 1972);

Hickman and Mayo, *Adventures in Towns* (London: Blackie, 1972);

Helen Piers, *Snail and Caterpillar* (London: Longman, Young, 1972; New York: American Heritage Press, 1972);

Enid Blyton, *The Land of Far-Beyond* (London: Methuen, 1973);

John Symonds, *Harold: The Story of a Friendship* (London: Dent, 1973);

The Butterfly, adapted from the text by Claude Nicolas (Edinburgh: Chambers, 1974);

The Frog, adapted from the text by Nicolas (Edinburgh: Chambers, 1974);

The Duck, adapted from the text by Nicolas (Edinburgh: Chambers, 1975);

Piers, *Grasshopper and Butterfly* (Harmondsworth: Kestrel, 1975; New York: McGraw-Hill, 1975);

Geoffrey Squire, *The Observer's Book of European Costume* (London: Warne, 1975);

The Bee and the Cherry Tree, adapted from the text by Nicolas (Edinburgh: Chambers, 1976);

The Salmon, adapted from the text by Nicolas (Edinburgh: Chambers, 1976);

The Dolphin, adapted from the text by Nicolas (Edinburgh: Chambers, 1977);

The Roe Deer, adapted from the text by Nicolas (Edinburgh: Chambers, 1977);

Richard W. Barber, *A Companion to World Mythology* (Harmondsworth: Kestrel, 1979; New York: Delacorte, 1980);

Eileen Hunter, *Tales of Waybeyond* (London: Deutsch, 1979);

Tolkien, *Poems and Stories* (London: Allen & Unwin, 1980);

Rumer Godden, *The Dragon of Og* (London: Macmillan, 1981; New York: Viking, 1981);

Rosemary Harris, *The Enchanted Horse* (Harmondsworth: Kestrel, 1981);

Piers, *Frog and Water Shrew* (Harmondsworth: Kestrel, 1981);

Mary Norton, *The Borrowers Avenged* (Harmondsworth: Kestrel, 1982);

Peter Dickinson, *The Iron Lion* (London: Blackie, 1983; New York: Bedrick/Blackie, 1983);

Godden, *Four Dolls* (London: Macmillan, 1983; New York: Greenwillow, 1983);

Rudyard Kipling, *How the Whale Got His Throat* (London: Macmillan, 1983; New York: Bedrick, 1987);

Anthea Peppin, *The National Gallery Children's Book* (London: National Gallery, 1983);

Anna Sewell, *Black Beauty* (Harmondsworth: Puffin, 1984);

Ursula Moray Williams, *The Further Adventures of Gobbolino and the Little Wooden Horse* (Harmondsworth: Puffin, 1984);

Cecil Frances Alexander, *All Things Bright and Beautiful* (Cambridge: Lutterworth, 1986);

George Macbeth, *The Story of Daniel* (Cambridge: Lutterworth, 1986);

Beatrix Potter, *Country Tales* (London: Warne, 1987);

Potter, *Wag-by-Wall* (London: Warne, 1987);

Rosemary Harris, *Love & the Merry-Go-Round* (London: Hamilton, 1988);

Harris, *Colm of the Islands* (London: Walker, 1989);

Jenny Koralek, *The Cobweb Curtain: A Christmas Story* (London: Methuen, 1989; New York: Holt, 1989);

Brian Sibley, *The Land of Narnia* (London: Collins, 1989; New York: Harper & Row, 1990);

Sibley, *The Magical World of Narnia* (London: Collins, 1990);

Tolkien, *Bilbo's Last Song* (London: Unwin Hyman, 1990; Boston: Houghton Mifflin, 1990);

Margaret Greaves, *The Naming* (London: Dent, 1992; San Diego: Harcourt Brace Jovanovich, 1993);

Lewis, *A Book of Narnians: The Lion, the Witch and the Others,* text compiled by James Riordan (London: Collins, 1994).

Pauline Baynes has had a long and distinguished, if largely unheralded, career. She is widely known only for her definitive illustrations for the Chronicles of Narnia by C. S. Lewis and for several works by J. R. R. Tolkien; in fact, she is a prolific artist who has produced hundreds of book and magazine illustrations, book covers, bookplates, posters, Christmas cards, advertising art – even designs for embroideries and biscuit tins. She has accepted a wide variety of commissions to earn a living.

Among these, children's books have been the most frequent, though she has never been particularly an illustrator for children and considers herself to be foremost a decorator and designer.

Pauline Baynes was born on 9 September 1922 in Brighton, one of two daughters of Frederic William Wilberforce Baynes and Jessie Harriet Maud Cunningham Baynes. Her earliest years were spent in India, where her father was in the civil service, but in the late 1920s she returned to England with her mother and sister. From the age of five she boarded in a convent school and then in the Beaufront School, Camberley. At age fifteen she attended the Farnham (Surrey) School of Art, where she concentrated on design. At sixteen she spent two terms at the Slade School of Art (then in Oxford), which her sister, Angela, also attended. This was her only formal art training, which she gave up to concentrate on war work.

In World War II Farnham Castle served as the Camouflage Development and Training Centre of the Royal Engineers. Both Baynes sisters were sent there in 1940 by the Women's Voluntary Service to be assistant model makers. Other people with artistic skills or backgrounds in art were there, among them Powell Perry, a flamboyant corporal whose family owned a printing firm in London. Perry organized some of the center artists to illustrate books for him, and thus Pauline Baynes received her first commission, a paperback titled *Question Mark* (which today unfortunately cannot be located). She followed this with art for the fairy tales *Beauty and the Beast, The Emperor's Nightingale,* and Oscar Wilde's *The Remarkable Rocket,* among other tales, in the Perry Colour Books, a series analogous to Noel Carrington's Puffin Picture Books for Penguin. Baynes recalls her work for Perry, executed in black and colored inks at night or on weekends, as abysmal in quality, but it shows an early flair for color and decoration and is not without charm. She illustrated for Perry even after she left the center in 1942 to draw charts for the Admiralty Hydrographic Department in Bath.

"I've had a charmed life," she remarked in a 1973 article; and though in truth it has been founded firmly on talent and hard work, her early career benefited from strokes of luck. A drawing in the margin of a letter to author Harry Price was shown by chance to Frank Whittaker of Country Life and led to a commission to illustrate three children's books by Victoria Stevenson. In the first two, *Clover Magic* (1944) and *Magic Footstool* (1946), Baynes's pen drawings are imaginative and vigorous in execution but reveal a weak knowledge of

Illustration by Baynes from "Thumbelina" in Stories from Hans Christian Andersen *(1972)*

anatomy (a result of her interrupted art education). By the third Stevenson volume, *The Magic Broom* (1950), however, she had improved her technique. In the interim she illustrated a book she had written, *Victoria and the Golden Bird* (1948), the story of a girl carried around the world by a great bird to visit children of many lands. The book contains splendid painted double-page spreads, flat in modeling but animated and colorful.

Baynes's good fortune continued in 1948 when a portfolio she had left with the London publisher George Allen and Unwin came to the attention of Tolkien, author of *The Hobbit* (1937). The artist originally hired to illustrate Tolkien's mock-medieval story *Farmer Giles of Ham* (1949) had been found unsuitable for the job, and Tolkien was shown the work of new candidates. He was impressed by several comical ink-and-watercolor cartoons Baynes had drawn after medieval manuscript decorations, and Baynes was commissioned for the job. In a short time she produced, without preliminary roughs, the required pen-and-ink drawings and three-color plates, derived in style from medieval manuscripts but with a touch of the Italian Renaissance in their fluid lines. Tolkien found her drawings to be in such perfect accord with his text that he declared in a letter to his publisher dated 16 March 1949 that "they are more than illustrations, they are a collateral theme." For the reprint of *Farmer Giles of Ham* in the Tolkien collection *Poems and Stories* (1980) Baynes redrew some of the illustrations,

added new pictures, and introduced a second color and gray tones. The original set of line drawings, however, cannot be improved, and though they date from early in Baynes's career while her skills were still developing, they are among the most effective examples of her work in black and white — in some ways they are typical of much of her work: decorative as well as illustrative, playful yet dignified, and meticulously drawn with flowing, rhythmic lines that suggest movement and life.

Her drawings for *Farmer Giles of Ham* won the admiration of Tolkien's friend Lewis, who had written a Christian fantasy for children but had neither the time nor the skill to illustrate it. Baynes was commissioned, and *The Lion, the Witch and the Wardrobe* appeared with her pictures in 1950. It proved the first of a hugely popular series of books by Lewis, the Chronicles of Narnia. The remaining six volumes, each illustrated by Baynes, followed at yearly intervals: *Prince Caspian* (1951), *The Voyage of the "Dawn Treader"* (1952), *The Silver Chair* (1953), *The Horse and His Boy* (1954), *The Magician's Nephew* (1955), and *The Last Battle* (1956). Author and artist shared an enthusiasm for Narnia, the fantasy world invented by Lewis, with its child heroes and heroines, talking animals, and creatures out of myth and legend.

Nevertheless, Lewis had distinct tastes in art and was never entirely satisfied with Baynes's work. He felt, for example, that the children's faces in *The Lion, the Witch and the Wardrobe* were plain and asked Baynes to "pretty them up." Privately he thought that she could not draw lions – a disadvantage for books in which the Christ figure Aslan appears as the king of beasts – but he found his artist too sensitive and shy to accept too much criticism, and perhaps he was aware of how much her pictures added to the appreciation of his texts. In fact, as the series progressed Baynes's skills improved, and her pen drawings became more ambitious, with added texture and detail. Unfortunately, current editions of the Chronicles of Narnia do not show Baynes's art at its best, the images having deteriorated through many printings. Nor do later editions include all of her pictures, omitting, for example, wash drawings made for *The Horse and His Boy,* which Lewis admired.

The Narnia books stand out among Baynes's work of the 1950s, which also includes illustrations for leading magazines such as the *Illustrated London News* and for many history books, another Baynes specialty, requiring extensive research. Her best work of the 1950s, however, is the set of sixty-four pen-and-ink head- and tailpieces and full-page pen-and-crayon plates she made for Henri Pourrat's *A Treasury of French Tales* (1953). These illustrations exhibit a decorative baroque style with great imagination and wit: for example, the headpiece to "The Tale of the Dead Man Who Was Warm" encloses a picture of the story's traveling doctor in his dogcart within a frame of forbidding twisted branches, festooned with icicles like thorns and surmounted by a skull wearing a fur hat. In style and technique the illustrations recall the work of Rex Whistler, whose art Baynes admires.

By 1960 Baynes was well established as an illustrator of fairy tales and fantasy. During the course of the year were published *Ali Baba and Aladdin* by A. G. Hughes, the third selection from the *Arabian Nights* to be illustrated by Baynes; *Fairy Tales from the British Isles* by Amabel Williams-Ellis, also with Baynes's art; and Dorothy Ensor's adaptation of the Persian story *The Adventures of Hatim Tai* with five color plates by Baynes. The latter is an especially striking example of the orientalism in which Baynes too rarely delights. In this work she was inspired by Persian miniatures but used the technique of negative space popularized by art nouveau and limited the printed color palette to black, red, lavender, and pale green.

In 1963 appeared Baynes's most ambitious project to that date: two hundred illustrations interspersed like playful musical accompaniment throughout *The Puffin Book of Nursery Rhymes,* compiled by Iona and Peter Opie. A few of the pictures are in the

manner of woodcuts; others are more delicately drawn. Many, in concept or style and in their generally pastoral atmosphere, resemble wood-engraved vignettes by Thomas Bewick.

After *Farmer Giles of Ham,* Tolkien wanted Baynes to illustrate his *Lord of the Rings,* but that book grew too large and production too costly, and Baynes was excluded from the project. However, Baynes and her husband, Fritz Gasch, a former German prisoner-of-war whom she married in 1961, became close friends with Tolkien, and he found other work for her. He thought of his *Farmer Giles of Ham* artist when forming his verse collection *The Adventures of Tom Bombadil* (1962); the book's sixteen poems are enlivened by Baynes's illustrations: head- and tailpieces, marginal, and full-page illustrations, some with orange color added. Tolkien objected only to her large picture for "The Hoard" because of the way she drew a knight and because the dragon is facing the wrong way in its cave. Eighteen years later Baynes redrew this picture for *Poems and Stories* so that it conformed to Tolkien's wishes.

She also illustrated Tolkien's small book *Smith of Wootton Major* (1967). Like *Farmer Giles of Ham, Smith of Wootton Major* has a medieval flavor which is reflected in Baynes's illustrations. But unlike the earlier book, which is set in a disguised medieval Oxfordshire, this tale of a gifted blacksmith who visits the perilous realm of faerie is not tied to a historical period or to familiar geography. Baynes therefore rejected the pastiche of *Farmer Giles of Ham* in favor of stylized images of village, household, and woodland scenes that transcend time and space. Also, for the most part, she deliberately avoided humor in her drawings to suit the bittersweet story. In 1980 Baynes redrew all but one of her *Smith of Wootton Major* pictures for the reprint of the tale in *Poems and Stories* to accommodate a different format, and she added brown and orange colors. The later versions are successful but lack some of the charm of the black-and-white, small-format originals.

Baynes has often been commissioned to illustrate books with a setting or subject in medieval times, a period in which she feels very much at home. Among her best work in this vein (besides her illustrations for Tolkien) are three books by Jennifer Westwood, especially *Medieval Tales* (1968); Constance B. Hieatt's *The Joy of the Court* (1971), a retelling of the Arthurian story of Sir Erec; *Good King Wenceslas* (1987), the history behind the Christmas carol retold by Baynes with robust gouache illustrations, decorations, and borders; and, most notably, Grant Uden's *A Dictionary of Chivalry* (1968), for which Baynes was awarded the Kate Greenaway Medal. The latter work took the artist two years to complete and is a masterly achievement, including a wraparound painted jacket, endpapers in the style of brass rubbings illustrating knights and their dogs, a pen-drawn title spread depicting Saint George and the dragon, and nearly six hundred other illustrations printed in the margins, most in line or line and tone but more than one hundred painted in jewel-like colors. Pleasing to look at, they are also accurate and detailed, as much a work of scholarship as the text they complement. Equally impressive and well researched are nearly seven hundred illustrations, some two hundred in color, that Baynes produced for Richard W. Barber's *A Companion to World Mythology* (1979). These were drawn in a variety of art styles according to the country or culture whose mythology is described in the text. The layout of the book is similar to that of the Uden volume; unfortunately, the printer was given the wrong dimensions for the finished book, and some of Baynes's pictures are cropped at the fore edge.

Baynes's talent for close observation extends to nature, and nowhere is this better demonstrated than in the three books she has illustrated for Helen Piers: *Snail and Caterpillar* (1972), runner-up for the Kate Greenaway Medal; *Grasshopper and Butterfly* (1975); and *Frog and Water Shrew* (1981). Each of these books presents a poignant story of friendship told against a detailed natural background and is enhanced by Baynes's gouache paintings of flowers, trees, insects, and other flora and fauna of the countryside. Her familiarity with country scenes and ways has also served her well in illustrating books such as the final Borrowers novel by Mary Norton, *The Borrowers Avenged* (1982), and four stories by Beatrix Potter published as *Country Tales* (1987) and *Wag-by-Wall* (1987).

Baynes's illustrations for Rosemary Harris's *The Enchanted Horse* (1981) is a late but superior example of her oriental style. Baynes responded to the book, set in India, with illustrations in the manner of Mughal paintings. For the more fantastic aspects of the story, notably a demon with eleven arms and nine feet (after Shiva), later disguised as a giant tiger, she drew upon Indian mythology. Her paintings of opulent fabrics, upholstery, rugs, blankets, wall ornaments, and carved screens beautifully convey the flavor of the text and further demonstrate Baynes's remarkable talent for decoration.

How Dog Began (1985) combines Baynes's text about the first dog to be tamed with her most un-usual illustrations. Inspired by cave paintings, the pictures are black and gray against backgrounds resembling stone, with abstract, near-stick-figure humans alongside animals more realistically drawn. The grayness of the illustrations, unrelieved by rich blacks or stark whites, unfortunately dulls their impact and makes one wish for the color that many real cave paintings have. The pictures, however, perfectly suit the prehistoric setting of the text.

Baynes's earliest illustrations for religious subjects (besides Lewis's Narnia tales) appeared in *And It Came to Pass: Stories from the Bible Selected and Arranged to be Read as Literature,* by W. G. Bebbington (1951) – three otherwise unremarkable drawings in line. In recent years she has made a specialty of religious books illustrated in full color. In *All Things Bright and Beautiful* (1986) she adds to the song by Cecil Frances Alexander a parade of beasts, flowers, birds, fish, insects, and trees across painted double-page spreads; she also contributes a medieval scene, a landscape with an erupting volcano, and a picture of Victorian children at play in a pastoral setting. The book is a visual treat, with a diversity of creatures and plants to catch young eyes as well as a song to sing.

Bayne's *The Song of the Three Holy Children* (1986), one of her most beautiful books, is another delight to see. Its brightly colored pictures, inspired by paintings in a medieval Spanish Beatus manuscript and paired with a hymn from the Apocrypha, illustrate the whole of Nature praising the Lord. People, animals, angels, and even the hills (painted with eyes) look up, the trees and other green things of the earth reach heavenward, and lightning forks appear like hands raised in prayer. A third book illustrated by Baynes and published in 1986, George Macbeth's *The Story of Daniel,* is well designed and in places superbly drawn, especially in its scenes of Nebuchadnezzar's pyre; but the paintings often resemble cels from animated cartoons, and though in style they are appropriate to Macbeth's simple rhyming couplets, they are less substantive than most of Baynes's other work in color.

Baynes first illustrated the Bible story of Noah (in the form of a poem by John Heath-Stubbs) in *All Along Down Along* (1971), a collection by Leonard Clark. She was restricted in that work, however, to only six pages in small format, and her pictures of many beasts are uncomfortably cramped. In 1988 she made her own adaptation of *Noah and the Ark,* with text from the Revised Standard Version, in a landscape format and with an ample number of pages. Baynes makes the most of this space, from a

Baynes with her husband, Fritz, 1988 (photograph by Cathy Courtney)

title page depicting men at war to a final picture of Noah and his extended family beneath a rainbow. Between are lavish, unrestrained paintings that often break through their own borders and, especially in the procession of the animals boarding the ark, spill across the two-page spreads.

Baynes's *In the Beginning* (1990) turns to the first part of Genesis, and instead of depicting the destruction of life as in the story of Noah, it shows life's creation and celebrates its diversity in a series of sweeping gouache illustrations, including an endpaper panorama of people and beasts living in harmony with nature – the whole earth as Eden. In contrast Baynes's paintings for *Thanks Be to God* (1990), a collection of prayers from around the world, are less impressive; however, the book provides interesting examples of Baynes's work in traditional, oriental, and medieval styles.

Despite her focus on religious subjects, Baynes has continued to work on projects in the areas of fantasy and mythology. Harris's *Colm of the Islands* (1989) is the story of a young man who wants a quiet life but must rescue his friend Selva from giants and escape the enchantment of a sea princess in her underwater kingdom. It is a romantic tale with a wide canvas, and Baynes rose to the occasion

with splendid gouache illustrations of Hebrides landscapes and seascapes, above and beneath the ocean. Her water effects are particularly fine, with droplets splashing beyond the confines of pictures into the margins, and waves beautifully blue and green with white swirling foam. *Colm of the Islands* also gave Baynes another opportunity to depict fabulous creatures, a talent she had demonstrated in the *Companion to World Mythology* and in earlier books such as Joseph Wood Krutch's *The Most Wonderful Animals That Never Were* (1969) and Rumer Godden's *The Dragon of Og* (1981).

Though production costs prevented Baynes from illustrating Tolkien's *Lord of the Rings,* she painted a fine triptych for the slipcase of the deluxe edition (1968) and two decorated maps of Middle-earth (the invented world of *The Hobbit* and *The Lord of the Rings*) which had wide circulation as posters. In 1990 she illustrated part of the final chapter of *The Lord of the Rings* for *Bilbo's Last Song,* the book version of a poem by Tolkien, first illustrated by Baynes as a poster in 1974. The book also includes, parallel to the main illustrations, paintings of the hobbit Bilbo sleepily recalling his life, and a third series of pictures by Baynes that depicts the story of *The Hobbit.*

In addition, Baynes has continued her association with the Narnia books long after the death of Lewis in 1963. She painted new cover illustrations for reprints of the Chronicles of Narnia, notably for the original Puffin paperback editions (1959–1965); a Narnia poster map (1972); color plates for Brian Sibley's *The Land of Narnia* (1989), a book about Lewis; a superb set of paintings for a large-format edition of *The Lion, the Witch and the Wardrobe* (1991), most of which were also reproduced as a calendar; and illustrations for *A Book of Narnians* (1994), accompanying selections from Lewis's books. In 1993 she completed art for a Narnia bestiary.

In recent years Pauline Baynes has wondered if she should retire from illustration. She apologizes that her eyes are no longer good and that she cannot draw with as much detail. But though some of her latest work, particularly her rendering of human figures, shows a lessening of skill, her eye for detail is as good as ever; her sense of design remains one of the best among contemporary illustrators; and her pictures continue to convey a youthful exuberance.

References:

Susan Forsyth, "The Loneliness of the Children's Book Illustrator," *Times* (London), 17 October 1973, p. 14;

Walter Hooper, *Past Watchful Dragons: The Narnian Chronicles of C. S. Lewis* (London: Collier-Macmillan, 1979), pp. 73, 76–80, 107;

John Morris, "The Flattery of Imitation?: Perry Colour Books," *Penguin Collectors' Society Newsletter,* 31 (December 1988): 21–33;

Elaine Moss, "Pauline Baynes: Mistress of the Margin," *Signal,* 11 (May 1973): 88–93;

Nancy-Lou Patterson, "An Appreciation of Pauline Baynes," *Mythlore,* 7 (Autumn 1980): 1–3;

Dorothy Wood, "Pauline Baynes, Mapmaker," *Puffin Post,* 6, no. 2 (1972): 10–11.

Papers:

Original art by Pauline Baynes is held by the Marion E. Wade Center, Wheaton College, Wheaton, Illinois; the Kerlan Collection, University of Minnesota, Minneapolis; and the Bodleian Library, Oxford.

Margery Williams Bianco

(22 July 1881 – 4 September 1944)

Harry E. Eiss
Eastern Michigan University

BOOKS: *The Late Returning* (London: Heinemann, 1902; New York: Macmillan, 1902);

Spendthrift Summer (London: Heinemann, 1903);

The Price of Youth (London & New York: Macmillan, 1904);

The Bar (London: Methuen, 1906);

Paris, illustrated by Allan Stewart (London: Black, 1910);

The Thing in the Woods (London: Duckworth, 1913);

The Velveteen Rabbit; or, How Toys Become Real, illustrated by William Nicholson (London: Heinemann, 1922; New York: Doran, 1922);

Poor Cecco: The Wonderful Story of a Wonderful Wooden Dog Who Was the Jolliest Toy in the House Until He Went Out to Explore the World, illustrated by Arthur Rackham (London: Chatto & Windus, 1925; New York: Doran, 1925);

The Little Wooden Doll, illustrated by Pamela Bianco (New York: Macmillan, 1925);

The Apple Tree, illustrated by Boris Artzybasheff (London & New York: Doran, 1926);

The Skin Horse, illustrated by Pamela Bianco (London: Doran, 1927; New York: Doubleday, 1927);

The Adventures of Andy, illustrated by Leon Underwood (London & New York: Doran, 1927);

The Candlestick, illustrated by Ludovic Rodo (New York: Doubleday, Doran, 1929; London: Doran, 1929);

All About Pets, illustrated by Grace Gilkison (New York: Macmillan, 1929);

Out of the Night: A Mystery Comedy in Three Acts, by Bianco and Harold Hutchinson (New York: French, 1929);

The House That Grew Smaller, illustrated by Rachel Field (New York: Macmillan, 1931);

A Street of Little Shops, illustrated by Grace Paull (New York: Doubleday, Doran, 1932);

The Hurdy-Gurdy Man, illustrated by Robert Lawson (London & New York: Oxford University Press, 1933);

Margery Williams Bianco

More About Animals, illustrated by Helen Torrey (New York: Macmillan, 1934);

The Good Friends, illustrated by Paull (New York: Viking, 1934);

Green Grows the Garden, illustrated by Paull (New York: Macmillan, 1936);

Winterbound (New York: Viking, 1936);

Tales from a Finnish Tupu, by Bianco and James Cloyd Bowmann, illustrated by Laura Bannon (Chicago: Whitman, 1936);

Other People's Houses (New York: Viking, 1939);

Franzi and Gizi, by Bianco and Gisella Loeffler (New York: Messner, 1941);

Bright Morning, illustrated by Margaret Platt (New York: Viking, 1942; London: Collins, 1945);

Illustration "Summer Days" by William Nicholson from The Velveteen Rabbit; or, How Toys Become Real *(1922)*

Penny and the White Horse, illustrated by Marjory Collison (New York: Messner, 1942);

Forward, Commandos!, illustrated by Rafaello Busoni (New York: Viking, 1944; Redhill: Wells Gardner, Darton, 1947);

Herbert's Zoo and Other Favorite Stories, by Bianco and others, illustrated by Julian (New York: Simon & Schuster, 1949).

OTHER: Blaise Cendrars, *The African Saga,* translated by Bianco (New York: Payson & Clarke, 1927);

René Bazin, *Juniper Farm,* translated by Bianco (New York: Macmillan, 1928);

Cendrars, *Little Black Stories for Little White Children,* translated by Bianco (New York: Payson & Clarke, 1929);

Georges Oudard, *Four Cents an Acre: The Story of Louisiana under the French,* translated by Bianco (New York: Brewer & Warren, 1931);

Hans Aanrud, *Sidsel Longskirt and Solve Suntrap: Two Children of Norway,* translated by Bianco and Dagny Mortenson, illustrated by Ingri and

Edgar Parin d'Aulaire (Philadelphia: Winston, 1935);

Samivel, *Rufus the Fox,* translated by Bianco (New York: Harper, 1937);

"Our Youngest Critics," in *Writing and Criticism: A Book for Margery Bianco,* edited by Anne Carroll Moore and Bertha Mahony Miller (Boston: Horn Book, 1951), pp. 47–57;

"De La Mare," in *Writing and Criticism: A Book for Margery Bianco,* edited by Moore and Miller (Boston: Horn Book, 1951), pp. 67–77;

"Poor Cecco Was a Member of Our Family," in *Writing Books for Boys and Girls,* edited by Helen Ferris (Garden City, N.Y.: Doubleday, 1952).

In a 1925 essay, "Our Youngest Critics," Margery Williams Bianco claimed to derive great satisfaction in writing for children because they are both "deeply appreciative and highly critical." Although she wrote in several genres and for adolescent and adult audiences as well, her reputation rests almost completely on one book for children, *The Velveteen Rabbit; or How Toys Become Real* (1922), which celebrates the love and loyalty of a child for his stuffed rabbit and the idea that only through love can people become truly alive. Most of her other books, including *Winterbound* (1936), for which she received the Newbery Honor Medal, are seldom read.

Born in London on 22 July 1881, the younger of two daughters, Margery Williams was introduced to literature at an early age by her father, a barrister and distinguished classical scholar. He believed that children should learn to read early and then be allowed to follow their own course of reading until they were ten years old. Two years after her father's death in 1888, Williams moved with her family to New York and then to a farm in Pennsylvania. She attended a day school in Philadelphia in 1891 and then spent the next few years traveling back and forth between the United States and England, receiving little formal schooling. She attended the Convent School in Sharon Hill, Pennsylvania, from 1896 to 1898, the last schooling she received. She then resumed her travels between England and the United States.

Her first novel, *The Late Returning* (1902), which she had written at the age of seventeen, was published in 1902. It and her other early adult novels, *Spendthrift Summer* (1903) and *The Price of Youth* (1904), brought little attention from the critics. In 1904 she married Francesco Bianco, a graduate of the University of Turin, who eventually turned his love of books into a managerial job at the rare book department of Brentano's in Paris. The pair lived in London from 1904 to 1907, where they had two children, Cecco in 1905 and Pamela in 1906. They moved to Paris in 1907 and then back to London in 1911.

From 1914 to 1918 the Biancos lived in Turin, Italy, where Francesco served in the Italian army during World War I. In summer 1919, as the war came to an end, Margery discovered Walter de la Mare's poetry, which affected her greatly. Later she wrote her essay "De La Mare," in praise of de la Mare's ability to recapture the child's "clear and unspoiled vision" filled with the elements of "wonder and miracle," qualities in her own writing for which she has since been praised.

Her daughter Pamela began to gain some recognition as an illustrator, having her works exhibited at the Leicester Galleries in London in 1919 and then at the Anderson Galleries in New York in 1921. By 1921 the entire family had settled in the United States. One year later Margery Bianco's central work, *The Velveteen Rabbit; or How Toys Become Real,* was published.

Bianco claimed to have disliked everything she had written before this work and said that she had been looking for something different. She happened to think of cherished toys from her childhood and toys that her children had loved. These memories led to *The Velveteen Rabbit* (inspired by a toy rabbit named Tubby) and formed the basis for all of Bianco's subsequent stories. The book proved successful, aided by William Nicholson's skillful illustrations. In this work Bianco discovered the wonder and sense of the miraculous invoked by the works of de la Mare and expressed it through a simplicity and directness matching a child's worldview. In the story a velveteen rabbit, received by a young boy as a gift in his Christmas stocking, is initially forgotten but later dearly loved by the boy, so much so that the rabbit eventually becomes real in the boy's mind. When the well-worn rabbit is to be burned because of the boy's infectious illness, a fairy turns him into an actual rabbit so that he can leap, run, and come to look at the boy who first made him feel real.

The story's poignancy, and its fairy-tale quality, often compared to work by Hans Christian Andersen, keep *The Velveteen Rabbit* from becoming overly sentimental. The story's simple message of the importance of love has endeared it to several generations of readers. Although some modern critics believe the story veers too far into sentimentality and find aspects of it to be dated, the book is generally regarded as a classic of children's literature.

Poor Cecco: The Wonderful Story of a Wonderful Wooden Dog Who Was the Jolliest Toy in the House Until He Went Out to Explore the World (1925) is a tale derived from Bianco's memories of her three favorite childhood toys: Cecco, the wooden dog; Tubby, the rabbit; and Bulka, the plush dog. As a child Bianco had created imaginary personalities for the three toys, and she developed these basic personalities in the story of Cecco. The characters, who feel human emotion but are limited in movement by their physical composition, set off from the toy cupboard to see the world. They become lost, amid other adventures, and are mailed back from their wanderings, tied together like a parcel. Though it has received less attention than *The Velveteen Rabbit, Poor Cecco* has received more consistently positive reviews. Critics have commented on the strength of the story's characters and dramatic action.

Bianco's *The Little Wooden Doll* (1925), illustrated by her daughter, has received little attention perhaps because it is such a short book or perhaps because of flaws in the narrative. The story involves a doll that never loses hope of being loved by a child. After being rejected and abused by two insensitive children, the doll is restored by some

Illustration by Arthur Rackham from Poor Cecco: The Wonderful Story of a Wonderful Wooden Dog Who Was the Jolliest Toy in the House Until He Went Out to Explore the World *(1925)*

friendly mice and spiders. The mice take the doll to a third, more loving child. The doll's clothes are transformed, abruptly and without adequate explanation, leaving a troubling narrative gap.

Three other short works followed *The Little Wooden Doll. The Apple Tree* (1926) has the quality of parable about it. Two children, waiting for the arrival of Easter, meet a stranger under an apple tree. The man breathes life into a seemingly dead sparrow and then disappears. The children decide that he must be Easter. The story presents spiritual values in a beautiful, fairy-tale style. *The Adventures of Andy* (1927), featuring a wooden doll, are all pleasant, and the book has a good sense of humor. *The Skin Horse* (1927) is about a sick child's love for his ancient toy and relates how their mutual wish comes true on Christmas Eve.

Bianco's *All About Pets* (1929), a nonfiction work, has been praised for its honest, friendly, obviously loving presentation of how to live with and take care of pets. It was followed by *More About Animals* (1934), a collection of fourteen short stories.

The Good Friends (1934) is another extension of Bianco's animal books, this one obviously fantasy, filled with eccentric, endearing, talking animals.

Bianco wrote two other books during this period. *A Street of Little Shops* (1932) is a collection of vignettes exploring the private lives of nonsensical and lovable characters who live in the little shops along the sides of a busy little street. *The Hurdy-Gurdy Man* (1933), praised by reviewers for the excellent illustrations provided by Robert Lawson, relates how a hurdy-gurdy man brings his own form of fun, kindness, and understanding to a town too steeped in thrift and tidiness.

Bianco's *Winterbound* (1936), intended for an adolescent audience, was awarded a Newbery Honor Book Medal but has since received mixed reviews, and contemporary critics praise it – along with Bianco's *Other People's Houses* (1939) – more as a precursor of young adult novels than for any lasting literary value. The novel does, however, offer a strong female character. The sixteen-year-old Garry, one of four urban children wintering in rural Connecticut, demonstrates unusual enterprise and resourcefulness as she runs the household when the children's mother is unexpectedly called away for the winter. *Other People's Houses* shows a more confident telling of a young woman's life than did *Winterbound,* and the setting of class against class and poor against rich presents strong social commentary. It is all handled well and is neither too sentimental nor didactic.

Bianco produced a series of picture books in the early 1940s. *Franzi and Gizi* (1941), illustrated by Gisella Loeffler, is a humorous story about two little chubs who have a happy adventure in the woods, spending a great deal of time eating. *Bright Morning* (1942) is a depiction of a Victorian childhood and childhood innocence. Nothing dramatic occurs, but Chris (age eight) and Emmie (age five) capture the quality of early childhood, and the world of Victorian England is brought to life in the story. *Penny and the White Horse* (1942), illustrated by Marjory Collison, concerns the love of a child, Penny, for a white horse on a carousel, describing the child's joy of the merry-go-round and, as in earlier works, invoking a child's love for a nonhuman toy or animal. In her final book, *Forward, Commandos!* (1944), Bianco portrays the restless energy and playfulness of boys eight to ten years of age. The spirit is well captured, though there is little plot.

Bianco died on 4 September 1944, after an illness lasting only three days. Although some present-day critics consider Bianco's writing dated, many praise her storytelling abilities and her insight into the child's mind. Her writing is a product of a time when children's literature presented an ethos that many children and critics find unrealistic today, an ethos combining love, beauty, health, nature, God, family, truth, and the natural goodness of the child's worldview. In this sense her writing represents the end of an era. There is more to her work, however, for important insights are revealed through Bianco's acceptance of the aesthetic perceptions and imagination of a child.

Creating a story that children will like results from seeing the world from a child's perspective, and that is what Bianco was able to accomplish. The purity of her childlike vision is frequently praised by critics. She is often compared to Andersen for her skill as a prose stylist, combining humor,

charm, poignancy, and wisdom in clear stories. And though her work is sometimes seen as overly sentimental today, it is often praised for its honest presentation of the viewpoint of a child.

References:

Marcia Dalphin, "Hearts of Oak in the Toy Cupboard," *New York Tribune Books,* 11 October 1925, p. 6;

Anne Thaxter Eaton, "Unicorns and Common Creatures," in her *Reading with Children* (New York: Viking, 1940), pp. 97–118;

Anne Carroll Moore and Bertha Mahony Miller, eds., *Writing and Criticism: A Book for Margery Bianco* (Boston: Horn Book, 1951).

Enid Blyton

(11 August 1897 – 28 November 1968)

Peter Hunt
University of Wales

BOOKS: *Child Whispers* (London: Saville, 1922);
Real Fairies: Poems (London: Saville, 1923);
Responsive Singing Games (London: Saville, 1923);
The Enid Blyton Book of Fairies (London: Newnes, 1924);
Songs of Gladness (London: Saville, 1924);
The Zoo Book (London: Newnes, 1925);
The Enid Blyton Book of Bunnies (London: Newnes, 1925);
Reading Practice, 8 volumes, numbered 1–5, 8, 9, and 11 (London: Nelson, 1925–1926);
Silver and Gold (London: Nelson, 1925; New York: Nelson, 1928);
The Bird Book (London: Newnes, 1926);
The Book of Brownies, illustrated by Ernest Aris (London: Newnes, 1926); republished as *Brownie Tales* (London: Collins, 1964);
Tales Half Told (London: Nelson, 1926);
The Animal Book (London: Newnes, 1927);
A Book of Little Plays (London: Nelson, 1927);
The Play's the Thing (London: Home Library Book, 1927); republished as *Plays for Older children* and *Plays for Younger Children,* 2 volumes (London: Newnes, 1940);
Aesop's Fables, Retold (London: Nelson, 1928);
Let's Pretend (London: Nelson, 1928);
Old English Stories, Retold (London: Nelson, 1928);
Pinkity's Pranks and Other Nature Fairy Tales, Retold (London: Nelson, 1928);
Tales of Brer Rabbit, Retold (London: Nelson, 1928);
Nature Lessons (London: Evans, 1929);
Tarrydiddle Town (London: Nelson, 1929);
The Knights of the Round Table (London: Newnes, 1930);
Tales from the Arabian Nights (London: Newnes, 1930);
Tales of Ancient Greece (London: Newnes, 1930);
Tales of Robin Hood (London: Newnes, 1930);
Cheerio! A Book for Boys and Girls (London: Birn, 1933);
Five Minute Tales (London: Methuen, 1933);
Let's Read (London: Birn, 1933);

Enid Blyton

My First Reading Book (London: Birn, 1933);
Read to Us (London: Birn, 1933);
The Adventures of Odysseus. Stories from World History Retold (London: Evans, 1934);
The Enid Blyton Poetry Book: Ninety-Six Poems for the Twelve Months of the Year (London: Methuen, 1934);
The Old Thatch, First Series, 8 volumes (London: W. & A. K. Johnston, 1934–1935);
The Red Pixie Book (London: Newnes, 1934);
Round the Year with Enid Blyton, 4 volumes (London: Evans, 1934);

The Story of the Siege of Troy. Stories from World History Retold (London: Evans, 1934);

Tales of the Ancient Greeks and Persians. Stories from World History Retold (London: Evans, 1934);

Tales of the Romans. Stories from World History Retold (London: Evans, 1934);

Ten Minutes Tales: Twenty-Nine Varied Stories for Children (London: Methuen, 1934);

The Children's Garden (London: Newnes, 1935);

The Green Goblin (London: Newnes, 1935); abridged and republished as *Feefo, Tuppeny, and Jinks* (London: Staple Press, 1951);

Hedgerow Tales (London: Newnes, 1935);

Six Enid Blyton Plays (London: Methuen, 1935);

The Famous Jimmy (London: Muller, 1936; New York: Dutton, 1937);

Fifteen Minute Tales (London: Methuen, 1936);

The Yellow Fairy Book (London: Newnes, 1936);

Adventures of the Wishing Chair (London: Newnes, 1937);

The Adventures of Binkle and Flip (London: Newnes, 1938);

Billy-Bob Tales (London: Methuen, 1938);

Heyo, Brer Rabbit! Tales of Brer Rabbit and His Friends (London: Newnes, 1938);

Mr. Galliano's Circus (London: Newnes, 1938);

The Old Thatch, Second Series, 8 volumes (London: W. & A. K. Johnston, 1938);

The Secret Island (Oxford: Blackwell, 1938);

Boys' and Girls' Circus Book (London: News Chronicle, 1939);

Cameo Plays, Book 4, edited by George H. Holroyd (Leeds: Arnold, 1939);

The Enchanted Wood (London: Newnes, 1939);

How the Flowers Grow, and Other Musical Plays (Exeter: Wheaton, 1939);

Hurrah for the Circus! Being Further Adventures of Mr. Galliano and His Famous Circus (London: Newnes, 1939);

School Plays: Six Plays for Schools (Oxford: Blackwell, 1939);

The Wishing Bean and Other Plays (Oxford: Blackwell, 1939);

Naughty Amelia Jane! (London: Newnes, 1940);

Birds of Our Gardens (London: Newnes, 1940);

Boys' and Girls' Story Book (London: Newnes, 1940);

The Children of Cherry Tree Farm (London: Country Life, 1940);

Children of Kidillin, as Mary Pollock (London: Newnes, 1940);

The Little Tree House, Being the Adventures of Josie, Click and Bun (London: Newnes, 1940); republished as *Josie, Click, and Bun and the Little Tree House* (London: Newnes, 1951);

Mr. Meddle's Mischief (London: Newnes, 1940);

The Naughtiest Girl in the School (London: Newnes, 1940);

The News Chronicle Boys' and Girls' Book (London: News Chronicle, 1940);

The Secret of Spiggy Holes (Oxford: Blackwell, 1940);

Tales of Betsy-May (London: Methuen, 1940);

Three Boys and a Circus, as Mary Pollock (London: Newnes, 1940);

The Treasure Hunters (London: Newnes, 1940);

Twenty Minute Tales (London: Methuen, 1940);

The Adventures of Mr. Pink-Whistle (London: Newnes, 1941);

The Adventurous Four (London: Newnes, 1941);

The Babar Story Book (London: Methuen, 1941); abridged and republished as *Tales of Babar* (London: Methuen, 1942);

A Calendar for Children (London: Newnes, 1941);

Enid Blyton's Book of the Year (London: Evans, 1941);

Five O'Clock Tales (London: Methuen, 1941);

The Further Adventures of Josie, Click and Bun (London: Newnes, 1941);

The Secret Mountain (Oxford: Blackwell, 1941);

The Twins at St. Clare's (London: Methuen, 1941);

The Children and Willow Farm (London: Country Life, 1942);

Circus Days Again (London: Newnes, 1942);

Enid Blyton Happy Story Book (London: Hodder & Stoughton, 1942);

Enid Blyton Readers, Books 1–3, 3 volumes (London: Macmillan, 1942);

Enid Blyton's Little Books, 6 volumes (London: Evans, 1942);

Five on a Treasure Island (London: Hodder & Stoughton, 1942; New York: Crowell, 1950);

Hello, Mr. Twiddle (London: Newnes, 1942);

I'll Tell You a Story (London: Macmillan, 1942);

I'll Tell You Another Story (London: Macmillan, 1942);

John Jolly at Christmas Time (London: Evans, 1942);

Mary Mouse and the Doll's House (Leicester: Brockhampton Press, 1942);

More Adventures on Willow Farm (London: Country Life, 1942);

The Naughtiest Girl Again (London: Newnes, 1942);

The O'Sullivan Twins (London: Methuen, 1942);

Shadow, The Sheep Dog (London: Newnes, 1942);

Six O'Clock Tales: Thirty-Three Short Stories for Children (London: Methuen, 1942);

The Adventures of Scamp, as Mary Pollock (London: Newnes, 1943);

Bimbo and Topsy (London: Newnes, 1943);

The Children's Life of Christ (London: Methuen, 1943);

Blyton with her pupils at Southerhay, Surbiton, in 1919

Dame Slap and Her School (London: Newnes, 1943);

Five Go Adventuring Again (London: Hodder & Stoughton, 1943; New York: Crowell, 1951);

John Jolly by the Sea (London: Evans, 1943);

John Jolly on the Farm (London: Evans, 1943);

The Magic Faraway Tree (London: Newnes, 1943);

Merry Story Book (London: Hodder & Stoughton, 1943);

More Adventures of Mary Mouse (Leicester: Brockhampton Press, 1943);

The Mystery of the Burnt Cottage (London: Methuen, 1943; Los Angeles: McNaughton, 1946);

Polly Piglet (Leicester: Brockhampton Press, 1943);

The Secret of Killimooin (Oxford: Blackwell, 1943);

Seven O'Clock Tales: Thirty Short Stories for Children (London: Methuen, 1943);

Smuggler Ben, as Mary Pollock (London: Laurie, 1943);

Summer Term at St. Clare's (London: Methuen, 1943);

The Toys Come to Life (Leicester: Brockhampton Press, 1943);

At Appletree Farm (Leicester: Brockhampton Press, 1944);

Billy and Betty at the Seaside (Dundee: Valentine & Sons, 1944);

A Book of Naughty Children: The Mystery of the Disappearing Cat (London: Methuen, 1944); republished as *The Mystery of the Disappearing Cat* (London & Los Angeles: McNaughton, 1948);

The Boy Next Door (London: Newnes, 1944);

The Christmas Book (London: Macmillan, 1944);

Claudine at St. Clare's (London: Methuen, 1944);

Come to the Circus (Leicester: Brockhampton Press, 1944);

The Dog That Went to Fairyland (Leicester: Brockhampton Press, 1944);

Eight O'Clock Tales (London: Methuen, 1944);

Enid Blyton Readers. Books 4–6 (London: Macmillan, 1944);

Enid Blyton's Nature Lover's Book (London: Evans, 1944);

Five Run Away Together (London: Hodder & Stoughton, 1944; Chicago: Reilly & Lee, 1960);

The Island of Adventure (London: Macmillan, 1944); republished as *Mystery Island* (New York: Macmillan, 1945);

Jolly Little Jumbo (Leicester: Brockhampton Press, 1944);

Jolly Story Book (London: Hodder & Stoughton, 1944);

Little Mary Mouse Again (Leicester: Brockhampton Press, 1944);

The Mystery of the Disappearing Cat (London: Methuen, 1944);

Rainy Day Stories (London: Evans, 1944);

The Second Form at St. Clare's (London: Methuen, 1944);

Tales from the Bible (London: Methuen, 1944);

Tales of Toyland (London: Newnes, 1944);

The Three Golliwogs (London: Newnes, 1944);

The Blue Story Book (London: Methuen, 1945);

The Brown Family (London: News Chronicle, 1945);

The Caravan Family (London: Lutterworth, 1945);

The Conjuring Wizard and Other Stories (London: Macmillan, 1945);

Enid Blyton Nature Readers, 20 volumes (London: Macmillan, 1945);

The Family at Red Roofs (London: Lutterworth, 1945);

Fifth Formers at St. Clare's (London: Methuen, 1945);

The First Christmas (London: Methuen, 1945);

Five Go to Smuggler's Top (London: Hodder & Stoughton, 1945; Chicago: Reilley & Lee, 1960);

Hallo, Little Mary Mouse (Leicester: Brockhampton Press, 1945);

Hollow Tree House (London: Lutterworth, 1945);

John Jolly at the Circus (London: Evans, 1945);

The Mystery of the Secret Room (London: Methuen, 1945; Los Angeles: Parkwood Press, 1950);

The Naughtiest Girl Is a Monitor (London: Newnes, 1945);

Round the Clock Stories (London: National Magazine, 1945);

The Runaway Kitten (Leicester: Brockhampton Press, 1945);

Sunny Story Book (London: Hodder & Stoughton, 1945);

The Teddy Bear's Party (Leicester: Brockhampton Press, 1945);

The Twins Go to Nursery-Rhyme Land (Leicester: Brockhampton Press, 1945);

Amelia Jane Again (London: Newnes, 1946);

The Bad Little Monkey (Leicester: Brockhampton Press, 1946);

The Castle of Adventure (London & New York: Macmillan, 1946);

The Children at Happy House (Oxford: Blackwell, 1946);

Chimney Corner Stories (London: National Magazine, 1946);

The Enid Blyton Holiday Book, 12 volumes (London: Sampson Low, 1946–);

Enid Blyton Nature Readers, Volumes 21–30 (London: Macmillan, 1946);

First Term at Malory Towers (London: Methuen, 1946);

Five Go Off in a Caravan (London: Hodder & Stoughton, 1946);

The Folk of the Faraway Tree (London: Newnes, 1946);

Gay Story Book (London: Hodder & Stoughton, 1946);

Josie, Click and Bun Again (London: Macmillan, 1946);

The Little White Duck and Other Stories (London: Macmillan, 1946);

Mary Mouse and Her Family (Leicester: Brockhampton Press, 1946);

The Mystery of the Spiteful Letters (London: Methuen, 1946);

The Put-em-Rights (London: Lutterworth, 1946);

The Red Story Book (London: Methuen, 1946);

The Surprising Caravan (Leicester: Brockhampton Press, 1946);

Tales of Green Hedges (London: National Magazine, 1946);

The Train That Lost Its Way (Leicester: Brockhampton Press, 1946);

The Adventurous Four Again (London: Newnes, 1947);

At Seaside Cottage (Leicester: Brockhampton Press, 1947);

Before I Go to Sleep: A Book of Bible Stories and Prayers for Children at Night (London: Latimer House, 1947; Boston: Little, Brown, 1953);

Enid Blyton's Treasury (London: Evans, 1947);

Five on Kirrin Island Again (London: Hodder & Stoughton, 1947);

The Green Story Book (London: Methuen, 1947);

The Happy House Children Again (Oxford: Blackwell, 1947);

Here Comes Mary Mouse Again (Leicester: Brockhampton Press, 1947);

The House at the Corner (London: Lutterworth, 1947);

Jinky Nature Books, 4 volumes (Leeds: Arnold, 1947);

Little Green Duck and Other Stories (Leicester: Brockhampton Press, 1947);

Lucky Story Book (London: Hodder & Stoughton, 1947);

More about Josie, Click and Bun (London: Newnes, 1947);

The Mystery of the Missing Necklace (London: Methuen, 1947);

Rambles with Uncle Nat (London: National Magazine, 1947);

The "Saucy Jane" Family (London: Lutterworth, 1947);

A Second Book of Naughty Children: Twenty-Four Short Stories (London: Methuen, 1947);

The Second Form at Malory Towers (London: Methuen, 1947);

The Secret of Cliff Castle, as Mary Pollock (London: Laurie, 1947);

The Smith Family At Home (Leeds: Arnold, 1947);

The Smith Family At the Zoo (Leeds: Arnold, 1947);

The Smith Family At the Circus (Leeds: Arnold, 1947);

The Valley of Adventure (London & New York: Macmillan, 1947);

The Very Clever Rabbit (Leicester: Brockhampton Press, 1947);

The Adventures of Pip (London: Sampson Low, 1948);

The Boy with the Loaves and Fishes (London: Lutterworth, 1948; New York: Roy, 1958?);

Brer Rabbit and His Friends (London: Coker, 1948);

Brer Rabbit Book, 8 volumes (London: Latimer House, 1948);

Come to the Circus (London: Newnes, 1948);

Enid Blyton's Readers, Book 7 (London: Macmillan, 1948);

Enid Blyton's Bedtime Series, 2 volumes (Leicester: Brockhampton Press, 1948);

Five Go Off to Camp (London: Hodder & Stoughton, 1948); republished as *Five on the Track of a Spook Train* (New York: Atheneum, 1972);

How Do You Do, Mary Mouse (Leicester: Brockhampton Press, 1948);

Just Time for a Story (London: Macmillan, 1948; New York: St. Martin's Press, 1952);

Jolly Tales (London: Johnston, 1948);

Let's Garden (London: Latimer House, 1948);

Let's Have a Story (London: Pitkin, 1948);

The Little Girl at Capernaum (London: Lutterworth, 1948; New York: Roy, 1958?);

Mister Icy-Cold (Oxford: Blackwell, 1948);

More Adventures of Pip (London: Sampson Low, 1948);

The Mystery of the Hidden House (London: Methuen, 1948);

Nature Tales (London: Johnston, 1948);

Now for a Story (Newcastle upon Tyne: Hill, 1948);

The Red-Spotted Handkerchief and Other Stories (Leicester: Brockhampton Press, 1948);

The Sea of Adventure (London & New York: Macmillan, 1948);

The Secret of the Old Mill (Leicester: Brockhampton Press, 1948);

Six Cousins at Mistletoe Farm (London: Evans, 1948);

Tales after Tea (London: Laurie, 1948);

Tales of the Twins (Leicester: Brockhampton Press, 1948);

They Ran Away Together (Leicester: Brockhampton Press, 1948);

Third Year at Malory Towers (London: Methuen, 1948);

We Want a Story (London: Pitkin, 1948);

The Bluebell Story Book (London: Gifford, 1949);

Bumpy and His Bus (London: Newnes, 1949);

A Cat in Fairyland and Other Stories (London: Pitkin, 1949);

Chuff the Chimney Sweep and Other Stories (London: Pitkin, 1949);

The Circus Book (London: Latimer House, 1949);

The Dear Old Snow Man (Leicester: Brockhampton Press, 1949);

Don't Be Silly, Mr. Twiddle (London: Newnes, 1949);

The Enchanted Sea and Other Stories (London: Pitkin, 1949);

The Enid Blyton Bible Stories, Old Testament, 3 volumes (London: Macmillan, 1949);

Enid Blyton's Daffodil Story Book (London: Gifford, 1949);

Good Morning Book (London: National Magazine, 1949);

Five Get into Trouble (London: Hodder & Stoughton, 1949); republished as *Five Caught in a Treacherous Plot* (New York: Atheneum, 1972);

Humpty Dumpty and Belinda (London: Collins, 1949);

Jinky's Joke and Other Stories (Leicester: Brockhampton Press, 1949);

Little Noddy Goes to Toyland (London: Sampson Low, 1949);

Mr. Trumpy and His Caravan (London: Sampson Low, 1949);

The Mountain of Adventure (London & New York: Macmillan, 1949);

My Enid Blyton Bedside Book, 12 volumes (London: Barker, 1949);

The Mystery of the Pantomime Cat (London: Methuen, 1949);

Oh, What a Lovely Time (Leicester: Brockhampton Press, 1949);

The Enid Blyton Nature Plates, 3 volumes (London: Macmillan, 1949);

Robin Hood Book (London: Latimer House, 1949);

The Rockingdown Mystery (London: Collins, 1949);

The Secret Seven (Leicester: Brockhampton Press, 1949); republished as *The Secret Seven and the Mystery of the Empty House* (Chicago: Children's Press, 1972);

A Story Party at Green Hedges (London: Hodder & Stoughton, 1949);

The Strange Umbrella and Other Stories (London: Pitkin, 1949);

Tales After Supper (London: Laurie, 1949);

Those Dreadful Children (London: Lutterworth, 1949);

Tiny Tales (Worcester: Littlebury, 1949);

The Upper Fourth at Malory Towers (London: Methuen, 1949);

The Astonishing Ladder and Other Stories (London: Macmillan, 1950);

A Book of Magic (London: Coker, 1950);

Enid Blyton's Little Book No. 1, numbers 2 through 6 follow in series (London: Brockhampton, 1950);

The Enid Blyton Pennant Series, 30 parts (London: Macmillan, 1950);

Enid Blyton Readers, Books 10–12 (London: Macmillan, 1950);

Five Fall into Adventure (London: Hodder & Stoughton, 1950; New York: Atheneum, 1972);

Hurrah for Little Noddy (London: Sampson Low, 1950);

In the Fifth at Malory Towers (London: Methuen, 1950);

The Magic Knitting Needles and Other Stories (London: Macmillan, 1950);

Mister Meddle's Muddles (London: Newnes, 1950);

Mr. Pinkwhistle Interferes (London: Newnes, 1950);

The Mystery of the Invisible Thief (London: Methuen, 1950);

The Pole Star Family (London: Lutterworth, 1950);

The Poppy Story Book (London: Gifford, 1950);

The Rilloby Fair Mystery (London: Collins, 1950);

Round the Year with Enid Blyton (London: Evans, 1950);

Round the Year Stories (London: Coker, 1950);

Rubbalong Tales (London: Macmillan, 1950);

The Seaside Family (London: Lutterworth, 1950);

Secret Seven Adventure (Leicester: Brockhampton Press, 1950); republished as *The Secret Seven and the Circus Adventure* (Chicago: Children's Press, 1972);

The Ship of Adventure (London & New York: Macmillan, 1950);

Six Cousins Again (London: Evans, 1950);

Tales About Toys (Leicester: Brockhampton Press, 1950);

Blyton with her daughters, Gillian, left, and Imogen

The Three Naughty Children and Other Stories (London: Macmillan, 1950);

Tricky the Goblin and Other Stories (London: Macmillan, 1950);

We Do Love Mary Mouse (Leicester: Brockhampton Press, 1950);

Welcome Mary Mouse (Leicester: Brockhampton Press, 1950);

What an Adventure (Leicester: Brockhampton Press, 1950);

The Wishing Chair Again (London: Newnes, 1950);

The Yellow Story Book (London: Methuen, 1950);

Boody the Great Goblin and Other Stories (London: Pitkin, 1951);

The "Queen Elizabeth" Family (London: Lutterworth, 1951);

Benny and the Princess and Other Stories (London: Pitkin, 1951);

The Big Noddy Book (London: Sampson Low, 1951);

The Buttercup Farm Family (London: Lutterworth, 1951);

The Buttercup Story Book (London: Gifford, 1951);

Down at the Farm (London: Sampson Low, 1951);

Father Christmas and Belinda (London: Collins, 1951);

Five on a Hike Together (London: Hodder & Stoughton, 1951);

The Flying Goat and Other Stories (London: Pitkin, 1951);

Gay Street Book (London: Latimer, 1951);

Hello Twins (Leicester: Brockhampton Press, 1951);

Here Comes Noddy Again (London: Sampson Low, 1951);

Hurrah for Mary Mouse (Leicester: Brockhampton Press, 1951);

Last Term at Malory Towers (London: Methuen, 1951);

Let's Go to the Circus (London: Odhams, 1951);

The Little Spinning House and Other Stories (London: Pitkin, 1951);

The Magic Snow-Bird and Other Stories (London: Pitkin, 1951);

The Mystery of the Vanished Prince (London: Methuen, 1951);

Noddy and Big Ears Have a Picnic (London: Sampson Low, 1951);

Noddy and His Car (London: Sampson Low, 1951);

Noddy Has a Shock (London: Sampson Low, 1951);

Noddy Has More Adventures (London: Sampson Low, 1951);

Noddy Goes to the Seaside (London: Sampson Low, 1951);

Noddy Off to Rocking Horse Land (London: Sampson Low, 1951);

Noddy Painting Book (London: Sampson Low, 1951);

Noddy's House of Books, 6 volumes (London: Sampson Low, 1951);

A Picnic Party with Enid Blyton (London: Hodder & Stoughton, 1951);

Pippy and the Gnome and Other Stories (London: Pitkin, 1951);

A Prize for Mary Mouse (Leicester: Brockhampton Press, 1951);

The Proud Golliwog (Leicester: Brockhampton Press, 1951);

The Runaway Teddy Bear and Other Stories (London: Pitkin, 1951);

The Six Bad Boys (London: Lutterworth, 1951);

A Tale of Little Noddy (London: Sampson Low, 1951);

"Too-Wise" the Wonderful Wizard and Other Stories (London: Pitkin, 1951);

Up the Faraway Tree (London: Newnes, 1951);

Well Done, Secret Seven (Leicester: Brockhampton Press, 1951); republished as *The Secret Seven and the Tree House Adventure* (Chicago: Children's Press, 1972);

Bright Story Book (Leicester: Brockhampton Press, 1952);

The Children's Jolly Book, by Blyton, W. E. Johns, and others (London: Odhams, 1952);

The Circus of Adventure (London: Macmillan, 1952; New York: St. Martin's Press, 1953);

Come Along Twins (Leicester: Brockhampton Press, 1952);

The Enid Blyton Bible Stories: New Testament, 16 volumes (London: Macmillan, 1952–1953);

Enid Blyton Tiny Strip Books, first of a series (London: Sampson Low, 1952);

Enid Blyton's Animal Lover's Book (London: Evans, 1952);

Enid Blyton's Color Strip Book (London: Sampson Low, 1952);

Enid Blyton's Omnibus (London: Newnes, 1952);

Five Have a Wonderful Time (London: Hodder & Stoughton, 1952);

The Mad Teapot (Leicester: Brockhampton Press, 1952);

Mandy, Mops, and Cubby Find a House (London: Sampson Low, 1952);

Mandy, Mops, and Cubby Again (London: Sampson Low, 1952);

Mary Mouse and Her Bicycle (Leicester: Brockhampton Press, 1952);

Mr. Tumpy Plays a Trick on Saucepan (London: Sampson Low, 1952);

My First Enid Blyton Book (London: Latimer, 1952);

My First Nature Book (London: Macmillan, 1952);

The Mystery of the Strange Bundle (London: Methuen, 1952);

Noddy and Big Ears (London: Sampson Low, 1952);

Noddy and the Witch's Wand (London: Sampson Low, 1952);

Noddy's Colour Strip Book (London: Sampson Low, 1952);

Noddy Goes to School (London: Sampson Low, 1952);

Noddy's Ark of Books (London: Sampson Low, 1952);

Noddy's Car Gets a Squeak (London: Sampson Low, 1952);

Noddy's Penny Wheel Car (London: Sampson Low, 1952);

The Queer Adventure (London: Staples Press, 1952);

Reference Book to New Testament Bible Plates (London: Macmillan, 1952);

The Rubadub Mystery (London: Collins, 1952);

Secret Seven on the Trail (Leicester: Brockhampton Press, 1952); republished as *The Secret Seven and the Railroad Mystery* (Chicago: Children's Press, 1972);

Snowdrop Story Book (London: Gifford, 1952);

The Two Sillies and Other Stories Retold by Enid Blyton (London: Coker, 1952);

The Very Big Secret (London: Lutterworth, 1952);

Welcome Josie, Click and Bun (London: Newnes, 1952);

Well Done, Noddy (London: Sampson Low, 1952);

Clicky the Clockwise Clown (Leicester: Brockhampton Press, 1953);

The Enid Blyton Bible Stories, New Testament, 14 volumes (London: Macmillan, 1953);

Enid Blyton's Christmas Story (London: Hamish Hamilton, 1953);

Five Go Down to the Sea (London: Hodder & Stoughton, 1953; Chicago: Reilly & Lee, 1961);

Go Ahead Secret Seven (Leicester: Brockhampton Press, 1953); republished as *The Secret Seven Get Their Man* (Chicago: Children's Press, 1972);

Gobo and Mr. Fierce (London: Sampson Low, 1953);

Here Come the Twins (Leicester: Brockhampton Press, 1953);

Mandy Makes Cubby a Hat (London: Sampson Low, 1953);

Mary Mouse and the Noah's Ark (Leicester: Brockhampton Press, 1953);

Mr. Tumpy in the Land of Wishes (London: Sampson Low, 1953);

My Enid Blyton Story Book (London: Juvenile Productions, 1953);

The Mystery of Holly Lane (London: Methuen, 1953);

The New Big Noddy Book (London: Sampson Low, 1953);

New Noddy Colour Strip Book (London: Sampson Low, 1953);

Noddy and the Cuckoo's Nest (London: Sampson Low, 1953);

Noddy at the Seaside, illustrated by Van Beek (London: Sampson Low, 1953);

Noddy's Cut-Out Model Book (London: Sampson Low, 1953);

Noddy Gets Captured (London: Sampson Low, 1953);

Noddy Is Very Silly (London: Sampson Low, 1953);

Noddy's Garage of Books, 5 volumes (London: Sampson Low, 1953);

Playways Annual, by Blyton and others (London: Lutterworth, 1953);

The Secret of Moon Castle (Oxford: Blackwell, 1953);

Snowball the Pony (London: Lutterworth, 1953);

The Story of Our Queen (London: Muller, 1953);

Visitors in the Night (Leicester: Brockhampton Press, 1953);

Well Really Mr. Twiddle! (London: Newnes, 1953);

The Adventure of the Secret Necklace (London: Lutterworth, 1954);

The Castle Without a Door and Other Stories (London: Pitkin, 1954);

The Children at Green Meadows (London: Lutterworth, 1954);

Enid Blyton's Friendly Story Book (Leicester: Brockhampton Press, 1954);

Enid Blyton Magazine Annual (London: Evans, 1954);

Enid Blyton's Marigold Story Book (London: Gifford, 1954);

Enid Blyton's Noddy Pop-up Book (London: Sampson Low, 1954);

Enid Blyton's Noddy Giant Painting Book (London: Sampson Low, 1954);

Good Work, Secret Seven! (Leicester: Brockhampton Press, 1954); republished as *The Secret Seven and the Case of the Stolen Car* (Chicago: Children's Press, 1972);

Five Go to Mystery Moor (London: Hodder & Stoughton, 1954; Chicago: Reilly & Lee, 1963);

The Greatest Book in the World (London: British & Foreign Bible Society, 1954);

How Funny You Are, Noddy! (London: Sampson Low, 1954);

Little Strip Picture Books, first of a series (London: Sampson Low, 1954);

The Little Toy Farm and Other Stories (London: Pitkin, 1954);

Mary Mouse to the Rescue (Leicester: Brockhampton Press, 1954);

Merry Mister Meddle! (London: Newnes, 1954);

More about Amelia Jane (London: Newnes, 1954);

The Mystery of Tally-Ho Cottage (London: Methuen, 1954);

Noddy and the Magic Rubber (London: Sampson Low, 1954);

Noddy's Castle of Books, 5 volumes (London: Sampson Low, 1954);

Enid Blyton's Sooty (London: Collins, 1955);

Away Goes Sooty (London: Collins, 1955);

Benjy and the Others (London: Latimer, 1955);

Bible Stories from the Old Testament (London: Muller, 1955);

Bible Stories from the New Testament (London: Muller, 1955);

Bimbo and Blackie Go Camping (London: Collins, 1955);

Bobs (London: Collins, 1955);

Christmas with Scamp and Bimbo (London: Collins, 1955);

Enid Blyton's Favourite Book of Fables. From the Tales of La Fontaine (London: Collins, 1955);

Blyton considering book illustrations at her last home, Green Hedges, Beaconsfield

Enid Blyton's Little Bedtime Books, 8 volumes (London: Sampson Low, 1955–1958);

Neddy the Little Donkey (London: Collins, 1955);

Enid Blyton's What Shall I Be? (London: Collins, 1955);

Finding the Tickets (London: Evans, 1955);

Five Have Plenty of Fun (London: Hodder & Stoughton, 1955);

Foxglove Story Book (London: Gifford, 1955);

Gobbo in the Land of Dreams (London: Sampson Low, 1955);

The Golliwog Grumbled (Leicester: Brockhampton Press, 1955);

Holiday House (London: Evans, 1955);

The Laughing Kitten (London: Harvill Press / New York: Roy, 1955);

Mandy, Mops and Cubby and the Whitewash (London: Sampson Low, 1955);

Mary Mouse in Nursery Rhyme Land (Leicester: Brockhampton Press, 1955);

Mischief Again (London: Collins / New York: Roy, 1955);

Mr. Pinkwhistle's Party (London: Newnes, 1955);

Mr. Sly-One and Cats (London: Evans, 1955);

Mr. Tumpy in the Land of Boys and Girls (London: Sampson Low, 1955);

More Chimney Corner Stories (London: Latimer, 1955);

Mother's Meeting (London: Evans, 1955);

Noddy in Toyland (London: Sampson Low, 1955);

Noddy Meets Father Christmas (London: Sampson Low, 1955);

Playing at Home (London: Methuen, 1955);

Ring o' Bells Mystery (London: Collins, 1955);

The River of Adventure (London: Macmillan / New York: St. Martin's Press, 1955);

Run-about's Holiday (London: Lutterworth, 1955);

Secret Seven Win Through (Leicester: Brockhampton Press, 1955); republished as *The Secret Seven and the Hidden Cave Adventure* (Chicago: Children's Press, 1972);

The Troublesome Three (London: Sampson Low, 1955);

Who Will Hold the Giant? (London: Evans, 1955);

You Funny Little Noddy! (London: Sampson Low, 1955);

Be Brave, Little Noddy! (London: Sampson Low, 1956);

Bom the Little Toy Drummer (Leicester: Brockhampton Press, 1956);

The Clever Little Donkey (London: Collins, 1956);

Colin the Cow-Boy (London: Collins, 1956);

A Day with Mary Mouse (Leicester: Brockhampton Press, 1956);

A Day with Noddy (London: Sampson Low, 1956);

Enid Blyton's Animal Tales (London: Collins, 1956);

Enid Blyton's Book of Her Famous Play Noddy in Toyland (London: Sampson Low, 1956);

Enid Blyton's Noddy Playday Painting Book (London: Sampson Low, 1956);

Five on a Secret Trail (London: Hodder & Stoughton, 1956);

Four in a Family (London: Lutterworth, 1956);

Let's Have a Party (London: Harvill Press, 1956; New York: Roy, 1957?);

The Mystery of the Missing Man (London: Methuen, 1956);

Noddy and His Friends (London: Sampson Low, 1956);

Noddy and Tessie Bear (London: Sampson Low, 1956);

Noddy Nursery Rhymes (London: Sampson Low, 1956);

The Noddy Toy Station Books, 5 volumes (London: Sampson Low, 1956);

The Rat-a-Tat Mystery (London: Collins, 1956);

Scamp at School (London: Collins, 1956);

A Story Book of Jesus (London: Macmillan, 1956);

Three Cheers Secret Seven (Leicester: Brockhampton Press, 1956); republished as *The Secret Seven and the Grim Secret* (Chicago: Children's Press, 1972);

Bom and His Magic Drumstick (Leicester: Brockhampton Press, 1957);

Children's Own Wonder Book, by Blyton and others (London: Odhams, 1957);

Do Look Out, Noddy! (London: Sampson Low, 1957);

Enid Blyton's Bom Painting Book (London: Dean, 1957);

Five Go to Billycock Hill (London: Hodder & Stoughton, 1957);

Mary Mouse and the Garden Party (Leicester: Brockhampton Press, 1957);

Mystery of the Strange Messages (London: Methuen, 1957);

New Testament Picture Books, 2 volumes (London: Macmillan, 1957);

Noddy and Bumpy Dog (London: Sampson Low, 1957);

Noddy's New Big Book (London: Sampson Low, 1957);

Secret Seven Mystery (Leicester: Brockhampton Press, 1957); republished as *The Secret Seven and the Missing Girl Mystery* (Chicago: Children's Press, 1972);

The Birthday Kitten (London: Lutterworth, 1958);

Bom Goes Adventuring (Leicester: Brockhampton Press, 1958);

Clicky Gets into Trouble (Leicester: Brockhampton Press, 1958);

Five Get into a Fix (London: Hodder & Stoughton, 1958);

Mary Mouse Goes to the Fair (Leicester: Brockhampton Press, 1958);

Mr. Pink-Whistle's Big Book (London: Evans, 1958);

My Big Ears Picture Book (London: Sampson Low, 1958);

My Noddy Picture Book (London: Sampson Low, 1958);

Noddy Has an Adventure (London: Sampson Low, 1958);

The Noddy Shop Book (London: Sampson Low, 1958);

Noddy's Own Nursery Rhymes (London: Sampson Low, 1958);

Puzzle for the Secret Seven (Leicester: Brockhampton Press, 1958); republished as *The Secret Seven and the Case of the Music Lover* (Chicago: Children's Press, 1972);

Rumble and Chuff, 2 volumes (London: Juvenile Productions, 1958);

The School Companion, by Blyton and others (London: New Educational Press, 1958);

You're a Good Friend, Noddy! (London: Sampson Low, 1958);

A. B. C. with Noddy (London: Sampson Low, 1959);

Bom and the Clown (Leicester: Brockhampton Press, 1959);

Bom and the Rainbow (Leicester: Brockhampton Press, 1959);

Dog Stories, republished collection of *Three Boys and a Circus* (1940) and *Adventures of Scamp* (1943) (London: Collins, 1959);

Hullo Bom and Wuffy Dog (Leicester: Brockhampton Press, 1959);

Mary Mouse Has a Wonderful Idea (Leicester: Brockhampton Press, 1959);

Noddy and Bunkey (London: Sampson Low, 1959);

Noddy Goes to Sea (London: Sampson Low, 1959);

Noddy's Car Picture Book (London: Sampson Low, 1959);

The Ragamuffin Mystery (London: Collins, 1959);

Secret Seven Fireworks (Leicester: Brockhampton Press, 1959); republished as *The Secret Seven and the Bonfire Mystery* (Chicago: Children's Press, 1972);

Adventure of the Strange Ruby (Leicester: Brockhampton Press, 1960);

Adventure Stories (London: Collins, 1960);

Bom Goes to Magic Town (Leicester: Brockhampton Press, 1960);

Cheer Up, Little Noddy! (London: Sampson Low, 1960);

Clicky and Tiptoe (Leicester: Brockhampton Press, 1960);

Five on Finniston Farm (London: Hodder & Stoughton, 1960);

Good Old Secret Seven (Leicester: Brockhampton Press, 1960); republished as *The Secret Seven and the Old Fort Adventure* (Chicago: Children's Press, 1972);

Happy Day Stories (London: Evans, 1960);

Here Comes Bom (Leicester: Brockhampton Press, 1960);

Mary Mouse Goes to Sea (Leicester: Brockhampton Press, 1960);

Mystery Stories (London: Collins, 1960);

Noddy Goes to the Fair (London: Sampson Low, 1960);

Noddy's One, Two, Three Book (London: Sampson Low, 1960);

Noddy's Tall Blue Book (London: Sampson Low, 1960);

Noddy's Tall Green Book (London: Sampson Low, 1960);

Noddy's Tall Orange Book (London: Sampson Low, 1960);

Noddy's Tall Pink Book (London: Sampson Low, 1960);

Noddy's Tall Red Book (London: Sampson Low, 1960);

Noddy's Tall Yellow Book (London: Sampson Low, 1960);

Old Testament Picture Books, 2 volumes (London: Macmillan, 1960);

Will the Fiddle (London: Instructive Arts, 1960);

Tales at Bedtime (London: Collins, 1961);

The Big Enid Blyton Book (London: Hamlyn, 1961);

Bom at the Seaside (Leicester: Brockhampton Press, 1961);

Bom Goes to the Circus (Leicester: Brockhampton Press, 1961);

Five Go to Demon's Rocks (London: Hodder & Stoughton, 1961);

Happy Holiday, Clicky (Leicester: Brockhampton Press, 1961);

Mary Mouse Goes Out for the Day (Leicester: Brockhampton Press, 1961);

Mr. Plod and Little Noddy (London: Sampson Low, 1961);

The Mystery of Banshee Towers (London: Methuen, 1961);

The Mystery That Never Was (London: Collins, 1961);

Noddy's Toyland Train Picture Book (London: Sampson Low, 1961);

Shock for the Secret Seven (Leicester: Brockhampton Press, 1961); republished as *The Secret Seven and the Case of the Dog Lover* (Chicago: Children's Press, 1972);

A Day at School with Noddy (London: Sampson Low, 1962);

Five Have a Mystery to Solve (London: Hodder & Stoughton, 1962);

The Four Cousins (London: Lutterworth, 1962);

Fun with Mary Mouse (Leicester: Brockhampton Press, 1962);

Look Out Secret Seven (Leicester: Brockhampton Press, 1962); republished as *The Secret Seven and the Case of the Missing Medals* (Chicago: Children's Press, 1972);

Noddy and the Tootles (London: Sampson Low, 1962);

Stories for Monday (London: Oliphants, 1962);

Stories for Tuesday (London: Oliphants, 1962);

The Boy Who Wanted a Dog (London: Lutterworth, 1963);

Brer Rabbit Again (London: Dean, 1963);

Five Are Together Again (London: Hodder & Stoughton, 1963);

Fun for the Secret Seven (Leicester: Brockhampton Press, 1963); republished as *The Secret Seven and the Case of the Old Horse* (Chicago: Children's Press, 1972);

Tales of Brave Adventure Retold (London: Dean, 1963);

Enid Blyton's Sunshine Picture Story Book (Manchester: World Distributors, 1964);

Happy Hours Story Book (London: Dean, 1964);

Mary Mouse and the Little Donkey (Leicester: Brockhampton Press, 1964);

Noddy and the Aeroplane (London: Sampson Low, 1964);

Storybook for Fives to Sevens (London: Parrish, 1964);

Storytime Book (London: Dean, 1964);

Tell-a-story Books (Manchester: World Distributors, 1964);

Trouble for the Twins (Leicester: Brockhampton Press, 1964);

The Boy Who Came Back (London: Lutterworth, 1965);

Easy Reader (London: Collins, 1965);

Enid Blyton's Brer Rabbit's a Rascal (London: Dean, 1965);

Enid Blyton's Sunshine Book (London: Dean, 1965);

Enid Blyton's Treasure Box (London: Sampson Low, 1965);

Learn to Count with Noddy (London: Sampson Low, 1965);

Learn to Go Shopping with Noddy (London: Sampson Low, 1965);

Learn to Read About Animals with Noddy (London: Sampson Low, 1965);

Learn to Tell the Time with Noddy (London: Sampson Low, 1965);

The Man Who Stopped to Help (London: Lutterworth, 1965);

Noddy and His Friends: A Nursery Picture Book (London: Sampson Low, 1965);

Noddy Treasure Box (London: Sampson Low, 1965);

Tales of Long Ago, Retold by Enid Blyton (London: Dean, 1965);

Enid Blyton's Bedtime Annual, first of several volumes (Manchester: World Distributors, 1966);

Enid Blyton's Playbook, first of several volumes (London: Collins, 1966);

The Fairy Folk Story Book (London: Collins, 1966);

Fireside Tales (London: Collins, 1966);

Gift Book (London: Purnell, 1966);

The Happy House Children (London: Collins, 1966);

John and Mary, series of 9 volumes (Leicester: Brockhampton Press, 1966–1968);

Pixie Tales (London: Collins, 1966);

Pixieland Story Book (London: Collins, 1966);

Stories for Bedtime (London: Dean, 1966);

Stories for You (London: Dean, 1966);

Holiday Annual Stories (London: Low Marston, 1967);

Magic Stories (London: Low Marston, 1967);

Pixie Stories (London: Low Marston, 1967);

Toy Stories (London: Low Marston, 1967);

Noddy and His Passengers (London: Sampson Low, 1967);

Noddy and the Magic Boots and *Noddy's Funny Kite,* cover titled as *Noddy's Funny Kite* (London: Sampson Low, 1967);

Noddy and the Noah's Ark Adventure Picture Book (London: Sampson Low, 1967);

Noddy in Toyland Picture Book (London: Low Marston, 1967);

Noddy Toyland ABC Picture Book (London: Sampson Low, 1967);

Page from The Big Noddy Book *(1951), illustrated by Beck*

Noddy's Aeroplane Picture Book (London: Sampson Low, 1967);

The Playtime Story Book, 4 volumes (Manchester: World Distributors, 1967);

Adventures on Willow Farm (London: Collins, 1968);

Brownie Tales (London: Collins, 1968);

The Playtime Book, 4 volumes (Manchester: World Distributors, 1968);

Once Upon a Time (London: Collins, 1968).

PLAY PRODUCTIONS: *Noddy in Toyland,* London, Stoll Theatre, 1954;

The Famous Five, London, 1955.

OTHER: *Treasure Trove Readers,* compiled by Blyton (Exeter: Wheaton, 1934);

Nature Observation Pictures, selected from T[homas] A. Coward, *The Birds of the British Isles,* with footnotes by Blyton (London: Warne, 1935);

Coward, *Birds of the Wayside and Woodland,* edited, with introductory chapters, by Blyton (London: Warne, 1936);

The Blyton-Sharman Musical Plays for Juniors, words by Blyton (Exeter: Wheaton, 1939).

It is easy to sum up Enid Blyton's place in children's literature. She was, and is, the most successful British children's book author ever to have written, quite probably the most successful children's author in the world. She wrote some six hundred books, and estimates of her annual sales twenty-five years after her death vary between four and eight million copies worldwide. More than four hundred editions are still in print in Britain, and about ten new editions appear every month. Her work has been translated into at least twenty-seven languages, and – along with Lenin, Agatha Christie, Simenon, and Chairman Mao – she is reputed to be among the top five most-translated authors. Her most famous creation, "Noddy," with more than seventy editions in print, gained a new life through a television series in 1992. Her most well-known series, The Famous Five, appeared in twenty-one volumes between 1942 and 1953 and had sold about six million copies by 1953. Such sales of the books are continuing, as in the 1970s they were supplemented by extra titles, books written in French and translated into English, which sold a million copies in two years in France. Another of her series of school stories, Malory Towers, has been extended with great success in titles written in German. Computer games based on her books are sold, and this would have pleased Blyton, as she was interested in new media. She is consistently at the top of British readership polls. Few British readers have escaped her influence, and her work is regarded by many educators as a basic stepping-stone to literacy.

Yet her name does not appear in lists of recommended books for children or in critical histories of children's literature, nor has she won awards. In fact, she epitomizes a division within the world of children's books, a division between the respectable and the popular. If her name has become synonymous with children's books, it is with children's books of the most simple and reductive kind. Her books have been accused of most forms of political incorrectness – sexism and racism, class prejudice and snobbery – and have periodically been withdrawn from circulation in some British libraries. New editions have appeared that have been "sanitized."

Paradoxically, unlike Roald Dahl, whose books have achieved a similar notoriety despite their small numbers, Blyton cannot well be accused of anarchy, sadism, or vulgarity. Instead, she is accused of coziness and conservatism, of trivializing everything from folklore and religion to women's place in society. She followed Edith Nesbit in adopting a tone of voice that addresses children directly and unpatronizingly but does this to the point of embracing childish values. She adopted an attitude to fantasy that was essentially sentimental and soft-centered; she placed the family at the center of her books, but a family that was solidly middle class. Consequently, her books retain an essentially nineteenth-century didactic outlook. Even the simplest nursery tale has a built-in moral – and thus preserves the reactionary values of a class and period.

Her immense popularity thus subverts many modern attitudes. This is perhaps ironic, for Blyton believed that she was writing to and for children, although her materials represent a debased adult view of what is fit for children. In simplifying and "making pretty" the fairy tradition, and in making fantasy safe in both primary and secondary worlds, she actually perpetuates a demeaning view of what childhood is and should be.

Barbara Stoney's authorized biography of Enid Blyton, *Enid Blyton: A Biography* (1974), is a masterpiece of the subtle subtext. It reveals a childlike woman, an obsessive writer who was highly successful with the world's children but not so successful with her own. In many ways Blyton repressed whole areas of her life and developed a compensatory fantasyland. While she was clearly dedicated to a straightforward moral view of children and childhood, she was also a shrewd businesswoman who appreciated clearly how series could be successfully developed and marketed. Yet although she outproduced whole syndicates, it is not easy to say how far her manipulation of the formulae of children's books was conscious. One is left with an impression of a low-key, almost tragic life behind the phenomenal success.

Enid Mary Blyton was born 11 August 1897, in East Dulwich, London, the eldest child of Thomas Carey Blyton and Theresa Mary Blyton. She had two brothers, Hanly and Carey. Shortly after her birth, the family moved to Beckenham, in Kent, then on the southern fringe of London. Enid was a bookish child; her early reading included fairy tales, George MacDonald's *The Princess and the Goblin, Alice in Wonderland, The Coral Island, Black Beauty,* and *Little Women.* In her autobiography (written for children) she said, "I read every single old myth and legend I could get hold of – the old Norse myths, the old Greek myths which I thought were beautiful but rather cruel."

Although Blyton later developed a fiery temper, she had a happy early childhood and was remembered at school as being lively and given to practical jokes. She was particularly attached to her father, who left the family when Enid was thirteen in 1909. This fact was kept secret from neighbors and friends by her mother, and although Enid reestablished a relationship with her father later, she seems clearly to have been emotionally affected.

In her teens she wanted to be a writer, but several hundred early literary efforts were returned by publishers at this time. Her parents wanted her to be a professional musician, but she had an affinity with children and in 1916 began to train as a teacher in Ipswich by taking the National Froebel Union course, based on an educational theory that encouraged freedom and creativity in children. Her biographer is unable to establish why at this period Blyton became estranged from her mother, but so strong was the alienation that Enid never saw Mary again and even refused to go to her funeral in the 1950s on the grounds that she was "too busy." It is interesting to speculate how much the comfortable domestic stories that she wrote might have offered some compensation for this alienation.

Her first published poem, "Have you . . . ?," appeared in a magazine for adults, *Nash's Magazine* (March 1917):

> Have you heard the night-time silence, just when all
>   the world's asleep,
> And you're curled up at your window, all alone?
> Have you held your breath in wonder, at the sky so
>   dark and deep?
> Have you wanted just *one* star for all your own?

This was followed by "My summer prayer" in August 1917 and "Do you . . . ?" in September 1918.

She passed her examinations by the time she was twenty-one and went to teach in a small school for boys, Bickley Park School in Kent, in 1919. After a year she became a nursery governess for a family in Surbiton, where she was very successful as a teacher and family friend – although after she left the family four years later, she hardly ever referred to this period of her life.

In 1921 she met the artist Phyllis Chase and began a partnership with her through an illustrated story in one of Cassell's magazines. The two worked on Christmas and Easter greeting cards, pieces for the journals *The Londoner* and *The Bystander,* and in 1922 began to write for children in the weekly *Teacher's World.* The first of these pieces was "Peronel and his Pot of Glue."

Her first books were also illustrated by Chase: *Child Whispers* (1922) and *Real Fairies: Poems* (1923). Many of the poems in these books were written from the child's viewpoint, as she wrote in the preface to *Child Whispers:* "In my experience of teaching I have found the children delight in two distinct types of verses. These are the humorous type and the imaginative poetical type – but the humour must be from the child's point of view and not from the 'grown up's' – a very different thing." These poems were well received by critics, for the poems were in the rather whimsical – not to say sugary – style popular at the time. They are similar to the work of A. A. Milne, Rose Fyleman, Walter de la Mare, and Eleanor Farjeon and have affinities with the chubby and "cute" pictures by Mabel Lucie Attwell. Blyton's sentimentality toward and simplification of childhood is indistinguishable from the approach of these writers.

Among her earliest books was *The Book of Brownies* (1926), which remained in print into the 1980s. In this work Blyton established her simple, brightly colored fairyland where goblins, brownies, fairies, dwarfs, and wizards exist in a small, bland world. These fairies, however debased they may seem to the critical adult eye, were derived from Shakespearean and pre-Raphaelite concepts of tiny creatures rather than those concepts of the tough school of the English and European folktale. Their type has, perhaps, been best described scathingly in Rudyard Kipling's *Puck of Pook's Hill* (1906). Puck, the oldest thing in England, trenchantly dismisses them: "Besides, what you call [fairies] are made-up things the People of the Hills have never heard of – little buzzflies with butterfly wings, and gauze petticoats, and shiny stars in their hair, and a wand like a school-teacher's cane for punishing bad boys and rewarding good ones. . . . Do you wonder that the People of the Hills don't care to be confused with that painty-winged, wand-waving, sugar-and-shake-your-head set of impostors?"

By 1923, when Blyton was still at Surbiton, her earnings from writing alone exceeded £300 per year. It is difficult to give a comparable figure for modern times, but £300 was then a very comfortable living wage for a family. To give some idea of her creative output, in 1923 she produced a series of storybooks and about 120 other published items. She began a weekly periodical column for *Teacher's World,* which not only obliquely chronicled her life but allowed her to write about natural history (an interest of her father), her holidays, and pets. She continued this column until 1945.

On 28 August 1924 she married Hugh Alexander Pollock, who worked for one of her publishers, Newnes, and continued to write. Her writing by 1925 averaged between four thousand and five thousand words each day, and she also answered, just the right house and just the right street. It's rather a nursery-rhyme sort of street, with latticed windows, coloured doors, and little stiff trees standing about in pots – just the sort of street you would expect the writer of 'The King's Breakfast' to live in. And certainly the right street for Christopher Robin."

In 1929 the Pollocks moved to the first of two houses that became world famous through their association with Blyton, "Old Thatch" at Bourne End in Buckinghamshire, west of London. Here she established her cheerful persona through her pieces for *Teachers' World,* which ranged from Arabian Nights stories to nature notes. Even her pets became famous – such as her dog Bobs, who had his own column on Enid's children's page. Some indication of her popularity is that when Bobs's "Letters" were privately printed and sold from "Old Thatch," ten thousand copies were sold in less than a week. (It is also perhaps significant that when Bobs died, his death was unacknowledged and his column continued.) Enid also established her habit of espousing worthy causes from her residence here, as she mobilized thousands of children to collect, for example, aluminum foil or to pick up wastepaper.

In 1930 her daughter Gillian was born, but after about a month Blyton installed a nanny and went back to her writing. Stoney loyally, or tactfully, wrote: "It was not that Enid did not love her daughter but, during this – to her – rather uninteresting stage of her child's development, other matters seemed more absorbing." Gillian appears to have survived her childhood without too much trauma, but her sister, Imogen, who was born in 1935, produced a very critical account in *A Childhood at Green Hedges* (1989). Not only had Enid been disappointed at not having a son but it is clear that the children did not get all the attention that they might have. This is particularly ironic in view of Blyton's strongly voiced opinions about "working mothers." She certainly "used" her daughters in her columns, and Gillian's rag doll became the hero of a series of books beginning with *Naughty Amelia Jane* (1940).

In 1932 Enid attempted to publish an adult book, "The Caravan Goes On," but it was rejected. Her only other attempt to write for an adult audience, a 1956 play titled *The Summer Storm,* was unable to be staged.

Her true career began to blossom fully in 1937 when *Adventures of the Wishing Chair,* after being serialized in *Sunny Stories,* appeared in book form. The book's fantasy world is simple and derivative, and the book features some slapstick comedy. It remains popular, but its fantasy differs much from that of

Blyton in her garden

by hand, hundreds of fan letters each week. At this period she was writing not only for educational journals but for a London newspaper, the *Morning Post.* She edited *The Teachers' Treasury* (three volumes, 1926) which, along with her writing for *Teachers' World,* provided materials for teachers of many different subjects. She was also general editor of *Modern Teaching* (six volumes, 1928).

The best-known magazine with which she was associated was *Sunny Stories for Little Folks,* which published two issues per month. She began to edit it in 1926 and continued to do so until 1952, by which time she was writing every word of it – except the competitions – and she gave it up then only to start her own magazine! One interesting article for *Teachers' World* at this period describes her meeting with A. A. Milne. It begins in the "cozy" style to which generations of British children became accustomed: "I went yesterday to see Mr. Milne of 'When We Were Very Young' fame. As I turned into the pretty Chelsea street and came up to his blue front door, I couldn't help thinking he lived in another book published in the same year, J. R. R. Tolkien's *The Hobbit,* an altogether more substantial and resonant piece – and one that has received much critical acclaim. In Blyton's story the wishing chair, bought by the children Mollie and Peter, takes them to a series of colorful and unproblematic lands – of dreams, of giants, of gnomes. The idea was continued in *The Enchanted Wood* (1939) and *The Magic Faraway Tree* (1943), which has the most readily identifiable source in Yggdrasil, the huge ash tree from the Norse legends with which Blyton was familiar. But the kind of humor that Blyton presents can be epitomized by the characters Mr. Watzisname, Dame Washalot, and the Saucepan Man. The books also employ typical Blyton settings, which are vague and idyllic.

In 1938, somewhat against her husband's wishes, the family moved to a second famous house which was named, after much interaction with her readers, "Green Hedges" at Beaconsfield, just to the north of Bourne End. Here Enid began a routine that allowed her regularly to produce between six thousand and ten thousand words a day.

One of the first books produced from the new home was *Mr. Galliano's Circus* (1938), part of a popular genre and, indeed, one of the better examples. With its anachronistic horse-drawn caravans and children having miraculous powers with animals, *Mr. Galliano's Circus* has a timelessness that balances the pervading atmosphere of child wish fulfillment. It is by no means a negligible book in comparison with Noel Streatfeild's *The Circus is Coming* (1938), which won the British Library Association's Carnegie Medal for the best children's book of the same year.

Much more characteristic of Blyton's later output is another 1938 book, *The Secret Island,* which had first appeared in *Sunny Stories.* This is, ironically, a branch of the "holiday adventure" story which had been established by Arthur Ransom's *Swallows and Amazons* (1930) as a realistic genre.

The basic structure of *The Secret Island* brings together core features of the nineteenth-century children's novel. The parents of Nora, Mike, and Peggy are disposed of (missing on a flight to Australia); the children are mistreated by relatives with whom they are left; they run away, aided by a working-class boy who (like Dickon in Frances Hodgson Burnett's 1911 novel *The Secret Garden*) knows about survival in the country; they live on an island; Peggy acts as mother figure; Mike and Nora are twins; the children build a house; and the parents return in time for Christmas. The final touch, that of the parents' buying the island for the

children, is typical of Blyton's tendency to "gild the lily."

The sequels employ a fine selection of time-honored literary devices. *The Secret Mountain* (1941), for example, owes much to H. Rider Haggard's *King Solomon's Mines* (1885); the children discover a secret African kingdom, and Blyton even uses the same climactic eclipse of the sun. *The Secret of Spiggy Holes* (1940) involves the rescue of the Prince of Baronia, and the ending of that book neatly sums up both Blyton's intentions and her style:

> The motor started up with a lovely whirring sound. The little boat leapt forward. Mike swung her out to sea, feeling as proud as could be. A motor-boat of their own. How lucky they were!
>
> Now they're off, all the way back to Peep-Hole. Good-bye, Mike – good-bye Jack! Good-bye, Nora and Peggy! You deserve your good luck, and we loved all your adventures. Maybe we'll hear more of them another day. Good-bye, good-bye!

Enid Blyton's contribution to the war effort is interesting. Not only did she give practical and patriotic advice through her columns, but such was her selling power that she continued to be published when restrictions on paper had forced other writers to fall silent. In 1940 she produced twelve books under her own name and two under the pseudonym of "Mary Pollock." Despite some skeptical rumors to the contrary, these pseudonymous works were equally successful. Characteristic of her "domestic" work is *The Children of Cherry Tree Farm* (1940), really little more than a series of nature notes strung together on a thin but comfortable plot line.

She also made her first contributions to what was at the time the most popular of genres for girls, the girls' school story. Although a relatively late development from the boys' school story, this genre had built a considerable following through the 1920s and 1930s, with writers increasingly relying on such features as secret passages, spies and crooks, and cheated heiresses. Perhaps surprisingly in view of her reputation but also predictably in view of her association with the teaching profession, Blyton's books did not use these devices.

The Naughtiest Girl in the School (1940) and its two sequels are set in a coeducational school with progressive ideas, and the whole plot motivation lies in the attitudes of the characters. Blyton's second work, *The Twins at St. Clare's* (1941), returned to a more traditional setting of the girls-only private school, but again, although there are jolly "japes," the story is concerned more with people than with props. (So popular has the St. Clare's series been that an animated cartoon version was screened on Japanese television in 1991.)

The world of St. Clare's had no place for the war, but, unlike some authors, Blyton took on the war directly with *The Adventurous Four* (1941). The children in this book (again, the first of a series) resemble those from Blyton's five-novel *The Secret . . .* series published between 1938 and 1953: the fisherman's son Andy; Tom, the "second male lead"; and twin sisters Jill and Mary. The topical and strongly patriotic plot includes not only shipwreck and survival but the exposure of a German submarine base. While serious fiction seemed to balk in the face of the reality of war, popular fiction saw itself as a weapon.

Some indication of Blyton's increasing grip on the children's book market is the fact that Jean de Brunhoff's character Babar the Elephant, who had first made his appearance in English in 1934, reappeared in 1941 in *The Babar Story Book,* where it was retold by Enid Blyton. This version appeared in a widely read and respectable series, Methuen's Modern Classics, in 1942. The anomalous nature of this retelling did not go unnoticed; as a reviewer in *Junior Bookshelf* observed in December 1941, "What in heaven's name can she have done to it? Did de Brunhoff's fine prose need rewriting?"

Another oddity was in the series of Mary Mouse books which began to appear in 1942. These were originally printed on magazine offcuts to save the publisher's wartime paper allocation, hence their unusual shape. The series continued until 1964 when, with the publication of *Mary Mouse and the Little Donkey,* the sales figures for the entire series were estimated to have reached four-and-a-half million copies.

In 1942 Blyton's most famous series also began: The Famous Five. The Five consist of the same team of boys and girls and superintelligent animals who appear elsewhere in her books. It may well be that the continuing great success of the series rests in its cheerful abandonment of any claims to probability. The characters, such as they are, include the leader Julian, rather inclined to be rude and contemptuous toward anyone of "inferior" class; Dick, the virtually invisible second male lead; "George" (really named Georgina), the "tomboy"; Anne, the stereotyped weak, domesticated, dependent girl; and, of course, Timmy the dog. As George and Timmy are being met at a train station, this typical opening scene demonstrates the straightforwardness of Blyton's prose, the argot of the time (and the social class), the sexism, and the animism:

They ran at top speed. The train drew in at the station just as they raced on to the platform. A head of short curly hair looked out from a window – and then another dark brown head just below it.

"George – and Timmy!" yelled Anne.

"Halloo!" shouted George, almost falling out of the door.

"WOOF!" barked Timmy and leaped down to the platform almost on top of Dick. Down jumped George, her eyes shining. She hugged Anne, and gave Julian and Dick a punch each. . . . Julian . . . linked his arm in hers. "Let me take that suit-case. We'll just slip into the village first and have a few ice-creams to celebrate. There's a shop here that has some jolly decent ones."

"Good. I feel exactly like ice-creams," said George happily. "Look, Timmy knows what you said. His tongue is hanging out for an ice-cream already. . . ."

"Woof," said Timmy, and licked Anne's hand for the twentieth time.

Perhaps some reader interest in George, in this series, lies in the fact that Blyton did not seem entirely to approve of her own creation: the text of *Five Go Off to Camp* (1948), for instance, presents a subversive element, as "George . . . hated doing all the things that girls had to do, such as making beds and washing-up. She looked sulky." Blyton admitted that George was in fact based on herself as a child. The adult reader might be forgiven for detecting Freudian symbolism in George's desire for a lighthouse to go with her island (she owns one!), quite apart from the books' preoccupations with tunnels and underground rivers.

The sexism of the narrative's attitudes to the girls, Anne especially, is obvious and has been toned down in the latest editions. But in 1949 there was no political correctness in such work as this from *Five Get Into Trouble:*

"Good old Anne," said Dick, when at last he and the others joined her, dressed again, with their blazers on for warmth. "Look, she's got the food all ready. Proper little housewife, aren't you, Anne? I bet if we stayed here for more than one night Anne would have made some kind of larder, and have arranged a good place to wash everything – and be looking for somewhere to keep her dusters and broom!"

For reasons not altogether clear from her biography, Blyton's marriage failed during the war, but apparently one problem lay in the effect of the war upon her husband, Major Pollock. His first wife had

Blyton at a party for the one hundred thousandth member of the Enid Blyton Magazine Club, 1957

left him while he was on active service in the 1914–1918 war, and, suspicious and possessive, he broke down. He and Enid were divorced in December 1942, and Enid married a surgeon, Kenneth Darrell Waters, in October 1943, the year in which she produced one of her best-loved fantasies, *The Magic Faraway Tree.*

That year also saw the beginning of a new mystery series with *The Mystery of the Burnt Cottage,* featuring the "five find-outers." This time the central character is the fat, and therefore not entirely admirable, Frederick Algernon Trotteville, a junior Sherlock Holmes. Although this first book has its merits, the series is flawed by the vulgar and spiteful treatment of the local policeman, ominously named Mr. Goon, by the children and the author. For some readers Blyton has gone too far in the direction of taking the child's point of view; the narrative attitude toward Goon is reprehensible, while the children's relationship with his superior, Inspector Jenks, becomes increasingly silly: Jenks ignores Goon and goes straight to the children. Inspector

Jenks was based on a real-life police officer, who objected mildly to Blyton's portrayal of Mr. Goon.

If Blyton has not always found favor with librarians, the series of stories which she began in 1944 with *The Island of Adventure* had a less frosty reception. A skeptic might say that this was because the books published by Macmillan were well presented, bulked out to more than three hundred pages by large print and excellent Stuart Tresilian illustrations. The stories themselves were no more probable than before, and this time there was an even more loquacious nonhuman, Kiki the parrot, and an even more ludicrous example of children's empathy with animals. In *The Mountain of Adventure* (1949) Philip demonstrates his talents with a herd of goats:

Philip made the noise again. The kid left its mother and came leaping to him. It sprang into his arms and nestled there, butting its soft white head against Philip's chin. . . . It was amazing the attraction that Philip had for creatures of any kind. Even a moth would rest contentedly on his finger.

Clearly Blyton is presenting a potent mixture of escapism and wish fulfillment, but one explanation of her success in spite of using this is in what stylisticians call "free indirect discourse" (FID). This is discourse which cannot be attributed directly either to the narrator or the character, or which conveys opinions or thoughts that could well come from the characters but that serve also to advance the narrative. The effect is to bridge the gap between the narrator's voice, which might otherwise seem overbearing, and the minds of the characters. Here is an example from the third of Blyton's "Adventure" series, *The Valley of Adventure* (1947), which illustrates her mature technique perfectly. This extract, with the stretches of "free indirect discourse" marked "FID," shows how she controls the telling of her story:

> Lucy-Ann was half afraid they might lose their way going back. But the boys had taken good note of everything [FID]. It was when they got to the wood that difficulty might have arisen, but here the notched trees soon set them right.

> They saw the plane was still down in the valley. So the men were somewhere about [FID]. It would be as well to be careful [FID] and Jack told Kiki to be quiet. The waterfall seemed to have gone to her head [FID?], and she had been very noisy coming back, singing and squawking loudly.

> "There's our shed," said Lucy-Ann thankfully. It felt quite like home, coming back to it from that enormous mountainside [FID]. "I hope all our things are safe."

> They went inside. Yes, their things were there, exactly as they had left them [FID]. Good! [FID]

The Island of Adventure was republished as *Mystery Island* in the United States, and the Boys' Club of America gave it an award as one of the six most popular junior books published in 1947. This award resulted in one of Blyton's rare trips abroad, a visit to the United States notable mainly for the fact that she argued violently with her American agent.

Blyton's Malory Towers series, her third series of school stories, began with *First Term at Malory Towers* in 1946 and produced what some critics feel is her most human character, Darrell Rivers. It is interesting that one of the most apparently improbable scenes in that book describes a tonsillectomy — a scene that in fact describes a real-life operation that Enid's eventual second husband, Darrell Wa-

ters, had performed on her daughter Imogen at Green Hedges in 1942.

By the late 1940s Blyton's position was unassailable. She was maintaining her output and at one time had contracts with more than twenty British publishers. Her husband took her financial affairs in hand, and in 1950 they formed Darrell Waters Limited, the company that still administers the books. Her income from investments alone was estimated at this time to be around £100,000 per year (which today would comfortably give her millionaire status). Enid took up golf and bought her own eighteen-hole course at Studland Bay in Dorset. But if she did not need to work, paradoxically she entered her most productive period: 1949 was something of an annus mirabilis.

First she began what may well have been her best series of mysteries with *The Rockingdown Mystery* (1949). Again there is a quartet of children, again a spaniel, and again an independent, very competent boy in charge — who this time has a pet monkey. Some Gothic features are evident in the series, although more familiar devices soon reappear: spies and submarines in *The Rubadub Mystery* (1952) and a gang of thieves in *The Ragamuffin Mystery* (1959).

Also in this postwar year of 1949 one of her publishers told Blyton a story about some children forming a secret society in a garden shed, and this inspired the The Secret Seven adventures, a kind of junior Famous Five series, but one that ran to fifteen volumes. To the uninitiated, the characters are as undifferentiated and indistinguishable as the acolytes of Nancy Drew, but the series of scaled-down encounters in caves and with crooks has maintained its popularity, although the names of some characters — for example, Doris and Hilda —have gone out of fashion.

Most serendipitously, in 1949 David White of the publishing house of Sampson Low was struck by the potential of the work of Dutch artist Harmsen Van der Beek and commissioned Blyton to write some stories for his pictures. This was the seed of one of her greatest successes, and anyone in doubt about her business acumen might note the letter that she wrote to White: "Now about the general title — at the moment this is 'All Aboard for Toyland,' and I imagine we might have as a 'motif' a toy train rushing along crowded with passengers — going all round the jacket top, sides and bottom or something like that — to give the books a 'series' look. The specific titles (which will all be different of course) will each contain the name 'Noddy.' In the end, if they are very successful, they'll probably be referred to and ordered as the 'Noddy' books."

This was an understatement. Forty years later more than seventy editions of Noddy were in print in Britain alone. Van der Beek died in 1953, but both the books and the extensive merchandising were continued through the use of a picture "dictionary." Curiously, the most regular artist following Van der Beek, Robert Tyndall, who illustrated the series for eleven years, did not actually use the dictionary, and he was never credited for his work.

Noddy, an apparently innocent creature, has received more criticism than any of Blyton's other creations. A small boy with a nodding head, he drives a car and is looked after by Mrs. Tubby from next door. He lives in a Toyland visualized by Van der Beek and has an older, bearded friend, Big-Ears. The relationship between the two has given rise to much ribaldry through the years. Noddy is not a particularly strong or admirable character; he tends toward cowardliness and relies on Big-Ears or Mr. Plod the Policeman to get him out of trouble. He performs no great deeds: his greatest excitement in life occurs when he is kidnapped by Golliwogs or when he drives Father Christmas around Toyland. Generally the plots are well constructed, but it is difficult to find anything but reductiveness in their relationships with folktales.

Noddy was memorably called by one critic "the most egocentric, joyless, snivelling and pious anti-hero in the history of British fiction," and an article in the journal *Encounter* (January 1958) compared him to a whining and cowardly sponger upon the welfare state. The expression "Noddy language" has entered the English language as a dismissive phrase for idiotic simplicity. The primary attack, however, has been on Blyton's use of the Golliwog, a doll originating at the turn of the century as an admirable character. In Blyton's work, and notably in the Noddy books, the equation of "black" with "bad" is fairly blatant; modern versions have toned this down considerably.

There can still be lapses, however. For example, in 1949 Blyton published, apparently without notice being taken, *A Story Party at Green Hedges,* which contained a story titled "The Little Black Doll." In this story the doll – named Sambo, no less – has his reward for a virtuous deed when magic rain washes his blackness away and the narrative remarks, "No wonder he's happy – little pink Sambo." Whatever one thinks of this as an attitude in 1949, the fact that the book was reissued in 1976 demonstrates either insensitivity or, more probably, carelessness on the part of the publisher.

Another controversial book was Blyton's one venture into social realism in 1951 with *The Six Bad Boys.* It has been called Blyton's most unpleasant story: her simplifying approach is not really appropriate or viable for a story about seriously deprived children. What is worse for some critics is that because most of the boys in the book are irredeemably of the lower class, they are therefore damned anyway. Equally unacceptable today is her laboring of the point that mothers who wantonly wish to go out to work are to blame for society's evils: the clear implication is that a woman's place is in the home. Critics who have been unamused by the sententiousness have not on the whole drawn parallels with Blyton's personal situation, as they might well have done. Her avowed aim in *The Six Bad Boys* was to "explain some of the wrong things there are in the world, and to help put them right," but the primitive morality that she displays has not worn well.

Be that as it may, from 1949 onward, surveys have continually shown Blyton to be the most widely read children's writer in Britain: she cannot be ignored. In 1954 she branched out into the theater with *Noddy In Toyland,* for which she wrote the lyrics (thirty-three of them); the musical director worked out "more or less" all of the music in a single day. At first she found writing for the theater difficult, but once she had adapted her technique, she was able to write a play, *The Famous Five,* at her usual speed in 1955.

In the 1950s, following the founding of *Enid Blyton Magazine* (1953–1959), she formalized her interaction with children by forming several clubs – for example, the Busy Bees, which was linked to the national People's Dispensary for Sick Animals. These clubs are now defunct, but at their peak in the 1970s they had a membership of around a quarter of a million children. The Famous Five Club raised money first for a babies' home at Beaconsfield and later for other children's hospitals; the Sunbeam Society contributed to homes for blind babies, and the Enid Blyton Magazine Club contributed to help what were then known as "spastic" children.

In 1957 she was taken ill with what specialists diagnosed as a digestive problem brought on by overwork but which her husband, in an attempt to slow her work rate, let her believe was a heart condition. Barbara Stoney suggests that in her last years Blyton was less able to retreat into her fantasy world, and her concentration slackened. Increasingly she may have felt guilty about her separation from her mother, brothers, and first husband, but she continued to work hard, apparently to shut out any unpleasant memories or ideas. Her husband Darrell Waters died in September 1967, after he had destroyed many of Enid's diaries – an action that naturally leads to speculation that their publication might have affected her public image. Her last year was one of mental confusion and physical decline. She died in 1968, a year in which she published only seven books.

Her life was summed up by Stoney: "I still believe that she was a talented, hard-working writer for children who, behind the public image which she guarded so carefully, was a very insecure, complex and often difficult, childlike woman whose life was at times far-removed from the sunny world she created for herself in her highly-successful writings. Emotionally she never matured beyond the unhappy little girl from Beckenham who was not allowed to tell anyone that her beloved father had deserted her for someone who appeared to mean more to him than herself. But this probably led on to one of the most important factors in her success – her ability to relate so closely to her child readers."

But how did Blyton do it? In 1955 she had written: "I have just finished a book for MacMillan's. . . . I began it on Monday, and finished it this afternoon (Friday). It is 60,000 words long and flowed like its title (*The River of Adventure*)." It is hardly surprising that she attracted some attention because of her methods. Psychologist Peter McKellar, in researching his book *Imagination and Thinking* (1957), had written to her about this question in 1953 and received these replies:

> I don't really understand how my imagination works. . . . I shut my eyes for a few minutes, with my portable typewriter on my knee – I make my mind blank and wait – and then, as clearly as I would see real children, my characters stand before me in my mind's eye. I see them in detail. . . . I always know their Christian names. . . . I know their characters. . . . As I look at them, the characters take on movement and life. . . . That's enough for me. My hands go down on my typewriter keys and I begin. The first sentence comes straight into my mind, I don't have to think of it – I don't have to think of anything. . . . The story is enacted in my mind's eye almost as if I had a private cinema screen there. . . . I am in the happy position of being able to write a story and read it for the first time.

This facility extended to the length of the books, too:

> Another odd thing is that my "under-mind" seems to be able to receive such directions as "the story must be 40,000 words long." Because, sure enough, no matter what length I have to write to . . . the book ends almost to the word – the right length.

Most of the critical controversy has centered upon whether her books are "good" for children or not. Because children's books have a long shelf life and because their transmission of ideas may well be subliminal, teachers and librarians have worried about what so seductive a writer as Enid Blyton has transmitted. Is the "obvious virtue" that she gets children to read counterbalanced by the dangers of how and what they read?

Blyton, as Stoney says, "always found it difficult to understand those who criticized her work. She sincerely believed that she was providing her young readers with enjoyable – but never frightening – stories, that at the same time laid down certain moral codes of behaviour." As Blyton herself added, "my public, bless them, feel in my books a sense of security, an anchor, a sure knowledge that right is right, and that such things as courage and kindness deserved to be emulated. Naturally the morals and ethics are *intrinsic* to the story – and therein lies their true power." Her response to critics was that she didn't take any notice of critics who were more than twelve years old – a disingenuous defense also used by Roald Dahl.

In fact, as far as serious criticism of children's literature is concerned, the characteristic critical tactic has been to ignore her. Blyton is scarcely mentioned. For example, Margery Fisher's *Intent Upon Reading* (1961), an influential critical appraisal of modern children's books, mentions Blyton only in contrast with Beatrix Potter: "In her books, if Beatrix Potter wanted to use a long or an unfamiliar word, she did. Enid Blyton and others think that children are taxed too much if they are confronted by so much as a polysyllable, but generations of them . . . have enjoyed [Potter] without too much intellectual effort."

Only in the last few years, when the concept of a "literary canon" has been strongly challenged, has Blyton received serious and balanced criticism. Literature is now seen in a wider sociological and linguistic context, and Blyton's importance is being recognized. For example, Barbara Wall, writing in 1991, has observed: "Blyton's are books for children to grow out of, not to grow into. Yet no one has written more positively and single-mindedly to and for children." This kind of critical assessment seems likely to set the tone for future readings of Blyton. Her books have become part of British culture: in a sense they have become part of the public domain. The fact that her books can be updated – the fact that publishers wish them to survive – is a positive attribute. Thus, in the first publication of *The Three Golliwogs* (1944) the eponymous characters are called Golly, Woggie, and Nigger, but in the 1973 editions their names have become Wiggie, Waggie, and Wollie. Society, as it were, needs Blyton. For good or bad, popular literature is what society genuinely measures itself by.

In a sense Blyton defines children's literature in terms of children – not in terms of adults. Her involved, childlike stance, her simple and repetitive style, her rapid pacing and episodic plot structures, her reductive uses of archetypal characters and stories, and her outlining of scenes and characters are all against the stream of adult writing and of adult concepts of literature. But in using them she liberates the anarchic in the child, the "narrative lust" that has been forgotten in adult writing. Unlike Dahl's books, hers are not offensive because of their content. Indeed, they appeal to the uncritical in their support of certain kinds of values.

Enid Blyton is in the British bloodstream, and there seems to be no reason her books should not sell for many years to come – and a good many reasons to think, as books become less influential in society, that her success will never be surpassed.

Bibliographies:
A Complete List of Books by Enid Blyton (Edinburgh: Menzies, 1950);

Barbara Stoney, "Books by Enid Blyton, 1922–1968," in her *Enid Blyton: A Biography* (London: Hodder & Stoughton, 1974), pp. 221–244.

Biographies:
Enid Blyton, *The Story of My Life* (London: Pitman, 1952);

Barbara Stoney, *Enid Blyton: A Biography* (London: Hodder & Stoughton, 1974);

Imogen Smallwood, *A Childhood at Green Hedges* (London: Methuen, 1989).

References:

Bob Dixon, "The Nice, the Naughty and the Nasty: the Tiny World of Enid Blyton," *Children's Literature in Education,* 15 (1974): 43–61;

Janice Dohm, "Enid Blyton and Others: an American View," *Journal of Education,* 87 (1955): 358–361;

Peter McKellar, *Imagination and Thinking* (London: Cohen & West / New York: Basic Books, 1957);

Bob Mullan, *The Enid Blyton Story* (London: Boxtree, 1987);

Sheila Ray, *The Blyton Phenomenon: The Controversy Surrounding the World's Most Successful Children's Writer* (London: Deutsch, 1982);

Ray, "Enid Blyton," in *Twentieth-Century Children's Writers,* edited by Tracy Chevalier, third edition (Chicago: St. James Press, 1989), pp. 101–110;

Nicholas Tucker, "The Blyton Enigma," *Children's Literature in Education,* 19 (1975): 191–197;

Colin Welch, "Dear Little Noddy," *Encounter,* 10 (January 1958): 18–22;

Michael Woods, "The Blyton Line: A Psychologist's View," *Lines,* 2, no. 7 (1969): 8–16.

Dorothy Kathleen Broster

(2 September 1877 – 7 February 1950)

Ruth Waterhouse
Macquarie University

BOOKS: *Chantemerle: A Romance of the Vendean War,* by Broster and Gertrude Winifred Taylor (London: John Murray, 1911; New York: Brentano, 1911);

A Vision Splendid, by Broster and Taylor (London: John Murray, 1913; New York: Brentano, 1914);

Sir Isumbras at the Ford (London: John Murray, 1918);

The Yellow Poppy (London: Duckworth, 1920; New York: McBride, 1922);

The Wounded Name (London: John Murray, 1922; Garden City, N.Y.: Doubleday, Page, 1923);

"Mr. Rowl" (London: Heinemann, 1924; New York: Doubleday, 1924);

The Flight of the Heron (London: Heinemann, 1925; New York: Dodd, Mead, 1926);

The Happy Warrior (London: Cayme Press, 1926);

The Gleam in the North (London: Heinemann, 1926; New York: Coward-McCann, 1931);

The Dark Mile (London: Heinemann, 1929; New York: Coward-McCann, 1934);

Ships in the Bay! (London: Heinemann, 1931; New York: Coward-McCann, 1931);

A Fire of Driftwood: A Collection of Short Stories (London: Heinemann, 1932);

Almond, Wild Almond (London: Heinemann, 1933);

World Under Snow, by Broster and G. Forester (London: Heinemann, 1935);

Child Royal (London: Heinemann, 1937);

The Sea Without a Haven (London: Heinemann, 1941);

Couching at the Door (London: Heinemann, 1942);

The Captain's Lady (London: Heinemann, 1947);

The Short Voyage and Other Verses (N.p.: Privately printed, 1950).

Collection: *A Jacobite Trilogy* (London: Penguin, 1984).

Dorothy Kathleen Broster's writing career spanned the period from just before World War I until just after World War II, and this turbulent pe-

riod of uncertainty and conflict may well have influenced the attitudes encoded in her work. Her books, most of them historical romances set during the French Revolution and the Napoleonic period or the Jacobite rebellion of 1745 and its aftermath, were very popular. Though not specifically written for adolescents they attracted a wide reading public including many young readers, and her most famous book, *The Flight of the Heron* (1925), was produced by BBC Scotland in 1976 as a six-part television serial and broadcast at a time suitable for children's viewing.

Broster wrote, in an undated typescript for a speech kept at St. Hilda's College, Oxford, that "it is not easy to make a good blend of history and fiction," yet she always strove to reconcile the two, for "it is one's own historical or artistic conscience which clamours for satisfaction." Though historical accuracy, "even in small details," was important to her, she firmly believed that "character makes plot," and especially "the clash of character." In most of her books the main character (perhaps reflecting the major problems of her own time) must deal with seemingly irreconcilable demands (love versus honor, conflicting loyalties to race or country, for example), and in some books she does not shrink from tragic endings. But comedy and parody pervade other books. She sometimes privileges and sometimes tantalizes her reader, sometimes sharing knowledge available to one character but not others, sometimes selectively withholding information from both character and reader. She makes no concessions to her reader; she uses a fair amount of French without translation, and her widespread use of intertexts, whether as epigraphs or as an integral part of the discourse, is a feature of her writing.

The eldest of three girls and one boy, Broster was born to Thomas Mawdsley and Emilie Kathleen Gething Broster at Grassendale near Liverpool, a port situated on the Mersey. Her first memories were of ships, which figure prominently in many of her books, especially the later ones. From

Dorothy Kathleen Broster

Cheltenham Ladies' College she won a scholarship to St. Hilda's College, Oxford, where she studied modern history from 1896 to 1899; she took an honors degree, though her master of arts was not conferred until 1920. In later years she was instrumental in starting the Old Students' Association at St. Hilda's and gave generously to the college. She was perceived there as having "little oddities," going through agonies of indecision about even practical affairs of life: "before venturing out provision must be made for sun and heat, cold and damp, and always for rain, however high and steady the barometer." Her friends were conscious of her lack of confidence, which may have had a bearing on her taking no steps to correct the assumption of many of her readers for some time that her novels were written by a man. She was averse to personal publicity, but when her gender was discovered she found it necessary to insist that women could write convincingly about men.

In 1900–1901 she was secretary to Edward Armstrong, history tutor and later acting provost of Queen's College and professor of history at Oxford. From 1901 to 1913 she was secretary to Sir Charles Firth, Regius Professor of modern history at Oxford, helping him with his research, a training that,

together with her degree, influenced her own fiction. During this time, apart from some short stories and verses, she began her writing career with two collaborative novels, *Chantemerle: A Romance of the Vendean War* (1911) and *A Vision Splendid* (1913). Needing constant encouragement to write, she owed much to her college friend and first collaborator, Gertrude Winifred Taylor (who was at St. Hilda's College during 1899–1902 and to whom *The Dark Mile* [1929] is dedicated). Both books, carefully contextualized within historical periods, and with historical personages appearing peripherally, try rather heavy-handedly to combine semipolitical, religious, and romantic themes.

Chantemerle is set in the early period of the French Revolution and culminates in the Vendean revolt, its initial success and its final disastrous suppression. *A Vision Splendid* is divided between the reign in France of Louis Philippe in the 1830s, with yet another abortive rising, and England during the gradual development of the Oxford movement. In both books the love of two men for the same woman is important and foreshadows the use of such a device in several of Broster's later books. But there are marked differences in each book's treatment of the relationship. In *Chantemerle* the two men are cousins, French nobles: Comte Gilbert de Château-Foix of Chantemerle in Poitevin Vendée, betrothed to Lucienne d'Aucourt, who is a passive minor character throughout; and Louis, Vicomte de Saint-Ermay. Louis is the first representative of the type of charming Frenchman that appears so frequently in later novels. In *A Vision Splendid* the two men are Tristram Hungerford, an Englishman who is a friend of Charles Dormer of the Oxford movement, and Armand, Comte de la Roche-Guyon, a Royalist opposed to Louis Philippe. Horatia Grenville is a vivacious and self-willed heroine in *A Vision Splendid.*

In both books the charming Frenchman sweeps the woman off her feet and one of the two lovers is killed (Gilbert and Armand respectively). But where Louis is preserved in the Vendean rising to escape to England to Lucienne, Horatia marries Armand but comes to hate him because of his affair with another woman, while Tristram, after many struggles, has accepted ordination and the clerical celibacy advocated by the Oxford movement.

As she does in her other books that deal with the French Revolution, Broster adopts the bias of the Royalist side in *Chantemerle.* A speech by the Girondin Vergniaud to the National Assembly does present the opposite point of view, and graphic details about the horrors of war in the Vendean rising foreshadow the implicit antiviolence that permeates later books. The role of the Curé, M. des Graves, who persuades Gilbert to give Lucienne her freedom and to return to religious faith (and is finally rescued from France to become a cardinal), is important, and with the somewhat didactic sermons of John Keble, John Henry Newman, and Dormer in *A Vision Splendid,* suggests an interest in religion that may have been Taylor's, since in Broster's later books – until the last – religion does not again play a major part.

Complex and contradictory emotions are explored in both books: both Gilbert and Louis save each other's life, yet each feels betrayed by the other over Lucienne. Tristram introduces Armand to Horatia and later has to plead Armand's case with her father, Reverend Grenville; Armand maintains his relationship (though not his adultery) with Mme de Vigerie, and Horatia does not forgive him until he is on his deathbed. Thematically both books focus on the conflict between love (between family and friends as well as with women) and honorable behavior, foreshadowing what becomes a major theme for Broster – that of irreconcilable demands on individuals caught up in momentous historical events not of their making.

During World War I Broster nursed soldiers in Kent and in France under the auspices of the Red Cross until she fell ill and returned home early in 1916. There she continued to work on *Sir Isumbras at the Ford* (1918), her first uncollaborative novel. The book asserts that a crucial incident (the main character's escape from being shot after the abortive Royalist invasion of Quiberon Bay in 1795) is historical fact. The book's title alludes to an 1857 Pre-Raphaelite painting by John Everett Millais, showing an aging knight with a boy and girl on his horse. The six-year-old French-Scottish Comte Anne-Hilarion de Flavigny is an important figure in the book. Kidnapped by two women acting for the Republic's convention and taken to France because he has overheard information about the forthcoming expedition to Quiberon, Anne is rescued by the Chevalier Fortuné de La Vireville, a Chouan leader. In this book the love triangle is part of La Vireville's past. Returning injured to France, he falls in love with Raymonde de Guéfontaine. After the fiasco of the landing at Quiberon Bay, the blunders of which are graphically described from the point of view of those who were under incompetent commanders, La Vireville and Raymonde are brought together by the child Anne. (La Vireville appears again in a later book, *Ships in the Bay!* [1931].)

As compared with the more didactic aspects of the collaborative novels, Broster's first solo book is more concerned with action. It continues the thematic exploration of the theme of how the individual deals with personal conflicts within a larger context of warfare. Her treatment of the historical aspects of the Quiberon expedition may owe something to the time when she was writing, especially her indirect attack on the leadership bungling that so senselessly sacrificed so many men. The child Anne, who opens the book and has a significant role in motivating the actions of adults, is (like most of Broster's child characters until Arabella in her last two books) rather too sweetly drawn.

Broster believed *The Yellow Poppy* (1920) to be her best book. It is dedicated to Gertrude Schlich, who shared a house with her for the last twenty-five years of her life and to whom (so the dedication states) the book owes a good deal. Broster recounts the germ idea of *The Yellow Poppy* as being a dream: "I have a habit of dreaming vividly – that I saw the house of a great French noble, deserted after the Revolution, and that noble's wife going to it, unknown and shabbily dressed, to drink tea with the caretaker in what had been her own proud mansion. I knew nothing else whatever; but hence came the chateau of Mirabel and Valentine Duchesse de Trélan and all that follows in that rather long book."

Set against the background of the antirepublican unrest in 1799–1800 in Finistère that led to Napoleon Bonaparte's rise to power as first consul, more than half the novel deals with the barriers between the Duc and Duchesse of Trélan and how they are surmounted. Each believes the other dead, and each is misled (wittingly and unwittingly) by those around them. Each goes under an assumed name: the Duc as Gaston (M. de Kersaint) having left France at the beginning of the Revolution and having fought with the Austrians as a leader of a Royalist guerrilla group, and the Duchesse as Valentine, having survived the September massacres of 1792, as concierge of her own former home of Mirabel. The three attempts to recover the treasure hidden at Mirabel bring Valentine into contact with Roland de Céligny (Gaston's illegitimate son), the Comte Artus de Brencourt (Gaston's rival for Valentine's affections), and the Abbé Pierre Chassin (Gaston's foster brother). Though the third attempt is successful, de Brencourt refuses to reveal Valentine's identity to Gaston (Chassin is bound by the seal of the confessional) and provokes him into a duel in which Gaston is wounded before Roland unwittingly proves that she is alive. Their brief idyllic reunion is ended when the rising in the west is put down, and Gaston is ordered to surrender. His safe conduct is ignored, and he is shot at Mirabel. (The historical model for Gaston was betrayed in the same way.) The novel ends tragically with the death of the hero but without the consolation that follows the deaths of Gilbert and Armand in the earlier books, foreshadowing the tragic power of the Jacobite trilogy.

Broster said that *The Wounded Name* (1922) was "perhaps my favourite." Its background is the period from April 1814 to August 1815, and it focuses on an incident taking place in Brittany during the hundred days between Napoleon's escape from Elba and the battle of Waterloo. In 1814 the Chouan leader, L'Oiseleur, the Vicomte Aymar de La Rocheterie, travels to England and meets Comte Laurent de Courtomer, who falls under La Rocheterie's spell. Captured by Bonapartists in May 1815, Laurent finds that Aymar is his fellow prisoner, shot by his own men. Laurent's devotion to Aymar, including nursing him both at the chateau of Arbelles and (when Aymar is released) as an escapee for whom Aymar suffers torture rather than give him away, is constantly tested by his gradual discovery of more and more of the background of

what led to the actions of Aymar's men. The central section of the book is a long flashback to April 1814 as it is recounted from Aymar's point of view. Aymar tries for some months to live down the reports of his treachery but eventually seeks a court of inquiry at which he is, with the surprise appearance of one of those involved in the incident, acquitted.

Aymar's love for his cousin (whose safety provides one motive for the action that precipitates the mistaken revenge of his men) is subordinated to the exploration of his relationship with Laurent. The book sets out to consider the subjectivity of perception and how the same event can be interpreted differently by friends and by enemies, and indeed the extent to which friendship is dependent upon trust. After a series of books in which a love triangle of male/female relationships were paramount, Broster, as well as inverting the triangle by making two women love Aymar, moves male friendship (earlier a subordinate strand) into the foreground of the book, intertexually recalling the role of Horatio in William Shakespeare's *Hamlet* (1603), the source of the book's title. She also makes much more dramatic use than in earlier novels of the device of withholding information from the reader and main character alike until its revelation has maximum impact because of its changed temporal context.

After a series of books in which France has been a major, if not always the total, setting, *"Mr. Rowl"* (1924) is set entirely in England, though Raoul des Sablières, the "Mr. Rowl" of the title, is another French charmer. In this book, however, he has fought as a hussar officer for Napoleon against the English, though his parental background is that of émigrés to England. Captured at Salamanca, he briefly breaks parole to rescue from attack Miss Juliana Forrest, daughter of Lord Fulgrave, and so activates the love triangle. Juliana's fiancé, out of jealousy, denounces Raoul, and because he seeks to safeguard Juliana's reputation, Raoul as a "broke-parole" is sent to Norman Cross. Involved in an unsuccessful escape bid, Raoul is sentenced to the hulks in Devon, from which he escapes through Juliana's help. After posing as a Spanish woman and then a French woman, Raoul is captured at Stowey by a naval officer on half pay, Capt. Hervey Barrington, but gradually wins him over, and all ends happily (in a section brazenly called "A Month of Miracles") with Barrington given a new ship and Raoul becoming betrothed to Juliana and receiving a cartel for having saved the life of an English officer in Spain.

Drawing especially on two historical books about prisoners of war in Britain during the late eighteenth century, Broster, writing before Jewish concentration camps were established, sketches the sheer inhumanity of how prisoners were treated in an earlier period. In spite of this aspect of the novel, her contrasts of English and French speech and behavior utilize some rather lighthearted stereotypes, including Barrington's softheartedness toward women in distress but bitterness over being outwitted by a man posing as a woman, and Lord Fulgrave's physical resemblance to Lord Wellesley associated with his inability to control his daughter.

The comic touches becoming apparent in Broster's romances reappear only after the Jacobite trilogy, which constitutes the next, and major, period of her writing. In June 1923, she records, she (together with her friend) made her first visit to Scotland, to Inverness. It rained almost constantly, but she visited Lochaber, Lochiel's land, where the 1745 rebellion began and ended. This was the period in which Bonnie Prince Charlie made his unsuccessful attempt to gain the throne of England. Though she had not intended to write about that "tragic and romantic venture," "the spirit of the place got such a hold upon me that before I left I had the whole story planned almost in spite of myself." The picture in her mind that proved the seed for the book was the scene from the middle of the book "where my English hero Keith Windham rescues my Scottish one, Ewen Cameron, from being shot by the English redcoats after Culloden in front of a mountain sheiling." She ruefully comments that she had great trouble with Windham, "who refused to be called anything but Keith, though he was not a Scot, and in fact disliked them." She also quotes the response of a Highland scholar and historian who queries how the author (he assumes a man) obtained such an "intimate, inside knowledge of the Highland character."

The Flight of the Heron is a powerful evocation of the Jacobite rising of 1745, centering upon the unlikely friendship that grows between Ewen Cameron of Ardroy, cousin of the chief of Clan Cameron, Lochiel, and Keith Windham, an English officer of the Royal Scots, who are brought together by the flight of a heron that is foreseen by Ewen's foster father, Angus MacMartin, who foretells that the two will meet five times and that the other will render Ewen great service and cause him bitter grief.

The main characters in the book are closely associated with historical figures and events, though Broster explains that she has taken certain liberties with the character of the earl of Loudoun. The contextualizing of the English and the Highland attitudes toward the Jacobite rising is a major feature of the book, for although sympathy is predominantly with the Jacobites, Keith Windham's viewpoint is an important means by which the behavior of both the Highlanders and the English is judged (especially the victors' shocking behavior after Culloden). The male friendship between those closely associated that characterized the previous novel is now explored in terms of a growing friendship and respect between enemies (Ewen's marriage to Alison Grant which takes place halfway through the book is a minor element). The fulfilling of the opening prophecy is the main plot technique, and the conflict of loyalties on both sides – familial, clan, racial – is a main theme.

The sequel, *The Gleam in the North* (1926), is probably the most historically based of all Broster's novels. Set six years later, in 1752 and 1753, it deals with the capture and subsequent hanging of Dr. Archibald Cameron, brother of Lochiel (now dead). For the purposes of the trilogy, Archie is made a cousin of Ewen Cameron of Ardroy, who seeks to protect Archie when he returns to Scotland to attempt to rekindle the earlier rebellion. Ewen is imprisoned with his brother-in-law Hector Grant at Fort William, but though he manages to escape, Archie is betrayed by Finlay MacPhair of Glenshian, who fulfills the historical role of Pickle, the spy who assisted the English in informing the government about Highland unrest. Archie is refused a trial, and, in spite of the efforts made by Ewen through the stepfather and stepbrother of Keith Windham, he is hanged at Tyburn for high treason. Ewen in disguise attends him as a minister and hears Archie's forgiveness of his enemies.

With a less intricate plot line than its predecessor, the book depends more upon exploring the character and subjectivity of Ewen Cameron and comparing and contrasting him with Hector and Finlay MacPhair, as well as with English characters. There are reminiscences of *The Yellow Poppy* toward the end, as both conclude with judicial execution, but with the emphasis now upon the male rather than on the female response to the barbarity.

The third book of the trilogy, *The Dark Mile* (1929), returns more to the mode of fictional romance, as Ewen Cameron's cousin, Ian Stewart, falls in love with Olivia Campbell, daughter of Campbell of Cairns who at Culloden ordered the massacre of Highlanders, including Ian's elder brother. Family loyalty (especially his father's attitude) conflicts with his own love. The book is also concerned with the revenge sought by Finlay MacPhair of Glenshian on Ewen Cameron and Hector Grant and with the identification of the actual informer who enabled the English to capture Archie Cameron as Olivia's godfather, David Maitland.

With a more obviously contrived plot than the two earlier books, *The Dark Mile* is concerned with exploring the agony in the minds of two men, one of whom loves and tries to give up a woman he cannot marry because of her father's actions, the other who has betrayed another for what seemed adequate motives at the time but in retrospect are not. The title *The Dark Mile* is at once literal and symbolic, and introspection plays a more important part in the discourse. In view of the tragic endings of the two previous books, it seems that Broster has manipulated the bittersweet ending of this novel to return to the happier endings that she gave to all her later books (perhaps in response to the worsening circumstances of her own world in the pre–World War II years).

Possibly in reaction to the dark tragedies of the Jacobite trilogy, Broster's next book, *Ships in the Bay!* (1931), is what she terms a "comic opera" (and the epigraphs of the first section are taken from W. S. Gilbert and Arthur Sullivan's *Pinafore* and *Patience*). Set in Wales in 1796 and 1797, it parodies all manner of romantic motifs as it traces the accidental meeting of and growing romance between Miss Nest Meredith, daughter of the precentor of St. David's, and Martin Tyrell (who is provided with three other aliases during the course of the book), who, charged wrongly with treason, escapes from a ship onto which he has been pressed only to be bitten on the ankle by Nest's dog at their first encounter. The retrospective flashback of *The Wounded Name* reappears to account for Martin's escapade in Altona, where he falls hopelessly in love with the wife of an Irish rebel, and the abortive French invasion of Fishguard in February 1797 (the ships in the bay that abandon the landing force) forms a hilarious climax, in which La Vireville from *Sir Isumbras at the Ford* also takes an important part.

Not only does the book delightfully parody romantic plot motifs, but it is also heavily intertextual, playing with the Nausicaa/Odysseus relationship as a comparison/contrast with Nest/Martin. Its most striking character, Jonas Salt, the antiquarian, provides a great deal of the fun, especially in his conversations, which are designed to carry two or more different levels of meaning, depending on the knowledge of the recipient (including the reader).

A different type of romance, *Almond, Wild Almond* (1933), though a return to the events of 1745, contrasts with the two previous books. Lacking the parodic element of *Ships in the Bay!* but also lacking

the psychological traumas of *The Dark Mile,* the book deals peripherally with some of the participants in the Jacobite trilogy. It concerns the love of Ranald Maclean of Fasnapoll in Askay and Bride Stewart of Inchrannoch House. While Ranald is on the run after Culloden, the two are married in the kitchen while Hanoverian officers are actually being entertained by Bride's uncle (a historical incident at a nearby house). The rise and fall of the Jacobite fortunes is again the backdrop, but this book returns to a love-triangle plot. The nub of the story is Bride's attempt to save her husband from capture by Lowlanders by allowing the searching soldiers to think that an English officer has been sharing her bed. Her husband's outraged rejection of her for this action almost leads him to his death twice at the hands of his rival Gregor MacGregor and is set against the constancy of Bride's love as she fearlessly journeys to rescue him in the company of a young French officer who has previously attempted to seduce her after she has saved him from capture.

A book concerned with contrasting how men and women regard their honor in relation to love (Ranald is inclined to privilege honor over love), it also shows the greater pragmatism and steadfastness and sacrifice of women and also their power; toward the end of the book Bride is several times compared with the Virgin Mary as if to stress her purity, and the wild almond of the title symbolizes not only spring but also the metamorphosis of the deserted Phyllis into an almond tree. As well as Ovid, however, the title alludes to a poem of Herbert Trench affixed as an epigraph to the book, which poignantly problematizes whether her lover is faithful.

Broster's last collaboration, with G. Forester, is another lighthearted parody, this time of a detective story. *World Under Snow* (1935) is (apart from some of the short stories) the only book with a contemporary setting, and it is the only one that claims that "All the characters in this book are entirely imaginary." It seems to be a pastiche of a Dorothy Sayers detective story, with the Lord Peter Wimsey–type character the suspected murderer, and the amateur detective falling for the suspect's fiancée and eventually winning her (and clearing his friend).

Broster's last two books form a pair, and both return in subject to the French Revolution in the period between 1793 and 1795 and to the romance mode. *The Sea Without a Haven* (1941) deals with the vicissitudes suffered by Charlotte d'Esparre, forced by her aunt to marry a Creole, M. de Marescot, who is murdered on the evening of their marriage day. Charlotte escapes from Toulon to Leghorn and is taken from there to Corsica and Farfalletta, from which she is eventually rescued by the naval captain Nugent Carew, who marries her. In the sequel, *The Captain's Lady* (1947), Carew brings her back to his parents' home in Devon. Told by her aunt that de Marescot is still alive and entangled with her brother's acquaintance who is a French spy, she leaves Carew. He reclaims her, and she rescues him from the aftermath of the spy's activities.

In these last two books Broster returns to some aspects of one of her earliest books, *A Vision Splendid,* though with a reversal of roles. Broster features marriages between a French girl and an English man, and again the role of religion is given an important place. Charlotte leaves Carew upon hearing wrongly that her first husband is still alive, not knowing that her first marriage is not binding (she was forced into it, and it was not consummated). Throughout both books, too, while there is a constant clash of loyalties, there is also an element of escapism, signaled in part by the series of coincidences that allow for the happy endings (perhaps a reaction at the end of her life against World War II and its aftermath). An unpleasant child, Arabella Mounsey, plays an important part in both books, in marked contrast to earlier child characters.

Broster published two collections of short stories. *A Fire of Driftwood* (1932) includes a group of six stories linked (all but one) to the French Revolution, ranging from the comic to the tragic, and each with a close link to (almost a rough draft of) one of her full-length novels. The other seven are by contrast all set in the twentieth century, and all but one involve the supernatural (and in three of them religion plays an important part). Her second collection of five stories, *Couching at the Door* (1942), is also predominantly set in the twentieth century, and again the supernatural (usually associated with violence, past or present) is foregrounded. This change in period and genre in most of the short stories provides a reaction against and complement to the historical basis of most of the novels.

Broster's last years were clouded by war and domestic difficulties, but a Cheltenham and Oxford friend said in an obituary printed in the *Chronicle of the Association of Senior Members* of St. Hilda's College (1949–1950) that "she became even more tolerant, more gentle and forbearing, mellowing into a kind of serenity which her youth had hardly promised." The same friend commented that "Her life did not bring her much into contact with small children but, as one would judge from her books, she was greatly attracted by them; she would play

the most hilarious games and to the end she retained a quick apprehension of their needs and characters." Broster recounts how she received letters from many children and found them "a perpetual joy." It is perhaps fitting, then, if somewhat ironic, that she is now perceived as being a writer for children – more correctly adolescents. Late in life when her work was labeled "old-fashioned," she defended it against a critic's sneer that in it chivalry and honor are at a premium. The two aspects are not unrelated. Throughout her work, whether collaborating or on her own, she foregrounds values such as loyalty and love and condemns their opposites, forthrightly valorizing aspects of liberal humanism in a way that may now be perceived as suitable for younger readers, whereas her original audience of adult readers may find the methods by which such values are advocated escapist and somewhat simplistic.

Yet in other ways her work does not avoid the problematics of history and its construction (too often by the winning side). From her first collaborative book, Broster has been concerned with the broader sociocultural context in which individuals are caught up and which poses problems that can seem irreconcilable. In exploring such events in the historical past (as in virtually all her full-length books in contrast to her short stories), she is implicitly commenting on her own period. Focusing in the main upon two earlier periods of upheaval and conflict not unlike her own, the French Revolution and the Jacobite rising of 1745, she has always brought out how her protagonists are part of a larger whole, and though her sympathies are with the losing side in each case, she does not neglect to sketch other perspectives on the events.

The overall development of Broster's writing is striking. She begins two early collaborative books with conventional love triangles, where plot and character are subordinated to the ideas (such as those of the Oxford movement) and the complexities of various strands are not neatly integrated. But in Broster's solo efforts the balance is reversed. Thematically she tends to portray characters who face cultural and personal conflicts because of mutually exclusive demands of a historical situation, such as loyalty to a loved one, set against family political, racial, or religious loyalties. The love of man and woman, which is a major focus in the early and late books, is in her midcareer balanced by a foregrounding of male friendships. While the earlier books emphasize the men, the later books are equally concerned with the women, how love affects them and how they respond (*Almond, Wild Al-*

mond is especially important here, though the last two novels use Charlotte as the preeminent focalizer). From the beginning of her career she is not afraid to climax a book with the death of a major character, though in her later books the death of major characters is avoided as romance and comic elements become more important and as she plays with novelistic conventions and stereotypes.

Broster is recorded as having a delightful wit and as being able to reveal the absurdities in daily happenings, and comic elements appear in most books, often within conversation, though only two are totally comic, *Ships in the Bay!* and *World Under Snow.* A major device that appears in many books can be used for both comic and more serious purposes: dialogue that carries multiple levels of meaning, depending on the extent of knowledge of speaker and recipient(s) – including the reader. There is also the challenge to the reader offered by a considerable use of intertextuality, as Broster alludes to Greek and Roman classics as well as a good deal of French and English literature (often not translating her French quotations).

On the whole Broster's style is not so highly wrought as to draw attention to itself, though she makes judicious use of symbolism, especially in midcareer, and on occasion of poetically described landscape (especially in the Scottish books). In her rendition of conversation, she does differentiate between the class of the speakers with a representation of dialect in some books for the lower-class protagonists. She asked, "why should not a good story be clothed in good English?," and she always set out to combine the two.

In dealing predominantly with the historical past in her novels, Broster has perhaps sought escape from but has also indirectly taken up some of the fundamental issues of culture and society that were of concern to her contemporaries. Her displaced exploration of problems of the interwar period is interesting for the insights it reveals about her own period as well as about the periods in which her novels were set.

Reference:

Vera Brittain, *The Women at Oxford. A Fragment of History* (London: Harrap, 1960).

Papers:

Some manuscripts by Broster are held by St. Hilda's College, Oxford University.

Richmal Crompton

(15 November 1890 – 11 January 1969)

Margaret J. Masson
St. John's College, Durham

BOOKS: *Just William* (London: Newnes, 1922);
More William (London: Newnes, 1922);
The Innermost Room (London: Melrose, 1923);
William Again (London: Newnes, 1923);
The Hidden Light (London: Hodder & Stoughton, 1924);
William the Fourth (London: Newnes, 1924);
Anne Morrison (London: Jarrolds, 1925);
Still William (London: Newnes, 1925);
The Wildings (London: Hodder & Stoughton, 1925);
David Wilding (London: Hodder & Stoughton, 1926);
The House (London: Hodder & Stoughton, 1926); republished as *Dread Dwelling* (New York: Boni & Liveright, 1926);
Kathleen and I, and, of Course, Veronica (London: Hodder & Stoughton, 1926);
William the Conqueror (London: Newnes, 1926);
Enter – Patricia (London: Newnes, 1927);
Leadon Hill (London: Hodder & Stoughton, 1927);
Millicent Dorrington (London: Hodder & Stoughton, 1927);
A Monstrous Regiment (London: Hutchinson, 1927);
William the Outlaw (London: Newnes, 1927);
William in Trouble (London: Newnes, 1927);
Felicity Stands By (London: Newnes, 1928);
The Middle Things (London: Hutchinson, 1928);
Mist and Other Stories (London: Hutchinson, 1928);
Roofs Off! (London: Hodder & Stoughton, 1928);
The Thorn Bush (London: Hodder & Stoughton, 1928);
William the Good (London: Newnes, 1928);
Abbot's End (London: Hodder & Stoughton, 1929);
The Four Graces (London: Hodder & Stoughton, 1929);
Ladies First (London: Hutchinson, 1929);
Sugar and Spice and Other Stories (London: Ward Lock, 1929);
William (London: Newnes, 1929);
Blue Flames (London: Hodder & Stoughton, 1930);
Naomi Godstone (London: Hodder & Stoughton, 1930);

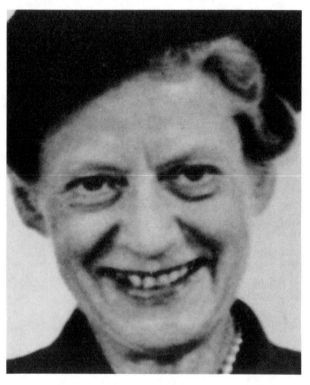

Richmal Crompton

William the Bad (London: Newnes, 1930);
William's Happy Days (London: Newnes, 1930);
The Silver Birch and Other Stories (London: Hutchinson, 1931);
William's Crowded Hours (London: Newnes, 1931);
Marriage of Hermione (London: Macmillan, 1932);
Portrait of a Family (London: Macmillan, 1932);
The Odyssey of Euphemia Tracy (London: Macmillan, 1932);
William the Pirate (London: Newnes, 1932);
The Holiday (London: Macmillan, 1933);
William the Rebel (London: Newnes, 1933);
Chedsy Place (London: Macmillan, 1934);
The Old Man's Birthday (London: Macmillan, 1934; Boston: Little, Brown, 1935);
William the Gangster (London: Newnes, 1934);

Quartet (London: Macmillan, 1935);

William the Detective (London: Newnes, 1935);

Caroline (London: Macmillan, 1936);

The First Morning (London: Hutchinson, 1936);

Sweet William (London: Newnes, 1936);

There Are Four Seasons (London: Macmillan, 1937);

William the Showman (London: Newnes, 1937);

Journeying Wave (London: Macmillan, 1938);

William the Dictator (London: Newnes, 1938);

Merlin Bay (London: Macmillan, 1939);

William and the A.R.P. (London: Newnes, 1939); republished as *William's Bad Resolution* (London: Newnes, 1956);

Steffan Green (London: Macmillan, 1940);

William and the Evacuees (London: Newnes, 1940); republished as *William and the Filmstar* (London: Newnes, 1956);

Narcissa (London: Macmillan, 1941);

William Does His Bit (London: Newnes, 1941);

Mrs. Frensham Describes a Circle (London: Macmillan, 1942);

Weatherley Parade (London: Macmillan, 1944);

William Carries On (London: Newnes, 1945);

William and the Brain Trust (London: Newnes, 1945);

Westover (London: Hutchinson, 1946);

The Ridleys (London: Hutchinson, 1947);

Family Roundabout (London: Hutchinson, 1948);

Just William's Luck (London: Newnes, 1948);

Jimmy (London: Newnes, 1949);

Frost at Morning (London: Hutchinson, 1950);

William the Bold (London: Newnes, 1950);

Jimmy Again (London: Newnes, 1951);

William and the Tramp (London: Newnes, 1952);

Linden Rise (London: Hutchinson, 1952);

The Gypsy's Baby (London: Hutchinson, 1954);

William and the Moon Rocket (London: Newnes, 1954);

Four in Exile (London: Hutchinson, 1955);

Matty and Dearingroydes (London: Hutchinson, 1956);

William and the Space Animal (London: Newnes, 1956);

William and the Artist's Model (London: J. Garnet Miller, 1956);

Blind Man's Bluff (London: Hutchinson, 1957);

William's Television Show (London: Newnes, 1958);

Wise Man's Folly (London: Hutchinson, 1959);

The Inheritor (London: Hutchinson, 1960);

William the Explorer (London: Newnes, 1960);

William's Treasure Trove (London: Newnes, 1962);

William and the Witch (London: Newnes, 1964);

Jimmy the Third (London: Armada, 1965);

William and the Pop Singers (London: Newnes, 1965);

William and the Masked Ranger (London: Newnes, 1966);

William the Superman (London: Newnes, 1968);

William the Lawless (London: Newnes, 1970).

It comes as a surprise to most fans of the popular Just William series that the creator of the quintessentially scruffy, ebullient, anti-intellectual, and antiestablishment eleven-year-old William was a woman. Richmal Crompton was in many ways the very opposite of the character whose creation made her famous. A private, self-effacing woman, she taught classics before illness forced her into retirement at the age of thirty-three. She never married and had no children of her own. Richmal Crompton's unusual Christian name, an amalgam of some distant forebears' Christian names, Richard and Mally (the latter a nickname for Mary), creates an ambiguity that no doubt contributed to the early mystique surrounding her identity. Her name was in fact Richmal Crompton Lamburn – known to her friends as "Ray" – and the early anonymity that her nom de plume afforded her was reluctantly relinquished with her growing fame. Indeed, Crompton was always a little coy about making her reputation as the writer of the William books. Her real aspiration was to be a successful novelist, and she published over forty novels for adults. Unfortunately, these tend toward the banal and sentimental in a way that her William stories hardly ever do, and to Crompton's chagrin her novels were often marketed on the basis of being by the same author as the William books.

In creating a character who was the antithesis of the conventional child-hero of the day, Crompton introduced a rambunctious antihero who is never willingly clean and is regularly baffled by grown-up logic and values. This subversive, anarchic spirit is probably the key to William's appeal. The "ideal child" – polite, obedient, and with a horror of dirtying his white silk suits – is pilloried along with other pompous or pretentious figures, and the besting of such conventional authority no doubt provides the kind of compensation that is important at certain stages in a child's fictive world. Yet adults, although more resigned to the constraints and hypocrisies of polite, middle-class culture, also relish the kind of free spirit embodied in William.

Indeed, the first stories were written with an adult audience in mind, and only much later in Crompton's writing life did she begin to write primarily for her younger audience. By this time the stories were already losing some of their wit. The irony that came from the gap in perception between child-character and grown-up reader diminished, and the liveliness and humor of the stories gradually waned. For the most part, however, the William stories seem to have been widely popular despite their middle-class, parochial English setting. William has been beloved by children and adults from a wide stratum of British society, and the series has been translated into seventeen languages. Yet only two of Crompton's novels – *Dread Dwelling* (1926), which first appeared in England as *The House,* and *The Old Man's Birthday* (1934) – were ever published in the United States, and only a few of her stories crossed the Atlantic. The lack of popularity of the Just William series in the United States may be due to the fact that America has its own slightly older version of William in the character of Penrod Schofield, the young tearaway created by Booth Tarkington. Crompton believed that the American child developed "straight from the cradle to adolescence" and therefore bypassed the prepubescent world of eleven-year-old William Brown.

Richmal Crompton Lamburn was born on 15 November 1890 in the old mill town of Bury, Lancashire. Her father, Edward J. S. Lamburn, came from a farming family in the Buckinghamshire area, but by the time he met Richmal's mother he was a licensed curate who had decided to be a schoolmaster and was teaching in Bury Grammar School. Clara Crompton Lamburn, Richmal's mother, was the daughter of a Bury chemist. Richmal was the couple's second child – seventeen months younger than her sister Gwen and two and a half years older than her brother, Jack. When Richmal was five, a younger sister, Phylis, died at the age of fourteen months.

Crompton's childhood was happy, with a secure and close-knit family which, although far from wealthy, was certainly not plagued with financial worries. Crompton was sensitive and shy, and her mother worried over her lack of natural assertion and her introspective temperament. Richmal was remembered as a highly imaginative child who would escape when she could to the attic, where she composed her first stories and poems in the privacy she found there. Her first "magazine" had only her young brother and her doll as its audience: even at a young age, Crompton shunned the attention that her literary achievements attracted.

For the first few years of her formal education, Crompton attended the local private school; then at the age of eleven she followed Gwen on to the Clergy Daughters' School in Warrington, some twenty-three miles away. The regime at this school was austere to the point of being spartan, and their father's strong sense of duty toward his daughters' moral training would have been soundly reinforced in their early years at Warrington. After an outbreak of scarlet fever in 1904, the school moved to Darley Dale. There, in the beautiful hill country of Derbyshire, a somewhat more relaxed regime was established, and the school became known as St. Elphin's after the parish church in Warrington. Crompton's school days were, by all accounts, happy and successful. She seems to have shed some of the shyness and introversion that sometimes had made her earlier childhood painful, and in an environment where the seriousness of education for girls was assumed, her scholarly gifts were also nurtured and bore fruit. Crompton's academic successes, notably in Latin, were recorded in the school magazine, and as she grew to share her father's love for the classics her relationship with him grew closer.

At St. Elphin's Crompton's writing took on a more public dimension. She became a member of the school's magazine committee and was a regular contributor of amusing rhymes and stories. Reports in the magazine comment appreciatively on a skit written by "Ray Lamburn" that was obviously a caricature of school life. This subversive talent was put to use in more-limited circles in the form of a satiric school diary which amused Crompton's friends. Her later literary exposé of St. Elphin's as the model for the school in her early autobiographical novel *Anne Morrison* (1925) was not considered amusing. The headmistress at that time, who had taught at the school when Crompton was a pupil, forbade any St. Elphin's pupil to read it; the consequent rift between headmistress and author was to last for forty years.

In 1911 Crompton was offered a place at Newnham College in Cambridge to read classics, but she had already accepted a scholarship to Royal Holloway College in London and went there to train as a classics teacher. She was remembered as a quiet, modest student with a marked sense of humor but with few intimate friends. Nevertheless, she was a keen athlete, was elected senior first-year student, and graduated as the best candidate of 1914. It was an interesting time to be at a woman's college: the suffragette campaign was at its height, and Crompton, although not a militant campaigner, was an active supporter in the cause. This is not a pronounced feature in her later writing, however; indeed, the William books, with an eleven-year-old boy as their hero, depend for much of their humor on the stereotypical disdain for the feminine. War

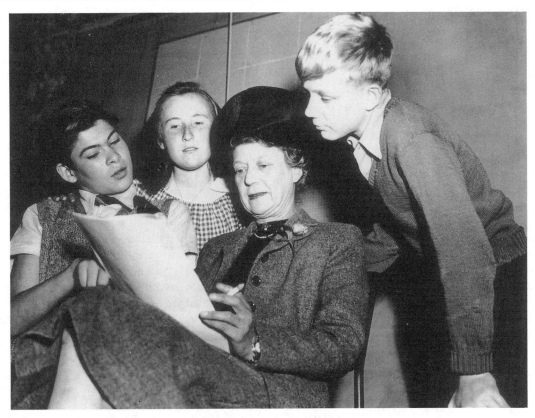

Crompton meeting with the young actors in the BBC radio series "Just William," 7 June 1948
(Hulton Deutsch Collection)

was declared against Germany a few weeks before Crompton's class sat for their final exams. Therefore, it is not surprising that no student that year gained a first-class degree.

After graduation Crompton returned to St. Elphin's, where she spent the next three years teaching classics. Her father died in 1915, and her mother moved to London to live with Gwen and her husband. To be nearer her mother and sister, Crompton took up the post of classics mistress at Bromley High School, a private girls' day school where she taught for six years. In this pleasant London suburb she bought a house in which she and her mother set up a home together, and in Bromley, Crompton started to submit her writing for publication. The first of her stories appeared in the *Girls Own Paper and Women's Magazine* and was titled "Thomas," an unremarkable debut with an utterly conventional young hero. It was followed by the story "One Crowded Hour," which was published in the September 1918 *Home Magazine*. The second story was a much livelier piece, with a protagonist who was clearly the prototype for William – although William's appearance proper did not come until February 1919 as the hero of "Rice Mould," also published in *Home Magazine*.

Beginning in 1919 Crompton, though she preferred writing romantic fiction, could only get the publisher to accept a love story if it were accompanied by a William story. For more than three years a William story appeared almost every month in *Home Magazine,* and, beginning with the character's second appearance, Thomas Henry provided the illustrations. Such a good fit was there between illustrations and stories that Henry's pictures became an almost integral part of the William series. Until his death in 1962 Henry was the only conceivable William illustrator; the most popular of his successors was Henry Ford. From 1922 until its collapse in 1940 the *Happy Mag* published the William stories. "Every story has a happy ending" was its motto, and the magazine was intended to appeal to the whole family. At this stage the William stories came to be read by children as well as their parents, and the publisher, Newnes, began to republish the stories in book form, thirty-eight volumes in total.

During her early days as a regular contributor to the *Happy Mag,* Crompton's dilemma about the growing conflict between her teaching and her writing was resolved. In the summer of 1923 she became ill with poliomyelitis and nearly died. Her convalescence left her without the use of her right leg and unable to return to full-time teaching. As she grew stronger, she turned her full energy to her writing career. Crompton had been a dedicated, imaginative, and successful teacher, and with great regret she was forced to give it up. Nevertheless, with her growing popularity as a writer, it would have been increasingly hard to keep up with her publisher's demands.

Crompton continued to pour the deepest part of herself into her full-length novels and yet continued to win acclaim for the William stories. More than once she tried to eliminate the troublesome boy, but the demand for the irrepressible character always won the day. Undoubtedly the love stories sustained and satisfied her in important ways; she continued to write them at the rate of about one a year — matching her output of the William books — even after it became obvious that the quality of these full-length novels was probably never going to rise above the mediocre. In some ways their world is an interesting complement to that of William. Crompton's early novels are highly autobiographical and offer many clues into the development of the character and inner life of their author. *The Innermost Room* (1923) and *Anne Morrison* are particularly interesting for these reasons. Family relationships in the novels reveal interesting aspects of Crompton's own family life. In particular, *Anne Morrison,* the most directly autobiographical, reveals much about Edward Lamburn in what amounts to a sympathetic portrait of the shy, austere schoolteaching clergyman with a passion for learning. It also offers an intriguing account of the heroine's school days, with what may well have been the damningly offensive insights into the "special friendships" at a girls' boarding school.

When Anne goes to college, the novel explores her response to the suffragette movement and early feminism. While broadly sympathetic and committed to winning the right to vote for women, the heroine feels a definite ambivalence toward feminism; she is suspicious of extremists, of those women who too wholeheartedly challenge the (male) status quo and thereby undermine their own femininity. A related ambivalence pervades Crompton's portrayal of the relationships between the sexes in the novels. These relationships are often entirely conventional: the men are strong and restless and not entirely to be trusted; the women are dependent, passive, and long-suffering. When there are more independent women, they are rarely at the center of the narrative and are never cast as positive role models. Sex is treated with discretion, but there

are hints of the traditional woman's fear and suspicion of it as something brutish and distasteful. In general, Crompton's novels accurately reflect the mores and values of Edwardian middle-class England; in no significant way do they challenge or radically question the culture within which they are written, and perhaps for this reason they would easily be forgotten — were it not for the fact that their author also wrote about a small boy called William.

The William stories are based on the same world as the novels, and it is their genius that they do not leave the reader's perception of that world as it was before. Like all good satire, they expose the absurdities in a world initially considered normal. Written over a period of some fifty years, the social world of William naturally changes. But the changes are relatively superficial and reflect the changing expectations of the English middle class. So in the early days the Brown household has a cook, a housemaid, and a gardener. By the 1960s only a single helper comes in each day to assist Mrs. Brown with the chores.

The Brown family consists of Mr. Brown, who goes off each day to work at an unspecified job in the city; the somewhat passive Mrs. Brown, who spends much of her time darning socks, knitting, or attending tea parties with the other worthy women of the village; and Robert and Ethel, William's elder siblings, who are among his regular adversaries in the tales. Ethel is about nineteen years old — vapid, vain, and, to judge from the reactions of the men who come into her orbit, one of the most attractive young women in the village. She has a succession of lovelorn suitors, and, while their regard for his sister baffles William, he is only too willing to aid or obstruct romance when it serves his purposes. Robert's age fluctuates between seventeen and twenty-one and, except for a short period during the war when he is in military service, he is perpetually a student. As aspiring intellectual and a cultured young man, his scruffy younger brother is a constant source of irritation. William is the dreaded saboteur of the plans Robert holds most dear, whether they be activities of the Young Bolsheviks or of the Society of Twentieth-Century Poets, or his attempts to woo the latest number on the ever-lengthening list of The One Great Love of Robert's life. Together, the Brown family provides the most immediate source of the grown-up, conventional normality that baffles and frustrates William. The animosity and incomprehension between William and his family is mutual — with the exception of his mother, who, against all odds, has a touching faith in her younger son.

Equally significant in William's supporting cast of characters is the group of friends who constitute the Outlaws. Apart from the ever-faithful Joan, who is one of the few females not tainted with complicity in the dubious world of civilization in the William stories, the Outlaws is a select and secretive group consisting of William and his three closest male friends: Ginger, Henry, and Douglas. Jumble, William's devoted and long-suffering mongrel, is also an indispensable member of William's inner cabinet. Kindred spirits, they are all bound together by a loyalty that is regularly strengthened by their exploits against their common foes: the Hubert Lane gang; their unreasonable, unappreciative families; the adult world at large; and girls. In this last group the particular bane of their lives is one Violet Elizabeth Bott, a six-year-old embodiment of manipulative feminine wiles. On her first encounter with the unprepared William in *Still William* (1925), her trembling lower lip and threats to "thcream and thcream until I'm thick. And I can" render him helpless to refuse her request to "Kith [her]." She even has the young hero – sworn enemy to all things feminine – dress up as a gnome to play "fairieth" with his new and terrifying antagonist. William's relation to members of the opposite sex is not altogether reliable, and he is from time to time capable of heroic infatuations, his steely manhood susceptible to being melted by a particularly attractive or appreciative female.

Violet Elizabeth's family, the Botts, quickly became regulars in the William stories. A modest, small-time grocer who concocts a sauce so wonderful that its advertisements convince many "that any food without Botts' sauce was rank poison," Botty finds himself one of the nouveau riche, master of the Hall and, from time to time, wilting under the onerous burdens of his new social position. The Botts are the perfect targets for a satire of the pretensions of social climbers. Yet Crompton's treatment of Mrs. Bott as she desperately tries to acquire some aristocratic relatives or invite some literary luminary to the Hall in hopes of attaining reflected glory for herself is not wholly unsympathetic. The Botts are, after all, not quite the pillars of the establishment they aspire to be in the tight-knit fabric of village life.

The William series also assembles a colorful cast of occasional characters who are more obviously outsiders bringing dramatic and thematic interest to the stories. Some of these include the burglars and desperadoes who from time to time inspire the Outlaws in their bold stands against the prevailing social order. Yet when these characters violate the fierce sense of fairness that inhabits the deepest recesses of the Outlaws' moral sensibilities, a display of heroism sometimes results, albeit briefly, in a truce between William and his would-be critics. William is always drawn to those on the fringes of respectable village life: his affection for tramps and the like is no doubt partly because they, like him, have no reason to be friends with established authority and will not prove a threat to his anarchic individualism. The more interesting outsiders are less predictable: the maiden aunt of strict religious convictions who enters into the delights of the fairground with an empathy and vigor that are out of character with what one expects from an elderly great-aunt; the current love of Robert's life, who turns out to take an intelligent interest in William's pursuits; the "Great Man" from the cabinet who is late for a political meeting because he is absorbed in one of William's plays; the scheming uncle who helps the Outlaws devise a plot to undermine his impossibly perfect nephew. Whenever an adult appears who can empathetically share the rich imaginative world of William and his friends – someone who sees, as they do, that not all is always just and authentic in the world of powerful adulthood – such a person is welcomed with a sense of vindicated justice.

But to suggest that William is a paragon of moral seriousness would be to do him a grave disservice. William adheres to a certain boyhood code which, while not always requiring that one be strictly truthful – for the enemy clearly does not always have the right to be told the full truth – prohibits cruelty. None of the darker boyish exploits involving cruelty to animals appear that one finds, for example, in Penrod Schofield, William's closest equivalent in the United States. William also does not have the self-awareness of the more sophisticated Penrod, and his innocence and inability to appreciate irony increase the comic dimension of much of the sarcasm displayed by some of the grown-up characters. Unlike the plans of the children in Enid Blyton's stories, William's seldom work out as he intends; the endings of the stories are not usually ones that William himself would have chosen. Crompton presents her readers with a world in which they are encouraged to laugh at the ridiculous situations in which many of William's exploits land him. He is a character who appeals to his audience partly because they can see why his plans fail and his grandiose schemes come to naught. It is not a smug child's world, self-congratulatory against all adults and all authority, but one that understands and identifies with the anarchic, egotistic, and unsocialized child even while it recognizes the ways in which such anarchy cannot finally triumph. William, then, invites both the reader's sympathy and judgment, his or her affinity with the hero mixed also with a nostalgic superiority over the young boy who has not yet come to terms with the conventions and limits of the adult social world.

The irritation of William's family with their youngest boy is also capable of eliciting sympathy in the reader: William is garrulous to a degree that tests the patience of even his ever-optimistic mother. Crompton brilliantly presents the monologues of the indignant, verbally persistent child who fails to appreciate that his litany of indignant justifications or requests, or even his attempts to be friendly, are extremely provocative. "Can't we do anything about William?" asks his exasperated sister on more than one occasion; "Can't we send him to an orphanage or anything?" William's rhetoric – with its strict childhood logic, its repetition of the particular overworked phrase, and its strategy of the aggrieved rhetorical question – is artfully evoked. In *William and the Evacuees* (1940), when he breaks much of the household's crockery in his attempts to become a juggler, his justification is typical: "D'you think jugglers can throw up plates like that without practisin? D'you think they're born throwing plates like that? They've gotter break a few plates an' things practisin. Stands to reason."

In the later stories William's grammar conforms more closely to Standard English, but by then the series is already in decline. At its best, Crompton's representation of the colloquial speech patterns of a child gives the William stories much of their effectiveness. Perhaps more than any other single feature, William's "dreaded eloquence" creates a memorable and unmistakable character. Its comic effect is foregrounded by its counterpointing with the narrator's tone and stance: through this, Crompton's authorial wit, irony, and gentle satire heighten the humor of the stories, as in this passage from *Just William* (1922):

> In all its activities the Society of Outlaws (comprising four members) aimed at a simple, unostentatious mode of procedure. In their shrinking from the glare of publicity they showed an example of unaffected modesty that many other public societies might profitably emulate. The parents of the members were unaware of the very existence of the society. The ill-timed and tactless interference of parents had nipped in the bud many a cherished plan, and by bitter experience the Outlaws had learnt that secrecy was their only protection. Owing to

the rules and regulations of an unsympathetic world that orders school hours from 9 to 4 their meetings were confined to half-holidays and occasionally Sunday afternoons.

Such a passage reveals the way in which Crompton uses the measured language of adult sobriety to articulate a view of anarchic youth. She skillfully exploits the juxtapositioning of such stylistically fine, balanced prose – poised, cultured, and serene – with the crumpled immediacy of William's own speech. In these jumps in tone, the irony is sharpened as the dissonance is widened. The adult reader appreciates this irony at a more sophisticated level, more quickly recognizes specific targets of satire, and is more likely than the child reader to pick up some of the allusions to classical literature that enrich Crompton's humor.

Yet on at least one occasion Crompton's humor, in retrospect, came to be considered in bad taste. In 1934 she wrote a story titled "William and the Nasties," republished as *William the Detective* (1935), in which William has learned that in Germany, Jewish shopkeepers were being thrown out of their shops by the "Nasties." With visions of himself chasing "Jew after Jew out of sweetshop after sweetshop and appropriating the precious spoils," William longs to join such a cause. Once the scale of Nazi anti-Semitism became apparent, Crompton, like most of her British contemporaries, was appalled, and her subsequent novels are replete with references to the "monstrous evil" of Nazi atrocities. But in her own prewar anti-Semitism and failure to appreciate the impending catastrophe of the Nazis' rise to power, Crompton was typical of her nationality and class.

Despite William's subversive nature, Crompton was a conservative by temperament. A lifelong supporter of and sometime campaigner for the Conservative Party in Britain, Crompton was generally bored with politics and was no great advocate of radical change. An unostentatiously religious woman, she was at home in the mainstream Anglican Church and contributed to numerous charities and good causes. She particularly supported the work of her cousin Canon Robin Lamburn, a saintly man (the only Englishman to be awarded the Albert Schweitzer Award) who spent his life working in a leprosy hospital in Tanzania. As she grew older, she became increasingly interested in meditation and mysticism and supported the work of the Church Fellowship of Psychic Study. It is indicative of the self-parodic style of Crompton's satire that psychic incidents – along with maiden aunts, well-meaning church ladies, heads-in-the-clouds intellectuals, and ineffectual clergymen – all provide popular targets for ridicule in the William stories.

Crompton's success meant that publishers were keen to encourage her to try her hand at creating other children's sagas. It is surprising, given her firsthand experience of girls' schools, that Crompton's attempt at a female equivalent of William was not a success, and her efforts to develop a new boy character, Jimmy, were also disappointing. Although Crompton continued to publish her novels, the William stories continued to be successful. In the 1960s, as Crompton's writing powers diminished and she began to feel "written out," more of her energy went into helping with film and television scripts of her stories, and William continued to delight new generations through such various modern media.

Crompton continued to live with her mother until the latter's death in 1939. When war broke out soon after Clara Lamburn's death, Crompton's sister Gwen moved in, bringing with her Margaret and Richmal, her two daughters. Her son, Tom, was already away at war. Gwen had divorced her husband in 1935, and she had, along with her own family, for some time been an integral part of her sister's household. Indeed, young Tom Disher was one of several models for William Brown: Crompton's brother, Jack, and, much later, Edward Ashbee, the son of her niece Richmal, were two other main sources of inspiration for William's exploits. Gwen and her family lived with Crompton until 1943, and Jack moved in for a few months after he was invalided out of the Royal Air Force. In general, however, Crompton preferred to live alone with her dog, Ming, after the death of her mother.

That Crompton never married has inevitably caused some speculation: her novels offer some evidence of a fear of and distaste for men and sex. Yet those who knew her have described her as a woman who enjoyed the company of men but did not have great opportunities, given her social circumstances, for courtship. No doubt her dearly guarded privacy, her permanent disability, her mother's watchful care, and the failure of her sister's marriage all acted as disincentives in the pursuit of romance. The sustenance of a warm network of friends and her close involvement in the families of both her sister and brother seemed to provide Crompton with all the companionship she needed.

Crompton negotiated life with her paralyzed leg with considerable success. Her work reveals no traces of self-pity or bitterness, and indeed, on three occasions in novels written after her illness, Crompton makes facetious references to deformed limbs. In 1960 she twice broke a leg, and her health became more precarious after a heart attack in 1961. Despite the threat of remaining a semi-invalid after a long hospitalization, Crompton was determined to live a full and relatively independent life until another heart attack finally killed her on 11 January 1969. Her last evening had been spent with the family of her niece and namesake, Richmal Ashbee. Crompton's funeral service was at Saint Nicholas Church in Chislehurst on 16 January, and she was cremated in the nearby town of Eltham.

As in life, so in death was Crompton acclaimed as the creator of the world of William Brown. Her obituaries bore testimony to the enormous affection in which this lovable rascal continued to be held: many of his fans had by now grown up to be politicians and journalists, college principals and lawyers, alternative comedians and pop stars. Michael Palin, of Monty Python fame, and John Lennon were both devoted fans. Neither the films nor the television series have been quite as successful as their literary originals. The stories themselves have been undergoing some revival in recent years in Britain and are read and reread on the radio. The books, regularly reprinted since the mid 1980s, continue to sell well, both to first-time readers and to wistful adults. Since the mid 1980s Richmal Crompton has attracted more serious critical attention: the first – and hitherto only – critical biographies of her were both published in 1986. The name Richmal Crompton or the mention of "Just William" still has power to bring nostalgic smiles to many adults, and allusions in newspaper columns, obituaries, and quiz shows confirm that the scruffy little boy from an unnamed village in England is as firmly a part of contemporary British culture as any other character from the world of British children's fiction.

Biographies:

Mary Cadogan, *Richmal Crompton: The Woman Behind William* (London: Unwin, 1986);

Kay Williams, *Just – Richmal: The Life and Work of Richmal Crompton Lamburn* (Guildford: Genesis, 1986).

Reference:

Mary Cadogan and David Schutte, *The William Companion* (London: Macmillan, 1990).

Eleanor Farjeon

(13 February 1881 – 5 June 1965)

David Barratt
Chester College

BOOKS: *Floretta,* music by Harry Farjeon (London: Henderson & Spalding, 1899);

The Registry Office: An Operetta in 1 Act, music by Harry Farjeon (London: Henderson & Spalding, 1900);

A Gentleman of the Road, music by Harry Farjeon (London: Boosey & Hawkes, 1903);

Pan-Worship and Other Poems (London: Elkin Matthews, 1908);

Dream Songs for the Beloved (London: Orpheus Press, 1911);

Trees (London: Batsford, 1914);

Arthur Rackham: The Wizard at Home (New York: Century, 1914);

Nursery Rhymes of London Town, illustrated by Macdonald Gill (London: Duckworth, 1916);

More Nursery Rhymes of London, illustrated by Gill (London: Duckworth, 1917);

Sonnets and Poems (Oxford: Blackwell, 1918);

All the Way to Alfriston, illustrated by Robin Guthrie (Bognor Regis, Sussex: Greenleaf Press, 1918);

Singing Games for Children, illustrated by J. Littlejohns (New York: Dutton / London: Dent, 1919); republished, with music (London: Oxford University Press, 1927–1930);

A First Chapbook of Rounds; A Second Chapbook of Rounds, music by Harry Farjeon, illustrated by John Garside, notation by Winifred How (New York: Dutton, 1919; London: Dent, 1919);

Gypsy and Ginger, illustrated by C. E. Brock (New York: Dutton, 1920; London: Dent, 1920);

Tomfooleries, as "Tomfool" (London: Daily Herald, 1920);

Moonshine, as "Tomfool" (London: Labour Publishing/Allen & Unwin, 1921);

Martin Pippin in the Apple Orchard (London: Collins, 1921; New York: Stokes, 1922);

Songs for Music and Lyrical Poems, illustrated by John Aveten (London: Selwyn & Blount, 1922);

Eleanor Farjeon

Tunes for a Penny Piper, illustrated by Aveten (London: Selwyn & Blount, 1922);

The Soul of Kol Nikon (New York: Stokes, 1923; London: Collins, 1923);

All the Year Round (London: Collins, 1923); republished as *Around the Seasons* (New York: Walck / London: Hamish Hamilton, 1969);

The Country Child's Alphabet, illustrated by William M. Rothenstein (London: Poetry Bookshop, 1924);

The Town Child's Alphabet, illustrated by David Jones (London: Poetry Bookshop, 1924);

Mighty Men, 2 volumes; *Book 1: Achilles to Julius Caesar,* illustrated by Hugh Chesterman (Oxford:

Blackwell, 1924); *Book 2: Beowulf to Harold,* illustrated by Chesterman (Oxford: Blackwell, 1925); republished in 1 volume as *Mighty Men: from Achilles to Harold* (New York: Appleton-Century, 1926; Oxford: Blackwell, 1928);

Faithful Jenny Dove and Other Tales (London: Collins, 1925); revised as *Faithful Jenny Dove and Other Illusions* (London: M. Joseph, 1963);

Nuts and May: a Medley for Children, illustrated by Rosalind Thornycroft (London: Collins, 1925);

Young Folk and Old (Shaftesbury, Dorset: High House Press, 1925);

Songs from "Punch" for Children, music by the author (London: Saville, 1925);

Tom Cobble, illustrated by M. Dobson (Oxford: Blackwell, 1925);

Singing Games from Arcady, music by the author (Oxford: Blackwell, 1926);

Italian Peepshow, and Other Tales, illustrated by Thornycroft (New York: Stokes, 1926); republished as *Italian Peepshow and Other Stories,* illustrated by Irene Mountfort (Oxford: Blackwell, 1934); revised as *Italian Peepshow,* illustrated by Edward Ardizzone (London: Oxford University Press, 1960);

Joan's Door, illustrated by Will Townsend (London: Collins, 1926; New York: Stokes, 1927);

The King's Barn: or, Joan's Tale (London: Collins, 1927);

The Mill of Dreams: or, Jennifer's Tale (London: Collins, 1927);

Young Gerard: or, Joyce's Tale (London: Collins, 1927);

Come Christmas, illustrated by Molly McArthur (London: Collins, 1927); republished, illustrated by Rachel Field (New York: Stokes, 1928);

The Wonderful Knight, illustrated by Doris Pailthorpe (Oxford: Blackwell, 1927);

The ABC of the B.B.C., illustrated by T. C. Derrick (London: Collins, 1928);

Snowfall (London: Favil Press, 1928);

A Bad Day for Martha, illustrated by Eugenie Richards (Oxford: Blackwell, 1928);

An Alphabet of Magic, illustrated by Margaret Tarrant (London: Medici Society, 1928);

Kaleidoscope (London: Collins, 1928; New York: Stokes, 1929); revised edition, illustrated by Ardizzone (New York: Walck, 1963; London: Oxford University Press, 1963);

The Perfect Zoo, illustrated by Kathleen Burrell (Philadelphia: McKay, 1929; London: Harrap, 1929);

A Collection of Poems (London: Collins, 1929);

The Tale of Tom Tiddler, with Rhymes of London Town, illustrated by Norman Tealby (London: Collins, 1929; New York: Stokes, 1930);

The King's Daughter Cries for the Moon, illustrated by May Smith (Oxford: Blackwell, 1929);

Tales from Chaucer, illustrated by W. Russell Flint (London: Medici Society, 1930; New York: Cape & Smith, 1932);

Westwoods, illustrated by Smith (Oxford: Blackwell, 1930; Poughkeepsie, N.Y.: Artists & Writers Guild, 1935);

Ladybrook (New York: Stokes, 1931; London: Collins, 1931);

Poems for Children (Philadelphia: Lippincott, 1931); republished as *Eleanor Farjeon's Poems for Children* (Philadelphia: Lippincott, 1984);

The Old Nurse's Stocking Basket, illustrated by E. H. Whydale (New York: Stokes, 1931; London: University of London Press, 1931);

The Fair of St. James: a Fantasia (New York: Stokes, 1932; London: Faber & Faber, 1932);

Katy Kruse at the Seaside: or, The Deserted Islanders (Philadelphia: McKay, 1932; London: Harrap, 1932);

Perkin the Pedlar, illustrated by Clare Leighton (London: Faber & Faber, 1932);

Kings and Queens, with Herbert Farjeon, illustrated by Thornycroft (London: Gollancz, 1932; New York: Dutton, 1933); republished, with the songs set to music by Eleanor Farjeon (London: Edward Arnold, 1938; revised edition, London: Dent, 1953; Philadelphia: Lippincott, 1955);

Heroes and Heroines, with Herbert Farjeon, illustrated by Thornycroft (New York: Dutton / London: Gollancz, 1933);

Pannychis, illustrated by Leighton (Shaftesbury, Dorset: High House Press, 1933);

Over the Garden Wall, illustrated by Gwendolin Raverat (New York: Stokes / London: Faber & Faber, 1933);

Ameliaranne and the Magic Ring, illustrated by S. B. Pearse (Philadelphia: McKay, 1933); republished as *Ameliaranne's Prize Packet* (London: Harrap, 1933);

Ameliaranne's Washing Day, illustrated by Pearse (Philadelphia: McKay / London: Harrap, 1934);

The Clumber Pup (Oxford: Blackwell, 1934);

The Old Sailor's Yarn Box, illustrated by Mountfort (New York: Stokes, 1934); republished as *Jim at the Corner and Other Stories* (Oxford: Blackwell, 1934); revised as *Jim at the Corner,*

Farjeon at age eleven

illustrated by Ardizzone (New York: Walck / London: Oxford University Press, 1958);

The Children's Bells: a Selection of Poems (Oxford: Blackwell, 1934);

And I Dance Mine Own Child, illustrated by Mountfort (Oxford: Blackwell, 1935);

A Nursery in the Nineties (London: Gollancz, 1935); republished as *Portrait of a Family* (New York: Stokes, 1936);

The Humming Bird (New York: Stokes, 1936; London: M. Joseph, 1936);

Jim and the Pirates, illustrated by Richard Naish (Oxford: Blackwell, 1936);

Ten Saints, illustrated by Helen Sewell (New York: Oxford University Press, 1936; London: Oxford University Press, 1953);

Lector Readings, illustrated by Ruth Westcott (New York: Stokes / London: Nelson, 1936);

Martin Pippin in the Daisy Field, illustrated by Isobel and John Morton-Sale (London: M. Joseph, 1937; New York: Stokes, 1938);

Paladins in Spain, illustrated by Katharine Tozer (London: Nelson, 1937);

The Wonders of Herodotus, illustrated by Edmund Nelson (London: Nelson, 1937);

Sing for Your Supper, illustrated by the Morton-Sales (New York: Stokes / London: M. Joseph, 1938);

One Foot in Fairyland: Sixteen Tales, illustrated by Robert Lawson (New York: Stokes / London: M. Joseph, 1938);

An Elephant in Arcady, with Herbert Farjeon (London: Ascherberg, Hopwood & Crewe, 1938);

Grannie Gray: Children's Plays and Games with Music and Without, illustrated by Joan Jefferson Farjeon (London: Dent, 1939);

A Sussex Alphabet, illustrated by Sheila M. Thompson (Bognor Regis, Sussex: Pear Tree Press, 1939);

Miss Granby's Secret (London: M. Joseph, 1940); republished as *Miss Granby's Secret: or, The Bastard of Pinsk* (New York: Simon & Schuster, 1941);

Brave Old Woman (London: M. Joseph, 1941);

Magic Casements (London: Allen & Unwin, 1941);

The New Book of Days, illustrated by Philip Gough and M. W. Hawes (London: Oxford University Press, 1941; New York: Walck, 1961);

Cherrystones, illustrated by the Morton-Sales (London: M. Joseph, 1942; Philadelphia: Lippincott, 1944);

The Fair Venetian (London: M. Joseph, 1943);

Golden Coney (London: M. Joseph, 1943);

The Dark World of Animals, illustrated by T. Stoney (London: Sylvan, 1945);

Ariadne and the Bull (London: M. Joseph, 1945);

A Prayer for Little Things, illustrated by Elizabeth Orton-Jones (Boston: Houghton Mifflin, 1945);

The Mulberry Bush, illustrated by the Morton-Sales (London: M. Joseph, 1945);

The Glass Slipper, with Herbert Farjeon, music by Clifton Parker, illustrated by Hugh Stevenson (London: Wingate, 1946);

First and Second Love: Sonnets (London: M. Joseph, 1947);

Love Affair (London: M. Joseph, 1947; New York: Macmillan, 1949);

The Starry Floor, illustrated by the Morton-Sales (London: M. Joseph, 1949);

Mrs. Malone, illustrated by David Knight (London: M. Joseph, 1950; New York: Walck, 1962);

Silver-Sand and Snow (London: M. Joseph, 1951);

Aucassin and Nicolette: a Lyric Drama, with Herbert Farjeon, music by Parker (London: Chappell, 1952);

The Silver Curlew, illustrated by Ernest Shepard (London: Oxford University Press, 1953; New York: Viking, 1954);

The Little Bookroom, illustrated by Ardizzone (London: Oxford University Press, 1955; New York: Walck, 1956);

The Glass Slipper, illustrated by Shepard (London: Oxford University Press, 1955; New York: Viking, 1956);

Elizabeth Myers (Aylsford, Kent: St. Albert's Press, 1957);

A Room at the Inn: a Masque, with Herbert Farjeon, music by Harry Farjeon (London: French, 1957);

Edward Thomas: The Last Four Years (London: Oxford University Press, 1958);

Then There Were Three, illustrated by the Morton-Sales (London: M. Joseph, 1958; Philadelphia: Lippincott, 1965);

A Puffin Quartet of Poets, compiled by Eleanor Graham, illustrated by Diana Bloomfield (London: Penguin, 1958);

Eleanor Farjeon's Book, edited by Graham, illustrated by Ardizzone (London: Penguin, 1960);

Mr. Garden, illustrated by Jane Paton (New York: Walck / London: Hamish Hamilton, 1966);

Morning Has Broken, illustrated by Gordon Stowell (Oxford: Mowbrays, 1981);

Invitation to a Mouse and Other Poems, edited by Annabel Farjeon, illustrated by Antony Maitland (London: Pelham, 1981);

Something I Remember, edited by Anne Harvey, illustrated by Alan Marks (London: Blackie, 1987);

Cats (Chicago: Calico Books, 1989).

Editions: *Nursery Rhymes of London Town; More Nursery Rhymes of London Town,* music by the author, 4 volumes (London: Oxford University Press, 1919–1926);

Martin Pippin in the Apple Orchard, illustrated by Robert Kennedy (London: Oxford University Press, 1952; Philadelphia: Lippincott, 1961);

Grannie Gray: Children's Plays and Games with Music and Without, illustrated by Peggy Fortnum (London: Oxford University Press, 1956);

Perkin the Pedlar, illustrated by Dodie Masterman (London: Oxford University Press, 1956);

The Old Nurse's Stocking Basket, illustrated by Margaret Walters (London: Oxford University Press, 1959);

Tales from Chaucer, illustrated by Walters (London: Oxford University Press, 1959);

The Children's Bells: a Selection of Poems, illustrated by Fortnum (London: Oxford University Press, 1957; New York: Walck, 1960);

The Old Nurse's Stocking Basket, illustrated by Edward Ardizzone (New York: Walck, 1965).

PLAY PRODUCTIONS: *Floretta, an Opera in 2 Acts,* London, St. George's Hall, July 1899;

The Registry Office, an Operetta in 1 Act, London, St. George's Hall, July 1900;

A Gentleman of the Roads, an Operetta, London, St. George's Hall, July 1902;

The Two Bouquets: a Victorian Comedy with Music, with Herbert Farjeon, music by the authors, London, Ambassadors Theatre, 13 August 1936;

An Elephant in Arcady, with Herbert Farjeon, music by Ernest Irving, London, Kingsway Theatre, 6 October 1938;

The Glass Slipper, with Herbert Farjeon, music by Clifton Parker, London, St. James Theatre, December 1944;

The Silver Curlew, Liverpool, Playhouse, 25 December 1948.

RADIO: *Six Masques for Broadcasting,* with Herbert Farjeon, music by Harry Farjeon, BBC, 25 December 1938.

OTHER: Carlo Goldini, *The Fan,* in *Four Comedies,* translated by Eleanor and Herbert Farjeon, edited by Clifford Bax (London: Cecil Palmer, 1922);

The Two Bouquets: a Victorian Comedy with Music, with Herbert Farjeon, in *Famous Plays of 1936* (London: Gollancz, 1936);

Charles Dickens, *Christmas Books,* introduction by Farjeon (London: Oxford University Press, 1954);

The Hamish Hamilton Book of Kings, edited by Farjeon and William Mayne, illustrated by Victor Ambrus (London: Hamish Hamilton, 1964); republished as *A Cavalcade of Kings* (New York: Walck, 1965);

The Hamish Hamilton Book of Queens, edited by Farjeon and Mayne, illustrated by Ambrus (London: Hamish Hamilton, 1965); republished as *A Cavalcade of Queens* (New York: Walck, 1965);

The Green Roads: Poems for Young Readers by Edward Thomas, edited by Farjeon, illustrated by B.

Brett (New York: Holt, Rinehart / London: Bodley Head, 1965).

Eleanor Farjeon's writing career spanned almost half a century. Although not exclusively a children's writer, her reputation and main claim to critical discussion and evaluation rest with her poetry, prose, and drama written for children.

Marcus Crouch in *The Nesbit Tradition* (1972) maintains that at a time when children's literature in Great Britain had fallen away from its "Golden Age," Eleanor Farjeon, together with Walter de la Mare and John Masefield, managed to continue the creative force of fantasy writing through the 1920s and 1930s until new writers revitalized the mode in the 1940s. Her best work was not done as longer prose fiction, the genre that garners the greatest prestige, but as children's poetry. With de la Mare, Farjeon established poetry as a significant subgenre of children's literature. In fact, Eileen Colwell claims in *Eleanor Farjeon: A Monograph* (1961) that there are only two real children's poets this century — Farjeon and de la Mare. Farjeon ventured into whimsical humor in a way de la Mare did not and in this is more directly comparable to her contemporary A. A. Milne, or to her predecessors Hilaire Belloc and G. K. Chesterton, as well as anticipatory to the more recent humorous verse of Ted Hughes, Spike Milligan, Adrian Henri, and others. While giving status to poetry and fantasy, she managed (as did de la Mare and Arthur Ransome) to give continued status to children's writing as a serious artistic profession and not just as a way of making a living.

Eleanor "Nellie" Farjeon was born into an unusual family and consequently had an unusual childhood. She relates this in some detail in *A Nursery in the Nineties,* which she did not publish until 1935, after her mother's death. A much briefer but more accessible account is given in her introduction to *The Little Bookroom* (1955), her award-winning collection of short stories. Her niece Annabel has also written an account in her biography, *Morning Has Broken* (1986).

Her father, Benjamin Farjeon, was Jewish. Born in poverty in the East End of London, he had been apprenticed to a printer and was largely self-educated. As a young man he immigrated to Australia during the gold rush of the 1850s and then moved on to New Zealand, where he founded the *Dunedin Daily News,* becoming a successful journalist. However, always a "Dickens idolator," he submitted a Christmas short story to the great man; and on receiving a letter in reply, even though it

was somewhat noncommittal, he gave up his promising newspaper career to return to England to set up as a fiction writer.

Farjeon's mother, born Margaret Jefferson, was American. The Jeffersons had for generations been actors, originally in eighteenth-century England before immigrating to the United States. Eleanor's grandfather eventually made a fortune playing the part of Rip van Winkle but as a younger man had toured New Zealand, briefly meeting Benjamin Farjeon. Margaret was introduced to Benjamin while on a visit to London. He was by now a popular novelist, and the young Margaret admired his novels. They married and lived briefly in the United States, where their first child, Harry, was born. The couple soon returned to London, eventually settling in South Hampstead. Here the remaining children were born: Charles (who died in infancy), Eleanor, Joseph (Joe), and Herbert (Bertie). Like the Brontës, all four children were extremely talented and confident with their gifts. Harry, after graduation from the Royal Academy of Music, London, became a professor there for the rest of his life; Joe became a popular detective novelist; and Bertie became a dramatist, producer, and critic.

As a girl and young woman Farjeon was painfully shy and withdrawn. *A Bad Day for Martha* (1928) reflects autobiographical accounts of childhood trauma in company. This shyness was reinforced by a sense of her own lack of physical attractiveness. It was not until she was thirty years old that she was drawn into various friendships by her outgoing youngest brother, Bertie. Farjeon suggests various reasons for her emotional immaturity, the chief one being her intense imaginative fantasizing.

This took two forms, the first being the game of TAR, which she played with Harry. She writes fully of its origins and development in *A Nursery in the Nineties:* "This game began when I was about five years old and for more than twenty years it continued to be the chief experience of my inward and outward life." TAR stands for "Tessy and Ralph," the two child characters in a pantomime to which Farjeon and her brother had been taken. Out of this replay an elaborate, almost hypnotic, role-play improvisation emerged, sometimes involving all four children, with Harry controlling its starts and stops. The other form was the fantasizing she did at nights, during her chronic insomnia. She imagined Greek gods and goddesses, creating ideal fantasies of beauty and power for them. In the end Harry stopped playing TAR, leaving Farjeon emotionally bereft and lacking in a strong sense of identity. Critics have argued whether TAR was as damaging to

Farjeon as she seems to suggest. It has been maintained, probably correctly, that the peculiar feature of her fantasy, the easy transition between reality and the fantasy world, and her many transitional tones have their origins in TAR.

The two older Farjeon children, Harry and Eleanor, were educated at home; in fact, they received little formal education but were encouraged to read widely in their father's eight-thousand-volume library. For a time their father gave them each a new book every Sunday, sitting with them while he introduced it. Writing was a natural activity in the household; and most of what Eleanor wrote she showed her father, who encouraged her, though not uncritically.

Family life was close, if emotionally charged. Even when their father became increasingly prone to fits of anger — partly on account of poor health, partly because of his failing success as his melodramatic and sentimental style fell out of fashion — he remained a dynamic and positive force. Farjeon was introduced to the cultural life of London, meeting many famous actors and singers of the day.

Her father's death in 1903 left Farjeon unsupported in her desire to be a writer. Her grandfather, who had been helping the family financially, died shortly afterward, leaving Farjeon with something of the financial and emotional support of her mother. She never married or had children and continued to live most of the rest of her life in the Hampstead area of north London. Although at the time of her father's death she felt she had achieved nothing because of her lack of discipline, her final production was enormous; more than eighty books can be credited to her name. Some of these are collections of previously published material, but this can be set against a mass of unpublished material, including eight plays, memoirs, and fragments of stories.

Farjeon did not set out to be a children's writer, nor did she ever see herself solely as one. Her first ambition was to be a poet; only reluctantly did she give up this hope. In fact, she did receive some small recognition here, but nothing in comparison to that which she received as a teller of tales and maker of verse for children. The variety of her work is enormous: adult and children's writing; poetry, drama, and prose fiction; varying modes of fantasy, ranging in tone from whimsicality to high seriousness. However, apart from reworking plays she wrote with her brother Bertie, she wrote no original long fiction for children, although she did for adults.

Farjeon in her studio (photograph by Helen Craig)

This variety in material is paralleled by the variety of publishers and illustrators with whom she worked. A typical example is that of *Martin Pippin in the Daisy Field,* which was first published in 1937 by Michael Joseph, a relatively new publisher at that time. Athough Joseph continued to publish much of her work over the next few years, he ceased printing *Martin Pippin.* In the 1950s Oxford University Press (and Walck in the United States) took over its publication. Hamish Hamilton then took over the copyright in 1964, and finally in 1966 Puffin bought the paperback rights. Often new editions meant new illustrators as well.

Farjeon was fortunate in her career to find two influential supporters of her work, Helen Dean Fish and Anne Carroll Moore, in the United States. Fish was responsible for having sixteen of Farjeon's titles published by Stokes, where she was children's editor from 1922 through 1941, when the company merged with Lippincott. Fish, a New York children's librarian, championed *Martin Pippin in the Apple Orchard* (1921) from the beginning. *Italian Peepshow* was listed in the *Horn Book* list of the twenty-five outstanding books for 1926. There were no equivalent institutional backers of Farjeon in the United Kingdom for many years.

Although a prolific writer who needed seclusion for her writing, she developed a large circle of friends. She put people before writing and always appeared to give friends her undivided attention. She was a stimulating, unorthodox person, somewhat eccentric, but sympathetic and compassionate, intensely involved in life and living.

Even so, she remained in many ways a private person. She never gave interviews or allowed her picture to be taken for publicity; nor did she give talks or visit schools. The children with whom she involved herself were nieces or friends or neighborhood children. And even while listening to other people's problems, she rarely divulged her own in return, though she did dramatize the everyday events of her own life. All this makes it more difficult to reconstruct her own creative processes or any philosophy of life apart from what is revealed in her books. Those who saw her at work commented on the great number of drafts she made — both handwritten and typed. The final draft would usually be sent to a professional typist. Given a lifelong history of poor eyesight, such application is remarkable and evidences a high sense of professionalism. Despite finding writing easy, with ideas pouring into her mind faster than she could deal with them, she would not release a final draft until completely satisfied.

When she did emerge into Bertie's friendship groups, it was to be among a set of young people actively involved in art and avant-garde ideas — emancipation and socialism particularly. These ideas rooted fast in her; for the rest of her life she considered herself a socialist and was reasonably liberated in her relationships for someone who had begun life as a shy young girl with a Victorian nursery upbringing.

Many of Farjeon's early books are written in the pastoral mode. Much of Farjeon's attachment to the pastoral stems from her love of Sussex, to which she was introduced by Bertie's friends. The county of Sussex lies south of London, at its nearest some thirty miles away, with its furthest reaches still being no more than seventy. With a good rail network, it was easily accessible to Londoners. Its main features are a long coastline full of sand and shingle beaches and the South Downs, gently contoured chalk hills that run parallel to the coast at some ten miles distance and at whose feet lie little sheltered valleys. Sussex had not yet become prey to suburban coastal sprawl, and the Downs were still grazed by sheep, whose shepherds lived in huts among them.

The Meynell estates lay at the foot of the Downs; Edward Thomas's cottage lay nearby on the Sussex-Hampshire border. Farjeon joined in the popular passion for hiking, or "tramping." She once had a memorable day's walking with D. H. Lawrence, and her early poem *All the Way to Alfriston* (1918) describes an extended tramp. The poem was originally written to be published by the young son of James Guthrie, a printer-artist living on the coast, at whose house she became a frequent and welcomed visitor.

The years between 1912 and 1917 are fully documented in her memoir *Edward Thomas: The Last Four Years* (1958). She traces her friendship with Thomas, a promising young literary critic who through the influence of Robert Frost, then living in England, found his true expression as a poet before being killed in World War I. There is, in fact, little doubt that she was deeply in love with Thomas. But as he was a reserved married man with three children, he kept her at an emotional distance, although intellectually and artistically there was great kinship. Farjeon was accepted into the Thomas family and enjoyed the company of the children and Thomas's wife, Helen.

The two other significant friendships Farjeon enjoyed during this period were of Dr. Maitland Radford and D. H. Lawrence. She met the latter at the home of the Meynells, an upper-class Catholic family with estates in Sussex. Alice Meynell was one of the leading poetesses in England at this time. Farjeon attributes to Maitland and Lawrence her maturation in terms of "truth without illusion." Lawrence praised the sonnets she was writing but criticized her for "a faint tinge of sentimentality, a dross of smallness, almost cowardice" that may have come from a desire to keep the peace, a trait deeply inbred within the Farjeon children in view of their father's irascibility.

At this time Farjeon had published little. Her earliest publication dates from 1891 — an essay on a pet sparrow published in *Little Wideawake: An Illustrated Magazine for Good Children*. She had contributed small pieces to various magazines and had written three librettos. She had also done a series of mock-Elizabethan poems for *Blackwood's Magazine* in 1913 and a long Celtic-twilight novel, *The Soul of Kol Nikon* (1923), that Thomas found unreadable, even if the *Irish Review*, which published it serially (1915–1917), did not. She also published two volumes of poetry at her own expense and a long essay titled

Trees (1914), which was her first paid commissioned work.

The first work of any significance began in 1915: Farjeon contributed a series of anonymous poems to the satiric humorous magazine *Punch*. In these poems she takes London place-names and fancifully weaves poetry in the style of nursery rhymes around them. Thus poems titled "Mayfair," "Cheapside," and "Hammersmith" appear. One of the assistant editors at *Punch* recognized the writer's talent and persuaded Duckworth to publish the poems in an augmented and illustrated form. They appeared in 1916 as *Nursery Rhymes of London Town,* and a sequel was published a year later. This led to a contract with the socialist *Daily Herald* to provide a daily verse, under the pseudonym "Tomfool." These were often humorous or whimsical poems of everyday events, observations, or ironies. Collections of these poems, *Tomfooleries* and *Moonshine,* were published in 1920 and 1921. The contract provided her with her first steady income, continuing until 1929. Her income was augmented in 1920 when she joined the staff of a serious weekly review, *Time and Tide,* to which C. S. Lewis also contributed some years later. For this she wrote under the pen name "Chimaera."

None of this work was specifically for children, although clearly *Nursery Rhymes of London Town* was based on a children's genre and was actually dedicated to her niece Joan (Joe's daughter): "And if little Joan had never been born / These songs would never have been sung." Her first collection of tales, *Martin Pippin in the Apple Orchard,* was also directed at adults. As stories of awakening sexuality and love they proved popular with a younger audience. The collection marks Farjeon's first use of a single storyteller to relate a cycle of stories, a technique she would employ in several subsequent collections.

What was more specifically designed for children were the music and singing games. Although she had not received any formal musical education, she shared some of Harry's gift of composition and set her two volumes of *Nursery Rhymes of London Town* to music herself as well as working with him on other songs. At the same time she was collecting and inventing singing games for children, which finally emerged complete with music between 1927 and 1930, together with other collections. Despite this activity, Colwell claims that her first real children's book was *Nuts and May: a Medley for Children,* published by Collins in 1925, with illustrations by Rosalind Thornycroft, the sister of Bertie's wife, Joan. That volume contains both poems and stories,

one of which is "Italian Peepshow," based on an Italian holiday. This story then became the title story of a volume published in the next year, which has proved to be one of her most popular collections of short stories for children.

After Thomas's death she briefly shared a Sussex cottage with Joe and his wife and then for two years rented The End Cottage, Mucky Lane, Houghton, Sussex. According to Annabel Farjeon, Farjeon saw these two years as possibly the most important in her life, a perfect pastoral existence with no set routine and simple country pleasures. She observed the local children and their rhymes and games. She was taught by her neighbors how to cook and bake – an activity of which she became increasingly fond, eventually becoming quite a gourmet. She returned to London in 1921; she did not return to Sussex until 1935, when she and George Earle bought a holiday cottage, Hammonds, near Lewes, retaining it till 1949.

The Martin Pippin books are the epitome of her main pastoral genre, the Sussex pastoral. In some ways these books are reminiscent of Rudyard Kipling's *Puck of Pook's Hill* (1906), likewise set in Sussex. *Martin Pippin in the Apple Orchard* was actually conceived in Brittany in 1907, but the places are based on the Meynell estates, and the stories were written for a Sussex soldier serving in France. Martin Pippin is a timeless, magical storyteller, gaining his quest through the charm of his stories. *Martin Pippin in the Daisy Field* was written much later; in the book Martin tells his stories to the young daughters of the girls in the first book. It is full of lovely whimsical dialogue, poetry, and nostalgia. Its construction is distorted at the end, however, and thus the book is less satisfying than the fulfilled quest depicted in *Martin Pippin in the Apple Orchard*.

Farjeon's own favorite was the story "Elsie Piddock Skips in her Sleep," found in *Martin Pippin in the Daisy Field* and based on one of the Mucky Lane children, Elsie Puttick. It tells of pastoralism challenged by industrialization and capitalism but defeating it by recourse to past feats. The technique is more like magic realism than anything, and the sentiment is akin to William Morris's rural socialism. Colwell claims it is "perhaps one of the best short stories of this generation."

Two other forms of Farjeon's pastoralism need to be noted: the urban pastoralism of *Nursery Rhymes of London Town* and the Arcadian or classical pastoralism of another of her favorite stories, *Pannychis* (1933). Unlike the traditional pastoral, Farjeon's makes no opposition between city and

Illustration titled "The Ugly Sisters" by E. H. Shepard from The Glass Slipper *(1955)*

country. Instead she pastoralizes the city; it becomes an urban garden through the power of linguistic fantasy. The pastoral may gain in magic, but it loses its tension and its ability to make social comment thereby. The Arcadian pastoral stems from her love of classical Greece but is the least used form of all three.

George Earle ("Pod") was English master at King Alfred's School, Hampstead – a progressive private school. He was the son of a professor of Anglo-Saxon at Oxford University and had inherited a tremendous feeling for words, to which he added a deep understanding of Keats. He was an inspirational teacher, as good at carpentry as at English. Farjeon had met him briefly in London in Edward Thomas's company and then again in 1920. Earle's marriage had failed, though there was no question of divorce since his wife was a devout Catholic. Earle and Farjeon fell in love and "decided to elope," in Farjeon's words. In practice this meant a holiday in Italy and then living together on weekends at Farjeon's rented house – an old coach house made into a small mews cottage – 20 Church Walk, Hampstead. Despite family opposition, Pod came to live with Farjeon permanently. *Kaleidoscope,* a story collection published in 1928, is based on Earle's childhood memories. In 1930 he had a slight stroke and retired from teaching – he was then sixty. In the meanwhile she had purchased the house, which had by now been renamed 20 Perrins Walk. She lived in it for the rest of her life.

It was still unconventional for unmarried couples to live together, but Farjeon was growing increasingly unconventional in her lifestyle. She would walk through the house naked at times, spend mornings in bed writing and typing, and wear Russian peasant dresses. She claimed that Earle gave to her his love of Romantic poetry and concern for words; in return she gave him invigorating companionship and maternal care.

One feature of Farjeon's life reflected in her books is her love of animals. When she and Earle went down to Hammonds, her four cats went with them. One of the four, her "marmalade girl," became famous by having a book written about her, *Golden Coney* (1943). She took in both strays and neighborhood cats in her Hampstead home; veterinarians were more honored than doctors; and fresh food, not canned, was always on the menu. Her poem "Mrs. Malone," about an old lady who welcomes every distressed animal because "There's room fer another" and who is then similarly welcomed into heaven by Saint Peter, seems to apply to Farjeon exactly.

One of Farjeon's notable works from the 1920s is *Faithful Jenny Dove and Other Tales* (1925). Although actually meant for adults, it is perfectly accessible to older children. These stories exploit the fantastic in terms of ambiguity and strangeness. "And a Perle in the Myddes" is perhaps the best, exploiting a real sense of the layers of history. Its success lies in its creation of atmosphere that is quite Dickensian at times. Farjeon's weakness, as always, is to iron out the problematic and to resolve too safely.

The early 1930s were probably the time of greatest productivity in a highly productive life.

Her publishers were asking for books, and she responded. Her works included *Tales from Chaucer* (1930), *Katy Kruse at the Seaside: or, The Deserted Islanders* (1932), *Ameliaranne and the Magic Ring* (1933), and *Ameliaranne's Washing Day* (1934). The terms offered were never generous. At this period her writing was almost entirely for children, and she was at the height of her popularity as a children's author.

Farjeon began collaborating with her brother Bertie in the 1930s, first with *Kings and Queens* (1932) and *Heroes and Heroines* (1933). These were burlesque poems about historical and legendary characters and set the style for their ensuing dramatic material – light, witty, controlled verse, caricaturing each personage portrayed. Thornycroft did the illustrations, and later Farjeon composed music for some of the songs.

Their next collaboration was *The Two Bouquets* (1936), a light comedy with lyrics written to fit existing melodies, mainly from the Victorian era. It is a deliberate turn-of-the-century pastiche, Wildean at moments, though the drawing-room comedy of Noel Coward is equally discernible. It enjoyed a success in the London theater, being revived after the war, but the effort to take it to New York two years after its London opening was marred by heavy-handed production and direction. Its sequel, *An Elephant in Arcady,* set in Italy, followed in 1938 and was less successful.

An exhilarating stay in the United States to work on a New York production of *The Two Bouquets* and to visit her American cousins ended in some emotional exhaustion. Annabel Farjeon suggests the ensuing depression could have been caused by menopause, financial worries, the threat of war, even a brief love affair, or by a combination of all these. But Farjeon had developed defensive techniques of not dwelling long on unpleasant things, and the depression does not seem to have lasted, although her decline in popularity did.

A major part of Farjeon's output was poetry written for and about children. *Joan's Door* (1926), *Come Christmas* (1927), *Over the Garden Wall* (1933), *Sing for Your Supper* (1938), and *Cherrystones* (1942) are examples of individual volumes, while several collections began to be built up, such as *Poems for Children* (1931) and *The Children's Bells: a Selection of Poems* (1934). The other two main collections came later: *Silver-Sand and Snow* in 1951 and *Then There Were Three* in 1958. After Eleanor's death Annabel Farjeon edited a selection of favorite poems, *Invitation to a Mouse and Other Poems* (1981).

Farjeon was a prolific poet, and it is difficult to obtain any clear overview of her enormous range and content. In "Mary's One" she writes,

Do you write one every day? said Mary
　　Well, I said, I try. . . .
After that I wrote Mary one
　　In less than half a minute –
And now that Mary's one is done
　　I see there's nothing in it.

A common criticism of the poetry is that there is just too much of it – that it needs excising. Her adult verse, especially in its use of the sonnet form, suggests an ability to work hard and long at a particular poem, an ability that may have been overwhelmed in her children's verse by the flow of her ideas.

Ultimately, though, the problem in her children's verse lies in the exclusion of certain areas of childhood experiences and the overemphasis (as defense or compensation) of the more spontaneous and joyous perceptions of childhood. That overconcentration echoes Wordsworthian innocence and wisdom without allowing adult perspectives to bring in ambivalences, nostalgia, or irony. It thus excludes tones, ambiguities, and tensions at the heart of Romanticism, which a poet such as de la Mare captures. Thus, a poem such as "Myfanwy among the Leaves" (1925) denies any tension between the nostalgia of the fallen leaves and the girl's careless joy. Even the traditional symbolism of poets such as Robert Herrick and Andrew Marvell is suppressed. Farjeon does not portray the losses, tragedies, nightmares, fears, and insecurities of childhood experience. But she does powerfully depict the joy and simplicity of the child's direct perception of reality, its humor, game playing, and whimsicality, not in just a line or a single poem but through the body of her poetry.

The tone is essentially pastoral rather than lyrical – delight in nature is generalized to the whole of childhood experience, and there is a suppression of any significant first-person narrator speaking of unique personal experience. Particular children may be described, but not the particular feelings of the poet. She shows a preference for using frames to structure poetry – alphabet frames, as in "The School Child's Alphabet" (1924) and "An Alphabet of Magic" (1928), or seasonal frames, as in the marvelous "Round the Year" cycle (1928). What emerges most clearly from her poetry is a deep sense of harmony, perhaps best captured in a stanza from "Spring Night in a Village":

And from a small, sweet garden I
    Can see in heaven a perfect moon,
On earth a perfect peony
    And hear no sound that's out of tune.

Farjeon was also one of the few children's writers who actually wrote plays for children to perform – *Grannie Gray* (1939) is her main collection of such plays, together with some sections of *Nuts and May*. Farjeon attempted little for radio, however; a series of masques in which both Harry and Bertie collaborated were broadcast in 1938 and subsequently published. This was the only serious work Farjeon contributed to this medium.

The 1940s saw a diminution of her work for children, although not in her overall output. She wrote several novels for adults: *Miss Granby's Secret* (1940), *Brave Old Woman* (1941) – based largely on the life of her old governess – *The Fair Venetian* (1943), and *Love Affair* (1947). Annabel suggests the latter novel is based on intimate relationships Farjeon had with an American actor and then a much younger émigré, Otto Lampel, during the war years. Certainly Farjeon saw Otto as her protégé, even if eventually unsuccessful, and he seems to have become emotionally dependent on her.

During the war Farjeon did some miscellaneous prose work, such as *The New Book of Days* (1941) and *A Prayer for Little Things* (1945). Her other activities included assisting in wartime productions and working for the P.E.N. Club, especially in seeking to get Jewish writers out of Europe and raising funds for impoverished émigré writers. Her efforts to work with Bertie came to little until 1944, when they were asked to do something for children, basically as a Christmas pantomime. They worked enthusiastically on a version of Cinderella, titled *The Glass Slipper* (1946). It was written mainly in rhyming couplets with songs and plenty of light-hearted knockabout humor. Thus it lacks the aristocracy of the Charles Perrault version and fails to gain the mysteriousness of the older folk versions (as in the Grimms' "Aschenputtel"). Despite slips into sentimentality (some arising from autobiographical material) and some tediousness with the many ordeals of the rejected princesses, it moves along at an easy pace and was generally considered a great success. Part of this was because of the music of a young composer, Clifton Parker, whom both the Farjeons took to greatly. There was one further collaboration before Bertie's death, *Aucassin and Nicolette: a Lyric Drama,* again with music by Clifton Parker, intended for adults. It was not published until 1952.

The year 1947 saw the publication of love poems written before and at the same time as her friendship with Edward Thomas – *First and Second Love: Sonnets*. These were well reviewed, and there was a momentary pang of regret that she had not become the serious poet that she had wanted to be at one point. But the course of English poetry had developed quite differently from her own Georgian style, and her inability to respond to the modernism of Ezra Pound, T. S. Eliot, and W. H. Auden consigned her adult poetry to the category of interesting anachronism.

The decade ended sadly for her. In 1945 Bertie had died suddenly after a fall. Then Harry, always afflicted with poor eyesight, developed Parkinson's disease and a painful stone. In 1948 he slipped and broke a thigh, dying shortly after. The next year Earle likewise suffered a fall, also dying shortly afterward. He had become somewhat demanding and restrictive, and his death was perhaps something of a relief for Farjeon.

Her brothers' deaths marked the end of a long period of collaboration with them. Her first public success had been in writing librettos for Harry's music during his student days – three light operas that were deemed so good that the Royal Academy of Music had them performed in public. Farjeon had also worked with Harry in producing two volumes of rounds (1919). Harry wrote many piano pieces for children, which proved to be popular as exam and music festival pieces.

Farjeon took over the writing of a second pantomime, *The Silver Curlew,* first produced in Liverpool in 1948. The piece was based on the Norfolk folktale of Tom Tit Tot, which has many resemblances to the German story "Rumpelstilzkin." It has been suggested that Bertie was one of the few people from whom Farjeon took criticism, and because of this he was able to discipline her fantasy. The suggestion is that without such discipline *The Silver Curlew* took off too much toward fantasy. What perhaps does not work is the mixing of the pantomime farce, often with feminist overtones, and nature mysticism. But it is a far more ambitious work than *The Glass Slipper,* and when *The Silver Curlew* was turned by Farjeon into prose fiction in 1953 it became much more readable than the prose version of *The Glass Slipper* (1955). The remembered experience of Norfolk holidays and the Norfolk dialect come over delightfully.

In the second London production of *The Silver Curlew,* the actor chosen to play the king was Denys Blakelock. Farjeon loved the theater and was never happier than in the rehearsals, which she would attend in their entirety, encouraging all and sundry with presents and flasks of coffee. Blakelock was as double-natured as the king he portrayed, even manic-depressive at times, and Farjeon spent much time cajoling him into sufficient self-confidence to go on with the part. As Annabel Farjeon tartly remarks, Farjeon was to play Nanny to Blakelock's king for the next fourteen years.

While Blakelock's memoirs of Farjeon – titled *Eleanor: Portrait of a Farjeon* (1966) and *In Search of Elsie Piddock* (1967) – are tiresomely self-conscious and egocentric, he was one of the few people to penetrate her walls of privacy and to write about what he found on the other side. It is possible from what he writes to see the sort of life the older Farjeon lived in all its eccentricity, warmth, muddle, cats, friends, and vitality. He also writes intimately and sympathetically of her conversion to Catholicism – being a devout Catholic himself who helped in her conversion process. Farjeon was baptized into the Roman Catholic Church in August 1951, having been reading the Bible, the writings of Saint Augustine, and *The Cloud of Unknowing,* a medieval mystical work.

Farjeon was not sure how her family would react to her conversion. Although her father had been Jewish, he had never practiced any sort of faith, and the young Farjeons underwent an entirely secular upbringing. Nevertheless, she appears always to have been spiritually open and had written several semireligious books, for example *Ten Saints* and *Lector Readings,* both published in 1936. She wrote to her nephew, Gervase, of "a progression to a form of faith which my own sense of spiritual life has been moving for the last thirty or forty years." Annabel Farjeon sees her niece's faith as having satisfied her idealism, enthusiasm, and innocence with a hope of a perfect hereafter. Letters to Blakelock trace Farjeon's rapidly growing spiritual understanding and maturity.

Ill health became increasingly insistent; a history of foot problems resulted in a toe amputation. She was a prey to bronchitis and continuing poor eyesight. Nevertheless, in her seventies she was still active and productive. After hearing a radio program on Edward Thomas, in which it was suggested she had been his mistress, Farjeon started to compile her memoirs and edit the letters she had had from him. As is clear from *Edward Thomas: The Last Four Years,* her memory of their relationship was crystal clear even after forty years.

But the main production of the 1950s was the publication of a uniform edition of her major children's works by Oxford University Press. Many

Farjeon and George Earle at their home, Hammonds

of these were out of print by this time, and the new editions led to the rediscovery of her work. The series culminated in a selection of her best stories in *The Little Bookroom,* published in 1955, for which she was awarded the Carnegie Medal in 1956. In the same year she also received the international Hans Christian Andersen Medal.

The Little Bookroom contains twenty-seven stories in all. It was dedicated to Blakelock, "who began to share my childhood in the Little Bookroom sixty years after." The tone of nostalgia and the image of the safe enclosed space of her childhood home recur constantly through the collection, with desire on the whole being resolved in terms of the fulfilled life of the imagination rather than of a fantasized return to childhood.

Four types of short fiction can be categorized in the volume: fairy story, folktale, fable, and short story. Several are also pastoral. All have a sense of being rooted in the past, either the mythic past or the nostalgic past. Of the fairy stories, the best are "Westwoods," "The Clumber Pup," "The Little Dressmaker," and "Leaving Paradise." They feature typical genre motifs, for example poor woodcutters or servant girls marrying the princess or prince. Underlying such motifs are explorations of female desire and the tension between the everyday and the imaginative, sometimes, as in "Westwoods," with Platonic echoes. The journey back to childhood dreams is to the place where desire was awakened, the only place it can be fulfilled. In "Leaving Paradise" the possibility is portrayed of missing this fulfillment and seeking unfulfillable satisfaction in the mundane or secular life of the city.

Two of the best-known stories are realistic short stories, though with something still magical about them – "And I Dance My Own Child," based on a story from her grandfather, and "The Connemara Donkey." Both are strongly pastoral, and in the former story the motif of the young girl looking after and telling stories to the old grandmother provides a strangeness, a symbolic otherness that reverses her usual old storyteller/young listener structure.

Blakelock's friendship with Farjeon went into decline from 1955 to 1962, owing to a homosexual infatuation on his part. When that relationship ended, he sought to resume his intimacy with Farjeon, now an old lady. The relationship did not resume as it had been before, however, for she needed considerable support and reassurance by this time. Two other old friendships were also briefly renewed, with the Meynells and also with Robert Frost on a brief visit to England in 1963.

Domestic arrangements had been worked out on the basis of a second house Farjeon had bought near Perrins Walk, which she let to domestic helpers. Most of these were devoted to her, but in the end she needed permanent help, and a full-time couple was installed. A cataract operation eventually restored her sight to the best it had ever been, but mobility was a problem. She kept mentally alert, however. One of her last stories, *Mr. Garden* (1966), demonstrates new tones and technique. The maternal stance of the narrator is marvelously economic, unsentimental, and uncondescending. Farjeon's nature mysticism emerges, a delicate symbiotic balance between Christian and pagan, garden and gardener, with the young boy at the fulcrum. It is a celebration of English gardens, such as Farjeon cultivated to the last. After yet another bout of bronchitis in May 1965, pneumonia set in. She died on 5 June 1965 and was buried on Hampstead Hill.

The illustrator of *Mr. Garden* was Jane Paton, one of the thirty or forty illustrators employed by Farjeon's publishers for her works. Some, like Paton, only illustrated one book; others did many more. Isobel and John Morton-Sale were a husband-and-wife team whom Farjeon first met in 1937 in connection with *Martin Pippin in the Daisy Field* and then in the next year with her collection of poems *Sing for Your Supper*. Thereafter they became good friends, and the Morton-Sales illustrated many of Farjeon's subsequent volumes of poems – *Cherrystones*, *The Mulberry Bush* (1945), *The Starry Floor* (1949), and the collection of these volumes in *Then There Were Three*. Colwell feels that their children are perhaps too wistful, particularly in *Martin Pippin in the Daisy Field*.

The choice of a good illustrator can often tip the balance in any children's book. It is beyond doubt that the choice of Edward Ardizzone to illustrate *The Little Bookroom* must have enhanced its chances of being a prizewinner. In fact, Ardizzone accepted the Carnegie Medal on Farjeon's behalf. Farjeon, and most critics since, have felt that Ardizzone was her best illustrator, capturing exactly the mood of Edwardian nostalgia, of delicate sensibility, and of magical enchantment. Sometimes his children seem a little too fragile, but the title-page illustration of *The Little Bookroom* captures exactly the myopic Farjeon as a small girl. Farjeon wrote of his pictures that "all I feel of childhood is in them." Ardizzone was asked to reillustrate many of the Oxford University Press editions, such as *Jim at the Corner* (1958), *Italian Peepshow* (1960), *Kaleidoscope* (1963), and *The Old Nurse's Stocking Basket* (1959). He also illustrated *Eleanor Farjeon's Book* (1960).

Other significant illustrators were Peggy Fortnum (*The Children's Bells*), Irene Mountfort (the original *Italian Peepshow*), Ernest Shepard (*The Silver Curlew*), and Macdonald Gill, whose woodcuts for *Nursery Rhymes of London Town* made it such an attractive volume to handle. Besides Rosalind Thornycroft, her sister-in-law's sister, Farjeon's artist niece, Joan Jefferson Farjeon, also did work for her. In the case of the first edition of *Tales from Chaucer*, the art press of the Medici Society commissioned no less an artist than W. Russell Flint to provide the illustrations.

Besides the Hans Christian Andersen and Carnegie Medals, Farjeon also accepted from the Catholic Library Association the Regina Medal in 1959. She refused to attend the ceremonies, however, and actually refused a D.B.E. (Dame of the British Empire – a royal award for public service). The Children's Book Circle instituted an award in her memory, the Eleanor Farjeon Award, "for writers who have worked for and with children by their books."

Critical opinion has been consistent, even if not overly analytical, concerning her work. A review of *Mr. Garden* by Selma Lanes is typical: "She successfully maintains a dual viewpoint: the sympathies and enthusiasms of childhood combined with the understanding and judgment of a wise and generous grownup" (*Book Week,* 7 August 1966). Ellin Greene notes how comfortable Farjeon is with a child's sense of time; her niece Joan saw her aunt always at the same age as herself. Margery Fisher notes her "power to compel truth out of (her)self that has grown slowly out of childhood's impressions." In Fisher's mind, therefore, Farjeon overcame D. H. Lawrence's early strictures, although others may not agree so readily.

Farjeon's own comments reveal her desire to tell children the truth as she sees it: "Don't write down to children . . . don't try to be on their level . . . don't think there is a special tone they will respond to. Don't be afraid of words and things you think they can't grasp." She writes out of an integration of childhood and adult language and perspective, a single consciousness that flows naturally, the very opposite of the self-consciousness of an adopted role, typical of poorer writers. In fact, Farjeon denied she ever wrote specifically for children: "the truth is, I write for anybody who will be kind enough to like it."

Several of her limitations have already been mentioned. The charge that her books are dated needs to be linked to her failure to open up all levels of childhood experience rather than just accepting this datedness as a change in taste. Ultimately it means her imagination is too much rooted in an idealized past, a pastoralism that is not vital enough to stand against the inroads of the modern, let alone against the fragmentation of the postmodern. On the other hand her joy, warmth, and altruism find genuine and abiding literary expression. "Our strength is our gift for the good of mankind," she wrote in *Ten Saints,* and the sentiment may stand as the final word for her dedication as a writer.

Biographies:
Denys Blakelock, *Eleanor: Portrait of a Farjeon* (London: Gollancz, 1966);

Blakelock, *In Search of Elsie Piddock* (London: Favil Press, 1967);

Annabel Farjeon, *Morning Has Broken: A Biography of Eleanor Farjeon* (New York: Watts, 1986; London: Julia MacRae, 1986).

References:
Eileen Colwell, *Eleanor Farjeon: A Monograph* (New York: Walck / London: Bodley Head, 1961);

Marcus Crouch, *The Nesbit Tradition: The Children's Novel in England 1945–1970* (London: Benn, 1972);

Crouch and Alec Ellis, eds., *Chosen for Children,* third edition (London: Library Association, 1977);

Margery Fisher, *Intent upon Reading* (Leicester: Brockhampton, 1961);

Ellin Greene, "Eleanor Farjeon," in *Writers for Children: Critical Studies of the Major Authors since the Seventeenth Century,* edited by Jane Bingham (New York: Scribners, 1988), pp. 227–234;

Greene, "Eleanor Farjeon: The Shaping of a Literary Imagination," in *The Child and the Story: An Exploration of Narrative Forms,* edited by P. Ord (Boston: Children's Literature Association, 1983);

Greene, "Literary Uses of Traditional Themes: From 'Cinderella' to *The Girl Who Sat by the Ashes* and *The Glass Slipper,*" *Children's Literature Association Quarterly,* 11 (Fall 1986): 128–132;

Grace Hogarth, "Remembering Eleanor Farjeon," *Signal,* 35 (May 1981): 76–81;

Naomi Lewis, ed., *The Eleanor Farjeon Book: A Tribute to her Life and Work,* with an introduction by Lewis, illustrated by Edward Ardizzone (New York: Walck / London: Hamish Hamilton, 1966);

Francis Clarke Sayers, "Eleanor Farjeon's 'Room with a View,'" *Horn Book,* 32 (October 1956): 335–344.

Rose Fyleman
(6 March 1877 – 1 August 1957)

Donald R. Hettinga
Calvin College

BOOKS: *Fairies and Chimneys* (London: Methuen, 1918; New York: Doran, 1920);

The Sunny Book, illustrated by Millicent Sowerby (London: Humphrey Milford, 1918);

The Fairy Green (London: Methuen, 1919; New York: Doran, 1923);

The Fairy Flute (London: Methuen, 1921; New York: Doran, 1923);

The Rainbow Cat, illustrated by Thelma Cudlipp Grosvenor (London: Methuen, 1922; New York: Doran, 1923);

Forty Goodnight Tales, illustrated by Grosvenor (London: Methuen, 1923; New York: Doran, 1924);

The Rose Fyleman Fairy Book (New York: Doran, 1923);

A Small Cruse (London: Methuen, 1923);

Eight Little Plays for Children (London: Methuen, 1924; New York: Doran, 1925);

The Adventure Club, illustrated by A. H. Watson (London: Methuen, 1925; New York: Doran, 1926);

Fairies and Friends (London: Methuen, 1925; New York: Doran, 1926);

Forty Good Morning Tales, illustrated by Erick Berry (London: Methuen, 1926; New York: Doubleday, Doran, 1929);

Letty: A Study of a Child, illustrated by Lisl Hummel (London: Methuen, 1926; New York: Doran, 1927);

A Little Christmas Book, illustrated by Hummel (London: Methuen, 1926; New York: Doran, 1927);

The Katy Kruse Dolly Book (New York: Doran, 1927);

A Princess Comes to Our Town, illustrated by Gertrude Lindsay (London: Methuen, 1927); illustrated by Berry (New York: Doubleday, Doran, 1928);

A Garland of Rose's (London: Methuen, 1928);

Seven Little Plays for Children (London: Methuen, 1928);

Old Fashioned Girls, and Other Poems, illustrated by Ethel Everett (London: Methuen, 1928);

Gay Go Up, illustrated by Decie Merwin (London: Methuen, 1929; New York: Doubleday, Doran, 1930);

Twenty Tea-Time Tales (London: Methuen, 1929);

The Doll's House, illustrated by Berry (London: Methuen, 1930; New York: Doubleday, Doran, 1931);

The Katy Kruse Play Book, illustrated by Katy Kruse (Philadelphia: McKay, 1930);

Tea Time Tales, illustrated by Berry (New York: Doubleday, Doran, 1930);

Fifty-One New Nursery Rhymes, illustrated by Dorothy Burroughes (London: Methuen, 1931; New York: Doubleday, Doran, 1932);

Hey! Ding-a-Ding (London: University of London Press, 1931);

The Strange Adventures of Captain Marwhopple (London: Methuen, 1931; New York: Doubleday, Doran, 1932);

The Easter Hare (London: Methuen, 1932);

The Rose Fyleman Birthday Book (London: Medici Society, 1932);

Happy Families (London: Methuen, 1933);

Jeremy Quince, Lord Mayor of London, illustrated by Cecil Leslie (London: Cape, 1933);

The Princess Dances, illustrated by Leslie (London: Dent, 1933);

Nine New Plays for Children, illustrated by Eleanor L. Halsey (London: Nelson, 1934);

Sugar and Spice, illustrated by Janet Laura Scott (Racine, Wis.: Whitman, 1935);

Bears, illustrated by Stuart Tresilian (London: Nelson, 1935);

Monkeys (London: Nelson, 1936);

Billy Monkey: A True Tale of a Capuchin, by Fyleman and E. M. D. Wilson, illustrated by Leslie (London: Nelson, 1936);

Six Longer Plays for Children, illustrated by Halsey (London: Nelson, 1936);

Rose Fyleman

Here We Come a'Piping (Oxford: Blackwell, 1936; New York: Stokes, 1937);

A'Piping Again (New York: Stokes, 1938);

The Magic Pencil, and Other Plays from My Tales (London: Methuen, 1938);

Bells Ringing (Oxford: Blackwell, 1938; New York: Stokes, 1939);

Pipe and Drum (Oxford: Blackwell, 1939);

After All (London: Methuen, 1939);

The Spanish Cloak (London: Methuen, 1939);

A Book of Saints (London: Methuen, 1939);

Folk Tales From Many Lands (London: Methuen, 1939);

Runabout Rhymes, illustrated by Margaret Tempest (London: Methuen, 1941);

Timothy's Conjuror (London: Methuen, 1942);

Hob and Bob: A Tale of Two Goblins, illustrated by Charles Stewart (London: Hollis & Carter, 1944);

Punch and Judy (London: Methuen, 1944);

The Timothy Toy Trust, illustrated by Marjorie Wratten (London: Methuen, 1944);

Adventures with Benghazi, illustrated by Peggy Fortnum (London: Eyre & Spottiswoode, 1946);

Number Rhymes (Leeds: Arnold, 1947);

The Smith Family, Books 4–6 (Leeds: Arnold, 1947);

Over the Tree-Tops: Nursery Rhymes from Many Lands (Oxford: Blackwell, 1949);

Red-Riding-Hood (London: Oxford University Press, 1949);

Rose Fyleman's Nursery Stories (London: Evans, 1949);

Rhyme Book for Adam (London: Methuen, 1949);

Lucy the Lamb (London: Eyre & Spottiswoode, 1951);

The Sparrow and the Goat (London: Eyre & Spottiswoode, 1951);

The Starling and the Fox (London: Eyre & Spottiswoode, 1951);

Daphne and Dick (London: Macdonald, 1952);

White Flower, illustrated by M. E. Stewart (Leeds: Arnold, 1953).

OTHER: *Songs Translated,* translated by Fyleman (London: Curwen, 1927);

Katharina Marie Bech Michaelis, *Bibi,* illustrated by Hedvig Collin, translated by Fyleman (London: Allen & Unwin, 1933);

Widdy-Widdy-Wurkey: Nursery Rhymes from Many Lands, illustrated by Valery Carrick, translated by Fyleman (Oxford: Blackwell, 1934); republished as *Picture Rhymes from Foreign Lands* (New York: Stokes, 1935);

Michaelis, *Bibi Goes Travelling,* translated by Fyleman (London: Allen & Unwin, 1934);

Michaelis, *The Green Island,* illustrated by H. Collin, translated by Fyleman (London: Allen & Unwin, 1935);

Lida, *Pere Castor's Wild Animal Books,* translated by Fyleman (London: Allen & Unwin, 1938);

Jan Karafiat, *Fireflies,* illustrated by Emil Weiss, translated by Fyleman (London: Allen & Unwin, 1942);

Alfred Flueckiger, *Tuck: The Story of a Snow-Hare,* illustrated by Grace Huxtable, translated by Fyleman (London: Bodley Head, 1949);

Marie-Louise Ventteclaye, *Simone and the Lilywhites,* translated by Fyleman (London: Museum Press, 1949);

Lillian Miozzi, *The Adventures of Tommy: The Cat Who Went to Sea,* illustrated by Charlotte Hough, translated by Fyleman (London: Bodley Head, 1950);

Lili Martini, *Peter and His Friend Toby,* illustrated by Wolfgang Fenten, translated by Fyleman (London: Bodley Head, 1955).

SELECTED PERIODICAL PUBLICATIONS –
UNCOLLECTED: Rose Fyleman, "Writing for Children," *Saturday Review of Literature,* 6 (1929): 391–392;

Fyleman, "Writing Poetry for Children," *Horn Book,* 16 (1940): 58–66.

Although she wrote, edited, or translated more than fifty books for children, Rose Fyleman is remembered primarily for her poems about fairies. For several decades she was known as the "accredited poet of fairies," but her publications extended far beyond poetry and far beyond fairies. She also wrote fiction – both fantasy and realistic – plays, information books, and opera librettos.

Born in 1877 in Nottingham, England, Rose Fyleman began writing as a young girl, functioning as the "poet laureate" of her family, not, she recalled in 1940, "that any particular fuss was made of my accomplishments." Still, on holidays and birthdays she "was expected to produce some sort of rhymed tribute of the event." Most of those early efforts have not survived, and, indeed, Fyleman's interest in writing was only occasional and recreational for approximately forty years.

After her early schooling she studied at the University College in Nottingham where she was, by her own admission, a rather undistinguished student. Then, with the financial support of an aunt, she studied singing in Germany, Paris, and London, a pursuit that she credits with aiding her in developing her ear for lyric poetry. Though she was not able to pursue her dream of becoming an opera singer, she did perform as a professional singer and gave voice lessons to students in London. During this period she began her first efforts at publishing verse. She discovered a "women's paper, of no great literary standing" that paid her sixpence per line for her poems. Since she was at this time commuting from Nottingham to London to give voice lessons, she would write on the train, frequently composing just enough lines to "prospectively cover the cost of a meal" in the dining car.

She still did not take her writing seriously until she began helping her sister in an elementary school. In that capacity she found it difficult to find poems that were appropriate for the children she was teaching. According to her, "the poems available were for the most part, with notable few exceptions, such as those of [Robert Louis] Stevenson and Lewis Carroll, either silly and feeble or of the 'Wreck of the Hesperus' or 'We are Seven' type; that is to say, totally unsuitable for children." Consequently, she began experimenting more seriously with her own poetry, focusing now on verse for children, specifically the children of this school.

Upon seeing one of the poems, "Fairies at the Bottom of Our Garden," another schoolteacher suggested that Fyleman submit the poem to *Punch.* She did, and it was accepted. That publication helped to establish connections with publishers on both sides of the Atlantic, leading to the publication of *Fairies and Chimneys* in England in 1918 and in the United States in 1920. With these publications, Fyleman's career as a writer was under way.

Though collecting folk and fairy stories from other cultures was common at the same time that she was writing her poems about fairies, Fyleman avoided the darkness and the evil that many of the Celtic and Germanic fairy stories contain. Her fairy world is a world in which fairies are visible to children but not to most adults, and in which the fairies seemingly exist for the delight of children. This avoidance of the darker and scarier side of human fantasies comes in part from Fyleman's theory of the nature of children's interests. "Children are not interested in a great number of things in which grown-up people are interested," she wrote in the *Horn Book* in 1929. "They do not want to hear about the problems of sex, about social and economic complications, about the reactions of men and women to the circumstances of life and to the characteristics and temperament of other men and women." They do not want to hear, in other words, about much of what the traditional world of fairy stories deals with.

THE ADVENTURE
CLUB

BY

ROSE FYLEMAN

WITH TEN ILLUSTRATIONS BY
A. H. WATSON

METHUEN & CO. LTD.
36 ESSEX STREET W.C.
LONDON

"YOU'RE IN CHARGE OF THE OTHERS REALLY."
Frontispiece]   [*See page* 5

*Frontispiece and title page for Fyleman's collection of stories about the Hastings family and their adventures in Spain
(Lilly Library, Indiana University)*

In the world of these poems fairies are the companions and peers of children, offering them a secret world of wish fulfillment. In "Fairies at the Bottom of Our Garden," which begins her first published volume, fairies dance at night and can sit on moonbeams. Significantly, the Queen of the fairies who accompanies the King in these mystical revels is the persona of the poem – a little girl. It is not surprising when fairies ride the city bus or go "a marketing." This is a world of wonder – peacocks and robins, cuckoos, and rooks serve the fairies in everything from housekeeping to government – but, clearly, the fairyland is a fanciful and imaginative extension of the child's normal and safe world.

In *The Fairy Flute* (1921) Fyleman continues her development of these themes. In the poem fairies are a consolation to children. Children who are ugly or awkward or intellectually slow, or children who are lonely or frightened are told that if the fairies love them everything will be all right. The novice fairy companion is assured that fairies will not hurt; they will only want to play; they are born to dance and enjoy themselves. Moreover, fairies help

their child companions to forget about dreary things like rainy days and lying sick in bed.

If Fyleman's fairies serve as companions to children, they also can, on occasion, serve more didactically to illustrate various lessons about good or bad behavior. For example, in one of the brief stories in *Forty Goodnight Tales* (1923), the fairy queen punishes a greedy fairy page by turning him into a frog. Then, too, in "Darby and Joan," a play in Fyleman's *Eight Little Plays for Children* (1924), the title characters are eternally separated because of their propensity for quarreling. But what is significant about these instances of moral instruction is that generally all the objects of punishment are either imaginary creatures or adults; never are they children. With the instruction thus implicit, the fairies remain attractive companions for the young readers of Fyleman's work.

The world of the fairies, however, seems particularly middle to upper class and particularly feminine, two factors that perhaps explain the history of Fyleman's critical reception in this century. The fairy poems were popular during the middle of the century, being reprinted again and again throughout the 1950s. Indeed, *Fairies and Chimneys* was recommended throughout the 1940s and 1950s by the American Library Association as an important part of any children's library, and it was only in the 1960s that the book disappeared from their list of recommendations. Part of the problem may well be that balls and fairy tea parties could not weather the cultural changes that were occurring in Britain and the United States. That, at least, is Patrick J. Groff's assessment in the *Horn Book* in 1966. There he complains about "going through highly-thought-of anthologies of children's verse poetry to find them full of 'my dears' and lyrical odes to fairies and nature." While he admits that "some very conventional modern girls might still like poetry such as that by Rose Fyleman," the modern boy will object. Yet in 1974 David McCord, also in the *Horn Book,* celebrated Fyleman for the same poems that Groff dismissed.

Fyleman's assumptions about class and audience are evident throughout her work but also notably in some of her best realistic fiction, *The Adventure Club* (1925). The collection of stories, told in the rather engaging voice of the thirteen-year-old participant-narrator, Selina Hastings, relates the tales of an upper-middle-class group of children that is spending the summer in the English countryside because their father, a doctor, had some type of breakdown and needs a lengthy vacation in Spain. The Hastings children form an adventure club with some neighboring children, but there is a serious question as to whether they should play together, until their caregiver discovers that the neighbors are truly gentry and have visited with the right sort of people in London. The adventures are quite lively and still hold the attention of young readers. But behind all of the adventures is a safety net of "local people" who serve the gentry and can help to save the children from any real mishaps.

In a typical episode, the children encounter a caravan, or travel trailer, parked in a local field and decide that it must belong to Gypsies. When they investigate they find that no one seems to be around except a baby. Since the baby wears "a pretty white frock and a tiny gold chain with a locket" and since it has "very blue eyes and golden hair," the children decide that the Gypsies must have stolen the child and that it must be rescued. They are rather surprised when the "Gypsies" appear, and that one of them "wore a tweed skirt and a white jumper and was quite young and very pretty." All ends well; it seems the baby's nurse had left it napping while she visited her boyfriend. The children rationalize their thinking in a childlike fashion:

But we couldn't possibly have known, could we? We'd heard of people who weren't gypsies going about in a caravan, but we'd never actually come across anyone who did it, and we certainly shouldn't have thought of their having a baby with them.

Like any children, they acted on the basis of their experience, but what is noteworthy is that their experience is thoroughly infused with the categories of social structure.

But while, because of Fyleman's narrative strategies, some of the fiction, like *The Adventure Club,* is relatively successful, other items of fiction do not succeed as well. Illustrated by Katy Kruse, *The Katy Kruse Play Book* (1930), for example, offers a plot so improbable that it seems to violate Fyleman's own dictum not to condescend to children. The plot begins when Great-Uncle James, the adventurer, writes from Australia that he wants his nieces and nephews to join him, but before they do, they must build up their muscles so that they will be strong and adventurous. He kindly gives them each £100 to aid them in this enterprise, and they spend it learning to play tennis, row boats, play football, drive cars, and ride motorcycles. However, at the end of the book, Great-Uncle James writes again to announce that he no longer wants to settle down with them and offers them an introduction to a movie producer instead. They become movie stars, the story being the reminder of "how it all came about, and how it was all owing to Great-Uncle James, who was determined to make them strong, brave, and adventurous."

The kind of wish fulfillment that lies behind the abrupt resolution of *The Katy Kruse Play Book,* and of the plots of *Forty Goodnight Tales,* also informs Fyleman's fantasy fiction such as *Adventures with Benghazi* (1946). Benghazi, a talking cat, can do all sorts of magic when the moon is full. He can travel through time, change shape, understand all languages, and be impervious to harm. With such powers, Benghazi takes the protagonist, Gardenia, on various adventures. He takes her beneath the sea to introduce her to mermaids. He rescues a mermaid that has been captured by a circus. Before she returns to the sea, however, he grants her one wish — to ride on the circus rides as she has seen humans do. When Gardenia's Christmas celebration is canceled, Benghazi takes her to see Borealis the Ice Prince and to meet Father Christmas. During that visit, however, they are attacked by Aquila, "the great enchantress of the north," whom Benghazi defeats by using his wits against her might. But it is Fyleman's beloved fairies that prove to be Benghazi's undoing. In the last adventure he takes Gardenia to a fairy party that puts the child right in the center of the world of the imagination. At the party Gardenia meets everyone from Titania to Sleeping Beauty, Cinderella, and Dick Whittington's cat. In fact, the two have so much fun that Benghazi forgets that he must return before sunrise or forfeit his magical powers. Fyleman resolves this dilemma as well as the problem of how to end the narrative by having Benghazi use the last of his powers to return Gardenia to her world, becoming through that act of sacrifice merely an ordinary cat.

Later on in her career Fyleman demonstrated an interest in animals both ordinary and extraordinary. While she continued on occasion to write of animals with fantastic powers, she also worked on information books about animals. Perhaps most notable is *Billy Monkey: A True Tale of a Capuchin* (1936), a prose work of more than 150 pages in which Fyleman relates anecdotes in the life of a pet monkey and his owner. Most of the anecdotes are designed to be entertaining to children as they recount Billy's humanlike idiosyncrasies – his play with toys and his initial fear of stuffed animals. The reader does get a bit of a sense of what a capuchin is like, but not much. Fyleman's translations offer much more

in the way of accurate information about animals. In the late 1930s she translated the Pere Castor series of books from the French, and these – whether they focused on Scaf, the Seal; Martin, the Kingfisher; or Frou, the Hare – did a good job of providing an engaging narrative while offering accurate information about the animal subject.

But whether she was translating books about animals or composing poems about fairies, Fyleman took her task seriously, working hard to make the literature engaging without being condescending to children. In reflecting on this task, she once said that she wrote as she felt the ideas, and if when finished "the work appeals to the mind and heart of a child I am content, for that in itself is surely the most satisfying reward we writers for children can know." On her death on 1 August 1957 she was remembered as the "poet of fairies."

References:

Patrick J. Groff, "Where Are We Going with Poetry for Children?," *Horn Book,* 42 (1966): 456–463;

David McCord, "I Went to Noke and Somebody Spoke," *Horn Book,* 50 (1974): 58–66.

Eve Garnett

(9 January 1900 – 5 April 1991)

Ian Wojcik-Andrews
Eastern Michigan University

BOOKS: *The Family from One End Street,* illustrated by Garnett (London: Muller, 1937; New York: Vanguard, 1939);

Is It Well with the Child?, foreword by Walter de la Mare (London: Muller, 1938);

In and Out and Roundabout: Stories of a Little Town (London: Muller, 1948);

Further Adventures of the Family from One End Street, illustrated by Garnett (New York: Vanguard, 1956);

Holiday at the Dew Drop Inn: A One End Street Story, illustrated by Garnett (New York: Vanguard, 1962);

To Greenland's Icy Mountains: The Story of Hans Egede, Explorer, Colonizer, Missionary (London: Heinemann, 1968);

Lost and Found: Four Stories (London: Muller, 1974);

First Affections: Some Autobiographical Chapters of Early Childhood (London: Muller, 1982).

Eve Cynthia Ruth Garnett's *The Family from One End Street* (1937), a pioneering novel about the life and times of the working-class Ruggles family, assured her and the Ruggleses a place in the history of children's literature. The book was really the first work of children's literature in the twentieth century that for a young audience (ages seven and upward) seriously represented working-class family life. E. Nesbit had touched briefly on working-class themes in *Harding's Luck* (1909). Books for young children, like Constance Howard's *Ameliaranne and the Green Umbrella,* had appeared in 1920. Howard's story is similar to Garnett's; both have daughters of washerwomen as child heroines. Despite these early efforts by Nesbit and Howard, it was Garnett's book that, at least in 1937, authentically reproduced working-class conditions in children's literature. Along with the middle-class Walker and the Blackett families from Arthur Ransome's famous Swallows and Amazons series (1930–1947), the Ruggleses became one of the most notable families in twentieth-century British children's literature:

Ransome's *Pigeon Post* (1936) had won the Carnegie Medal in its inaugural year, while Garnett's *The Family from One End Street* won the award in 1938 over J. R. R. Tolkien's *The Hobbit.*

Garnett wrote and illustrated literature for children and adults throughout the remainder of her life; as recently as 1982 she wrote and published *First Affections: Some Autobiographical Chapters of Early Childhood.* However, it is the fortunes and misfortunes of the Ruggles family from One End Street in Otwell that, rightly or wrongly, have assured her place in children's literary history in general and in any discussion of the family in particular.

After eight other publishers had turned the novel down as "unsuitable" for children, her publisher Frederick Muller had agreed to publish it and wrote to her, asking her how she knew the poor so well — presumably because Garnett's own middle-class childhood and adulthood bore little resemblance to the working-class life of the Ruggles family depicted so convincingly in her novel. The daughter of Lt. Col. F. H. Garnett (little is known of her mother), Eve Garnett was born in Worcestershire, England, where she received a thoroughly middle-class education at the Convent at Bideford in Devon; the West Bank School, also in Devon; and the Alice Ottley School in Worcester. After this she studied at two prestigious art schools in London: the Chelsea Polytechnic School of Art and the Royal Academy School of Art.

Garnett's early and distinguished career as an artist — she completed forty murals for Children's House in London and had her work exhibited at the Le Fevre Gallery, the New English Art Club, and the Tate Gallery in London — began at these art schools where, though often ill, she was nonetheless awarded both the Creswick Prize and a silver medal for her landscape painting. Not surprising, she illustrated her own books as well as those of other writers. For example, she was commissioned to illustrate Evelyn Sharp's *The London Child* (1927). In 1948 she illustrated Robert Louis Stevenson's *A*

Eve Garnett (Gale International Portrait Gallery)

Child's Garden of Verses. Her illustrations for her *The Family from One End Street* and *Is It Well with the Child?* (1938) are both numerous and memorable, and clearly demonstrate her skills in plain line drawing.

Though Garnett's social and cultural milieu was distinctly middle-class, she in fact frequently came into contact with, and often deliberately sought out, the working class. She later recalled in a 1938 letter to the editor of *The Junior Bookshelf* that "While my contemporaries were enjoying *Peter Pan* or *The Wind in the Willows,* I was absorbing . . . the life story of *Lost Gyp* and her bare-footed brother who . . . would endeavour to make a living selling damp fusees . . . or the fortunes of little Meg . . . eternally shivering outside a gin palace awaiting Father." These images of poor, working-class children moved her as a child. As an art student she frequently visited London's East End slums to observe and draw the poor.

Whether she truly felt that her literary skills could ameliorate working-class deprivation is not clear, though obviously she was deeply shocked by what she saw. Much of her 1938 letter to *The Junior Bookshelf* is ambiguous: "I am not sure what originally led me, as a child, to take an interest in the poor. . . . It may have been the story, told me by a well-meaning governess, that the first-class coaches

on railways were always sandwiched in the middle of the train between the two third [class coaches] . . . the idea being, presumably, that the lives of the first-class passengers were of greater value than those of their proletarian or less wealthy brethren in the thirds . . . but on the whole I think my interest was chiefly aroused by a small collection of books ["The Poor"]." What is clear, however, is that her sketches of the poor East End children were the bases of the illustrations commissioned for Evelyn Sharp's *The London Child.* Moreover, the working-class life she witnessed – often squalid but always resilient, according to Marcus Crouch in *The Nesbit Tradition* – so affected her that it became the basis of her famous first novel – *The Family from One End Street.*

The working-class Ruggles family lives in Otwell at No. 1 One End Street. The immediate family consists of Mr. Ruggles the Dustman, Mrs. Ruggles the Washerwoman, and their several children – Lily Rose, Kate, twins James and John, Peggy, and William the youngest, all of whom we meet in the first chapter, "The Christenings." Early in this chapter Garnett comments that the neighbors "pitied Jo and Rosie for having such a large family, and called it Victorian . . . but the Dustman and his wife were proud of their numerous boys and girls."

Despite a large family that is clearly an anachronism in the eyes of the other members of the Otwell community, the Ruggleses live their lives from day to day, cheerfully confronting whatever problems life may present them.

In fact, while each family member is "afflicted with Ideas" — Mr. Ruggles dreams of owning a pig; Lily Rose wants to open a steam laundry; James (the elder of the twins) longs to have adventures and travel around the world — the Ruggles family leads a largely uneventful life. As Nicholas Bagnall wrote in his 10 April 1991 obituary of Eve Garnett in *The Independent,* "The book's climax involves a day trip to London. . . . One of the twins stows away on a barge . . . the other [twin] is invited to a rich family's party. The twins do belong to a Gang, but it defeats no villains. How did such humdrum stuff catch on?" The book's success is probably due to the ordinariness of the adventures, dreams, and aspirations of the Ruggles family as a collective unit and as individuals. In many ways they are heroic, not in the grand epic style of the classical period, but in the smaller novelistic style of the modern age.

Given their working-class conditions, the problems that the Ruggles family must continually confront are economic. For example, in chapter 2 Mrs. Ruggles becomes angry with Lily Rose upon discovering that Lily Rose's attempts to help her mother by doing the ironing have backfired, resulting in a customer's burnt silk petticoat. The customer is Mrs. Beaseley, and Mrs. Ruggles knows that the petticoat will have to be replaced, "and a nice expense *that's* going to be." Later, in chapter 3, Kate passes her eleven-plus examination and wins a scholarship to the secondary school. Mrs. Ruggles, a practical woman who is also sympathetic to her daughter's future, remarks to her husband, "I say, government or no government, clothes have got to be found right now straight away . . . things have to be bought and bills paid *now.*" When Garnett focuses her attention on Mr. Ruggles, money again is central: Mr. Ruggles finds £41 that he returns to the Lost Property Department at the local police station. The result of Mr. Ruggles's honesty is "*Two quid*" from Mr. Short, the money's rightful owner: Garnett's italicizing the two words clearly suggests the importance of money to Mr. Ruggles. As Mary Rayner writes in the third edition of *Twentieth-Century Children's Literature,* "These are real parents up against real pressures."

But *are* they real, or just realistic from a middle-class point of view? Garnett's depiction of the Ruggles family in 1937 as representative of the working class sparked a critical debate within children's literature — a traditionally conservative canon despite the contemporary emphasis on multiculturalism, for example — that continues today. Essentially, the question is whether or not a middle-class person — in this case Eve Garnett — can honestly and accurately represent working-class life. Critics argue both sides. In *Children's Books — History and Trends* Crouch writes, "*The Family From One End Street* in 1937 showed a different aspect of naturalism. It was one of the few books for children written successfully with a purpose. It was, and remains, unique in drawing an attractive and convincing picture of British working-class life." But is it *too* attractive a picture of working-class life? As Crouch remarks in *The Nesbit Tradition,* the book dealt *humorously* with working-class life. Thus, is *The Family from One End Street* merely a stereotypical portrait of a working-class family written from a distinctly bemused, middle-class point of view, and thus, in fact, an immensely patronizing work? The financial problems that the Ruggles family face *are* resolved by the patronage of others, and the Ruggleses *do* always know their place: few working-class people, if any, are in reality so deferential to their "betters."

Frank Eyre wrote in 1971 that "We praised too highly *The Family from One End Street* because it was all we could find of that sort to praise. . . . Unhappily the shadow of One End Street hangs over much contemporary realistic writing for children." But surely the shortsightedness of critics like Eyre cannot be transferred to the novel itself. Other critics like Mary Rayner argue that the "Ruggles family members are still refreshingly real." Nicholas Bagnall's comments are interesting in this debate. He remarked in his obituary of Garnett that, "in her old age she spoke to tradespeople in patrician tones. . . . Though to us her work may seem old-fashioned, she was ahead of her time. Readers had to wait another 30 years before the 'realist' children's story became ideologically acceptable with the work of authors such as Leila Berg, who wrote about disadvantaged families and was much praised for it by progressive people who had forgotten that in her own way Eve Garnett had done it all already." Of course, this begs the questions: what *did* she do, and did she do it patronizingly? Nonetheless, Bagnall's point of view seems a sensible one. A writer cannot be held responsible for changing critical perceptions, even though critics can.

In a sense, all of the above critics are correct. The book obviously does not represent working-class life accurately, if only because it does not show the squalor that she saw and, presumably, experienced. An accurate representation of working-class life would (for a start) insist on setting the constant cheerfulness and stoicism of the Ruggles family in the context of that squalor. The book pays no attention to broader social, economic, and political issues that might explain class struggle, though Garnett has Mr. Ruggles puzzlingly refer to communists, and there are several references to welfare. But these do not make Garnett a social realist or her novel proletarian.

On the other hand, Garnett's *The Family from One End Street* more than realistically portrays one family's sense of constant financial hardship, particularly when compared to the financially comfortable middle-class fantasies of Ransome (fiction) and Tolkien (fantasy). In these utopian contexts, Garnett's work is real, though by no means dystopian. Perhaps one of the book's characters reveals as much about middle-class condescension as several of the book's critics do. Mr. Ruggles has just received a small financial reward from Mr. Short, the writer whose lost money Mr. Ruggles had found and returned to the police station. After Mr. Ruggles offers his profuse thanks for the reward and leaves, Mr. Short closes the door, thinking to himself: "Eight human beings . . . achieving complete happiness and their life's ambition for five shillings a head; *five shillings! Thanks* . . . Did one pity or envy Mr. Ruggles?" Is that last question asked by Mr. Short or by Ms. Garnett? Is condescension implicit in the question, regardless of who asks it?

The two sequels to *The Family from One End Street* are better books, though they are less well known and read. As narratives, they remain flawed, almost what Henry James, speaking of George Eliot's work, famously called "loose baggy monsters." *The Family from One End Street* is a series of "homely" episodes loosely tied together, John Rowe Townsend wrote in *Written for Children* (1965). *Further Adventures of the Family from One End Street* (1956) and *Holiday at the Dew Drop Inn* (1962) are not much different. The former is almost two separate books, one about Kate's adventures in the country and the other about the rest of the family's adventures in Otwell. Plotting techniques are not Garnett's strong point, as all critics agree.

Ironically, an uneven plot and narrative structure led Garnett to greater character development. Whereas *The Family from One End Street* was clearly written with what Crouch in *Children's Books – History and Trends* calls a "purpose," that purpose being to expose social and economic deprivation among the working class, Garnett's sequels focus less on external conditions and more on the development of the characters. Townsend, in *Written for Children*, says

that we see the Ruggleses, "from above and outside." In the sequels we begin to see them from the inside. Thus, while economic issues continue to make their presences felt, a good portion of *Further Adventures* concerns Kate's adventures and misadventures as she travels to the country with Peg and Jo, her younger sister and brother. From chapter 3, when Kate and her two small charges leave Mrs. Ruggles and board the train to visit Mrs. Wildgoose in Kent, to chapter 8, when Garnett again picks up the narrative threads of daily life at One End Street, the reader remains with Kate and the children at the Dew Drop Inn, the home of Mrs. Wildgoose. There the children learn to live in the country, a field, a metonymic device in children's literature that functions as a utopian space by becoming their favorite place to play. The children learn all kinds of "agricultural lore," as Garnett calls it in chapter 7 – Kate in particular becoming far more realized. Caught between her own desires for play and her responsibility for the children, she becomes increasingly real as a child, let alone a working-class child. Kate's character is further developed in *Holiday at the Dew Drop Inn*.

Eve Garnett continued to base her writing on her own life experiences. Perhaps tired of the Ruggles family and of writing and illustrating books that reflected social concerns, in 1968 Garnett wrote *To Greenland's Icy Mountains: The Story of Hans Egede, Explorer, Colonizer, Missionary,* a work that stemmed from her research and travels in northern Norway. Intended for older children – eleven to fourteen – the fascinating *To Greenland's Icy Mountains* concerns the life of explorer and missionary Hans Egede. During her travels Garnett met Nils Egede Bloch-Hoell, a direct descendant of Egede's sister.

Travel also clearly allowed her to expand her creative activities. Her work on Egede, for example, was turned into a radio play entitled *The Doll's House in the Arctic.* This radio script was just one of many she did throughout the 1950s for the then-distinctly middle-class British Broadcasting Corporation, the Australian National Broadcasting Corporation, and the New Zealand Broadcasting Company.

In 1982 Garnett brought together in her autobiography many more of these connections between her life and her art. *First Affections: Some Autobiographical Chapters of Early Childhood* was, however, described in *The Daily Telegraph* obituary of Garnett as "completely unrevealing." In her 1938 letter to the editor of *The Junior Bookshelf* Garnett had written, "What *The Family From One End Street* is, its readers must decide." Perhaps the same might be applied to her autobiography, though history might determine otherwise. She lived most of her life in Lewes, Sussex, a thinly-disguised setting for her fiction. A friend and colleague, writing her obituary in the London newspaper *The Independent* (10 April 1991), described her as "slim, delicately made, always elegant [with] a beautiful face with enormous grey eyes." She died on 5 April 1991 in a nursing home in Lewes, and her £400,000 estate is presently being executed by Haywards Health solicitors Houseman, Rohan, and Benner. She was unmarried.

Garnett's work as a whole, though in particular *The Family from One End Street,* is important because it raises relevant and continuing critical issues. Studies of Garnett's work might raise questions about authorial intention and thus psychoanalytic readings of literature, though perhaps the kind that Garnett herself might shy from, as her 1938 letter suggests. She wrote: "The idea of such literature [*Peter Pan* and *The Wind in the Willows*] in the modern nursery where the shadow of Dr. Freud flickers . . . is, of course, unthinkable. What hope, in an age that has turned the searchlights of psychoanalysis on *Peter Rabbit* and his cousin Benjamin."

But perhaps most important of all, the issue of middle-class condescension (and this issue is not just confined to her one famous novel) raises important and lasting questions about the representation of class, race, and gender in children's literature. In short, Garnett's illustrations and written work throughout her career raised questions that literary theorists, educational psychologists, and social theorists are only now coming to terms with — the influence of society and culture on behavior. Moreover, whether Garnett's book is condescending is largely beside the point, like questions such as whether Disney's animations are good or bad, likable or unlikable, faithful or unfaithful reproductions of the classic fairy tales. A more important question might be raised about what the historically determined conditions of literary production that excluded working-class writers from representing themselves were and whether or not those same conditions exist today. Garnett linked literature to history all her life.

J. B. S. Haldane

(5 November 1892 – 1 December 1964)

G. G. Harper
Calvin College

SELECTED BOOKS: *Daedalus: or, Science and the Future* (New York: Dutton, 1924; London: Kegan Paul, 1924);

Callicinicus: A Defence of Chemical Warfare (London: Kegan Paul, 1925);

Animal Biology, by Haldane and Julian Sorell Huxley (Oxford: Clarendon, 1927);

The Last Judgment: A Scientist's Vision (New York: Harper, 1927);

Possible Worlds, and Other Essays (London: Chatto & Windus, 1927);

Science and Ethics (London: Watts, 1928);

Enzymes (London: Longmans, 1930); enlarged and edited by Haldane and Kurt G. Stern as *Allgemeine Chemie der Enzyme* (Dresden & Leipzig, 1932);

The Causes of Evolution (London: Longmans, Green, 1932);

The Inequality of Man, and Other Essays (London: Chatto & Windus, 1932); republished as *Science and Human Life* (New York: Harper, 1933);

Materialism (London: Hodder & Stoughton, 1932);

Biology in Everyday Life, by Haldane and John Randal Baker (London: Allen & Unwin, 1933);

Fact and Faith (London: Watts, 1934);

Human Biology and Politics (London: British Science Guild, 1934);

The Outlook of Science, edited by William Empson (London: Kegan Paul, 1935);

Science and the Supernatural: A Correspondence between Arnold Lunn and J. B. S. Haldane (N.p.: Sheed, 1935);

My Friend, Mr. Leakey (London: Cresset, 1937; New York: Harper, 1938);

Science and Everyday Life (London: Lawrence & Wishart, 1939);

The Marxist Philosophy and the Sciences (London: Allen & Unwin, 1939);

Keeping Cool, and Other Essays (London: Chatto & Windus, 1940);

Adventures of a Biologist (New York: Harper, 1940);

J. B. S. Haldane

Science in Peace and War (London: Lawrence & Wishart, 1940);

New Paths in Genetics (London: Allen & Unwin, 1941);

A Banned Broadcast, and Other Essays (London: Chatto & Windus, 1946);

Science Advances (London: Allen & Unwin, 1947);

What Is Life? (New York: Boni & Gaer, 1947; London: Lindsay Drummond, 1949);

Everything Has a History (London: Allen & Unwin, 1951);

Haldane in Monaco, 1961 (Associated Newspapers)

The Biochemistry of Genetics (London: Allen & Unwin, 1954).

John Burdon Sanderson Haldane was born in 1892 in Oxford. He was the only son of John Scott Haldane, an Oxford physiologist and colleague of John Burdon Sanderson, for whom Haldane was named, and of Louisa Kathleen Trotter Haldane. Haldane's only sister was the novelist Naomi Mitchison. A studious and sometimes intellectually arrogant boy, he went to Eton and then on scholarship to New College, Oxford, where he achieved first-class honors in both mathematics and *literae humaniores*. He served in the Black Watch regiment in World War I and was wounded. He was later sent to Mesopotamia and again wounded. In 1919 he became a fellow of New College, where he did research in physiology and began his studies in genetics. He went to Cambridge University in 1922 as a reader in biochemistry, married journalist Charlotte Franken Burghes, and continued his investigations in genetics. At University College, London, he was given a chair in genetics in 1933 and later a chair in biometry.

He moved to India in 1961 to head an institute in genetics and biometry, became a citizen, and died in 1964 of rectal cancer. He published prolifically during his lifetime, mainly in genetics and also on the general topic of science and life. He also wrote on politics; he was at one time a Marxist but gradually disengaged himself from the Communist Party after the scientific scandal involving Trofim Denisovich Lysenko. He is recognized as "one of the most effective popularizers of science, as indicated by his books, *Daedalus* (1924), *Possible Worlds* (1927), *The Inequality of Man* (1932), and by his weekly articles in the *Daily Worker*." His reputation in children's literature is dependent on *My Friend, Mr. Leakey* (1937), which is characterized by the same wit, scientific insight, and appeal to everyday experience that make his other writings noteworthy. The children's book appeared somewhat unexpectedly: his reputation as a geneticist was large and solid, and there had been no indication in print that he was capable of such writing, but it stands as a valuable contribution to the field.

One of the most interesting features of *My Friend, Mr. Leakey* is the frequent introduction of scientific terminology. For example, one of the characters uses cheese to attract and kill rats by means of a poison mixed with the cheese: "He made a lot of this poison, and he also made a lot of the stuff that gives the smell to Roquefort cheese. . . . This is called methyl-heptadecyl ketone, and I think it has a lovely smell." Haldane also introduces difficult scientific concepts that are made to fit the story, but they actually counter the ostensible subject, the use of magic to effect change. It is as if he were trying to equate magic with science in some sense; it gives the impression that the narrator is giving his bona fides as a scientist while still remaining a believer in magic. Ronald W. Clark, author of a life of Haldane, attributes the book to "the romantic in his own nature, the imaginative potentiality one can discern in some of his writings, and which continued to bob to the surface." But this does not square with Haldane's reputation as a rationalist and scientist of the most rigorous kind — indeed, his training was actually in mathematics and the classics, a mixture of the rigorously rational and the antiquarian but hardly productive of rich fancy. In this respect he is like Charles Lutwidge Dodgson (Lewis Carroll), also a mathematician and also fanciful.

The novel, like Carroll's Alice books, is the work of a mathematician at play. The problem is, however, that the child as reader cannot know this. Grown-ups can, of course — it is not long before an adult reader sees the rather awkward fun that Haldane is having. Some children might find the intrusion of real science into a standard retelling of an Arabian Nights tale unsettling. A low-key experiment involving several children who are accustomed already to magic stories indicates that the scientific matter is mystifying but hardly unsettling. To the grown-up reader, however, the sudden appearance of a jawbreaking chemical term is amusing. It is possible, then, that Haldane's perhaps unconscious intent is to interest grown-ups first, almost as if he were talking to young readers but with his eye on the attendant adults to see how they are taking the performance, to see if any of them giggle or show consternation.

Haldane wrote the story for his own amusement. The narrator resembles the author – he is somewhat donnish, insists on scientific or mathematical exactness, and yet has a puckish humor. The scientific asides may be merely self-congratulatory, perhaps even narcissistic – the seer gazing into his own mirror to find his own identity again. Whatever the motive, Haldane has left an interesting, even compelling, story that appeals to precocious youngsters even though many of the behaviors of the characters seem outlandish. The mixture of fantasy and common, or perhaps more precisely uncommon, sense is still interesting, probably more to grown-ups than to children. Some precocious children might also enjoy Haldane's self-ironizing references to science, including his peculiar footnotes.

My Friend, Mr. Leakey is a collection of short stories, unified by the presence of the narrator and Mr. Leakey, the magician. The narrator is clearly modeled on Haldane himself. He is a scientist, has been trained in classical languages and literature, and is quirky and sometimes combative. Mr. Leakey, however, is also partly modeled on Haldane, or at least on a professor: he is sometimes pedantic, sometimes forgetful, and sometimes also combative – like Haldane, he has an animosity toward Western capitalism and its vanities. In another story there is a John Milton–like diatribe against gold: "people waste an awful lot of time and trouble making mines for gold; and when they have got it, it isn't really as useful as iron, or chocolate, or india-rubber, and not as pretty as glass, or flowers, or pictures." Yet Mr. Leakey is also avuncular – a good host, jovial at times, and patient in explaining what he is about. He enjoys performing magic tricks yet can be offhand about some of the wonders of his world. His sangfroid while traveling on a magic carpet is well described – the reader gets a sense of unbelievable speed by being told almost in the same breath what parts of the world are passing beneath the fly-

Haldane working at the Indian Statistical Institute, Calcutta, India, circa 1962 (Mrs. Naomi Mitchison)

ing carpet. His explanation of why jinn find it difficult to work in certain parts of the Middle East is instructive; they are inhibited by the presence of radio waves: "The wireless messages go right through them and give them pains in the stomach, which makes them still angrier." Almost sybaritic in his tastes, Mr. Leakey puts his strange servants – including a dragon that lives in a hot fire, a jinni, and an octopus that has been trained as a table waiter – to work providing feasts that include even strawberries fetched from as far away as Ceylon by the jinni. Mr. Leakey is the narrator's friend; it is not long before Haldane has established him as the child-reader's friend also, and the reader is thus induced to ingest scientific information with the usual expenditure of intellectual energy.

A close look at the stories reveals Haldane's method of integrating scientific information in the narratives. In "Rats" a greengrocer named Smith has four sons. Three find their way to professions, one of them as successor to his father in the shop; the fourth, Jack, is not good in school but spends his time making radio tubes and devising contraptions to outwit the electric company. One day the brothers see an advertisement about the need for a device to catch and destroy the rats that are plaguing the London docks. None of the hundreds of devices that are submitted by the public work well. Jim, one of the brothers, submits a device that works well for a bit, but then fails. Then Charles, with a scheme that involves the chemical that gives the smell to Roquefort cheese, tries but also fails. Finally Jack, the youngest, tries. He borrows heavily and goes to work creating his solution to the rat problem. His method is simple: baking iron filings into biscuits and leaving them all over the docks and then turning on several powerful magnets. The rats eat the biscuits, are attracted to pits in which the magnets have been placed, and die of starvation. The magnet also catches a night watchman who has ignored the warnings and worn shoes with iron nails, but he is rescued. Jack Smith receives the £100,000 reward and marries the daughter of the director of the docks.

The next story, "The Snake with the Gold Teeth," begins with a whimsical indicator of Haldane's political stance – it features Paolo Maria Encarnaçao Esplendido, who owns many gold mines in Brazil but makes most of his money from silver mines. "One reason why he was so rich," the narrator says, "was that he paid the miners very badly. So people didn't like him very much." Also, he does not spend his money on hospitals and universities, as many rich people do. He spends it on motor boats with silver fittings and on toothbrushes with golden handles – things that Haldane's narrator calls "useless things." He also has a private menagerie, with seven caimans, some of them twenty feet long, and a giant anaconda whose eggs Esplendido eats from a golden egg cup. One of his snakes, called Joao, develops trouble with his teeth, so the man has them capped with gold. Haldane then continues with a learned disquisition on the uses of gold by the rich:

> . . . all sorts of people have gold spoons and watches and salt-cellars, and things like that. And some of the kings

and princes in India have the oddest things made of gold. The Akoond of Swat had seven wives with gold nose-rings. The Jam of Las Bela has seventeen golden toothpicks, five golden parrot cages, and a golden footscraper. The Begum of Bhopal had a golden sewing machine. She was an old lady, and quite intelligent, but she always went about with her head in a bag because she thought it would never do if people saw her face. And the Nono of Spiti has a golden spittoon. (You may think I have made up the Nono of Spiti, but I haven't. There really is a place called Spiti in the Himalaya mountains . . . and the king of it is called the Nono. I can't help it if people and places have funny names like that.)

One day the snake loses one of the gold teeth. His owner accuses his keeper of stealing the tooth. A chase ensues during which the owner falls into his swimming pool and is eaten by Joao "so quickly that he [the snake] burnt his tongue on the cigar the Senhor was smoking." The keeper convinces a judge that he did not kill his employer and is hired by a rich American to train a caiman and exhibit her in a circus.

This one book admits Haldane to the ranks of successful authors of children's books. The book still charms the reader, though it makes inordinate demands on the reader's store of knowledge. Many of its jokes are no longer resonant, dependent as they often are on knowledge of cultural matters among the English middle and professional classes of Haldane's time. Some of the magic has now become technological commonplace, but small adjustments still allow the charm to show.

References:

Ronald W. Clark, *The Life and Work of J. B. S. Haldane* (London: Hodder & Stoughton, 1968; New York: Coward-McCann, 1969);

Krishna R. Drunamraju, *Haldane: The Life and Work of J. B. S. Haldane with Special Reference to India* (Aberdeen, Scotland: Aberdeen University Press, 1985).

Kathleen Hale

(24 May 1898 –)

Gary D. Schmidt
Calvin College

BOOKS: *Orlando the Marmalade Cat: A Camping Holiday* (London: Country Life, 1938; New York: Scribners, 1938);

Orlando the Marmalade Cat: A Trip Abroad (London: Country Life, 1939; New York: Transatlantic Arts, 1939);

Orlando's Evening Out (London & New York: Penguin, 1941);

Orlando's Home Life (London & New York: Penguin, 1942);

Orlando the Marmalade Cat Buys a Farm (London: Country Life, 1942; New York: Transatlantic Arts, 1947);

Henrietta the Faithful Hen (London & New York: Transatlantic Arts, 1943);

Orlando the Marmalade Cat Becomes a Doctor (London & New York: Transatlantic Arts, 1944);

Orlando the Marmalade Cat: His Silver Wedding (London: Country Life, 1944; New York: Transatlantic Arts, 1958);

Orlando's Invisible Pyjamas (London: Transatlantic Arts, 1947);

Orlando the Marmalade Cat Keeps a Dog (London: Country Life, 1949; New York: Transatlantic Arts, 1949);

Orlando the Judge (London: John Murray, 1950);

Orlando's Country Peep Show (London: Chatto & Windus, 1950);

Orlando the Marmalade Cat: A Seaside Holiday (London: Country Life, 1952);

Manda the Jersey Calf (London: John Murray, 1952; New York: Coward-McCann, 1953);

Orlando's Zoo (London: John Murray, 1954);

Orlando the Marmalade Cat: The Frisky Housewife (London: Country Life, 1956);

Orlando's Magic Carpet (London: John Murray, 1958; Hollywood, Fla.: Transatlantic Arts, 1960);

Orlando the Marmalade Cat Buys a Cottage (London: Country Life, 1963);

Orlando and the Three Graces (London: John Murray, 1965; revised edition, London: Warne, 1992);

Orlando the Marmalade Cat Goes to the Moon (London: John Murray, 1968);

Orlando the Marmalade Cat and the Water Cats (London: Cape, 1972);

Henrietta's Magic Egg (London: Allen & Unwin, 1973);

A Slender Reputation: An Autobiography (London: Warne, 1994).

OTHER: Mary Rachel Harrower, *I Don't Mix Much with Fairies,* illustrated by Hale (London: Eyre & Spottiswoode, 1928);

Harrower, *Plain Jane,* illustrated by Hale (New York: Coward-McCann, 1929);

Charles Perrault, *Puss-in-Boots: A Peep-Show Book,* illustrated by Hale (Boston: Houghton Mifflin, 1951);

Evelyn Waugh, *Basil Seal Rides Again,* illustrated by Hale (London: Chapman & Hall, 1963).

Much of Kathleen Hale's early life is in distinct contrast to the books for which she is known. Her father, Charles Edward Hale, died when she was only five. When her mother, Ethel Alice Aylmer Hale, was unable to care for them, the three children were divided; Hale went to live with her grandparents and an insensitive aunt, with whom she felt terribly neglected, especially emotionally. After her mother was able to bring the children together again in Manchester in 1907, Hale never found the loving family for which she yearned and that she wrote about in the Orlando books. Her one outlet was art, a talent inspired at an early age by the works of Edmund Dulac and Arthur Rackham, though her drawings did not resemble theirs. After World War I her artwork was exhibited in a series of art exhibitions and reproduced in art journals. In 1926 she married Douglas McClean, a bacteriologist, and soon after began designing book jackets and illustrating several children's books. Hale then turned to writing her own children's books, creating

Kathleen Hale (Hulton Deutsch Collection)

an imaginative vision of what she thought a family should be.

Hale is today remembered principally for the Orlando the Marmalade Cat series. Perhaps what is most extraordinary about this series is its longevity. The series began in 1938 with *Orlando the Marmalade Cat: A Camping Holiday* and concluded in 1972 with *Orlando the Marmalade Cat and the Water Cats.* The texts for the nineteen books of the series grew longer and longer, at first to match the aging of Hale's two children, for whom the first books were written. In addition, the stories grew more and more fantastic, adding magic carpets and even – during 1968 – a trip to the moon. But neither Orlando nor his wife, Grace, nor the three kittens, Tinkle, Pansy, and Blanche, ever change; their ages seem to be eternally fixed.

The first two books in the series – *Orlando the Marmalade Cat: A Camping Holiday* and *Orlando the Marmalade Cat: A Trip Abroad* (1939) – were not particularly successful. The third book, *Orlando's Evening Out* (1941), published under the severe paper shortages of World War II, was enormously successful and brought the first two volumes into popularity along with it. From then until 1958 a new Orlando book was published at least every other year;

around 1950 they were released at the rate of every six months. Some series can boast a longevity of thirty-four years, but none have appeared in such variety. The books were printed in a variety of formats: oversized, horizontal picture book, miniature sizes, pop-up. They were produced both in lavishly large printings and small printings marked by the economies of war. They have been adapted for British Broadcasting Corporation radio and for the ballet stage.

Like so many children's books, Hale's books began as stories for the author's children. After Hale's second son, Nicholas, was born in 1933, she grew tired of the children's literature that she found available. She found inspiration in the family cat. In fact, much of the Orlando series is based on Hale's family life. The early books were based upon trips that she and her husband had taken – camping in the country and a trip to the coast of France. *Orlando the Marmalade Cat Buys a Farm* (1942) is based on a farm located near Hale's home, and the story benefits from her farm experience during World War I. *Orlando the Marmalade Cat Buys a Cottage* (1963) deals with Hale's own house. The result is that Hale works out of her own immediate experience. This extends to the character of Orlando himself, who is modeled upon Hale's husband.

118

Hale illustrated all of the Orlando books with lithographs, pictures drawn directly onto stone plates; the process is an inexpensive way of producing books for the publisher but one requiring many painstaking hours by the artist. The illustrations fill the pages, seeming to play with the text. In *Orlando the Marmalade Cat: A Camping Holiday,* for example, the text sometimes moves vertically, sometimes horizontally across a double-page spread, sometimes in large chunks scattered wherever there is room between illustrations. At times the illustrations set a large scene; at times each page holds several smaller scenes to be read almost as a narrative. This creative interplay between text and illustration was to lessen over the years, but in the early books it is pronounced.

The illustrations successfully blend the human and feline worlds successfully. Orlando may be shown distinctly as a cat, but his green visor and sturdy position behind a steering wheel suggest his human capabilities. If the art seems elementary and disproportioned, Hale uses those qualities to suggest a child's-eye view of Orlando's world, filled with incongruities of size and details disproportioned according to the child's interest.

The books were originally modeled on Jean de Brunhoff's Babar books and, in fact, appeared in much the same folio format. But while the Babar books are still enjoying a lively existence, the Orlando series has faded from popularity. The usual forces for this kind of decline are not evident here: the books are not especially tied to a particular time, nor do references to World War II, during which so many of these were written, date the texts. Perhaps the books have faded because of a want of invention; there is no sense that each book represents some new idea on the part of the author, some new way of handling material that is potentially delightful. In fact, the Orlando books become progressively less interesting as the fantasy is stretched further and further and the interplay between the human and feline worlds is pushed further from the center.

But these problems are not evident in the early books of the series. *Orlando the Marmalade Cat: A Camping Holiday* deals with the adventures of the family as they set up a tent on the banks of a river by a farm and a small village. The book opens with a full-page illustration of Orlando draped around his rather severe Master, and the text suggests that Orlando is wheedling something out of him. "As Orlando told him they must have a holiday, his Master said he would think about it. He walked up and down the lawn, thinking deeply, anxiously

watched by all the family. At last he went indoors and telephoned for a pale green tent, and the cats knew he was going to let them go." This situation represents Hale at her best. The humor comes from the interplay between the human world – the Master, who does not want the cats to go so that they will continue to control the mischievous mice – and the cats, who want to wander, in this case to a campground. The fantasy and realism are mixed together seamlessly. Hale maintains this delicate balance between the two worlds throughout the book. The cat family drives away in a car, but they drink milk in a farmyard. They camp by a stream because of its lovely wild orchids, but also because it is full of little fish. They climb a small mountain to play with caterpillars, but they also have to hide from the sheepdog. They win prizes at a local fair, visit a ruined castle, and go to the shore, but they return to Master and instantly take up their role of catching mice. Both the human and feline sides are working simultaneously, and the interplay between them creates much of the delightful humor of the book.

Orlando's Evening Out works on a similarly simple concept. Here the cat family goes not to a campground but to a circus. And again it is the setting that provides much of the context for Orlando's adventures. Hale seems to pose a question: What would happen if a cat became involved with the circus acts? The result is that Orlando leaps from one act to another, frustrating the performers and delighting the audience. In the end he is awarded a golden medal for his performance.

This book suggests problems that will become manifest with the later books. Much of the book is a discursive journey to the circus; the last few pages deal with Tinkle's capture of his first mouse (out from the folds of the elephant's ear). Both these framing sections meander pointlessly; they seem to exist only to provide the opportunity for Hale to include some jokes, none of which truly connects to the circus experience. Pansy, for example, weeps because, having looked the wrong way through her binoculars, she thinks her family has abandoned her. Blanche disturbs a weather vane, confusing the directions of some birds heading for Africa. These are irrelevant to the story and break the unity of the book, so that it becomes merely episodic, with one thing happening after another without any sense of completion or wholeness.

When the later books lose the unity of place that mark the early books, this discursive quality becomes pronounced. *Orlando's Home Life* (1942), which sounds as though it should be marked by unity of place, is a jumble of short, page-long epi-

Front cover for one of Hale's nineteen books about Orlando; his wife, Grace; and their three kittens
(Lilly Library, Indiana University)

sodes that are disparate. It begins with the need to make money for the children to attend school and moves to various inventive ways of making that money, then to the kittens actually attending school, and then to a set of tutors who come once the school seems ineffective. But once the tutors are dismissed, the book becomes merely silly, with the cats wandering around the town encountering various adventures, none of which is developed or recalls the opening or in fact exploits the potential interest of the character. *Orlando and the Three Graces* (1965), in which Orlando's wife is mysteriously multiplied into three, is similar in its rapid movement from home to shops to home again to the sky on a magic carpet and finally to the castle of Santa Claws. *Orlando the Judge* (1950), in which Orlando takes over the case of missing cheese, also is unable to generate any kind of unity other than that suggested by its plot situation.

In the end these works are unremarkable. If one compares them to the Babar series, or even to H. A. Rey's Curious George series, one sees the same attempt at generating a rapid series of episodes that are loosely held together. Neither the

Babar nor the Curious George books are unified by setting, but they are unified by a strong central character and vivid language. Babar is the somewhat stolid, stern, but loving king and father, sometimes addled and sometimes confused but always taken up with his children. George is creative, imaginative, and spontaneous, quick to repent, quick to play.

The largest disappointment of these books must be the character of Orlando himself. The first book in the series is suggestive of some interesting possibilities for developing the character of Orlando. His relationship with his Master in that volume seems interesting and manipulative. He is inventive (witness his use of his whiskers to imitate flies), loving and playful with his family, and always pleased with himself – a quality that might have been usefully exploited. He seems to dwell on the borders of the human and feline worlds, and his free movement between those two worlds is intriguing. But Hale develops none of these qualities, and too often Orlando is bland and uninteresting.

In *Orlando the Judge* the crowded courtroom whispers, as Orlando takes the high seat, that "it's

Orlando. . . . Now everything will be all right." If it had been Babar taking the seat — a character who had been developed and given strong qualities over a series of books — this would be understandable. In this text the line seems self-indulgent. There is nothing in any of the texts to suggest that everything will be all right because Orlando is present. Hale is sometimes able to present him as a character whose resourceful ideas lead to comic and exaggerated situations, but there is nothing there beyond the simple comedy.

Yet these books did indeed survive for almost a generation. In part World War II might account for some of this. Perhaps the two strongest elements of these books are their vision of the life of the family and their insistence upon normality in a world filled with the unexpected. It is this latter quality which would be important in a world at war. No matter what the situation, Orlando and his family end up together and at some sort of peace. At the end of *Orlando the Marmalade Cat Becomes a Doctor* (1944) Orlando and Grace purchase and run a hospital. "However busy Grace might be, she never allowed a day to pass without spending an hour with her kittens. She called them to her and they gathered round beneath the magnolia blossom in the Maternity ward to hear the wonderful stories she was waiting to tell them. Sometimes they romped with the insects, or they discussed the day's events, and they always ended by falling asleep and dreaming of each other." No matter how hectic the books might be — and they are all remarkably hectic — they end on a peaceful note like this. The unexpected moments and crises of life do not upset this final peace.

The books are marked by a celebration of the family, an element tied closely to the final peaceful scenes. Perhaps surprising for the late 1930s and 1940s, Orlando and Grace share equally the child-rearing responsibilities. In *Orlando's Evening Out* it is Orlando who takes charge of the three kittens when they travel to the circus. In *Orlando's Home Life* Orlando and Grace work together to earn the money for the children's education. In fact, there is never a sense of Orlando alone; he is always pictured in conjunction with his family. In part this may come out of Hale's perception of her own childhood as one marked by unhappiness and neglect. Perhaps she is picturing the kind of family that she wished to have had. "Tinkle," she notes in an interview for *Something About the Author* (volume sixty-six, 1991) "who is a little bit of a rebel, was based on me, though he had to be softened not to appear too subversive from the parents' point of view. Through

Tinkle I wanted to convey a message of tolerance and understanding, that if a child is being difficult it may not be because he is 'naughty' but because something creative inside of him is steaming up. When writing my books I kept in mind children who were deprived of family love and always tried to portray a warm happy life."

Certainly this is the case in the Orlando books. The children get into mischief, but they are never in any serious trouble. When, in *Orlando the Judge,* they are arrested for trespassing, it is their own father who is the courtroom judge, and he opens their case by winking at them. Tinkle may be missing for a time in *Orlando the Marmalade Cat: The Frisky Housewife* (1956) but there is never any question that he will be found. Orlando may be separated from his family for a time in *Orlando the Marmalade Cat: A Trip Abroad,* but it is no surprise to find him parachuting from a plane crossing the English Channel so that he might land on the beach where his family is bathing, responding to their questions with an "Oh la la!" In the end the family remains happily and securely together.

The Orlando books have been praised for their verbal humor, but the puns that mark these books are hardly memorable and not enough to carry the humor of the books. In *Orlando's Invisible Pyjamas* (1947) Tinkle refers to the mouse being held in his father's mouth as a mustache. In *Orlando's Three Graces* Santa Claus is transformed into Santa Claws. Sliding down a drainpipe in *Orlando the Judge* becomes eavesdropping. Readers of the series might be more inclined to watch for the repeating characters, such as the Persian king and his multiple wives, or Hale's husband clutching a *New Statesman,* or Mr. Gorgon, or Mr. Cattermole.

Perhaps the most successful fusion of strong elements comes in *Orlando the Marmalade Cat Buys a Farm.* Here the cat family, out for a drive, comes upon a small farm they had once visited. It is for sale, and their Master wires the money to them. Orlando finds that all the animals have taken up residence in the house because of the dilapidated state of the barns, and the cats and the rest of the animals clean and polish the stables to make them more attractive. The book follows them through the seasons, showing the cows being milked, the sheep herded, the grain threshed, the hay made into stacks, and the sheep sheared. Orlando and his family are quite successful, selling their goods at market and winning blue ribbons for their stock. In the fall they gather fruit, plow for winter wheat, set up hedges, and clean the ditches to prevent flooding. In the winter they go skating as the cows warm them

Hale finishing one of her Orlando paintings, February 1949 (photograph by Hubsch, Hulton Deutsch Collection)

with their breath. And as the snow melts a lamb is born. In the end, "Orlando sat and planned the future, gazing at the fire with eyes as green as the coming springtime."

Here is a satisfying union of the human and feline worlds, unity of place that provides a credible and attractive context for the adventure, a sense of restraint in holding back a too elaborate fantasy. Their adventures and chores are intimately tied to the life of the farm, and the humor and delight of the book lie in how cats perform human chores. The full illustrations mirror the changing of the seasons and reflect the complexity of farm life, while at the same time exploiting the potential humor in personifying animals. Orlando's family works successfully and playfully together, so that every item in the book hangs together.

Hale wrote children's books about two other animals. *Henrietta the Faithful Hen* was first published in 1943; it was followed by *Henrietta's Magic Egg* thirty years later in what is Hale's last children's work. Despite a rather curious illustration in *Orlando the Marmalade Cat: The Frisky Housewife* where Henrietta is elected to a pantheon including Babar, the White Rabbit, Black Beauty, Toad of Toad

Hall, and Squirrel Nutkin, she is not a memorable character. Hale is unable to blend the human and hen worlds as she had done in the Orlando series, though she does humorously portray the Mistress, Mrs. Fowler, as a very large and somewhat dowdy chicken. The adventures are as episodic as those in the Orlando series, and the later book suffers from a too elaborate fantasy that seems to have little point. A tree grows out of a fantastic egg and blossoms into flowers that seem to have eyes and mouths. It arouses – for no apparent reason – the ire of a mob, and is saved from destruction only when Henrietta acts as an oracle and answers to the future come from birds hidden in the branches. Lacking the qualities of resourcefulness and caring found in Orlando, Henrietta is an unappealing character and, today, is assigned to the oblivion of the unpublished.

Manda the Jersey Calf (1952), Hale's longest book, was written after a journey to Ireland. It follows Manda as she leaves England on a holiday to Ireland. She wanders along by ruined cottages, admiring scenery and sights, until she is befriended by Meg, a jennet who belongs to a poor family. Manda stays with the family for a time, but soon it is clear that the family can support neither Manda nor Meg. They both leave, tearfully, and return to the coast of Ireland. There, by accident, they accept money from a crowd who believes that Manda is predicting races, and they must make their escape. Back home, Manda's family accepts the jennet and sends two sheep to the poor Irish family to help them make their fortunes.

The book is marked by much more text than any other Hale book, and with it comes more description. Manda, for example, "had beautiful eyes like deep, dark pools, fringed by long lashes like rushes growing by the water's edge. Her face was dark as a piece of burnt toast." Ireland is depicted as a land of color: "Hills changed to mountains and huge grey rocks like sleeping elephants lay in the green turf, with lacey caps of white and yellow lichen, posies of sea-pinks and collars of heaters." The illustrations are correspondingly fewer, with less narrative information than the Orlando illustrations.

This work is marked by some of the Orlando problems, however. Manda is a flat character, with little to make her memorable. She seems a passive observer who is acted upon, and it is the landscape around her which is more interesting. The adventures are episodic, with little connection between one and another. The reason for the holiday itself is stretched, so that the fantasy does not encourage that willing suspension of disbelief which makes any fantasy work.

Hale will be remembered for those books in which she most successfully encourages that willing suspension, where the disparity between the human and animal world is not too apparent but is easily bridged. The more fantastic the story, the wider the gap becomes, the less successfully it is bridged.

Captain W. E. Johns

(5 February 1893 – 21 June 1968)

Gary D. Schmidt
Calvin College

BOOKS: *The Camels Are Coming,* as W. E. Johns, illustrated by Johns (London: J. Hamilton, 1932);

Mossyface, as William Earle (London: Mellifont, 1932);

The Pictorial Flying Course, by Johns and Harry M. Schofield, illustrated by Johns (London: J. Hamilton, 1932);

Fighting Planes and Aces, illustrated by Howard Leigh (London: J. Hamilton, 1932);

The Spy Flyers, illustrated by Leigh (London: Hamilton, 1933);

The Cruise of the Condor, illustrated by Leigh (London: J. Hamilton, 1933);

Biggles of the Camel Squadron, illustrated by Leigh (London: J. Hamilton, 1934);

Biggles Flies Again, illustrated by Leigh (London: J. Hamilton, 1934);

The Raid (London: J. Hamilton, 1935);

The Black Peril: A "Biggles" Story (London: J. Hamilton, 1935);

Biggles Flies East, illustrated by Leigh and Alfred Sindall (London: Oxford University Press, 1935);

Biggles Hits the Trail, illustrated by Leigh and Sindall (London: Oxford University Press, 1935);

Some Milestones in Aviation (London: J. Hamilton, 1935);

The Air VC's (London: J. Hamilton, 1935);

Biggles in France (London: Boys' Friend Library, 1935);

Biggles Learns to Fly, illustrated by Leslie Stead (London: Boys' Friend Library, 1935);

Steeley Flies Again (London: Newnes, 1935);

Sky High (London: Newnes, 1936);

Blood Runs Thin, as John Early (London: Newnes, 1936);

Biggles in Africa, illustrated by Leigh and Sindall (London: Oxford University Press, 1936);

Biggles & Co., illustrated by Leigh and Sindall (London: Oxford University Press, 1936);

Captain W. E. Johns

Murder by Air (London: Newnes, 1937);

The Passing Show: A Garden Diary by an Amateur Gardener, illustrated by Leigh (London: My Garden, 1937);

Biggles Flies West, illustrated by Leigh and Sindall (London: Oxford University Press, 1937);

Biggles – Air Commodore, illustrated by Leigh and Sindall (London: Oxford University Press, 1937);

Desert Night (London: Hamilton, 1938);

Champion of the Main, illustrated by H. Gooderman (London: Oxford University Press, 1938);

Biggles Flies South, illustrated by Leigh and Jack Nicolle (London: Oxford University Press, 1938);

The Murder at Castle Deeping (London: Hamilton, 1938);

Biggles Goes to War, illustrated by Leigh and Martin Tyas (London: Oxford University Press, 1938);

The Biggles Omnibus (London: Oxford University Press, 1938) – includes *Biggles Flies East, Biggles Hits the Trail,* and *Biggles & Co.;*

The Rescue Flight: A Biggles Story, illustrated by Leigh and Sindall (London: Oxford University Press, 1939);

Wings of Remembrance (London: Newnes, 1939);

The Modern Boy's Book of Pirates, as W. E. Johns (London: Amalgamated, 1939);

Biggles Flies North, illustrated by Leigh and Will Narraway (London: Oxford University Press, 1939);

Biggles in Spain, illustrated by Leigh and J. Abbey (London: Oxford University Press, 1939);

Biggles – Secret Agent, illustrated by Leigh and Sindall (London: Oxford University Press, 1940);

The Biggles Flying Omnibus (London: Oxford University Press, 1940) – includes *Biggles Flies North, Biggles Flies South,* and *Biggles Flies West;*

Biggles in the South Seas, illustrated by Norman Howard (London: Oxford University Press, 1940);

Biggles in the Baltic, illustrated by Leigh and Sindall (Toronto: Oxford University Press, 1940);

The Unknown Quantity (London: Hamilton, 1940);

The Third Biggles Omnibus (London: Oxford University Press, 1941) – includes *Biggles in Spain, Biggles Goes to War,* and *Biggles in the Baltic;*

Biggles Defies the Swastika, illustrated by Leigh and Sindall (London: Oxford University Press, 1941);

Biggles Sees It Through, illustrated by Leigh and Sindall (London: Oxford University Press, 1941);

Spitfire Parade: Stories of Biggles in War-Time, illustrated by Ratcliffe Wilson (London: Oxford University Press, 1941);

Worrals of the WAAF (London: Lutterworth, 1941);

Worrals Flies Again (London: Hodder & Stoughton, 1942);

Worrals Carries On (London: Lutterworth, 1942);

Sinister Service, illustrated by Stuart Tresilian (London: Oxford University Press, 1942);

Biggles Sweeps the Desert, illustrated by Stead (London: Hodder & Stoughton, 1942);

Biggles in the Jungle, illustrated by Terence Cuneo (London: Oxford University Press, 1942);

Biggles "Fails to Return," illustrated by Stead (London: Hodder & Stoughton, 1943);

Biggles Charter Pilot, illustrated by Mendoza (London: Oxford University Press, 1943);

Biggles in Borneo, illustrated by Tresilian (New York: Oxford University Press, 1943);

King of the Commandos, illustrated by Stead (London: University of London Press, 1943);

Worrals on the War-Path (London: Hodder & Stoughton, 1943);

Worrals Goes East (London: Hodder & Stoughton, 1944);

Gimlet Goes Again (London: University of London Press, 1944);

Biggles in the Orient, (London: Hodder & Stoughton, 1944);

Worrals of the Islands: A Story of the War in the Pacific (London: Hodder & Stoughton, 1945);

Biggles Delivers the Goods (London: Hodder & Stoughton, 1946);

Gimlet Comes Home (London: University of London Press, 1946);

Sergeant Bigglesworth CID (London: Hodder & Stoughton, 1946);

Worrals in the Wilds (London: Hodder & Stoughton, 1947);

Comrades in Arms, illustrated by Stead (London: Hodder & Stoughton, 1947);

Gimlet Mops Up (London: Brockhampton, 1947);

Worrals in the Winds (London: Hodder & Stoughton, 1947);

Worrals Down Under (London: Lutterworth, 1948);

Gimlet's Oriental Quest (London: Brockhampton, 1948);

The Rustlers of Rattlesnake Valley (Nashville: T. Nelson, 1948);

Biggles' Second Case (London: Hodder & Stoughton, 1948);

Biggles Hunts Big Game (London: Hodder & Stoughton, 1948);

Biggles Breaks the Silence (London: Hodder & Stoughton, 1949);

Biggles Takes a Holiday (London: Hodder & Stoughton, 1949);

Gimlet Lends a Hand (London: Brockhampton, 1949; reissued, London: May Fair Books, 1964);

Worrals Goes Afoot (London: Lutterworth, 1949);

Worrals in the Wastelands (London: Lutterworth, 1949);

Dr. Vane Answers the Call (London: Latimer House, 1950);

Worrals Investigates (London: Lutterworth, 1950);

Gimlet Bores In (London: Brockhampton, 1950);

Biggles Gets His Men (London: Hodder & Stoughton, 1950);

Johns at his writing table, 1960 (Hulton Deutsch Collection)

Biggles Goes to School (London: Hodder & Stoughton, 1951);

Another Job for Biggles (London: Hodder & Stoughton, 1951);

Biggles Works It Out (London: Hodder & Stoughton, 1951);

Gimlet Off the Map (London: Brockhampton, 1951);

Gimlet Gets the Answer (London: Brockhampton, 1952);

Biggles – Air Detective (London: Latimer House, 1952);

Biggles Follows On (London: Hodder & Stoughton, 1952);

Biggles Takes the Case (London: Hodder & Stoughton, 1952);

The First Biggles Omnibus (London: Hodder & Stoughton, 1953) – includes *Biggles Sweeps the Desert*, *Biggles in the Orient*, *Biggles Delivers the Goods*, and *Biggles "Fails to Return"*;

Biggles in the Blue (London: Brockhampton, 1953);

Biggles and the Black-Raider (London: Hodder & Stoughton, 1953);

Short Stories (London: Latimer House, 1953);

Biggles in the Gobi (London: Hodder & Stoughton, 1953);

Biggles of the Special Air Police (London: Thames, 1953);

Biggles, Foreign Legionnaire (London: Hodder & Stoughton, 1954);

Gimlet Takes a Job (London: Brockhampton, 1954);

Biggles Pioneer Air Fighter (London: Thames, 1954);

Biggles and the Pirate Treasure and Other Biggles Adventures (London: Brockhampton, 1954);

Biggles Cuts It Fine (London: Hodder & Stoughton, 1954);

Kings of Space: A Story of Interplanetary Exploration (London: Hodder & Stoughton, 1954);

Return to Mars (London: Hodder & Stoughton, 1955);

Adventure Bound, illustrated by Douglas Relf (Nashville: T. Nelson, 1955);

Biggles Follows On (London: Transworld, 1955);

Biggles' Chinese Puzzle and Other Biggles Adventures (London: Brockhampton, 1955);

Biggles in Australia (London: Hodder & Stoughton, 1955);

The Biggles Air Detective Omnibus (London: Hodder & Stoughton, 1956) – includes *Sergeant Bigglesworth CID, Biggles' Second Case, Another Job for Biggles,* and *Biggles Works It Out;*

No Rest for Biggles (London: Hodder & Stoughton, 1956);

Biggles of 266 (London: Thames, 1956);

Biggles Takes Charge (London: Brockhampton, 1956);

Now to the Stars (London: Hodder & Stoughton, 1956);

To Outer Space (London: Hodder & Stoughton, 1957);

Adventure Unlimited, illustrated by Relf (Nashville: T. Nelson, 1957);

Biggles Makes Ends Meet (London: Hodder & Stoughton, 1957);

Biggles of the Interpol (London: Brockhampton, 1957);

Biggles on the Home Front (London: Hodder & Stoughton, 1957);

Biggles Presses On (London: Brockhampton, 1958);

Biggles Buries a Hatchet (London: Brockhampton, 1958);

Biggles on Mystery Island (London: Hodder & Stoughton, 1958);

No Motive For Murder (London: Hodder & Stoughton, 1958);

The Edge of Beyond (London: Hodder & Stoughton, 1958);

The Man Who Lost His Way (London: Macdonald, 1959);

The Death Rays of Ardilla (London: Hodder & Stoughton, 1959);

Biggles in Mexico (London: Brockhampton, 1959);

Biggles' Combined Operation (London: Hodder & Stoughton, 1959);

Biggles at World's End (London: Brockhampton, 1959);

The Biggles Book of Heroes (London: M. Parrish, 1959);

Adventures of the Junior Detection Club (London: M. Parrish, 1960);

Biggles and the Leopards of Zinn (London: Brockhampton, 1960);

Biggles Goes Home (London: Hodder & Stoughton, 1960);

Where the Golden Eagle Soars, illustrated by Colin Gibson (London: Hodder & Stoughton, 1960);

To Worlds Unknown (London: Hodder & Stoughton, 1960);

Biggles and the Missing Millionaire (London: Brockhampton, 1961);

Biggles Forms a Syndicate (London: Hodder & Stoughton, 1961);

Biggles and the Poor Rich Boy (London: Brockhampton, 1961);

The Quest for the Perfect Planet (London: Hodder & Stoughton, 1961);

Worlds of Wonder: More Adventures in Space (London: Hodder & Stoughton, 1962);

Biggles Goes Alone (London: Hodder & Stoughton, 1962);

Orchids for Biggles (Brockhampton, 1962);

Biggles Sets a Trap (London: Hodder & Stoughton, 1962);

The Biggles Book of Treasure Hunting, illustrated by William Randell (London: M. Parrish, 1962);

Biggles and the Plane That Disappeared: A Story of the Air Police (London: Hodder & Stoughton, 1963);

Biggles Takes It Rough (London: Brockhampton, 1963);

Biggles' Special Case (London: Brockhampton, 1963);

Biggles Flies to Work (London: Dean, 1963);

Biggles Takes a Hand (London: Hodder & Stoughton, 1963);

The Man Who Vanished into Space (London: Hodder & Stoughton, 1963);

Biggles and the Black Mask (London: Hodder & Stoughton, 1964);

Biggles Investigates and Other Stories of the Air Police (London: Brockhampton, 1964);

Biggles and the Lost Sovereigns (London: Brockhampton, 1964);

Biggles and the Plot That Failed (London: Brockhampton, 1965);

Biggles and the Blue Moon (London: Brockhampton, 1965);

Biggles Looks Back: A Story of Biggles and the Air Police (London: Hodder & Stoughton, 1965);

Biggles Scores a Bull (London: Hodder & Stoughton, 1965);

The Biggles Adventure Omnibus (London: Hodder & Stoughton, 1965) – includes *Biggles Gets His Men, No Rest for Biggles, Another Job for Biggles,* and *Biggles Takes a Holiday;*

Biggles and the Gun Runners (London: Brockhampton, 1966);

Biggles in the Terai (London: Brockhampton, 1967);

Biggles and the Penitent Thief (London: Brockhampton, 1967);

Biggles Sorts It Out (London: Brockhampton, 1967);

Biggles and the Dark Intruder (London: Knight, 1967);

Biggles in the Underworld (London: Brockhampton, 1968);

The Boy Biggles (London: Dean, 1968);

Biggles and the Deep Blue Sea (London: Brockhampton, 1969)

No Surrender, by Johns and R. A. Kelley (London: Harrap, 1969);

Biggles and the Little Green God (London: Brockhampton, 1969);

Biggles and the Noble Lord (London: Brockhampton, 1969);

Biggles Sees Too Much (London: Brockhampton, 1970);

Biggles of the Royal Flying Corps, selections, edited by Piers Williams (London: Purnell, 1978).

OTHER: *Wings: A Book of Flying Adventures,* edited by Johns (London: J. Hamilton, 1931);

The Modern Boy's Book of Aircraft, edited by Johns (London: Amalgamated, 1931);

Thrilling Flights, edited by Johns, illustrated by Howard Leigh (London: J. Hamilton, 1936).

If one went by sheer productivity, then Capt. W. E. Johns would be one of the most prominent names in English literature, composing literally hundreds of volumes. Yet today Johns is virtually unread, his books, being out of print in North America and almost out of print in Britain, are now the stuff of collectors frequenting dark bookstores.

It is not insignificant that Johns's books were listed as being authored by Captain Johns, for much of his personal life is tied up in the books he wrote. His is a life of which Biggles or Gimlet would have approved; in fact, Johns himself saw Biggles as a kind of alter ego. Like Biggles, Johns led an extraordinarily adventurous life. He enlisted in the army in World War I and was engaged in night patrols across no-man's-land, dodging shells and bullets to garner information. Attached to the air force, he was engaged in numerous dogfights, finally being shot down behind enemy lines while flying alone. He crashed in a field but was caught and sent to a prison camp. While trying to escape, he was caught by a German farmer while trying to steal an apple, and then he was returned to an even stronger prison camp to face days of solitary confinement. He remained at this camp until the end of the war. But the experience of those days was not to be lost on him. His time in the air, fighting dogfights and evading anti-aircraft fire, led to the Biggles books

about a resourceful, daring, adventurous pilot fighting, among other enemies, Germans.

To call these novels quickly paced is to name their principal feature. Written not long after Buck Rogers and Flash Gordon had dominated the silver screens of the United States, these novels showed a similar intensity, rushing from one adventure to the next, from one hair-raising scene to another. In *Worrals Goes East* (1944) Worrals is not in Aleppo for ten minutes before she is being followed by a hook-nosed Arab with, one presumes, a dagger under his cloak. In *Biggles Flies North* (1939) Biggles is in Fort Beaver even less time before he is shot at and in a brawl. In *Gimlet Goes Again* (1944) (Johns was not inventive in his titles) the novel opens with Cub Peters being picked up by a Nazi searchlight as he is parachuting into France. The pace only accelerates from there.

Certainly this is not the stuff of modern realism, but these novels were never meant to be completely realistic. They were on one level meant to be thrillers, peopled with starkly good and brave characters as well as starkly evil and pernicious characters. The novels presents a world in which the moral choices are clear, the enemies always obvious, the motivations always plain. One is simply to act heroically. It is a terrible burden but one that is at the same time noble.

In *Biggles in the Baltic* (1940), for example, Biggles is asked to man a base within enemy lines just after the outbreak of World War II. He and his small squadron hide out on a tiny island, from which they fly out to harass German defenses; the British command does not last more than twenty-four hours. In just a short time, expecting to be found out at any moment, they sink a submarine from the air, blow up two munitions depots, swamp a cruiser and a destroyer with a million gallons of water, and end with a great cataclysm that leads to the destruction of another destroyer. That they are themselves in constant danger is of no moment; they are fighting for Britain, and that is enough.

This is a British world that Johns depicts. Many of the novels are tied to World War II, where characters such as Biggles and Worrals and Gimlet fight against the Nazi menace. The villains are, for the most part, stereotyped; they hate and destroy for the pleasure of hating and destroying. Their destruction is devoutly to be wished, but only in a war situation; Biggles will not kill a group of Nazi airmen in a hanger when they do not see him or have a chance; "too much like murder," he says politely.

The Nazis are hardly different than the other villains in a Johns book. McBain of *Biggles Flies*

North is as dreadful a villain as any Nazi. He is a saboteur, an assassin in the dark, and a sheer bully. His actions are always hidden, and he kills by proxy, inciting a mob against Biggles, for example, rather than facing him himself. But Biggles is the stiff-upper-lip British hero. "C'mon, let's get it over with," he tells a Nazi firing squad that faces him. (He escapes; the Nazis are poor shooters.) Gimlet, after rescuing one hundred British airmen from a concentration camp in occupied France, is not content with the escape; he must first use this body of men to destroy an enemy airfield. During the attack he calmly discusses foxhounds with Biggles, who has flown down to join in the show. This calm is the distinction between a Johns villain and hero; the one fighting fanatically for the wrong reasons, the other fighting for Britain with a kind of *sprezzatura* that would have humbled Sir Philip Sidney.

In this British world it is not only the Nazis that are suspicious; in fact, any ethnic group outside of the British is questionable. The hook-nosed Arab at Aleppo is suspicious principally because he is an Arab; the only Arab who seems trustworthy is pictured as something of a buffoon. In *Gimlet's Oriental Quest* (1948), a novel that begins in Scotland and ends in Siam, the Siamese are seen as strange and foreign and simply other. Cub and Tony, the young male characters, are kidnapped while searching for treasure. They are brought to a dark and mysterious opium den by swarthy criminals, where they are to be tortured by someone who comes in with red-hot instruments to practice a trade passed down from one generation to another. Escaping with the help of Gimlet, they hack their way through pathless jungles and find a hideously deformed Indian living in a shack; he eventually kills off two of the villains while being killed himself – a tidy solution to their presence. The other villain is killed by a crocodile.

It is hard to imagine a book like this being written today, with characters so stereotyped, so demeaned. And yet, Johns's main purpose here is to focus not on his non-British villains, but instead on his British protagonists. Against the meanness and pettiness and horror and greed and bullying of the villains is set the loyalty of Biggles, the tenaciousness of Gimlet, the intuition and fortitude of Worrals. Though the settings may be exotic, the virtues Johns celebrates are those familiar to any British audience. Gimlet cannot let Biggles be gunned down by the Nazi firing squad; alone, he finds a machine gun and rescues him against all odds, because he is loyal. Cub has little chance of rescuing Gimlet from the Nazi trap in *Gimlet Goes*

Biggles, Johns's adventure hero, as depicted on the title page of Biggles Sweeps the Desert *(1942)*

Again, but he must try nonetheless. Roy's first thought when the Nazis invade the hidden base in *Biggles in the Baltic* is not for himself, nor even for his comrades; it is to hide the codebooks so that the Germans will not be able to break Britain's code. Loyalty to country, loyalty to comrades, nobility in the face of dreadful circumstances, staunch perseverance, fortitude and inventiveness – all are qualities that Johns celebrates. And these are, of course, the same qualities that Winston Churchill was calling for in his wartime speeches.

For the most part the world of Johns's novels is a male one. Perhaps because of the settings, Biggles and Gimlet especially seem isolated from anything female. In Fort Beaver of *Biggles Flies North,* there seems to be not a single female in the town, perhaps because it is in a most harsh country – Canada – which is, in the world of this novel, mostly north of the Arctic circle and inhabited by hardly anyone civilized. Both Gimlet and Biggles have around them a core of trustworthy male associates, some of whom are comic – a cook who tells stories that he is never allowed to finish, a pilot who is wondering what his mother would think of all of this – but who are quietly and completely competent. They live in what is essentially a closed world. Had Johns not written the Worrals books, one wonders if he would have had a single interesting female character. Certainly Worrals never duplicates the physical feats of a Biggles or Gimlet – no jumping off four-hundred-foot cliffs with a parachute for her. Worrals is more intuitive.

Worrals is a member of the British Women's Auxiliary Air Force (WAAF), and in *Worrals Goes East* she is assigned to uncover a printing press publishing propaganda that could set the entire Arab world aflame, thus forcing the necessity of sending British troops, thus weakening the war effort in Britain. This domino effect is, of course, precisely what the Nazis are counting on, but Worrals is able to ascertain the ringleader principally through her intuition; she knows right away that the suave Dr. Bronfield is a baddie. Except for an encounter with a snake, Worrals and Frecks hardly depend upon Nimrud, their Arab guide, who is constantly frustrated by the role that these women are taking. "It is very much not good for a woman to lead, so that a man must follow," he complains. Worrals's response is telling: "This is a war on which rests not only the fate of men, but women. Therefore, it is only right and just that women should do their share." Nimrud agrees reluctantly but is cheered when Worrals suggests that there may be "real fighting" ahead, a curious equivocation on Johns's part. Apparently what Worrals is doing is not "real fighting."

Whether they engage in "real fighting" or not, certainly there is the same rapid set of adventures here that marks the books on Biggles and Gimlet. "It's queer to think that had it not been for the war, at this moment I should probably be cleaning a typewriter in a dingy office, or perhaps going off to the cinema," muses Frecks just before they sneak into the enemy camp. If the Worrals books lack the physical dangers and adventures of the Biggles books, they lack none of the suspense, for Worrals and Frecks find themselves in repeated tight spots: Arabs hanging onto the tail of their plane, caught in a dead-end cave and forced to hide in an ancient coffin, snakes under their sheets, poisoned candies. They exude the same calm and competence of Biggles, and if they lack his raw physical skills, they exceed his intuitive abilities – an important ability, for their baddies are not as open and obvious as those that Biggles faces.

In establishing his settings, Johns stressed the exotic, the other. Nothing could be much different from the landscapes of Britain than the settings that Johns creates as a context for the adventures to be played out. Aleppo, in *Worrals Goes East,* is a dark and sinister city with side alleys held in shadow, set on the edge of the desert, itself a place of desolation. Canada, in *Biggles Flies North,* seems to be mostly a land of rock and ice. Siam, in *Gimlet's Oriental Quest,* is a land of jungle and snake and flood and alligators. In their oddity, their differences, the landscapes of these novels seems to make possible the adventures. Dark and sinister things would naturally happen in Aleppo, and one could only expect that Biggles will be downed and have to survive on the great frozen landscape of Canada – as in fact he does.

In his science-fiction novels, this propensity for the exotic setting is something that Johns could indulge. In *Kings of Space: A Story of Interplanetary Exploration* (1954), Johns has Tiger Clinton and his son Rex meet up with the Professor among the highlands of Scotland; he takes them on voyages to the Moon, to Venus, and then to Mars. In each case Johns spends a great deal of time remarking upon the landscapes, which are never uninteresting. That of the Moon is desolate and craggy; that of Venus is a tropical primeval forest; and that of Mars blasted by an interplanetary explosion and now besieged by clouds of poisonous mosquitoes. In *Now to the Stars* (1956), the third in a series with the same characters, Johns exploits this propensity immoderately, creating planetoids of grass, of glass, of ice, of jungles, of barren rock, of forests.

Despite the potentialities of science fiction, this is not a genre in which Johns is comfortable. The plot situations are incredibly contrived and manipulated by coincidence. Rex and Tiger meet the Professor by absolute chance, yet despite the Professor's usual wariness they are taken into his confidence and are soon making interplanetary jaunts with him. Lacking the skill of an H. G. Wells, Johns is unable to populate his worlds convincingly, and each episode is so separate, so quick, so pointless that the whole is rather loosely strung. Perhaps most disturbing is the way in which Johns unconsciously shows over and over again that his central thesis – that life develops differently according to the conditions in which it finds itself – is wrong. Despite remarkably different conditions, each planet is populated by humanoid characters – some short, some hairy, some primitive, but all humanoid. The books are perhaps most remarkable for their didacticism. Rex again and again learns that the earth is only a tiny world, one among uncounted worlds and one whose population is certainly not unique. It is a world that at any moment might be destroyed by a cosmic accident, suggesting that life is tenuous. But even as humanity faces this discomforting danger, Johns points out, it threatens to destroy itself

Johns, 1960 (Hulton Deutsch Collection)

through its atomic experiments. These novels, written during such experiments, suggest the potential danger of splitting the atom and warn of human arrogance and impetuousness.

The exotic setting is something that Johns also employed in his Westerns, another genre into which he ventured. Johns began *The Rustlers of Rattlesnake Valley* (1948) as he began many other works – with establishing such an exotic setting:

> Purple twilight settled softly over the thirsty mesa. Towards the gaunt indigo mountains that cut into the western sky like a row of broken teeth, the blood-red desert sun sank like a toy balloon, filling the hollows with shadows and painting the billowing sage and mesquite until they glowed like a sea of smoky gold. Silence unfolded the monotonous emptiness of the Arizona wilderness, a bewildering chaos of sand, cactus, and sun-splintered crags that quivered eerily as they flung back the furnace heat of the day.

The images here are disturbing: thirsty mesas, mountains like broken teeth, a blood-red desert. But this is a self-indulgent passage, drawn with purple ink. How might silence unfold emptiness? How could the landscape be filled with color and changing images and dramatic scenes yet still be monotonous? Would the crags quiver eerily to one accustomed to heat waves, as is the first viewer of the scene to which the reader is introduced?

Johns will indulge himself in other equally dramatic settings in *The Rustlers of Rattlesnake Valley* – hidden valleys and trails obscured by hot lava and such – but he is at home in this genre, in the sense that it allows him to play out a series of quickly paced adventures. Two young boys – Pash and Tony – stop a set of rustlers, escape from being gunned down, cross the desert in search of cattle and survive without water, escape from a hut while being surrounded by those intent on their destruction, ride cattle being stampeded across a barrier they had erected, and in short avoid death a score or so of times. They are young Gimlets and Biggleses, set in the context of the American West.

This is all fluffy stuff, filled with impossibilities and even silliness. Tex, quick with a gun, as one might expect, really does say, "This place ain't big enough for the two of us, and I ain't leaving" in complete seriousness, though it is hard to read this without a chuckle today. There are some disturbing elements in the book as well, such as references to the "coon" who cooks for the cowboys and the "greasers" who rustle cattle and bring them south of the border.

But there is, despite all of this, something beyond the sheer adventure, that makes this novel rather interesting: it is in fact a rewrite of Frances Hodgson Burnett's *The Secret Garden* (1911), where Pash is Dickon, close to nature, close to the cowboys, easy with a gun, comfortable on a horse, nonchalant in his outdoor expertise. Tony is Colin, the sickly Britisher who has spent most of his life in bed, a pampered invalid. Within minutes of arriving in the West, however, he seems to change. He grows strong and tanned, he is natural on a horse, and can ride at a gallop through a hailstorm of bullets, heading off stampeding cattle. He grows strong on hard food and hard living and grows close to Pash as he grows close to the landscape. "We'll make a cowboy out of you," says the ranch boss to Tony at the end of the adventures. "By Japers! He's one already!" asserts Pash. When the sheriff sees Tony soon after this assertion, he cannot understand how this change has come about, "for Tony's face was already a healthy brown, and in Pash's clothes he looked as if he had been born and bred on the range."

Now all of this is inordinately abrupt; Johns did not have the skill at character depiction that marks Burnett's best work. But the course of this change is an important motif through the novel. Tony learns what Biggles and Gimlet and Worrals already know: that life is itself a grand adventure. After eating food that he would not have given to dogs in his past life, and after drinking deeply from a muddy river, Tony sits back and "wiped his mouth with his sleeve, and laughed for the sheer joy of living." That last phrase — "the sheer joy of living" suggests Johns's approach to his adventures.

Johns wrote several works of nonfiction, principally relating to aviation. *Some Milestones in Aviation* (1935) begins with eighteenth-century hot-air balloon experiments and continues through the work of the Wright brothers, the improvements during World War I, and the flight of Charles Lindbergh. Focusing principally on British aviation feats, Johns shows an enormous optimism and appreciation for the early pilots, with whom he undoubtedly felt some kinship.

This kinship is especially evident in *Fighting Planes and Aces,* a work that was published in 1932 and that extolled the British pilots and planes, while giving due as well to the German pilots. Johns presents them as he would present Biggles — as great adventurers:

> As the first glimmer of dawn lightens the eastern sky a party of sleepy-eyed mechanics drag back the doors of a hanger and wheel out a drab-colored camel or S.E.5. The lone eagle of the skies, the knight of 1918, steps out of the squadron office and examines his battlefield, the sky, closely. He is fearless, a distinguished fighter, and devoted to the service of his country.

Johns thus presents not only the specifics of the planes used during the war — he presents the details with great relish — but he especially focuses on the aces, recounting their adventures and escapes with all the suspense of a Biggles story. Lieutenant Insall, for example, forces a German plane to land behind enemy lines and destroys it with an incendiary bomb. But while returning he is hit by ground fire and is downed in no-man's-land. While the German artillery opens fire, Insall and his co-pilot rig up blankets and wait for night. The light of his candles shielded by the blankets, the pilot repairs the machine, fills in shell holes on the grand, and, at dawn, flies off, to the consternation of the German soldiers. Of Col. W. A. Bishop, Johns writes what may summarize all his aces:

> The story of his progress reveals judgment, utter fearlessness, considerable skill, and a fair amount of luck. Time and time again he found himself in predicaments from which not even his skill and courage alone could have extricated him. He preferred to fight single-handed, many of his combats taking place far over the line. He was a real roving free-lance ace and a true knight of the air.

Johns may have just as easily been speaking of his own characters.

As works of children's literature, Johns's novels are attractive principally for the rapidity of their adventures. But one large element distinguishes them from, say, the Horatio Hornblower novels being written by C. S. Forrester at around the same time, about a similar character, having similarly fast-paced adventures. While the Hornblower narratives leave the protagonist in a kind of splendid isolation and focus on his interior consciousness, the Johns novels surround the protagonists with companions and focus on sheer adventure; Biggles never thinks as much as Hornblower about what he is doing and what image he is projecting. Instead, the reader sees Biggles acting, and usually this seeing is mediated by an admiring companion.

In the Gimlet books Cub Peters is in fact quite close to the reader of the novel. One never identifies so much with Gimlet or Biggles; they are so heroic as to seem unreal and unapproachable. But the more modest Cub, or Ginger in the Biggles books, are closer to the reader chronologically as well as in exploits; here are characters with whom readers might identify. So in *Gimlet Goes Again,* for example, the perspective is almost always that of Cub, who follows and assists Gimlet in his espionage. In the Worrals books, Frecks plays this role, despite the fact that she too is a flight officer. Cub and Frecks are the characters who support the protagonists, who provide a kind of approach for readers to characters frequently presented as more than ordinary mortals.

If Johns is forgotten today, it is because his novels stand only a single reading. There is no depth to Biggles or Worrals; they do not grow or develop. They are what they are from the first page of the first novel. The qualities they show – courage, resourcefulness, cool confidence, unbending wills – these mirror those qualities every British citizen needed during the days in which these books were written. Perhaps in his insistence on the "sheer joy of living," Johns struck a note that needed to be struck then. If the note does not ring as clear for the present generation of child readers, it may be because Johns did not see himself as writing to them.

C. S. Lewis

(29 November 1898 – 22 November 1963)

David L. Russell
Ferris State University

See also the Lewis entries in *DLB 15: British Novelists, 1930–1959* and *DLB 100: Modern British Essayists, Second Series.*

BOOKS: *Spirits in Bondage: A Cycle of Lyrics,* as Clive Hamilton (London: Heinemann, 1919; San Diego: Harcourt Brace Jovanovich, 1984);

Dymer [as Clive Hamilton] (London: Dent, 1926; New York: Dutton, 1926);

The Pilgrim's Regress: An Allegorical Apology for Christianity, Reason and Romanticism (London: Dent, 1933; New York: Sheed & Ward, 1935; reprinted with new preface, London: Bles, 1943);

The Allegory of Love: A Study in Medieval Tradition (Oxford: Clarendon, 1936; New York: Oxford University Press, 1936);

Out of the Silent Planet (London: John Lane, 1938; New York: Macmillan, 1943);

Rehabilitations and Other Essays (London & New York: Oxford University Press, 1939);

The Personal Heresy: A Controversy, by Lewis and E. M. W. Tillyard (London & New York: Oxford University Press, 1939);

The Problem of Pain (London: Centenary, 1940; New York: Macmillan, 1940);

The Screwtape Letters (London: Bles, 1942; New York: Macmillan, 1958); reprinted with additional material as *The Screwtape Letters and Screwtape Proposes a Toast* (New York: Macmillan, 1959; London: Bles, 1961);

A Preface to Paradise Lost (London: Oxford University Press, 1942; New York: Oxford University Press, 1942);

Broadcast Talks: Reprinted with some alterations from two series of Broadcast Talks ("Right and Wrong: A Clue to the Meaning of the Universe" and "What Christians Believe") given in 1941 and 1942 (London: Bles, 1942); republished as *The Case for Christianity* (New York: Macmillan, 1943);

C. S. Lewis (Wade Collection)

Christian Behaviour: A Further Series of Broadcast Talks (London: Bles, 1943; New York: Macmillan, 1943);

Perelandra (London: John Lane, 1943; New York: Macmillan, 1944);

The Abolition of Man: Reflections on Education with Special Reference to the Teaching of English in the Upper Forms of Schools, Riddell Memorial Lectures, Fifteenth Series (London: Oxford University Press, 1943; New York: Macmillan, 1947);

Beyond Personality: The Christian Idea of God (London: Bles, Centenary, 1944; New York: Macmillan, 1945);

That Hideous Strength: A Modern Fairy-Tale for Grown-Ups (London: John Lane, 1945; New York: Macmillan, 1946);

The Great Divorce: A Dream (London: Bles, Centenary, 1945; New York: Macmillan, 1946);

Miracles: A Preliminary Study (London: Bles, Centenary, 1947; New York: Macmillan, 1947); revised edition (London: Collins, 1960);

Arthurian Torso: Containing the Posthumous Fragment of The Figure of Arthur by Charles Williams and A Commentary on The Arthurian Poems of Charles Williams by C. S. Lewis (London: Oxford University Press, 1948; New York: Oxford University Press, 1948);

Transposition and Other Addresses (London: Bles, 1949); republished as *The Weight of Glory and Other Addresses* (New York: Macmillan, 1949);

The Lion, the Witch, and the Wardrobe (London: Bles, 1950; New York: Macmillan, 1950);

Prince Caspian: The Return to Narnia (London: Bles, 1951; New York: Macmillan, 1951);

Mere Christianity (revised and enlarged edition of *Broadcast Talks, Christian Behaviour,* and *Beyond Personality*) (New York: Macmillan, 1952; London: Bles, 1961);

The Voyage of the Dawn Treader (London: Bles, 1952; New York: Macmillan, 1952);

The Silver Chair (London: Bles, 1953; New York: Macmillan, 1953);

The Horse and His Boy (London: Bles, 1954; New York: Macmillan, 1954);

English Literature in the Sixteenth Century Excluding Drama (The Oxford History of English Literature, vol. 3) (Oxford: Clarendon Press, 1954; New York: Oxford University Press, 1954);

The Magician's Nephew (London: Bles, 1955; New York: Macmillan, 1955);

Surprised by Joy: The Shape of My Early Life (London: Bles, 1955; New York: Harcourt, Brace & World, 1956);

The Last Battle (London: The Bodley Head, 1956; New York: Macmillan, 1956);

Till We Have Faces: A Myth Retold (London: Bles, 1956; New York: Harcourt, Brace & World, 1957);

Reflections on the Psalms (London: Bles, 1958; New York: Harcourt, 1958);

The Four Loves (London: Bles, 1960; New York: Harcourt, 1960);

Studies in Words (Cambridge: Cambridge University Press, 1960; New York: Cambridge University Press, 1990);

The World's Last Night and Other Essays (New York: Harcourt, Brace & World, 1960); revised and expanded edition (New York: Macmillan, 1980);

A Grief Observed, as N. W. Clerk (London: Faber & Faber, 1961; New York: Harper & Row, 1961);

An Experiment in Criticism (Cambridge: Cambridge University Press, 1961; New York: Cambridge University Press, 1992);

They Asked for a Paper: Papers and Addresses (London: Bles, 1962);

The Discarded Image: An Introduction to Medieval and Renaissance Literature (Cambridge: Cambridge University Press, 1964);

Poems, edited by Walter Hooper (London: Bles, 1964; New York: Harcourt, Brace & World, 1965);

Screwtape Proposes a Toast and Other Pieces (London: Collins, 1965);

Studies in Medieval and Renaissance Literature, edited by Hooper (Cambridge: Cambridge University Press, 1966; New York: Cambridge University Press, 1979);

Letters of C. S. Lewis, edited by W. H. Lewis (London: Bles, 1966; New York: Harcourt, 1966);

Of Other Worlds: Essays and Stories, edited by Hooper (London: Bles, 1966; New York: Harcourt, Brace & World, 1967);

Christian Reflections, edited by Hooper (London: Bles, 1967; Grand Rapids, Mich.: Eerdmans, 1967);

Spenser's Images of Life, edited by Alastair Fowler (Cambridge: Cambridge University Press, 1967);

Letters to an American Lady [Mary Willis Shelburne], edited by Clyde S. Kilby (Grand Rapids, Mich.: Eerdmans, 1967);

A Mind Awake: An Anthology of C. S. Lewis, edited by Kilby (London: Bles, 1968);

Narrative Poems, edited by Hooper (Cambridge & New York: Cambridge University Press, 1969);

Selected Literary Essays, edited by Hooper (Cambridge & New York: Cambridge University Press, 1969);

God in the Dock: Essays on Theology and Ethics, edited by Hooper (Grand Rapids, Mich.: Eerdmans, 1970);

Fern-Seed and Elephants and Other Essays on Christianity, edited by Hooper (London: Fontana, 1975);

Lewis, standing, with his father, Albert, and his brother, Warren

The Dark Tower and Other Stories, edited by Hooper (London: Collins, 1977; New York: Harcourt Brace Jovanovich, 1977);

The Joyful Christian: 127 Readings from C. S. Lewis (New York: Macmillan, 1977);

They Stand Together: The Letters of C. S. Lewis to Arthur Greeves (1914–1963), edited by Hooper (London: Collins, 1979; New York: Macmillan, 1979);

On Stories, and Other Essays in Literature, edited by Hooper (San Diego & London: Harcourt Brace Jovanovich, 1982);

Boxen: The Imaginary World of the Young C. S. Lewis, edited by Hooper (San Diego, New York & London: Harcourt Brace Jovanovich, 1985);

Present Concerns, edited by Hooper (London: Fount, 1986; San Diego, New York & London: Harcourt Brace Jovanovich, 1986).

Once best known as a Christian apologist and the author of *The Screwtape Letters,* and admired by at least two generations of scholars as a teacher and literary historian, C. S. Lewis may eventually be most famous for the seven books, collectively referred to as the Narnian Chronicles, that he wrote for children. Clive Staples Lewis was born in Belfast, Ireland, on 29

November 1898, the younger son of Albert Lewis, a solicitor of Welsh extraction, and Flora Hamilton, a brilliant mathematician of an old Irish family. His family was addicted to nicknames, and he was called Jack all his life. He had a close relationship with his older brother, Warren ("Warnie"), with whom he was to live for the better part of his adult life. Lewis was only nine when his mother died of cancer, an event about which he rarely talked or wrote but one of profound impact on his entire life.

Almost immediately after his mother's death Lewis was sent off to England to a succession of schools, first to Wynyard, which proved an intolerable place run by a tyrannical staff, then to Campbell College and to Cherbourg. He never quite forgave his father for this harsh and abrupt severing of the family at a time when it was needed most, and their relationship would remain strained forever after. He matriculated at Malvern College in 1913 where he began to master both Latin and Greek. However, the most significant educational experience of his youth began when he withdrew from school altogether in 1914 and entered under the tutelage of his father's former headmaster, William Kirkpatrick – "the Great Knock" as he was affectionately called. Kirkpatrick was a brilliant and demanding teacher, perfectly suited to the task of preparing Lewis for the Oxford entrance examinations. Lewis had already demonstrated that he was a prodigy; he read broadly and thought deeply. This time with Kirkpatrick he was later to refer to as "those blessed days."

In 1917 Lewis matriculated at University College, Oxford, but after but a single term there he was called to the war front. On 15 April 1918 he was wounded at the Battle of Arras in France and convalesced for several months after. The war having ended later that year, Lewis was finally able to return to Oxford, which, in various capacities, he would call home for the rest of his life. There he met his idol, William Butler Yeats, and he was steeped in classical learning as well as in English history and literature. He eventually took an English degree and in 1925 was elected a Fellow of Magdalene College, Oxford. He was particularly drawn to early English literature, and his finest literary criticism focused on medieval and Renaissance literature. His love of things medieval surfaced later in his Narnia books, as did his fondness for what he called "Northernness" – the Norse, Icelandic, and Germanic legends, epics, and sagas. For him "Northernness" also seemed to represent robust and upright character, fierce independence of mind, and devotion to duty. In addition, he favored things medieval, and seemed to pride himself on being a traditionalist. He read modern literature but cared little for most of it, and in fact, when he was a faculty member, his syllabus (not surprisingly, along with J. R. R. Tolkien's) stopped at 1832.

From his parents Lewis had inherited both a lively imagination and an intensely pious sentiment, the latter of which he was to deny until he was over thirty. Lewis had been an atheist throughout much of his late youth and early adulthood, perhaps largely because it was the fashionable stance for a young intellectual to take. Lewis was always to see the year 1929 as the turning point of his life, for that was when he began moving away from atheism toward Christianity. On a bus trip during that summer he went through a mystical experience, in which he viewed himself as if encased in a constraining suit of armor that he must remove. It was, he remarked, as if he were a snowman "at last beginning to melt." A short time after, back in his rooms at Oxford, he knelt and prayed, "the most dejected and reluctant convert in all England," as he described himself. His turn to religion was perhaps hastened by the death, that autumn, of his father. As is often so in the case of strained relationships,

this death had a devastating effect on Lewis, and he was long plagued with remorse.

In the following year, 1930, Lewis bought a house near Oxford, called The Kilns. Partners with him in this venture were his brother, Warnie, and Janie Moore, the mother of a college friend who had been killed in the First World War. Lewis and Moore had maintained a close, perhaps intimate, relationship for several years, and their relationship has been the subject of much idle speculation and wild curiosity. Moore was twenty-eight years Lewis's senior, and she originally had a small house in Oxford where she offered Lewis domestic comforts in return for companionship. Certainly Lewis was the surrogate son, in the very least, and quite likely Moore replaced Lewis's own dead mother, with whose loss he seems never to have been fully reconciled. Lewis, his brother, and Moore spent most of the rest of their lives together at The Kilns.

Moore was an unschooled woman with a penchant for psychosomatic illnesses, making her a rather surprising companion for someone of Lewis's intellect. But her influence can be seen in many of his most popular works, such as *The Screwtape Letters* (1942) and the Narnian Chronicles, for as his biographer A. N. Wilson remarks, "[Lewis] is the great chronicler of the minor domestic irritation," and with Moore he shared "a rich enjoyment of the comedy of human character." Some of the most memorable scenes in Lewis's novels are those detailing domestic life – we need only recall the chapters from *The Lion, the Witch, and the Wardrobe* (1950) recounting in rich detail the pleasant day the Pevensie children spent with the Beavers. Moore quite likely provided Lewis with a measure of emotional and domestic stability that he welcomed as an escape from the daily rigors of academe. Although by the end of her life (Moore died in 1951) she had come to be a particular burden on the household and Warnie had come to resent her, Lewis himself had a singular appreciation for her qualities and her influence on his life.

During the 1930s Lewis settled into the scholar and teacher's life at Oxford. The outward aspects of his life were to be uneventful – he went abroad only once, to Greece in 1960, and seldom even visited London. The intellectual side of his life was multifarious. As a teacher Lewis generally earned the respect, and sometimes the admiration, of his students. He was demanding, but occasionally abrasive and insensitive; some of his pupils had the distinct feeling that their sessions with him were simply annoying interruptions in his day. One of his first students was a future poet laureate of England, John Betjeman, and their relationship was not particularly happy; in fact, Lewis passed up the opportunity to save Betjeman from failing out of the university. But other pupils found him extremely conscientious, astonishingly well-read, astute in judgment, and generous in character. His lectures were popular, both for their lively delivery and their rich content, for he drew from the great breadth of his voracious reading.

It was also during this time that Lewis and his circle of friends assembled an informal literary group called the Inklings, which included among others the medieval scholar and author of The Lord of the Rings cycle, J. R. R. Tolkien. The group met weekly, usually at the Eagle and Child pub, and with a changing membership throughout the late 1930s and 1940s, before it finally dissipated. It was at the meetings of the Inklings that The Lord of the Rings cycle and the Chronicles of Narnia both had their first hearings. This club was suited to Lewis's attachment to cronyism, and the "good old boy" network still thrived at Oxford. Later, these associations worked both for and against him.

Over the years Lewis produced, in addition to numerous essays and commentaries, four major works of literary criticism: The Allegory of Love: A Study in Medieval Tradition (1936), a history of medieval and Renaissance love literature; A Preface to Paradise Lost (1942), a commentary on John Milton's masterpiece; English Literature in the Sixteenth Century Excluding Drama (1954), perhaps the magnum opus of Lewis's critical output, a learned, but adroitly written, volume in the Oxford History of English Literature series; and The Discarded Image: An Introduction to Medieval and Renaissance Literature (1964), a sort of summing-up and retrospective of his own views as developed during a lifetime of reading. His approach to literary criticism was historical, and his works are marked by an almost matchless breadth of reading. The critic William Empson believed that Lewis was "the best read man of his generation, one who read everything and remembered everything he read." Most literary criticism is dated within its own generation, but Lewis's remains highly readable, provocative, and, perhaps more significantly, in print more than three decades after his death – a forceful testimonial to his powers as a scholar.

Although Lewis had always dabbled in literary composition (he wrote a long narrative poem called Dymer during the 1920s), his earliest fictional work of note was in the area of science fiction, which for him was largely a vehicle for conveying his religious sentiments and philosophical speculations. Out of the Silent Planet (1938), the first of his science-fiction trilogy, is heavily laden with religious allegory. The novel is the story of a philologist named Ransom (his name is, naturally, significant) who is kidnapped and taken to the distant planet of Malacandra, which we call Mars. The planet is ruled by the eldila, elusive creatures of light, highly suggestive of the angelic beings of traditional Christian belief, and the chief eldil is Oyarsa, who is both wise and compassionate. The Malacandrians have no fear of death, and Oyarsa remarks of the "bent lord" of Earth, that he made his people "wise enough to see the death of their kind approaching, but not wise enough to endure it." The novel is, of course, a thinly disguised theological treatise, a genre at which Lewis excelled.

In the sequel, Perelandra (1943), Ransom is summoned to the planet of Venus (called Perelandra) to save that planet from a fall similar to that of Eden. Ransom must protect the Eve-like Green Lady from Weston, who has lost his own identity and become the "Un-man," an embodiment of the forces of Evil. Like Satan, the "Un-man" tempts the Green Lady, and Ransom – not so much an Adam as a Christ – struggles to thwart the temptation.

That Hideous Strength: A Modern Fairy-Tale for Grown-Ups (1945), the third novel in the trilogy, is a mixture of fantasy and realism demanding more of readers than many are willing to give. Its convoluted plot involves an elaborate bureaucratic pseudoscientific organization in cahoots with the state and tied to the evil eldila, and this circumstance is woven into a tale of marital difficulties between a college don and his wife. The portrayal of the grim and powerful organization, carrying out its secret and inhumane experiments, was surely fueled by the atrocities of Adolf Hitler's Germany, and the book has been described by Margaret Hanney as "a powerful, if oblique, critique of fascism."

In a lighter vein, although with no less serious underlying purpose, Lewis wrote The Screwtape Letters, destined to be one of his most popular works, and a book that made his name a household word in wartime Britain. Originally published in installments in the Guardian in 1941, these are ostensibly letters from an elder devil instructing a younger one how to corrupt a good Christian. The Screwtape Letters reveals Lewis as a talented satirist and humorist. He was to employ these talents again in The Great Divorce: A Dream (1945), the story of an allegorical bus trip in which a group of souls from hell travel to the outskirts of heaven. The guide for the trip is George MacDonald, the celebrated Victorian fantasist and writer of literary fairy tales.

Although Lewis wrote religious essays throughout his life, he fairly abandoned his role as a self-proclaimed theologian after being trounced in a debate by the Christian philosopher Elizabeth Anscombe, an experience that caused him to reevaluate his own philosophy and brought him to the conclusion that his own religious writings were spurious. He ceased writing Christian apologetics and struck upon the idea of using children's fantasy as a vehicle for his religious message. Given Lewis's firm grounding in medieval romance, it is not surprising that he should choose heroic fantasy as the medium for his allegory.

It seems now that C. S. Lewis's lasting reputation may rest chiefly upon the Chronicles of Narnia. As with so much of the greatest imaginative writing, these books seem to have grown out of a period of spiritual and personal despair for Lewis. It was not only his defeat at the hands of Anscombe but a variety of personal and professional afflictions that brought him to this crisis in midlife. His long-time friendship with Tolkien was cooling considerably; his daily routines of teaching, writing, and managing his household were weighing heavily on him; and, perhaps most significantly, some of his own fundamental Christian beliefs had been called into question by his colleagues at Magdalene College. In short, he was facing something of a crisis of faith.

As a result, he turned to literary fantasy, and, as so often happens, out of great personal suffering grew the finest art. But writing the Chronicles is not to be seen as a refuge – this was not to escape; on the contrary, Lewis was simply seeking a more effective vehicle by which to explore what were for him the great truths. He was quite aware of the advantages offered by fantasy for exploring philosophical concepts and hypotheses. The medium proved ideal for Lewis's purpose, for he was able to avoid preaching and yet to portray with great clarity his own vision of Christian faith. The Chronicles of Narnia are unabashedly Christian apologetics in fictional guise.

Some find it curious that Lewis should choose to write for children, for he remained a bachelor for most of his life, was absorbed in the academic life at one of the world's great universities, and had little actual contact with young people. Lewis, however, had a great respect for children's reading: "When I was ten, I read fairy tales in secret and would have been ashamed if I had been found doing so. Now that I am fifty I read them openly. When I became a man I put away childish things, including the fear of childishness and the desire to be very grown up," he

Lewis, left, and Warren Lewis at Annogassan, Ireland, 1949

wrote in *On Stories, and Other Essays in Literature* (1982). There are, of course, Christian implications in this statement and, as the Chronicles demonstrate, Lewis did indeed have a great respect for the ingenuous quality of childhood, its vigor and enthusiasm, its purity and hopefulness. But Lewis also recognized the sharp distinction between the reading tastes of children and adults. He wrote:

> Fashions in literary taste come and go among the adults, and every period has its own shibboleths. These, when good, do not improve the taste of children, and, when bad, do not corrupt it; for children read only to enjoy. . . . Juvenile taste is simply human taste, going on from age to age, silly with a universal silliness or wise with a universal wisdom, regardless of modes, movements, and literary revolutions.

Lewis perhaps betrays his distaste for modern adult literature in this remark, but his conviction that writing for children is a serious undertaking, neither frivolous nor simplistic, was genuine. He identified two sorts of writers for children: the wrong sort –

those who seem to believe that children are a distinct race and who, therefore, make up their taste in stories; and the right sort — those who recognize the common humanity of children and adults and who "label their books 'For Children' because children are the only market now recognised for the books they, anyway, want to write." How close these sentiments must be to those of all the greatest children's writers. And, finally, of his own books for children, Lewis noted that "I was writing 'for children' only in the sense that I excluded what I thought they would not like or understand; not in the sense of writing what I intended to be below adult attention."

The Chronicles consist of seven books all dealing with the mythical land of Narnia, heavily imbued with medieval romance elements and rich in Christian allegory and symbolism. Each book is capable of standing alone, and, indeed, the books, taken in order of their publication dates, do not represent chronological sequence. The sixth book, *The Magician's Nephew* (1955), describes the beginning of Narnia, whereas the first book, *The Lion, the Witch, and the Wardrobe,* begins, as it were, in medias res. Nor do the same characters appear throughout the books. Taken as a whole, they relate the history of a land, describing its heroes, its villains, its triumphs, its defeats.

The Lion, the Witch, and the Wardrobe was in fact begun as early as 1939, but then laid aside by Lewis, to be resumed about 1948, when the accumulated personal crises described above seem to have reached a pitch. It is the tale of the four Pevensie children — Peter, Susan, Lucy, and Edmund — who, while staying in the large country house of an eccentric professor during the Second World War, discover that they can enter into another land through the back of a large wardrobe in one of the many bedrooms. They soon learn that the land, the magical Narnia, which is peopled largely by talking animals; dwarfs; half-goat, half-human fauns; and other fanciful creatures, is in grave danger from its cruel tyrant, the White Witch, who has cursed the country with a hundred years of winter. They also learn that they are the chosen instruments by which Narnia is to be released from the Witch's evil power.

The two elder children, Peter and Susan, are appropriately dutiful and brave, if rather uninteresting as characters. Their younger sister, Lucy, is blessed with intuitive sight (her name, derived from the Latin for light, seems obviously symbolic) and whenever she appears throughout the Chronicles she represents a purity of faith by which they all

may become closer to Aslan, the great lion, who is a thinly disguised Christ figure. Edmund is the dynamic character in this story, for he succumbs to the Witch's temptations and betrays his siblings. The temptation for Edmund are some magical Turkish Delights, sweet confections that have mind-altering powers. His eating of the delights puts him in the Witch's power and leads him to betray his siblings. Aslan, who is ascribed to be the Son of the Emperor-Beyond-the-Sea, must sacrifice himself; he is slain by the White Witch upon a Stone Table, and the children know the depths of despair, for this is their Calvary. But with the coming of the next dawn, the children witness the miracle of Aslan's resurrection from the dead, and both Edmund and Narnia are redeemed. Appropriately for Christian symbolism, the two girls discover that the Stone Table "was broken into two pieces by a great crack that ran down it from end to end; and there was no Aslan." It is, of course, the two Marys discovering the empty tomb, and like them they believe that someone has stolen Aslan's body; Lucy weeps, "they might have left the body alone." What follows is a fairly conventional battle scene in which the Witch is defeated, and the establishment of the four children as Kings and Queens of Narnia. The battle scenes, which are found in every book in the series, are part of the convention of medieval romance to which these books owe so much.

The joint reign of the four children lasts for many years and will be remembered as the Golden Age of Narnia. But in the end they must return through the wardrobe back to England. It is one of the fundamental tenets of Lewis's fantasy that Narnian time does not flow with English time; that while the children are in Narnia, though many Narnian years may pass, on Earth no time at all goes by.

In this story Lewis gives life to the deepest principles of his Christian faith. He presents a world corrupted with a powerful evil, full of dangerous temptations; humanity is seen as often weak and prone to erring ways, but with the capacity for devotion and even heroism if guided by the unconditional love of the godhead, who is also the redeemer. The Emperor-Beyond-the-Sea, Aslan's father, is never portrayed in the Chronicles but is rather a mythical, pervasive presence, suggesting the transcendent and omnipotent quality of God, just as Aslan, the son, reveals the vastness of God's

Lewis draws on his deep knowledge of the medieval romance tradition, incorporating the series of trials and adventures with a specific goal to be ac-

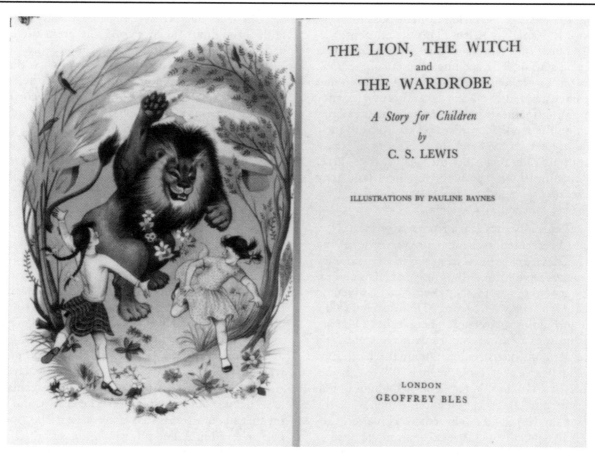

Frontispiece and title page for the first volume of the Chronicles of Narnia

complished in the end. Whereas the romance typically concludes with a matrimonial celebration, Lewis concludes with spiritual renewal, well-suited not only to the child reader but to the deeper purpose of his story. From the medieval romance he also borrows character types – a witch whose beauty belies her wickedness; dauntless heroes; fair damsels; unassuming helpers in the form of talking animals, fauns, and similar creatures. He borrows story details and plot devices – magic swords, potions, transformations, heroic battles, and temptations. And he borrows the fundamental assumption of the existence of a worldly order, as critic Peter Schakel puts it, "a sense of unity, and of immanent meaning in the universe."

The Lion, the Witch, and the Wardrobe is also imbued heavily with the influence of Edmund Spenser, one of Lewis's favorite poets. At one point in the story the children encounter in Narnia the figure of Father Christmas – the traditional English folk figure, an inclusion to which the noted scholar Roger Lancelyn Green (himself a reteller of myths and folktales for children) had objected as an inap-

propriate juxtaposition. But Lewis insisted on retaining the scene much as Spenser included such familiar figures as St. George alongside the creatures of his own imagination. And, of course, the allegorical nature of the work is strongly reminiscent of Spenser. Incidentally, Tolkien disliked *The Lion, the Witch, and the Wardrobe* partly because he never liked allegory and partly because he found it sloppily constructed – the land of Narnia seemed not to him to be thoroughly and coherently conceived (an objection that has troubled few of the millions of child readers who have enjoyed the books since their publication).

Prince Caspian: The Return to Narnia (1951), the second book of the Chronicles, has as its theme the necessity of surrendering to trust, the faith that is the foundation of religion. Like the first book, *Prince Caspian* is written in the spirit of the traditional medieval romance, but it is the familiar initiation tale, the story of a youth leaving the safe haven of home to meet the world's bitter realities by which maturity is ultimately achieved. Once again the four Pevensie children are summoned to Narnia (for, we learn, the passage to Narnia is made possible only when it is desired by Aslan). This time they are virtually swept into Narnia as they await a train in a deserted station. The opening chapters of the book focus on the gradual revelation to the children that they have arrived in Narnia several centuries after their glorious joint reign and that some new evil has fallen on the land. They discover the ruins of their castle of Cair Paravel and slowly realize the truth and nostalgically remember their happy lives there; it is an unsettling experience for them (and they surely must be among the few children in all of literature ever touched by nostalgia).

Eventually they learn from a dwarf that Narnia has been ruled by Telmarine tyrants for many years. These Telmarines, from the western country of Telmar, have silenced the talking animals and exhibit a hatred of nature; they destroyed the splendid royal city by the sea and moved their capital to the more forbidding mountains. The so-called Old Narnians must carry on the old traditions in secret, and there is much distrust throughout the land. The children learn that the true heir to the throne, Prince Caspian, has, in fact, Narnian blood in him and is inclined to accept the old Narnian ways (including the Narnian faith in Aslan). However, Caspian is in danger from his wicked uncle, the usurper Miraz, who seeks to dispatch him. A series of adventures follows, and, with the help of Aslan and the Pevensies, Caspian conquers the Telmarines and reestablishes the old realm of Narnia.

The entire first portion of the book is devoted, then, to establishing a longing for that long-past Golden Age, when magic ruled and the trees and animals talked. Here also is introduced one of the major conflicts of the story – belief versus disbelief. The children require physical evidence of the great passage of time, but so do the dwarfs and other creatures they encounter require evidence that these children were indeed once the Narnian kings and queens and that the old stories about the Golden Age were not just stories, but truth. Lewis is reminding us that most of what we believe is based on faith rather than the existence of concrete evidence, but the skepticism of humanity often demands more. Surely Lewis had his own skeptical age in mind, an age seemingly overrun by tyrants – he had seen Hitler and Joseph Stalin and the atrocities that accompanied their regimes. To many in the twentieth century, the day of miracles had passed, and that is the sentiment suggested by the dwarfs, Trumpkin and Nikabrik. Trumpkin will eventually regain his faith, but Nikabrik remains the doubter and at last despairs and is killed as he commits treason against his king.

In fact, only Lucy clings steadfastly to her faith throughout the story. At one point the children have lost their way in the mountains, and Lucy stubbornly insists that they follow her direction, despite the strenuous objections of the rest. They soon find that Lucy's intuition was correct, for, of course, it had been Aslan all along guiding her. In her absolute faith in the Lion and the messages he gives her, Lucy demonstrates Lewis's belief, expressed in *Mere Christianity* (1952), that everyone must, in the movement toward Christian maturity, experience a change "from being confident about our own efforts to the state in which we despair of doing anything for ourselves and leave it to God."

Lewis also remarks in *Mere Christianity*, "Enemy-occupied territory – that is what this world is. Christianity is the story of how the rightful king has landed, you might say landed in disguise, and is calling us all to take part in a great campaign of sabotage." This is the central story of *Prince Caspian*. This book is also the farewell to Peter and Susan, who have now grown too old to return to Narnia. Actually, in many respects Susan (who seems to have matured more rapidly than Peter) was too old for this adventure. Always the practical one, Susan had believed in Aslan, but would not let herself act on those beliefs. Her reason overpowered her faith. Susan will be the only one of the Pevensies not brought back to Narnia at the final day in the last book of the series, for she, in Peter's words, "is no longer a friend of Narnia." She has grown up and, worse, denies the fantasies of childhood, the fantasies that, in fact, hold the greatest truths.

The Voyage of the Dawn Treader (1952) is the third book of the Narnia series, and it introduces Eustace Clarence Scrubb, a cousin of the Pevensies. The story opens in the Scrubb household, where Lucy and Edmund Pevensie are guests while their parents travel to the United States along with Susan. Peter, the eldest of the Pevensies, is away at school. But their absence is a convenience, for both Susan and Peter are too old for another Narnia adventure. We cannot help being reminded of Christ's admonition: "Except ye be converted, and become as little children, ye shall not enter into the kingdom of heaven" (Matt. 18:3). Eustace, who is to become a major character in the series, is portrayed at the outset as something of a pest to the Pevensies. He has been brought up by two "very up-to-date and advanced people [who] were vegetarians, non-smokers and teetotalers and wore a special kind of underclothes." Lewis's own prejudices are quite blatant here, for he himself was a passionate smoker ("sixty cigarettes a day between pipes," according to Wilson) and was a rather bullish drinker. He had little use for fanaticism of any sort, but his principal objection to the Scrubbs is undoubtedly that they are thoroughly "modern." Eustace has received an experimental, modern education, heavily scientific in its orientation with little use for the "impractical" humanistic studies. He prefers his animals, "especially beetles . . . dead and pinned on a card" and likes only nonfictional books. He is what Lewis would call a pseudointellectual. Consequently, he is a boy lacking in any sort of imaginative wonder and views his cousins with their incredible tales of Narnia with not mere skepticism, but disdain.

One day, in a bedroom of the Stubbs' home, as the children are staring, mesmerized, at a picture of an old sailing ship, the sea suddenly washes out of the picture and overtakes them. They next find themselves floundering in the sea to be rescued by none other than their old friend, Caspian, now King Caspian X. The young king, glad to see his old friends Lucy and Edmund, explains that he is on a journey to explore the unknown Eastern Seas and to either find or avenge the deaths of seven lords, his father's friends, who were exiled by Caspian's wicked uncle. Eustace, naturally, is incorrigible, refusing to believe he is in another world and demanding to be taken to the nearest British consul. The rest endure him. The voyage proceeds with a variety of adventures, most reminiscent of episodes from such other famous voyages as those of the *Odyssey* and the *Aeneid*. The travelers encounter a giant sea serpent, a dark island where dreams come alive (with unpleasant consequences), an island populated by strange life forms called Dufflepuds, an island with a pool that turns objects into gold, and an island of dragons.

On Dragon Island, which they discover early in their journey, Eustace is physically transformed into a dragon. Up to this time, Eustace had been a constant complainer, cynic, and general wet blanket. But this harrowing experience awakens him to the reality of his situation, and he is rescued from that fate only by the intervention of Aslan. Eustace describes the almost mystical scene where Aslan removes the dragon shell that encases him and bathes (or baptizes) Eustace in a pool and clothes him anew. It is, of course, Eustace's spiritual as well as physical rebirth, and he emerges a more sensitive and balanced human being, prepared for the adventures that await him not only in this book, but in its sequels.

Also accompanying Caspian on the trip is his faithful captain, Drinian, steady and strong, and the irrepressible Reepicheep, the king of the mice. Drinian and Reepicheep are, in many respects, on the opposite ends of the spectrum, with Caspian in the middle. Drinian is the voice of reason and caution, always to be relied on for sound advice. Reepicheep is the very symbol of daring and bravery; he frequently seems foolhardy and is certainly zealous. Reepicheep's purpose is to find the land of Aslan and the diminutive mouse king perched on the prow of the ship, his eyes fixed to the east, is the image of the martyr-saint, anxious to make the ultimate sacrifice on his spiritual quest. Caspian, who has been compared to Odysseus, Aeneas, Huckleberry Finn, and other literary heroes who grow as a result of physical, emotional, and spiritual tests in the course of a journey, learns from both his friends. The good ruler must have intuitive foresight and a lively imagination as well as sound common sense. In fact, one of the overriding themes of this book is the importance of balance and moderation in life. Caspian, to be an effective king, must resist the fanatical spirituality demonstrated by Reepicheep (who surrenders his own kingship), but he also must temper logic and practicality, as demonstrated by Drinian, with a deeper humanity.

As in all the Narnia books, *The Voyage of the Dawn Treader* is heavily laden with Christian symbolism. On one island Lucy is called upon to break a spell of invisibility that had been cast upon the inhabitants by a powerful Magician. She must enter his quarters and search through his great book of spells to find one that will undo the magic. She bravely undertakes this fearful task and discovers the Magician's Book to be a Book of Life in which she read "the loveliest story [she] ever read or ever shall read in [her] whole life." But all she can recall of the story when she is finished are the images of a cup, a sword, a tree, and a green hill – the Christian symbolism is pervasive. Then, at the end of the voyage, the children see a Lamb roasting a fish on an open fire and they are invited to share the feast. The Lamb is transformed into Aslan before their eyes and Lucy asks, "Will you tell us how to get into your country from our world?" and Aslan replies, "I shall be telling you all the time." This is a testament to Lewis's conviction that the world is permeated with divine messages; if we do not hear them, it is only that we do not always listen.

True to the romance tradition, *The Voyage of the Dawn Treader* is the only one of the Chronicles to end with a marriage – King Caspian's. Also at the end, Lucy and Edmund are told that they will not return to Narnia; like Susan they have grown too old for it. But Eustace is destined to return, indicating the extent of his personal growth throughout the book. All the major characters have reached a significant new stage of maturity as a result of this voyage, and we leave the book with the bittersweet emotions that accompany every passing stage of life.

The fourth book of the Narnia series is *The Silver Chair* (1953), which introduces Jill Pole, a schoolmate of Eustace Scrubb. It is the tale of the rescue of Prince Rilian, the son and heir of King Caspian X, from the clutches of the Green Witch who has imprisoned him in an underground realm. Eustace, fresh from his experiences in Narnia as related in *The Voyage of the Dawn Treader* and now a lively and imaginative character, takes Jill with him through a door in a wall into Aslan's kingdom. In this way they escape the insensitive taunts of the other students at Experiment House, a "modern" school that fosters the pseudointellectualism and narrow dehumanization Lewis so despised. Passing through the door, Eustace and Jill find themselves not in Narnia, however, but on an extraordinarily high mountain, off which Jill, in her rashness, accidentally pushes Eustace, who is, of course, saved by Aslan. Jill herself first meets Aslan on this mountain, and he gives her four Signs for which she must watch. He cautions her to "remember, remember, remember the Signs" – recalling Moses' words to the Israelites about the Law. Indeed, Aslan's mountain is suggestive of Mount Sinai or Mount Horeb. It is on the mountain that Jill learns of the purpose for her visit, for the Sons and Daughters of Adam and Eve are never brought to Narnia without specific reasons. She and Eustace are to find the lost Prince Rilian.

Once Jill reaches Narnia (blown by Aslan's gentle breath over the Eastern Sea) and joins Eustace, they discover that King Caspian, whom Eustace knew as a young man, is now aged and feeble and about to embark on a journey to the Seven Isles. Almost immediately, the first Sign is muffed – for Eustace was to greet an old friend, but he failed, of course, to recognize Caspian. After inquiries, the children learn that ten years before an evil Witch, taking the form of a green serpent, stung and killed the Queen, Caspian's wife and Rilian's mother. The grief-stricken Rilian set out to avenge his mother's death and has not been heard from since.

Eustace and Jill soon enlist the help of one of Lewis's more charming characters, Puddleglum, a Marsh-wiggle, a tall, lanky, froglike creature who wears a pointed hat and invariably sees the glass as half empty. His prognostications of doom and gloom soon become a source of humor, and

Puddleglum assumes the role of the sage guide as the trio sets out to the north in search of the other three Signs that are to lead them to Rilian. On the way they meet a knight and a beautiful lady in a "long, fluttering dress of dazzling green." Astute readers recognize her immediately as the Green Witch, but the travelers are mesmerized by her beauty and unwittingly take her advice to lodge at Harfang House, the abode of giants who are preparing for a great feast (a feast to include, among other things, cooked humans). They promptly fail to heed the second Sign, which is to journey north until they come to the ruined city of the ancient giants, for they virtually stumble over the ruins without recognizing them. They soon realize their error and do manage to escape from the giants' clutches before they are served up for the feast, but they have ignored the third Sign in the meantime, which was to do as the writing on a stone in the ruined city tells them. Those words say "Under Me" – a rather cryptic message indicating that they must go underground, beneath the city. By accident they fall into the underground world as they are escaping from the giants, and there they encounter the curious creatures – called Earthmen – who inhabit the sunless realm. This is the land ruled by the Green Witch, and the travelers soon encounter Prince Rilian, who is kept under the enchantment of Witch by means of a Silver Chair in which he is periodically strapped, the powers of which strip him of his memory and therefore his identity. There is a scene in which the Witch attempts to persuade Puddleglum, the children, and Rilian that the Upper World does not in reality exist, that it is all illusion. At least one critic sees this as Lewis's "nursery nightmare of [his] debate with Miss Anscombe." It is Puddleglum who counters the Witch with the notion that if all those things are made up – including the "trees and grass and sun and moon and stars and Aslan himself" – then those "made-up things seem a good deal more important than the real ones [and] I'm on Aslan's side even if there isn't any Aslan to lead it. I'm going to live as like a Narnian as I can even if there isn't any Narnia. . . ." Wilson suggests that this is "Lewis the wounded Christian, unable to think out his position but determined, in a moving and dogged way, to be loyal to it.

Rilian is recognized by the three travelers when he invokes the name of Aslan – the fourth Sign. With their help he is released from his bondage, and when the Witch transforms herself into the serpent that killed Rilian's mother, she is slain by the prince and his newfound compatriots. The Witch's death also frees the Earthmen whom she

Lewis and his wife, Joy, 1958

has kept enslaved, and they return to their land of Bism, deep within the bowels of the earth. The four ultimately find their way to the Upper World where they encounter the dwarfs in the midst of an annual ritual, the Great Snow Dance, which in its complexity becomes a symbol of the bonds of loyalty and trust that the heroes have just demonstrated. The joy of Rilian's return to Cair Paravel is diminished by father's death. Caspian dies on a couch down by the sea that had played so important a role in his life. But the water is also an image of rebirth. As the children are given a glimpse of Aslan's country, they see a thinly disguised Christian heaven, where old King Caspian is resurrected in both body and spirit from Aslan's baptismal stream. Caspian arises youthful and radiant, having put on the cloak of immortality, and Lewis has managed to assuage our grief over Caspian's death by showing us that Aslan has wiped away death. Back home Jill and Eustace take a stand against the incorrigible youths that bullied them and, with Aslan's help, manage to effect some significant changes in the horrible Experiment House, repeating on a mundane level the heroic adventures in Narnia.

It has been pointed out that *The Silver Chair* possesses the cyclical movement of the romance, the

descent into the netherworld, and the triumphal return. The heroes – chiefly Rilian and Jill – have achieved a greater sense of their own identity (Rilian literally regains his; Jill finds in herself the strength and resolve to stand up to her taunting schoolmates, and, incidentally, helps to bring about complete reform at the school). Finally, the marriage that traditionally concludes a romance is replaced curiously by Caspian's death, which becomes, the children learn, an event of ultimate happiness – for Caspian. This particular theme would be played out in fuller detail in *The Last Battle* (1956).

The fifth book is *The Horse and His Boy* (1954), one of only two that open in the Secondary Fantasy World. *The Horse and His Boy,* as do the other books, contains many familiar devices from romance literature, including the missing twin, the lost child, and the return of the hero to his homeland, but it is principally the tale of the loss and regaining of identity. Set in the time when Peter, Susan, Edmund, and Lucy are reigning as kings and queens of Narnia, the story opens in Calormen, Narnia's wicked southern neighbor, a totalitarian empire with many cultural characteristics of the Middle East – it is largely a desert land with occasional oases. The Calormenes are dark and swarthy in appearance, wear turbans, loose-flowing robes, and shoes that curl upward at the toes; the soldiers fight with curved scimitars. Calormene society is highly stratified; its women are little more than chattels, and it relies heavily on slave trade. In short, it is the very antithesis of its free northern neighbor of Narnia. Lewis is, of course, betraying his blatant prejudice here, his "Northernness."

The hero of the story is Shasta, whom we find in a remote fishing hut, the presumed son of a cruel and base fisherman. But he discovers quite by accident that this fisherman in fact found him as a babe drifting in an open boat and raised him more as a slave than as a son. Just as the fisherman sells him to a Calormene lord, Shasta manages to escape with the help of a Narnian Talking Horse named Bree, who had been kidnapped, and they set out for the freedom of the North. The two fugitives soon meet two more fugitives, a Calormene girl of noble birth named Aravis and her Talking Horse, Hwin, who are also seeking freedom, Aravis escaping from the prospects of a miserable arranged marriage. The foursome reaches the great Calormene city of Tashbaan, which is dazzling from a distance, but inside the gates it is a squalid place with narrow, crowded, and dirty streets, rancid odors, and everywhere the presence of Calormene oppression, most evident in a single traffic regulation: "Everyone who is less important has to get out of the way for everyone who is more important."

It is in Tashbaan that Shasta chances to encounter the visiting Narnian king and queen, Edmund and Susan, who are being entertained by the repulsive Calormene Prince Rabadash, who is courting Susan. Shasta is mistaken by the Narnians for Crown Prince Corin of Archenland, who is traveling with them and unwittingly becomes privy to a Narnian plan to flee the Calormene capital, thus rescuing Susan from an unpleasant alliance with Rabadash. Although Shasta does not yet discover his true identity, he does know he belongs to the North and is more eager than ever to reach the free lands. Shasta eventually manages to reach the appointed rendezvous point near the Tombs of the Ancient Calormene Kings, but Aravis, Bree and Hwin are not there, and he must spend a terrifying night alone among the eerie tombs on the edge of the desert. His fears are assuaged by the company of a mysterious yellow cat, and he subsequently dreams of a large and gentle lion who provides him further comfort. Experienced Lewis readers will recognize, of course, the presence of Aslan.

Meanwhile, Aravis has been having her own adventures in the city, encountering a childhood friend Lasaraleen, now a Calormene noblewoman, who helps her escape from the city, but not before she fortunately overhears the Calormene ruler, the Tisroc, plotting an invasion of Narnia in retaliation for Queen Susan's spurning of Prince Rabadash. However, this excuse is only convenient, for the Tisroc confesses, "Every morning the sun is darkened in my eyes, and every night my sleep is the less refreshing, because I remember that Narnia is still free."

Aravis finally joins the rest, and the four companions head out across the desert to Archenland in another test of strength and endurance. On the way they are attacked by a fierce lion, and Aravis is wounded; Bree, up to this point a self-assured, at times haughty creature, loses his nerve and runs; but Shasta boldly chases after the lion. Shortly, Shasta learns that this lion was Aslan, as was the cat and the lion of the dream, and that all these appearances were not without purpose. Luck is referred to more than once in the book. Shasta, when he finds himself traveling alone, lost in Archenland, remarks: "I *do* think . . . that I must be the most unfortunate boy that ever lived in the whole world." Aravis says to the Hermit of the Southern March when he offers her hospitality after an accident, "I *have* had luck." But perhaps it is to the Hermit, who is a famous seer, that we should lend our credence: "I have now lived a hundred and nine winters in this world and have never yet met any such thing as Luck." Indeed, it is Providence behind all actions in the world, as Shasta finally concedes, "at least it wasn't luck, at all really; it was *Him*." When Shasta encounters Aslan, we are reminded of Moses on the mountain when to Shasta's question "Who are you?" Aslan responds three times: "Myself." This is the revelation scene, found in every one of the books, and in it Aslan also tells Shasta: " . . . I was the lion you do not remember who pushed the boat in which you lay, a child near death, so that it came to shore where a man sat, wakeful at midnight, to receive you." Aslan too makes it clear that his purpose is not always understood by mortals, for when Shasta questions why Aslan caused Aravis to be wounded, the lion replies, "Child, . . . I am telling you your story, not hers. I tell no-one any story but his own."

Aravis, Bree, and Hwin have remained with the Hermit while Shasta sought help from Narnia for King Lune of Archenland to defeat Rabadash's army. Here is where Shasta proves himself, of course, and he successfully gets word to King Edmund and Queen Lucy. A battle ensues and Rabadash and his troups are utterly defeated at the gates of King Lune's castle. After the victory King Lune reveals to all what the readers have undoubtedly long suspected, that Shasta is really Cor, the twin son of Lune, elder brother of Corin, and heir to the throne of Archenland. Typical of the romance ending, Shasta eventually marries Aravis and they live long and happy lives. Rabadash too finds his identity, for Aslan transforms him into a donkey following the defeat at the hands of the Narnians and prophesies that the only way to undo this spell is for him to "stand before the altar of Tash in Tashbaan at the great Autumn Feast this year and there, in the sight of all Tashbaan, your ass's shape will fall from you and all men will know you for Prince Rabadash." Only through this humble submission will he regain his own identity. *The Horse and His Boy* is one of the most consistently exciting of the Chronicles, and is not without its share of good comic scenes.

The last two books of the series deal with the beginning and the ending of Narnia respectively, and so seem to frame the Chronicles. *The Magician's Nephew* opens in London at the turn of the century, and its principal characters are Digory Kirke (who we learn is to grow up to be the professor of *The Lion, the Witch, and the Wardrobe*) and his neighbor, Polly Plummer. Digory and his mother, who is very ill, live with an aunt and an eccentric Uncle Andrew who dabbles in the occult and possesses some magic rings that have the power to transport the bearer (and anything physically touching the bearer) to an enchanted Wood Between the Worlds, from which it is possible to enter other worlds. The children are taken against their wills to the Wood, and in their attempt to return home they arrive in the dismal Land of Charn. Charn is permeated with images of death – it is dark, cold, and still, and in one room they discover hundreds of figures in, as it were, a state of suspended animation. They are drawn to a bell on which is inscribed an ominous warning against ringing it, but the temptation is too much for Digory. In ringing the bell he awakens the Queen Jadis, the powerful embodiment of evil – and the one who would become the hated White Queen of the first book.

As with all the Narnia books, Lewis includes the underlying theme of maturation. In *The Magician's Nephew,* it is Digory whose emotional and personal growth we are to witness. Digory's yielding to temptation brings considerable sorrow, for Queen Jadis manages to escape Charn with the children and ends up in London, where she causes considerable havoc, as described in one of Lewis's finest comic scenes in the Chronicles. The escapade results in an accident by which the children, Uncle Andrew, Queen Jadis, a cabby and his wife (Frank and Helen), not to mention the cabby's horse, Strawberry, and a London lamppost all end up in Narnia, just prior to its creation.

It is the creation scene, when the great lion Aslan calls all of Narnia into being through a song (certainly one of the loveliest of creation stories), for which this book is best remembered, and indeed the description is poetic. Narnia is a land of peace and plenty, a land of talking animals and spectacular beauty, and its contrast with the decaying land of Charn is evident. But there is also a social commentary here, for Narnia is rural, free and good; whereas Charn is a city, evil and oppressive. (It is interesting to note that Narnia, in all its history as told by Lewis, has no real cities, but is rather thoroughly pristine and rural.) Frank, the cabby, and his wife, Helen, are made the first king and queen of Narnia, but they are not in every respect the Adam and Eve of Narnia, for it is Digory who is responsible for allowing Evil to enter Narnia. The Evil is in the person of Queen Jadis and casts a shadow on the very first day of Narnia's existence.

Digory must redeem himself by becoming the means for Narnia's salvation from this Evil, and so Aslan sends him on a journey for a silver apple which will protect the land. Accompanying him is Strawberry, who is now transformed into a winged horse named Fledge. The Christian symbolism is difficult to miss when Digory nearly succumbs to temptation in the garden containing the apple tree. Queen Jadis is the temptress and three times attempts to persuade Digory to take the apple for himself – he readily refuses the first two times, but when Jadis points out that he could take the apple home to his own desperately ill mother, Digory nearly falters. But he finally makes the choice he must make, and that is for the greater good of Narnia – for that must take precedence over the well-being, even the life, of his mother. Digory's resistance is the triumphal moment of the story and is evidence of the fullness of Digory's emotional and spiritual growth.

Of course, the Evil is still in the Garden that is Narnia, and it will resurrect some day (as readers of the series well know), but Digory has made it possible for the young land to enjoy many generations of peace and happiness. As his own reward Digory is given another apple from the tree by Aslan, and his mother is miraculously cured. From a seed of that apple a tree grew in London, and from that tree the wardrobe was made, a wardrobe that stood in a back bedroom of Digory's large country house when he was host to the Pevensies some forty-five years later. And the London lamppost that was accidentally transported to Narnia marked the spot for Lucy and the other Pevensies when they made their first visit to Narnia. *The Magician's Nephew* is a book of contrasts, reminding us that in this world (as in Narnia) the struggle between good and evil, light and dark, demands our own steadfastness, resolve, and unshakable faith in order that ultimately the good may triumph. And that is, of course, the story of *The Last Battle*.

As *The Magician's Nephew* describes the beginning of Narnia, *The Last Battle* describes the end of Narnia. Like *The Horse and His Boy, The Last Battle* takes place entirely in the fantasy world, opening in Narnia, which has, once again, fallen upon evil times. A deceitful ape named Shift has exerted tremendous influence over the realm by disguising a foolish donkey, Puzzle, in a lion's skin and passing him off as Aslan. Among the early victims of Shift's deceit is the last king of Narnia, Tirian, who is taken into bondage. It is Tirian who beseeches the children to come from England to Narnia once again to help the kingdom in its time of trial, and Jill and Eustace are swept from a speeding train into Narnia to Tirian's service. Although they capture Puzzle and expose the deception of the Ape, Tirian and the children find to their dismay that, having been deceived once, the Narnians have now come to doubt the true Aslan. The kingdom has reached a crisis in faith. At the same time, a Calormene invasion is taking place – all made possible by the duplicity of Shift – and Tirian and the children prepare for the greatest of the battles. For the first time in the entire series, the children contemplate that if they were to die while in Narnia, would they also be dead in England?

The focus of the conflict is a Stable in which the terrible god Tashlan – a union between the Calormene god Tash and Aslan fabricated by Shift – is supposedly residing. Those who enter the Stable emerge in various states of terror, and one Calormene soldier falls down dead upon leaving the Stable. The Stable door comes to symbolize death. When ultimately Tirian and the children are thrust through the Stable doors to meet their own deaths, they discover not the darkness that they glimpsed from the outside but a stunning brightness and, instead of the narrow confines of a stable, the endless expanse of a country far richer and more beautiful than anything they had ever dreamed of before. The doors were not an exit, but an entrance into

Eternity. Awaiting them are not only Aslan himself, but the Professor, Aunt Polly, Peter, Edmund and Lucy. Susan Pevensie is excluded from Narnia not because she grows up, but because she rejects childhood – in Jill's words, "she's interested in nothing now-a-days except nylons and lipstick and invitations." And Polly laments that Susan "wasted all her school time wanting to be the age she is now, and she'll waste all the rest of her life trying to stay that age. Her whole idea is to race on to the silliest time of one's life as quick as she can and then stop there as long as she can." This is Lewis reminding us again of Christ's exhortation to become as children that we might inherit the kingdom of God.

We learn that all of them (excepting Susan) had been on the same train, along with the children's parents – and all of whom had been killed in a train accident that happened at the same moment the children were called to Narnia. The question of what would happen to Eustace and Jill if they died in Narnia is resolved by having their deaths in Narnia and England coincide. They also find in their midst a Calormene soldier who also enjoys this eternal life, because he believed in a God of goodness; it matters little by what name that God is called. Lewis's own faith was magnanimous, and one of the great distinctions between his concept of heaven (as described in *The Great Divorce*) and Dante's is that in Lewis's anyone may enter who truly desires to do so.

But with them Narnia must die too. With the same drama as its creation with Aslan's song, Narnia comes to an end. The moors and mountains crumble, and the ocean covers all the land, a feeble sun shines upon the waters, and then, at Aslan's command, the Time-giant "took the Sun and squeezed it in his hand as you would squeeze an orange. And instantly there was total darkness." It is as if, its purpose having been fulfilled, Narnia is simply taken up by Aslan, gently folded and then put away forever. Lewis gives us one of the most hopeful conclusions in all children's literature: "All their life in this world and all their adventures in Narnia had only been the cover and the title page: now at last they were beginning Chapter One of the Great Story, which no one on earth has read: which goes on for ever: in which every chapter is better than the one before." *The Last Battle* won the 1957 Carnegie Medal for the most distinguished contribution to children's literature published in Great Britain. Many critics consider it the finest of the Chronicles, although none has acquired the fame of *The Lion, the Witch, and the Wardrobe*.

Lewis ceased writing children's stories with *The Last Battle.* He had begun writing them because they were perfectly suited to his purpose, and now, that accomplished, he turned to other ventures. Much like Lewis Carroll or E. B. White, whose reputations in children's literature rest on a very small body of unforgettable works, Lewis's reputation among children is secure. He has influenced a great many of his successors in the field of heroic fantasy, including Lloyd Alexander (*The Prydain Chronicles*), Ursula Le Guin (*The Earthsea Cycle*), Anne McCaffrey (*The Dragonwing Trilogy*), Susan Cooper (*The Dark is Rising Trilogy*), and others who have written heroic fantasies in series, drawn on medieval romance and folk elements for inspiration, and focused on serious, even exalted purposes.

In the midst of his writing of the Narnia Chronicles, he was also working on his *English Literature in the Sixteenth Century,* and he at last received the honor of a professorship, which was to come to him, not from his own Oxford, but from Cambridge. He taught for the rest of his professional life at Magdalene College, Cambridge, although he continued to live at The Kilns near Oxford, commuting to Cambridge every week.

Lewis had remained a bachelor until he was nearly sixty, when he married an American, Joy Davidman Gresham, in a civil ceremony on 23 April 1956. He dedicated his novel for adults, *Till We Have Faces: A Myth Retold* (1956), a reworking of the Cupid and Psyche myth, to Joy. And the title of his own autobiographical work, *Surprised by Joy: The Shape of My Early Life* (1955), took on added significance with his marriage. Within months of the marriage, Joy Lewis was diagnosed with terminal cancer. The disease went into remission for a period, but she died on 13 July 1960, after a long struggle.

Lewis was devastated and perhaps never really recovered from the loss. But as the true writer, he dealt with his grief by writing, and his *A Grief Observed* (1961) is still admired for its profoundly personal examination of bereavement.

Lewis himself was in failing health by this time, and in the summer of 1963 he was forced to resign from Cambridge because of a heart and bladder condition. At The Kilns to be cared for by his brother, he continued his lifelong passion of reading. He died quietly on the afternoon of 22 November 1963. Few days in history can claim so great a loss to humanity, for on the other side of the Atlantic another writer, Aldous Huxley, died and President John F. Kennedy was assassinated. Lewis, who labored intensely over his scholarly writings but seldom wrote more than one draft for his children's stories, might likely be bemused to learn that his celebrity now rests largely with the young readers of his Narnia books. But somehow we must also suspect that Lewis himself would have believed that, after all, the message of his Narnia books was the greatest message one could ever hope to write.

Biographies:

Robert Lancelyn Green and Walter Hooper, *C. S. Lewis: A Biography* (New York: Harcourt Brace Jovanovich, 1974);

Margaret Patterson Hanney, *C. S. Lewis* (New York: Ungar, 1981);

A. N. Wilson, *C. S. Lewis: A Biography* (New York: Norton, 1990).

Reference:

Paul F. Ford, *Companion to Narnia* (New York: Harper & Row, 1980).

Hugh Lofting

(14 January 1886 – 27 September 1947)

Francis J. Molson
Central Michigan University

BOOKS: *The Story of Doctor Dolittle, Being the History of his Peculiar Life at Home and Astonishing Adventures in Foreign Parts* (New York: Stokes, 1920); republished as *Doctor Dolittle: Being the History of his Peculiar Life at Home and Astonishing Adventures in Foreign Parts* (London: Cape, 1922);

The Voyages of Doctor Dolittle (New York: Stokes, 1922; London: Cape, 1923);

Doctor Dolittle's Post Office (New York: Stokes, 1923; London: Cape, 1924);

The Story of Mrs. Tubbs (New York: Stokes, 1923; London: Cape, 1924);

Doctor Dolittle's Circus (New York: Stokes, 1924; London: Cape, 1925);

Porridge Poetry: Cooked, Ornamented, and Served (New York: Stokes, 1925; London: Cape, 1925);

Doctor Dolittle's Zoo (New York: Stokes, 1925; London: Cape, 1926);

Doctor Dolittle's Caravan (New York: Stokes, 1926; London: Cape, 1929);

Zingo and the Magic Beasts (Jersey City: Colgate, 1926);

Doctor Dolittle's Garden (New York: Stokes, 1927; London: Cape, 1928);

Doctor Dolittle in the Moon (New York: Stokes, 1928; London: Cape, 1929);

Noisy Nora: An Almost True Story (New York: Stokes, 1929; London: Cape, 1929);

The Twilight of Magic (New York: Stokes, 1930; London: Cape, 1931);

Gub-Gub's Book: An Encyclopedia of Food (New York: Stokes, 1932; London: Cape, 1932);

Doctor Dolittle's Return (New York: Stokes, 1933; London: Cape, 1933);

Doctor Dolittle's Birthday Book (New York: Stokes, 1935);

Tommy, Tilly and Mrs. Tubbs (New York: Stokes, 1936; London: Cape, 1937);

Victory for the Slain (London: Cape, 1942);

Doctor Dolittle and the Secret Lake (New York & Philadelphia: Lippincott, 1948; London: Cape, 1953);

Hugh Lofting (courtesy of Christopher Lofting)

Doctor Dolittle and the Green Canary (New York & Philadelphia: Lippincott, 1950; London: Cape, 1951);

Doctor Dolittle's Puddleby Adventures (New York & Philadelphia: Lippincott, 1952; London: Cape, 1953);

SELECTED PERIODICAL PUBLICATION –
UNCOLLECTED: "Children and Internationalism," *Nation,* 118 (13 February 1924): 172–173.

In the judgment of some commentators, Hugh Lofting's books chronicling Doctor Dolittle's adventures should be off-limits to youngsters today for two reasons. First, some of the stories, in particular *The Story of Doctor Dolittle, Being the History of His Peculiar Life at Home and Astonishing Adventures in Foreign Parts* (1920), *The Voyages of Doctor Dolittle* (1922), and *Doctor Dolittle's Post Office* (1923) are judged to be racist. Second, even if the racial stereotyping is eliminated, the books are still objectionable because the doctor represents the patronizing attitude of Eurocentric imperialism. Thus, according to these commentators, the Dolittle books should be removed from library shelves and relegated to the dustbin of children's literature as relics of a bygone and unlamented era. But the dustbin is not the appropriate location for the considerable creative achievement of Lofting.

Hugh Lofting was born 14 January 1886 at Maidenhead in Berkshire to John Brien and Elizabeth Agnes Lofting, both Roman Catholic. One of six siblings – five boys and one girl – he acquired early in his life a love for animals. When eight years old, Lofting was sent to Mount Saint Mary, a Catholic public school, which he attended for almost a decade – a stay about which little is known.

Since all the Lofting boys were expected to select professions that provided a dependable means of support, Hugh decided upon civil engineering, although he might have preferred a career as a writer. In 1904 he traveled to the United States and enrolled at the Massachusetts Institute of Technology. Two years later he returned to England, attended London Polytechnic, and there completed his studies. The next several years he worked prospecting for gold and surveying in Canada and for railroads in West Africa and Cuba.

In 1912 Lofting came back to the United States and, settling in New York and rejecting engineering as a career, began to write professionally. That same year he married Flora Small; within several years two children, Elizabeth and Colin, were born. When World War I began in 1914, Lofting went to work for the British Ministry of Information in New York. Two years later, having enlisted in the British army and having been commissioned a captain of the Irish Guards, he spent two years on active duty in Flanders and France, where he was wounded.

Lofting's wartime experience in Flanders was seminal. What he observed of war engendered in him a lifelong antipathy to it. His love of animals contributed further to his suffering as he became aware that animals, pressed into military service, were not medically treated when wounded but were summarily killed.

When he wrote home, he sought to divert attention from the horrors of war through creating stories about a physician who, because he had learned to talk with animals, was able to provide the medical assistance they required. After the war Lofting returned to the United States in 1919 and took up residence in Connecticut, where he concentrated on his writing. With his family urging him to make a book out of the stories he sent home, Lofting received assistance from Cecil Roberts, a popular British author, who provided an introduction to Frederick A. Stokes, a publisher. Lofting completed a book-length manuscript. Upon publication in 1920, *The Story of Doctor Dolittle, Being the History of his Peculiar Life at Home and Astonishing Adventures in Foreign Parts,* enjoyed a favorable reception – so much so that, when a British edition was planned (1922), Hugh Walpole wrote a complimentary preface that hailed the novel as a classic, comparable to the Alice in Wonderland narratives.

The most successful of Lofting's novels, *The Story of Doctor Dolittle* features distinctive and original characters, an attractive secondary world, rapidity of incident, and a childlike disregard for plausibility. In Puddleby-on-the-Marsh, Doctor John Dolittle not only has come to prefer doctoring animals in doctoring humans but, discovering that animals speak, learns their languages through the aid of Polynesia, his parrot. Eventually the doctor is able to help animals in extraordinary ways and acquires fame from as far away as Africa, where monkeys, threatened by a mysterious ailment, urgently request his aid before they all die. Accompanied by a few animal friends, Dolittle journeys to Africa, lands, sets out into the jungle, is captured by a native tribe, but escapes. Reaching the land of the monkeys and organizing a hospital, he saves many of his patients. As payment for his services, the doctor accepts a rare Pushmi-Pullyu that has a head at both ends of its body. Returning to the coast, Dolittle is again captured but once more escapes, helped by a prince who is repaying the favor of having his black face whitened so that a sleeping princess might not be frightened by what she sees when she awakes. Homeward bound, Dolittle is chased by pirates, but he captures them, forcing them to become birdseed farmers. After rescuing others, Dolittle finally comes home.

In his study of Lofting, *Hugh Lofting* (1992), Gary D. Schmidt argues that *The Story of Doctor Dolittle* is the "kind of story a child would create, in a world a child would create." He also acknowledges that this putative child-author is a Victorian child

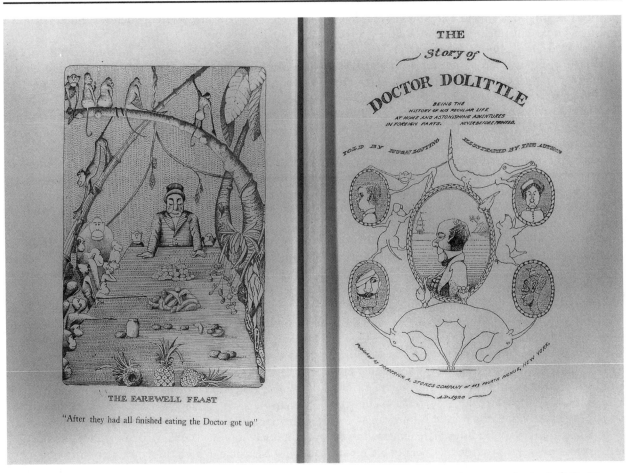

THE FAREWELL FEAST

"After they had all finished eating the Doctor got up"

Frontispiece and title page of the first of Lofting's books about the English doctor who can speak the languages of animals (Lilly Library, Indiana University)

who, not unexpectedly, reflects Victorian views and values. Schmidt's comments are perceptive and do speak to the genuine power of the novel, as well as to the critical problem it poses today. A child's imagination shapes a plot that is unconcerned with plausibility — for example, the best way for a doctor to find out what ails an animal is to ask, and the easiest way to do that is to speak that animal's language, and the way to accomplish that is to learn animal talk, and so forth. A child's imagination peoples a story with characters familiar to children — a portly, nonthreatening adult like a generous bachelor uncle — propels it by means of rapid-fire incidents — an African voyage, a jungle trek, capture by natives, escape, a second capture and escape — and invents outlandish adventures — monkeys, coming to Dolittle's assistance when he is being pursued, make themselves into a bridge. A child's sense of humor gives the characters names like Dab-Dab and Gub-Gub and relishes burlesque — pirates rehabilitated as birdseed farmers. Finally, a child's notion of justice dispenses rewards and punishments — riches

to the "good" doctor and frustration to the "bad" king.

At the same time, because it is a child's imagination that conceives and furnishes the secondary world of *The Story of Doctor Dolittle,* its geography and population reflect what a Victorian child knows, accepts, dreams about, hopes for, and fears. Thus the setting is "dark" and exotic Africa, which the "white man" has explored and civilized. Or, when monkeys need medical assistance, they do not ask their neighbors, because the neighbors do not speak monkey language. Instead, they go to the only person who can communicate with them; that Dolittle also practices a Western medical technology unknown to a native person is coincidental. The real point is that in this fantasy world Dolittle is the only individual who combines animal language fluency and medical skills.

It is ironic that the reason for the success of *The Story of Doctor Dolittle* is also the source of what today bothers some commentators. Lofting imaginatively re-created Victorian racial and cultural attitudes. No wonder some admirers, believing that rewriting would not compromise the author's success in re-creating the child's view of the world, have attempted to eradicate the most objectionable elements in the novel. For instance, in the afterword to the centennial edition of *The Story of Doctor Dolittle* (1988), Christopher Lofting, the author's son, takes the position that striking allegedly racist words, phrases, and sections is appropriate. He even claims that his father, if alive, would have done the same. Other admirers, not convinced that such editing is appropriate or even something that should be encouraged, argue for retaining the novel as originally written. They prefer to offset supposed negative effects by either forewarning young readers of the racist passages or providing opportunity for discussing the novel and its racism. Further, Schmidt questions why children's books should be considered fair game for rewriting to ensure the correctness of their political or cultural content. An unwillingness to edit *The Story of Doctor Dolittle,* therefore, does not necessarily reflect racial bigotry or cultural insensitivity; it may signal instead a refusal to concede that children's literature must first of all be a means of socializing young people.

The popular and critical success of *The Story of Doctor Dolittle* demonstrated to Lofting that he could effectively write sustained fiction. He began to believe that he had made the right choice in deciding to become a professional writer. This seemed to be confirmed when his next novel, *The Voyages of Doctor Dolittle* proved successful, receiving the 1923 Newbery Medal. After his success Lofting focused solely on children's literature; during the next six-year period he completed a new Dolittle novel each year. He also published during this creative outburst a book of nonsense poems, *Porridge Poetry: Cooked, Ornamented, and Served* (1925), and an essay, "Children and Internationalism," in which Lofting states that a prime intention of his writing was to assist in the breaking down of barriers between nations and peoples.

The Voyages of Doctor Dolittle is a much longer and richer novel than its predecessor, partly because a major new character, young Tommy Stubbins, is introduced and partly because justification for another voyage is required, along with a new ship's company. In particular, Lofting needed to depict Tommy's introduction to the doctor; his visits to the Dolittle household; and his becoming an assistant, learning animal language, and finally acting as the doctor's secretary. At the same time Tommy is being assimilated into the Dolittle family, the doctor has been attempting to learn the lan-

guage of shellfish. Unsuccessful in doing so, he realizes that he requires the assistance of Long Arrow, the world's greatest naturalist, and asks Miranda, the Purple Bird-of-Paradise, to track him down. When Long Arrow cannot be found, Dolittle decides to sail to Spidermonkey Island, somewhere off the coast of Brazil, where the naturalist was last reported to be.

Getting to the island, however, is delayed by the discovery of stowaways; an unscheduled stop at Monteverde in the Cape Blanca Islands, where Dolittle participates in a most unusual bullfight; and a tremendous storm and shipwreck. When the reunited company reaches Spidermonkey Island, Dolittle finds a Jabiza beetle upon which Long Arrow has inscribed a plea for help and enlists the beetle to help locate the cave entrapping the naturalist and his friends.

Just as the doctor and Long Arrow are set to exchange information, they are caught up in a war between the Popsipetels and their more numerous and hostile neighbors, the Bag-jagderags. Coming again to the aid of the former – a people the doctor previously helped by introducing them to fire and arranging with porpoises to stop the island's drift towards the South Pole – Dolittle, along with Long Arrow and Bumpo, faces defeat, despite fighting valiantly as "The Terrible Three." An army of black parrots, alerted by Polynesia, comes to Dolittle's aid, descends upon the Bag-jagderags, pecks at their heads, and forces their surrender. After the Peace of the Parrots uniting the tribes is drawn up and the floating island is stabilized by dropping a huge rock into its hollow center to force it to settle on the ocean floor, the united tribes ask Dolittle to become their king. He agrees reluctantly, and the new King Jong begins to discharge his duties with fairness and compassion, installing modern sanitation, curing the sick, dispensing justice, and setting a democratic example.

Aspects of Dolittle's characterization do smack of the stereotypical white man's acceptance of a "burden" to "civilize" the "lesser peoples." Yet the overall portrait of King Jong's reign is not as stereotypical as some would have it. Dolittle is quite aware of the ways in which the cultural differences between white and Indian do not necessarily imply the latter's inferiority. Probably reflecting what he has learned from his master, Stubbins remarks about the schooling which King Jong began: "You see, these Indians were ignorant of many of the things that quite small white children know – though it is also true that they know a lot that white grown-ups never dreamed of." Moreover, Dolittle

Front cover for Lofting's 1923 Newbery Medal–winning book (Lilly Library, Indiana University)

simplest structure upon which an author still relatively inexperienced in constructing plots can build a children's story – the journey. (This structural device, by the way, can be found in most of Lofting's subsequent fiction.) Second, Lofting employed amplification and variation. For instance, he included additional detail about Dolittle's life and adventures; he devised purpose and destination for a second journey; he invented additional adventures, some even more outlandish than the first ones; and he expanded the number and kind of individuals accompanying the doctor on his travels.

Augmenting the Dolittle family by including a boy was significant. Although young readers might have been able to identify with either the doctor or the animals, the addition of Stubbins as a major character enhanced the novel's capacity to encourage and accommodate young reader identification. Moreover, Stubbins functions as both participant and narrator; in this way, Lofting, by abandoning the generalized childlike point of view he adopted in *The Story of Doctor Dolittle,* added immediacy and intimacy to his storytelling. Finally, Stubbins is just one of several marginalized characters introduced as prospective crew members of the ship, the *Curlew.* In addition to the boy, there are Matthew Mugg, the cat's meat man; Joe, the mussel man; Ben Butcher, a sinister able seaman; Luke the Hermit, a suspected murderer; and Bumpo, the African prince. As it turns out, the two characters who do become crew members are the most marginalized: Stubbins (who is twice dismissed as unimportant by Colonel Bellows, the representative of a society that has no time or attention to devote to children), and Bumpo. A significant part of the enduring appeal of *The Voyages of Doctor Dolittle,* as well as all Dolittle stories, is Lofting's interest in characters situated on the margins of society. Margins are familiar to many youngsters who feel that adults unfairly dismiss them as unimportant or incapable of accomplishments they consider significant.

It is easy to understand why *The Voyages of Doctor Dolittle* was awarded the Newbery Medal in 1923 and continues to deserve a wide readership. There is the additional information provided about one of the most distinctive and engaging characters in children's literature, John Dolittle, who, as a result, begins to acquire a kind of history. In particular, readers realize that Dolittle is committed to doing good whenever he can; moreover, the good he accomplishes is the unambiguous kind youngsters understand and appreciate – for example, helping to alleviate the sufferings of animals as well as humans. There are the new adventures that, be-

agrees to relinquish the patriarchal role forced upon him. He does seem reluctant to give up his kingship, but not because he seeks power or wishes to exploit or destroy. The prime motive in his agreeing to become king was to help the needy – the motive one expects of a physician. Further, because he has a strong sense of duty and obligation, he feels that leaving the tribes may be an irresponsible act, a betrayal of their trust. Once he is convinced by Polynesia and Long Arrow that the Indians are capable of taking charge of their lives, moreover, he is willing to return home via the great shellfish to renew his search for animal-language proficiency and to acquire information about life on the ocean floor.

It is instructive to observe what steps Lofting took in achieving success in *The Voyages of Doctor Dolittle.* First, he retained the two key features that made his first novel distinctive and refreshing. He continued the focus on John Dolittle and his family of talking animals. He also continued to utilize the cause they are as interesting and fanciful as those in the first novel, provide genuine excitement. There is a new major character for young readers to relish, Tommy Stubbins, the boy who becomes assistant to the famous doctor and acquires a variety of skills and opportunities both to do good and to embark on adventures. In this fashion Lofting was able to dramatize without sermonizing or moralizing that adventure, discovery, and learning do not necessarily exclude doing good.

Edward Blishen argues in *Hugh Lofting* (1968) that the four novels appearing immediately after *The Voyages of Doctor Dolittle* "form the ebullient, happy center of the series. . . . They bear all the marks of Lofting's headlong delight in his own creation and in the world of fantastic creation to which it gave him entrance." Lofting's creativity was indeed headlong: a new Dolittle novel appeared annually over the course of four years. Although this creative output was remarkable, these novels are of uneven quality and of varying degrees of interest. In these novels Lofting is not always consistent in his use of narrative point of view. Sometimes he implies that Stubbins is the narrator who is retelling what had been relayed to him by other family members. At other times Stubbins is clearly the narrator who is recounting incidents in which he himself was involved years after they have happened. Still, by and large the humorous, lighthearted, and engaging tone readily discerned in these novels and an emphasis on a variety of adventures involving talking animals make for entertaining reading.

Doctor Dolittle's Post Office begins with the doctor, having returned to West Africa because the Pushmi-Pullyu was homesick, coming to the aid of a black woman, Zuzama, who is grief-stricken over her husband's enslavement. The historical setting Lofting has chosen for the Dolittle series is that period in the early nineteenth century when Great Britain had outlawed slavery and instructed its navy to intercept all slavers. In the episode Lofting is careful to acknowledge both the culpability of white people for fostering slavery and the fact that some blacks preyed on other blacks and sold them into slavery. Dolittle's reaction to Zuzama's plight and his decision to assist her obviously reflect his outrage over the cruel treatment some humans exhibit toward other humans.

Not so obvious is that the doctor, although preferring animals to humans, has not closed his heart to the suffering of his fellow human beings. The injustice of slavery, moreover, becomes part of the evidence that justifies Dolittle's pessimism concerning humanity, pessimism that surfaces in the last novels. Most of the plot of *Doctor Dolittle's Post Office,* however, describes Dolittle's setting up in the African kingdom of Fantippo a postal system that utilizes birds.

Some commentators, asking why a black tribe needs a white person to organize its postal system, find the treatment of King Koku and his people condescending and racist. Yet placed in its historical and fantastic setting, the whole episode is not as offensive as it might seem at first glance. Dolittle does not impose his postal system upon the people, nor does he gain any monetary profit. Rather, King Koku asks him for assistance, and all profits are returned to the tribe, which begins to prosper. Moreover, the system Dolittle sets up is a cooperative arrangement: while birds take care of the foreign mail, the tribe is responsible for local deliveries. Finally, the disdain that Lofting is supposedly expressing is in no way focused just on people of color; it should be recalled that the reliable forecasts originating in the bird-staffed weather bureau Dolittle organized are all rejected out of hand by white experts.

In *Doctor Dolittle's Circus* (1924) Lofting recounts events immediately subsequent to *The Story of Doctor Dolittle.* Needing money for food and to replace a boat lost at sea, Dolittle decides to join a circus in order to take advantage of the crowd appeal of the Pushmi-Pullyu. The story goes on to depict the family's various adventures as it slowly comes to enjoy a modicum of financial success, the doctor's deepening concern over the inhumane treatment of the circus animals, and his determination to ameliorate living conditions in the circus. The most engaging segment of the narrative is a droll episode in which Dolittle assists Sophie the Seal to escape. Highlights include Sophie's masquerading as a woman traveling in the doctor's company, the odd couple's journey across the countryside to the sea, Dolittle's participation in a most peculiar foxhunt, and the seal's actual return to the sea. The novel concludes with Dolittle's taking on the duties of circus manager, his arranging for the animals to run their own shows, and the family's beginning to make money.

Tommy Stubbins reappears as the narrator of *Doctor Dolittle's Zoo* (1925), the opening scene of which is a surprise welcome-back party thrown by those family members who had not accompanied the doctor on his search for Long Arrow. Asked to take charge of the zoo, which had been neglected during Dolittle's prolonged oversea adventures, Stubbins then establishes Animal Town to provide decent housing for the many animals who have

Illustration by Lofting from The Story of Mrs. Tubbs *(1923)*

come uninvited to be near the famous doctor. When the discovery of gold nearby enables the family to live without the constant threat of poverty, the animals, particularly members of the Rat and Mouse Club, are at leisure to tell stories. The remainder of the novel consists of recitations of these stories, except for a final episode involving fire at a neighboring house, the successful attempt to rescue a family of mice from the fire, a lost will, and the setting up of an animal welfare trust. *Doctor Dolittle's Zoo* is mildly entertaining if readers are content with additional details about Dolittle's animal friends. On the other hand, if readers hope to learn more about the doctor or his ideas, the story is disappointing.

Perhaps the least interesting novel of this group is *Doctor Dolittle's Caravan* (1926), most of which Lofting gives over to the doctor's desire to establish a bird opera and chorus. Prominent in the plot is the canary Pippinelli's narrative of her adventures before joining the opera. (These adventures reappear expanded and in greater detail years later in *Doctor Dolittle and the Green Canary,* 1950.) Depending on one's tastes in animal fantasy, one might consider the novel as either humorous, as the various animals prepare to go on stage, or interminable, since so much of the narrative concerns unexciting rehearsals and performances.

In most respects, the novel is typical of Lofting's achievement at this time. Plot is linear and episodic, hence easy to read and follow, although it does seem once or twice that the author achieves closure not because logic dictates it but because he has reached a previously determined page limit. In this connection, one can appreciate the observation that the Dolittle novels are perhaps best approached as one long series. The stories are humorous, and a fondness for puns is obvious. Readily manifest is a respect for animals, their dignity, and their desire for freedom. Present too is a variety of sallies launched against human foibles, especially those of high society. Finally, the predominating tone is best described as British – evidence that Lofting, regardless of his residing permanently in the United States, always remained British at heart.

Marring the success of these years was the death of Lofting's wife in 1927. In 1928 Lofting married Katherine Harrower, who died several months after the wedding of influenza. Perhaps because of the emotional losses and understandable creative exhaustion, after 1927 Lofting's output declined both in quantity as well as quality. *Noisy Nora: An Almost True Story* (1929), *The Twilight of Magic* (1930), and *Gub-Gub's Book: An Encyclopedia of Food* (1932) are all inconsequential children's books. Exceptions to the drop-off in quality are *Doctor's Dolittle's Garden* (1927) and *Doctor Dolittle in the Moon* (1928), books that make up two-thirds of the moon trilogy.

Doctor Dolittle's Garden is clearly a transitional novel. Because the first third consists of a series of tales told by animals in the presence of Dolittle and Stubbins, the novel is related to the previous narratives that provide details about the Dolittle family or contain blocks of tales told by the animals. In the last two-thirds, however, a marked shift in content and intent occurs. Lofting, who seems to have allowed his protagonist to drift into passivity, returns to depicting Dolittle as an active naturalist who once more takes up his studies of insect language and feels increasingly frustrated by a lack of progress. The doctor complains that he might learn so much more if only he could travel – not just to uncharted lands on Earth but to the Moon.

A mysterious visitor suddenly appears in the Dolittle garden – a gigantic moth who has managed somehow to voyage from the Moon to Earth and is on a special mission requesting the doctor's services. Dolittle is excited because the moth's presence proves the reality of life on the Moon and provides the means of getting there. In the remaining part of the novel, Dolittle prepares for a lunar journey, decides on his companions, and takes off, unaware that Stubbins, overwhelmed by a desire to travel (a trait he shares with his mentor), has disobeyed orders and become a stowaway. Surviving the rigors of space travel, the Dolittle team, now augmented by Stubbins, lands on the Moon. Seeing an abundance of living plants, the doctor has answered an important question concerning what kind of life is possible on the Moon.

Science fiction elements are paramount in the second part of the moon trilogy, *Doctor Dolittle in the Moon*. Lofting shows Dolittle engaged in several scientific activities: exploring the lunar surface, speculating over the various forms of plant and animal

life encountered, seeking to make sense of the evidence pointing to the presence of other humans, and discerning the principles behind the apparently peaceful and cooperative organization of life on the Moon. Pleased that lunar life eschews violence and disharmony – phenomena of which he is all too aware on Earth – and anxious to learn the reasons, Dolittle makes two important discoveries. One is that the lunar atmosphere allows for astonishing growth and longevity, necessitating some kind of organization. The other is the existence of Otho Bludge, a stone-age artist who was blown off Earth onto the surface of the Moon. Becoming king, Bludge has convinced all living things on the Moon to cooperate and to restrain their tendencies for aggrandizement. The ensuing peace has allowed the kingdom to prosper. Taking care of Bludge's health becomes Dolittle's paramount concern, since he believes Bludge is necessary for stability and peace. He also suspects that, whether he wants to or not, he may have to stay indefinitely on the Moon. The novel ends as Bludge makes it clear that he wants Dolittle to stay as his personal physician, and arranges for Stubbins to be returned to Earth.

Whether or not *Doctor Dolittle in the Moon* is well-crafted fiction, it is an interesting novel. With its depiction of lunar life and society organized on principles different from those on Earth, the novel brings a seriousness and didacticism new to the Dolittle series. The doctor is once more an active protagonist, but he is not a savior who can set matters right because he already has answers or solutions. Instead, he is a learner. As he learns, he gathers further evidence justifying his unhappiness over humanity, which seems incapable of cooperating and living in peace.

Further, *Doctor Dolittle in the Moon* belongs to a small group of early children's fantasies that are a form of children's science fiction. Because it presupposes a real journey to the Moon, depicts alien life, and describes a utopian society, the novel can be considered science fiction. At the same time, because the journey and the existence of lunar life are not scientifically rationalized, one may prefer to categorize the novel as science fantasy. In any case, the novel did play a role in the development of children's science fiction.

Five years passed before Lofting satisfied reader curiosity concerning Dolittle's fate by releasing *Doctor Dolittle's Return* (1933), the last segment of the moon trilogy and the last significant children's book the author saw published before his death. In the first chapters Stubbins and the other family members are looking for a signal on the Moon's sur-

Illustration by Lofting from Doctor Dolittle and the Secret
Lake *(1948)*

face indicating the doctor's return. In the meantime, because money is scarce, Stubbins reorganizes the household and finds outside employment. Finally one night the signal is observed, and shortly after the lunar moth deposits a weary and elongated Dolittle in the garden.

As he gradually adjusts to earth atmosphere and regains his normal size, the doctor shares what he has learned about lunar conditions. Because he longs for time to write up his adventures, Dolittle arranges for his arrest and imprisonment. Unsuccessful in his attempt to find in prison an opportunity to write, he returns home. When Stubbins offers to take over much of the medical practice, the doctor is able to study and experiment with seeds brought back from the Moon. Dolittle's ambition is lofty – "I hope to discover some of the really big Secrets – such as the great length of life up there, almost everlasting life. Yes, perhaps even that itself – with scientific guidance – everlasting life!" In the final scene the doctor is "writing away furiously" while Matthew and Stubbins speculate whether he might succeed in his determination to "set the world to right." Here Lofting seems to be casting Dolittle as the hero who learns and seeks answers not just for learning's sake but to use that learning for the benefit of society.

As a kind of compensation for the dearth of quality work Lofting was producing in these years, personal happiness again materialized when he met

and married Josephine Fricker in 1935 and moved to Topanga, California, where a son, Christopher, was born in 1936. In subsequent years Lofting's health began to deteriorate, a situation paralleled by a decline in his mental and emotional state as he confronted the rising threat, and reality, of war in Europe. During these declining years, however, he began and finished one more Dolittle book, *Doctor Dolittle and the Secret Lake* (1948), but he did not live to see its publication. Lofting died on 27 September 1947 in Santa Monica, California. Additional narratives, *Doctor Dolittle and the Green Canary* and *Doctor Dolittle's Puddleby Adventures* (1952) appeared posthumously but added little to his critical reputation.

The final appearance of Dolittle in a novel of any significance occurs in *Doctor Dolittle and the Secret Lake*. The novel is interesting in spite of the fact that Lofting was unable to meld effectively the two distinct strands in the plot. One strand is a relatively uneventful narrative of domestic affairs and the doctor's decision to embark on one more voyage, this time to locate Mudface, the ancient turtle, and interrogate him about antediluvian times. Mudface's recollections constitute the second plot strand, and in it is perhaps the most intriguing material Lofting ever produced. Unfortunately, a relatively bland style and the use of a narrative frame featuring banter among the Dolittle family as it listens to Mudface's recollections seem inappropriate to the seriousness of the material. Yet stylistic disharmony cannot obscure Lofting's startling mythopoeia, in which he recounts some of the events of the biblical flood from the perspective of the animals caught up in that flood. Included too are a cast of human characters different from those familiar from Genesis and an imaginary setting in Shalba. Located in what is now Africa, Shalba is a land of high civilization and prosperity: because there is plenty of food, no one kills animals for meat. But it is a land where injustice and iniquity reign because its king, Mashtu, seeks to impose his power upon the entire world. In this account Noah has been forced to become a zookeeper in Shalba and is responsible for the turtles.

When torrential rains come – attributed by Mudface to a design he senses but cannot further identify – the turtle seeks to save Eber and Gaza, a young human couple whom he has befriended. The chief motive for "good" behavior Mudface appears to accept is the Golden Rule – do unto others as you would have them do unto you – and not any supernatural sanction or imperative. During the turmoil of the flood and its aftermath, Mudface goes to great lengths to save the young couple, who appear to be the only human survivors except for those, along with a large collection of animals, aboard the ark built by Noah. Under the leadership of elephants and other grass-eating species, the animals organize the rule of animals and, at Mudface's urging, decide to enslave, rather than kill, Eber and Gaza. When the meat eaters overthrow the elephants and wish to kill the humans, Mudface again rescues his friends, transporting them to the new world where the couple begins to establish a new family. Eber and Gaza's attempt at repopulating the world on terms of love and mutual respect between humans and animals has failed.

Doctor Dolittle and the Secret Lake probably reflects its author's pessimism over the outbreak of World War II and its witness to the continuing acceptance of war as the preferred method of settling differences among nations. Actually, the mythopoeic strand of the novel is as pessimistic as any children's book was ever allowed to be at the time. In spite of this the moon trilogy constitutes a plea that society should be grounded in peace, harmony, and respect for all living beings on Earth. The whole point of the entire Dolittle series is to model in miniature a form of utopia. The Dolittle family is an authentic community where white and black, young and old, the privileged and the marginalized, animals and humans, meat eaters and grain eaters all live in peace and harmony.

Lofting's accomplishment is real and meritorious. His legacy encompasses the creation of one of the most memorable characters in children's literature; the shaping of an enticing secondary world children enthusiastically enter; a group of remarkable talking animals; Tommy Stubbins, with whom many young readers have identified and thereby have gone adventuring beyond their dreams; the adopting of a narrative point of view that successfully approximates some of the ways children comprehend the world; and a celebration of the noble idea that disparate peoples and species can live harmoniously.

References:

Edward Blishen, *Hugh Lofting* (London: Bodley Head, 1968);

Margaret Blount, *Animal Land: The Creatures of Children's Fiction* (New York: Morrow, 1975): 198–201;

Eleanor Cameron, *The Green and Burning Tree* (Boston: Little, Brown, 1969): 49–56;

Helen Dean Fish, "Doctor Dolittle, His Life and Work" *Horn Book,* 24 (September–October, 1946): 339–346;

Gary D. Schmidt, *Hugh Lofting* (New York: Twayne, 1992).

Patricia Lynch

(7 June 1898 – 1 September 1972)

Judith Gero John
Southwest Missouri State University

BOOKS: *The Green Dragon* (London: Harrap, 1925);

The Turf-Cutter's Donkey, illustrated by Jack B. Yeats (London: Dent, 1935); republished as *The Donkey Goes Visiting* (New York: Dutton, 1936);

King of the Tinkers, illustrated by Katherine C. Lloyd (New York: Dutton, 1938; London: Dent, 1938);

The Turf-Cutter's Donkey Kicks Up His Heels, illustrated by Eileen Coghlan (New York: Dutton, 1939; London: Dent, 1952);

The Grey Goose of Kilnevin, illustrated by John Keating (London: Dent, 1940; New York: Dutton, 1940);

Fiddler's Quest, illustrated by Isobel Morton-Sale (London: Dent, 1941; New York: Dutton, 1943);

Long Ears: The Story of a Little Grey Donkey, illustrated by Joan Kiddell-Monroe (London: Dent, 1943);

Strangers at the Fair and Other Stories, illustrated by Coghlan (Dublin: Browne & Nolan, 1945; London: Penguin, 1949);

Lisheen at the Valley Farm and Other Stories, by Lynch, Helen Staunton, and Teresa Deevey (Dublin: Gayfield, 1945);

The Cobbler's Apprentice, illustrated by Alfred Kerr (London: Hollis & Carter, 1947);

A Story-Teller's Childhood (London: Dent, 1947; New York: Norton, 1962);

Brogeen of the Stepping Stones, illustrated by Kerr (London: Kerr Cross, 1947);

The Mad O'Haras, illustrated by Elizabeth Rivers (London: Dent, 1948); republished as *Grania of Castle O'Hara* (Boston: L. C. Page, 1952);

The Dark Sailor of Youghal, illustrated by Jerome Sullivan (London: Dent, 1951);

The Boy at the Swinging Lantern, illustrated by Kiddell-Monroe (London: Dent, 1952);

Brogeen Follows the Magic Tune, illustrated by Peggy Fortnum (London: Burke, 1952; New York: Macmillan, 1968);

Delia Daly of Galloping Green, illustrated by Kiddell-Monroe (London: Dent, 1953);

Brogeen and the Green Shoes, illustrated by Fortnum (London: Burke, 1953);

Orla of Burren, illustrated by Kiddell-Monroe (London: Dent, 1954);

Brogeen and the Bronze Lizard, illustrated by Grace Golden (London: Burke, 1954; New York: Macmillan, 1970);

Tinker Boy, illustrated by Harry Kernoff (London: Dent, 1955);

Brogeen and the Princess of Sheen, illustrated by Christopher Brooker (London: Burke, 1955);

The Bookshop on the Quay, illustrated by Fortnum (London: Dent, 1956);

Brogeen and the Lost Castle, illustrated by Brooker (London: Burke, 1956);

Fiona Leaps the Bonfire, illustrated by Fortnum (London: Dent, 1957); republished as *Shane Comes to Dublin* (New York: Criterion, 1958);

Cobbler's Luck, illustrated by Brooker (London: Burke, 1957);

The Old Black Sea Chest: A Story of Bantry Bay, illustrated by Fortnum (London: Dent, 1958);

Brogeen and the Black Enchanter, illustrated by Brooker (London: Burke, 1958);

The Stone House at Kilgobbin, illustrated by Brooker (London: Burke, 1959);

Jinny the Changeling, illustrated by Fortnum (London: Dent, 1959);

The Runaways (Oxford: Blackwell, 1959);

The Lost Fisherman of Carrigmor, illustrated by Brooker (London: Burke, 1960);

Sally from Cork, illustrated by Elizabeth Grant (London: Dent, 1961);

Ryan's Fort, illustrated by Grant (London: Dent, 1961);

The Longest Way Round, illustrated by D. G. Valentine (London: Burke, 1961);

The Golden Caddy, illustrated by Juliette Palmer (London: Dent, 1962);

Frontispiece for The Turf-Cutter's Donkey *(1935), Patricia Lynch's episodic tale of two Irish children and their magical adventures*

Brogeen and the Little Wind, illustrated by Beryl Sanders (London: Burke, 1962);

The House by Lough Neagh, illustrated by Nina Ross (London: Burke, 1963);

Brogeen and the Red Fez, illustrated by Sanders (London: Burke, 1963);

Holiday at Rosquin, illustrated by Mary Shillabeer (London: Dent, 1964);

Guests at the Beech Tree, illustrated by Sanders (London: Burke, 1964);

The Twisted Key and Other Stories, illustrated by Kiddell-Monroe (London: Harrap, 1964);

Mona of the Isle, illustrated by Shillabeer (London: Dent, 1965);

Back of Beyond, illustrated by Susannah Holden (London: Dent, 1966);

The Kerry Caravan, illustrated by James Hunt (London: Dent, 1967).

OTHER: *Knights of God: Stories of the Irish Saints,* collected by Lynch, illustrated by Alfred Kerr (London: Hollis & Carter, 1945; Chicago: Regnery, 1955);

The Seventh Pig and Other Irish Fairy Tales, collected by Lynch, illustrated by Jerome Sullivan (London: Dent, 1950); revised as *The Black Goat of*

Slievemore and Other Irish Tales (London: Dent, 1959);

Tales of Irish Enchantment, collected by Lynch, illustrated by Fergus O'Ryan (Dublin: Clonmore & Reynolds, 1952; London: Burns & Oates, 1952).

Patricia Lynch is especially important in the scope of children's literature for her incorporation of Irish folklore and Celtic magic into her stories for children. Not only did she bring to print many Irish legends, but she also introduced a country and a way of life to children who otherwise might have had no contact with leprechauns, country fairs, or turf fires. Her books of Irish fantasy with her descriptions of the Irish countryside have been translated into French, Gaelic, Dutch, German, Swedish, and Malay.

Married to Richard Michael Fox, also a writer, before her first book was published, Lynch was the daughter of an Irish businessman, Timothy Patrick, and an Irish lace maker and storyteller, Nora Lynch. She published all of her books as either Patricia Lynch or Patricia Nora Lynch. In *A Story-Teller's Childhood* (1947), Lynch recounts being moved from place to place, making and losing friends, losing her father, and watching her mother search for the money she believed he had left (this money eventually paid for Lynch's boarding school). Instead of dwelling on feelings of abandonment and loss, Lynch reflects on this time in her life as giving her the necessary background for collecting stories. Her book explains the variety of locales for her stories – her father had business in Egypt; she attended schools in Ireland, Scotland, England, and Belgium; and she spent time in Paris.

In addition to her travels outside Ireland, Lynch also lived in several different locations within Ireland and fell in love with the Irish country life. It is her recollections of country fairs and her preservation in print of the rustic lifestyle that makes her books important as a source of tales of Ireland as a place of charm, leprechauns, and legends. A member of P.E.N. and a delegate to the P.E.N. congress in Vienna, Lynch received the 1947 Silver Medal of Aonac Tailteann, a London Junior Book Club Award, and the 1941 Irish Women's Writers' Club award for her writing. In 1967 she was elected to the Irish Academy of Letters.

As is the case of many storytellers, Lynch has basically one story, but by changing the locale, the characters, and the magic, she is able to be entertaining in a variety of ways. Frequently reliving the experiences of her own childhood, Lynch's characters are usually young children who leave their homes and have amazing adventures. Sometimes the children are miserable at home and must find new homes; sometimes they reunite with their scattered families; often they have magical adventures or meet one or more of the Fair Folk of Irish legend.

Although her first book, *The Green Dragon* (1925), was not overly successful, *The Turf-Cutter's Donkey* (1935) was a critical success. Eileen and Seamus, the young children of a turf cutter, have amazing adventures after a leprechaun repairs Eileen's boots and instills in them the power that allows her to jump great distances. An episodic collection of stories connected by characters, *The Turf-Cutter's Donkey* includes Eileen and Seamus in such situations as confronting some tinkers; meeting an eagle looking for a shamrock that Eileen possesses; meeting the ancient hero Finn MacCool and the men of Fianna; and getting pulled into a picture book.

The Turf-Cutter's Donkey was initially a serial in *The Irish Press* and illustrated by G. Altendorf; Jack B. Yeats illustrated the book version. A winner of the London Junior Book Award, this book exemplifies the mixture of homespun Irish life and Celtic legend that is the hallmark of most of Lynch's writing. She returns to the characters Eileen and Seamus in several of her other books, including *The Donkey Goes Visiting* (1936) and *The Turf-Cutter's Donkey Kicks Up His Heels* (1939). Most of the motifs that are familiar in Lynch's work can be found in these early books. Characters – Princess Goldilocks, bands of tinkers, a leprechaun and his magic pig, the silver man and his airplane, and mythic Irish heroes and settings – bogs, country fairs, and dusty roads – reappear throughout Lynch's works. Lynch's stories usually have happy endings and incorporate the idea that all roads (and all children) will eventually reach home.

King of the Tinkers (1938) focuses on Miheal Fahy's adventures with a band of tinkers. Along the way he is helped by a girl named Nora, an old woman, a changeling baby, and a mysterious higgler named Red Lantry. Miheal is trying to recover his possessions stolen by the tinkers (especially the fiddle that belonged to his father), and Nora is looking for a home. The value given by the depicted culture to the man (woman, boy, or girl) who can play the fiddle is clear in this book and becomes another important key to Lynch's books. In this case, Yellow Handkerchief, head of a tinker band and a recurring character in Lynch's works, believes that the ability to play Miheal's father's fiddle will give him the advantage he needs to become king of the tinkers. Through Nora's quest and the thwarted stops in the secret valley of Finn MacCool, a distinct yearning to belong emerges. In the end Nora is welcomed by Miheal's mother and loved as a daughter in her rustic country home. She is finally safe and has a place to belong. While the adventure of the stories is treated as a lark, this book tells the story of a child without a home and a great desire to belong. There is excitement in the traveling life, and there are wonderful people on the road, but each traveler needs to go home, and each child needs to belong.

The Grey Goose of Kilnevin (1940) and *Fiddler's Quest* (1941) also take up this theme of needing a place to belong, but the books vary in style and delivery. *The Grey Goose of Kilnevin* chooses to go on her journey, and she eventually helps Sheila find her grandfather and helps her grandfather find his memory and his home. Complete with animal helpers, a wicked guardian, and a talking scarecrow, Sheila travels to the legendary home of Bridgie Swallow to bring home butter.

Fiddler's Quest tells a similar story of a search for a grandfather, but apart from some happy coincidences, there is no magic other than the spell of the story itself. Ethne Cadogan is pulled out of

Frontispiece and title page for Lynch's story of Ethne Cadogan's search for her grandfather (Lilly Library, Indiana University)

school by her father and left at a ship that will take her to Dublin in the hopes that she will find her grandfather. Miles Cadogan, the father, leaves for America to make his fortune and does not have time to accompany his daughter in her search. Having no head for details, Miles assumes that everyone will care for the little girl. Sheila's claim to fame is her ability to play the fiddle. Her quest is to find her grandfather. The grandfather is King Cadogan of Inishcoppal Island, one of the great Irish fiddlers, and Sheila hopes to please him with her accomplishments. The barriers to completing her quest are many and great. She becomes involved with some Irish rebels, including Neil Desmond, and finds she must flee with the "Widda" Rafferty and her family when they help Neil. Finally they meet King Cadogan, and Sheila finds the family she has sought.

Another not so childlike aspect of Lynch's work is her concern for the families of the men forced to leave Ireland in search of work. In this story, Tim Rafferty finally writes his wife after many long years of silence to tell her he is coming home with one thousand dollars.

Knights of God: Stories of the Irish Saints (1945), *Strangers at the Fair and Other Stories* (1945), and *Lisheen at the Valley Farm and Other Stories* (1945) came from the storehouse of myths and legends that Lynch had been hoarding since her childhood. It is difficult to tell which of her stories are authentic Irish tales and which originated with Lynch. *Knights of God* is a collection of the stories of some of the Irish saints, and authentic or not, the other collections owe their beginnings to the folklore of Ireland.

Two years later, in 1947, Lynch produced three books that define and reserve her place in the worlds of both Irish literature and children's books. *The Cobbler's Apprentice* received the Silver Medal at the Aonac Tailteann festival. Lynch's autobiography, *A Story-Teller's Childhood,* offered adult readers and critics a blueprint by which to examine all of Lynch's works. The book is Lynch's way of thanking all of the people on whose kindness she was forced by circumstance to depend; of showing off Irish resilience and camaraderie; and of fulfilling her own search for a home and a place to belong. Her wish-fulfilling fantasies of fathers coming home, of untold wealth being misplaced but eventually recovered, and of returning to the Irish countryside to live must have certainly grown out of her childhood. And yet, when she writes about it, these things become secondary to the adventures she has and the friends she makes.

While this book is not often included among her writings for children, the story is similar to many of her children's stories but told in a more authentic form. The child alone can be resilient, strong, and happy and can eventually find a home. As in her other books, deep-rooted feelings of abandonment and loss take a backseat to her conviction that traveling is exciting and that everyone will eventually find home.

Stories that seem like fun as fiction suddenly take on shades of sadness when read in the light of Lynch's autobiography. The third book to appear during 1947 is the first of Lynch's Brogeen books, *Brogeen of the Stepping Stones*. Before she died in 1972, Lynch completed thirteen books featuring Brogeen the Leprechaun: *Brogeen Follows the Magic Tune* (1952); *Brogeen and the Green Shoes* (1953); *Brogeen and the Bronze Lizard* (1954); *Brogeen and the Princess of Sheen* (1955); *Brogeen and the Lost Castle* (1956); *Cobbler's Luck* (1957), a series of short stories; *Brogeen and the Black Enchanter* (1958); *The Stone House at Kilgobbin* (1959); *The Lost Fisherman of Carrigmor* (1960); *The Longest Way Round* (1961); *Brogeen and the Little Wind* (1962); and *Brogeen and the Red Fez* (1963).

The books in this series are her most often translated books. By trade Brogeen is a shoemaker — as are all leprechauns — but Brogeen loves to travel and visit the world of humans. He has obligations as the best shoemaker at the fairy Fort of Sheen, but he is also allowed (sometimes required) to visit the outside world. He collects companions; sometimes he has a pig, but more often he is accompanied by a tiny elephant named Trud. In several stories he is bothered by a strange man named the Black Enchanter, who turns out to be neither black nor too much of an enchanter. The Brogeen books offer many readers a chance to view Ireland's fairyland and long for a brief visit to the Fort of Sheen.

The Mad O'Haras (1948) is another of Lynch's successful but rare attempts to examine Irish life without resorting to magic or flights of fancy. In the book Grania O'Hara discovers that her missing mother is alive but that they have been separated out of her mother's desire to protect her from the O'Hara madness. The O'Haras were tinkers, and Kevin, Grania's father, had tried to set down roots. When he died, the O'Hara madness (primarily their temper and stubbornness) alienated them from the rest of the community. Grania, an artist of some talent, joins her mother and discovers both the problems and the freedom associated with her new life. Although Kevin's brothers feel they must go away in order to earn a living, the community also begins to accept the family's presence, so that these traveling tinkers, like so many of Lynch's travelers, might eventually find a home.

The Seventh Pig and Other Irish Fairy Tales (1950) is another collection of authentic Irish stories, this set dedicated to Mrs. Hennessy, one of Lynch's early caregivers who was herself an Irish storyteller. The close association between the Irish "folk" and the supernatural inhabitants of the countryside who are a part of each of these tales explains why such occurrences happen naturally in much of Lynch's work. Throughout her writing, Lynch includes collections of short stories; some are original, and some have been collected, but her interest in these stories explains, in part, her style of writing. Although she had been during her life affiliated with newspapers, the episodic nature of most of her work owes much to these short tales of enchantment.

While Lynch continued writing a variety of fantasy stories, two stories exemplify the best of what Lynch was able to accomplish. *The Bookshop on the Quay* (1956) borrows heavily, as most of her stories do, from the experiences of Lynch's childhood. Shane Madden is orphaned by the deaths of his parents and abandoned by his Uncle Tim, a good-hearted drover. Leaving his Uncle Joseph and Aunt Maureen because he is not happy and is tired of waiting for Uncle Tim to return, Shane makes his way to Dublin in hopes of finding Tim. In Dublin, Shane is taken in by the O'Clerys, who own a bookstore and allow him to work for them. Shane finally finds his Uncle Tim, but he feels he has found a home working in the shop full of stories, and he is asked to return after he has visited Uncle Joseph and Aunt Maureen.

As charming as Lynch's books of magic are, her power as a storyteller rests with her real experiences. She can reconstruct the fear, the hunger, the weariness, and the hopes of a child alone far better than anything else she does. Her memories of her own childhood helped to create so many books of hope and fear and longing.

Still, her stories of magic and enchantment are Lynch's trademark, and *Jinny the Changeling* (1959) is effective in turning all of the fear and frightened longings of childhood into a magical journey of success. The Clerys find a baby in a clump of bushes, and almost immediately their lives and luck begin to change. The father of the family has disappeared, and so the quest to find a father and become a family is taken up once again. Jinny proves to be a fairy's child, and Mr. Clery has been working for the Queen of the Hills, who finally rewards him generously and sends him home to his family.

Fantasy, frequently an escape medium for those who have suffered great loss, is able to restore, in part, what Lynch lost in the real world. Her tendency to straddle the line between the world of reality and the world of fantasy reflects her hopes of a father who might return from the land of the dead (perhaps he is trapped inside a fairy fort), a mother who will spend time with her daughter instead of hunting for a fortune, and a brother who wants to go exploring with his little sister. But these fears and concerns that hover in the background of Lynch's stories are the dark images that haunt many children. The fear of being left alone, abandoned, and hungry are the fears that haunt childhood. Lynch's books frequently admit that life is hard but that even if the worst happens, there are wonderful people to meet and exciting adventures to be had on the road to a new home.

Bessie Marchant

(12 December 1862 – 10 November 1941)

Donald R. Hettinga
Calvin College

BOOKS: *The Old House by the Water* (London: Religious Tract Society, 1894);

In the Cradle of the North Wind (Edinburgh: Nimmo, 1896);

Weasel Tim (London: Culley, 1897);

Among the Torches of the Andes (Edinburgh: Nimmo, 1898); revised as *On the Track* (London: Sampson Low, 1924);

The Bonded Three, illustrated by William Rainey (London: Blackie, 1898);

Yuppie (London: Culley, 1898);

The Girl Captives, illustrated by Rainey (London: Blackie, 1899);

The Humbling of Mark Lester (London: Simpkin Marshall, 1899);

Winning His Way (London: Gall & Inglis, 1899);

The Half-Moon Girl; or The Rajah's Daughter (London: Partridge, 1899);

Tell-Tale-Tit (London: Culley, 1899);

The Ghost of Rock Grange (London: S. P. C. K., 1900);

Held at Ransom (London: Blackie, 1900);

Cicely Frome, The Captain's Daughter (Edinburgh: Nimmo, 1900);

In the Toils of the Tribesmen (London: Gall & Inglis, 1900);

From the Scourge of the Tongue (London: Melrose, 1900);

Among Hostile Hordes (London: Gall & Inglis, 1901);

The Fun o' the Fair (London: Culley, 1901);

In Perilous Times (London: Gall & Inglis, 1901);

That Dreadful Boy! (London: Culley, 1901);

Tommy's Trek (London: Blackie, 1901);

Three Girls on a Ranch [in Morocco, in Mexico], 3 volumes, illustrated by Rainey (London: Blackie, 1901–1911);

The Bertrams of Ladywell, illustrated by John Jellicoe (London: Wells Gardner, 1902);

A Brave Little Cousin (London: S. P. C. K., 1902);

Fleckie (London: Blackie, 1902);

The House of Brambling Minster (London: S. P. C. K., 1902);

Leonard's Temptation (London: Culley, 1902);

The Secret of the Everglades (London: Blackie, 1902; New York: Mershon, 1915);

A Heroine of the Sea (London: Blackie, 1903);

Lost on the Saguenay (London: Collins, 1903);

The Owner of Rushcote (London: Culley, 1903);

The Captives of the Kaid (London: Collins, 1904);

Chupsie (London: Culley, 1904);

The Girls of Wakenside (London: Collins, 1904);

Hope's Tryst (London: Blackie, 1904);

Yew Tree Farm (London: S. P. C. K., 1904);

Caspar's Find (London: Culley, 1905);

A Daughter of the Ranges, illustrated by A. A. Dixon (London: Blackie, 1905);

The Debt of the Damerals (London: Clarke, 1905);

The Mysterious City, illustrated by W. S. Stacey (London: S. P. C. K., 1905);

The Queen of Shindy Flat, illustrated by Charles Sheldon (London: Wells Gardner, 1905);

Athabasca Bill (London: S. P. C. K., 1906);

The Girl of the Fortunate Isles, illustrated by Paul Hardy (London: Blackie, 1906);

Kenealy's Ride (London: Gall & Inglis, 1906);

Maisie's Discovery, illustrated by R. Tod (London: Collins, 1906);

Uncle Greg's Man Hunt (London: Culley, 1906);

Darling of Sandy Point, illustrated by Harold Piffard (London: S. P. C. K., 1907);

Juliette, The Mail Carrier, illustrated by Tod (London: Collins, 1907);

The Mystery of the Silver Run (London: Wells Gardner, 1907);

No Ordinary Girl, illustrated by Frances Ewan (London: Blackie, 1907; New York: Caldwell, 1911);

Sisters of Silver Creek, illustrated by Robert Hope (London: Blackie, 1907);

The Apple Lady, illustrated by G. Soper (London: Collins, 1908);

A Courageous Girl, illustrated by Rainey (London: Blackie, 1908);

Daughters of the Dominion (London: Blackie, 1908);

Rolf the Rebel, illustrated by Stacey (London: S. P. C. K., 1908);

An Island Heroine, illustrated by W. H. Margetson (London: Collins, 1909);

Jenny's Adventure (London: Butcher, 1909);

The Adventures of Phyllis, illustrated by F. Whiting (London: Cassell, 1910);

The Black Cockatoo, illustrated by Lancelot Speed (London: Religious Tract Society, 1910);

A Countess from Canada, illustrated by Cyrus Cuneo (London: Blackie, 1910);

Greta's Domain, illustrated by Rainey (London: Blackie, 1910);

Molly of One Tree Bend (London: Butcher, 1910);

The Deputy Boss, illustrated by Oscar Wilson (London: S. P. C. K., 1910);

The Ferry House Girls, illustrated by W. R. S. Stott (London: Blackie, 1911);

Redwood Ranch, illustrated by Piffard (London: S. P. C. K., 1911);

A Girl of the Northland, illustrated by N. Tenison (London: Hodder & Stoughton, 1912);

His Great Surrender, illustrated by Gordon Browne (London: S. P. C. K., 1912);

A Princess of Servia, illustrated by Rainey (London: Blackie, 1912);

The Sibyl of St. Pierre, illustrated by Rainey (London: Wells Gardner, 1912);

The Western Scout, illustrated by Stacey (London: S. P. C. K., 1912);

The Youngest Sister, illustrated by Rainey (London: Blackie, 1912);

The Adventurous Seven, illustrated by Stott (London: Blackie, 1913);

The Heroine of the Ranch, illustrated by Cuneo (London: Blackie, 1914);

Denver Wilson's Double, illustrated by W. Douglas Almond (London: Blackie, 1914);

Helen of the Black Mountain (London: Blackie, 1914);

The Loyalty of Hester Hope, illustrated by Rainey (London: Blackie, 1914);

A Mysterious Inheritance (London: Blackie, 1914);

A Girl and a Caravan (London: Blackie, 1915);

Joyce Harrington's Trust (London: Blackie, 1915);

Molly Angels' Adventures (London: Blackie, 1915);

A Canadian Farm Mystery; or, Pam the Pioneer (London: Blackie, 1916);

A Girl Munition Worker (London: Blackie, 1916);

The Unknown Island (London: Blackie, 1916);

The Gold-Marked Charm (London: Blackie, 1917);

Lois in Charge; or, A Girl of Grit, illustrated by Cuneo (London: Blackie, 1917);

A V.A.D. in Salonika (London: Blackie, 1917);

Cynthia Wins, illustrated by John E. Sutcliffe (London: Blackie, 1918);

A Dangerous Mission, illustrated by Wal Paget (London: Blackie, 1918);

Norah to the Rescue, illustrated by Stott (London: Blackie, 1919);

A Transport Girl in France (London: Blackie, 1919);

Sally Makes Good, illustrated by Leo Bates (London: Blackie, 1920);

The Girl of the Pampas (London: Blackie, 1921);

Island Born, illustrated by Bates (London: Blackie, 1921);

The Mistress of Purity Gap (London: Cassell, 1921; New York: Funk & Wagnalls, 1922);

Harriet Goes a-Roaming (London: Blackie, 1922);

The Fortunes of Prue (London: Ward Lock, 1923);

Rachel Out West, illustrated by Henry Coller (London: Blackie, 1923);

A Bid for Safety (London: Ward Lock, 1924);

Diana Carries On (London: Nelson, 1924);

The Most Popular Girl in the School (London: Partridge, 1924);

Sylvia's Secret, illustrated by W. E. Wightman (London: Blackie, 1924);

By Honour Bound (London: Nelson, 1925);

Her Own Kin (London: Blackie, 1925);

To Save Her School, illustrated by H. L. Bacon (London: Partridge, 1925);

Delmayne's Adventures (London: Collins, 1925);

Cousin Peter's Money (London: Sheldon, 1926);

Di the Dauntless, illustrated by Wightman (London: Blackie, 1926);

Millicent Gwent, Schoolgirl (London: Warne, 1926);

Molly in the West, illustrated by F. E. Hiley (London: Blackie, 1927);

The Two New Girls (London: Warne, 1927);

Glenallan's Daughters (London: Nelson, 1928);

Lucie's Luck, illustrated by Hiley (London: Blackie, 1928);

The Bannister Twins, illustrated by E. Brier (London: Nelson, 1929);

Hilda Holds On, illustrated by Hiley (London: Blackie, 1929);

How Nell Scored (London: Nelson, 1929);

Laurel the Leader (London: Blackie, 1930);

Cuckoo of the Log Raft (London: Newnes, 1931);

Two on Their Own, illustrated by Hiley (London: Blackie, 1931);

The Homesteader Girl, illustrated by V. Cooley (London: Nelson, 1932);

Silla the Seventh (London: Newnes, 1932);

Jane Fills the Breach, illustrated by Hiley (London: Blackie, 1933);

Illustration by Paul Hardy from The Girl of the Fortunate
Isles *(1906)*

Deborah's Find, illustrated by Coller (London:
    Blackie, 1933);
The Courage of Katrine (London: Warne, 1934);
Erica's Ranch (London: Blackie, 1934);
Lesbia's Little Blunder (London: Warne, 1934);
Hosea's Girl (London: Hutchinson, 1934);
Felicity's Fortune (London: Blackie, 1936);
Nancy Afloat (London: Nelson, 1936);
A Daughter of the Desert (London: Blackie, 1937);
Anna of Tenterford, illustrated by J. A. May (London:
    Blackie, 1938);
Miss Wilmer's Gang, illustrated by May (London:
    Blackie, 1938);
Waifs of Woollamoo (London: Warne, 1938);
A Girl Undaunted; or, The Honey Queen, illustrated by
    May (London: Blackie, 1939);
Marta the Mainstay (London: Blackie, 1940);
Two of a Kind (London: Blackie, 1941);
The Triumphs of Three (London: Blackie, 1942).

Borneo, Greece, Canada, Bolivia, Mexico, France, Argentina, Australia, Serbia, the western United States — Bessie Marchant took her readers on adventures all around the globe in her more than 130 novels. Yet for all the varieties of settings, the worlds of Marchant's novels appear remarkably the same, for readers see these settings through the eyes of Marchant's female heroines, the vision of the only slightly modern British woman.

Certainly that vision comes out of Marchant's own development. Born in 1862 in Pentham in Kent, Bessie Marchant received a typical Victorian education at private schools. She married Jabez Ambrose Comfort at age thirty-seven. The couple had one daughter together and lived in Charlbury, Oxfordshire, where Marchant wrote most of her adventures. Her first novel, *The Old House by the Water* (1894), was published before she married, but it was as a married woman that her career blossomed. A prolific writer, she published an average of three to four novels per year between 1899 and 1940, virtually all of them marketed as "books for girls."

Marchant's early novel *The Half-Moon Girl; or, The Rajah's Daughter* (1899) employs motifs that characterize Marchant's fiction for girls. Half of the plot is set in Borneo, though as is typical throughout Marchant's work, that setting is significant mainly for the exotic contrast it presents to British life and culture. Borneo is a place that produces specimens for British curiosity, and snakes, monkeys, and natives are killed off with similar dispassion. The principal indigenous characteristic of the Rajah's daughter is her half-moon tattoo; otherwise she displays the virtues of a polite young Englishwoman. She is useful and subservient to the English naturalist who befriends her, yet she is somehow less human than her British counterparts. By a contrivance of plotting, the Rajah's daughter is wearing the skin of an orangutan when the British expedition first spots her, and in a somewhat comic moment they think they have discovered the missing link in the evolutionary chain. Their mistake, however, reveals something of Marchant's attitude toward this native character: her main function in the plot is to deliver a treasure to a disinherited, but virtuous, Englishwoman. After she does so, the Rajah's daughter dies, an event in striking contrast to the numerous sick westerners of other novels who almost always make miraculous returns from the brink of death.

The real focus of this and many novels is the inheritance of a young woman. Marchant shows a significant sympathy for the plight of her gender under the conventions of property law. Here a young Englishwoman is endangered by the idiosyncratic will of her uncle until the surprising will of the British naturalist in Borneo provides for her by leaving her an enormous diamond. The scenario appears repeatedly. In *A Mysterious Inheritance* (1914), for example, three sisters in western Canada begin living on an inheritance from an uncle only to discover that his son is still alive and that their base of income is threatened.

Marchant uses the situation of these sisters to develop virtues that consistently appear in her characters: honesty and self-reliance. When the sisters discover the possible existence of their cousin, they immediately notify their solicitor of that fact and set off to begin a business of their own — a butter factory. When, through some clever twists of the plot, the sisters receive both the inheritance and the factory, Marchant's point is clear: honesty pays off. Consequently Marchant presents characters who are honest even if their honesty reflects poorly on them. There is an awkward moment, for example, when the heroine of *A V.A.D. in Salonika* (1917) comes face to face with the aunt she has been snubbing because the aunt takes in roomers; yet the heroine can do nothing but be honest. When she explains her supercilious motives to her aunt, her aunt forgives her, and the heroine learns the lesson that Marchant intended.

Women are weak, yet capable, in these novels, and in that paradox contemporary readers can see something of the flux that women's roles were in during the first part of the twentieth century. Again and again female characters are stranded because they may not in themselves make significant decisions about property or some aspects of lifestyle. In *A Girl of the Northland* (1912) a mother and three sisters are impoverished even though the family owns land made instantly valuable by the discovery of copper; because the male of the family is not home, they cannot sell or mine the land. In that instance, however, the women prove themselves to be perfectly capable of providing for themselves in a harsh frontier environment.

In some instances, however, societal mores are not to blame for the apparent frailty of the heroines. Some make themselves seemingly inadequate through self-pity and self-indulgence. Several heroines, when confronted with an urgent decision or an emergency, wonder to themselves why they are women when the task before them seems so obviously to cry out for a man. One such heroine, Joan, the protagonist of *A V.A.D. in Salonika,* overcomes her feelings of inadequacy to save a man who has been crushed by a landslide, but she immediately slips back into a feminine stereotype. When the object of her rescue asks her to hurry to his cottage to take care of some important papers, Joan feels his request impertinent and pauses first to purchase a new hat and gloves. As a result the papers, which later turn out to contain military secrets, are stolen by a German spy, and the man's life is ruined. Marchant clearly intends her readers to eschew such foibles, a point that is underlined by how she reshapes Joan in the conclusion of the novel. Joan, who is serving as a volunteer nurse in Greece, proves that she is a better motorcycle rider and mechanic than any of the men in the military unit, and she uses her skills to identify a spy and to save the unit from betrayal. Through this and other incidents Marchant wanted her readers to value self-reliance and independence for women, but she did not feel secure enough about the values of her readers to create characters who were consistently strong.

Whatever her motives, Marchant's readers could not have taken her novels seriously. They are at best escapist melodramas, filled with outrageous coincidences, offering the young women who read them safe, uplifting adventures that seemed exotic but which were, in actuality, not at all far from home.

John Masefield

(1 June 1878 – 12 May 1967)

Susan R. Gannon
Pace University

See also the Masefield entries in *DLB 10: Modern British Dramatists, 1900–1945; DLB 19: British Poets, 1880–1914*; and *DLB 153: Late-Victorian and Edwardian British Novelists, First Series.*

BOOKS: *Salt-Water Ballads* (London: Richards, 1902; New York: Macmillan, 1913);

Ballads (London: Elkin Mathews, 1903);

A Mainsail Haul (London: Elkin Mathews, 1905; enlarged edition, London: Elkin Mathews, 1913; New York: Macmillan, 1913);

Sea Life in Nelson's Time (London: Methuen, 1905);

On the Spanish Main (London: Methuen, 1906);

A Tarpaulin Muster (London: Richards, 1907; New York: Dodge, 1908);

Captain Margaret: A Romance (London: Richards, 1908; Philadelphia: Lippincott, 1909);

Multitude and Solitude (London: Richards, 1909; New York: Kennerley, 1910);

The Tragedy of Nan and Other Plays (New York: Kennerley, 1909; London: Richards, 1909);

The Tragedy of Pompey the Great (London: Sidgwick & Jackson, 1910; New York: Macmillan, 1910);

Ballads and Poems (London: Elkin Mathews, 1910);

Martin Hyde, The Duke's Messenger (Boston: Little, Brown, 1910; London: Wells, Gardner, Darton, 1910);

A Book of Discoveries (London: Wells, Gardner, Darton, 1910; New York: Stokes, 1910);

Lost Endeavour (London: Nelson, 1910; New York: Macmillan, 1917);

My Faith in Woman Suffrage (London: Woman's Press, 1910);

The Street of To-Day (London: Dent, 1911; New York: Dutton, 1911);

Jim Davis (London: Wells, Gardner, Darton, 1911; New York: Stokes, 1912);

The Street of Today (London: Dent, 1911; New York: Dutton, 1911);

William Shakespeare (London: Williams & Norgate, 1911; New York: Holt, 1911);

John Masefield

The Everlasting Mercy (London: Sidgwick & Jackson, 1911; Portland, Maine: Smith & Sale, 1911);

Jim Davis (London: Wells, Gardner & Darton, 1911; New York: Stokes, 1912);

The Everlasting Mercy and The Widow in the Bye Street (New York: Macmillan, 1912);

The Widow in the Bye Street (London: Sidgwick & Jackson, 1912);

170

The Story of a Round-House and Other Poems (New York: Macmillan, 1912);

The Daffodil Fields (New York: Macmillan, 1913; London: Heinemann, 1913);

Dauber: a Poem (London: Heinemann, 1913);

Philip the King and Other Poems (London: Heinemann, 1914; New York: Macmillan, 1914);

Job M. Synge: A Few Personal Recollections, With Biographical Notes (Churchtown, Dundrum: Cuala Press, 1915; New York: Macmillan, 1915);

The Faithful: A Tragedy in Three Acts (London: Heinemann, 1915; New York: Macmillan, 1915);

Good Friday: A Dramatic Poem (New York: Macmillan, 1915); republished as *Good Friday: A Play in Verse* (Letchworth, Hertfordshire: Garden City Press, 1916);

Good Friday and Other Poems (New York: Macmillan, 1916);

Sonnets (New York: Macmillan, 1916);

Sonnets and Poems (Letchworth, Hertfordshire: Garden City Press, 1916);

The Locked Chest; The Sweeps of Ninety-Eight (Letchworth, Hertfordshire: Garden City Press, 1916; New York: Macmillan, 1916);

Gallipoli (London: Heinemann, 1916; New York: Macmillan, 1916);

Lollingdon Downs and Other Poems (New York: Macmillan, 1917); republished as *Lollingdon Downs and Other Poems, With Sonnets* (London: Heinemann, 1917);

The Old Front Line (London: Heinemann, 1917; New York: Macmillan, 1917); republished as *The Old Front Line, or, the Beginning of the Battle of the Somme* (London: Heinemann, 1917);

Rosas (New York: Macmillan, 1918);

The War and the Future (New York: Macmillan, 1918);

Collected Poems and Plays, 2 volumes (New York: Macmillan, 1918);

A Poem and Two Plays (London: Heinemann, 1918);

St. George and the Dragon (London: Heinemann, 1919);

The Battle of the Somme (London: Heinemann, 1919);

Reynard the Fox: or, The Ghost Heath Run (New York: Macmillan, 1919; London: Heinemann, 1919);

Enslaved and Other Poems (London: Heinemann, 1920; New York: Macmillan, 1920);

Right Royal (New York: Heinemann, 1920; London: Heinemann, 1920);

King Cole (London: Heinemann, 1921; New York: Macmillan, 1921);

The Dream (London: Heinemann, 1922; New York: Macmillan, 1922);

Melloney Holtspur (London: Heinemann, 1922; New York: Macmillan, 1922);

King Cole and Other Poems (London: Heinemann, 1923); republished as *King Cole, The Dream, and Other Poems* (New York: Macmillan, 1923);

The Taking of Helen (London: Heinemann, 1923; New York: Macmillan, 1923);

A King's Daughter: A Tragedy in Verse (New York: Macmillan, 1923; London: Heinemann, 1923);

The Collected Poems of John Masefield, 2 volumes (London: Heinemann, 1923);

Recent Prose (London: Heinemann, 1924; revised, 1932; New York: Macmillan, 1933);

Sard Harker (London: Heinemann, 1924; New York: Macmillan, 1924);

The Trial of Jesus (London: Heinemann, 1925);

Collected Works, 4 volumes (New York: Macmillan, 1925);

Odtaa (New York: Macmillan, 1926; London: Heinemann, 1926);

Tristan and Isolt: A Play in Verse (London: Heinemann, 1927; New York: Macmillan, 1927);

The Midnight Folk (London: Heinemann, 1927; New York: Macmillan, 1927);

The Coming of Christ (New York: Macmillan, 1928; London: Heinemann, 1928);

Midsummer Night and other tales in Verse (London: Heinemann, 1928; New York: Macmillan, 1928);

Easter: a Play for Singers (New York: Macmillan, 1929; London: Heinemann, 1929);

The Hawbucks (London: Heinemann, 1929; New York: Macmillan, 1929);

The Wanderer of Liverpool (London: Heinemann, 1930; New York: Macmillan, 1930);

Poetry Essays (London: Heinemann, 1931);

Minnie Maylow's Story and Other Tales and Scenes (London: Heinemann, 1931; New York: Macmillan, 1931);

A Tale of Troy (London: Heinemann, 1932; New York: Macmillan, 1932);

The End and Beginning (London: Heinemann, 1933; New York: Macmillan, 1933);

The Bird of Dawning (London: Heinemann, 1933; New York: Macmillan, 1933);

The Taking of the Gry (London: Heinemann, 1934; New York: Macmillan, 1934);

The Box of Delights; or, When the Wolves Were Running (London: Heinemann, 1935; New York: Macmillan, 1935);

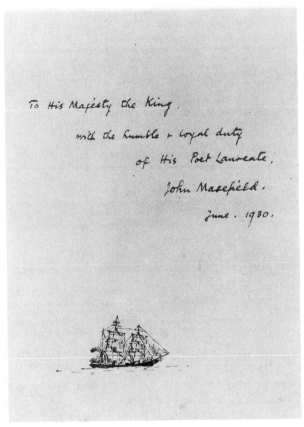
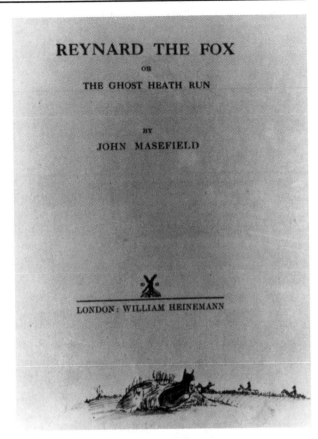

Inscription and title page from the copy of the verse drama presented to King George V (Windsor Castle Library, by permission of Her Majesty the Queen)

Victorious Troy; or, The Hurrying Angel (London: Heinemann, 1935; New York: Macmillan, 1935);

Plays, 2 volumes (London: Heinemann, 1936);

A Letter from Pontus and Other Verse (London: Heinemann, 1936; New York: Macmillan, 1936);

Eggs and Baker (London: Heinemann, 1936; New York: Macmillan, 1936);

The Square Peg; or, The Gun Fella (London: Heinemann, 1937; New York: Macmillan, 1937);

Dead Ned (New York: Macmillan, 1938; London: Heinemann, 1938);

Some Verses to Some Germans (London: Heinemann, 1939; New York: Macmillan, 1939);

Live and Kicking Ned (London: Heinemann, 1939; New York: Macmillan, 1939);

Basilissa: A Tale of the Empress Theodora (London: Heinemann, 1940; New York: Macmillan, 1940);

Some Memories of W. B. Yeats (New York: Macmillan, 1940);

In the Mill (London: Heinemann, 1941; New York: Macmillan, 1941);

Conquer: A Tale of the Nika Rebellion in Byzantium (London: Heinemann, 1941; New York: Macmillan, 1941);

The Nine Days Wonder (London: Heinemann, 1941; New York: Macmillan, 1941);

Guatama the Enlightened and Other Verse (London: Heinemann, 1941; New York: Macmillan, 1941);

A Generation Risen, by Masefield and Edward Seago (London: Collins, 1942);

Natalie Maisie and Pavilastukay: Two Tales in Verse (London: Heinemann, 1942; New York: Macmillan, 1944);

Wonderings: Between One and Six Years (London: Heinemann, 1943; New York: Macmillan, 1943);

New Chum (London: Heinemann, 1944; New York: Macmillan, 1945);

Thanks Before Going (London: Heinemann, 1946); enlarged as *Thanks Before Going with Other Gratitude for Old Delight including A Macbeth Production and Various Papers Not Before Printed* (London: Heinemann, 1947; New York: Macmillan, 1947);

A Book of Pooth Sorts (London: Heinemann, 1947);

Badon Parchments (London: Heinemann, 1947);

A Play of St. George (London: Heinemann, 1948; New York: Macmillan, 1948);

On the Hill (London: Heinemann, 1949; New York: Macmillan, 1949);

St. Katherine of Ledbury and Other Ledbury Poems (London: Macmillan, 1951);

So Long to Learn: Chapters of an Autobiography (London: Heinemann, 1952; New York: Macmillan, 1952);

The Bluebells and Other Verse (London: Heinemann, 1961; New York: Macmillan, 1961);

Old Raiger and Other Verse (London: Heinemann, 1964; New York: Macmillan, 1965);

In Glad Thanksgiving (London: Heinemann, 1966; New York: Macmillan, 1967);

Grace before Ploughing: Fragments of Autobiography (London: Heinemann, 1966; New York: Macmillan, 1966).

Today John Masefield is best known for his poetry, especially for his *Salt-Water Ballads* (1902) and for having been Poet Laureate of England from 1930 to 1967. But Masefield produced an amazingly wide and diverse body of work during a long career, including plays, short stories, historical studies, novels, memoirs, and a few memorable books for children. Outstanding among Masefield's children's books are two fresh and original fantasies, *The Midnight Folk* (1927) and *The Box of Delights; or, When the Wolves Were Running* (1935). But he also wrote a couple of historical adventure yarns for younger readers, *Martin Hyde, The Duke's Messenger* (1910) and *Jim Davis* (1911), as well as *A Book of Discoveries,* (1910) a rambling account of how two boys learn to investigate the natural history of their country neighborhood. Some of Masefield's adventure fiction for the general reader has always been read by younger readers, and his novels about Ned Mansell, *Dead Ned* (1938) and *Live and Kicking Ned* (1939), and the stories *The Bird of Dawning* (1933) and *Lost Endeavour* (1910) have been published in editions aimed at older children and adolescents.

Masefield was born in Ledbury, Herefordshire, on 1 June 1878. When he was very young, his family lived in a Victorian house with a garden and an orchard. His first six years seem to have been spent in a paradisal world in which his creative imagination was nurtured by a delight in nature, music, and the poetry his mother read to him. However, Caroline Masefield died in January 1885, soon after giving birth to her sixth child. The mental stability of Masefield's solicitor father, Edward

Masefield, was severely affected by her death, and by other personal and financial losses. For a time the children were looked after by a governess Masefield disliked, and at the age of ten he was sent to Warwick School. On his father's death in 1891, the Masefield children were consigned to the care of Edward Masefield's brother and sister-in-law, William and Kate.

In 1891 at the age of thirteen, Masefield was sent to study seamanship on the instructional ship HMS *Conway.* On graduation in 1894 he joined HMS *Gilcruix* as an apprentice seaman. The voyage proved difficult; conditions aboard the ship were brutal, and his health, both mental and physical, seems to have broken down. Discharged and hospitalized in Valparaiso, Chile, he returned home in the fall of 1894. In the spring of 1895 he sailed to New York to sign on to the *Bidston Hill,* but he thought better of the idea and did not report to his ship. Instead, he stayed in New York, working at various odd jobs, including a job in the Alexander Smith carpet factory in Yonkers. During his stay in New York he became interested in poetry and began to write.

When he returned to England in 1897, Masefield continued to write while working for a business firm and then a bank. In 1899 one of his poems was published in the *Outlook,* and during the following year he met William Butler Yeats and Lady Gregory. A regular at Yeats's Monday evening gatherings, Masefield began to meet members of the Bloomsbury literary world. In 1901 he left his bank job to begin a long and successful career as a professional writer in many genres. His first book, *Salt-Water Ballads,* was a great success. In the following year he was married to Constance Crommelin. Their first child, Isabel Judith, was born in 1904, and their second, Lewis, in 1910.

In 1909 Masefield had become infatuated with an older woman, Elizabeth Robins, to whom he confided much about his early life which he did not elsewhere acknowledge, particularly the cruel difficulty of his life at sea. Masefield was hurt when the relationship was broken off by Robins, and some of his feeling about it was probably reflected in *The Everlasting Mercy,* a narrative poem written in 1911 about the spiritual conversion of a reprobate named Saul Kane. The poem was controversial because of its harsh naturalism, but, together with three more long narratives, *The Widow in the Bye Street* (1912), *Dauber: a Poem* (1913), and *The Daffodil Fields* (1913), it made Masefield quite famous.

At a time when he was experimenting with fiction for adults, Masefield wrote three adventure

Masefield, portrait by Sir John Lavery

novels for a teenage audience. In each of these, an essentially decent boy finds himself on his own in very dangerous company. *Martin Hyde, The Duke's Messenger* is a fast-moving historical novel about an orphaned boy of twelve caught up in the Monmouth Rebellion against James II. Young Martin feels the stresses of his situation and comes to believe that "war wastes more energy . . . than any other form of folly" and that "no sane creature" likes adventure. At last, in an ending that is pure wish fulfillment, Martin's life is saved by a girl of twenty, a lovely, daring, athletic secret agent who becomes the love of his life. *Lost Endeavour* is a darker fiction in which young Charles Harding is kidnapped, sold into slavery, and captured by pirates. Though full of action and adventure, and sometimes considered a children's story, this is a sobering tale of a young boy trapped in a brutal and hateful way of life that he fears will destroy him, body and soul. This novel has a bitter edge and offers little consolation to the young reader. In *Jim Davis,* on the other hand, readers are offered a softer, more hopeful version of Masefield's familiar kidnap plot. An orphan boy living in Devon discovers the lair of local smugglers, who force him to go to sea with them. Jim escapes from the smugglers,

only to be captured by gypsies who believe he will bring them luck. Fortunately, one of the smugglers turns up and helps him to get away. Though the story is vividly told, its violence is distanced, and the resilient young hero manages to rise above all his problems. In the end, Jim finds a mother figure and a home, and looks forward to further adventures.

In a rather different vein Masefield produced *A Book of Discoveries,* in which two young brothers explore Masefield's favorite corner of England. During a busy summer vacation Mac and Robin Shenstone go boating, camping, and treasure hunting. A friendly retired sailor teaches them how to interpret the archaeological traces of earlier inhabitants: Ancient Britons, Romans, pirates, and smugglers. Masefield demonstrates in this book something of Arthur Ransome's gift for describing children caught up in imaginative play and interesting tasks, and though this is a realistic story, some of the boys' imaginative games and the tales of pirates and smugglers suggest material that Masefield was to use later in his fantasy novels set in the same region.

During World War I Masefield undertook four trips to France on behalf of the war effort. His letters from the front have recently been published (*Letters from the Front, 1915–1917* [1984]). In 1916 and in 1918 he also traveled to America to lecture on literature and to promote American support for the Allies. After the war Masefield wrote another verse narrative, *Reynard the Fox: or, The Ghost Heath Run* (1919). During the 1920s he became increasingly interested in drama and in the oral recitation of poetry.

The two undoubted classics for children written by Masefield are both fantasies about a boy named Kay Harker, from the same family as the hero of Masefield's popular novel for adults, *Sard Harker* (1924). In *The Midnight Folk* (1927) young Kay enters a nighttime world of dream and imaginative adventure to find a treasure his great-grandfather had won and lost and to restore the honor of his family. Though by day the orphaned Kay lives an ordinary life, by night he is drawn into a magical world in which past and present, reality and illusion, blend strangely.

Kay finds he can move into a painting on the wall to interview an ancestor, get advice from his cat Nibbins, fly through the air on a borrowed broomstick, or visit a friendly fox in his lair. In his dreamy night world Kay resolutely faces danger after danger in order to see the injustices that marred his great-grandfather's life put right at last.

Each move of the fantasy takes the dreamer-hero closer to an understanding of the mysterious events surrounding the loss of the Treasure of Santa Barbara and closer to the wonderful moment in which his beloved old toys march home with it. The logic of the story makes it seem natural that in the end Kay defeats not only his great-grandfather's enemies but his own.

What makes *The Midnight Folk* an exceptional children's book is the deft telling of the tale, the taste and discipline with which Masefield keeps delicately to his own rules, producing an unusually convincing blend of fantasy and realism. Kay's openness to experience and readiness to trust in a kind of fairy-tale providence make him an appealing hero. And he is surrounded by vividly realized characters: animals, toys, other-worldly creatures, and a wonderful assortment of villains. No two of these characters speak in quite the same voice, and there is rich humor in their self-revelation through accent, manner, and rhetorical flourish.

In 1930, when Robert Bridges died, Prime Minister Ramsay MacDonald chose Masefield to be Poet Laureate. During the 1930s Masefield traveled widely, received many honorary degrees, lectured, and worked to help younger writers.

In 1933 he wrote the appealing sea story *The Bird of Dawning,* which some young readers have enjoyed. In it "Cruiser" Trewsbury, a "forceful young man of nearly twenty-two" is shipwrecked, yet manages to commandeer *The Bird of Dawning,* a China clipper he and his shipmates find adrift, and sail her home to win a race and make his name and fortune. The story is full of danger; it celebrates the young sailor's steadfastness and courage in the face of what seem incredible odds.

In the fantasy *The Box of Delights; or, When the Wolves Were Running,* Kay Harker, now several years older and on his way home from school for Christmas vacation, meets a mysterious stranger with a marvelous box and is drawn into a battle between the forces of good and evil. Some of the characters from the earlier book make return appearances, including the witch-governess Sylvia Daisy Pouncer, now married to the stagy arch-villain Abner Brown, who is pretending to be the head of a local theological college. The fantasy here – presented as a dream – is less delicately blended into reality, less psychologically subtle than *The Midnight Folk,* but the story is full of wonderful inventions like the "box of delights" that lets its owner "go small" or "go swift." The vivid dream sequences in which Kay visits the past or, in the company of Herne the Hunter, runs as a stag, flies as a wild duck, swims as

a fish, are unforgettable. The snowy Christmas-tide country setting, the battle between good and evil conducted with the aid of mythic figures might suggest something of the sort of thing later done by Susan Cooper in her Dark Is Rising series.

Dead Ned and its sequel, *Live and Kicking Ned,* tell the story of Ned Mansell, a young medical student in eighteenth-century England. Falsely accused of murder, Ned is convicted and hanged. The sequence describing this experience – told in the first person – is powerful and disturbing. But Masefield based his story on the tradition that London doctors did in fact attempt to restore life to executed felons. Ned is revived and forced to flee the country, working as a surgeon on a slave ship. Reborn into a new life, he undergoes many adventures in Africa and finds his way home, where he is cleared at last of the crime for which he had been wrongfully punished.

Masefield's son Lewis died in Africa during World War II, and his wife died in 1960. In his later years Masefield was the recipient of many honors from all over the world. He died on 12 May 1967, and his ashes were buried in the Poets' Corner in Westminster Abbey.

Of all Masefield's work, a few lively historical adventure tales (rather in the vein of Leon Garfield) and perhaps a few poems or stories about the sea are still read with pleasure by younger readers. *A Book of Discoveries,* though now out of print, remains entertaining and original. It is his fantasies about Kay Harker, *The Midnight Folk* and *The Box of Delights,* that probably constitute Masefield's best claim to permanent fame as a first-rate writer of fiction for children. In the freshness and precision of their language, their vivid sense of place, the delicacy of their structure, these novels are very much the work of a poet.

Letters:

The Letters of John Masefield to Florence Lamont, edited by Corliss and Lansing Lamont (London: Macmillan, 1979; New York: Columbia University Press, 1979);

Letters to Reyna, edited by William Buchan (London: Buchan & Enright, 1983);

Letters to Margaret Bridges, 1915–1919, edited by Donald E. Stanford (Manchester: Carcanet, 1984);

Letters from the Front 1915–1917, edited by Peter Vansittart (London: Constable, 1984);

Brangwen: The Poet and the Dancer, edited by John Gregory (Lewes, Essex: Book Guild, 1988).

Bibliographies:

Charles Herbert Simmons, *A Bibliography of John Masefield* (New York: Columbia University Press, 1930);

Henry Wood Nevinson, *John Masefield: an Appreciation, Together With a Bibliography* (London: Heinemann, 1931);

Geoffrey Handley-Taylor, comp., *John Masefield, O. M.: The Queen's Poet Laureate, a Bibliography and Eighty-first Birthday Tribute* (London: Cranbrook Tower Press, 1960);

I. A. Williams, *Bibliography of John Masefield* (Belfast, Maine: Porter, 1979);

Crocker Wight, *John Masefield, a Bibliographical Description of his First, Limited, Signed and Special Editions* (Boston: The Library of the Boston Athenaeum, 1986).

References:

Francis Berry, *John Masefield: The Narrative Poet* (Sheffield: University of Sheffield, 1967);

Fraser B. Drew, *John Masefield's England: A Study of the National Themes in His Work* (Cranbury, N.J.: Associated University Presses, 1973);

June Dwyer, *John Masefield* (New York: Ungar, 1987);

Margery Turner Fisher, *John Masefield* (London: Bodley Head, 1963);

William Hamilton, *John Masefield: A Critical Study* (London: Allen & Unwin, 1922);

Corliss Lamont, *Remembering John Masefield* (Rutherford, N.J.: Fairleigh Dickinson University Press, 1971);

John Edward Mason, *John Masefield* (Exeter: Paternoster Press, 1938);

Constance Babington Smith, *John Masefield: A Life* (Oxford: Oxford University Press, 1978);

Muriel Spark, *John Masefield* (London & New York: Peter Nevill, 1953; revised edition, London: Hutchinson, 1991);

Sanford Sternlicht *John Masefield* (Boston: Twayne, 1977);

Leonard Strong, *John Masefield* (London: Longmans, Green, 1952).

Papers:

Masefield's papers are in the Bodleian Library, Oxford; the Harry Ransom Humanities Research Center, University of Texas at Austin; Houghton Library, Harvard University; The Berg Collection, New York Public Library; Beinecke and Sterling Libraries, Yale University; and in other libraries and private collections.

A. A. Milne

(18 January 1882 – 31 January 1956)

Charlotte F. Otten
Calvin College

See also the Milne entries in *DLB 10: Modern British Dramatists, 1900–1945; DLB 77: British Mystery Writers, 1920–1939;* and *DLB 100: Modern British Essayists, Second Series.*

BOOKS: *Lovers in London* (London: Rivers, 1905);

The Day's Play (London: Methuen, 1910; New York: Dutton, 1925);

The Holiday Round (London: Methuen, 1912; New York: Dutton, 1925);

Once a Week (London: Methuen, 1914; New York: Dutton, 1925);

Happy Days (New York: Doran, 1915);

Once on a Time (London: Hodder & Stoughton, 1917; New York & London: Putnam, 1922);

First Plays (London: Chatto & Windus, 1919; New York: Knopf, 1920) – includes *Wurzel-Flummery, The Lucky One, The Boy Comes Home, Belinda: An April Folly,* and *The Red Feathers;*

Not That It Matters (London: Methuen, 1919; New York: Dutton, 1920);

If I May (London: Methuen, 1920; New York: Dutton, 1921);

Mr. Pim (London: Hodder & Stoughton, 1921; New York: Doran, 1922);

Second Plays (London: Chatto & Windus, 1921; New York: Knopf, 1922) – includes *Make-Believe, Mr. Pim Passes By, The Camberley Triangle, The Romantic Age,* and *The Stepmother;*

The Sunny Side (London: Methuen, 1921; New York: Dutton, 1922);

The Red House Mystery (London: Methuen, 1922; New York: Dutton, 1922);

Three Plays (New York: Putnam, 1922; London: Chatto & Windus, 1923) – includes *The Dover Road, The Truth about Blayds,* and *The Great Broxopp;*

The Artist: A Duologue (London & New York: French, 1923);

The Man in the Bowler Hat: A Terribly Exciting Affair (London & New York: French, 1923);

A. A. Milne

Success (London: Chatto & Windus, 1923; New York: French, 1924);

When We Were Very Young (London: Methuen, 1924; New York: Dutton, 1924);

A Gallery of Children (London: Paul, 1925; Philadelphia: McKay, 1925);

Ariadne; or, Business First: A Comedy in Three Acts (London & New York: French, 1925);

For the Luncheon Interval: Cricket and Other Verses (London: Methuen, 1925; New York: Dutton, 1925);

To Have the Honour: A Comedy in Three Acts (London & New York: French, 1925);

Portrait of a Gentleman in Slippers: A Fairy Tale in One Act (London & New York: French, 1926);

Winnie-the-Pooh (London: Methuen, 1926; New York: Dutton, 1926);

Now We Are Six (London: Methuen, 1927; New York: Dutton, 1927);

The Ascent of Man (London: Benn, 1928);

The House at Pooh Corner (London: Methuen, 1928; New York: Dutton, 1928);

The Ivory Door: A Legend in a Prologue and Three Acts (London & New York: Putnam, 1928; London: Chatto & Windus, 1929);

Toad of Toad Hall: A Play from Kenneth Grahame's Book The Wind in the Willows (London: Methuen, 1929; New York: Scribners, 1929);

The Secret and Other Stories (New York: Fountain Press / London: Methuen, 1929);

By Way of Introduction (London: Methuen, 1929; New York: Dutton, 1929);

The Fourth Wall: Played in America under the Title of "The Perfect Alibi." A Detective Story in Three Acts (London & New York: French, 1929);

Michael and Mary: A Play in Three Acts (London: Chatto & Windus, 1930; London & New York: French, 1932);

When I Was Very Young (New York: Fountain Press / London: Methuen, 1930);

Two People (London: Methuen, 1931; New York: Dutton, 1931);

Four Days' Wonder (London: Methuen, 1933; New York: Dutton, 1933);

Peace with Honour (London: Methuen, 1934; New York: Dutton, 1934; revised, 1935);

More Plays (London: Chatto & Windus, 1935) – includes *The Ivory Door, The Fourth Wall,* and *Other People's Lives;*

Miss Elizabeth Bennet: A Play from "Pride and Prejudice" (London: Chatto & Windus, 1936);

Miss Marlow at Play: A One-Act Comedy (London & New York: French, 1936);

The Magic Hill, and Other Stories (New York: Grosset & Dunlap, 1937);

The Princess and the Apple Tree, and Other Stories (New York: Grosset & Dunlap, 1937);

It's Too Late Now: The Autobiography of a Writer (London: Methuen, 1939); republished as *Autobiography* (New York: Dutton, 1939);

Behind the Lines: A Book of Poems (London: Methuen, 1940; New York: Dutton, 1940);

Sarah Simple: A Comedy in Three Acts (London & New York: French, 1940);

War With Honour (London: Macmillan, 1940);

War Aims Unlimited (London: Methuen, 1941);

The Ugly Duckling: A Play in One Act (London: French, 1941);

Chloe Marr (London: Methuen, 1946; New York: Dutton, 1946);

Books for Children, a Reader's Guide (London: Cambridge University Press, 1948);

Birthday Party, and Other Stories (New York: Dutton, 1948; London: Methuen, 1949);

The Norman Church (London: Methuen, 1948);

A Table near the Band, and Other Stories (London: Methuen, 1950; New York: Dutton, 1950);

Before the Flood: A Play in One Act (London & New York: French, 1951);

Year In, Year Out (London: Methuen, 1952; New York: Dutton, 1952);

Prince Rabbit and the Princess Who Could Not Laugh (London: Ward, 1966; New York: Dutton, 1966);

Five Minutes of Your Time (London: League of Nations Union, n.d.).

Editions and Collections: *Four Plays* (London: Chatto & Windus, 1926) – comprises *To Have the Honour; Ariadne, or Business First; Portrait of a Gentleman in Slippers;* and *Success;*

The Christopher Robin Story Book (London: Methuen, 1929); republished as *The Christopher Robin Reader* (New York: Dutton, 1929);

Those Were the Days (London: Methuen, 1929; New York: Dutton, 1929) – includes *The Day's Play, The Holiday Round, Once a Week,* and *The Sunny Side;*

Very Young Verses, preface by Milne (London: Methuen, 1929) – includes selections from *When We Were Very Young* and *Now We Are Six;*

The Christopher Robin Birthday Book (London: Methuen, 1930; New York: Dutton, 1931);

Four Plays (New York: Putnam, 1932) – includes *Michael and Mary, To Have the Honour* as *Meet the Prince, The Fourth Wall* as *The Perfect Alibi,* and *Portrait of a Gentleman in Slippers;*

A. A. Milne, edited by E. V. Knox (London: Methuen, 1933);

The Pocket Milne (New York: Dutton, 1941; London: Methuen, 1942);

The Old Sailor, and Other Selections (New York: Dutton, 1947);

Sneezles, and Other Selections (New York: Dutton, 1947);

The King's Breakfast, and Other Selections (New York: Dutton, 1947);

Introducing Winnie-the-Pooh, and Other Selections (New York: Dutton, 1947);

Pooh's Birthday Book (New York: Dutton, 1963);

The Pooh Story Book (New York: Dutton, 1965; London: Methuen, 1967);

The Christopher Robin Book of Verse (New York: Dutton, 1967); republished as *The Christopher Robin Verse Book* (London: Methuen, 1969); *Winnie-the-Pooh,* facsimile edition (London: Methuen, 1971; New York: Dutton, 1971).

SELECTED PERIODICAL PUBLICATIONS – UNCOLLECTED: "The Rape of the Sherlock: Being the Only True Version of Holmes's Adventures," *Vanity Fair* (London), 70 (15 October 1903): 499;

"This England – According to Milne," *New York Times Magazine,* 25 July 1943, pp. 7, 17;

"New Explorations in Baker Street," *New York Times Magazine,* 9 March 1952, pp. 10ff;

"Always Time for a Rhyme," *New Herald Tribune Book Review,* 12 October 1952, p. 10.

Four books by one author became classics almost as soon as they were published in the 1920s: *When We Were Very Young* (1924), *Winnie-the-Pooh* (1926), *Now We Are Six* (1927), and *The House at Pooh Corner* (1928). Names such as "Pooh Bear" and "Poohsticks" are firmly lodged in the English language; the adventures of Pooh are not only well known but recapitulated in the lives of children; and the poems are recited by children all over the world in many different languages. Their phenomenal popularity is owing in part to the illustrations of E. H. Shepard, which capture the subtle humor, the generous spirit, and the amiable style of the author.

Alan Alexander Milne (he was first named Alexander Sydney but his parents changed their minds and named him Alan Alexander instead) was born at Henley House, Mortimer Road, Hampstead, London, the third and last child of John Vine Milne and Sarah Maria Heginbotham Milne. His first school was Henley House, the private fee-paying school where his father was headmaster and where H. G. Wells was one of his instructors. At age eleven he went to Westminster School as a scholarship student. In 1900 he was enrolled as an undergraduate at Trinity College, Cambridge University, where he was elected editor of *Granta.* After leaving Cambridge he became an assistant editor of *Punch,* in which some of his essays and poetry had been appearing regularly. On 4 June 1913 he married Dorothy ("Daphne") de Sélincourt, and in 1914 he joined the army as a signaling officer in the Fourth Royal Warwickshire Regiment. While serving in the army in France, he began to write plays and farces for the soldiers. Having contracted a serious fever, he was sent back to England to recuperate. Officially discharged in 1918, he resigned his editorship at *Punch* to become a full-time playwright. His plays brought him success in both England and the United States, with *Mr. Pim Passes By* (1920) and *The Truth About Blaydes* (1921) achieving early critical and popular acclaim. He had already in 1917 tried his hand at writing a fairy story, *Once on a Time,* "not for children," but for his wife and himself. In a later edition he claimed not to know whether it was a children's book or an adults'. In 1929 he dramatized Kenneth Grahame's *The Wind in the Willows,* which had to wait until 1930 for its first performance. Milne's solid reputation was built on the four children's books; already in the 1930s interest in his plays for adults began to wane, while response to the children's books swelled, somewhat to Milne's chagrin. In 1952 Milne suffered a stroke. He died in 1956 at age seventy-four.

Milne never quite understood how the four thin books he had written for children could have catapulted him into long-lasting fame, while his major works for adults had brought him only short-lived recognition. Describing in his autobiography, *It's Too Late Now: The Autobiography of a Writer* (1939), the embarrassment he felt at being considered only a writer for children, Milne observes:

> It is easier in England to make a reputation than to lose one. I wrote four "Children's books," containing altogether, I suppose, 70,000 words – the number of words in the average-length novel. Having said good-bye to all that in 70,000 words, knowing that as far as I was concerned the mode was outmoded, I gave up writing children's books. I wanted to escape from them as I had once wanted to escape from *Punch;* as I have always wanted to escape. In vain.... As a discerning critic pointed out: the hero of my latest play God help it, was "just Christopher Robin grown up."

A prolific professional writer, Milne wrote thirty-four plays, six novels, three books of verse, and three books of short stories; in addition, his essays and miscellaneous pieces were collected into approximately nineteen volumes. Although most of his writing for adults is out of print, his poetry for children and his Pooh books continue to sell internationally, in English and in translations. When *The House at Pooh Corner* was published in London and New York in October 1928, sales figures appeared on the British jacket: *When We Were Very Young,* 179,000; *Winnie-the-Pooh,* 96,000; *Now We Are Six,* 109,000. These figures did not include sales in the United States. *When We Were Very Young* alone sold 500,000 copies in the first ten years. The sales of all four books quickly escalated to millions of copies.

Christopher Robin Milne in March 1928 (photograph by Marcus Adams, Trinity College, Cambridge University)

When We Were Very Young, Milne's first book of poems for children, was dedicated to his three-year-old son, Christopher Robin, "or as he prefers to call himself Billy Moon." Addressing the question of who is the speaker in the poems, Milne, somewhat coyly in his preface, deflects attention from himself as author, "that strange but uninteresting person," to Christopher Robin "or some other boy or girl, or Nurse, or Hoo." Of the forty-four poems in the book, eighteen are spoken by the omniscient third-person adult author, twenty-three by the first-person voice of Christopher Robin, two by Nurse, and one may be the voice of Hoo (the fairy or the butterfly of "Twinkletoes").

Most of the poems appeared in magazines before being published in *When We Were Very Young.* "Vespers," undoubtedly the best-known of all Milne's verses, had a curious publication history. As Milne recounts in *It's Too Late Now:*

> while at work on a play, I had wasted a morning in writing a poem called "Vespers." I gave it to Daphne, as one might give a photograph or a valentine, telling her that if she liked to get it published anywhere she could stick to the money. She sent it to Frank Crowninshield of *Vanity Fair* (N.Y.) and got fifty dollars. Later she lent it to me for the Queen's Doll's House Library, and later

still collected one-forty-fourth of all the royalties of *When We Were Very Young,* together with her share of various musical and subsidiary rights. It turned out to be the most expensive present I had ever given her.

"Vespers" appeared in the center column of page 45 of the January 1923 issue of *Vanity Fair;* it is flanked on both sides by an article titled "The High-Low Controversy" (subtitled "To Just What Lengths Should a Skirt Go?"). On the opposite page are sketches of New York "Between Eleven and Three," with glimpses of cabarets and the "New York That Hates to Go Home." In this inauspicious setting "Vespers" began its unpredictably complicated critical reception, with Milne himself denouncing what he regarded as its misperceived sentimentality. Recognizing that even "hard-headed reviewers have been sentimental over it," Milne insisted years later in his autobiography "that prayer means nothing to a child of three, whose thoughts are engaged with other, more exciting matters." Milne regarded the child in his poem as egocentric, as one who focused only on himself and who interrupted himself at prayer by recalling the delights of his bath and the blue of Nanny's gown. However much Milne insisted that a three-year-old child is ruthlessly egotistic rather than naturally pious, the prayer brought (and continues to bring) a lump to the throats of his readers – especially to parents and to those who remember their own confident early prayers.

The stanza that opens and closes the poem is spoken by the author-father; it, rather than the actual prayers of the child, is the most susceptible of all the stanzas to the accusation of sentimentality. The diction is almost precious as the speaker hushes the audience and describes the "little boy" whose "little gold head" droops on "little hands" as he prays. The stanzas spoken by Christopher Robin are the authentic voice of a child at prayer: First he prays for Mummy, then Daddy, and then Nanny. He does what children at prayer were (and are) forbidden to do in the presence of the Almighty – to peek. He spreads his fingers, opens his eyes to the surrounding temporal sights, and sees Nanny's dressing gown through his parted fingers. He prays for God to "make her good" – a petition that reflects a child's moral anxiety about himself. Then, by deft association with his own dressing gown, he pretends to pull the hood over his head and to make himself disappear, finding comfort in the childish notion that he can't be seen because he cannot see, "And nobody knows that I'm there at all." In the penultimate stanza Christopher Robin remembers to pray for himself, "Oh! Now I remember. *God bless me.*" Perhaps unwittingly Milne captures not so much the egotism of a child at prayer but the erratic concentration of all people at prayer, whether child or adult. As John Donne, the famous seventeenth-century preacher and dean of St. Paul's (himself no slouch at prayer) admitted, a straw under his knee could quickly call him from the presence of the eternal God to the trivial realities of the temporal world.

Like many famous poems, "Vespers" has been parodied. Even the title of J. B. Morton's "Now We Are Sick" (itself the most famous of the parodies) invokes ridicule. Echoing "Christopher Robin is saying his prayers," Morton's "Christopher Robin Has/Fallen/Down-Stairs."

Readers of the twenty-three poems spoken by a child frequently make the assumption that Milne's son, Christopher Robin, actually experienced what is described so artlessly in the poems. Milne was quick to say that the voice of the child is a fictive voice; that the experiences described could be the experiences of any child, not just those of Christopher Robin; that Christopher Robin is mentioned in only three of the poems; that some of the experiences were those of Milne himself as a child; and that, although Milne was credited by his publishers as having "wonderful insight into a child's mind," he was "not inordinately fond of or interested in children."

The topics narrated by the child have the narrow range of experiences that engage a child on an ordinary day: playing with toys and with a puppy and a mouse, going places, eating, growing up, feeling the pressures of conforming to the behavioral expectations of adults. Throughout the poems the child broaches the question of the power that adults command. The child's dawning awareness of his own individuality and of the disadvantages of being in the state of childhood is subtly hinted at in several of the poems. In "Nursery Chairs," for example, the child-narrator, while sitting on the Second Chair, pretends to be a lion who frightens Nanny – obviously an empowering strategy. In the Fourth Chair the child has an internal debate and teeters on the brink of three-year-old self-acceptance, with all its enfeebling characteristics, wondering whether to go to sea, or whether to pretend to be a lion or tiger, or whether to, in his words, "be only me."

Although Peter Hunt regards "Nursery Chairs" as "reminiscent of the worst of Robert Louis Stevenson's *A Child's Garden of Verses* in its archness and artificiality," Milne has captured the need of a young child to fantasize about independence. Through the fantasy the child prepares himself for the ultimate realization of the fantasy: freedom from adult supervision. In "Disobedience" the child reverses roles with his mother. Assuming his mother's power, the child parrots her commands to him: "You must never go down to the end of the town, / if you don't go down with me." The mother disobeys, goes to the end of the town alone, and "James James / Morrison's mother / Hasn't been heard of since." Recognizing that the punishment is the inevitable consequence of the crime, the child expresses no regrets at losing her.

Although Milne disclaimed any special insights into the psyche of a three-year-old, psychologists and parents know the universality of the emotions expressed by the child-narrator of the poems. He dreams of being self-sufficient enough to live alone in "The Island": "There's nobody else in the world, and the world / was made for me."

Of the eighteen poems narrated by the author-father, two are perhaps the best known: "Buckingham Palace" and "Hoppity." In her biography of Milne, *A. A. Milne, The Man Behind Winnie-the-Pooh* (1990), Ann Thwaite records the enthusiastic responses of adults to "Hoppity": "The most bizarre report was from the Hon. Edwin Samuel, who said he had read some Milne verses at a Jaffa Chamber of Commerce lunch. 'All those busy Arab merchants took the afternoon off for endless repeats of 'Christopher Robin goes hoppity, hoppity, hop'. . . . A New York woman reported, 'We had had to hop. We kept it up until I was overcome by exhaustion and avoirdupois. Then just the children hopped.' "

The poems in *When We Were Very Young* are not only danceable but singable. When they first appeared in *Punch,* before they were gathered into *When We Were Very Young,* a number of composers offered to set them to music. Milne chose Harold Fraser-Simson, who published first *Fourteen Songs* (1924) and subsequently sixty-seven songs.

When We Were Very Young prepared the way for *Winnie-the-Pooh* and helped to immortalize the name "Christopher Robin," to the lifelong embarrassment of the actual Christopher Robin Milne. Born on 21 August 1920, Christopher Robin, as soon as he was old enough to know himself by name, called himself Billy Moon (his pronunciation of "Milne" being "Moon"). He has spent many years of his life attempting to disentangle himself from the semi-biographical, fictional character named after him in *Winnie-the-Pooh.* The Christopher Robin in the book shares many of the identifiable traits of the real Christopher Robin. Biography and fantasy are intertwined and, hence, cannot easily be separated.

Of course as soon as Kanga unbuttoned her pocket, she saw what had happened. Just for a moment she thought she was frightened, and then she knew she wasn't; for she felt quite sure that Christopher Robin would never let any harm happen to Roo. So she said to herself, "If they are having a joke with me, I will have a joke with them."

"Now then, Roo, dear," she said, as she took Piglet out of her pocket. "Bed-time."

"Aha!" said Piglet, as well as he could after his terrifying journey. But it wasn't a very good "Aha!" and Kanga didn't seem to understand what it meant.

"Bath first," said Kanga in a cheerful voice.

"Aha!" said Piglet again, looking round anxiously for the others. But the others weren't there. Rabbit was playing with baby Roo in his own house, and feeling more fond of him every minute, and Pooh, who had decided to be a Kanga, was still at the sandy place on the top of the forest, practising jumps.

"I am not at all sure," said Kanga in a thoughtful voice, "that it wouldn't be a good idea to have a cold bath this evening. Would you like that, Roo, dear?"

Piglet, who had never been really fond of baths, shuddered a long indignant shudder, and said in as brave a voice as he could:

"Kanga, I see that the time has come to speak plainly."

"Funny little Roo," said Kanga, as she got the bath-water ready.

Page from Milne's manuscript for Winnie-the-Pooh *(by permission of the Estate of A. A. Milne; from Ann Thwaite,* A.A. Milne – His Life, *1990)*

Readers have searched (and continue to search) for the "real" Christopher Robin. It is not surprising that children are confused when the Christopher Robin they meet in the flesh is even older than their parents. In Bruno Bettelheim's *The Uses of Enchantment* (1976) Christopher Milne (he has eliminated "Robin" from his name) explains his attitude toward being one of the six most famous children in the world: "If the Pooh books had been like most other books – published one year, forgotten the next – there would have been no problem. If I had been a different sort of person there might well have been no problem. Unfortunately the fictional Christopher Robin refused to die and he and his real-life namesake were not always on the best of terms. For the first misfortune (as it sometimes seemed) my father was to blame. The second was my fault."

Winnie-the-Pooh was dedicated to the wife/mother by the dual authors: "Hand in hand we come / Christopher Robin and I / To lay this book in your lap." From the dedication to the final words of the last chapter, Milne includes Christopher Robin in its authorship. One of the most complex approaches to narration in all of children's literature is Milne's use of the child who is narrator to the father, who then recounts what the child has told him back to the child and to all the readers. Two voices are frequently heard: Christopher Robin's young inchoate words and stories are woven into A. A. Milne's articulate words and narratives. Milne is purportedly telling Christopher Robin the stories that Christopher Robin remembers, and then doesn't remember, and then wishes to be told again. Both father and son agree to the fiction that Christopher Robin remembers but that Pooh doesn't: "I do remember," he said, "only Pooh doesn't very well, so that's why he likes having it told to him again. Because then it's a real story and not just a remembering."

Not all critics regard the authorial conferences between Milne and Christopher Robin as flattering to the child, who expresses delight in finding himself elevated into a creative authorial role. Alison Lurie, for example, regards these dialogues as "condescending conversations between the author and Christopher Robin." She bolsters her argument by referring to A. A. Milne as "another and more powerful deity" and Christopher as his "godlike child."

Further complicating the identity of Christopher Robin is the presence of the animals in the story, most of whom actually belonged to Milne's son. Justly famous (and replicated all over the world), Pooh was a present to Christopher Robin on his first birthday. Pooh, Piglet, Eeyore, Kanga, Roo, and Tigger were all a part of Christopher

Robin's menagerie, but Rabbit and Owl were, according to Milne, "my own unaided work." Five of the surviving animals are in the Donnell Library Center of the New York Public Library; Roo has disappeared.

Winnie-the-Pooh has ten chapters, with each chapter being complete in itself as an episode. Beginning with Pooh's insatiable appetite for honey, the first chapter establishes Pooh's character. He is inventive but not intellectual; adventuresome but blundering; obtuse but the most faithful friend a child ever had. The origin of the name "Pooh" is given at the end of the first chapter. After holding onto the string of a balloon in his descent from a honey-bearing tree, Pooh's arms "stayed up straight in the air for more than a week, and whenever a fly came and settled on his nose he had to blow it off. And I think – but I am not sure – that *that* is why he was always called Pooh." The subsequent chapters deal with trying to catch a woozle, meeting a heffalump, leading an "exposition to the North Pole," rescuing Piglet who "is entirely surrounded by water," seeing Pooh out of a tight place, helping Eeyore find his tail, celebrating Eeyore's birthday, observing the interaction between Kanga and Baby Roo, giving a Pooh Party, and saying Good-bye.

Although Pooh is the main character, Christopher Robin is obviously the character on whom all others (especially Pooh) depend. Undergirding the narrative and the characterization is the father/son relationship. The father-author confers upon his son the insight, strength, and ingenuity required to solve the problems that his toy animal friends have created. By taking on adult responsibility in each episode, the son escapes the powerlessness that causes so much frustration in childhood. He exercises his power by rescuing his friends – often from both physical and psychological danger. Christopher Robin, however, does not abuse his power by dominating his friends. It is his unfailing tolerance of his friends and his undiminished love for them, in spite of their flawed personalities and their propensity for creating disaster, that endear him to his friends and that have endeared him to his many readers.

Each character has a recognizably stable personality throughout the book. Their child-owner finds them familiar and predictable and, hence, comfortable companions. Although some critics have regarded the animals as stereotypes of human qualities – Pooh is unintelligent, Piglet apprehensive, Eeyore pessimistic, Kanga overprotective of her baby, Roo stifled by her mother, Rabbit dictatorial, Owl pseudointellectual – the animals are more

Milne and Christopher in 1934

complex and more subtle than any stereotype. (Tigger, with his bouncy, erratic behavior, does not enter the narrative until *The House at Pooh Corner*.) And yet the animals suggest human stereotypical characteristics. College students have even called themselves and their friends by the names of Christopher Robin's animals, because they discovered much about themselves – and their friends – in Milne's portrayal of these stuffed animals.

Apart from the gravity of the situations in which Christopher Robin and his friends find themselves, there is the underlying humor that sustains them – the humor that in turn charms the readers. Milne does not ridicule or humiliate his characters. Because Milne treats each character with respect and understanding, Christopher Robin's treatment of them reflects the author's generosity. Each character is buoyed up by Milne's sense of their individuality.

Several reasons have been given for the popularity of *Winnie-the-Pooh*. Among the reasons are that

the book shows how essential the capacity for friendship is to human life, and reveals how critical the ability to overlook the foibles and weaknesses of one's friends is to joyful human existence. Because Pooh is a Bear of "No Brain at All," he engages in self-deprecation after each bumbling episode. When Pooh is shown by Christopher Robin that there is no menacing Woozle, for example, but that Pooh and Piglet have simply followed their own tracks, Pooh says, "I have been Foolish and Deluded." Christopher Robin reassures him, "You're the Best Bear in All the World." Milne valued loyalty to one's friends and relations, displaying his own loyalty to and love for his brother Ken by supporting him financially during his debilitating illness. Milne continued to support Ken's family after Ken's death.

Other reasons for its enduring popularity are, as Hunt observes, its "sophisticated writing, the pace, the timing, and the narrative stance all contributing to the comic effect." Thwaite finds that "part of the strength and charm of the stories comes from the juxtaposition of toy animal and forest."

It was, however, *The Pooh Perplex* by Frederick C. Crews (1963) that managed, as Lurie observes, "to stifle almost all critical comment on *Winnie-the-Pooh* for a decade" – but not to stifle the sales of the book itself. *The Pooh Perplex* created a market for *Winnie-the-Pooh* on college campuses, where Pooh Societies sprang up and where Hummalongs and Heffalump Hunts became regular features of campus life. In his preface to *The Pooh Perplex,* Crews writes: "*Winnie-the-Pooh* is, as practically everyone knows, one of the greatest books ever written, but it is also one of the most controversial. Nobody can quite agree as to what it really means." Using the critical approaches to texts current in 1963, Crews created fictitious critics who dazzle their readers with the brilliance of their readings and the ingenuity of their interpretations. Included are various approaches to literary criticism: psychoanalytic, biographical, materialist, stylistic, cultural, archetypal. *The Pooh Perplex* seems to have inflicted no permanent damage on *Winnie-the-Pooh* (nor was that Crews's intent), but Crews did manage to stimulate a whole generation of college students to reread it, or read it for the first time.

Much of the delight of *Winnie-the-Pooh* comes from the illustrations by E. H. Shepard. Since Milne acknowledged that part of the success of *When We Were Very Young* was owing to Shepard's illustrations, Shepard was asked to illustrate *Winnie-the-Pooh.* To assure the authenticity of the illustrations, Milne invited Shepard to his home in Sussex to meet the characters in Christopher Robin's nursery and to walk in Ashdown Forest, where many of the adventures took place. Shepard's illustrations are realistic presentations of the Sussex landscape and of the domestic life of Christopher Robin: forest, trees, branches, grass are matched by the actual Eeyore, Kanga, Roo, Piglet, Tigger. (There were apparently no objections to the substitution of Graham Shepard's Growler for Christopher Robin's Pooh; Shepard had been drawing his son's bear for a long time.) The original illustrations were black-and-white. When Shepard was in his eighties, he undertook the task of coloring the original illustrations, perhaps to compete with the Disney "takeover" of illustrations in the United States.

One of the most memorable of Shepard's illustrations is close to the end of *Winnie-the-Pooh.* Pooh and Piglet are walking together, companionably, with only their backs visible to the reader. Their body postures indicate that they are close friends. Deep in conversation, they are discussing what only true friends can talk about – what is closest to their hearts:

> "When you wake up in the morning, Pooh," said Piglet at last, "what's the first thing you say to yourself?"
> "What's for breakfast?" said Pooh. "What do *you* say, Piglet?"
> "I say, I wonder what's going to happen exciting *to-day?*" said Piglet.
> Pooh nodded thoughtfully.
> "It's the same thing," he said.

The spinoffs of *Winnie-the-Pooh* began soon after publication and continue to flourish. According to Thwaite, the first of the spinoffs was "*Tales of Pooh* (selections of the stories), *The Hums of Pooh* (yet another song book), *The Christopher Robin Birthday Book* (Milne took a considerable interest in that: 'The quotations should hope to apply to the person who writes in it rather than to the day . . . '), the Very Young Calendar, the Pooh Calendar – and so on, not to mention Pooh birthday cards and Christmas cards and games and toys and china. In the early 1930s Pooh had already become an industry." *The Tao of Pooh* (1982) and *The Te of Piglet* (1992) are among the more recent additions to the Pooh industry.

Translations of *Winnie-the-Pooh* also appeared soon after its publication and continue to appear. There are editions in German, Danish, Finnish, Dutch, Hebrew, Spanish, French, Polish, Slovenian, Hungarian, Swedish, Latin, Russian, Portuguese, Latvian, Ukrainian, Greek, Japanese, Afrikaans, Czech, and Slovak. Russian children know Winnie as "Vinni-Pukh"; Spanish children as "El Osito Pu"; Portuguese children as "Joanica-Puff." Each language has attempted to capture the uniqueness of Milne's original.

Now We Are Six was dedicated to Anne Darlington "because she is so speshal." (Anne Darlington was a neighbor girl who went to school with Christopher Robin and whom Milne hoped Christopher Robin would marry.) Adopting the spelling and the voice of a six-year-old, and using the first-person-plural "we" in his introduction to the sequel to *When We Were Very Young,* Milne explains, again using the dual voice:

> We have been nearly three years writing this book. We began it when we were very young . . . and now we are six. So, of course, bits of it seem rather babyish to us, almost as if they had slipped out of some other book by mistake. On page whatever-it-is there is a thing which is simply three-ish, and when we read it to ourselves just now we said, "Well, well, well," and turned over rather quickly. So we want you to know that the name of the

Milne

book doesn't mean that this is us being six all the time, but that it is about as far as we've got at present, and we half think of stopping there.

Milne did stop there. This was to be his final book of poems for children. As for the use of "we" in *When We Were Very Young* and *Now We Are Six,* Christopher Milne has his own explanation: "We grew up side by side and as we grew the books were written. . . . When I was three he was three. When I was six he was six." Writing the children's books, according to Christopher Milne, enabled his father to relive his childhood – a golden time that was shared with his beloved brother Ken, under the benevolent care of their dearly loved father.

Of the thirty-five poems in the book, eight are spoken by an omniscient third-person adult, two by the father, twenty-four by Christopher Robin, and one by a girl. The subjects covered range from kings, knights, and emperors (third-person omniscient); to "Buttercup Days," a poem about Anne written from the perspective of a father, "Where is Anne? / Close to her man," (the "man" being six-year-old Christopher Robin), and "Journey's End," a poem that asks, "*Christopher, Christopher, where are*

you going, Christopher Robin?" (from the father's perspective); to poems about having the "Sneezles," being busy, requiring solitude, having an imaginary friend "Binker," sharing a life with Pooh and being six (as Christopher Robin is). The poem spoken by the girl is uncharacteristic of Milne; critics have observed that the world Milne created in his four children's books is almost all male. "The Good Little Girl" is a psychologically sophisticated response to a female child to what she regards as the eternal question adults pester her with, "Have you been a *good* girl, Jane?"

The two most famous poems spoken by Christopher Robin are "Us Two" and "The End." In "Us Two" Christopher Robin again reveals the close friendship that exists between him and Pooh. The last stanza in which they promise always to stick together reaffirms the bond between them. *Now We Are Six* concludes, appropriately enough, with "The End," a poem in which Christopher Robin celebrates being six: "But now I am Six, I'm as clever as clever as clever. / So I think I'll be six now for ever and ever." Shepard's illustration shows Christopher Robin in the center jumping for joy, with Pooh and Piglet, suspended in midair on each side of him, joining in animated celebration.

The sales reception of *Now We Are Six* was just what the publishers had counted on. In the United States ninety thousand copies "had already been ordered on publication day in October 1927." *The Retail Bookseller* announced, "For the third time A. A. Milne has demonstrated that a book for children can outsell all other books in the country."

Although the critical response to *Now We Are Six* was generally laudatory, Dorothy Parker, a writer for *The New Yorker,* expressed distaste. Writing as "Constant Reader," she says, " Of Milne's recent verse, I speak in a minority amounting to solitude. I think it is affected, commonplace, bad. I did so, too, say bad. And now I must stop to get ready for being ridden out of town on a rail." She was to launch an even more expressive attack on *The House at Pooh Corner.*

The House at Pooh Corner, sequel to *Winnie-the-Pooh,* is a continuation of the earlier book and is Milne's way of saying goodbye to childhood – his own childhood as well as the one he lived through Christopher Robin. In his introduction Milne states explicitly, "An introduction is to introduce people, but Christopher Robin and his friends, who have already been introduced to you, are now going to say Good-bye." The book is ostensibly the keeping of the promise made by Milne to Christopher Robin at the end of *Winnie-the-Pooh*:

"And what did happen?" asked Christopher Robin.
"When?"
"Next morning."
"Could you think and tell me and Pooh some-
time?"
"If you wanted it very much."
"Pooh does," said Christopher Robin.

Like its predecessor, *The House at Pooh Corner*
has ten chapters. Beginning with a chapter on building a house at Pooh Corner for Eeyore, the subsequent chapters deal with welcoming Tigger to the
forest; nearly encountering the Heffalump again;
discovering that tiggers don't climb trees; following
Rabbit through a busy day and Christopher Robin
through a morning; observing Pooh inventing a
game; assisting in the unbouncing of Tigger;
applauding Piglet as he does a very grand thing;
finding the Wolery by Eeyore for Owl to move
into; and discovering the Enchanted Place where
Christopher Robin and Pooh promise never to forget each other.

The characters remain essentially the same as
they were in *Winnie-the-Pooh*. Pooh is still addicted to
honey and is just as addle-brained. Eeyore is just as
gloomily self-effacing and pessimistic. Rabbit is still
the quintessential organizer. Owl is just as skillful in
disguising his intellectual vacuities. Piglet is as faithful and as fearful. Tigger is a new, uncontrollably
bouncy presence. And Christopher Robin remains
the companion, savior, and friend of them all. As in
Winnie-the-Pooh, the humor springs from the situations in which the characters inevitably find themselves, either because of their personal limitations
or because of their ineptitudes and follies.

Pooh's songs, a part of the texture of the stories, and eminently singable (as the many musical
arrangements of them attest to), are also his psychologically creative way of handling pressure and
stress. One of the most famous songs (which Parker
was to pounce upon) is the one Pooh devised as an
"Outdoor Song which Has To Be Sung In the
Snow." Explaining the intricate rhythms of his song
to Piglet, Pooh says:

> "Well, you'll see, Piglet, when you listen. Because
> this is how it begins. *The more it snows, tiddely pom* — "
> "Tiddely what?" said Piglet.
> "Pom," said Pooh. "I put that in to make it more
> hummy."

The word *hummy* disgusted Parker: "And it is that
word 'hummy,' my darlings, that marks the first
place in *The House at Pooh Corner* at which Tonstant
Weader fwowed up." Although Milne was insulted

by Parker's response, it was not until he wrote his
autobiography that he responded in writing to her
ridicule:

> The books were written for children. When, for in-
> stance, Dorothy Parker, as "Constant Reader" in *The
> New Yorker,* delights the sophisticated by announcing
> that at page 5 of *The House at Pooh Corner* "Tonstant Wea-
> der fwowed up" (*sic,* if I may), she leaves the book,
> oddly enough, much where it was.... no writer of
> children's books says gaily to his publisher, "Don't
> bother about the children, Mrs. Parker will love it." As
> an artist one might genuinely prefer that one's novel
> should be praised by a single critic, whose opinion one
> valued, rather than be bought by "the mob;" but there is
> no artistic reward for a book written for children other
> than the knowledge that they enjoy it.

Apart from the enormous sales of *The House at
Pooh Corner,* which indicate the wide readership it
continues to have, there are critics who, after fifty
years, still disagree with Parker. As recently as
1978, Roger Sale admits in *Fairy Tales and After* that
the end of *The House at Pooh Corner* can still bring
tears to his eyes.

The final paragraph of *The House at Pooh Corner*
is Milne's way of not saying goodbye to childhood:
"So they went off together. But wherever they go,
and whatever happens to them on the way, in that
enchanted place on the top of the Forest, a little boy
and his Bear will always be playing." Writing in his
autobiography some years later, Milne finds himself
reflecting on the nature of childhood: "Childhood is
not the happiest time of one's life, but only to a
child is pure happiness possible." Truth lies deep
beneath the surface of Milne's statement. Happiness
for Milne was making stories of his own childhood
and of his son's childhood because then both became for him "not just a remembering." Milne
wrote in his autobiography, "Whatever subject an
author chooses or has chosen for him, he reveals no
secret but the secret of himself." This "secret of himself" he shared with the readers most capable of receiving it – children.

Interviews:
Henry Albert Phillips, "The Author of *Winnie-the-
Pooh,*" *Mentor* (December 1928): 49;
S. J. Woolf, "The Hardest Job Is Being a Father,"
New York Times Magazine, 8 November 1931, p.
8;
Janet Mabie, "Christopher Robin's Father," *Pictorial
Review* (February 1932): 2, 26, 30;
John K. Hutchens, "Christopher Robin's Candid
Father," *New York Herald Tribune Book Review,*
30 November 1952, p. 2.

Bibliography:

Tori Haring-Smith, *A. A. Milne, A Critical Bibliography* (New York: Garland, 1982).

Biographies:

Christopher Milne, *The Enchanted Places* (London: Eyre Methuen, 1974; New York: Dutton, 1975);

Milne, *The Path Through the Trees* (London: Methuen, 1979; New York: Dutton, 1979);

Ann Thwaite, *A. A. Milne, The Man Behind Winnie-the-Pooh* (London: Faber & Faber, 1990; New York: Random House, 1990).

References:

Bruno Bettelheim, *The Uses of Enchantment: the Meaning and Importance of Fairy Tales* (New York: Knopf, 1976);

Humphrey Carpenter, *Secret Gardens, A Study of the Golden Age of Children's Literature* (Boston: Houghton Mifflin, 1985);

Frederick C. Crews, *The Pooh Perplex* (New York: Dutton, 1963);

Benjamin Hoff, *The Tao of Pooh* (New York: Dutton, 1982);

Hoff, *The Te of Piglet* (New York: Dutton, 1992);

Peter Hunt, "A. A. Milne," in *Writers for Children,* edited by Jane Bingham (New York: Scribners, 1988): 397–405;

Alison Lurie, "Back to Pooh Corner," in *Children's Literature,* edited by Francelia Butler (Storrs, Conn.: Journal of The Modern Language Association Seminar on Children's Literature, 1973): 11–17;

Roger Sale, *Fairy Tales and After* (Cambridge, Mass.: Harvard University Press, 1978);

Thomas Burnett Swann, *A. A. Milne* (New York: Twayne, 1971).

Naomi Margaret (Haldane) Mitchison

(1 November 1897 –)

Carol Y. Long
University of North Dakota

BOOKS: *The Conquered* (London: Cape / New York: Harcourt, Brace, 1923);

When the Bough Breaks and Other Stories (London: Cape / New York: Harcourt, Brace, 1924);

Cloud Cuckoo Land (London: Cape, 1925; New York: Harcourt, Brace, 1926);

The Laburnum Branch (London: Cape, 1926);

Black Sparta: Greek Stories (London: Cape, 1928; New York: Harcourt, Brace, 1928);

Anna Comnena (London: Gerald Howe, 1928);

Nix-Nought-Nothing: Four Plays for Children (London: Cape, 1928; New York: Harcourt, Brace, 1929) – includes *My Ain Sel, Hobyay! Hobyah!, Elfen Hill,* and *Nix-Nought-Nothing*;

Barbarian Stories (London: Cape, 1929; New York: Harcourt, Brace, 1929);

The Hostages and Other Stories for Boys and Girls, illustrated by Logi Southby (London: Cape, 1930; New York: Harcourt, Brace, 1931);

Comments on Birth Control (London: Faber & Faber, 1930);

Kate Crackernuts: A Fairy Play (Oxford: Alden Press, 1931);

Boys and Girls and Gods (London: Watts, 1931);

The Price of Freedom (London: Cape, 1931);

The Corn King and the Spring Queen (London: Cape, 1931; New York: Harcourt, Brace, 1931;

The Powers of Light (London: Cape, 1932; New York: Peter Smith, 1932);

The Delicate Fire: Short Stories and Poems (London: Cape, 1933; New York: Harcourt, Brace, 1933);

The Home and a Changing Civilization (London: John Lane, 1934);

Vienna Diary (London: Gollancz, 1934; New York: Smith & Haas, 1934);

Beyond This Limit (London: Cape, 1935);

We Have Been Warned (London: Constable, 1935; New York: Vanguard, 1936);

The Fourth Pig: Stories and Verses (London: Constable, 1936);

An End and a Beginning and Other Plays (London: Constable, 1937);

Socrates, by Mitchison and Richard Crossman (London: Hogarth Press, 1937; Harrisburg, Pa.: Stackpole, 1938);

The Moral Basis of Politics (London: Constable, 1938; Port Washington, N.Y.: Kennikat Press, 1971);

The Kingdom of Heaven (London: Heinemann, 1939);

As It Was In The Beginning (London: Cape, 1939);

The Blood of the Martyrs (London: Constable, 1939; New York: McGraw-Hill, 1948);

The Alban Goes Out (Harrow, Middlesex: Raven Press, 1939);

The Bull Calves (London: Cape, 1947);

Men and Herring: A Documentary, by Mitchison and Denis Macintosh (Edinburgh: Serif, 1949);

The Big House (London: Faber & Faber, 1950);

Lobsters on the Agenda (London: Gollancz, 1952);

Travel Light (London: Faber & Faber, 1952);

Graeme and the Dragon, illustrated by Pauline Baynes (London: Faber & Faber, 1954);

The Swan's Road, illustrated by Leonard Huskinson (London: Naldrett Press, 1954);

The Land the Ravens Found, illustrated by Brian Allderidge (London: Collins, 1955);

To the Chapel Perilous (London: Allen & Unwin, 1955);

Little Boxes, illustrated by Louise Annand (London: Faber & Faber, 1956);

The Far Harbour, illustrated by Martin Thomas (London: Collins, 1957);

Behold Your King (London: Muller, 1957);

Five Men and a Swan: Short Stories and Poems (London: Allen & Unwin, 1958);

Other People's Worlds (London: Secker & Warburg, 1958);

Judy and Lakshmi, illustrated by Avinash Chandra (London: Collins, 1959);

The Rib of the Green Umbrella, illustrated by Edward Ardizzone (London: Collins, 1960);

Naomi Margaret (Haldane) Mitchison

A Fishing Village on the Clyde, by Mitchison and G. W. L. Patterson (London: Oxford University Press, 1960);

The Young Alexander the Great, illustrated by Betty Middleton-Sandford (London: Parrish, 1960; New York: Roy, 1961);

Karensgaard: The Story of a Danish Farm (London: Collins, 1961);

Presenting Other People's Children (London: Hamlyn, 1961);

The Young Alfred the Great, illustrated by Shirley Farrow (London: Parrish, 1962; New York: Roy, 1963);

Memoirs of a Spacewoman (London: Gollancz, 1962);

The Fairy Who Couldn't Tell a Lie, illustrated by Jane Paton (London: Collins, 1963);

Alexander the Great, illustrated by Rosemary Grimble (London: Longmans, Green, 1964);

Henny and Crispies (Wellington, New Zealand: Department of Education, 1964);

Ketse and the Chief, illustrated by Christine Bloomer (London: Nelson, 1965; New York: Nelson & Nashville, 1967);

When We Become Men (London: Collins, 1965);

A Mochudi Family, illustrated by Stephen John (Wellington, New Zealand: Department of Education, 1965);

Friends and Enemies, illustrated by Caroline Sassoon (London: Collins, 1966; New York: Day, 1968);

Return to the Fairy Hill (London: Heinemann, 1966; New York: Day, 1966);

Highland Holiday, photographs by John K. Wilkie (Wellington, New Zealand: Department of Education, 1967);

The Big Surprise (London: Kaye & Ward, 1967);

African Heroes, illustrated by William Stobbs (London: Bodley Head, 1968; New York: Farrar, Straus, 1969);

Don't Look Back, illustrated by Laszlo Acs (London: Kaye & Ward, 1969);

The Family at Ditlabeng, illustrated by Joanna Stubbs (London: Collins, 1969; New York: Farrar, Straus, 1970);

The Africans: A History (London: Blond, 1970);

Sun and Moon, illustrated by Barry Wilkinson (London: Bodley Head, 1970; Nashville: Nelson, 1973);

Cleopatra's People (London: Heinemann, 1972);

Small Talk: Memories of an Edwardian Childhood (London: Bodley Head, 1973);

A Life for Africa: The Story of Bram Fischer (London: Merlin Press, 1973; Boston: Carrier Pigeon, 1973);

Sunrise Tomorrow (London: Collins, 1973; New York: Farrar, Straus, 1973);

The Danish Teapot, illustrated by Patricia Frost (London: Kaye & Ward, 1973);

Oil for the Highlands? (London: Fabian Society, 1974);

All Change Here: Girlhood and Marriage (London: Bodley Head, 1975);

Stittlichkeit (London: Birkbeck College Press, 1975);

Solution Three (London: Dobson, 1975; New York: Warner, 1975);

Snake!, illustrated by Polly Loxton (London: Collins, 1976);

The Little Sister, with works by Ian Kirby and Keetla Masogo, illustrated by Angela Marrow (Cape Town: Oxford University Press, 1976);

The Wild Dogs, by Mitchison and Megan Biesele, illustrated by Loxton (Cape Town: Oxford University Press, 1977);

The Brave Nurse and Other Stories, illustrated by Loxton (Cape Town: Oxford University Press, 1977);

The Two Magicians, by Mitchison and Dick Mitchison, illustrated by Danuta Laskowska (London: Dobson, 1978);

The Cleansing of the Knife and Other Poems (Edinburgh: Canongate, 1978);

You May Well Ask: A Memoir 1920–1940 (London: Gollancz, 1979);

The Vegetable War, illustrated by Loxton (London: Hamish Hamilton, 1980);

Images of Africa (Edinburgh: Canongate, 1980);

Mucking Around: Five Continents Over Fifty Years (London: Gollancz, 1981);

What Do You Think Yourself? Scottish Short Stories (Edinburgh: Harris, 1982);

Not By Bread Alone (London: Boyars, 1983);

Among You, Taking Notes: The Wartime Diary of Naomi Mitchison 1939–1945, edited by Dorothy Sheridan (London: Gollancz, 1985);

Beyond This Limit: Selected Shorter Fiction of Naomi Mitchison, edited by Isobel Murray (Edinburgh: Scottish Academic Press, 1986);

Naomi Mitchison (Edinburgh: Saltire Society, 1986);

Early in Orcadia (Glasgow: Drew, 1987).

OTHER: *An Outline for Boys and Girls and Their Parents,* edited by Mitchison (London: Gollancz, 1932);

Re-educating Scotland, edited by Mitchison, Robert Britton, and George Kilgour (Glasgow: Scoop, 1944);

What the Human Race Is Up To, edited by Mitchison (London: Gollancz, 1962).

PLAY PRODUCTIONS: *Full Fathom Five,* London, 1932;

The Price of Freedom, Cheltenham, 1949;

The Corn King, music by Brian Easdale, London, 1950;

Spindrift, Glasgow, 1951.

SELECTED PERIODICAL PUBLICATIONS – UNCOLLECTED: "How to Educate Children," *Saturday Review of Literature,* 17 (14 November 1931);

"Writing Historical Novels," *Saturday Review of Literature,* 41 (17 April 1935).

Naomi Mitchison, journalist, poet, storyteller, novelist, and essayist, is known for her "sensitive imagination" and "curious fidelity" to others, regardless of century or place. From early childhood Mitchison knew what she liked and disliked in works written for children. In addition to fairy tales and stories depicting faraway places, among her favorites were the works of Thomas Hardy and E. Nesbit. If, however, she "began to suspect that the book [she] was reading was meant to improve [her] or teach [her] anything, [she] immediately looked at it with the most fierce suspicion and often refused to go on with it."

Born 1 November 1897 in Edinburgh, Scotland, Naomi Haldane spent her early years attending Dragon School. Her first career choice was to become a scientist like her father, John Scott Haldane, and her brother, J. B. S. Haldane. Though she did not graduate, her time at St. Anne's College, Oxford, sparked further interests in classical mythology and history. Work as a Volunteer Aid Detachment (VAD) nurse in London in 1915 broadened her interests to include social and political concerns. In 1916 she married barrister and Labour politician G. Richard Mitchison (later Baron Mitchison), with whom she shared many of her social and political endeavors. Since 1937 she has claimed residence at Carradale in Kintyre, but from the beginning of her marriage Mitchison has divided her time between being wife, mother, grandmother, great-grandmother, writer, teacher, and social and political activist. Mitchison was an Honorary Fellow at Oxford – St. Anne's in 1980 and Wolfson College in 1983 allowed brief periods of teaching; at the University of Stirling, Scotland, in 1976; the University of Dundee, Scotland in 1985; and the University of Strathclyde, Glasgow, Scotland, in 1983.

Her social and political concerns, both local and global, are myriad. She has fought against all nuclear weapons. Though she had six children of

Mitchison, center, with her mother; her father, John Scott Haldane; and her brother, J. B. S. Haldane (courtesy of Naomi Mitchison)

her own – four boys and two girls (her eldest son died at an early age) – she was instrumental in helping to establish the first birth-control clinics in London. She was named an officer of the French Academy in 1924, was a Labour candidate for Parliament, and was named to the Scottish Universities constituency in 1935. She was a member of the Argyll County Council during 1945–1966, a member of the Highland Panel from 1947 to 1954, and a member of the Highlands and Islands Development Council from 1966 to 1976. Some of her other activities included the counterrevolution in Austria in 1934 and the sharecroppers' struggle in Arkansas in 1935. She also visited the Soviet Union twice (1932 and 1952), using its setting for later historical works. Friendship with the Bakgatha tribe of Botswana led to Mitchison's being adopted as its adviser and *Mmarona* (mother) in the 1960s.

Mitchison's own works, whether written for children or adults, reflect her likes and are as diverse in nature as they are in kind. For those works written specifically for, or adapted for, children she employs such genres as poetry, drama, short fiction, fantasy, and historical fiction. Moreover, interests in classical mythology, history, science, travel, and social and political concerns often serve as backdrops for her works. Yet each work has a distinct common bond: though her characters often lived in times past, in foreign lands, and in times of conflict, all exemplify the expression of the human condition – the hope, the fear, the love, the grief, the sorrow, the joy – all that constitutes life. It is a common bond inviting readers to live and feel through the characters' eyes.

Although later known primarily for her historical fiction, Mitchison's first writing for children was poetry. The subject matter of *Cloud Cuckoo Land* (1925) finds roots in classical mythology. Typical entries, such as the following, explore ideas such as glory and honor in connection with individual internal conflict during war:

Troy is taken: Gather Hellenes, on the shore,
Troy is taken, now once more
In to Asia goes the war.

Here forget we strife and hate,
Here is none too proud or great,
Here is none to challenge fate.
Here at last let all be wise,
Deep the sacred truce – time lies
On our hearts and lips and eyes.

Regarded as a well-written work, it remains in print, and many portions appear in numerous anthologies of children's as well as adults' poetry. The collection is best liked for the attention to historical detail and for the nonsentimental portrayal of humankind's plight in an ever-changing world.

Nix-Nought-Nothing: Four Plays For Children (1928) is a collection of versions of Grimms' tales (favorites of Mitchison's), written with the intent that they be performed by children – something Mitchison herself loved to do as a child. Decision and humor are of utmost importance in these plays. Specific stage directions are given for each, but the directions also instruct that the characters' lines must remain current with the times. For example, Jack's lines in Mitchison's version of *Hobyay! Hobyah!* should include an ironic commentary on a current economic stance or condition that is abominable at the time of presentation. This quite blatant interspersing of social commentary is indicative of Mitchison's political interests.

Over the next several years, in addition to writing historical fiction for children and adults, Mitchison became increasingly active in pursuing her interests in social and political problems. As these interests often required travel and time away from her writing, literary critics began to see problems in her books. On one hand, Mitchison was characterized as an "efficient but self-effacing enthusiast who took too much time away from her writing to do practical work for causes she believed in." Yet on the other hand, for staunch supporters such as Henry Seidel Canby (as he wrote in the 19 September 1931 *Saturday Review of Literature*), she was "the most interesting historical novelist now writing in English," bringing the reader "closer to the lost ancient world than . . . history and poems."

Others agreed with Canby, especially concerning *The Hostages and Other Stories for Boys and Girls* (1930), which is the first of Mitchison's historical fictions for children. *The Hostages* is a collection of nine stories that span ancient times from about the fourth century B.C. to around 1100 A.D., some of which came from her adult works *When the Bough Breaks and Other Stories* (1924), *Black Sparta: Greek Stories* (1928), and *Barbarian Stories* (1929). "The First Breaking of England" is an expanded version

of "The Swallows' Path," which first appeared in serialized form in *Home and Country*.

What is so compelling about the stories in *The Hostages* is Mitchison's presentation of individual lives of Greek, Roman, and Gaelic boys in their struggles to come to terms with their physical and emotional surroundings, while pointing out the obvious resemblances to present time. Moreover, detailed sensory imagery such as the vivid descriptions of dress, lodging, and landscape, combined with the descriptions of the smells of culture-specific foods as well as the smell of the sweat that comes with hours of toil, creates a certain kind of historicity that allows the reader to join and identify with the emotional and physical needs of the protagonists.

The next two works Mitchison wrote for children draw their roots from her childhood interest in fairy tales and later interest in mythology. *Kate Crackernuts: A Fairy Play* (1931), in true fairy-tale fashion, depicts a journey through which the protagonist must travel before coming to an understanding of herself and her place in this world. *Boys and Girls and Gods* (1931) is a collection of stories of the lives of young people from faraway lands who "might have lived" thousands of years ago. They, too, must journey in life to find understanding in their worlds.

A continuing concern for Mitchison was how children were educated and what textbooks were available to them. Memories of childhood disappointments in works resurfaced when her own children expressed the same disappointment. In an attempt to reconcile this fault, Mitchison elaborated on her concerns in "How to Educate Children," an essay that appeared in the *Saturday Review of Literature* in 1931. Mitchison entreats adults to show children that learning does not have to be dry or boring. Several renowned scholars of the time agreed to contribute to the task at hand. *An Outline For Boys and Girls and Their Parents* (1932) was the result, with Mitchison as its editor.

The structure of *An Outline For Boys and Girls and Their Parents* was not that of an encyclopedia, but rather that of a critical look at contemporary knowledge. The intent of the work was not to preach or lecture, but to encourage the reader to think critically. The subject matter was written with the idea that children would be interested in all aspects of knowledge, from the origins of life to acts of government and communication through the arts. Major contributors included W. H. Auden; Hugh Gaitskell, a young economist who later was Labour Party leader; and Richard Hughes, a physicist, astronomer,

Mitchison in Greece in 1928 (courtesy of Naomi Mitchison)

and mathematician. All the contributors presented their work "newly and excitingly" and in a way that connected them with the rest of life. *An Outline for Boys and Girls and Their Parents* pointed to a way of developing informative books for children, feeding their "curiousity about the world around," that is still highly respected today.

This feeding of curiosity is also apparent in *An End and a Beginning and Other Plays* (1937), which portrays the lives of young heroes (Constantine, Charlemagne, Cortez, Akbar, and American Britons) of both local and distant places, especially their difficulties in coming to terms with their emerging importance. Sensory imagery again plays an important role in creating the atmosphere and time in which these young heroes lived.

From 1938 until 1950 Mitchison's works for children came to a halt. This period also marked the family's move back to Scotland. Much of her and her husband's time and energy were spent on the many social and political concerns they shared, especially the issue of feudalism. The transition to Scotland was an uneasy one, as neither wanted to return, and the struggles of this period appear as underlying tensions in her later works. Mitchison's nonfiction writing did not cease during this period,

but it was more specifically geared toward adults and dealt with Scottish, American, Austrian, and African affairs. Places to which she traveled during this time also served as backdrops for later works written for children and adults alike.

When Mitchison began once again to write for children, her works showed a shift in perspective. Instead of one character in relation to others, two or more characters are juxtaposed in their relationships with others in past and in present times. Tensions and diversity in beliefs, customs, cultures, and lore abound. *The Big House* (1950), a Nesbit-like fantasy with actual historical and autobiographical implications, commingles stories of the past with the present. Protagonists Susan and Winkie eventually realize the necessity of acknowledging past family differences as part of themselves before they can move forward to the time of mending that each has been seeking but unable to reach. Passages of "haunting beauty and melancholy" are somewhat undermined by varying "imperfect and unreconciled elements."

Graeme and the Dragon (1954) followed a few years later, as did *The Swan's Road* (1954) and *The Land the Ravens Found* (1955). The latter two come from the *Landamabok*, the historical account (written

Mitchison's home, Carradale House (courtesy of Naomi Mitchison)

down some four hundred years later) of families who settled in Iceland during the ninth and tenth centuries A.D. The English translation, *Origines Icelandicae,* is available in most English city or county libraries and in many American metropolitan and university libraries.

The characters in *The Swan's Road* and *The Land the Ravens Found* were real, and Mitchison's portrayal of their trials and tribulations in settling a new land gives the curious effect of an "insider looking out on" the rest of the world. The works also complement each other, for Vivill in *The Land the Ravens Found,* a work that chronicles the Vikings' arrival and settling of Iceland, is the grandfather of Gudrid, wife of Thorfinn Karlsefini in *The Swan's Road,* a work depicting Thorfinn's many adventures into America.

Tensions of another kind appear in *Little Boxes* (1956). Sally and her grandmother find their worlds so different that they have great difficulty in talking to one another. Mitchison is praised for her ability to show that "letting go of the past" does not mean that later it should not be remembered. Sally and her grandmother share a portion of each other's childhood, boxes used for "preserving things."

The focus on returning to remote or distant places comes in *The Far Harbour* (1957), *Judy and Lakshmi* (1959), and *The Rib of the Green Umbrella* (1960). In all three attention to "social and historical

facts or probabilities [are] as minutely correct as possible." *The Far Harbour,* in its picture of a remote Scottish community, is filled with numerous legends. Folkloric interweavings of past and present enhance the "satisfactory if unconventional home life."

It is in *Judy and Lakshmi* and *The Rib of the Green Umbrella* that Mitchison best captures her interest: "how people react to new situations, as many of us have had to do over the last half century. Doing this entails the imaginative gymnastic[s] of getting into other people's bodies and minds in these situations." For example, Mitchison's depiction of the strained friendship between Judy and Lakshmi because of religious and political differences among their families brings the reader to the "here and now" turmoil in India at the time of the book's publication. Yet the reader feels the comforting "coolness" of the floor on bare feet as, along with Judy, he or she steps into a traditional Hindu home for the first time.

Mitchison's re-creation of World War II Italy, where previously feuding communities join together to fight a common enemy, in *The Rib of the Green Umbrella,* involves the reader in seeing, hearing, and doing with the young hero, who is ever protective of his family yet willing to reach out and do all he can for others.

The Young Alexander the Great (1960) is perhaps the most widely known of Mitchison's works, and it is generally considered one of her best. Alexander, in living the Greek ideas of "self-discipline, the middle way, and brotherhood," illuminates activities and thinking of fourth-century B.C. at the court of Philip of Macedon. Alexander's interaction with his peers and his tutor, Aristotle – "the best brain of his generation," with whom Alexander was willing to argue and disagree – is enhanced by Mitchison in "What Happened Afterward": "What is so exciting is that [Alexander's] ideas went far beyond those of his tutor." Critics find Mitchison's portrayal of Alexander "wholly believable" and "authentic" in his "eager, curious, hotheaded, spoiling for battle but surprisingly merciful" personality.

Mitchison's works for children after 1960 follow the same conflict-tension-resolution pattern. Her authenticity in reconstructing history with accuracy, her carefulness and sensitivity in depicting customs other than her own, and her special attention to what it must have been like to be the protagonist are considered her greatest assets.

References:

Mabel A. Bessey, "Naomi Mitchison: Who Hears the Acaeans Shout and Rebuilds Sparta's Towers," *Scholastic* (10 February 1934): 6, 12;

Henry Seidel Canby, "Pattern of the Ancient World," *Saturday Review of Literature,* 9 (19 September 1931);

Marcus Crouch, *Treasure Seekers and Borrowers* (Rochester, Kent: Staples, 1962), pp. 67–68, 81, 116, 121–122;

"*Young Alexander the Great,*" 37 *Horn Book* (June 1961), p. 277;

"*Young Alexander the Great,*" *New York Times Book Review,* 28 May 1961.

Mary Norton

(10 December 1903 – 29 August 1992)

Jon C. Stott
University of Alberta

BOOKS: *The Magic Bed-Knob: or, How to Become a Witch in Ten Easy Lessons,* illustrated by Waldo Pierce (New York: Hyperion Press, 1943); republished as *The Magic Bed-Knob,* illustrated by Joan Kiddell-Monroe (London: Dent, 1945);

Bonfires and Broomsticks, illustrated by Mary Ahshead (London: Dent, 1947);

The Borrowers, illustrated by Diana Stanley (London: Dent, 1952); illustrated by Beth and Joe Krush (New York: Harcourt, Brace, 1953);

The Borrowers Afield, illustrated by Stanley (London: Dent, 1955); illustrated by Beth and Joe Krush (New York: Harcourt, Brace, 1955);

Bed-Knob and Broomstick, revised and combined versions of *The Magic Bed-Knob* and *Bonfires and Broomsticks,* illustrated by Erik Blegvad (London: Dent, 1957; New York: Harcourt, Brace, 1957);

The Borrowers Afloat, illustrated by Stanley (London: Dent, 1959); illustrated by Beth and Joe Krush (New York: Harcourt, Brace, 1959);

The Borrowers Aloft, illustrated by Stanley (London: Dent, 1961); illustrated by Beth and Joe Krush (New York: Harcourt, Brace & World, 1961);

Poor Stainless: A New Story about the Borrowers, illustrated by Stanley (London: Dent, 1971); illustrated by Beth and Joe Krush (New York: Harcourt Brace Jovanovich, 1971);

Are All the Giants Dead?, illustrated by Brian Froud (London: Dent, 1975; New York: Harcourt Brace Jovanovich, 1975);

The Borrowers Avenged, illustrated by Pauline Baynes (London: Kestrel, 1982); illustrated by Beth and Joe Krush (New York: Harcourt Brace Jovanovich, 1982).

Collections: *The Complete Adventures of the Borrowers* (New York: Harcourt, Brace & World, 1967);

The Borrower's Omnibus (London: Dent, 1990).

Although she wrote only eight novels in a career that extended from 1943 to 1982, Mary Norton is rightfully considered one of the major midcentury

Mary Norton (photograph by Angus McBean, by permission of Harcourt, Brace & Company)

British children's authors. *The Borrowers* (1952), winner of the distinguished Carnegie Medal, quickly assumed status as a classic. The five sequels to that book developed what critic Gillian Avery called "a powerful mythology." *Are All the Giants Dead?* (1975) offered an ingenious contrast to the author's previous works. From the time of the appearance of her first novel, *The Magic Bed-Knob: or, How to Become a Witch in Ten Easy Lessons* (1943), Norton demonstrated a superb fusion of what T. S. Eliot called "tradition and the individual talent." She combined elements of her own experiences, transformed to meet the needs of her fantasies, with recognizable aspects of genres popular in British children's fiction of the first half of the twentieth century to create narratives that still maintain their freshness, originality, and vitality.

Born in London 10 December 1903, the only daughter of Reginald and Mary Pearson, Mary Pearson spent most of her childhood in Leighton Buzzard, a small country town in Bedfordshire County. With her brothers, the nearsighted girl wandered through the countryside and, on rainy days, joined them in homemade theatricals. Her house and the surrounding area were to form the settings for the five novels and one short story of the Borrowers Series, *The Borrowers, The Borrowers Afield* (1955), *The Borrowers Afloat* (1959), *The Borrowers Aloft* (1961), *Poor Stainless: A New Story about the Borrowers* (1971), and *The Borrowers Avenged* (1982). At this time, according to Norton in an interview with Jon C. Stott, the idea for her most famous creations came into being: "I think the first idea – or first feeling – of *The Borrowers* came through my being short-sighted: when others saw the far hills, the distant woods, the soaring pheasant, I, as a child, would turn sideways to the close bank, the tree roots, and the tangled grasses." Trailing along after her brothers, she often daydreamed: "Moss, fern-stalks, sorrel stems, created the mise-en-scène for a jungle drama. . . . But one invented the characters – small, fearful people picking their way through the miniature undergrowth." Norton did not discuss her childhood reading, but echoes in her novels of the works of E. Nesbit, Kenneth Grahame, Frances Hodgson Burnett, and J. M. Barrie suggest their influence.

As a young adult living with her parents in Lambeth, a suburb of London, Mary audaciously suggested to a dinner guest, the actor-impressario Arthur Rose, her wish to become an actress, and, indeed, her wish came true. During the 1925–1926 season, she performed as an understudy at London's Old Vic theater. These experiences, which she described as the most memorable of her life, influenced her writing. For example, in *The Borrowers Afield* she says of her heroine: "Arrietty wandered out to the dim-lit platform; this, with its dust and shadows – had she known of such things – was something like going back stage." Often episodes in her novels resemble dramatic scenes, with two or three characters interacting in an indoor or confined set.

In 1927 she married Robert Norton, a member of a wealthy shipowning and trading family from Portugal. Until the outbreak of World War II, she lived with her four children in a relatively iso-

lated country estate several miles from Lisbon. When the war began she moved back to London with her children, while her husband remained in Portugal. Her life in Portugal, cut off as it was from extended family and friends, seems to have influenced her portrayal of Homily, the mother of the central character in the Borrowers Series. Arriving back in London, she may well have felt like that woman: "homeless and destitute. . . . And strange relations . . . who didn't know she was coming and whom she hadn't seen for years."

As the political conditions in Europe worsened during the late 1930s, Norton remembered the tiny imaginary people of her childhood: "It was only just before the 1940 war . . . that one thought again about the Borrowers. There were human men and women who were being forced to live . . . the kind of lives a child had once envisaged for a race of mythical creatures." Unable to support her family on the income she received first from the British War Office in London and then from the British Purchasing Commission in New York, she began writing essays, translations, and children's stories, including her first novel, *The Magic Bed-Knob*.

Drawing on the experiences of herself and her children, Norton presents the story of three children, Carey, Charles, and Paul Wilson, who live in the country during the bombing of London. They befriend Miss Price, a shy neighbor who is taking a correspondence course in witchcraft and who places a spell on a bed-knob, thus allowing the three to travel magically anywhere they wish. With her, they are transported to a South Seas island where, through the agency of her magic, they narrowly escape being eaten by cannibals. The book was a critical success. "This story has all the makings of [a classic]," declared the *New York Times Book Review*. The *Library Journal* acclaimed it a "modern masterpiece."

The novel draws on three popular types of children's novels: stories, such as those written by E. Nesbit at the turn of the century, of ordinary children encountering magic; tales, such as P. L. Travers's *Mary Poppins* (1934) about gruff, but kind witches; and narratives, like Kitty Barnes's *Visitors from London* (1940), about children evacuated from London because of the bombing. However, Norton does not slavishly follow the conventions of these genres. Her originality, which early reviewers praised, is found in the way she uses the conventions for her own purposes. Indeed, she may well have been parodying the traditions within which she was writing. Although the Wilsons' means of

traveling may not be as glamorous as the magic carpet used in Nesbit's books, their adventures are
equally exciting and equally brave. Miss Price may
seem like a failed Mary Poppins, but she is extremely courageous when she uses her untried skills
to rescue herself and the children from cannibals.

Norton does not parody the evacuation novel;
however, the war background enhances characterization. The children's loneliness away from their
mother is genuine and the dangers of London to
which they return at the end of the novel are great.
Miss Price is genuinely worried for them at this
point. Contemporary readers of the novel may have
found that the courage, gentleness, and friendliness
of Miss Price and the Wilsons were important attributes to possess during the frightening times.

An important element of the novel is its portrayal of the relationship between Miss Price and
the children. Unlike the other adults, who are what
early-twentieth-century children's writer Kenneth
Grahame called "Olympians," aloof and generally
uncaring, she is genuinely concerned for them. She
also helps them to develop as individuals. Carey,
who cares for her deeply, moves toward young
womanhood. Paul, the baby, becomes a child.
Charles overcomes the timidity he exhibited when
they first came to the country. Like a fairy godmother, which she little resembles outwardly, Miss
Price has helped them develop their inner poten-
tials.

In addition, Miss Price herself grows through
her interaction with the children. She had led a double life — a proper village spinster and an inept, apprentice witch — but she had achieved little success
with magic. She had, in fact, repressed her talents,
using them only to grow better flowers in her garden. The children are the first people to know about
her secret profession, and at first she is suspicious
and distrustful of them. However, she develops real
affection for them and worries more about them
than about herself during the dangerous trip to the
South Seas.

At the conclusion of the novel, the children's
aunt sends them back to wartime London. However, there is a hint of further adventures: Paul has
brought a magic bed-knob with him. More than the
plot and the genre demands a sequel, though. The
children, especially Charles, and Miss Price are capable of further character growth. In fact, as *The
Magic Bed-Knob* was published, Norton was writing a
sequel.

Bonfires and Broomsticks appeared in England in
1947 but not in the United States until 1957, combined with, when it was revised, and combined with

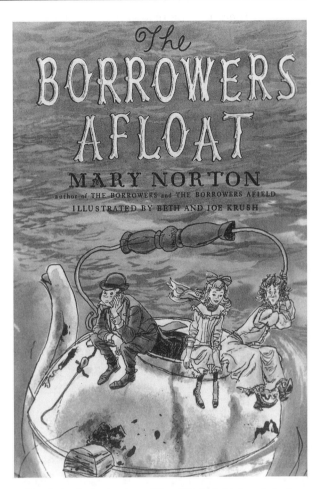

*Dust jacket for the American edition of Norton's third novel about a
family of tiny people who live beneath the floorboards of country houses*

her first book under the title *Bed-Knob and Broomstick*.
The *New York Times Book Review* found it "just as
good as the first," while poet John Betjeman believed it to be "quite the best modern fairy story I
have read." Back in the country to spend the summer with Miss Price, the Wilsons discover that the
bed-knob can be used for time as well as space
travel and wish themselves into the later seventeenth century, where they meet Emelius Jones, an
inept sorcerer whom they bring back to their own
time. When he returns to his own era, he is con-
demned to be burned at the stake for witchcraft.
Miss Price and the children rescue him, and the two
adults marry and live in the seventeenth century.

Just as the Wilsons arrive at Miss Price's with
expectations based on their memories of their earlier experiences, so readers approach the novel with
expectations based on their reading of *The Magic
Bed-Knob*. However, the sequel is no mere formulaic
repetition of characters and events; readers' awareness of how the story differs from its predecessor

will help them to understand its specific themes. Not only is the travel in time rather than in space, but the adventures are more serious. Whereas the escape from the cannibals was described with a humorous tone in *The Magic Bed-Knob,* the rescue of Emelius is presented as being extremely dangerous and filled with terror in *Bonfires and Broomsticks.* Moreover, both Charles and Miss Price are considered in greater detail than they were in the first book, and they undergo considerable character development. Finally, the conclusion of *Bonfires and Broomsticks* achieves definite closure. With the bedknob attached to the bed, which is now forever in the seventeenth century, there can be no further magical travel.

With the exception of Paul, the youngest sibling, who is of little importance in the novel, the children, now two years older, undergo further character growth and development. Carey, nearly a young lady, becomes fonder of Miss Price and works actively to bring her friend and Emelius together; she is becoming a matchmaker. Charles, who had been so quiet and shy during the previous adventures, takes a far greater role in events, becoming a brave leader and a courageous rescuer of Emelius. Miss Price, whose growing concern for the children was seen in *The Magic Bed-Knob,* is presented in considerable depth. Norton reveals with sympathy and understanding the woman's loneliness, her happiness and awkwardness when she begins to befriend Emelius, and her emotional flowering as she decides to sell her home and marry him.

While Norton's first two novels are certainly not major works of children's literature, they are very well written and give promise of the excellence of the books to come. The adventures she depicts are fast-paced and exciting. Her characterization is precise, especially in the case of Miss Price. Moreover, she understands the development patterns of children, particularly as they mature in their relationships with adults. Finally, she displays a sense of humor, as in her frequent references to Miss Price's long, pointed nose, which reveals her changing emotions. It is variously referred to as "a reassuring nose" and "a pink-tipped banner of indignation and wrath."

The Borrowers, Norton's third and greatest novel, was published in 1952 to almost instant critical acclaim. Marcus Crouch comments that, "of all the winners of the Carnegie Medal [awarded annually by the British Library Association to the best children's novel of the preceding year], it is the one book of unquestioned, timeless genius." Still widely read, it has been made into two television specials,

one in England, one in the United States. The novel is about a species of tiny people, identical to human beings, who live beneath the floorboards of old country houses, borrowing food and supplies left lying about by the large occupants of the dwellings; specifically the novel focuses on Pod and Homily Clock and their daughter, Arrietty, the last three Borrowers living in a house reminiscent of that in which Norton spent her childhood. The events of their lives are recounted to a young girl, Kate, by Mrs. May, an aging relative who had learned of them from her brother, who, as a child, had met and interacted with the little people.

The narrative begins one spring day as Arrietty, bored, restless, and unhappy, awaits her father's return from a borrowing expedition in the main house. When she learns that he has been discovered by a boy and that the family must emigrate to ensure their safety, she is overjoyed at the prospect of the freedom such a move could offer. However, the family delays their departure and, several days later, when she accompanies her father on her first borrowing excursion, she too is seen by the boy. The two strike up a friendship, and, in exchange for her teaching him to read, he agrees to take a letter into the fields where she thinks her relatives, the Hendrearys, live. The family, which again delays emigration when the boy, much to Homily's delight, brings them gifts of dollhouse furniture, is discovered by Mrs. Driver, the housekeeper, who then sets about to exterminate the Borrowers. Only when the boy breaks open a grating that leads from the Clocks' home to the outdoors is their escape made possible.

At this point Mrs. May ends her narration of events, explaining that her brother never saw the Borrowers again and never knew if they escaped. Together, the old woman and the young girl create a hypothetical ending to the Clocks' adventure, imagining their new life in the Hendrearys' home in the field.

Norton makes the existence of her tiny characters convincing through her skilled description of the settings, their actions, and the objects they use. Articles small to human beings are presented as huge from a Borrower's point of view. Discarded sheets of writing paper are made into wallpaper; a wire fly swatter is transformed into a safety door, keeping their apartments safe against mice. The world outside is gigantic and potentially dangerous to them. Insects are the size of birds; a drop of dew is as large as a marble; a clump of wood violets and clover is "a jungle."

More important for the achievement of credibility than Norton's descriptive skills is her ability to create fully realized characters and to present dramatically the conflicts they experience. Her focus is on Arrietty and, to a lesser extent, the boy. However, they are understood partly in relation to the adults in their lives.

Arrietty's father, Pod, exerts a benevolent, patriarchal control over his family. Although he is a kind and caring parent and a good provider, he asserts his position as the head of the family, believing that his wife and child should stay at home not only because of the dangers beyond it but also because borrowing has always been a strictly male occupation. He is also overprotective of his daughter, placing restrictions on her life as if he fears her growing up. When his daughter befriends the boy, he is unable to adapt to the changed conditions of their lives, hiding behind long-held, conservative notions about correct Borrower behavior. At one point, when he sees his daughter standing close to a candle, he warns, "Be careful of the light," a remark that symbolizes his attitude toward new ways of approaching experience.

Homily, Arrietty's mother, is fussy, distracted, emotional, house-proud, snobbish, self-centered, and manipulative; she is also extremely devoted to her family. She has lived her adult life confined to the apartments, her only company her husband and her daughter, and her only sense of fulfillment and self-worth is an outgrowth of pride in the home she has created for them. However, as she told her daughter (in an episode recounted in *Poor Stainless*, a short story published in 1971), she had gone outside frequently as a girl and had loved the freedom she had felt during her trips. Perhaps the negative qualities she displays during much of *The Borrowers* are products of the repression of the joyous sense of liberty she had experienced as a child. If this is so, it may explain why she insists that Pod take Arrietty on one of the borrowing expeditions he makes to the front porch of the house. She wishes the girl to experience the feelings she once had. In making it possible for Arrietty to leave the confines of their dwelling, she is assisting the girl's maturing process.

The three adult human beings who live in the house are "Olympians." Great-Aunt Sophy, the bedridden owner of the house, lives on past memories and her nightly bottle of Fine Pale Old Madeira and sees the boy only in the mornings when she is cranky. The housekeeper, Mrs. Driver, who "ruled supreme" wishes to control all aspects of life in the house, thereby providing her with a sense of security. She treats the boy roughly, and, after she sees the Clock family, seeks to maintain her dominance

by exterminating them. Crampfurl, the gardener, takes little notice of the boy. In contrast to Arrietty's parents, who offer their daughter love and support, the adults virtually ignore the boy.

Arrietty and the boy mature greatly during the novel. As Norton writes, "In each generation, only youth is restless and brave enough to try to get out from under the floorboards." At the edge of adolescence, Arrietty wants to escape not only from her cramped, dimly lit home but also from the psychological constraints of her parents' way of life. When she learns of the possibility of emigration, she angrily tells them, "I don't think it's so clever to live on alone, forever and ever, in a great, big, half-empty house; under the floor with no one to talk to, no one to play with, nothing to see but dust and passages, no light but candlelight and firelight and what comes through the cracks."

The girl's physical journey with her father symbolizes the first major steps in her inward journey toward adulthood. Having passed through the literal gates constructed by Pod, she prepares to pass through metaphorical gates that liberate her into a world of imaginative fulfillment and freedom. As she looks at her father, "suddenly she saw him as small." She is beginning to move away from what feminist critic Annis Pratt has called "enclosure in the patriarchy." Going across the porch, around the corner, and to the grating that looks in on their home, she has crossed a threshold, turned a corner, stood on the outside looking in, and wandered out of sight (and possibly out of mind) of her father. Her meeting with the boy a few moments later shatters her ethnocentric view (human beings, she thinks, exist for the benefit of Borrowers) and introduces her to worlds that exist beyond the narrow confines of the area beneath the floorboards. However, when the boy tells her that he thinks the Borrowers are a vanishing race, she becomes frightened and finds a new focus for her discontentment. Emigration now means more than personal freedom, it means a search for others of her kind to ensure the survival of the race. "I don't want us to die out," she thinks. "I don't want to be the last Borrower. I don't want . . . to live forever and ever like this . . . in the dark . . . under the floor."

When the family is discovered by Mrs. Driver and immediate emigration becomes a necessity, Arrietty is filled with joy. Having learned more about the larger world through her conversations with the boy and believing that the Hendrearys are to be found living in a nearby field, she faces her future with hope and excitement. It seems possible that her goals for herself and for the race can be fulfilled.

Dust jacket for the American edition of Norton's book about the place where fairy-tale characters live after their adventures

In addition to the clarity of description, the exciting plot, and the detailed character development, *The Borrowers* is also distinguished for the way Norton uses point of view to develop the novel's many themes. Events within the Clock household were told to the boy by Arrietty; he in turn, as a child, told them to his sister; as an adult she told them to Kate. As principal narrator, Mrs. May does not simply repeat what she heard from her brother many years earlier. Instead, she reports most of the events from the point of view of Arrietty, using her own feminine knowledge and experiences to interpret not only the girl's inner thoughts and emotions but also those of Mrs. Driver and Homily. In many ways she is like a Borrower herself. Using her brother's information, her own childhood visit to the house, and her mature wisdom, she creatively adapts old materials to make something new and purposeful.

In telling the story Mrs. May is like a crone, the wise old female keeper of lore and wisdom who in traditional societies was often responsible for helping young girls make the passage from childhood to adulthood. She seems to tell Kate the story because she recognizes that her listener is not unlike Arrietty and can profit from it. However, she does not present a complete, rigidly defined story, and she frequently casts doubt on the factuality of events she has recounted. She calls forth from her auditor a creative, questioning response. Kate, as she does in the final two chapters, must re-create the story for herself, understanding it in her own terms. Interestingly, Mrs. May tells Kate the story while teaching the girl quilt making. Thus, she teaches the girl both literally and symbolically. During the last two chapters, as they sew together the crocheted patches into a quilt, Mrs. May helps Kate gather together the pieces of information and understanding she has acquired from hearing the direct narrative to create a unified, seamless narrative to conclude the Clocks' adventures. Just as Arrietty and the boy learn and develop during the summer, Kate grows in sensitivity as she responds to and then cocreates the story.

The frame narrative with Kate and Mrs. May and the inner narrative about the Borrowers and human beings are linked thematically. Who sees the Borrowers and how they react to them determines much of the meaning of the story. Great-Aunt Sophy thinks that Pod is a product of her sherry drinking. Mrs. Driver believes in what she sees, but her response is exaggerated and vindictive. The boy gradually develops qualities of sympathy and understanding. His response to what he sees makes his summer with the Borrowers a turning point in his life. He is also one of the three people who tell the story and, as such, is part of the link in which point of view moves steadily from actually seeing the Borrowers to imaginative insight about them. Accordingly, Mrs. Mays greatest achievement is her transmission of her imaginative sympathy and insight to Kate. By the end of the novel, Kate, who has never sighted a Borrower, has, perhaps, as complete a comprehension of Pod, Homily, and Arrietty as anyone in the novel.

While the last two chapters create an emotionally satisfying conclusion to *To Borrowers,* questions remain. What were the details of the family's life after the escape, and did Arrietty, who had matured so much in a few weeks, continue to develop? It seems probable that having created a sequel to *The Magic Bed-Knob,* Mary Norton was leaving the way open for further stories about the Clock family.

In many ways these books, recounting as they do the wanderings and many temporary homes of the Clocks, reflect Norton's life after World War II. Although she gave little personal information about the period from 1945 onward, she lived in many different places before her death at Hartland, England, on 29 August 1992. London; Essex; West Cork, Ireland; and Bideford, England, all have been listed as her residences.

The Borrowers Afield opens the year after the telling of the first story, as Kate and Mrs. May depart for Firbank Hall, the house where the Clocks lived. The girl meets old Tom Goodenough who, when he was a boy, had been told by Arrietty about her family's escape and travel to the old cottage where Tom lived. He gives Kate the diary Arrietty had kept during their odyssey, and she uses this, along with his reports, to create a narrative that she records for her own children.

The Clocks' journey was not at all as Kate and Mrs. May had hypothesized at the end of *The Borrowers.* When they arrive at the badger set, the supposed home of the Hendrearys, it is empty, and the family is required to set up temporary residence in an old boot. They meet and befriend Spiller, a young Borrower who lives alone in nature; are captured by Mild Eye, a gypsy; and are rescued from his caravan by Spiller and his young human friend, Tom Goodenough. At the story's conclusion, they are reunited with the Hendrearys, who live within the walls of the boy's home, and Arrietty initiates a conversation with Tom.

The novel, which the *Times Literary Supplement* called "that rare thing, an entirely successful sequel" and *The New York Times Book Review* considered "in some ways even better [than *The Borrowers*]," answered many of the questions presumably asked by readers of the first volume but also raised new ones. If Kate and Mrs. May were incorrect in their hypotheses, how accurate is the account that the now-adult Kate gives her children? Her story is, after all, several times removed from the actual events. And how happy will the Clocks be living with the Hendrearys; has a satisfying closure to their odyssey been achieved? At best, an uneasy peace exists between Homily and Aunt Lupy, and Arrietty feels confined in the dark apartments. Will Arrietty's talking to a human being lead to emigration as it had after her meetings with the boy?

In *The Borrowers Afloat,* the last of the series to use a narrative framework, the opening chapters indicate that Kate has taken the lead in preserving the memory of the Clock family. She has told Mrs. May about the Borrowers' encounters with the Hendreary family, and she shows the old lady the tiny archway used by the family to enter the Hendrearys' home. The direct narrative continues the theme of a quest for a safe, stable home. The uneasy relationships between the Clocks and the Hendrearys continue and, when the human occupants of the house leave, Homily realizes that her family must once again emigrate. The three find another temporary home, this time in a discarded kettle that is soon washed down the river during a flood. The Borrowers are seen and nearly recaptured by Mild Eye but are again rescued by Spiller, who takes them toward a new home at Little Fordham, a nearby model village. Given the tenuousness of their lives in their two dwelling places in this novel and the uncertain conclusions of the first two books in the series, readers may wonder how suitable their proposed home will be.

The Borrowers Aloft, the fourth novel of the series, is the least successful, falling into predictable plot patterns of setting up house, capture, escape, and relocation. It is, as one reviewer stated, "somewhat more contrived," including as it does far more detailed but less functional accounts of the technical activities of borrowing. Having arrived at the model village of Little Fordham, the Clock family is delighted at the apparent freedom and increased opportunities for borrowing. However, their lives are influenced more than they realize by two groups of human beings: Mr. Pott, the owner of the village, and his friend Miss Menzies, who take a benevolent interest in the tiny people; and Mr. and Mrs. Platter, owners of a rival village, who kidnap the Clocks. Imprisoned for the winter in the Platters' attic, Pod, Homily, and Arrietty seem destined to spend the rest of their lives on display in the Platters' model village where they will stay permanently. However, the family escapes in a tiny balloon ingeniously created by Pod and Arrietty from discarded objects and returns to Little Fordham, where Spiller awaits them. When Pod learns that Arrietty has been talking to another human being, Miss Menzies, the family prepares to depart to another, more remote location. In an epilogue, the narrator announces that, as she has no further information about the Clocks, there will be no further stories about Borrowers.

What makes the novel markedly different from the earlier three is the greater attention given to the human beings in the Clocks' lives. Although Mr. Pott and Miss Menzies are kindly people, wishing only the best for the three tiny occupants of the model village, and Mr. and Mrs. Platter seek to control them for economic gain, contact with any human being is dangerous. As Pod tells Arrietty, depending on them not only robs the family of the independence of borrowing but, more important, he says, "They're never tamed. . . . One day, they'll break out — one day, when you least expect it." He explains that, when Arrietty becomes a mother, she will not want to endanger her family by contacting human beings. When she promises not to make contact with Miss Menzies, whom she dearly loves, it appears that the family has made its last contact with a human being. If there is no danger from being seen, there will be no dangerous experiences, and, accordingly, no more novels in the series.

Although there were to be two more stories about the Clocks, one published in 1971 and another in 1982, Norton's next major work, *Are All the Giants Dead?*, published in 1975, marked a completely new direction in her children's fiction. It is the story of James, an average boy who is taken, by Mildred, a middle-aged writer, to the land where famous fairy-tale characters live after their major adventures have been completed. He meets Jack-of-the-Beanstalk and Jack-the-Giant-Killer who are depressed because the former cannot grow a beanstalk for the latter to climb to the land of the last, apparently invincible giant. With James's assistance, the two recover their self-esteem, and Dulcibel, the

princess who must marry a frog, learns to control her own future. The adventures over, James finds himself back in his own bedroom. The distinguished British children's literature reviewer Margery Fisher was delighted with the new direction of Norton's writing, saying that the novel "is unexpected, but as brilliant, beguiling, and original as could possibly be wished."

While the novel does deal with themes found in the Borrowers Series — the maturing of a child who learns to understand another young person of the opposite sex, as well as with the adults with whom he interacts and the quiet heroism of a young boy — it is significantly different in that it involves a journey to a world of pure fantasy. Whereas the Clocks lived in turn-of-the-century Bedfordshire County, James visits a land and characters that exist only in the literary imaginations of authors and readers.

Norton stresses the ordinariness of James's character. He likes typical boys' activities and enjoys reading science fiction; he is bored when his guide, Mildred, introduces him to the people from tales he considers for little children and is ignorant of the conventions and plots of traditional stories. However, when he learns of Dulcibel's problems with the frog and the unhappiness of the two Jacks, he becomes concerned, responding to them as human beings whose well-being he cares about. He learns, however, that although he can offer assistance and emotional support, he cannot direct the lives of his friends. This realization marks the end of his adventure; it is implied that it is his last trip with Mildred. He is ready for new experiences, ready to explore new realms of the imagination. Appropriately, he falls asleep "dreaming a long, lovely dream about cosmonauts."

Mildred, James's adult guide, is one of Norton's most interesting adult characters. While Pod and Homily were fairly typical parents to Arrietty, Mildred is more like Miss Price of *The Magic Bed-Knob* and *Bonfires and Broomsticks,* an unusual woman who introduces children to new realms of experience. She is not unlike a fairy godmother, assisting the central character to grow and develop, helping him to realize his inner potential. Significantly, she leaves James behind with the two Jacks while she attends a royal wedding, thus giving him the opportunities to interact with the old men and Dulcibel without her guidance. In some ways she is also like Mrs. May, who has guided Kate into the story of the Borrowers, helped her to tell part of it, and then left the girl to tell more of it by herself. She may symbolize the role of a children's author, even Norton herself, a person who creates a narrative into which young readers can enter, exploring and creating meaning on their own. Mildred is somewhat sensitive about her age, and the two Jacks worry about being "past it." However, as events prove, Mildred still performs a valuable role for James, and the two Jacks bring satisfying closures to their stories, working together to destroy the last giant. Mary Norton, striking out in original directions after fourteen years without publishing a novel, proved that she was not past it. She displayed her typical sense of humor in the story, her ability to create strong characters, and her keen abilities to describe new settings and new actors.

In 1982 Norton returned to the saga of the Clock family. With the encouragement of her English editor, she published a manuscript she had been working on for several years, *The Borrowers Avenged*. As the adjective indicates, this story deals with completed action and brings the series to closure. Spiller leads Pod, Homily, and Arrietty to a new home in the semideserted rectory of the village church. The Hendrearys live nearby, in the church itself, and Arrietty is rejoined with Timmus (the spelling of whose name has been inexplicably changed). She also meets and befriends Peagreen, a lame, artistic young Borrower who assists the family in settling in. The main action of the story takes place in the church, as the Platters, attempting to seize Timmus, are arrested as robbers. Arrietty, for the first time in the series, does not make contact with a human being and develops a fuller understanding of Spiller and her relationship with him. The novel ends with Peagreen stating that Borrowers are never really safe; such is the nature of their lives. However, because of Arrietty's keeping her promise not to speak to Miss Menzies, the family does not have to emigrate. The series is over.

What immediately strikes a reader of *The Borrowers Avenged* is the length of the novel, nearly three hundred pages in the American edition — much longer than any of the four previous books. Much of the space is taken with descriptions of the Clocks' new home and with how-to-do-it accounts of their routine activities. Although English critic Marcus Crouch said that "on the evidence of this book, the author is at the height of her powers still," the novel lacks the tightness of construction and intensity of its predecessors.

When the Clocks first enter the rectory, Pod announces, "we're home," and, indeed, the rectory is the most secure place the family has lived in since leaving Firbank Hall. Their first and latest homes are similar: both are on the ground floors of large buildings containing few people; both have a grating looking to the outside; and both provide ample opportunities for borrowing. However, the rectory is superior to Firbank Hall: the human occupants seldom enter the area near the Clocks' home; the grating opens into the outdoors; and there are other Borrowers nearby. Though they may never be completely safe, their quest for a suitable home seems to have ended.

Arrietty, who is overjoyed with the prospects of living in this home, has no dangerous adventures during the novel. However, she continues to mature, achieving a sense of independence and an awareness of her interdependence with the other Borrowers in her life. She thinks of her family's safety and happiness, understands the emotions of her new friend Peagreen, takes an active role in the upbringing of Timmus, and, finally, realizes that she must accept Spiller on his own terms. In the novel's concluding paragraphs, Peagreen helps her to understand how important Spiller is to her and how much he will do for her. Although it is not stated, the implication is that she will marry the young man who has been so kind to her and her family during their dangerous odyssey.

The Borrowers Avenged is unlike the earlier works in the series in that it contains a great deal of satire about conditions of twentieth-century English life. In the earlier books, there had been generalized satire of human nature. However, with the move to the village, the Clocks come into closer contact with life of the twentieth century which, at best, is unaesthetic and artistically tasteless. Peagreen comments critically on the tasteless renovations made to the rectory, and the author comments on the shoddy buildings constructed by the money-grubbing Mr. Platter. The Clocks are more comfortable with traditional ways of life and have difficulty understanding the concepts of money and banking. By living in an isolated part of the rectory, they can avoid as much as possible the modern world and its evils.

In reading Mary Norton's novels, readers can acquire a greater understanding of English life of the twentieth century. In addition to their implicit comments on modernization, the "Borrowers Series" presents a picture of English country life at the time of the author's childhood. The Clocks' frequent moves reflect the increasingly unsettled social conditions of the period after World War I. *The Magic Bed-Knob* relates to the dangers of World War II. More important, readers can learn about timeless aspects of human nature: the difficulties of coming of age, defining oneself in relation to and in opposition against the conservative values of one's parents; the necessities of fulfilling oneself without giving in to selfishness, mean-spiritedness, and greed; and the need to understand and accept the natures of other people. Finally, they can acquire greater understanding of the nature and importance of stories and storytelling, the value of creative interactions with narratives.

All of these aspects of Mary Norton's novels would be of little importance, if she were not a superb stylist, sensitively presenting and exploring her themes and characters, using humor, sympathy, and her powers of precise observation to create novels that have delighted readers since their first publication. Small though her literary output was, she is certainly a major writer of children's literature.

References:

Julia Davenport, "The Narrative Framework of *The Borrowers:* Mary Norton and Emile Brontë," *Children's Literature in Education,* 49 (1983): 75–79;

Nigel Hand, "Mary Norton and 'The Borrowers,' " *Children's Literature in Education,* 7 (1972): 38–55;

Lois Kuznets, "Permutations of Frame in Mary Norton's 'Borrowers' Series," *Studies in the Literary Imagination,* 18 (1985): 65–78;

Michael and Margaret Rustin, "Deep Structures of Fantasy in Modern British Children's Books," *Lion and the Unicorn,* 10 (1986): 60–82;

Jon C. Stott, "Anatomy of a Masterpiece: *The Borrowers,*" *Language Arts,* 55 (1976): 538–544;

Margaret Thomas, "Discourse of the Difficult Daughter: A Feminist Reading of Mary Norton's *Borrowers,*" *Children's Literature in Education,* 84 (1992): 39–48;

Virginia L. Wolf, "From the Myth to the Wake of Home: Literary Houses," *Children's Literature,* 18 (1990): 53–67.

Mervyn Laurence Peake

(9 July 1911 – 17 November 1968)

Alice Mills
University of Ballarat

See also the Peake entry in *DLB 15: British Novelists, 1930–1959.*

BOOKS: *Uriel for President,* illustrated by Franz Bergman (Boston: Hale, Cushman & Flint, 1938);

Captain Slaughterboard Drops Anchor (London: Country Life, 1939; New York: Macmillan, 1967);

Shapes and Sounds (London: Chatto & Windus, 1941; New York: Transatlantic, 1941);

Rhymes without Reason (London: Eyre & Spottiswoode, 1944);

Titus Groan (London: Eyre & Spottiswoode, 1946; New York: Reynal & Hitchcock, 1946);

The Craft of the Lead Pencil (London: Wingate, 1946);

Letters from a Lost Uncle (from Polar Regions) (London: Eyre & Spottiswoode, 1948);

Drawings by Mervyn Peake (London: Grey Walls, 1949; New York: British Book Center, 1949);

The Glassblowers (London: Eyre & Spottiswoode, 1950);

Gormenghast (London: Eyre & Spottiswoode, 1950; New York: British Book Center, 1950);

Mr. Pye (London: Heinemann, 1953);

Figures of Speech (London: Gollancz, 1954);

Titus Alone (London: Eyre & Spottiswoode, 1959; New York: Weybright & Talley, 1967; revised by Langdon Jones, London: Eyre & Spottiswoode, 1970);

The Rhyme of the Flying Bomb (London: Dent, 1962; New York: British Book Center, 1976);

Poems and Drawings (London: Keepsake, 1965);

A Reverie of Bone and Other Poems (London: Rota, 1967);

Selected Poems (London: Faber & Faber, 1972);

A Book of Nonsense (London: Owen, 1972; New York: Dufour, 1975);

The Drawings of Mervyn Peake (London: Davis-Poynter, 1974);

Mervyn Peake: Writings and Drawings, edited by Maeve Gilmore and Shelagh Johnson (Lon-

Mervyn Peake

don: Academy Editions, 1974; New York: St. Martin's Press, 1974);

Twelve Poems (Hayes, Middlesex: Bran's Head, 1975);

Boy in Darkness (Exeter: Wheaton, 1976);

Peake's Progress, edited by Gilmore (London: Allen Lane, 1979; Woodstock, N.Y.: Overlook, 1981; corrected edition, London: Penguin, 1981).

TELEVISION: *Letters from a Lost Uncle (from Polar Regions)*, adaptation by Mervyn Peake, BBC, 1955.

RADIO: *Book Illustration*, BBC, 1947;
Alice and Tenniel and Me, BBC, 1954.

OTHER: *Ride a Cock-Horse and Other Nursery Rhymes*, illustrated by Peake (London: Chatto & Windus, 1940; New York: Transatlantic, 1944);

Lewis Carroll, *The Hunting of the Snark*, illustrated by Peake (London: Chatto & Windus, 1941);

Samuel Taylor Coleridge, *The Rime of the Ancient Mariner* illustrated by Peake (London: Chatto & Windus, 1943);

Quentin Crisp, *All This and Bevin Too*, illustrated by Peake (London: Nicholson & Watson, 1943);

Cyril Edwin Mitchison Joad, *The Adventures of the Young Soldier in Search of the Better World*, illustrated by Peake (London: Faber & Faber, 1943; New York: Arco, 1944);

Allan M. Laing, *Prayers and Graces*, illustrated by Peake (London: Gollancz, 1944);

Christina Hole, *Witchcraft in England* (London: Batsford, 1945; New York: Scribners, 1947);

The Brothers Grimm, *Household Tales*, illustrated by Peake (London: Eyre & Spottiswoode, 1946; revised edition, London: Methuen, 1973; New York: Schocken, 1979);

Maurice Collins, *Quest for Sita*, drawing by Peake (London: Faber & Faber, 1946; New York: Day, 1947);

Carroll, *Alice's Adventures in Wonderland and Through the Looking Glass*, illustrated by Peake (Stockholm: Continental Book, 1946; London: Allan Wingate, 1954; revised edition, London: Methuen, 1978; New York: Schocken, 1979);

Robert Louis Stevenson, *Treasure Island*, illustrated by Peake (London: Eyre & Spottiswoode, 1949; New York: Everyman, 1993);

Dorothy Haynes, *Thou Shalt Not Suffer a Witch and other Stories*, illustrated by Peake (London: Methuen, 1949);

Johann Rudolf Wyss, *The Swiss Family Robinson*, illustrated by Peake (London: Heirloom Library, 1950);

H. B. Drake, *The Book of Lyonne*, illustrated by Peake (London: Falcon Press, 1952; New York: British Book Center, 1952);

E. Clephan Palmer, *The Young Blackbird*, illustrated by Peake (London: Allan Wingate, 1953);

"Boy in Darkness," in *Sometimes Never: Three Tales of Imagination* (London: Eyre & Spottiswoode, 1956; New York: Ballentine, 1957);

H. B. Drake, *The Oxford English Course for Secondary Students Book One: Under the Umbrella Tree*, illustrated by Peake (London: Oxford University Press, 1957);

Aaron Judah, *A Pot of Gold and two other tales*, illustrated by Peake (London: Faber & Faber, 1959);

Robert Louis Stevenson, *Dr. Jekyll and Mr. Hyde*, illustrated by Peake (London: Dent, 1974).

Mervyn Laurence Peake's reputation during his lifetime as an outstanding illustrator of children's books is based on his illustrations for the *Alice* books (1946), *Treasure Island* (1949), and the Grimm brothers' *Household Tales* (1946). He is also a distinguished author and illustrator of nonsense verse and of two highly idiosyncratic illustrated stories for children, *Captain Slaughterboard Drops Anchor* (1939) and *Letters from a Lost Uncle* (1948). Since his death Peake's reputation as an artist has steadily grown. His Gormenghast trilogy for adults has attained the status of a classic, but little attention has been given to his writings by literary critics. While most of his works for children have been reprinted, as a writer and illustrator for children he has been almost completely neglected by the critics since his death.

Mervyn Peake was born in Kuling in central southern China in 1911. His father, Ernest Cromwell Peake, had come from Scotland as a missionary surgeon and set up the first European medical practice in that district. His mother, Amanda Elizabeth Powell, was a missionary nurse in Canton before marrying Ernest Peake in 1903. Mervyn's only sibling, his brother, Leslie, was born in 1904. Mervyn Peake was only fifteen months old when a bloody Chinese uprising against the Manchu dynasty forced the family to move far north to Tianjin, a northern Chinese city of sandstorms and icy winters, camels and mules, in the desert close to Beijing. The Peake family's privileged life as exotic foreigners, the mingled hostility and neediness of the Chinese people among whom they lived, and the remote location of Mervyn's birthplace in the European settlement high and isolated on a mountain were determinants of his later imagined worlds.

In 1914 the family left for London on furlough. There was little rest here for Ernest after his years of tropical medicine, for on the outbreak of the First World War he volunteered for medical service and was sent first to Belgium and then to France. Peake meanwhile lived in Kent with his mother and his brother, Leslie, now a schoolboy at Eltham School for the Sons of Missionaries (also known as Eltham College). It was here that his mother first noticed, and greatly encouraged, his talent for drawing.

These early years set a pattern of risk and isolation that Mervyn Peake took as themes for art and literature throughout his life. The image of a lost boy or man, separated from his family, wandering through an unfamiliar and dangerous landscape, is one of his favorite motifs. While his own life was relatively free from physical hazard, the themes of risk and isolation reflect Ernest's absences, in danger of being killed whether in China or at war in Europe. The theme of the lost boy was lived out momentarily by Leslie on the trip back from China by Trans-Siberian Railway. The train stopped many times in the dark woods, and the children were forbidden to climb down from their carriage. Leslie was on the track; the train began to move; and he was just able to run fast enough to catch hold of his father's hand and be pulled to safety. In Peake's versions of the lost boy motif, though, the father is not there to rescue his child.

In 1916 the Peake family returned to Tianjin where they stayed until 1923. Mervyn began school here and discovered Robert Louis Stevenson's *Treasure Island* (1883). His son Sebastian recalled from his own childhood that "my father loved *Treasure Island* especially, and as he could quote passages by heart, later, when I could read, I would test him. I would read the first word or two, 'Squire Trelawney, Dr. Livesey and the rest of these gentlemen . . . ' and he would then go on and on, faultlessly, with the story for pages if I had wanted."

In 1921, when Leslie was sent back to Eltham College in England, Peake began to write his first complete story, "The White Chief of the Umzimbooboo Kaffirs," published posthumously in *Peake's Progress* (1979). This is an ingenious mixture of autobiography and *Treasure Island,* added to a paraphrase of Drayson's "The White Chief of the Umzimvubu Caffres" from *Everyboy's Annual* for 1885. For his hero, Hugh, Peake contributes anguished parents – Dr. and Mrs. Silver, who are attacked by Hottentots and left for dead at the start of the story. Unlike his later lost children, Peake's Hugh promptly gains a new family, wins a treasure, and finds his way home.

The story was finished at Eltham College, after the Peake family's return to England in 1923, and ends with Hugh also at "Eltham College which he thoroughely [*sic*] enjoyed and got into the rugby fifteen, and had many special chums." Peake's spelling did not improve, and though, like his hero, he took to sport and made a lifelong friend in Gordon Smith, he came to be in danger of expulsion for un-

Illustration by Peake from his unpublished "The Moccus Book," 1930 (from John Watney, Mervyn Peake, *1976)*

satisfactory academic progress. The school's art master recognized his talents, however, and he was allowed to stay on.

His English master, Eric Drake, also recognized Peake's exceptional skills as writer and especially as draughtsman, "quite brilliant in both perception and vitality." With Drake's encouragement he wrote and illustrated cowboy stories. Stanley L. Wood, a prolific writer and illustrator of *Boys' Own* adventures, became his "secret god." In 1947, speaking about his own career as a book illustrator, Peake recalled Wood's illustrations for a *Treasure Island*-style serial called "Under the Serpent's Fang" as "so potent upon my imagination that I can recall them now almost to their minutest detail."

His first move away from this highly derivative, formulaic material took the form of a collaboration with his friend Smith. At school they created monsters together, Smith supplying a short rhyme and a nonsense name and Peake the drawing. Mokus was Smith's name for these creatures (to rhyme with hocus-pocus), Mocus or Moccus, Peake's variant spellings. The joint creation of monsters persisted after Peake left school in 1929 to become a student first at the Croydon School of Art and then at the Royal Academy Schools. He and

Smith put together a book of drawings and rhymes, the Moccus Book, with a view toward publication, but the only publisher to whom it was offered declined. Of these Moccus monsters, the Dusky Birron (reproduced in *Peake's Progress*) became the hero of a sustained, largely descriptive story for which Peake contributed drawings and a map and Smith the text.

Captain Slaughterboard Drops Anchor is like the Dusky Birron in its slightness of narrative and luxuriance of comic invention. Perhaps it was the reputation that he had developed as a talented artist that induced *Country Life* to risk publishing such an idiosyncratic, quirky book. Peake left art school in 1932 to join an artists' colony that was being set up on the island of Sark by his old Eltham teacher Eric Drake. During his three-year stay he womanized, painted, and exhibited. After Sark's successes he was offered a job as teacher of life-drawing at the Westminster School of Art and returned to England in 1935 to teach, write, sketch, paint, design for the theater, and live a pleasantly unconventional life on little money. At the Westminster School of Art he met a shy new sculpture student, Maeve Gilmore, and at once began to court her. They were married in 1937. Until his last illness Peake was extremely attractive to women. From his first meeting with Maeve, though, she was his comfort, the subject of his love poems and his principal female model, while continuing to work and exhibit in her own right as an artist. Together they moved frequently, doing their best to manage their ever-shaky finances. In 1940 their first son Sebastian was born; in 1942 Fabian; and in 1949 their daughter and last child, Clare. Sebastian grew up with stories; he remembered shivering with fright at his father's tales of wild men who "stalked my bedroom long after he'd said good night. With the wind sometimes outside howling, I imagined the voices of Blind Pew or his own Captain Slaughterboard." Some critics of children's literature, such as the reviewer for *Punch*, equated scariness with unsuitability, judging *Captain Slaughterboard Drops Anchor* to be "quite unsuitable for sensitive children."

Yet it is the restraint from horror in text and illustrations that is most remarkable in this pirate story. In Peake's earlier version of the story, "Mr. Slaughterboard" (published posthumously in *Peake's Progress*), the central character is an aesthetic psychopath, a parody of Melville's Captain Ahab. In the published story Captain Slaughterboard's name is his most sinister attribute, and although he and his men are depicted with all the piratical paraphernalia of guns, knives, swords, and cannon, their main occupations are eating and drinking, snoozing, and performing acrobatics for fun. Before the story begins, many of the crew "had been eaten by sharks or killed in battle, and hundreds had been made to walk the plank." At the end brief mention is made of terrible battles in which all the pirates except the captain are lost. The cheerful story line, however, concerns Captain Slaughterboard's discovery of a Yellow Creature on a pink island, the Creature's capture, and the Captain's transformation from pirate to tranquil island dweller with his yellow friend.

Captain Slaughterboard Drops Anchor is highly experimental in format for its period. In the pictures simply outlined shapes and crosshatching contrast with elaborate textures like those of the Chinese-style fish. The text is handwritten in spaces above, below, between, and around the pictures. Almost all copies of the first, black-and-white edition were burned in a warehouse fire. When the book was republished in 1945, some pages were tinted pastel pink, blue, yellow, or gray, with touches of a second color. Coloring the pages in this way produced some discrepancies with the text. The island is said to be pink, but it is shown variously as pink, blue, or yellow. Its inhabitants are said to be nearly all purple, except for the Yellow Creature, but are shown as yellow.

Captain Slaughterboard was republished again in reduced format in 1967 with a new, bright mustard-yellow coloring and some unacknowledged rewriting of the text and redrawing of the pictures. The innovations of the original book are much diminished, with text separated from pictures, handwritten letters replaced by letterpress, and punctuation normalized.

The year after *Captain Slaughterboard,* another commissioned work, *Ride a Cock-Horse and Other Nursery Rhymes* (1940), was published. This book is conventional in format, with the text of its fourteen nursery rhymes in large print, each on a separate page from its illustration on the facing page. The variety of Peake's styles and techniques, characteristic of his children's books, is less conventional. Pictures are crosshatched or outlined, sketchy or precise in detail, black and white or tinted. The book is laden with visual allusions: to Sir John Tenniel in the caricature of human bodies, to Goya in the Spanish princess, to Piranesi in the massive walls, and to Rembrandt in the shadowy obscurity of some pictures.

The baby in the frontispiece is modeled on Peake's newborn son, Sebastian. Critics have remarked how surprisingly the children in the illustrations foreshadow Sebastian and the yet-to-be-born Fabian as children. Yet with her sweep of dark hair the woman holding the baby does not overly resemble Maeve, nor does the enormous woman with a widow's peak of dark hair and elongated hands in "How Many Miles to Babylon?" The discrepancy in scale between woman and child in these pictures, and in little Jack Horner sitting in the corner of a large bare room, is the most idiosyncratic feature of the book. Perhaps it was this element which the *Nursery World* reviewer found sinister in denouncing the book as one "presumably for children but which ought never to find its way within a mile of them." The combination of fantasy and the sinister, though, was the book's main pleasure for Walter de la Mare who helped select the nursery rhymes.

Following the success of *Ride a Cock-Horse*, Peake was commissioned to illustrate Lewis Carroll's *The Hunting of the Snark* (1941), a small-format book designed to accommodate the scarcity of paper during the war. The publishers were also issuing Peake's first collection of poems, *Shapes and Sounds* (1941).

As in *Captain Slaughterboard* and *Ride a Cock-Horse*, *The Snark*'s human characters are caricatured, with disproportionate, swollen, or emaciated features, often dehumanized toward animal or reptile. The landscape, too, is a caricature of rocky cliffs looking back to Sark and further back to China. Its stones are stacked in unstable pillars like a child's untidy attempt at building with blocks. Similar but less extravagantly unstable stone structures can also be seen in both the earlier books and remain a favorite motif until his last tale for children, *Letters From a Lost Uncle*.

Little opportunity is afforded by the text for the creation of monsters apart from the Bandersnatch. Peake's version swoops and turns, long in tail, claw, beak, and eyelashes, in comic contrast to the foreshortened Banker underneath. In illustrations like this a new sense of depth and movement is achieved. The edge of the page cuts off part of the bird's body and so conveys vigorous, unconfined motion. In contrast the completely visible human bodies in the smaller pictures, however mobile or distorted, tend to function as representative images summing up a character rather than as dramatic vignettes.

None of the Snark hunters is shown as heroic in shape or attitude. The effect of the Bellman's Roman-nosed profile as he poses on the front cover is undercut by carpet slippers much too large for his feet and by the crags that mirror his craggy features, literalizing metaphor in a characteristic Peakian

Peake in his garden at Wallington, 1932

joke. The others epitomize the loser in their bare and stockinged feet, seedy clothes, and bent-over bodies.

Ride a Cock-Horse and *The Hunting of the Snark* were produced with some difficulty during the war years. In 1939 the Westminster School was evacuated, and Peake was out of work. He was keen to volunteer for the army, but despite the efforts of his friend Augustus John, who wrote "to recommend Mr. Mervyn Peake as a draughtsman of great distinction who might be most suitably engaged in war records," he had to wait until 1940 to be called up for military service. He worked on the pen-and-ink pictures for *Ride a Cock-Horse* and the manuscript that was to become *Titus Groan* (1946) in his small barrack room but no longer had the space to paint. These working conditions, he claimed later, turned him into an illustrator, for "I could do my work anywhere, in cafes, in fields, in billets . . . because I had no need of other impedimenta than a pencil, a pen, some paper and a bottle of indian ink."

Peake's first brief army posting within England was as an antiaircraft gunner but, as he knew how to drive, he was soon transferred to the Anti-Aircraft Driver Training Unit. Here he was given nominal duties painting lavatory notices because he was "artistic" once it became obvious that he was a most inept driving instructor. In 1941 he was transferred to a bomb disposal company for which he was no better suited. His military duties were light, and he was able to spend time with his family, painting and writing.

In 1942 his second son, Fabian, was born. A few weeks later Peake was in the hospital suffering from a nervous breakdown. He had been refused compassionate leave for the baby's birth, had forged a pass, and gone absent without leave. His punishment seems to have brought on the collapse. According to Smith he "suddenly realized that I could never obey another order again, not ever in my whole life!" He was sent home on sick leave, where he continued to work on the *Titus Groan* manuscript and produced illustrations for the 1943 publication of Coleridge's *The Rime of the Ancient Mariner*. That year his extended sick leave ended with discharge from the army.

Peake's creative energies were now at their height. As well as painting and exhibiting, he published a collection of his own nonsense verse, *Rhymes Without Reason* (1944); *Titus Groan*; the illustrated Alice books; and the Grimms' *Household Tales*; as well as six minor publications. *Titus Groan*, his long novel for adults, is characteristically Peakian in its range of grotesque characters, its child hero, and his lost father. The iron rituals of Gormenghast and Titus's rebellion reflect Peake's own decision never again to obey an order. The novel received mixed reviews, but with the 1943 publication of *The Rime of the Ancient Mariner* (*The Snark* having received little critical attention), Peake became recognized as the greatest living English illustrator.

When it was published in 1944, *Rhymes without Reason* was also hailed as a masterpiece, though reviewers were unsure whether it was an outstanding book for children, as John Betjeman claimed, or for adults, as Robert Lynd thought. Like nonsense verse of his models, Edward Lear, Lewis Carroll, and Hillaire Belloc, Peake's work defies such characterization. The format of *Rhymes without Reason*, however, marks it out as children's literature, with each poem printed in large type on its own page facing a brightly colored page of illustration. In the En-

glish tradition, the verses abound with talking animals, puns, alliteration, repetition, and parody, like this Wordsworthian uncle's lament:

There'll *never* be another Niece
As innocent as mine!

Mine was the One! Mine was the Two;
Mine was the Three and Four,
And I have heard her parents say
She rose to Seven or more!

Rhymes without Reason has not attained the status of a classic. As Quentin Crisp comments, the text is far superior to the illustrations. Compared with the technical brilliance of present-day color illustrations and with his own pen-and-ink work, these pictures are crude, their colors sometimes ugly, their backgrounds flat. There is little comic tension between picture and text, and few of the poems suffer unduly from being anthologized without their illustration. An exception is the lament of the elephant whose ears are destined to be chopped off by pirates to make sails. Only the picture reveals the unlikely speaker's identity and the equally unlikely function for the ears still attached to the living elephant.

Anthropomorphic animals and caricatured human beings are far more successfully depicted in the illustrations for the Grimm Brothers' *Household Tales*. "What an inspiration!" Elizabeth Bowen wrote, reviewing the first edition, although Maurice Collis complained that "Grimm's *Tales*, though they call for some of his gifts, hardly extend his talent." As usual, *Nursery World* thought the book unsuitable for children, a judgment on the fairy tales' mischief and menace, which Peake so skillfully evokes.

It is true that his comic invention was not stretched by the book's orthodox format or by his human characters: foolish peasants, wicked witches, child heroes, Maeve-like princesses. He worked hard, however, to "get all the costumes, etc., authentic mediaeval, and change my technique from the cross-hatching stuff I've used so far." His general technique in the sixty black-and-white pictures is to use broken outline, fine pen-and-ink work that sometimes turns to scribble for the shadows. The full-page illustrations explore chiaroscuro, framing a light-filled scene with a dark wall, archway, or tree. The illustration to "Our Lady's Child," of a little girl lost in a dark bare-branched wood, is Peake's closest equivalent to Blake's *Sons of Experience*, though his nervous detail is different from Blake's strong sense of boundaries. In terms of subject matter, the talking animals are his chief innovation.

They are less like human beings, livelier and lighter than the creatures of *Rhymes without Reason.* Some wear clothes and stand and sit like people; others are all animal apart from an expressively human eye.

If there is a weakness in these illustrations, it is in the conventionally imagined, idealized princesses of the colored pages. When Peake was commissioned in 1945 to illustrate the Alice books, he avoided sentimentalizing his heroine, and the result is a triumph of black humor that rivals Tenniel's version. In 1946 the Alice books with illustrations by Peake were published in a European edition not for sale in Britain or the United States. A British edition was not available until 1954, at which time Peake redrew twenty-two of the illustrations. "Even Tenniel-charmed eyes should be captivated" was Frances Sarzano's judgment upon the first edition, and reviewers of the third (1978) edition were equally lavish in their praise for the "classic edition for our time," the "visual feast of the year." Graham Greene wrote privately to compliment Peake on equaling Tenniel, apart from an element of the gamine in Alice herself that he did not like. Yet it is this touch of tomboy that rescues Peake's Alice from big-eyed, long-haired sentimentality.

Despite his high reputation as an illustrator, Peake was not the Swedish publisher's first choice for the Alice books. They wanted Tenniel but were unable to secure publishing rights. Tenniel remains in popular and academic opinion the supreme illustrator for Alice despite the excellence of Peake's version. Just as with *The Ancient Mariner,* Peake's illustrations equal but do not surpass those of his great predecessor. In his own opinion, though, his version is better. Speaking in a 1954 radio talk he complained of Tenniel's monopoly: "it doesn't seem to matter that his superb powers of invention are to some degree negated by a dreary technique." Peake's own proud claim is to catch the book's spirit better, its gentleness, madness, and nonsense.

Peake's techniques include the use of solid and broken outline, densely crosshatched shadows and expanses of white paper. Occasionally he adds a joke, as in the White King's struggle with a pencil that in the picture carries Alice's name. It is a mark of the artist's achievement that, conscious as he was of the need to differ from Tenniel, his pictures are so unconstrained in their comic energy. The characters bear a family resemblance to those of *Household Tales* but with a far greater emotional range from ridiculous inanity to comic menace, from pathos to monstrosity.

Peake in Battersea Park, 1938

"But in *Alice* there is no horror," he commented in his radio talk, discussing the issue of suitability for children. By 1946 he was well acquainted with horror. At the end of the war he was appointed war artist and sent to Western Europe where he visited the concentration camp at Belsen. The shock of what he saw, his wife believed, altered him "as if he had lost, during that month in Germany, his confidence in life itself."

Nevertheless, his next publication for children, *Letters From a Lost Uncle (from Polar Regions)* (1948) is exuberantly comic. The book is even more experimental in layout than *Captain Slaughterboard.* The back cover of the first edition is like an envelope with a seal marked "Sebastian, Fabian, Maeve." The lost uncle's letters are a mixture of poor typing, food stains, thumb prints, and pencil illustrations. The manuscript had been prepared in 1945 but was held up for publication, paper being in short supply after the war. When the book was fi-

Peake in 1966

nally published, Peake was highly critical of its printing and withdrew as many copies as he could. In 1955 he drew much clearer pictures for a television adaptation, but neither the scripts nor the new drawings have been published. All editions of the book require some puzzling-out of the illustrations and occasional dimly penciled additions to the text.

Letters From a Lost Uncle is a comic compendium of adventures on the ice, at sea, and in the jungle. The lost uncle has traveled alone through regions beloved by *Boys' Own* storytellers, losing a leg to a swordfish, twice using his new swordfish-spike leg to save his life. Of all Peake's lost wanderers the uncle is the most lost in terms of geography, but the most fulfilled in purpose. He quests for a mysterious White Lion, a search that echoes Captain Slaughterboard's delight in the Yellow Creature and parodies *Moby Dick*.

Apart from his artificial leg, the lost uncle resembles one of the characters in *Rhymes without Reason* who is also bearded, smokes a pipe, wears a bowler hat, and sails the sea on a table. The nonsense character, however, travels with his wife, while the lost uncle rejoices to be free of his wife,

her angry brothers, and sour sisters. Instead he travels with a turtledove named Jackson. "I could see that he would be useful at once as a beast of burden — and possibly as a friend . . . he didn't want to come with me at first." Judging by his stooped posture and drooping beak, Jackson remains reluctant to accompany the uncle; to pull the sledge; to carry the typewriter, camera, saucepans and portmanteaus; and to be blamed for all the brown stains on the letters. The uncle behaves as an egotistical tyrant toward Jackson, parodying the formula of heroic white adventurer with faithful but savage servant. His character is the most complex in Peake's work, as the death of the White Lion by freezing is the most mysteriously symbolic event. Perhaps for this reason Marcus Crouch, the *Junior Bookshelf* reviewer, was cautious in his praise: "a brilliant idea, and consistently carried out, but it remains a freak."

Peake never surpassed the fluency of line in the soft pencil drawings for *Letters from a Lost Uncle*. Against the curves of animal and reptile and the van Gogh swirls of the snowstorm, the straight lines of human artifacts are comically juxtaposed — table, pipe, and artificial leg. On the final page the dark and unheroic figures of the uncle and Jackson pose against a background of wheeled stars, man against nature, straightness against curve, tiny twentieth-century questers against the divine order of Dante's universe.

In 1946 the Peake family moved back to Sark, where Mervyn worked on the sequel to *Titus Groan, Gormenghast* (1950), and illustrations for Stevenson's *Dr. Jekyll and Mr. Hyde* (1974) and *Treasure Island,* as well as Dorothy Haynes's *Thou Shalt Not Suffer a Witch and Other Stories* (1949). In two of the eight black-and-white illustrations for this collection of macabre and sentimental stories, Peake uses solid black shapes for the hair of a malign female spirit and the black suit of a cheating merchant. The stories do not match their illustrations in quality, and the book has not been reprinted.

In *Treasure Island,* though, Peake found a text neither trivial nor already the property of a major illustrator like Gustave Dore or Tenniel. The *Scotsman* reviewer thought Peake's talents an excellent match for Stevenson's: "his drawings – tense, eerie and dramatic – abate nothing of the power of the narrative." The 1976 edition received more praise from the *Sunday Times* reviewer for its "extraordinary" illustrations from "one of the finest draughtsmen of his day" and from the *Times* reviewer as "one of the few editions that have come near to meeting the demands of the author's text." According to Bernard Miles, it was "one of the great books of the world."

Instead of making an effort to differ from earlier illustrators, Peake reworked and improved stock scenes from the first edition, with particular emphasis on Jim and the pirates rather than the good men. For at least one of his scenes of action, the struggle in the Hispaniola's cabin, his model was a Stanley L. Wood picture, now robbed of its heroism. For backgrounds he reverts to his early technique of crosshatching and densely textured shadow, with some masterly effects of chiaroscuro. The pirates come as close to talking animals as his talking animals did to men, low-browed, prognathous, and crouched. In his career as a book illustrator, Peake's only sustained study in character development is Long John Silver, who moves from likable rogue to villain. If *Alice* is his masterpiece in fantasy illustration, *Treasure Island* is its equal in the adventure genre.

Peake was commissioned to illustrate Johann Rudolf Wyss's *The Swiss Family Robinson* in 1950, but the publishers were not pleased with his work and his pictures were interspersed with others by an unacknowledged hand. The color plates and black-and-white illustrations are in realist style. His animals are sometimes vivid, but little is done to enliven Wyss's morally admirable human beings. Beside the exuberant caricatures of his earlier work, his human figures are pallid.

The Book of Lyonne (1952) by H. Burgess Drake, brother of Eric Drake, is a lengthy fantasy about talking animals including a child's pajama bag that comes to life as a lion. Lyonne, notable among Peake's illustrations, is a fine comic creation, all mane, staring eyes, and zip fastener, but elsewhere the artist recycled old ideas. Torpus the tortoise, for example, looks much like Jackson in *Letters From a Lost Uncle.*

Minor commissions for children's books followed, for E. Clephan Palmer's *The Young Blackbird* (1953), with its realist drawings squeezed into the margins to save paper, and a few illustrations for H. Burgess Drake's *Oxford English Course for Secondary Students Book One: Under the Umbrella Tree* (1957) and Aaron Judah's collection of moral tales, *The Pot of Gold and two other tales* (1959). *Letters From a Lost Uncle* was converted to a children's television series in 1955, and he wrote but did not finish a children's play, *Noah's Ark* (published in *Peake's Progress*), in about 1960. Its themes of betrayal and death are echoed from the unfinished third volume of the Titus trilogy, *Titus Alone* (1959).

Peake's career declined after 1950, when an unwise house purchase put him in severe financial difficulties. By 1953, overworking, he developed a tremor that slowed his production of drawings. The novel *Mr. Pye* (1953) failed to rescue his finances, and he put his hopes increasingly on a new career as playwright. When his play *The Wit to Woo* opened in 1957 to poor reviews, his health collapsed.

Doctors did not know what was wrong with him; Parkinson's disease, encephalitis lethargica, nervous breakdown, or premature senility. The tremor worsened and was only temporarily helped by a brain operation. His memory failed. As long as he could he wrote and illustrated, Maeve reminding him of the subject as he drew. He was ill for twelve years and died in 1968.

Mervyn Peake's work has attained both cult and classic status without being greatly popular. Although he draws upon popular fiction and art, his children's stories are darker and more mysterious, not altogether consoling. Among his illustrations for other writers, some are for minor works, now forgotten; the Alice pictures did not supplant Tenniel's; and his excellent *Treasure Island* and *Household Tales* illustrations have been almost lost in the outpouring of illustrated classics since his death.

Nevertheless, his books continue to be republished and to sell well. His imaginative achievement has been overshadowed by J. R. R. Tolkien's, but for those readers who enjoy the grotesque and macabre, caricature and comic energy, Mervyn Peake's works for children are the finest of his generation.

Biographies:

Maeve Gilmore, *A World Away: A Memoir of Mervyn Peake* (London: Gollancz, 1970);

John Batchelor, *Mervyn Peake: A Biographical and Critical Exploration* (London: Duckworth, 1974);

John Watney, *Mervyn Peake* (London: M. Joseph, 1976);

Gordon Smith, *Mervyn Peake: A Personal Memoir* (London: Gollancz, 1984);

Sebastian Peake, *A Child of Bliss* (Oxford: Lennard, 1989).

References:

Hugh Brogan, "Peake on *Treasure Island,*" *Mervyn Peake Review,* 3 (Autumn 1976): 24–26;

Quentin Crisp, "The Genius of Mervyn Peake," *Mervyn Peake Review,* 14 (Spring 1982): 37–42;

Belinda Humfrey, "Peake's Enchanting Whimsy," *Mervyn Peake Review,* 5 (Autumn 1977): 34–36;

Bruce Hunt, "Peake's Polar Regions: In Search of Whiteness," *Mervyn Peake Review,* 4 (Spring 1977): 32–36;

Alice Mills, "Queer Creatures in 'Captain Slaughterboard' and 'Mr. Slaughterboard,'" in *Peake Papers* (London: Mervyn Peake Society, 1994), pp. 49–59;

Isobel Murray, "I cannot give the reasons / I only sing the tunes," *Mervyn Peake Review,* 8 (Spring 1979): 27–29;

Brian Sibley, "Peaks and Chasms," *Mervyn Peake Society Newsletter,* 2 (Spring 1976): 17–22;

Sibley, "Through a Darkling Glass: An Appreciation of Mervyn Peake's Illustrations to *Alice,*" *Mervyn Peake Review,* 6 (Spring 1978): 25–28.

Papers:

A collection of Peake's correspondence and manuscripts is at University College, London.

Arthur Ransome

(18 January 1884 – 3 June 1967)

Catherine M. Lynch
Penn State, McKeesport Campus

BOOKS: *The ABC of Physical Culture* (London: Henry J. Drane, 1904);

The Souls of the Streets (London: Brown Langham, 1904);

The Stone Lady (London: Brown Langham, 1905);

A Child's Book of the Garden (London: Anthony Treherne, 1906);

Pond and Stream (London: Anthony Treherne, 1906);

Things in Season (London: Anthony Treherne, 1906);

Highways and Byways in Fairyland (London: Alston Rivers, 1907; New York: McBride, 1909);

Bohemia in London (New York: Dodd, Mead, 1907; London: Chapman & Hall, 1907);

A History of Storytelling: Studies in the Development of Narrative (London: T. C. & E. C. Jack, 1909; New York: Stokes, 1910);

Edgar Allan Poe, a Critical Study (London: Secker, 1910; New York: Kennerley, 1910);

The Hoofmarks of the Faun (London: Secker, 1911);

Oscar Wilde, a Critical Study (London: Secker, 1912; New York: Kennerley, 1912);

Portraits and Speculations (London: Macmillan, 1913);

The Elixir of Life (London: Methuen, 1915);

Old Peter's Russian Tales, illustrated by Dmitri Mitrokhin (London: T. C. & E. C. Jack, 1916; New York: Stokes, 1917);

The Truth about Russia (London: Workers' Socialist Federation, 1918);

Aladdin and His Wonderful Lamp (London: Nisbet [1919]; New York: Bretano's, 1920);

Six Weeks in Russia 1919 (London: Allen & Unwin, 1919); republished as *Russia in 1919* (New York: Huebsch, 1919);

The Soldier and Death (London: Wilson, 1920; New York: Huebsch, 1922);

The Crisis in Russia (New York: Huebsch, 1921; London: Allen & Unwin, 1921);

"Racunda's" First Cruise (New York: Huebsch, 1923; London: Allen & Unwin, 1923);

The Chinese Puzzle (London: Allen & Unwin, 1927; Boston: Houghton Mifflin, 1927);

Arthur Ransome

Rod and Line (London: Cape, 1929);

Swallows and Amazons, with illustrations by Clifford Webb and maps by Stephen Spurrier (London: Cape, 1930); with illustrations by Helene Carter (Philadelphia: Lippincott, 1931);

Swallowdale with illustrations by Webb (London: Cape, 1931); with illustrations by Carter (Philadelphia: Lippincott, 1932);

Peter Duck (London: Cape, 1932; Philadelphia: Lippincott, 1933);

Winter Holiday (London: Cape, 1933; Philadelphia: Lippincott, 1934);

Coot Club (London: Cape, 1934; Philadelphia: Lippincott, 1935);

Rod and Line (London: Cape, 1935);

Pigeon Post (London: Cape, 1936; Philadelphia: Lippincott, 1937);

We Didn't Mean to Go to Sea (London: Cape, 1937; New York: Macmillan, 1938);

Secret Water (London: Cape, 1939; New York: Macmillan, 1940);

The Big Six (London: Cape, 1940; New York: Macmillan, 1941);

Missee Lee (London: Cape, 1941; New York: Macmillan, 1942);

The Picts and the Martyrs: Or, Not Welcome at All (London: Cape, 1943; New York: Macmillan, 1943);

Great Northern? (London: Cape, 1947; New York: Macmillan, 1948);

Fishing (Cambridge: National Book League Reader's Guide, 1948);

Mainly About Fishing (London: A. C. Black, 1959);

The Autobiography of Arthur Ransome, edited by Hart-Davis (London: Cape, 1976);

The War of the Birds and the Beasts and Other Russian Tales, edited by Hugh Brogan (London: Cape, 1984);

Coots of the North and Other Stories, edited by Brogan (London: Cape, 1988);

The Blue Treacle (Kendal, U.K.: Amazon, 1993).

OTHER: *Stories by Cervantes,* edited by Ransome (New York: Dutton, 1909);

Stories by the Essayists, edited by Ransome (New York: Dutton, 1909);

Stories by Chateaubriand, edited by Ransome (New York: Dutton, 1909);

The Book of Friendship: Essays, Poems, Maxims & Prose Passages, arranged by Ransome (London & Edinburgh: T. C. & E. C. Jack, 1909);

The Book of Love, arranged by Ransome (London & Edinburgh, 1910);

"The Poetry of Yone Noguchi" in *The Pilgrimage,* by Yore Naguchi (New York: Kennerly / London: Matthews, 1912);

Rémy de Gourmont, *A Night in Luxembourg,* translation by Ransome (London: Swift, 1912; Boston: Luce, 1912);

Albert Rhys Williams, *Lenin: The Man and His Work,* "impression" by Ransome (New York: Scotland Seltzer, 1919);

Iury Libedinsky, *A Week,* translation and introduction by Ransome (London: Allen & Unwin, 1923);

Erling Tambs, *The Cruise of the Teddy,* introduction by Ransome (London: Cape, 1933);

Katharine Hull and Pamela Whitlock, *The Far-Distant Oxus,* introduction by Ransome (London: Cape, 1937);

Joshua Slocum, *Sailing Alone Around the World,* introduction by Ransome (London: Hart-Davis, 1948);

E. F. Knight, *The Falcon on the Baltic,* introduction by Ransome (London: Hart-Davis, 1951);

Knight, *The Cruise of the Alerte,* introduction by Ransome (London: Hart-Davis, 1952);

E. E. Middleton, *The Cruise of the Kate,* introduction by Ransome (London: Hart-Davis, 1953);

John Macgregor, *The Voyage Alone in the Yawl Rob Roy,* introduction by Ransome (London: Hart-Davis, 1954).

SELECTED PERIODICAL PUBLICATION –
UNCOLLECTED: " 'Swallows and Amazons': How it Came to be Written," *Horn Book,* 7 (February 1931): 38–43.

Arthur Ransome was forty-six when *Swallows and Amazons* was published in 1930. He was at a turning point in a career as a journalist in which he had covered many important stories, most notably the Russian Revolution. He had been publishing books since he was twenty on subjects as diverse as narrative technique, Oscar Wilde, cruising on the Baltic, and fishing. His friend and employer, the editor of the *Manchester Guardian,* offered him a salaried job with possible future advancement. Ransome turned the offer down to try writing the book that became *Swallows and Amazons,* a different sort of book for him, a children's book unlike others being written at that time. The experiment worked. *Swallows and Amazons* was widely reviewed and well received. Before the year was over it had sold 1,656 copies, and the publisher and the public wanted a sequel.

In the next seventeen years Arthur Ransome wrote eleven more novels for children that won him a continually increasing audience. All twelve books have gone through many editions. All are currently either in print or being reissued in England and the United States. They continue to attract enthusiastic readers, both children and adults. Ransome was one of the most notable children's authors of the 1930s and 1940s. In 1936, when the Carnegie Medal for the best children's book of the year was established by the British Library Association, the first book honored was Arthur Ransome's *Pigeon Post*. In 1952 Arthur Ransome was awarded an honorary doctorate by the University of Leeds. In a recent biography, *Arthur Ransome,* Peter Hunt observes, "By the time of his death, Ransome was a national figure and his books classics."

Arthur Ransome was born 18 January 1884 in Leeds, England, the eldest of four children of Cyril and Edith Ransome. His father was a history professor at the institution which later became the University of Leeds. He was also an avid fisherman. Ransome's mother was a talented watercolor painter. Spending the academic year in Leeds, the family went for its holidays to the Lake District. A note that Ransome wrote in 1958 for inclusion in new Puffin editions of *Swallowdale* (1931) and *Winter Holiday* (1933) sums up his memories of those days, "We adored the place. Coming to it we used to run down to the lake, dip our hands in and wish, as if we had just seen a new moon. Going away from it we were half drowned in tears. While away from it, as children or grown ups, we dreamt about it."

Although several years of his early schooling were spent in the Lake District (including the time of the Great Frost of February 1895 that is reflected in *Winter Holiday*), school was not a happy time for the young Ransome. Matters improved when he entered Rugby in 1897. His nearsightedness was discovered and corrected with glasses. Being able to see the ball greatly improved his success at games, and in the classroom he met some good and sympathetic teachers.

Ransome's father died the year that Ransome started at Rugby. Ransome's mother seems to have felt that it was her duty to her dead husband as well as to their eldest son to guide him into a stable, respectable profession. Ransome's personal preference — writing — was not in that category. As a result, in 1901 Ransome enrolled in his father's university to study science. He left after two terms to take a job as an errand boy for a London publisher, the first of a series of publishing jobs he took while trying to establish himself as a writer. His book *Bohemia in London* (1907) is the record of that time, recounting the friendships of aspiring writers and artists — living on cheese and apples, inspiration, and words. Many of the people he met during this period remained his lifelong friends.

He continued to go to the Lake District whenever possible. On one of these trips he encountered W. G. Collingwood and his wife Edith, and he was soon virtually adopted by them. A painter, antiquarian, and writer, Collingwood was the author of a book about Vikings in the Lake District, *Thorstein*

Ransome as a newspaper correspondent, circa 1920

of the Mere (1895), which had been a favorite of Ransome's in childhood. Artistic and literary themselves, the Collingwoods encouraged Ransome in his writing career.

Ransome proposed marriage to, but was rejected by, the Collingwoods' daughter Barbara. But he continued to be a friend of all the family. In the writing of *Pigeon Post* (1936) Ransome consulted Barbara's geologist husband, Oscar Gnosspelius, for scientific details and dedicated the book to him. Another Collingwood daughter, Dora, married Ernest Altounyan, and they had five children whose ages and activities in many ways mirror the Walkers of *Swallows and Amazons*. Toward the end of Ransome's life a coolness developed between him and the Altounyans and after that time he tried to deny their part in his inspiration. But his biographers find too many parallels and too much evidence – such as letters to and from the family and a sailboat named "Swallow" – not to feel that the real Altounyan children had some influence on the creation of the fictional Walkers. In all, the Collingwood family was as close to Ransome as his own and probably a more important influence on his writing.

In the course of his life in London's bohemia, Ransome met and married Ivy Constance Walker. His biographers agree that she was a woman who tried to stage her life as a melodrama with herself as the star. Perhaps she was attracted to Ransome as the writer of her story. Their story together did not last long, and Ransome did not write it except to record the necessary facts in his 1976 autobiography. Ivy and Arthur were married in 1909. He started his first trip to Russia in May 1913. Although he visited his wife and daughter on his periodic returns to England, sometimes with the hope of reconciliation, the marriage had ended. In spite of the difficulties, Ransome tried to maintain a friendly relationship with his daughter. Ransome's divorce from Ivy was finalized in 1924.

Ransome went to Russia for reasons beyond escaping an unhappy home situation. He intended to learn Russian and collect material for a book of Russian folktales. He was also commissioned to write a guidebook to St. Petersburg. He wrote the book, but it was never published because the Russian Revolution was in process and the city was being transformed into Leningrad. In 1916 Ransome became the Russian correspondent for the *Daily News*. Some of the rapidly shifting political movements and his part in them as well as his friendships with some of the major figures in the Russian political drama are the subject of many chapters of his autobiography and the basis for his books and pamphlets on Russia. In 1917 Ransome met Evgenia Petrovna Shelepina. In his autobiography he introduces her as "the tall jolly girl whom later on I was to marry and to whom I owe the happiest years of my life." Among other jobs for the revolution, Evgenia served for a time as personal secretary to Leon Trotsky.

In the pages of the autobiography that describe Arthur and Evgenia's departure from Russia in 1919 through territory that was controlled in turns by Red Russian, White Russian, or Estonian forces, one must read between the lines to understand their courage. Ransome's description focuses on the rapid flow of events, a lucky chess game, and Evgenia's presence of mind. They settled on the shores of the Baltic and were soon putting their courage to the test again by sailing on the Baltic Sea. The literary result of one summer under sail was *"Racunda's" First Cruise* (1923). Still well regarded as a cruising report, in its content it is Ransome's most immediate predecessor to the Swallows and Amazons books.

Amid all his varied activities Ransome gave some indications of developing into a writer of children's books. Even in the turmoil of the Russian Revolution and World War I, he had not lost his interest in narrative. *Old Peter's Russian Tales* appeared in 1916 and enjoyed steady sales. (In his autobiography Ransome reports that by 1956 combined sales of regular and cheap editions came to more than forty-nine thousand copies.) Ransome's method of retelling these tales was to study as many versions of the tale as he could and then to create his own version from the elements he thought best. In order to give the tales some context for English children, whose culture was so different from that in which the tales originated, Ransome created the peasant Old Peter to tell these tales to his two orphaned grandchildren, Vanya and Maroosia. Although little more than a linking device through most of the book, in the final chapter, "A Christening in the Village," these children appear as characters in a charming sketch of peasant Russia. These children are the first faint foreshadowings of the tribes of child characters in the later books.

The War of the Birds and the Beasts and Other Russian Tales (1984) was edited by Hugh Brogan from material collected by Ransome but not used in *Old Peter's Russian Tales*. Ransome's verse retelling *Aladdin and his Wonderful Lamp* (1919) has not lasted as well as *Old Peter's Russian Tales*, though it too is evidence of Ransome's interest in storytelling for a child audience.

After Ransome's divorce was final he married Evgenia in 1924, and they returned to England to live. By this time he was a special correspondent for the *Manchester Guardian*. He was sent by them at various times to cover political unrest in Egypt and China. Of the trip to China he reports, "I was later to get a great deal of pleasure from using some of the war-lords as models for Chinese pirates, and in taking hints from Madame Sun Yat-sen herself for my portrait of the Chinese girl graduate who, while hankering for academic life in Cambridge, does, from her filial piety, keep order in her community of tough characters."

Aside from this borrowing, little of Ransome's adventure-filled career in journalism appears directly in the Swallows and Amazons books. His ability to analyze motives and follow the tangled threads of parallel lines of action certainly was developed while reporting complex political and military situations. His clear, vigorous prose was honed by sending word-sparing telegrams to the *Daily News*. His journalist's eye, trained for catching telling detail, can be seen in all his work. But otherwise readers of *Swallows and Amazons* will not detect Ransome's wide journalistic experience in his stories. Readers will, however, meet deeper aspects of Ransome's life – his passion for the Lake District, his deep knowledge of sailing, his love of outdoor adventure, and his understanding of how observation and experience slowly map one's life.

Ransome did not set out to write a series of books. He wrote the first book as an experiment and then, encouraged by its reception, continued to attempt other books like it. As a result, to say that Ransome's Swallows and Amazons books are a series is inaccurate. Although most of the books do center on the same group of child characters, each novel can stand by itself without reference to the others. The cast of child characters varies from book to book, and each of the books offers a new situation. The reader can start with any book and previous or subsequent ones and still enjoy each fully. However, both characters and the narrator do refer to events or experiences from previous books.

Because Ransome brought the skills of his lifetime of writing to the creation of Swallows and Amazons, the strengths of all his work are fully present from the first. Chief among these is his characterization of children. He always works with a large cast, from eleven in *Secret Water* (1939) to four in *We Didn't Mean to Go to Sea* (1937). In the first of the books, *Swallows and Amazons,* the reader meets the two families of children who appear in ten of the twelve books. The Walker family: John, Susan, Titty, Roger, (and when she gets old enough in a later book, baby Bridget) sail on *Swallow*. Nancy Blackett and her sister, Peggy, sail on *Amazon*.

As the name for her ship suggests, Nancy is a woman of action. She is definitely the captain, and her younger sister, Peggy, travels gamely in her wake. The plots of the books in which Nancy appears usually involve the execution of one of Nancy's many plans. In *Swallows and Amazons* it is her idea that the two families of children should try to capture the other's ship to determine which will

Ransome, the defendant, leaving the court during the Alfred Douglas libel case in 1914 (Hulton Deutsch Collection)

be flagship of their two-ship fleet. Ransome peppers Nancy's speeches with her idea of nautical language: "Jibbooms and bobstays," "Don't be a galoot!" and "Shiver my timbers."

In the Walker family John and Susan, the two oldest, function as mother and father in all the children's adventures. John makes careful, thoughtful plans, considers the younger children, and generally tries to do as his naval officer father would, especially in matters of navigation. Susan cooks, sees that the younger ones get to bed on time, and that everyone has dry socks and meals. Titty is thoughtful and imaginative. Her sympathy for other people's feelings and her artistic talents are often important assets. Roger is in some ways a younger version of John. Usually the youngest, he sometimes stirs up events by trying to assert himself. Often Roger and Titty are companions. Roger's special interests are engines and food, especially chocolate. Although curiously lacking in sibling rivalry and generally more responsible than most children one encounters, Ransome's children are fully realized characters who interact with each other in complex ways.

In *Swallows and Amazons* the Swallows first meet the Amazons when the Walkers, visitors to the Lake, camp on an island that Nancy and Peggy are used to having to themselves. The novel is the story of the things that happen when these two groups of children come together. An additional complication occurs when Captain Flint's houseboat is broken into and a trunk containing his book in progress is stolen. Captain Flint, in "native" life Nancy and Peggy's Uncle Jim, functions as a member of the crew and an adult facilitator in many of the books. Because of his worldwide travel, his physical appearance, and the way he enters into the children's world, many see in Captain Flint Ransome's presence in the books.

The reader, however, sees only Captain Flint's actions, rarely what is going on in his mind. Ransome keeps his narrative focused on the children, moving it forward by telling his story first from one child's point of view and then another. Having given each his or her own individual talents, he gives each character his or her moment of making a unique contribution to the shared adventure of the plot.

Examples can be found in any of the books. In chapter 18 of *Swallows and Amazons,* Titty, left alone in the island camp to set signal lights, has a conversation with her mother, who has rowed over to visit. They speak in the characters of Robinson Crusoe and Man Friday, and Titty's mother, a "native," as the children call adults, demonstrates her understanding of the children's imagined life on the island. A few chapters later, again alone, Titty overhears men burying what turns out to be, when she insists on looking for it, Captain Flint's stolen trunk. Titty's imagination, creativity, and courage are all highlighted in these events – and they are needed for the satisfactory conclusion of the plot. Meanwhile the rest of Titty's family are being challenged by the dangers of sailing on the lake at night. By this technique of shifting from one child's experience to the next Ransome achieves the simultaneous development of individual and interrelated child characters.

Titty's afternoon with her mother as Robinson Crusoe and Man Friday illustrates another characteristic of Ransome's work – his portrayal of fantasy in the children's worldview. Here and elsewhere Titty and the rest bring to bear what they have read about or dreamed about and apply it to their activities. For example, the positions of the crew of the *Swallow* – Captain, First Mate, Able-Sea-

man – represent real responsibilities the children take on as well as the fantasy they harbor of playing their roles in the adult world. By always being aware of their real circumstances, Ransome's children stay happily balanced between the real world and fantasy in a way only possible in childhood.

The continuing interplay between fantasy and reality can be seen in the maps that are important in each of the books. The real landscape – harbors, islands, farms, roads – is faithfully recorded by the young explorers, but the places often are given names of longed-for geography – "North Pole," "Rio," "Amazon River."

Mapping is a fundamental metaphor for what Ransome's stories are about. Near the end of *Swallows and Amazons* John says, "There's one thing we must do now. . . . And that's make our chart. The Amazons will be here tomorrow and they've got their own names for everywhere." Mapmaking is the sign that the children have the right to claim this territory by virtue of their experience with it.

Accurate description is the essence of making such maps. Ransome and his child characters are always acute observers of the world around them. For example, in the middle of Titty's solo adventure, the reader is told, "After mother had gone, Able-Seaman Titty thought it well to go over her island. . . . The dipper had come back to a stone outside the harbour and bobbed to her again and again, and Able-Seaman Titty bobbed to him in return, but this time was so far away that he did not fly off but stood on his stone bobbing two or three times a minute." Like careful individual brushstrokes the details layer on each other to build up the scene. In Titty's isolation, even the bird is further from her now, but the landscape continues to be friendly. Titty's situation – and the lake and land – are all summed up in the bird. Titty's noticing the bird (as opposed to, say, the wind direction, which John would notice) is characteristic of her. In later books Ransome developed her affinity with birds by giving her a pet parrot and, in *Missee Lee* (1941), allowing her to communicate with a bird-loving Chinese pirate.

Ransome weaves a rich texture of detail not only in character and landscape but also in the experience of everyday camp life, especially campfire meals. He explains boats and sailing gear for children who may never have seen them. He takes a special delight in describing inventions and contrivances of his child characters. In *Swallows and Amazons,* for example, the leading marks, which Nancy and Peggy have devised for the entrance to the island's harbor, receive detailed description as

Nancy demonstrates them to John, who in turn explains to her what a nautical chart is.

With variations in theme and plot, the eleven books that followed *Swallows and Amazons* continued to explore this same world of realistic imagination. In *The Life of Arthur Ransome* (1984) Hugh Brogan documents through references to letters and notebooks some of the struggles Ransome went through in finding plots for the books that followed *Swallows and Amazons*. He seems to have made a real effort to keep the characters and their world without resorting to formula fiction.

Swallowdale is set in the "next summer" looked forward to at the end of *Swallows and Amazons*. Except for the ill-fated voyage at the beginning and a race between the two boats at the end, there is no sailing in the book, for the *Swallow* suffers a "shipwreck" and needs to be repaired. The Amazons are sidetracked by a visit from Great-aunt Maria, whose iron will is law for the younger members of her family, including Mrs. Blackett and Uncle Jim. At first only the Swallows, now including the parrot Polly in Titty's care, camp on the hill above Swainson's farm. Nancy's plan this time is for all of them to scale "Kanchenjunga" by a route that requires making overnight camp before going for the final ascent. Through individual effort and cooperation Nancy's plan succeeds, in spite of difficulties. Another mark can be made on the map of the landscape of experience.

One of the features of the camp in *Swallowdale* is what the Swallows call "Peter Duck's Cave." The reader is told, "[Peter Duck] had been the most important character in the story they had made up during those winter evenings in the cabin of the wherry with Nancy and Peggy and Captain Flint." Clearly it had been Ransome's intention, when he was writing *Swallowdale,* to make a book that was a story from the children's fantasy life. Perhaps *Peter Duck* (1932) is. Although it begins rather matter-of-factly – "Peter Duck was sitting on a bollard on the north quay of Lowestoft Inner Harbour, smoking his pipe in the midday sunshine" – the Swallows and Amazons and Captain Flint sail with this honest old salt to the New World to find the place on Crab Island where Peter Duck once saw some men bury something. Their ship, *Wild Cat,* is pursued every league of the way by the *Viper* under the command of Black Jake. If the experience is real, it is *Treasure Island* come to life. When the bullets fly, they seem real enough, and it takes a waterspout to finish off the *Viper*. Both Peter Duck and Captain Flint are models of seamanship, with Peter Duck represented as the more experienced. Captain

Illustration by Ransome from The Picts and the Martyrs: Or, Not Welcome at All *(1943)*

Flint's eagerness to find the treasure is contrasted with Peter Duck's indifference to it. But bags of pearls are far from ordinary experience. *Peter Duck* immediately became even more popular than its predecessors. Real or imagined, or a little of both, it is a suspense-filled adventure tale.

In *Peter Duck* the ship has a new crew member, the Cabin Boy, Bill, who escapes from mistreatment aboard the *Viper*. In his working-class attitudes and accent, he foreshadows the "Death and Glories" of later novels. Gibber, Roger's monkey, starts his career of mischief in this book too.

Ransome and his wife were visiting the Altounyan family at their home in Aleppo while Ransome was writing *Peter Duck*. He read parts to them as they were written, and Titty and Roger Altounyan even helped Ransome with the illustrations. Since he intended this to be a story told by the children, he thought it should be illustrated by drawings such as the children would have made, and so he made his own. Everyone, including publisher and author, was so satisfied with these illustrations that Ransome did his own illustrations for all the books that followed. He also prepared illustrations for *Swallows and Amazons* and *Swallowdale,* which had originally appeared with illustrations by other artists.

Winter Holiday is a departure from *Peter Duck* and a return to the lake reality of *Swallowdale.* It is different from all three previous books in that it is set in winter, and there is no sailing at all. It is the familiar lake, but some names on the map have changed to allow for "Eskimo Settlement," "Spitzbergen," and "High Greenland." Captain Flint's ice-locked houseboat becomes the *Fram* of a polar expedition, as the children explorers make plans to go to the North Pole. All of the Swallows and Amazons are present, but, although his houseboat is essential, Captain Flint is absent until the end.

The new children arrive – Dick and Dorothea Callum, visitors at one of the farms on the lake. Dick shares with his creator nearsightedness and a schoolboy passion for science. Dorothea shares her creator's literary vocation. She is always thinking up titles of books and sentences to render her experiences into the sort of purple prose she admires. In the end the "Two D's" prove themselves when, thanks to genuinely heroic effort, they reach the North Pole first.

Of course, it is Nancy who orchestrates the march across the frozen lake. The amazing thing is that she does it from her sickbed, quarantined with mumps. Ransome may have been experimenting in writing a book without Nancy in it, but she is still there, issuing her orders in a stream of coded messages. In her absence Peggy is for once given a chance to become a personality in her own right.

In setting and characters *Coot Club* (1934) is a departure from the books that preceded it. None of the original Swallows and Amazons appear except by allusion. The book is set on the Norfolk Broads, far from the Lakes. The elements of water, boats, and children – and Ransome's excellent prose – link it to the others. And *Coot Club* shares two characters with *Winter Holiday,* Dick and Dorothea Callum. This early spring holiday they are visiting their mother's former teacher and her pug dog William (certainly a character in this book). They meet a group of local children who have banded together to form a bird protection society, "The Coot Club."

When polite requests have failed, in a desperate attempt at bird protection the Coot Club's leader, Tom Dudgeon, casts adrift a motor launch full of "Hullabaloos," crass and noisy visitors to the quiet waters The Broads. The struggle is on between the Coots and the visitors. Among the Coots are Port and Starboard, twin girls who crew for their father's racing sailboat, and "The Death and Glories," three boatbuilders' sons who sail an old boat of that name. It is a skirmish in the war between the traditional and the new, motor launch and sail, summer visitor and native. When the *Death and Glory* rescues a drifting motor launch, the victory is for native coots.

Traditional skill won in *Coot Club,* but science and technology has its day in *Pigeon Post.* This book returns us to summer in the Lake District and the full cast (Swallows, Amazons and the two D's) of *Winter Holiday.* The project this time is gold mining, and Dick, who seems to be older now, is an important resource person. He has designed the bell system that allows the Blackett carrier pigeons to announce their arrival with a message, and he is responsible for the process by which the children refine the gold they seem to have found. The combined talents of the children solve one problem after another in this effort. A fire in the dry summer fells, for which the children are briefly unjustly blamed, provides a tense and exciting climax. There is only a token appearance by a sailboat.

In all but four of the Swallows and Amazons books the area of action is confined to the distance children can sail or walk in a day. Most of the time they are back in camp for tea. Four of the books (*We Didn't Mean to Go to Sea, Great Northern?* [1947], *Peter Duck,* and *Missee Lee*) take place in distant waters. Although the other three of these faraway books have a strong element of fantasy, *We Didn't Mean to Go to Sea* is all realistic. The action and terror is like that of the fire in *Pigeon Post,* but they are sustained for the entire book. Ransome seems to have said to himself, "What would happen if I set my young sailors on the North Sea?" To get them there in a large enough ship, he invented a rather lame accident for the young skipper of the *Goblin,* but, once he is out of the way and the anchor starts dragging in the fog, there is no turning back. *We Didn't Mean to Go to Sea* is a book of all sailing, and it belongs to the Swallows alone.

John, Susan, Roger, and Titty have to give their all to the problems of wind, tide, channel steamers, and seasickness. Ransome focuses on each child in turn as each surmounts the real challenges presented by their extreme situation. Everyone is called to go beyond his or her normal limits. Susan at last is able to leave the stove and, overcoming seasickness, proves herself John's equal as a sailor. Having survived, they are able to rescue Sinbad the kitten and enjoy a perhaps too-coincidental meeting with their homeward-bound father in Holland. There is no doubt that this is the most unified dramatic narrative of the series. Many have called it the masterpiece.

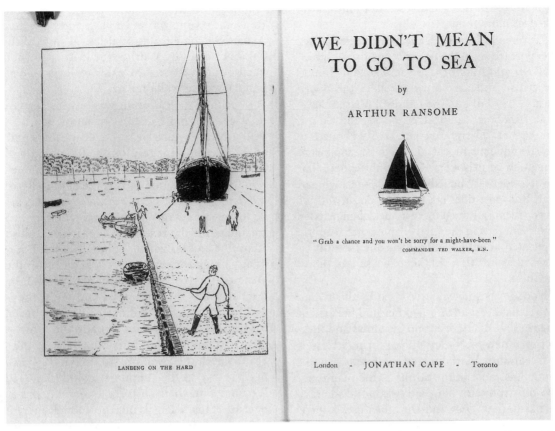

WE DIDN'T MEAN
TO GO TO SEA

by

ARTHUR RANSOME

" Grab a chance and you won't be sorry for a might-have-been "
COMMANDER TED WALKER, R.N.

London　-　JONATHAN CAPE　-　Toronto

LANDING ON THE HARD

Frontispiece and title page for Ransome's book about young sailors on the North Sea (Lilly Library, Indiana University)

Secret Water is the calm after the storm. In contrast to *We Didn't Mean to Go to Sea,* it has calmer water and fewer tense moments. It is set in the days immediately after *We Didn't Mean to Go to Sea* when naval orders prevent the Walkers from going on a planned family sailing trip. Commander Walker offers to allow the children to camp on an island in a tidal flats region. The island is surrounded by water at high tide, but most of this "sea" turns to mud flats at low water. The Swallows are left a small sailing boat and the project of mapping the island. In the process, they make friends with a local boy camped in a mired boat, who with Daisy and her two brothers forms another tribe, "The Eels." Like the Swallows, they have their own language and customs. Nancy and Peggy sail in to bring the total of children to eleven, for Bridget has been judged old enough at last. She brings Sinbad the kitten with her so that she will not be the youngest in camp. Bridget's experiences are often the focus of the attention in the story, especially the moment when she is captured by the Eels for "human sacrifice." Everyone learns a lot about tidal mud and tidal channels and how to relate to one's own tribe and another tribe's members. When Commander and

Mrs. Walker sail in to collect their family, the group has just completed the map.

The Big Six (1940) returns to the locale and characters of *Coot Club.* The twins, Port and Starboard, are away at school, but Dick and Dorothea are again visiting Mrs. Barrable and William, the heroic pug. Named after a famous team at Scotland Yard, this is a detective novel. False accusation, which appeared as a minor theme in some previous books, is the central problem here. The Death and Glories are not only falsely accused but actively framed for the serious crime of casting boats adrift. Adults are concerned, including the local policeman. In an attempt to prove that the young members of the Coot Club are innocent, Tom Dudgeon and Dick and Dorothea combine their talents and expertise to collect evidence with the adults. Class differences among the children are evident, but the children themselves ignore them in working for their shared goal.

Those who criticize Ransome for writing only about middle-class children whose families can afford to have sailboats seem to forget the Death and Glories. The young Coots in this book, so soon to be apprenticed to their fathers' trade, remind us of a sociological fact of the time: the time limit on a working-class childhood.

A far remove from such everyday reality, *Missee Lee* is the most exotic of the books set in distant water. The Swallows and Amazons crew for Captain Flint on a world cruise and are shipwrecked in the South China Sea. They fall into the hands of Missee Lee — lady pirate, onetime Cambridge student, and would-be Latin teacher. There are some highly comic moments as she attempts to teach Latin to her somewhat unwilling class of prisoners. One might expect that Nancy would identify immediately with a real woman pirate, but Ransome does not have her do so, and for once Nancy seems a muted force in the action. Missee Lee herself emerges in the final chapters between the role she wanted in her life in England and her duty to her deceased father that will keep her sailing pirate junks in China.

If Nancy was somewhat eclipsed by the events in China, Ransome made it up to her in *The Picts and The Martyrs* (1943). There are no Swallows and little sailing, but much of Nancy. The plot pits Nancy against Great-aunt Maria in a clash of wills. By the end Nancy has most of the adults in the neighborhood in collusion with her plan to conceal the fact that she has hidden Dick and Dorothea in a cottage in the woods instead of sending them home or asking Aunt Maria's permission for them to continue their visit. To distract Aunt Maria, Peggy and Nancy don their best frocks, recite poetry, and admire flowers. The skillfully written comic finale demonstrates that Nancy is like no one so much as she is like Great-aunt Maria.

Great Northern? brings together elements from the other books with new twists. The ship is the *Sea Bear,* sailing off the Hebrides with Captain Flint, a crew of the original Swallows and Amazons, and Dick and Dorothea Callum. Naturalist Dick spots what he thinks are a pair of rare birds, Great Northern Divers. Black Jake makes a reappearance in the character of Mr. Jemmerling, an evil egg collector who will stop at nothing to add these divers' eggs to his collection, unconcerned that by doing so he will harm both the birds themselves and the bird population of the British Isles. While the *Sea Bear* is brought to shore in a deserted cove for scrubbing, Dick hopes to get a photograph of the birds, Mr. Jemmerling hopes to get the eggs, and the laird of this island and his people, who think that the crew of the *Sea Bear* have been harassing their deer, hope to punish them. Nancy's plan gets altered as the events sweep all of the characters over the small area of rugged gullies, hills, and lakes in a conclusion that brings them all together for the first time.

By the time *Great Northern?* was published, Ransome's fame was at its peak and he was earning a steady income from royalties, in spite of the difficulties brought by World War I. After the book had been out for a year, the sales of Ransome's books had passed the million mark.

Although Ransome was no longer covering political hot spots in foreign lands, his life in the years during which he wrote "Swallows and Amazons" was not entirely quiet. Ransome had been troubled by ulcers for years and had had one operation for this condition during his days in Russia. Immediately after *Swallows and Amazons* was published, he underwent surgery again and was under medical treatment for the rest of his life. During these years Ransome and his wife bought a series of houses and boats, living for several years at a time in the Lake District, the Norfolk Broads, and, less often, London. In boats they designed and built, they sailed and fished on lakes, and, in their larger boats, lived for periods of time on the Broads and other waters. Ransome sailed one of his boats across the North Sea to check the Swallows' route for *We Didn't Mean to Go to Sea.* In the summers of 1938 and 1939 the Ransomes in their ship *Nancy Blackett* led a small fleet of ships, each flying the Jolly Roger, mostly crewed by young friends, on a week's cruise on the Norfolk Broads.

Many readers, child and adult, wrote Ransome with praise, questions, and suggestions. One of these letters in 1936 came from Pamela Whitlock and Katharine Hull (ages sixteen and fifteen), who, inspired by Ransome's work, had written a novel of their own. Ransome not only read it and encouraged them, he recommended it to his own publisher, advised the authors on all the details of seeing it through publication, and wrote its introduction. *The Life of Arthur Ransome* by Hugh Brogan quotes several of the lively letters of encouraging advice that Ransome sent the young authors during their preparation of *The Far-Distant Oxus* (1937).

There is no indication in *Great Northern?* that it was intended to be the last of his children's books, but no more tales about Swallows and Amazons appeared, although Ransome lived another twenty-nine years. In that time, he wrote introductions to a series of cruising books and *Mainly About Fishing* (1959), a final tribute to another of his lifelong passions. He died on 3 June 1967 after a long decline.

Many who have read the Swallows and Amazons books have shouted with their heroes, "Swallows and Amazons forever!" But a childhood "forever" is an extremely short time. By the time of *Great Northern?* the eldest of Ransome's fictional children had had about as many holidays as one gets before leaving school. It was time for them to grow up, and Ransome chose not to write about them on that adventure. They had, of course, grown and changed across the ten novels in which they sailed.

Ransome's legacy to readers is this series of adventures in which his literary skills, special knowledge, and love united to create a unique fictional world. Time will tell if these books will continue to find new child readers in an era when the motor launches of Hullabaloos have won the waters and safe camping places are hard to find.

Some critics feel that the length of Ransome's novels alone is enough to daunt the modern child reader. Others contend that readers will make allowances for such "old-fashionedness" because they will see beyond it and will find in the Swallows and Amazons' adventures in Ransome's created world the very essence of their own childhoods.

Ransome seems to have regarded the Swallows and Amazons books as the major achievement of his long and amazingly varied writing career. In a final note in his *Autobiography* (1976), he thanks Evgenia for "thirty years of unclouded happiness" and then for her "resolute courage" without which "I should never have dared to take the step that gave me, towards the end of my life, the twenty years in which I have been able to write those books that may seem to some children the excuse for my existence."

Biography:

Hugh Brogan, *The Life of Arthur Ransome* (London: Cape, 1984).

References:

Christian Hardyment, *Arthur Ransome and Captain Flint's Trunk* (London: Cape, 1984);

Peter Hunt, *Arthur Ransome* (Boston: Twayne, 1991);

Fred Inglis, "Class and Classic – the Greatness of Arthur Ransome" in his *The Promise of Happiness* (New York & London: Cambridge University Press, 1981), pp. 124–145;

Hugh Shelley, *Arthur Ransome* (London: Bodley Head, 1960; New York: Walck, 1964).

Papers:

The Brotherton Collection at the University of Leeds has the most important collection of Ransome's letters, diaries, unpublished manuscripts, notebooks, sketchbooks, photographs, and newspaper articles. The Lakeland Museum, Abbot Hall, Kendal, has some typed drafts and other papers. Letters and business papers are also in the hands of some of Ransome's friends and his publisher, Jonathan Cape.

(Leonard) Malcolm Saville

(21 February 1901 – 30 June 1982)

Gary D. Schmidt
Calvin College

BOOKS: *Mystery at Witchend,* illustrated by G. E. Breary (London: Newnes, 1943); republished as *Spy in the Hills* (New York: Farrar & Rinehart, 1945);

Seven White Gates, illustrated by Bertram Prance (London: Newnes, 1944);

Country Scrap Book for Boys and Girls (London: National Magazine Company, 1944; revised edition, London & Chesham: Gramol, 1945);

The Gay Dolphin Adventure (London: Newnes, 1945);

Open-Air Scrap Book for Boys and Girls (London & Chesham: Gramol, 1945);

Trouble at Townsend (London: Transatlantic Arts, 1945);

Jane's Country Year, illustrated by Bernard Bowerman (London: Newnes, 1946);

Seaside Scrap Book for Boys & Girls (London & Chesham: Gramol, 1946);

The Secret of Grey Walls (London: Newnes, 1947);

The Riddle of the Painted Box, illustrated by Lunt Roberts (London: Noel Carrington, 1947);

Redshank's Warning, illustrated by Roberts (London: Lutterworth, 1948);

Two Fair Plaits, illustrated by Roberts (London: Lutterworth, 1948);

Lone Pine Five, illustrated by Prance (London: Newnes, 1949);

Strangers at Snowfell, illustrated by Wynne (London: Lutterworth, 1949);

The Adventure of the Life-Boat Service (London: Macdonald, 1950);

The Master of Maryknoll, illustrated by Alice Bush (London: Evans, 1950);

The Sign of the Alpine Rose, illustrated by Wynne (London: Lutterworth, 1950);

The Flying Fish Adventure, illustrated by Roberts (London: John Murray, 1950);

All Summer Through, illustrated by Joan Kiddell-Monroe (London: Hodder & Stoughton, 1951);

The Elusive Grasshopper, illustrated by Prance (London: Newnes, 1951);

Malcolm Saville

The Buckinghams at Ravenswyke, illustrated by Bush (London: Evans, 1952);

Coronation Gift Book For Boys & Girls (London: Daily Graphic/Pitkins, 1952);

The Luck of Sallowby, illustrated by Tilden Reeves (London: Lutterworth, 1952);

The Ambermere Treasure, illustrated by Marcia Lane Foster (London: Lutterworth, 1953); republished as *The Secret of the Ambermere Treasure* (New York: Criterion, 1967);

Christmas at Nettleford, illustrated by Kiddell-Monroe (London: Hodder & Stoughton, 1953);

The Secret of the Hidden Pool, illustrated by Roberts (London: John Murray, 1953);

The Neglected Mountain, illustrated by Prance (London: Newnes, 1953);

228

Spring Comes to Nettleford, illustrated by Kiddel-Monroe (London: Hodder & Stoughton, 1954);

The Long Passage, illustrated by Bush (London: Evans, 1954);

Susan, Bill and the Ivy-Clad Oak [Wolf-Dog, Golden Clock, Vanishing Boy, Dark Stranger, "Saucy Kate," Bright Star Circus, Pirates Bold], 8 volumes, illustrated by Ernest Shepard and T. R. Freeman (London: Nelson, 1954–1961);

Saucers Over the Moon, illustrated by Prance (London: Newnes, 1955);

Where the Bus Stopped (Oxford: Blackwell, 1955);

The Secret of Buzzard Scar, illustrated by Kiddell-Monroe (London: Hodder & Stoughton, 1955);

Young Johnnie Bimbo, illustrated by Roberts (London: John Murray, 1956);

Wings Over Witchend (London: Newnes, 1956);

Lone Pine London (London: Newnes, 1957);

Treasure at the Mill, illustrated by Harry Pettit (London: Newnes, 1957);

The Fourth Key, illustrated by Roberts (London: John Murray, 1957);

King of Kings (London: Nelson, 1958; revised edition, Berkhamsted, Hertfordshire: Lion, 1975; Huntingdon, Ind.: Our Sunday Visitor, 1977);

The Secret of the Gorge (London: Newnes, 1958);

Mystery Mine (London: Newnes, 1959);

Four-and-Twenty Blackbirds, illustrated by Lilian Buchanan (London: Newnes, 1959); republished as *The Secret of Galleybird Pit* (London: Armada, 1968);

Small Creature, illustrated by John Kenney (London: Ward, 1959);

Sea Witch Comes Home (London: Newnes, 1960);

Malcolm Saville's Country Book (London: Cassell, 1961);

Malcolm Saville's Seaside Book (London: Cassell, 1962);

Not Scarlet But Gold, illustrated by A. R. Whitear (London: Newnes, 1962);

A Palace for the Buckinghams, illustrated by Bush (London: Evans, 1963);

Three Towers in Tuscany (London: Heinemann, 1963);

The Purple Valley (London: Heinemann, 1964);

Treasure at Amorys, illustrated by Freeman (London: Newnes, 1964);

Dark Danger (London: Heinemann, 1965);

White Fire (London: Heinemann, 1966);

The Thin Grey Man, illustrated by Desmond Knight (London: Macmillan, 1966; New York: St. Martin's Press, 1966);

The Man With Three Fingers, illustrated by Michael Whittlesea (London: Newnes, 1966);

Come to London: A Personal Introduction to the World's Greatest City (London: Heinemann, 1967);

Strange Story (London: Mowbray, 1967);

Power of Three (London: Heinemann, 1967);

Come to Cornwall (London: Benn, 1969);

Come to Devon (London: Benn, 1969);

Rye Royal (London: Collins, 1969);

Come to Somerset (London: Benn, 1970);

Strangers at Witchend (London: Collins, 1970);

The Dagger and the Flame (London: Heinemann, 1970);

Good Dog Dandy (London: Collins, 1971);

The Secret of Villa Rosa (London: Collins, 1971);

Where's My Girl? (London: Collins, 1972);

Diamond in the Sky (London: Collins, 1974);

Eat What You Grow, illustrated by Robert Micklewright (London: Carousel, 1975);

Portrait of Rye, illustrated by Michael Renton (East Grinstead, Sussex: Goulden, 1976);

The Countryside Quiz Book, illustrated by Micklewright (London: Carousel, 1978);

Marston, Master Spy (London: Heinemann, 1978);

Home to Witchend (London: Armada, 1978);

Wonder Why Book of Exploring a Wood, illustrated by Elsie Wrigley (London: Corgi, 1978);

Wonder Why Book of Exploring the Seashore, illustrated by Jenny Heath (London: Corgi, 1979);

Wonder Why Book of Wildflowers Through the Year (London: Corgi, 1980);

The Seashore Quiz Book, illustrated by Micklewright (London: Carousel, 1981).

OTHER: *Words for All Season,* edited by Saville, illustrated by Elsie and Paul Wrigley (Guildford, Surrey: Lutterworth, 1979).

In his *Tellers of Tales* (1965), Roger Lancelyn Green devotes a single sentence to one of the most prolific writers of British children's literature: "Popular exponents of the holiday adventure story are headed by Malcolm Saville, whose *Mystery at Witchend* (1943) began as a series of rather improbable but entertaining tales of children foiling spies and burglars with the greatest of ease." In a highly subjective book, this is a curiously detached sentence. The judgment seems mixed — "entertaining but improbable" — an illogical pairing perhaps. The last clause might be read as almost disdainful if it were not that the tone of the entire sentence seems so entirely factual.

Any assessment of Malcolm Saville must in the end be mixed. An extremely popular writer — he

Saville reading a story to children at the Rainbow Bookshop, Walton-on-Thames, England, January 1967 (Hulton Deutsch Collection)

is said to have received three thousand letters a year from his readers – he wrote eighty works for children, principally mysteries in which a plucky group of children find an adventure and thereby solve a mystery or thwart the nasty spy out to undermine Britain and its way of life. Green links Saville to the holiday adventure story, in which the adventures come to students while the term is out. But here lies the difficulty with this writer. He is indeed the representative writer – along with Enid Blyton – in the holiday adventure genre as it was developed in the middle of the twentieth century. But he followed conventions almost slavishly, never rising above them, never redefining them, never challenging them, never using them in new or unexpected ways.

Great writers use the conventions of a genre to give shape to, but not to limit, their work. For Saville, the conventions of the holiday adventure were absolute boundaries that defined everything about his books. Anyone who has read a single holiday adventure knows – without getting too far into a Saville book – who the bad guys are, who the good guys are, and how each is likely to act over the next two hundred pages. The result is a read that is entertaining and pleasant in part because it is familiar. The good children will win out over the nasties

without the help of the seemingly obtuse friendly adults. But there will be a few suspenseful moments along the way until the inevitable end is reached.

It is perhaps inevitable itself that a writer producing two or three novels each year must become either repetitive or generic. And at times Saville could be both. Still, on one level sheer productivity has to be admired, and Saville's is all the more impressive when one sees that for the first twenty-three years of his career he worked as a sales promotion manager for three publishers: Cassell and Company, Amalgamated Press, and George Newnes. At the last he edited books during the twenty years he was most active as a writer, and, in addition, he worked as an associate editor for *My Garden* magazine (1949–1952) and as a publicity and feature writer for Kemsley newspapers (1952–1955). He continued to work as an editor for George Newnes until 1966.

Saville began his writing career with what is arguably his best-known book: *Mystery at Witchend,* published two years later in the United States with the inaccurate title *Spy in the Hills.* This mystery set the pattern for much of his later work. In fact, it established a group of children, the Lone Piners, who would figure in subsequent novels such as *Seven White Gates* (1944), *The Gay Dolphin Adventure* (1945), and *The Secret of Grey Walls* (1947). In each, the group of five children thwart spies (whether against Britain's wartime interests or against its industries), bedevil kidnappers and jewel thieves, and bring to justice malefactors who forge paintings or threaten Britain's people. The central crises of the novels are reached as the group, or a part of the group, is threatened because of what has been discovered. It is the ingenuity of the Lone Piners that leads to their eventual rescue and the turning of the tables.

Mystery at Witchend introduces the Lone Piners; they are all in Shropshire because of the war. David (distinguished for his common sense and good will) and the twins (known for complicating situations) have come to Witchend, a manorial house, while their father has gone off to war. Tom Inglis has been evacuated to a nearby farm because of the Blitz. Petronella lives with her father, who watches over the reservoir in Shropshire that sends London its daily water supply. For much of the novel the children are exploring the wild hill country around their homes. During these explorations they come upon several hikers who appear soon after fog has blanketed the countryside and the sound of a low-flying plane has been heard. They are all heading toward the home of the severe Mrs. Thurston.

The children soon discover that these are German spies who plan to blow up the reservoir, thus damaging the British will to fight. In discovering this the twins are captured but soon rescued by other Lone Piners who have roused the countryside. The spies are caught, one by a flood that he has created, and the Lone Piners are extolled. All ends happily and in utter security, as though it had all been a game all along: "[Petronella] was very happy. It had been a wonderful day and the end of a perfect adventure. None of the girls at school could ever imagine an adventure like it." David begins to plan a new adventure — "I want to explore dark Hollow properly one day soon. Shall we, Tom?" — and the twins announce that they have already come up with a new mystery. It is all as if the danger were not very real after all; this has just been an adventure that children play at, and the new day will bring a new game.

If the plots are somewhat improbable, Saville has nonetheless created a credible cast of characters. It is in fact his characterization that marks Saville's work as worthy of attention for more than mere historical purposes. In *Mystery at Witchend*, Saville introduced characters remarkable for their diversity, even if they do fit into the expected roles of

holiday adventures. David is indeed a leader, good and true and loyal, but Saville has given him a moving role: while his father is away at war, David takes on some of his duties — purpose that fills David with determination. The twins show the uncanny perception that marks many twins. Petronella is the plucky girl who seems utterly self-reliant but who is overwhelmingly glad to have, finally, a group of friends. Tom, the most enigmatic, is a boy out of his element. He has been evacuated to a farm, where he works hard at unfamiliar tasks, all the while missing the life of London. Here is a cast of characters who fill stereotyped roles but who are not themselves stereotyped and flat.

Margery Fisher disagrees with this assessment:

> The personalities, realistic enough in themselves, are deliberately standardized so that they will fit the unexacting nature of the adventures and will exist in a vacuum of time. Each boy or girl is given a set description, repeated at the beginning of each story; they have been permitted to grow a year or two older through the years so that certain sentimental attachments may be introduced to vary the predictable scenes ... but it is essential to the nature of the stories that the children shall not be sufficiently individual to react in any but the most superficial way to danger.

The lack of growth that Fisher decries is certainly evident through the eighteen novels in which the Lone Piners explore and track and spy. However, this is not so much the fault of Saville's as of the series form. One of the pleasures of a series lies in the return to known characters. This necessitates standardization of characters, even at the sacrifice of realism. Time does become something of a vacuum so that the characters may be preserved. That preservation is not a flaw but an accepted convention.

Saville's other strength lies in his use of setting. "All fiction is influenced by 'Place,' " he wrote, and so most of his work is set in Britain, particularly Shropshire, the place most familiar to him. For some books he traveled through Europe so that he could establish accurate settings, placing some of his plots in Holland, Spain, Italy, France, and Luxembourg. In *Mystery at Witchend,* he used the setting as more than just a backdrop — a pattern he would follow in later novels. When he begins the novel by having a native warn against the dangers of the wild terrain, he is suggesting that the setting will itself be a character. And so it is. The plot is filled with threatening bogs, sudden valleys, mysterious rock formations that have given rise to local legends,

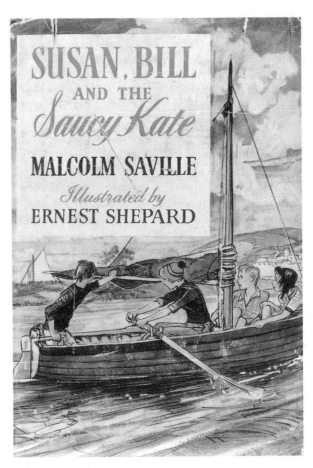

Dust jacket for one of Saville's books in the eight-volume Susan and Bill series

deadly mists, and trackless heights. Even the sabotage of the spies is directed against the terrain, and it is the terrain that captures at least one of them.

But even more, Saville uses his various sites as a medieval dramatist used his seats. The plot is spread around four different houses, each distinguished. Witchend, despite its name, is a big, homey house, full of kitchen and mother and family. Hatch Holt, Petronella's home, is marked by quirky tidiness and a loving paternalism. The Ingles farm is the site of all British virtues, aside, perhaps, from the domestic ones: hard work, duty, responsibility, and self-reliance. Appledore, despite its appealing name, is the undomestic site of spies and saboteurs. All the action swirls around these very different locales.

In later novels Saville retained this focus on location though at times he would narrow his attention considerably, as in *The Ambermere Treasure* (1953), published in 1967 in the United States as *The Secret of the Ambermere Treasure*. Here the spotlight is on Ambermere, a three-story medieval house with secret rooms, hidden treasure, and a bloody history. A group of children known as the Jillies are trying to get the house in order so that it may be opened to the public and the income used to keep it up; at the same time they are searching for a three-hundred-year-old treasure and battling two thieves who are also eager to find it. All of these goings-on occur in the house and on its grounds, and it is the house itself that strides prominently across the novel. "Doesn't this place with all these twisty passages and closed doors remind you of the corridors in the castle where the little princess used to go to find her wonderful grandmother?" Prue echoes, referring to George MacDonald's "Princess and Curdie" books, and of course it is a deliberate echo on Saville's part.

Margery Fisher is harsher on Saville, however: "[T]he dialogue is still characterized by a curious flabby profuseness which pads out the stories, as each character discusses or describes either what has happened or what may happen in the future. These mechanical exchanges are the main form of communication between characters. . . ." Here Fisher is on strong ground; few writers have called out so obviously for editing as Saville. His stories, though active and intriguing, always seem to take longer than they should. His characters are eternally gathering to tell and retell their stories in ways that are patently unrealistic and even, at times, silly. If Saville could create believable characters, he was unable to have them interact believably, nor could he allow a story to unfold without having his characters continually butting in to take over the narrator's job.

In addition to the clumsy and stilted narrative technique, Saville frequently demonstrates a flaw fatal to mysteries: a lack of subtlety in both his plot situations and depiction of relationships between characters. One is not far into *The Ambermere Treasure* before it is clear that Prue will find the treasure, nor are readers many chapters into *Mystery at Witchend* before they realize that sabotage is afoot and it has something to do with the Hatch Holt reservoir. Though every adult in the novel seems innocent and naive, the reader quickly suspects that Mrs. Thurston's frequent hikes around the reservoir and her rapidly drawn maps suggest more than birdwatching – her rationale, readily accepted by all adults in the novel. The same lack of subtlety extends to relationships between the characters. Of course the reader expects the close-knit friendships that develop within the groups that Saville creates. But the difficulty is that the villains especially are so patently devious. In *Mystery at Witchend* Mrs. Thurston's servant Joseph arrives at the train station at Onnybrook at the same time as David and the twins; his rude and accusatory stance mark him instantly as one of the villains – not exactly the subtlety one would expect from a spy. Mrs. Thurston herself is slim and severe; she kicks dogs, slaps children, scowls, and speaks German – a pattern for Amy Blunt in *The Ambermere Treasure,* who is a mirror villain except for her linguistic abilities. All the villains are transparent to the children of the novel, and it is only an adventure to thwart them.

To some measure the lack of subtlety may be expected in a mystery set for children. Those who are clearly villainous are pitted against those who are clearly virtuous, and the latter is composed chiefly of the clever children of the novel. Those are the conventions of the holiday adventure mystery. And there is a pleasure in pursuing the familiar and the expected. Yet certainly one reason for Saville's inability to produce a lasting novel is that his plots are so completely predictable. The cast of characters is laid out clearly and obviously; the mystery is

then introduced. All that remains is to follow the workings out of the adventure to its inevitable and expected conclusion.

Saville began his writing career at the height of World War II, at a time when the war was particularly grim for Britain. In one sense his writings were consciously meant to support and encourage British children, who after all are clever and resourceful enough to detect the Nazi spies here at home. Pitted against the treachery of the Nazi spies are all the British virtues that the children so adeptly and unconsciously embody, particularly loyalty and duty and perseverance.

Saville continued to celebrate this spirit in later years and in other genres to which he turned. He begins his *The Adventure of the Life-Boat Service* (1950), for example, with an affirmation of Britain's role in world affairs: "I have written this book because I believe that the leadership which Britain has given to the world in the past is primarily due to the belief that each human has a soul, a will and an individuality of his own." The rest of this short book is filled with examples of British heroism and ingenuity, the qualities that helped Britain survive the Blitz. For example:

> The Royal National Life-boat Institution was inspired by high-principled men who realized that here was urgent work which ought to be done and those who set themselves to do it did so without thought of personal gain but because they knew it was right. Perhaps today they would have been accused of not minding their own business and taking too much upon themselves, but nothing can alter the fact that the spirit of these few pioneers not only succeeded in overcoming innumerable obstacles but inspired the men who went out to face death in little boats to save the lives of those they had never seen.

It is hard not to hear in these words an echo of Dunkirk. But dominant is the paean of praise for the individuality and self-sacrifice that marks the British way of life.

In later years Saville did experiment with other genres and with fiction for older children. Most of these ventures are today forgotten, with perhaps one exception: *King of Kings* (1958), an overtly evangelical retelling of the life of Christ. Freed from the constraints of inventing dialogue, Saville drafted a moving interpretation of this life, using resources, staying close to the Gospels, and speculating (within strict boundaries) when the Gospels do not provide full details. His is a retelling filled with charity: there is forgiveness in the face of Judas's repentance, understanding of Peter's rashness and betrayal, peace in the face of Thomas's doubts. The dramatic story is provided; what Saville adds is a weaving together of disparate threads and a fleshing out of character and event that is wholly consistent with the text.

Writing of Saville's contributions, Fred Inglis has suggested in *Twentieth-Century Children's Writers* (1989) that Saville might best be remembered for his character types:

> [H]is faithful bands of chums repeat the unkillable, splendid rituals of secret oaths, perfect campsites, night stalking, kidnapped twins, and mysterious watches with torches and binoculars and cliff edges at the very mid of night. . . . Much is to be said for such delights; so much, that perhaps we may say that without them – without creaking Elizabethan Inns, lone pines and fog on the Stiperstones, without the landscapes of the English late Romantic movement (Housman, Kipling) – children cannot be said to have entered the culture, any more than they can if they know no old songs or fairy stories.

Saville is nothing if not a writer writing about the British culture, using familiar images and characters to tell familiar stories that made a way of life familiar to more than one generation.

Ernest Howard Shepard

(10 December 1879 – 24 March 1976)

Patricia J. Cianciolo
Michigan State University

BOOKS: *Fun and Fantasy: Punch Anthology* (London: Methuen, 1927);

Drawn From Memory (London: Methuen, 1957; Philadelphia: Lippincott, 1957);

Drawn From Life (London: Methuen, 1961; New York: Dutton, 1962);

Pooh: His Art Gallery: Anthology of Drawings (New York: Dutton, 1962);

Ben and Brock (London: Methuen, 1965; Garden City, N.Y.: Doubleday, 1966);

Betsy and Joe (London: Methuen, 1966; New York: Dutton, 1967).

BOOKS ILLUSTRATED: Thomas Hughes. *Tom Brown's Schooldays* (London: Partridge, circa 1904; Boston: Ginn, 1956);

Harold Avery, *Play the Game* (London: Partridge, circa 1904–1914);

Charles Dickens, *David Copperfield* (London: Partridge, circa 1904–1914);

Evelyn Everett Green, *Smouldering Fires* (London: Partridge, circa 1904–1914);

Rev. G. Henslow, *Aesop's Fables* (London: Partridge, circa 1904–1914);

Henry Walpole, *Jeremy* (London: Cassell, 1919);

A. C. Benson and Sir Lawrence Weaver, eds., *Everybody's Book of the Queen's Doll's House* (London: Methuen, 1924);

A. A. Milne, *When We Were Very Young* (London: Methuen, 1924; New York: Dutton, 1924; revised edition, London: Methuen, 1934; New York: Dutton, 1935); republished with a foreword by Sir James Pitman (New York: Dutton, 1966);

E. V. Lucas, *Playtime and Company* (London: Methuen, 1925);

Lucas, *A Book of Children's Verse* (London: Doran, circa 1925);

Milne, *Fourteen Songs from 'When We Were Very Young,'* music by H. Fraser-Simson (New York: Dutton, 1925);

Milne, *The King's Breakfast from 'When We Were Very Young,'* music by Fraser-Simson (New York: Dutton, 1925);

Milne, *Teddy Bear from 'When We Were Very Young,'* music by Fraser-Simson (New York: Dutton, 1926);

Dickens, *The Holly-Tree and Other Christmas Stories* (New York: Scribners, 1926);

Samuel Pepys, *Everybody's Pepys,* abridged and edited by O. F. Morshead (London: G. Bell, 1926; New York: Harcourt Brace, 1926);

Milne, *Winnie-the-Pooh* (New York: Dutton, 1926; London: Methuen, 1926; revised edition, London: Methuen, 1934; New York: Dutton, 1934; full color edition, London: Methuen, 1973; New York: Dutton, 1974; new edition handcolored by Eleanor Kwei, New York: Dutton, 1991);

Milne, *Songs from 'Now We Are Six,'* music by Fraser-Simson (New York: Dutton, 1927);

Eva Violet Isaacs Erleigh, *The Little One's Log* (London: Partridge, 1927);

Milne, *Now We Are Six* (London: Methuen, 1927; New York: Dutton, 1927; revised edition, New York: Dutton, 1934; London: Methuen, 1934; revised edition, New York: Dutton, 1961);

Georgette Agnew, *Let's Pretend* (London: Methuen, 1927; New York: Putnam, 1927);

Kenneth Grahame, *The Golden Age* (London: John Lane, 1928; New York: Dodd, 1929; edition with new pictures, New York: Dodd, 1954);

Lucas, *Mr. Punch's County Songs* (London: Methuen, 1928);

Milne, *The House at Pooh Corner* (London: Methuen, 1928; New York: Dutton, 1928; revised edition, London: Methuen, 1934; New York: Dutton, 1935; revised edition, New York: Dutton, 1961; full-color edition, London: Methuen, 1973; new edition hand colored by Kwei, New York: Dutton, 1991);

Ernest Howard Shepard

Anthony Armstrong (pseudonym of Anthony Armstrong Willis), *Livestock in Barracks* (London: Methuen, 1929);

Milne, *The Christopher Robin Story Book* (New York: Dutton, 1929);

Milne, *The Very Young Calendar* (New York: Dutton, 1929);

Grahame, *Dream Days* (London: John Lane, 1930; New York: Dodd, Mead, 1931; edition with new pictures, New York: Dodd, Mead, 1954);

F. V. Morley, ed., *Everybody's Boswell* (London: G. Bell, 1930; New York: Harcourt, Brace, 1930);

Milne, *Tales of Pooh* (London: Methuen, 1930);

Milne, *The Christopher Robin Birthday Book* (London: Methuen, 1930; New York: Dutton, 1931);

Grahame, *The Wind in the Willows* (London: Methuen, 1931; New York: Scribners, 1933; new edition, New York: Scribners, 1953; edition with new plates in full color, London: Methuen, 1971);

John Drinkwater, *Christmas Poems* (London: Sidgwick & Jackson, 1931);

Milne, *The Christopher Robin Verses* (New York: Dutton, 1932); republished as *The Christopher Robin Book of Verse* (New York: Dutton, 1962);

Jan Struther (pseudonym of Joyce Maxtone Graham), *Sycamore Square* (London: Methuen, 1932; New York: Oxford University Press, 1932);

Richard Jefferies, *Bevis* (London: P. Smith, 1932);

J. Boswell, *The Great Cham (Dr. Johnson)* (London: G. Bell, 1933);

A. C. Ward, ed., *Everybody's Lamb* (London: G. Bell, 1933; New York: Harcourt, Brace, 1933); republished with a new title page by Shepard (London: G. Bell, 1950);

Patrick Chalmers, *The Cricket in the Cage* (London: Macmillan, 1933);

Laurence Housman, *The Goblin Market* (London: Cape, 1933);

Housman, *Victoria Regina* (London: Cape, 1934; New York: Scribners, 1935);

Winifred Fortescue, *Perfume Provence* (London: Blackwood, 1935);

Struther, *The Modern Struwelpeter* (London: Methuen, 1935);

Milne, *Songs from 'Now We Are Six'* (New York: Dutton, circa 1935);

Milne, *More 'Very Young' Songs* (New York: Dutton, 1937);

Milne, *The Hums of Pooh,* music by Fraser-Simson (New York: Dutton, 1937);

Lucas, *As the Bee Sucks,* edited and illustrated by Shepard (London: Methuen, 1937);

John Collings Squire, *Cheddar Gorge* (London: Collins, 1937; New York: Macmillan, 1938);

Fortescue, *Sunset House,* frontispiece only by Shepard (London: Blackwood, 1937);

Housman, *The Golden Sovereign* (New York: Scribners, 1937; London: Cape, 1937);

Grahame, *The Reluctant Dragon* (New York: Holiday House, 1938);

Housman, *We Are Not Amused* (London: Cape, 1939);

Housman, *Happy and Glorious* (London: Cape, 1939);

Housman, *Bedchamber Plot* (London: Cape, 1939);

Housman, *Suitable Suitors* (London: Cape, 1939);

Housman, *Stable Government* (London: Cape, 1939);

Housman, *Promotion Cometh* (London: Cape, 1939);

Housman, *Primrose Way* (London: Cape, 1939);

Housman, *Go-Between* (London: Cape, 1939);

Housman, *Firelighters* (London: Cape, 1939);

Housman, *Enter Prince* (London: Cape, 1939);

Housman, *Comforter* (London: Cape, 1939);

Housman, *Great Relief* (London: Cape, 1939);

Housman, *Gracious Majesty: Scenes From the Life of Queen Victoria* (London: Cape, 1941; New York: Scribners, 1942);

Grahame, *Bertie's Escapade* (Philadelphia: Lippincott, 1945; London: Methuen, 1949);

Milne, *Old Sailor and Other Stories* (New York: Dutton, 1947);

Milne, *Sneezles and Other Selections* (New York: Dutton, 1947);

Roland Pertwee, *The Islanders* (London: Oxford University Press, 1950);

Anna B. Stewart, *Enter David Garrick* (Philadelphia: Lippincott, 1951);

Housman, *Palace Plays: Episodes from the Life of Queen Victoria* (London: Methuen, 1951);

Milne, *Year In, Year Out* (London: Methuen, 1952; New York: Dutton, 1952);

Eleanor Farjeon, *The Silver Curlew* (London: Oxford University Press, 1953; New York: Viking, 1954);

Malcolm Saville, *Susan, Bill, and the Wolf-Dog* (London: Nelson, 1954);

Saville, *Susan, Bill, and the Ivy-Clad Oak* (London: Nelson, 1954);

Juliana Ewing, *The Brownies and Other Stories* (London: Dent, 1954; New York: Dutton, 1954);

Mary Louisa Molesworth, *The Cuckoo Clock* (London: Dent, 1954; New York: Dutton, 1954);

Susan Colling, *Frogmorton* (London: Collins, 1955; New York: Knopf, 1956);

Roger Lancelyn Green, ed., *Modern Fairy Tales* (London: Dent, 1955; New York: Dutton, 1955);

Saville, *Susan, Bill, and the Vanishing Boy* (London: Nelson, 1955);

Saville, *Susan, Bill, and the Golden Clock* (London: Nelson, 1955);

Farjeon, *The Glass Slipper* (London: Oxford University Press, 1955; New York: Knopf, 1956);

Saville, *Susan, Bill, and the 'Saucy Kate'* (London: Nelson, 1956);

Saville, *Susan, Bill, and the Dark Stranger* (London: Nelson, 1956);

B. C. Rugh, *The Crystal Mountain* (New York: Riverside Press, 1956);

Frances Hodgson Burnett, *The Secret Garden* (London: Heinemann, 1956);

Shirley Goulden, *Royal Reflections* (London: Methuen, 1956);

George MacDonald, *At the Back of the North Wind* (London: Dent, 1956; New York: Dutton, 1956);

J. Fassett, ed., *The Pancake* (Boston: Ginn, 1957);

Milne, *The World of Pooh* (New York: Dutton, 1957; London: Methuen, 1958);

Milne, *The World of Christopher Robin* (New York: Dutton, 1958);

Fassett, ed., *The Briar Rose* (Boston: Ginn, 1958);

Green, *Old Greek Fairy Tales* (London: Bell, 1958);

J. Compton, ed., *A Noble Company* (Boston: Ginn, 1961);

Milne, *Pooh's Library: 'Now We Are Six,' 'When We Were Very Young,' 'Winnie-the-Pooh,' 'The House at Pooh Corner'* (New York: Dutton, 1961);

Hans Christian Andersen, *Fairy Tales,* translated by L. W. Kingsland (London: Oxford University Press, 1961; New York: Walck, 1962);

Milne, *The Pooh Song Book* (New York: Dutton, 1961; London: Methuen, 1977);

E. V. Rieu, *The Flattered Flying Fish* (London: Methuen, 1962; New York: Dutton, 1962);

Milne, *Pooh's Birthday Book* (New York: Dutton, 1963);

Milne, *The Pooh Story Book* (New York: Dutton, 1965; London: Methuen, 1967);

Milne, *The Christopher Robin Verse Book* (New York: Dutton, 1967; London: Methuen, 1969);

Milne, *Pooh's Pot O'Honey* (New York: Dutton, 1968);

Virginia Ellison, *The Pooh Cook Book* (New York: Dutton, 1969; London: Methuen, 1971);

Ellison, *The Pooh Party Book* (New York: Dutton, 1971; London: Methuen, 1975);

One of Shepard's preliminary sketches for A. A. Milne's
Winnie-the-Pooh *(1926) (Victoria & Albert Museum)*

Ellison, *The Pooh Get-Well Book* (New York: Dutton, 1973);

Milne, *Pooh's Alphabet Book* (New York: Dutton, 1975);

Carol S. Friedrichsen, *The Pooh Craft Book* (New York: Dutton, 1976);

Milne, *Pooh's Quiz Book* (New York: Dutton, 1977);

Milne, *Pooh's Bedtime Book* (New York: Dutton, 1980);

Milne, *Pooh's Counting Book* (New York: Dutton, 1982);

Milne, *Winnie-the-Pooh: A Pop-up Book,* Shepard's illustrations adapted by C. Murphy, paper engineering by Keith Moseley (New York: Dutton, 1984);

Milne, *The House at Pooh Corner: A Pop-up Book* (New York: Dutton, 1986);

Milne, *The Pooh Book of Quotations,* compiled by Brian Sibley, decorations by Shepard (London: Methuen, 1986; New York: Dutton, 1991);

Milne, *Piglet Is Entirely Surrounded by Water,* Shepard's illustrations adapted for the pop-up presentation by Robert Cremins (New York: Dutton, 1991);

Milne, *Pooh Invents a New Game,* Shepard's illustrations adapted for the pop-up presentation by Robert Cremins (New York: Dutton, 1991).

Ernest H. Shepard, a prolific, thoroughly professional illustrator of fiction and nonfiction for children and adults, has been referred to as the last of the great Victorian black-and-white men. Some literary and art critics lauded his black-and-white line drawings for children's stories and poems; others minimized them. It is best to say that he excelled in some of his work as an illustrator, particularly as an illustrator of children's literature. In this field he is most widely known and lauded for his drawings for A. A. Milne's collection of verses *When We Were Very Young* (1924) and *Now We Are Six* (1927) and for Milne's *Winnie-the-Pooh* (1926) and *The House at Pooh Corner* (1928), collections of fanciful adventures about Christopher Robin and his friends; for Hans Christian Andersen's *Fairy Tales* (1961); for Kenneth Grahame's *The Wind in the Willows* (1931); and for Richard Jefferies's *Bevis* (1932). His drawings for literary works by Frances Hodgson Burnett, George MacDonald, Charles Dickens, Eleanor Farjeon, and Samuel Pepys are also noteworthy for the deft characterization that appeared in his best work.

Shepard was born on 10 December 1879, in St. John's Wood, London. His father, Henry Dunkin Shepard, was an architect, and his mother, Jessie Harriet Lee, was the daughter of William Lee, a successful watercolor painter; his brother, Cyril, was two years his elder, and his sister, Ethel, was four years his elder. About 1883 the Shepard family moved to Kent Terrace (on the westward outskirts of Regent's Parkway) where he said he spent the happiest days of his early boyhood years. When his mother died in 1890 after a prolonged illness, Ernest, Cyril, and Ethel went to live with his father's four sisters. Almost a year later the three Shepard children and their father moved into a Georgian home in Hammersmith among a colony of artists where talk about art was as natural as politics or business. It was in the studio in their new home, the site of frequent visits between artists and Shepard's father, that Ernest Shepard began to consider a future as an artist seriously.

He married Florence Chaplin, a fellow art student, in 1904, and they had two children: in 1907 their son, Graham, was born in Arden Cottage at Shamley Green in Surrey (he was killed in 1943 when the British ship on which he was stationed sank); and in 1909 their daughter, Mary, was born in Red Cottage, Holbrook Lane, in Surrey. His wife died suddenly in 1927. He married Norah Carroll in 1944. He died on 24 March 1976 at the age of ninety-six, in the midst of the preparation for the celebration of the fiftieth anniversary of the publication of *Winnie-the-Pooh*.

Ernest Shepard began his formal education in a neighborhood kindergarten in Allsop Place near the Baker Street Underground. When his family moved to Hammersmith he was enrolled in Oliver's, a preparatory school in Acacia Road in St. John's Wood, where his uncle Willie was a senior master and where Ernest said he learned little else "beyond an apprenticeship in self preservation." Subsequently he was enrolled in Bewsher's, the preparatory school for St. Paul's. When he entered St. Paul's proper, where much attention was paid to the special aptitudes of the students, his talent singled him out for special treatment in art instruction, and he was encouraged to put his own visual thoughts on paper. The last year of the two and a half years he attended the school was spent largely in the special drawing class; at one point during that year he was the only student enrolled in the class. He then went on to Heatherley's Art School where he spent much of his time drawing from the antique; he was not encouraged to do any painting, nor did he learn anything of construction or design in this school. It was while he was enrolled at Heatherley's that he was called "Kipper," a nickname by which his family, friends, and colleagues (except Milne) addressed him thereafter.

Shepard competed for and was subsequently awarded a three-year tuition scholarship to the Royal Academy Schools, which he entered in July 1897, the youngest student there. He was given special help and attention by Frank Dicksee and Edwin A. "Ned" Abbey, two teachers at the schools who influenced Shepard's work. Dicksee, a family friend who sponsored his entry into the schools and supplied him with an easel for his first studio, was a master of the balance of black-and-white wood engravings within the frame. Abbey, a visiting American (Philadelphian) artist, who taught at the Academy Schools for a block of time and was a great believer in the apprentice system, is said to have helped Shepard introduce grace and

charm in his work and to create an atmosphere that was quiet and soft.

There were other artists whom Shepard admired and who, he said, influenced his work. He held Sir John Tenniel in high esteem because his imagination enabled him to make grotesque fantasies seem like realities; he respected Arthur Hughes because of the "lyrical qualities" of his designs; he valued Arthur Boyd Houghton's sense of the dramatic, his insight into the life of children, and his use of white; and he respected Charles Keene's ability to bring his characters to life and show action in his pictures.

Shepard began to exhibit at the academy before he finished his formal training at the schools; his first exhibit was at the Royal Academy's 1901 Summer Exhibition, in which he showed two paintings. He began to illustrate books for adults around 1900 through 1914; the first publisher to give him steady work as a book illustrator was Thomas Nelson, and his first illustrations were to *Tom Brown's Schooldays* by Thomas Hughes (circa 1904). After numerous rejections, he finally succeeded in 1907 in having two drawings placed in *Punch*, but it was not until 1921 that he joined the roundtable, which meant an appointment to the regular staff – with a regular income. He was associated with *Punch* for fifty years: by 1914 he was a regular contributor of political cartoons, subsequently attaining the positions of second cartoonist and principal cartoonist. He was elected to its editorial board in 1921 and continued working for *Punch* until his dismissal in 1953.

In 1924 he was invited by E. V. Lucas, a member of the roundtable and a director at Methuen, to illustrate eleven verses from Milne's *When We Were Very Young* for *Punch* and then for the complete book later that year. Thus began the successful collaboration between author Milne and illustrator Shepard. When Milne began to plan *Winnie-the-Pooh*, he told Shepard he must draw the pictures for the book; it was published in 1926. His illustrations for *Now We Are Six*, another book of verses, and then *The House at Pooh Corner* followed in 1927 and 1928 respectively.

The text and drawings in *Drawn From Memory* (1957) and *Drawn From Life* (1961) detail innumerable facts that he recalled about his relationships with members of his immediate family (father, mother, brother and sister), close relatives (especially his father's sisters), and family friends, as well as his educational experiences. In *Drawn From Memory* he tells about his childhood, and in *Drawn From Life* he focuses on his life from age ten, when his mother

Shepard's original design for the dust jacket for his autobiographical
volume (1957)

died, to age twenty-four (1904), the year of his marriage to his first wife. From these detailed memoirs and from *The Work of E. H. Shepard,* edited by Rawle Knox (1979), which was published to mark the one hundredth anniversary of Shepard's birth, one gets the impression that he was a humble, gentle, stable, and pleasantly caring person. He was not especially demonstrative in action or words and was very private; he seemed to value, appreciate, and accept members of his family, friends, and fellow authors and artists. He approached his work with high professional standards in mind. He was indeed a perfectionist and conscientiously tried to interpret accurately and with the exactitude and precision of a draftsman the action, mood, and personality of the characters.

In addition to mastering the technique of detailed pen-and-ink drawings, Shepard was highly respected for the professionalism with which he approached his work: he met his deadlines; sketched more details and many more versions than were required for the final product; was carefully observant of the setting, people, and animals that served as the models for his drawings; and tried not to allow his own personality to interpose in his work, for he believed his role as an illustrator was "a form of accompaniment."

Shepard worked from original models. After Milne's death and the death of his own son, Graham, Shepard said that Graham was the model for Christopher Robin. An examination of Shepard's drawings of Christopher Robin, photographs of Graham, and the sketches Shepard made of his son — all included by Knox in *The Work of E. H. Shepard* — reveals a strong likeness in their posture, physical characteristics, clothes, and hairstyle. But Christopher Milne claimed in his autobiography, *The Enchanted Places* (1975), that Shepard drew him from life and that he did indeed look like the drawings in *Winnie-the-Pooh*. Christopher Milne's posture and physical characteristics, his clothes, and his hairstyle as shown in a photograph as a child and included in his memoirs look much like Shepard's drawings of Christopher Robin. It is almost impossible to discount either Shepard's or Christopher Milne's claims, so the actual model for Christopher

Robin remains a mystery. In contrast, there is little doubt that Graham's teddy bear Growler was the model for Christopher Robin's teddy bear, Winnie-the-Pooh, and the drawings of Piglet were modeled after Christopher's real-life pet pig and had to be made different in shape and smaller in size for the incidents in the book. The sketches of the other characters (namely, Owl, Rabbit, Kanga and Roo, and Tigger) were close likenesses of the toys in the Milne household. Shepard visited Ashdown Forest and other places close to Milne's home in the Cotchford, Sussex; his sketches of these landscapes served as the actual settings for the outdoor scenes of Christopher's and his friends' escapades.

To prepare for the task of illustrating the thirty-eighth edition of *The Wind in the Willows* in 1931, Shepard visited and sketched the countryside and riverbanks around Kenneth Grahame's home near Pangbourne, England, where the adventures of Mile, Rat, Badger, and Toad occurred. The hundred-plus illustrations he made for this wonderful fantasy about animals of the woods, fields, and water so overshadowed those by illustrators in earlier editions that readers tend to think of him as the only illustrator of this classic.

Shepard's black-and-white line and occasionally crosshatched drawings, and to some extent those rendered in color, belong to perpetual childhood rather than to the Victorians. His sketches of the untidy landscapes, gnarled and odd trees, foliage, and people of all ages are rendered in loose line, but those of the animals are outlined in a heavier line, suggesting rather matter-of-factly their exterior texture, the felt or fur of Christopher's toys and the leathery skin and thick fur of Grahame's real-life animals. Although Shepard was said to have a problem depicting a range of feeling and emotions in the human face, he was especially successful in conveying feeling and attitude of humans and animals through bodily posture. Shepard was a communicative, humanistic artist, and his work was widely appealing. His small drawings were straightforward rather than sweet or soft; they have something to say, and they say it quietly and with real humor.

Reference:

Rawle Knox, ed., *The Work of E. H. Shepard* (London & New York: Methuen, 1979).

Noel Streatfeild

(24 December 1895 – 9 September 1986)

Nancy Huse
Augustana College

BOOKS: *The Whicharts* (London: Heinemann, 1931; New York: Coward-McCann, 1932);

Parson's Nine (London: Heinemann, 1932; New York: Doubleday, 1933);

Tops and Bottoms (London: Heinemann, 1933; New York: Doubleday, 1933);

The Children's Matinée: 8 Plays for Children (London: Heinemann, 1934);

A Shepherdess of Sheep (London: Heinemann, 1934; New York: Reynal & Hitchcock, 1935);

It Pays to Be Good (London: Heinemann, 1936);

Ballet Shoes, A Story of Three Children on the Stage (London: Dent, 1936; New York: Random House, 1937);

Caroline England (London: Heinemann, 1937; New York: Reynal & Hitchcock, 1938);

Tennis Shoes (London: Dent, 1937; New York: Random House, 1938);

The Circus Is Coming (London: Dent, 1938; revised, 1948); republished as *Circus Shoes* (New York: Random House, 1939);

Clothes-Pegs, as Susan Scarlett (London: Hodder & Stoughton, 1939);

Luke (London: Heinemann, 1939);

Sally-Ann, as Susan Scarlett (London: Hodder & Stoughton, 1939);

Dennis the Dragon (London: Dent, 1939);

The House in Cornwall (London: Dent, 1940); republished as *The Secret of the Lodge* (New York: Random House, 1940);

Peter and Paul, as Susan Scarlett (London: Hodder & Stoughton, 1940);

Ten Way Street, as Susan Scarlett (London: Hodder & Stoughton, 1940);

The Winter is Past (London: Collins, 1940);

Baddacombe's, as Susan Scarlett (London: Hodder & Stoughton, 1941);

The Children of Primrose Lane (London: Dent, 1941); republished as *The Stranger in Primrose Lane* (New York: Random House, 1941);

The Man in the Dark, as Susan Scarlett (London: Hodder & Stoughton, 1941);

Noel Streatfeild

I Ordered a Table for Six (London: Collins, 1942);

Under the Rainbow, as Susan Scarlett (London: Hodder & Stoughton, 1942);

Harlequinade (London: Chatto & Windus, 1943);

Summer Pudding, as Susan Scarlett (London: Hodder & Stoughton, 1943);

Curtain Up (London: Dent, 1944); republished as *Theatre Shoes; or, Other People's Shoes* (New York: Random House, 1945);

Murder While You Work, as Susan Scarlett (London: Hodder & Stoughton, 1944);

Myra Carroll (London: Collins, 1944);

Saplings (London: Collins, 1945);

Party Frock (London: Collins, 1946); republished as *Party Shoes* (New York: Random House, 1947);

Grass in Piccadilly (London: Collins, 1947);

Pirouette, as Susan Scarlett (London: Hodder & Stoughton, 1948);

Poppies for England, as Susan Scarlett (London: Hodder & Stoughton, 1948);

The Painted Garden (London: Collins, 1949; revised edition, London: Penguin, 1961); republished as *Movie Shoes* (New York: Random House, 1949);

Mothering Sunday (London: Collins, 1950; New York: Coward-McCann, 1950);

Osbert (Chicago: Rand, McNally, 1950);

Love in a Mist (London: Hodder & Stoughton, 1951);

The Picture Story Book of Britain (New York: Watts, 1951);

The Theater Cat (Chicago: Rand, McNally, 1951);

White Boots (London: Collins, 1951); republished as *Skating Shoes* (New York: Random House, 1951);

Aunt Clara (London: Collins, 1952);

The Fearless Treasure (London: M. Joseph, 1952);

The First Book of Ballet (New York: Watts, 1953; London: Bailey Brothers & Swinfen, 1956; revised edition, London: Ward, 1963);

The Bell Family (London: Collins, 1954); republished as *Family Shoes* (New York: Random House, 1954);

The Grey Family (London: Hamish Hamilton, 1956);

Judith (London: Collins, 1956);

Wintle's Wonders (London: Collins, 1957); republished as *Dancing Shoes* (New York: Random House, 1958);

The First Book of England (New York: Watts, 1958; London: Bailey Brothers & Swinfen, 1958; revised edition, London: Ward, 1963);

Magic and the Magician: E. Nesbit and Her Children's Books (London: Benn, 1958; New York: Abelard Schuman, 1958);

Queen Victoria (New York: Random House, 1958; London: W. H. Allen, 1961);

Ballet Annual (London: Collins, 1959);

Bertram (London: Hamish Hamilton, 1959);

The January Baby, The February Baby, The March Baby, The April Baby, The May Baby, The June Baby, The July Baby, The August Baby, The September Baby, The October Baby, The November Baby, The December Baby, 12 volumes (London: Barker, 1959);

The Royal Ballet School (London: Collins, 1959);

Look at the Circus (London: Hamish Hamilton, 1960);

New Town (London: Collins, 1960); republished as *New Shoes* (New York: Random House, 1960);

The Silent Speaker (London: Collins, 1961);

Apple Bough (London: Collins, 1962); republished as *Traveling Shoes* (New York: Random House, 1962);

Lisa Goes to Russia (London: Collins, 1963);

A Vicarage Family (London: Collins, 1963; New York: Watts, 1963);

The Children on the Top Floor (London: Collins, 1964; New York: Random House, 1964);

The Thames: London's Royal River (Champaign, Ill.: Garrard, 1964; London: Muller, 1966);

Away from the Vicarage (London: Collins, 1965); republished as *On Tour: An Autobiographical Novel of the Twenties* (New York: Watts, 1965);

Let's Go Coaching (London: Hamish Hamilton, 1965);

Enjoying Opera (London: Dobson, 1966); republished as *The First Book of the Opera* (New York: Watts, 1966);

The Growing Summer (London: Collins, 1966); republished as *The Magic Summer* (New York: Random House, 1967);

Old Chairs to Mend (London: Hamish Hamilton, 1966);

Before Confirmation (London: Heinemann, 1967);

Caldicott Place (London: Collins, 1967); republished as *The Family at Caldicott Place* (New York: Random House, 1968);

The First Book of Shoes (New York: Watts, 1967; London: Watts, 1971);

Gemma (London: Armada, 1968: New York: Dell, 1968);

Gemma and Sisters (London: Armada, 1968; New York: Dell, 1968);

The Barrow Lane Gang (London: BBC Publications, 1968);

Gemma Alone (London: Armada, 1969; New York: Dell, 1969);

Goodbye Gemma (London: Armada, 1969; New York: Dell, 1969);

Thursday's Child (London: Collins, 1970; New York: Random House, 1970);

Red Riding Hood (London: Benn, 1970);

Beyond the Vicarage (London: Collins, 1971; New York: Watts, 1972);

Ballet Shoes for Anne (London: Collins, 1972);

The Boy Pharaoh, Tutankhamen (London: M. Joseph, 1972);

When the Siren Wailed (London: Collins, 1974; New York: Random House, 1977);

A Young Person's Guide to Ballet (London & New York: Warne, 1975);

Far to Go (London: Collins, 1976; New York: Dell, 1976);

Gran-Nannie (London: M. Joseph, 1976);

Meet the Maitlands (London: W. H. Allen, 1978);
The Maitlands: All Change at Cuckly Place (London: W. H. Allen, 1979).

OTHER: *The Years of Grace,* edited by Streatfeild (London: Evans, 1950; revised, 1956);
By Special Request: New Stories for Girls, edited by Streatfeild (London: Collins, 1953);
Growing Up Gracefully, edited by Streatfeild (London: Barker, 1955);
The Day Before Yesterday: Firsthand Stories of Fifty Years Ago, edited by Streatfeild (London: Collins, 1956);
Confirmation and After, edited by Streatfeild (London: Heinemann, 1963);
Merja Otava, *Priska,* translated by Elizabeth Portch, edited by Streatfeild (London: Benn, 1964);
E. Nesbit, *Long Ago When I Was Young,* introductory essay by Streatfeild (London: Whiting & Wheaton, 1966; New York: Watts, 1966);
Marlie Brande, *Nicholas,* translated by Elisabeth Boas, edited by Streatfeild (London: Benn, 1968; Chicago: Follett, 1968);
Brande, *Sleepy Nicholas,* translated by Boas, edited by Streatfeild (London: Benn, 1970; Chicago: Follett, 1970);
The Christmas Holiday Book, The Summer Holiday Book, The Easter Holiday Book, The Birthday Story Book, The Weekend Story Book, 5 volumes, edited by Streatfeild (London: Dent, 1973–1977).

SELECTED PERIODICAL PUBLICATIONS –
UNCOLLECTED: "Myself and My Books," *Junior Bookshelf,* 3 (July 1939): 121–124;
"Why Did I Ever Write a Children's Book?," *Writer* (December 1949);
"Writing for Children," *Schoolmaster* (3 November 1956).

Mary Noel Streatfeild called herself a misfit in the vicarage family of her birth. In more than eighty children's and adults' books, however, she often drew on an imaginative, rebellious girlhood. Born in the day before Christmas 1895 to William and Janet Venn Streatfeild in Amberly, Sussex, Noel was the second daughter in a family of five daughters and a son. She built a life as a children's writer after careers on stage and as a novelist for adults, and moved from writing fiction to radio scripts and historical works. In explaining to the Streatfeild daughters that they would have to earn their own livings, her mother had remarked that Noel would be the one to surprise them all.

Expelled from her first school, St. Leonard's Ladies' College in St. Leonards-on-Sea, for resisting the authority of the headmistress, Streatfeild found outlets for her talents in parish pageants and in training for the stage. Part of her inspiration came from her delight in an unusual source, watching a troupe of child dancers called Lila Field's Little Wonders on their annual visit to the boardwalk at Eastbourne. In 1913 Streatfeild saw the young Ninette de Valois dance with this troupe. Her novels about child dancers, actors, and musicians – novels known in the United States as her "shoe" books, whose successive titles were based on the best-selling *Ballet Shoes, A Story of Three Children on the Stage* (1936) – comprise her best-known works today, but Streatfeild retained a sense of wonder toward the arts throughout her long life. Credited with originating the widespread trend of "career" and "theater" novels for children, Streatfeild is more properly defined as a writer about vocation, especially about dedication to the arts. Her books include careful description of the work it takes to act Shakespearean roles, to dance in the chorus of a ballet, to sing in ways suited to a genre. *Ballet Shoes* in particular is an example of a classic "girls' book," a work many times reissued, imitated, and discussed.

Other influences on Streatfeild's vicarage youth besides her imaginative play and resistance to schooling included guidance from her saintly father and dispositions of detachment and of appreciation for some deviation from routine offered by her mother. Janet Streatfeild skillfully synthesized long passages when she read aloud to her children, aware that they became restive listening to Scott, for example. Streatfeild and her sisters chafed under the vicar's spiritual discipline, loving as it was. In many of her novels she used memories of wearing out-of-fashion clothing and money worries as a basis for a story, although at the same time that the household was constrained by poverty, it was a relative poverty. Nannies and housekeepers were considered indispensable to a vicarage family, and these figures, as well as governesses and teachers, people her children's books. In fact, Streatfeild's last significant book, *Gran-Nannie* (1976), is a memoir about her father's nanny. This nanny originated the saying, common in the children's novels, "It will all be Sir Garnet," a nonsensical but comforting reassurance when children were apprehensive.

After working in a munitions factory during World War I, Streatfeild had little difficulty getting her parents to support her education as an actress. For a decade she supported herself by acting and modeling; twice she toured abroad, using the name Noelle Sonning. When William Streatfeild died suddenly in 1929 shortly after being appointed a bishop, Streatfeild took a year, with her mother's encouragement, to make the transition from being an actress to becoming a writer. Living in a London boardinghouse, she used her father's old typewriter to produce a novel about the theater, *The Whicharts* (1931). Finding it difficult to resist friends' invitations to lunch or matinees, she devised a structure for her day that proved productive: she wrote in bed until midafternoon, able to explain to callers that she could not see them because she was not dressed. In her later, affluent years this schedule was sustained by household help and secretaries; Streatfeild would dress late in the day, walk her dog, and be available for ballet and theater in the evening.

A close woman friend, Daphne Ionides, put Streatfeild in touch with a literary network. Her manuscript was accepted by Charles Evans of Heinemann, who encouraged a decade of adult novels from this new talent. Reviewers noted how children in various novels such as *Parson's Nine* (1932) and *A Shepherdess of Sheep* (1934) were depicted with empathy. Even *The Whicharts,* with its focus on some of the seamier sides of theater life, included rich portrayals of three girls adopted by a former mistress of their father.

In 1936 Mabel Carey, editor at Dent publishing, persuaded Streatfeild to write a children's book about the stage. Reluctantly she turned *The Whicharts* into a children's book about three little girls – Pauline, Petrova, and Posy – who take the surname Fossil because the old gentleman who "found" them was a fossil hunter. Even though none of them is without faults, the sisters in *Ballet Shoes* vow to get their family name into history books, and each supports the others' efforts. In transforming her adult novel into a children's book, Streatfeild managed to create a compelling story. Without the sexual implications of the adult novel's plot, *Ballet Shoes* nonetheless assumed that child readers would be interested in presumably adult concerns, such as how to act and dance for professional performances. Pauline, as the frontispiece explains, becomes a film star, in part so that Posy can train as a great ballerina. Petrova pursues her dream of flying airplanes, freed from the drudgery of her minimal talents for the stage. Together the girls finance the household that sustains them: their guardian Garnie, their nurse Nana, other servants, and boarders who contribute to their educations by sharing their talents in Shakespearean interpreta-

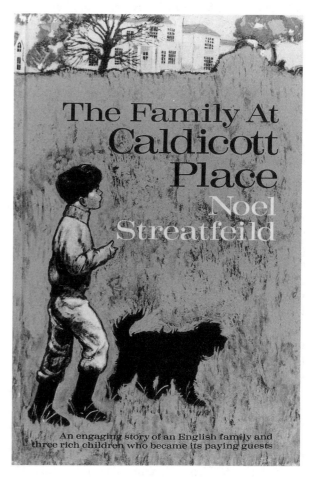

Dust jacket for the American edition of Streatfeild's novel about a family who cares for three wealthy but neglected children

tion or in dance. As scholarship students at Madame Fidolia's school, the girls prove their competence through hard work over time, each girl valued for her different talent.

Helped by a display of pink ballet shoes in the window, including those of a famous ballerina named Karsavina, Bumpus's Bookstore in London sold out of *Ballet Shoes* at Christmastime in 1936. Sadler's Wells Ballet School had been founded in 1931, and devotion to the ballet was growing in London. Streatfeild was taken aback by the rationing of the book until Dent's could bring out new editions. The early success of the book has continued, with sales of editions adding up to more than ten million copies by the early 1990s.

Even though Mabel Carey persuaded her to write *Tennis Shoes* (1937) and *The Circus Is Coming* (1938) as successive children's novels, Streatfeild thought of this writing as a sideline until the war altered both her opportunities and her outlook. A Carnegie Medal in 1939 for *Circus Shoes* (published in England as *The Circus Is Coming*) found her in the south of France, where she was working on an adult novel, *Luke* (1939), and making plans for several others. Without much change in her basic interests — the links between family life and competence in the arts, themes variously repeated in most of her adult fiction — Streatfeild seems to have recognized a key concern of the twentieth century in the attention her works have for issues of gender and class. Using traditional storytelling methods such as playful fairy-tale frameworks, she evolved a patterned plot linking the family story with the apprentice novel.

Many works hinge on economic necessity, in which siblings ranging in ages from about eight through fourteen combine their efforts to keep a family intact. In so doing, they become productive and self-assured. Many of the younger children in the novels are humorous figures; there are few villains, and a range of parental figures, usually women of different classes, make the children's environment safe and stimulating. With these components, Streatfeild raised crucial questions in nonthreatening ways. How money and family are connected, how girls and boys are educated, and whether personal loyalties can extend across class structures are parts of an ongoing analysis of childhood and its meanings, an analysis Streatfeild played a major role in furthering. Her representations of working-class people are based on her own observations and commitments. For many years she volunteered as a social service worker in Deptford in southeastern London, an activity fostered by Daphne Ionides.

Despite the formulaic themes and characters in her work, each of Streatfeild's children's novels can be appreciated on its own terms. The two immediate successors to *Ballet Shoes* seem particularly distinctive examples of her work. *Tennis Shoes,* for example, presents a mischievous self-portrait in Nicky Heath. Nicky's development into a tennis champion is the focus, but Streatfeild tells the story of a whole family — from that of the intervening wealthy grandfather and his notions of how money should be earned and spent, to that of the cook Annie, who once worked as a trapeze artist and manages to coach and cajole the rebellious Nicky. Based on her memories of her landed grandparents, of a cook who had always observed Streatfeild's Christmas Eve birthday even though the family tended to forget it, and of her own penchant for getting into trouble at home and at school, the novel also records Streatfeild's own struggle to perfect her tennis game as a child. Building to a chaotic climax in which Nicky's winning match is overshadowed

by the effects of her carelessness that result in a house burglary, the novel humorously allows Nicky to be self-centered. In such respects as this Streatfeild often deviated from conventional norms for girls' behavior and attitudes. Rather than simply reversing gender roles, however, she sturdily combined care and competence as dual themes to be resolved dialogically. Though Nicky does not show empathy for others as part of her story, the network of family relationships shows her woven into their ways of engaging the world.

Streatfeild's third children's book, *The Circus Is Coming,* depends less on her personal experience and more on research and basic fairy-tale patterns than do her previous works. It opens with a distorted world in which two children, Peter and Santa, have been reared by their aunt, a retired servant, to emulate the gentry. Their hollow education has left them just enough common sense to find their Uncle Gus, a circus performer, after their misguided aunt dies. The naive children are initiated into responsibility and interdependence through circus work. Their transformation is heightened by a father/son conflict between Gus and Peter, by the boys' actions in understanding and rescuing circus animals, and by a deus-ex-machina ending. The big top burns down, and this forces the circus owner to decide to allow the children to train for his next venture rather than to be schooled as office workers, as Gus had planned. With its vision of an ordered world peopled with varied groups, the book has a conservative and mythic tone resonant with Streatfeild's vicarage worldview in ways that her other books are not. Notions of home and family are examined through the social reality of the circus. A competent cook and housekeeper who is allied with his neighbors in other caravans and focused on his vocation as artiste, Gus is content in his trailer. The children initially have none of his simple ability to function and to thrive; they alienate others with their foolish manners. Much of what they learn in the course of the novel deals with material culture; their skills as acrobats and equestrians develop because the children must develop skills to live in the community. Unlike *Ballet Shoes,* in which learning to dance and to act means keeping a household going, or *Tennis Shoes,* in which saving for lessons allows a family activity to include all, *The Circus Is Coming* probes the relationship between production and reproduction. To grow up means to discover a culture's norms and values, to choose constructively a work and a manner of living. Less humorous than the first two children's novels, *The Circus Is Coming* is suspenseful and psychologically complex.

World War II affected Streatfeild deeply. Her flat at 10 Bolton Street, luxuriously furnished by the proceeds of her popularity, was destroyed in an air raid. Well before this she had committed herself to a grueling schedule, laboring full time as a canteen worker for the Women's Voluntary Service and driving a truck she had gotten a family friend to buy and outfit for her. Homeless for a time and staying in the houses of friends to sleep and write, she produced under the name Susan Scarlett a remarkable round of novels and romances during and after the war. Shortages of paper and the destruction of the plates of her early adult novels affected both her long-term reputation as a writer and her income.

The nearly twenty books produced during the early 1940s included varied children's novels. Two of them, *The House in Cornwall* (1940) and *The Children of Primrose Lane* (1941), use conventions of children's mystery novels to tell fast-paced stories; the Primrose Lane story is a wartime spy intrigue using humor. An interesting illustrated book, *Harlequinade* (1943), uses a metaphoric framework of the circus world to renew the lives of five children billeted in a remote part of the country for the duration of the war. Through rigorous practice born of desperate sadness and boredom, the children become a sustaining community able to renew the storytelling traditions of the past. All three of these books demonstrate Streatfeild's increasing intertextual knowledge; she was becoming a deliberate participant in the community of children's literature, rather than an accidental and impressionistic contributor to the field.

Streatfeild kept a diary of her wartime experience, during which she demonstrated great physical energy and moral courage. The book, "London Under Fire," remains unpublished: initial interest in it was diverted by postwar scarcity. Streatfeild's biographer Angela Bull notes that the writer's diaries generally credit the assistance of her household staff with sustaining her writing. *Curtain Up* (1944) reflects her ability to parlay the disorders of the war into a continuity of her own. Using the story of a family broken by the war and by an old quarrel between the children's mother and her theater family, Streatfeild drew on Pauline, Petrova, and Pauline of *Ballet Shoes* to act as mentors to a new set of almost-orphans. Scholarships to Madame Fidolia's school allow the Forbes children to develop the competence and understanding that fold them into their mother's family. Filled with humor and exaggeration, the book combines several strands of Streatfeild's knowledge. One main accomplishment

is the depiction of a multigenerational, multihousehold family passionately committed to the life of the theater. Through the pageantry and ritual of stage and family, the homeless children are re-created as participants in a proud, if eccentric, tradition. In adult fiction, too, she explored themes depicting the horror of random death (*I Ordered a Table for Six,* 1942) or validating tradition (*Saplings,* 1945). A 1947 novel, *Grass in Piccadilly,* suggests that the act of sheltering children may be exempt from ordinary assumptions about rights and decency.

When she moved into a flat at 51A Elizabeth Street in 1946, Streatfeild dug up a bomb site and turned it into a neighborhood garden. *Party Shoes* (1947), published earlier as *Party Frock* (1946), depicts an England recovering from war by drawing from the past and present heroism of its people. A young girl, Selina, staying with her noisy cousins in a country vicarage, becomes producer of a major pageant involving all classes and even the American troops in the neighborhood. From a real-life incident — her young niece's frustration at having outgrown a party dress before wartime restrictions permitted any occasion to wear it — Streatfeild shaped this tale in which Selina's creative and social skills help produce a major occasion for wearing the party dress sent by her godmother in America. Echoing some themes of Virginia Woolf's *Between the Acts* (1941), the novel explores gender role shifts in the postwar era. It also captures the survivors' yearning for community. Brilliant in its depiction of the group dynamics needed to put on the historical pageant, the book extends the family formula to all of England. The pageant preserves the threatened manor house and, as a hostel, it will once again belong to the common people, as the monks who built it had planned.

Party Shoes, with its positive treatment of Americans, is characteristic of Streatfeild's fascination with the United States. Hoping to write for motion pictures, she had visited New York and California in 1937 and 1938, and in 1947 she visited California again. As would become characteristic of her career in the 1950s and 1960s, Streatfeild created a children's novel based on her travel experience. *Movie Shoes* (1949; published in England as *The Painted Garden*) followed her having seen Margaret O'Brien filmed in *The Secret Garden* (1949). Admiring O'Brien's discipline, Streatfeild imagined a rebellious child like Mary of Frances Hodgson Burnett's 1911 novel of that same title in the role. Although in some respects not equal to the rich historical and artistic treatment of earlier books, *Movie Shoes* does convey the unglamorous side of film act-

Streatfeild (courtesy of W. H. C. Streatfeild)

ing, and it satirizes some aspects of California life. Streatfeild returned to England with a new sense of her vocation as children's writer. Though she continued to write for adults until 1961, the postwar years brought her a sense of urgency about children, about their potential and their need for competence and security.

White Boots (1951) afforded Streatfeild another opportunity to base a novel on research – this time about ice skating – but to draw from archetypal themes and figures (country/city, Cinderella, poor little rich girl) as well as her own experience. At the opening of the story Harriet is too thin, unable to recover from a long illness; her nickname is Daddy Longlegs. A kind doctor helps her genteel but impoverished family arrange to rent skates so that Harriet can skate free at the rink owned by a friend of the doctor. There Harriet meets, and learns from, Lalla, whose Aunt Claudia is determined that the child will be the skating star Lalla's father was before his early death. Gradually it becomes clear that Harriet is the skating star; Lalla is a comedienne on skates. Part of the intensity of the book comes from a psychological truth about competition and the vulnerability of friendship. Harriet's mother is able to intervene so that the friendship does not disintegrate. As in other

Streatfeild novels for children, a set of funny yet honorable siblings makes the action possible.

Shortly before Streatfeild wrote *White Boots,* her own life had changed. Her friendship with Daphne Ionides had faded, but a new friend and companion, Margot Grey, had begun to share Streatfeild's life in 1948. Adventurous and somewhat unconventional, Margot inspired two of Streatfeild's 1970s books for children, Victorian tales named *Thursday's Child* (1970) and *Far to Go* (1976), about a spunky orphan girl whose life is modeled on Margot's reputed birth as the illegitimate daughter of a gentlewoman. During the 1950s Streatfeild and Margot established their routines, which included sharing a dog, a small poodle named Pierre. Engaging in behavior the vicarage family would not have expected, Streatfeild and Margot indulged an interest in race horses and greyhound races. One adult novel of the period, *Aunt Clara* (1952), pokes fun at possible family concerns by having an elderly, churchgoing spinster inherit a relative's "estate," including a brothel and greyhounds.

Streatfeild's usual vein of storytelling for the adult market, domestic fiction, called upon her ironic skills in such novels as *Judith* (1956) and *The Silent Speaker* (1961), but she preferred the comic skills given free rein in a new medium. Radio drew on her strengths in dialogue and action; a series on a vicarage family provoked both laughter at and insight into England's values in a time of continuing postwar scarcity and rationing. *The Bell Family* (1954) and *New Town* (1960) are successful children's novels based on the radio series about the Bells, especially the mischievous Miss Virginia Bell, as the central character refers to herself. Streatfeild added to her prominence through the radio series by adopting the roles of advice giver, anthologizer, lecturer about children's books, and standard-bearer for literature and the arts. She began to be a "national monument" in the postwar years, as she reviewed books monthly for *Collins Magazine* and in other ways remained very much in the public eye. In 1952 she assumed the role of social historian, telling the story of England in *The Fearless Treasure.* In that narrative children from all social groups travel in time through their ancestors' lives; a cockney child inherits the responsibility for defending freedom. Streatfeild also edited advice books such as *The Years of Grace* (1950) and *Growing Up Gracefully* (1955) that aimed to help children, especially girls, grow up without suffering the awkwardness Streatfeild recalled from her own youth, and with esteem for the value of tradition and ritual like that she gleaned from her father's guidance.

Many historical books occupied Streatfeild throughout the remainder of her career, and writing them sustained that career for more than twenty years. These books are generally vivid and interesting because of her sure narrative sense and precise language. *The Royal Ballet School* (1959) allowed her to support an art form she loved while delineating the history of an institution. In 1972 an outstanding work, *The Boy Pharaoh, Tutankhamen,* appeared as one of the last examples of her ability. Her own memories were integrated into *When the Siren Wailed* (1974), a novel about cockney children evacuated to the countryside during the war but determined to be with their own parents in a dangerous London.

Although Streatfeild had ceased writing adult fiction by the early 1960s, she continued to improvise children's novels from both new and old materials. *Dancing Shoes* (1958; originally published as *Wintle's Wonders* in 1957) received some of her first bad reviews; yet its depiction of a girl growing into her own identity, becoming able to wear bright colors again after recovering from her mother's death, has a compelling strength. Coping with changing times, Streatfeild wrote a family story about a girl discovering her skills as homemaker for artistic siblings in *Traveling Shoes* (1962); the novel's English title, *Apple Bough* (1962), evokes an image of the house she reclaimed. In a humorous departure Streatfeild created a metafictional parody of her family formula: *The Children on the Top Floor* (1964) depicts foundlings reared by television. Another novel of a child who saves a household is *Caldicott Place* (1967). In a reversal of her usual formula, the house saves a family by providing the means to earn a living through taking in neglected children from wealthy families.

Often viewed as one of Streatfeild's triumphs, *The Magic Summer* (1967; originally published in England as *The Growing Summer,* 1966) makes excellent use of her habit of visiting Ireland every summer to stay on the coast with a friend, Rachel Leigh-White. Four children are forced to stay with a great-aunt they have never met. Nearly a recluse, great-aunt Dymphna lives in a great empty seaside house without electricity or plumbing. The summer involves struggle with daily necessities, but it is punctuated by the aunt's poetic insights. Unsentimental and sharp edged, the book is dedicated to Elizabeth Enright, author of family stories in which children cope with life on their own. Demonstrating Streatfeild's ability to improvise — there are no nannies or governesses — the book scrutinizes important adult/child relationships. Dymphna refuses to coddle, yet she nurtures the children by sharing her environment and love of the sea.

Another new line of stories resulted in a series during the late 1960s, the Gemma Bow novels: *Gemma* (1968), *Gemma and Sisters* (1968), *Gemma Alone* (1969), and *Goodbye Gemma* (1969). They relate the story of a "has-been," a child who had starred in films but has reached the awkward age at which she cannot get parts. Gemma must live with her aunt and uncle's family while her mother's film career soars. She deals with rejection by her mother and finds a partial reconciliation, gains singing and acting skills for the stage by working hard in her new environment, and brings into the spotlight with her the cousins she had dreaded to live with. Sensitive though sentimental, the novels depend less on dialogue and more on narration than Streatfeild's best-known works. Like many other Streatfeild novels, the Gemma Bow stories have been reissued in several paperback editions.

The 1960s extended Streatfeild's writing into the domain of memoir. At the invitation of Helen Hoke Watts, whom she had regaled with stories of the vicarage, she began a fictionalized series with an autobiographical basis in *A Vicarage Family* in 1963. Calling herself Victoria Strangeway, Streatfeild recounted the misadventures of her girlhood. In a dramatic finish to the story when Vicky's father insists on her early confirmation as a way of calming her, she throws an inkwell at her governess. Successive volumes, *Away from the Vicarage* (1965) and *Beyond the Vicarage* (1971), deal with Streatfeild's stage and writing careers. One important strand of the second and third volumes is Vicky's nostalgia for the life she had chafed under as a child. Another is the insight the vicarage stories provide into Streatfeild's relationships with her family, especially her mother, whom she represents with empathy but with some bitterness at the rejection Streatfeild had received as the clumsy, recalcitrant surplus daughter. The final volume of such memoirs, *Gran-Nannie* is the last book in which Streatfeild's powers are firmly under her control. The story of the nanny effectively draws together the themes of a writer who had placed the care of children, and their potential, at the center of her imaginative life.

Although Streatfeild's reputation declined among reviewers during the early 1960s when the class implications of her nannies and governesses seemed unacceptable for contemporary children, her name continued to garner a wide readership. She astutely adapted her vision by moving into new genres such as autobiography. With the rise of interest in women writers brought by feminist criticism and theory, Streatfeild's work takes on added import. Methods drawn from popular culture criticism and cultural studies also find significance in her life and work. Her books continue to appear in new editions marketed to today's children through changes in iconography; the stories remain resonant, cheerful, and focused on both daily domestic matters and the dreams of beauty and transcendence implicit in the arts.

Biographies:
Barbara Ker Wilson, *Noel Streatfeild* (London: Bodley Head, 1961);
Angela Bull, *Noel Streatfeild: A Biography* (London: Collins, 1984).

References:
Mary Cadogan and Patricia Craig, *Women and Children First: The Fiction of Two World Wars* (London: Gollancz, 1978);
Cadogan and Craig, *You're a Brick, Angela!: The Girls' Story 1839–1985* (London: Gollancz, 1986);

Marcus Crouch, *The Nesbit Tradition: The Children's Novel in England 1945–1970* (Totowa, N.J.: Rowman & Littlefield, 1972);
Anne W. Ellis, *The Family Story in the 1960s* (London: Clive Bingley, 1970);
E. M. Exley, "Noel Streatfeild: Carnegie Medal Winner," *Junior Bookshelf,* 3 (1939);
Nancy Huse, *Noel Streatfeild* (New York: Twayne, 1994);
Lois R. Kuznets, "Family as Formula: Cawelti's Formulaic Theory and Streatfeild's 'Shoe' Books," *Children's Literature Association Quarterly,* 9 (Winter 1984–1985): 147–149, 201;
Carol McDonnell, "A Second Look: *Ballet Shoes,*" *Horn Book Magazine,* 54 (April 1978): 191–193;
Nicholas Tucker, "Two English Worthies," *Children's Literature in Education,* 17 (Fall 1986): 191–197.

Barbara Euphan Todd

(9 January 1890 – 2 February 1976)

Joanne Lewis Sears
California State University, Fullerton

BOOKS: *The 'Normous Saturday Fiction Book,* by Todd, Marjory Royce, and Moira Meighn (London: Stanley Paul, 1924);

The 'Normous Sunday Story Book, by Todd, Royce, and Meighn (London: Stanley Paul, 1925);

The Very Good Walkers, by Todd and Royce (London: Methuen, 1925);

Hither and Thither (London: Harrap, 1927);

Mr. Blossom's Shop (London: Nelson, 1929);

Happy Cottage, by Todd and Royce (London: Collins, 1930);

The Seventh Daughter (London: Burns Oates, 1935);

South Country Secrets, as Barbara Euphan, with Klaxon [John Graham Bower] (London: Burns Oates, 1935);

The Touchstone, by Euphan and Klaxon (London: Burns Oates, 1935);

Worzel Gummidge; or, The Scarecrow of Scatterbrook (London: Burns Oates, 1936); republished, with *Worzel Gummidge Again,* in *Worzel Gummidge, The Scarecrow of Scatterbrook Farm* (New York: Putnam, 1947);

Stories of the Coronations, as Euphan, with Klaxon (London: Burns Oates, 1937);

Worzel Gummidge Again (London: Burns Oates, 1937); republished with *Worzel Gummidge; or, The Scarecrow of Scatterbrook,* in *Worzel Gummidge, The Scarecrow of Scatterbrook Form* (New York: Putnam, 1947);

The Mystery Train (London: University of London Press, 1937);

The Splendid Picnic (London: University of London Press, 1937);

More About Worzel Gummidge (London: Burns Oates, 1938);

Mr. Dock's Garden (Leeds: E. J. Arnold, 1939);

Gertrude the Greedy Goose (London: Muller, 1939);

The House That Ran Behind, by Todd and Esther Boumphrey (London: Muller, 1943);

Miss Ranskill Comes Home: A Novel, as Barbara Bower (London: Chapman & Hall / New York: Putnam, 1946);

Worzel Gummidge and Saucy Nancy (London: Hollis & Carter, 1947);

Worzel Gummidge Takes a Holiday (London: Hollis & Carter, 1949);

Aloysius Let Loose, by Todd and Klaxon (London: Collins, 1950);

Earthy Mangold and Worzel Gummidge (London: Hollis & Carter, 1954);

Worzel Gummidge and the Railway Scarecrows (London: Evans, 1955);

Worzel Gummidge at the Circus (London: Evans, 1956);

The Boy with the Green Thumb (London: Hamish Hamilton, 1956);

The Wizard and the Unicorn (London: Hamish Hamilton, 1957);

Worzel Gummidge and the Treasure Ship (London: Evans, 1958);

The Shop Around the Corner (London: Hamish Hamilton, 1959);

Detective Worzel Gummidge (London: Evans, 1963);

The Shop by the Sea (London: Hamish Hamilton, 1966);

The Clock Shop (Kingswood, Surrey: World's Work, 1967);

The Shop on Wheels (Kingswood, Surrey: World's Work, 1968);

The Box in the Attic (Kingswood, Surrey: World's Work, 1970);

The Wand from France (Kingswood, Surrey: World's Work, 1972).

RADIO: *The Frog Prince,* by Todd and Mabel and Denis Constanduros (London: French, 1956);

The Sleeping Beauty, by Todd and Mabel and Denis Constanduros (London: French, 1956).

Barbara Euphan Todd's reputation in children's literature rests primarily on her creation of one striking character, the animated scarecrow Worzel Gummidge. Though Todd published more than thirty-five works – novels, stories, games, poems, and plays — under three different names, the Scarecrow of Scatterbrook and his rural friends brought her modest recognition during her lifetime and considerable fame as television characters after her death.

Born in Doncaster, Yorkshire, to Anglican minister Thomas Todd and Alice Maud Mary (Bentham) Todd, Barbara Euphan Todd spent her youth in the rural Hampshire village of Soberton. Educated at a girls' school in Guildford, Surrey, she published during the 1920s many children's stories in collaboration with other writers. Her stepdaughter, Mrs. U. V. G. Betts, recalls enjoying one of these tales, *The Very Good Walkers* (1925), before becoming acquainted with Barbara Todd as her stepmother. Todd married John Graham Bower in 1932.

The couple moved to Blewbury, a rural literary and artistic colony south of Oxford, where Bower, a naval officer, wrote fiction and essays under the pseudonym Klaxon. As Barbara Euphan, Todd collaborated with her husband on *South Country Secrets* and *The Touchstone,* both published in 1935. In 1946, as Barbara Bower, Todd published her only adult novel, *Miss Ranskill Comes Home.* Perhaps because it was published after World War II, the novel enjoyed more success in the United States than in England. Throughout what was to be a long career, Todd continued to write other material — folktales adapted for radio, more plays and stories written in collaboration with others, and two volumes of poetry, *Hither and Thither* (1927) and *The Seventh Daughter* (1935).

In a 1980 letter to Todd's agent at A. M. Heath, Betts recalled that Barbara Todd "seems first to have had the idea of a walking talking scarecrow called Worzel Gummidge" in the 1930s. Between 1936 and 1963 she published the ten Worzel Gummidge novels on which her fame rests today. Betts notes that at first these books "made no very great impact," but for Todd they were labors of love: she named her own pets after characters in Worzel Gummidge country.

Most of the Worzel Gummidge novels render in closely observed detail the rural setting that Todd knew and loved. Clear sensory evocation of country scenes provides background for the adventures of John and Susan, visiting city children privy to a lively community of scarecrows unknown to the adult world. The opening chapter of *Worzel Gummidge Again* (1937) characterizes Todd's attention to seasonal details of rural life: John and Susan's "last visit had been made in the spring when moss and bricks were damp, and hens walked in a finicking way through the mud, and even the hay in the lofts had a faint musty tang about it. Now the lavender was dry on the hedge and the straw smelled hot and summery." Todd describes closely the "white scuts" on her rabbits, and the November garden has "blackened dahlias."

Todd's scarecrow characters grow literally out of their agricultural milieu. The mangel-wurzel, a cross between a white and a red beet, supplies the scarecrows' carved, wrinkled faces. Worzel (a dialect form of *wurzel*) and Eartha Mangold (an obsolete form of *mangel*) marry to become the Gummidges. (*Gummage* itself designates a resiny product of orchard trees.) Hannah Harrow (whose surname denotes the rake that breaks soil behind a plow), "sad because she was stuffed with sawdust," suffers not from rheumatism but from "the mice." "It's all along of sleeping in the haystack," explains her friend Eartha.

Such dialect jokes and wordplay, as well as Worzel Gummidge's mad logic and Todd's gentle satire of pretentiousness, comprise Todd's humor. Some of Worzel's dialect makes reading hard for modern child audiences, but contexts keep parodies such as this one amusing and appealing:

> Christmas comes but once a year,
> Rabbits wants new scuts to weer.
> Robins what've got no vests
> Needs some flannel for their chests.

Worzel teaches young scarecrows their job with his own homespun verse:

> One rook's same as t'other —
> If it isn't ask your mother.
>
> Two rooks never matter.
> Three rooks is much more fatter.
> Six rooks'll make their double.
> Eight rooks means lots of trouble.
>
> Ten rooks is past all bearing
> Twelve rooks means scarecrows scaring.
> Flap! FLAP! FLAP! FLAP! FLAP!

The scarecrow's literal-mindedness produces more verbal humor. When Worzel says to Susan that he has "taken on [a] job," she asks, "Who gave it to you?" Indignant, Worzel retorts, "I took it. That's what I said, didn't I? Nobody gave it to me." As gardener to nearsighted Miss Duffy, Worzel plants nettles and weeds and neglects the vegetables: "When I wants to take care of the lettuces, I moves the slugs back to the cabbages. They all gets their turns."

Todd directs her mild social satire not at a class system, but at pretension and lack of imagination. Ridiculously self-important, Mrs. Bloomsbury-Barton and Lady Piddingfold are foiled repeatedly by Worzel's forthright contrariness. When John and Susan arrive at a costume party dressed as scarecrows, two pompous gentlemen take them for real, poking at their straw with canes. The men ignore John's "OW!" and walk away "talking very determinedly about the British Empire because they were the sort of people who couldn't see jokes or believe in anything unlikely."

Todd observes the world accurately, with sympathy for a child's perception. Susan notices "that when ants are carrying their grubs about, they look awfully like washerwomen with big bundles of clothes." When Lady Lippindore loses her pearls, Worzel Gummidge finds them and thinks they are "a string of tapioca pudding."

In the 1950s Mabel and Denis Constanduros collaborated with Barbara Todd on a series of radio plays for children. For the Constanduroses she wrote scripts of the Worzel Gummidge stories. She continued to produce novels into the 1960s and into the 1970s, but her best work was by then behind her. She died in 1976, just as negotiations were in progress for television rights to the Worzel Gummidge books. Her stepdaughter remembers her as "warm and kind" but recalls chiefly her "dry – and sometimes wry – sense of humor," the earmark of her Worzel Gummidge books.

J. R. R. Tolkien

(3 January 1892 – 2 September 1973)

Colin Duriez
Inter-Varsity Press

See also the Tolkien entry in *DLB 15: British Novelists, 1930–1959.*

BOOKS: *A Middle English Vocabulary* (Oxford: Clarendon Press, 1922);

Beowulf: The Monsters and the Critics (London: Oxford University Press, 1937);

The Hobbit, or There and Back Again (London: Allen & Unwin, 1937; Boston: Houghton Mifflin, 1938; revised edition, London: Allen & Unwin, 1951; Boston: Houghton Mifflin, 1952);

Farmer Giles of Ham (London: Allen & Unwin, 1949; Boston: Houghton Mifflin, 1950);

The Fellowship of the Ring: Being the First Part of The Lord of the Rings (London: Allen & Unwin, 1954; Boston: Houghton Mifflin, 1954; revised edition, London: Allen & Unwin, 1966; Boston: Houghton Mifflin, 1967);

The Two Towers: Being the Second Part of The Lord of the Rings (London: Allen & Unwin, 1954; Boston: Houghton Mifflin, 1955; revised edition, London: Allen & Unwin, 1966; Boston: Houghton Mifflin, 1967);

The Return of the King: Being the Third Part of The Lord of the Rings (London: Allen & Unwin, 1955; Boston: Houghton Mifflin, 1956; revised edition, London: Allen & Unwin, 1966; Boston: Houghton Mifflin, 1967);

The Adventures of Tom Bombadil and Other Verses from The Red Book (London: Allen & Unwin, 1962; Boston: Houghton Mifflin, 1963);

Tree and Leaf (London: Allen & Unwin, 1964; Boston: Houghton Mifflin, 1965);

The Tolkien Reader (New York: Ballantine, 1966);

Smith of Wootton Major (London: Allen & Unwin, 1967; Boston: Houghton Mifflin, 1967);

The Road Goes Ever On: A Song Cycle, music by Donald Swann (Boston: Houghton Mifflin, 1967; London: Allen & Unwin, 1968);

The Father Christmas Letters, edited by Baillie Tolkien (London: Allen & Unwin, 1976; Boston: Houghton Mifflin, 1976);

The Silmarillion, edited by Christopher Tolkien (London: Allen & Unwin, 1977; Boston: Houghton Mifflin, 1977);

Unfinished Tales of Numenor and Middle-earth, edited by Christopher Tolkien (London: Allen & Unwin, 1980; Boston: Houghton Mifflin, 1980);

Finn and Hengest: The Fragment and the Episode, edited by Alan Bliss (London: Allen & Unwin, 1982; Boston: Houghton Mifflin, 1983);

Mr Bliss (London: Allen & Unwin, 1982; Boston: Houghton Mifflin, 1983);

The Monsters and the Critics and Other Essays, edited by Christopher Tolkien (London: Allen & Unwin, 1983; Boston: Houghton Mifflin, 1984);

The History of Middle-earth, edited by Christopher Tolkien, published in eleven volumes: *The Book of Lost Tales, Part One* (London: Allen & Unwin, 1983; Boston: Houghton Mifflin, 1984); *The Book of Lost Tales, Part Two* (London: Allen & Unwin, 1984; Boston: Houghton Mifflin, 1984); *The Lays of Beleriand* (London: Allen & Unwin, 1985; Boston: Houghton Mifflin, 1985); *The Shaping of Middle-earth* (London: Allen & Unwin, 1986; Boston: Houghton Mifflin, 1986); *The Lost Road and Other Writings* (London: Unwin Hyman, 1987; Boston: Houghton Mifflin, 1987); *The Return of the Shadow* (London: Unwin Hyman, 1988; Boston: Houghton Mifflin, 1988); *The Treason of Isengard* (London: Unwin Hyman, 1989; Boston: Houghton Mifflin, 1989); *The War of the Ring* (London: Unwin Hyman, 1990; Boston: Houghton Mifflin, 1990); *Sauron Defeated* (London: HarperCollins, 1992; Boston: Houghton Mifflin, 1992); *Morgoth's Ring* (London: HarperCollins, 1993; Boston: Houghton Mifflin, 199?); *The War of the Jewels* (London:

J. R. R. Tolkien

HarperCollins, 1994; Boston: Houghton Mifflin, 199?).

OTHER: *Sir Gawain and the Green Knight,* edited by Tolkien and E. V. Gordon (Oxford: Clarendon Press, 1925);

Ancrene Wisse: The English Text of the Ancrene Riwle, edited by Tolkien (London: Oxford University Press, 1962);

Sir Gawain and the Green Knight, Pearl, and Sir Orfeo, translated by Tolkien, edited by Christopher Tolkien (London: Allen & Unwin, 1975; Boston: Houghton Mifflin, 1975);

Pictures by J. R. R. Tolkien, edited by Christopher Tolkien (London: Allen & Unwin, 1979; Boston: Houghton Mifflin, 1979);

The Old English Exodus, translation and commentary by Tolkien, edited by Joan Turville-Petre (Oxford: Clarendon Press, 1981).

J. R. R. Tolkien's most familiar creation, the hobbits of Middle-earth, belonged only to his private world until September 1937. Before then they were known only to his children, his great friend C. S. Lewis, and a few other people. The print run of what is now a children's classic — *The Hobbit, or There and Back Again* (1937) — in its first edition was fifteen hundred copies. Forty years later, in 1977, the initial print run for the first U.S. edition of Tolkien's *The Silmarillion* was over three hundred thousand copies, and two years later the run for the first U.S. paperback edition was reportedly over two and a half million copies.

John Ronald Reuel Tolkien was born on 3 January 1892 in Bloemfontein, South Africa, the first son of English citizens Arthur Reuel and Mabel Tolkien. At the time of his father's death in 1896, John Tolkien and his brother Hilary were in England with his mother because of John's health. They remained in England after his father's death and occupied a rented house in Sarehole, Warwickshire, outside Birmingham. In Sarehole there was an old brick mill with a tall chimney. Though it was powered by a steam engine, a stream ran under its great wheel. The mill, with its frightening miller's son, made a deep impression on Tolkien's imagination. In *The Lord of the Rings* (1954–1955) he wrote of a mill in Hobbiton, located on the Water, which was torn down and replaced by a brick building which polluted both the air and water.

In his letters Tolkien remembered his mother as "a gifted lady of great beauty and wit, greatly stricken by God with grief and suffering, who died in youth (at 34) of a disease hastened by persecution of her faith." Her nonconformist family was opposed to her move to Roman Catholicism, which took place in 1900. "It is to my mother," wrote Tolkien, "who taught me (until I obtained a scholarship . . .) that I owe my tastes for philology, especially of Germanic languages, and for romance." The boys' education required that the family move into Birmingham.

Father Francis Morgan was a Roman Catholic parish priest attached to the Birmingham Oratory, founded by John Henry Newman. He provided friendship and counsel for the fatherless family. Half-Spanish, Father Morgan was an extrovert whose enthusiasm helped the Tolkien family. With the boys often ill and the mother developing diabetes, Father Morgan helped to move them to Rednal, in the countryside, for the summer of 1904. The feeling there was like that of Sarehole. Mabel Tolkien died there later that year, and Father Morgan was left with the responsibility of the boys. He helped them financially, found them lodgings in Birmingham, and took them on holidays.

In 1908 Father Morgan found better lodgings for the orphaned brothers on Duchess Road in Birmingham. Here Tolkien fell in love with another lodger, Edith Bratt. She was attractive, small, and slender, with gray eyes. Father Morgan (like King Thingol in Tolkien's tale of Beren and Luthien) disapproved of their love. He was fearful that Tolkien would be distracted from his studies, and ordered Tolkien not to see Edith until he was twenty-one. It meant a long separation, but Tolkien was loyal to his benefactor, the only father he had really known. When Tolkien wrote of their eventual engagement, Father Morgan accepted it without a fuss. The two were formally engaged when Tolkien was twenty-two, after Edith was received into the Roman Catholic Church.

While Tolkien was a schoolboy in King Edward VI Grammar School, he formed a club with several friends, the key members aside from Tolkien being G. B. Smith, R. Q. "Rob" Gilson, and Christopher Wiseman. Only Wiseman and Tolkien survived World War I. The group was called the Tea Club (T.C.) at first, and then later the Barrovian Society (B.S.), the last because the tearoom in Barrow's Stores on Corporation Street in Birmingham became a favorite place to meet. Gilson was the son of the head teacher at King Edward's School. G. B. Smith was also a close friend who commented on some of Tolkien's early poems, including his original verses about Earendil (then written "Earendel"). Smith was killed on active service in the winter of 1916. He wrote to Tolkien shortly before his death, speaking of how the T.C.B.S. – the "immortal four" – would live on, even if he died that night. Tolkien's biographer Humphrey Carpenter writes that Smith concluded: "May God bless you, my dear John Ronald, and may you say the things I have tried to say long after I am not there to say them, if such be my lot."

Though he was from a Methodist family, Wiseman found a great affinity with the Roman Catholic Tolkien. According to Carpenter, Wiseman and Tolkien shared an interest in Latin and Greek, Rugby football, and a zest for discussing anything under the sun. Wiseman was also sympathetic with Tolkien's experiments in invented language, as he was studying the hieroglyphics and language of ancient Egypt. Tolkien and Wiseman continued to meet after Wiseman entered Cambridge University. Wiseman served in the Royal Navy during World War I and later became head of Queen's College, a private school in Taunton. Although the two men did not meet frequently, the friendship with Wiseman was never entirely forgotten.

Tolkien's friends enjoyed his interest in Norse sagas and medieval English literature. After leaving school the four continued to meet occasionally, and to write to each other, until the war destroyed their association. The T.C.B.S. left a permanent mark on Tolkien's character, which he captured in the idea of "fellowship," as in the fellowship of the Ring. Friendship later with C. S. Lewis helped to satisfy this important side of his nature.

After graduating from Exeter College, Oxford, in 1915 and marrying Edith in 1916, Tolkien had his share of bitter action at the front lines. It was during the years of World War I that Tolkien began working on *The Silmarillion* (1977), writing "The Fall of Gondolin" in 1917 while convalescing. In fact most of the legendary cycle of *The Silmarillion* was already constructed before 1930 – before the writing and publication of *The Hobbit,* the forerun-

First page of Tolkien's 1928 Father Christmas letter to his children. Copyright ©
George Allen & Unwin, 1976. Reprinted by permission of Houghton Mifflin.

ner of *The Lord of the Rings*. In the latter books there are numerous references to matters covered by *The Silmarillion:* ruins of once-great places, sites of battles long ago, strange and beautiful names from the deep past, and elfish swords made in Gondolin, before its fall, for the Goblin Wars.

In a letter written many years later, Tolkien outlined to an interested publisher the relationship between his life and his imaginary world. He emphasized that the origin of his fiction was in language. "I do not remember a time," he recalled, "when I was not building it. Many children make up, or begin to make up, imaginary languages. I have been at it since I could write. But I have never stopped, and of course, as a professional philologist (especially interested in linguistic aesthetics), I have changed in taste, improved in theory, and probably in craft. Behind my stories is now a nexus of languages (mostly only structurally sketched). . . . Out of these languages are made nearly all the names that appear in my legends. This gives them a certain character (a cohesion, a consistency of linguistic style, and an illusion of historicity) to the nomenclature."

Tolkien's lifelong study and teaching of languages was the source of his imaginative creations. Just as science-fiction writers generally make use of plausible technological inventions and possibilities, Tolkien used his deep and expert knowledge of language in his fiction. He created in his youth two forms of the Elfish tongue, inspired by his discovery of Welsh and Finnish, starting a process which led to the creation of a history and a geography to surround these languages, and peoples to speak them (and other tongues). He explains: "I had to posit a basic and phonetic structure of Primitive Elvish, and then modify this by a series of changes (such as actually do occur in known languages) so that the two end results would have a consistent structure and character, but be quite different." In a letter to W. H. Auden Tolkien confessed that he always had had a "sensibility to linguistic pattern which affects me emotionally like colour or music."

Equally important to language in Tolkien's complicated makeup was a passion for myth and for fairy story, particularly, he says in his letters, for "heroic legend on the brink of fairy-tale and history." Tolkien revealed that he was an undergraduate before "thought and experience" made it clear to him that story and language were "integrally related." His imaginative and scientific interests were not on opposite poles. Myth and fairy story, he saw, must contain moral and religious truth, but implicitly, not explicitly or allegorically.

Both in his linguistic and his imaginative interests he was constantly seeking "material, things of a certain tone and air." Myths, fairy stories, and ancient words constantly inspired and sustained the unfolding creations of his mind and imagination – his Elfish languages and the early seeds of *The Silmarillion*. The tone and quality that he sought he identified with northern and western Europe, particularly England. He sought to embody this quality in his fiction and invented languages.

The stories he invented in his youth – such as "The Fall of Gondolin" – came to him as something given, rather than as conscious creation. This sense of givenness and discovery remained with him throughout his life. Paradoxically, *The Silmarillion* belongs to this period even though a full and developed version was not published until after Tolkien's death, edited by Tolkien's son Christopher who is the person closest to his thinking. The published *Silmarillion* is based on Tolkien's unfinished work and is not intended to suggest a finished work, though Christopher Tolkien's editorial work is highly skilled and faithful to his father's intentions. The unfinished nature of the book is most apparent in several independent tales therein, such as "Beren and Luthien the Elfmaiden," "Turin Turambar," and "Tuor and the Fall of Gondolin." These are in fact summaries of tales intended to be on a larger, more detailed scale but which were never completed. The condensed, summary nature of much of the published *Silmarillion* presents difficulties for many readers. This difficulty is compounded by the plethora of unfamiliar names. When J. E. A. Tyler updated his *Tolkien Companion* in 1976 to include *The Silmarillion,* he had to add about eighteen hundred new entries.

The ideas and structure of *Silmarillion* evolved throughout Tolkien's adulthood. The story chronicles the ancient days of the First Age of Middle-earth and before. It begins with the creation of the Two Lamps and concludes with the great battle in which Morgoth is overthrown. The unifying thread of the annals and tales of *The Silmarillion* is, as its title suggests, the fate of the Silmarils.

The published *Silmarillion* is divided into several sections. The first is the "Ainulindale" – the account of the creation of the world. This is one of Tolkien's finest pieces of writing, perfectly taking philosophical and theological matter into artistic form. The second section is the "Valaquenta" – the history of the Valar. Then follows the main and largest section, the "Quenta Silmarillion" – *The Silmarillion* proper (the history of the Silmarils). The next section is the "Akallabeth," the account of the downfall of Numenor. The final section concerns the history of the Rings of Power and the Third Age. Tolkien intended all these sections to appear in one book, giving a comprehensive history of Middle-earth.

The mythology, history, and tales of Middle-earth are, in fact, found in unfinished drafts dating over half a century, with considerable developments and changes in narrative structure. Some of the great tales have poetic and prose versions. The published *Silmarillion* provides a stable point of reference by which to read the unfinished publications (collected by Christopher Tolkien in *Unfinished Tales of Numenor and Middle-earth* (1980) and *The History of Middle-earth* (1983–1992). Further stability is provided by Tolkien's own often lengthy commentaries on *The Silmarillion* in his letters.

The seeds of *The Silmarillion* and Tolkien's other fantasies lay in his childhood, his schooldays, and his undergraduate fascination with language. As a schoolboy Tolkien was delighted to acquire a secondhand copy of Joseph Wright's *Primer of the Gothic Language* (1892). As a student at Oxford Tolkien chose comparative philology as his special subject, so he had Wright as a lecturer and tutor. One of Wright's achievements was the six large volumes of his English dialect dictionary. Wright communicated to Tolkien his love for philology and was a demanding teacher and a formative influence on his life. After the interruptions of war, Tolkien returned to Oxford, working on a new edition of the *Oxford English Dictionary*.

Over the years Tolkien was associated with three Oxford colleges: Exeter, Pembroke, and Merton. Between 1911 and 1915 he was an undergraduate at Exeter College, studying at first classics and then English language and literature. In 1925 he returned from Leeds University to become Professor of Anglo-Saxon at Pembroke College. After he changed chairs to become professor of English language and literature in 1945, he became a fellow of Merton College.

It was at Leeds, not Oxford, however, that Tolkien began his distinguished career as a university teacher. E. V. Gordon, a Canadian who had been a Rhodes scholar at Oxford, was appointed soon after Tolkien to teach in the English department at Leeds University. The two men became firm friends and were soon collaborating on a major piece of scholarship, a new edition of *Sir Gawain and the Green Knight* (1925). This presentation of the text of the finest of all the English medieval romances helped to stimulate study of this work, much loved by Tolkien. The edition also contains a major glossary.

In 1975, two years after Tolkien's death, *Sir Gawain and the Green Knight, Pearl, and Sir Orfeo,* including Tolkien's own translations of three major medieval English poems, was published. Both *Sir Gawain and the Green Knight* and *Pearl* are thought to be by the same unknown author from the West Midlands, an area of England with which Tolkien identified and upon which he based The Shire. Tolkien's area of teaching at Leeds University, and later Oxford, was essentially philology. According to T. A. Shippey, in his book *The Road to Middle-earth* (1982), Tolkien's fiction results from the interaction between his imagination and his professional work as a philologist. In his science-fiction novel *Out of the Silent Planet* (1938) C. S. Lewis put something of his friend into the fictional character of the philologist Elwin Ransom. In 1944 Tolkien wrote to his son Christopher: "As a philologist I may have some part in him, and recognize some of my opinions Lewisified in him."

The name Elwin means "elf friend" and is a version of the name of the central character in Tolkien's unfinished story, "The Lost Road." In that story he is named Alboin. From a child he has invented, or rather discovered, strange and beautiful words, leading him to the theory that they are fragments from an ancient world. This slightly autobiographical story tells us much about the love which motivated Tolkien's work in philology, and how it was intimately tied up with his invented mythology of Middle-earth. Owen Barfield said of Lewis that he was in love with the imagination. It could be said of Tolkien that he was in love with language.

When he moved south from Leeds to Oxford in 1925, Tolkien taught mostly Old English, Middle English, and the history of the English language. This work was intimately related to his construction of the languages, peoples, and history of the three Ages of Middle-earth. He commented in a letter that he sought to create a mythology for England, but it might be argued that he also tried to create a mythology for the English language. The earliest expression of the mythology embodied in *The Silmarillion*, a poem written in 1914 about the voyage of Earendil, was inspired by a line from Cynewulf's Old English poem *Crist,* "Eala Earendel engla beorhtost" (Behold Earendel brightest of angels).

In the year Tolkien took up the chair of Anglo-Saxon, W. H. Auden came to Oxford as an undergraduate. There Auden developed a particular liking for Old English literature. Like Tolkien, Auden had a deep interest in northern mythology and was influenced by Tolkien while at Oxford. In later years Tolkien was greatly encouraged by Auden's enthusiasm for *The Lord of the Rings.* He wrote on the quest hero in Tolkien's work, corresponded about and discussed with him the meaning of his work, and counteracted through reviews some of the negative criticism of the trilogy. In Carpenter's biography of Auden (1981) there is a photograph from the 1940s of him absorbed in reading *The Hobbit.*

In 1926 Tolkien met C. S. Lewis, who had been teaching at Magdalen College for one year. They met at the English faculty meeting on 11 May, and Lewis was not amused, recording in his diary his first impression of Tolkien:

> He is a smooth, pale, fluent little chap. Can't read Spenser because of the forms – thinks language is the real thing in the English School – thinks all literature is written for the amusement of men between thirty and forty – we ought to vote ourselves out of existence if we are honest. . . . No harm in him: only needs a smack or two.

Any initial antipathy, however, was soon forgotten. Within a year or so they were meeting in each other's rooms and talking far into the night.

These conversations proved crucial both for the two men's writings and for Lewis's conversion to Christianity. As Lewis remarked in *Surprised by Joy* (1955): "Friendship with Tolkien . . . marked the breakdown of two old prejudices. At my first coming into the world I had been (implicitly) warned never to trust a Papist, and at my first coming into the English Faculty (explicitly) never to trust a philologist. Tolkien was both." A typical note of the time occurs in a letter from Lewis to his Ulster friend Arthur Greeves in December 1929: "Tolkien came back with me to college and sat discoursing of the gods and giants of Asgard for three hours."

Tolkien recalled sharing with Lewis his work on *The Silmarillion,* influencing Lewis's science-fiction work. The pattern of their future lives, including their later club, the Inklings, was being formed. Tolkien remembered that "In the early days of our association Jack used to come to my house and I read aloud to him *The Silmarillion* so far

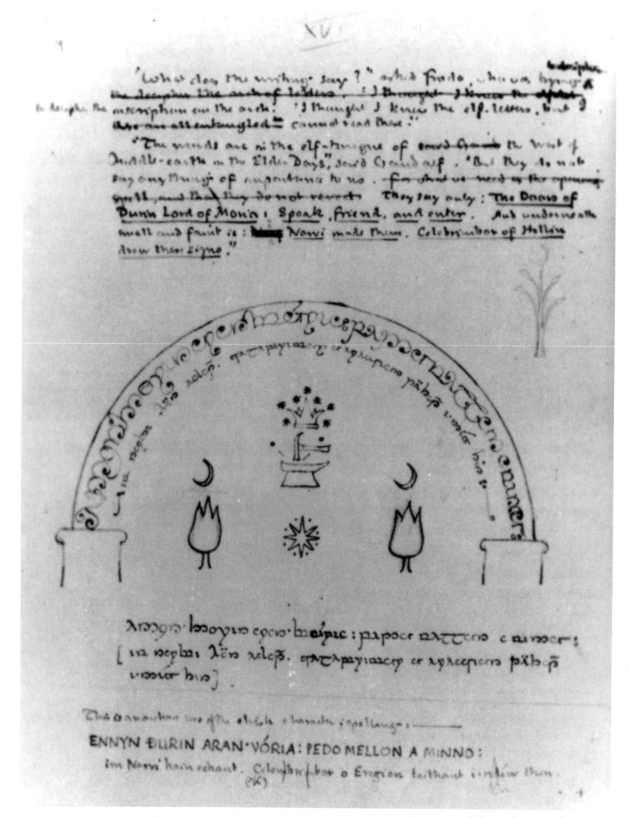

A page from the manuscript for The Lord of the Rings *(Marquette University, Milwaukee)*

as it had then gone, including a long poem: 'Beren and Luthien.' " Lewis was given the unfinished poem to take home to read and was delighted by it, offering Tolkien suggestions for improvement.

The gist of one of the long conversations between Lewis and Tolkien was recorded in October 1931 by Lewis in another letter to Arthur Greeves. It was a crucial factor in Lewis's conversion to Christianity. Tolkien argued that human stories tend to fall into certain patterns and can embody myth. In the Christian Gospels there are all the best elements of good stories, including fairy stories, with the astounding additional factor that everything is also true in the actual, primary world. They combine mythic and historical, factual truth, with no divorce between the two. Lewis's conversion deepened the friendship, a friendship only later eclipsed by Lewis's acquaintance with Charles Williams and what Tolkien called his "strange marriage" to Joy Davidman.

Also important in Tolkien's life at this time was The Kolbitar, an informal reading club he initiated soon after beginning to lecture at Oxford. Its purpose was to explore Icelandic literature such as the Poetic Edda. The name referred to those who crowd so close to the fire in winter that they seem to "bite the coal." Lewis attended meetings, as did Nevill Coghill. In some ways it was a forerunner of the Inklings.

What Tolkien writes in his literary criticism of *Beowulf* is also strikingly true of his own stories: "The significance of myth is not easily to be pinned on paper by analytical reasoning. It is at its best when it is presented by a poet who feels rather than makes explicit what his theme portends; who presents it incarnate in the world of history and geography, as our [*Beowulf*] poet has done." Tolkien points out the danger and difficulty of accounting for the mythical mode of imagination in a work like *Beowulf*:

> Its defender is thus at a disadvantage: unless he is careful, and speaks in parables, he will kill what he is studying by vivisection, and he will be left with a formal or mechanical allegory, and, what is more, probably one that will not work. For myth is alive at once and in all its parts, and dies before it can be dissected. It is possible, I think, to be moved by the power of myth and yet to misunderstand the sensation, to ascribe it wholly to something else that is also present: to metrical art, style, or verbal skill.

Tolkien's conclusion is that "In *Beowulf* we have, then, an historical poem about the pagan past, or an attempt at one. . . . . It is a poem by a learned man writing of old times, who looking back on the heroism and sorrow feels in them something permanent and something symbolical. So far from being a confused semi-pagan – historically unlikely for a man of this sort in the period – he brought probably first to his task a knowledge of Christian poetry."

There are parallels between the author of *Beowulf,* as understood by Tolkien, and Tolkien himself. Tolkien is a Christian scholar looking back to an imagined northern European past. The *Beowulf* author was a Christian looking to the imaginative resources of a pagan past. Both made use of dragons and other potent symbols, symbols which unified their work. Both are concerned more with symbolism than allegory. As with the *Beowulf* author, what is important is not so much the sources but what Tolkien did with them. Like the ancient author, also, Tolkien at his most successful created an illusion of history and a sense of depths of the past.

On 8 March 1939 Tolkien gave his Andrew Lang lecture at Saint Andrews University. "On Fairy Stories" was later published in *Essays Presented to Charles Williams* (1947) – the Inklings' tribute to the writer who had a great deal in common with Tolkien and Lewis. It set out Tolkien's basic ideas concerning imagination, fantasy, and subcreation.

This lecture is the key source for Tolkien's theological ideas behind his creation of Middle-earth and its stories. He links God and mankind in two related ways. In the first he, as an orthodox Christian, sees mankind – male and female – as being made in the image of God. This makes a qualitative difference between mankind and all other things which exist in the universe. The human ability to speak, love, and create fantasy originates in this imageness of God. The second way Tolkien links God and mankind is in similarities that exist by necessity between the universe of God's making and human making. Human making derives, that is, from our being in God's image. The actual course of Tolkien's essay does not so starkly highlight these two related links between God and mankind, but they underlie both the essay and Tolkien's fiction.

"On Fairy Stories" is concerned to rehabilitate the idea of the fairy story, which had been relegated to children's literature, and fantasy in general. To regard fairy stories as trivial, suitable only for telling to children, failed to do justice either to such stories or to real children. Tolkien, who had by then written much of *The Silmarillion* and published *The Hobbit,* attempted to set out a structure which belonged to good fairy tales and fantasies. This structure demonstrated that fairy tales were worthy of serious attention. Fairy tales, he pointed out, were stories about "faerie": "the realm or state where fairies have their being." Readers familiar with his essay *Beowulf: The Monsters and the Critics* (1937) will notice a similarity with Tolkien's portrayal of the Old English poem. Tolkien wrote of the *Beowulf* poet making his theme "incarnate in the world of history and geography." Fairy tales were fantasy, allowing their hearers or readers to move from the details of their limited experience to "survey the depths of space and time." The successful fairy story in fact was "sub-creation," the ultimate achievement of fantasy, the highest art, deriving its power from human language itself. The successful writer of the fairy story "makes a Secondary World which your mind can enter. Inside it, what he relates is 'true': it accords with the laws of that world."

In addition to offering a Secondary World, with an "inner consistency of reality," a good fairy tale has three other key structural features. In the first place, it helps to bring about in the reader what Tolkien called recovery – that is, the restoration of a true view of the meaning of ordinary and humble things which make up human life and reality, things like love, thought, trees, hills, and food. Second, the good fairy story offers escape from one's narrow and distorted view of reality and meaning. This is the escape of the prisoner rather than the flight of the deserter. Third, the good story offers consolation, leading to joy (what Lewis called *sehnsucht*).

The consolation, argued Tolkien, only had meaning because good stories pointed to the greatest story of all. This story had all the structural features of a fairy tale, myth, or great story, with the additional feature of being true in actual human history. This was the Gospel, the story of God coming to earth as a humble human being, a king, like Aragorn, in disguise, a seeming fool, like Frodo and Sam, the greatest storyteller entering his own story.

Tolkien's fundamental idea of the consolation is related to his view of nature, which was deeply theological. He saw nature in terms of a natural theology which was sacramental. His own created elves – which are the central concern of *The Silmarillion*, and his invented languages – were natural creatures, or, at least, their destinies were tied up with the natural world. Elves are his name for fairies, and thus are central to this essay. His main fiction, like this essay, was concerned to rehabilitate the fairy tale and to provide consolation for his readers. The three features of recovery, escape, and consolation focus on the effect that good fairy tales have on their readers. For Tolkien, the effect of a work of literature on its reader is clearly an important dimension of literary meaning.

Also belonging to this period of Tolkien's life – it was not in fact published until 1982 – was the writing of *Mr Bliss*. This is a children's story, illustrated throughout by Tolkien in color, about a man, noted for his tall hats, who lives in a tall house. In 1932 Tolkien bought a car (he later abandoned car ownership on principle, because of the environmental effect of massive car ownership and production). The consequences of having a car suggested the story of Mr Bliss's adventures after buying a bright yellow car for five shillings. The story was shown to Tolkien's publishers in 1937, when the publication of *The Hobbit* had created a demand for more from Tolkien's pen. The costs of color printings, however, were prohibitive, and Tolkien eventually sold the manuscript to Marquette University.

Of more abiding significance from this period is his creation of the strange figure of Tom Bombadil, "Master of wood, water and hill." He was a nature spirit, mastered by none and refusing possession himself. Like the biblical Adam, he was a name-giver. In *The Lord of the Rings* he gave to the ponies of the hobbits names that they "answered to for the rest of their lives." Like the wizards, he appeared like a man, though, unlike them, he had been in Middle-earth from earliest days. Tom Bombadil was the name given to him by hobbits; he was known by other names to elves, dwarves, and men.

He was also well known to Tolkien's children. Tom Bombadil was a Dutch doll belonging to Michael Tolkien as a young child. He became the hero of a poem, "The Adventures of Tom Bombadil," published in 1934 in the *Oxford Magazine*. Tom Bombadil eventually reemerged in *The Lord of the Rings*. The early Tom Bombadil poem was included, many years later, in the collection *The Adventures of Tom Bombadil* (1962) which was made up of light verses from *The Red Book of Westmarch*, supposedly written by Bilbo Baggins, Sam Gamgee, and other hobbits, and rendered into English from Westron (the Western speech of Middle-earth) by Tolkien, who adds an explanatory note. They are mainly concerned with legends and jests of The Shire at the end of the Third Age. Tolkien's talent for songs, ballads, and witty riddles fits well into the hobbit setting.

Tolkien's *The Hobbit* was published on 21 September 1937. Tolkien recalled the story beginning

He has well repaid my trust. For if Elrond had not yielded to me, neither of you would have set out, and then far more grievous would the evils of this day have been'. He sighed. 'And yet

40—Return of the King.   000

climbing up to the Citadel. Step by step they went, while Merry swayed and murmured as one in sleep.

'I'll never get him there,' thought Pippin. 'Is there no one to help me? I can't leave him here.' Just then to his surprise a boy came running up behind, and as he passed he recognized Bergil Beregond's son.

'Hullo, Bergil!' he called. 'Where are you going? Glad to see you again, and still alive!'

'I am running errands for the Healers,' said Bergil. 'I cannot stay.'

'Don't!' said Pippin. 'But tell them up there that I have a sick hobbit, a *perian* mind you, come from the battle-field. I don't think he can walk so far. If Mithrandir is there, he will be glad of the message.' Bergil ran on.

'I'd better wait here,' thought Pippin. So he let Merry sink gently down on to the pavement in a patch of sunlight, and then he sat down beside him, laying Merry's head in his lap. He felt his body and limbs gently, and took his friend's hands in his own. The right hand felt icy to the touch.

It was not long before Gandalf himself came in search of them. He stooped over Merry and caressed his brow; then he lifted him carefully. 'He should have been borne in honour into this city,' he said. ~~Greater was the wisdom of Elrond than mine; for if I had had my way, neither you, Pippin, nor he would have set out; and then far more grievous would the evils of this day have been.~~ But here is another charge on my hands, while all the time the battle hangs in the balance.'

So at last Faramir and Éowyn and Meriadoc were laid in beds in the Houses of Healing; and there they were tended well. For though all lore was in these latter days fallen from its fullness of old, the leechcraft of Gondor was still wise, and skilled in the healing of wound and hurt, and all such sickness as east of the Sea mortal men were subject to. Save old age only. For that they had found no cure; and indeed the span of their lives had now waned to little more than that of other men, and those among them who passed the tale of five score years with vigour were grown few, save in some houses of purer blood. But now their art and knowledge were baffled; for there were many sick of a malady that would not be healed; and they called it the Black Shadow, for it came from the Nazgûl. And those who were

Corrected galley proofs for The Return of the King *(Melissa and Mark Hime,* The Hobbitiana *catalogue, 1980)*

many years earlier, when he came across a blank page on an exam he was marking. On it he wrote the words "In a hole in the ground there lived a hobbit." The writing of the book probably began in 1930 or 1931. Lewis was shown a draft before the end of 1932. Tolkien's eldest sons remember the story being told to them before the 1930s. Perhaps various oral forms of the story merged into the more finished written draft. What is significant is that *The Hobbit* begins as a tale told by Tolkien to his children.

It is also clear that at first the story was independent of his burgeoning mythological cycle, *The Silmarillion,* and only later became drawn into the single invented world and history. The tale introduced hobbits into this mythological world and its history, dramatically affecting the course of the greater structure. *The Hobbit* belongs to the Third Age of Middle-earth and chronologically precedes *The Lord of the Rings.*

The title of the book refers to its hero, Bilbo Baggins. An unnamed critic in the *New Statesman* quoted on the dust jacket of the second British edition (1951) of *The Hobbit* remarked of Tolkien that "It is a triumph that the genus Hobbit, which he himself has invented, rings just as real as the time-hallowed genera of Goblin, Troll, and Elf." Lewis believed that the hobbits "are perhaps a myth that only an Englishman (or, should we add, a Dutchman?) could have created." Instead of a creation of character as is found in novels, much of what is known of Bilbo, Frodo, Sam, and other hobbits is known because they are known in character as hobbits, as Gandalf is known as a wizard or Treebeard in character as an Ent. Tolkien sustains the character of these different races with great skill.

Bilbo's house was a typical dwelling place of a wealthy hobbit. It was not a worm-filled, dirty, damp hole, but a comfortable, many-roomed underground home. Its hall, which connected all the rooms, had "panelled walls, and floors tiled and carpeted, provided with polished chairs, and lots and lots of pegs for hats and coats – the hobbit was fond of visitors." Hobbits generally liked to be thought respectable, not having adventures or behaving in an unexpected way. At the time portrayed in *The Hobbit* and *The Lord of the Rings,* in the Third Age, hobbits mainly lived in The Shire, but they had migrated from the east, from the other side of the Misty Mountains, in the Vale of Anduin. Originally, they were closely related to mankind, created in the First Age. Gollum – a foil to Frodo Baggins in *The Lord of the Rings* – was originally a stoor hobbit of the Anduin region.

In the story a party of dwarves, thirteen in number, are on a quest for their long-lost treasure, which is jealously guarded by a dragon. Their leader is the great Thorin Oakenshield. They employ Bilbo Baggins, at the recommendation of the wizard Gandalf the Grey, as their burglar to steal the treasure. The reluctant Baggins would rather spend a quiet day with his pipe and pot of tea in his comfortable hobbit hole than partake in any unrespectable adventure. Despite initial misgivings, the dwarves become increasingly thankful for the fact that they employed him, as he gets them out of many scrapes. He seems to have extraordinary luck, but there is an underlying sense of providence at work in events.

At one point in the adventure Bilbo is knocked unconscious in a goblin tunnel under the Misty Mountains and is left behind in the darkness by the rest of the party. Reviving, Bilbo discovers a ring lying beside him in the tunnel. It is the ruling ring that forms the subject of *The Lord of the Rings,* but Bilbo is to discover only its magical property of making its wearer invisible at this stage. After putting the ring in his pocket, Bilbo stumbles along the black tunnel. Eventually he comes across a subterranean lake, where Gollum dwells, a luminous-eyed corruption of a hobbit, his life preserved over centuries by the ring he has now lost for the first time. After a battle of riddles Bilbo escapes, seemingly by luck, by slipping on the ring and becoming invisible. Following the vengeful Gollum, who cannot see him, he finds his way out of the mountains, to the other side.

Bilbo's discovery of the ring provided Tolkien with the link between *The Hobbit* and its large sequel, *The Lord of the Rings.* However, it proved necessary for Tolkien partially to rewrite chapter 5 of the former book to provide proper continuity between the two works over the great significance of the ruling ring. He drafted this in 1947, in the midst of composing *The Lord of the Rings.* The new edition, incorporating the revised chapter, first appeared in 1951.

Bilbo eventually leads the party successfully to the dragon's treasure, and the scaly monster perishes while attacking nearby Lake-town. Bilbo and Gandalf journey back to the peaceful Shire. Bilbo has refused most of his share of the treasure, having seen the results of greed. The events have changed him forever, but even more, the ring he secretly possesses will shape the events recorded in *The Lord of the Rings.*

Significant information about the background to "The Quest of Erebor" (the events of *The Hobbit*) is found in *Unfinished Tales of Numenor and Middle-earth* (published posthumously in 1980). There we learn of the reluctance of the dwarves to take along a hobbit, the great persuasion Gandalf had to muster for Thorin, and the place that Providence played in the unfolding of events. What is striking about *The Hobbit* is Tolkien's skill in adjusting the scale of his great mythology of the earlier ages of Middle-earth to the level of children. Names are simple, in complete contrast to the complexities of *The Silmarillion*. Erebor is simply The Lonely Mountain. Esgaroth is usually called Lake-town. Elrond's home in Rivendell is described as the Last Homely House west of the Mountains.

Tolkien continued with the adult sequel to *The Hobbit, The Lord of the Rings,* more and more leaving aside his first love, *The Silmarillion.* The writing of the sequel was a long, painstaking task. In the midst of the writing of *The Lord of the Rings* he wrote "Leaf by Niggle" and "Farmer Giles of Ham" (1949). "Leaf by Niggle," a short allegory, was first published in January 1945 in the *Dublin Review* and was republished in *Tree and Leaf* (1964). The allegory, an unusual form for Tolkien, is also atypical in that it has autobiographical elements.

Niggle, a little man and artist, knows that he will one day have to make a Journey. Many matters get in the way of his painting, such as the demands of his neighbor, Mr. Parish, who has a lame leg. Niggle is concerned to finish one painting in particular. This started as an illustration of a leaf caught in the wind and then became a tree. Through gaps in the leaves and branches a Forest and a whole world open up. As the painting grows (with other, smaller paintings tacked on) Niggle has to move it into a specially built shed on his potato plot.

Eventually Niggle falls ill after getting soaked in a storm while running an errand for Mr. Parish. Then the dreaded Inspector visits to tell him that the time has come for him to set out on the Journey. Taking a train, his first stop (which seems to him to last for a century) is at the Workhouse. Later, after a long spell there, Niggle is allowed to resume his Journey in a small train which leads him to the familiar world depicted in his painting of long ago, and to his tree, now complete. "It's a gift!" he exclaims.

Eventually Niggle feels that it is time to move on into the Mountains. Long before, back in the town near where Niggle lived before the Journey, a fragment of Niggle's painting survived and was hung in the Town Museum, entitled simply "Leaf by Niggle." It depicts a spray of leaves with a glimpse of a mountain peak.

Tolkien's little story suggests the link between art and reality. Even in heaven there will be a place for the artist to add his or her own touch to the created world. The allegorical element could be interpreted with Niggle the painter signifying Tolkien the writer, and Niggle's leaf *The Hobbit.* Such interpretation emphasizes the autobiographical aspect of the story. The tale has equal applicability to the artist in general, however. In particular, there is a poignancy to the unfinished nature of Niggle's work. The story may appeal to some children even though its allegory may not be noticed.

"Farmer Giles of Ham" is more obviously of interest to children. This lighthearted short story is subtitled "The Rise and Wonderful Adventures of Farmer Giles, Lord of Tame, Count of Worminghall and King of the Little Kingdom." It begins with a mock-scholarly foreword about its supposed authorship and translation from Latin, and the extent of the "Little Kingdom" in "a dark period of the history of Britain." Tolkien concludes that the setting is before the days of King Arthur, in the valley of the Thames.

This humorous story, though on the surface very different from the tales of Middle-earth, is characteristic in its themes of Tolkien's other work. The story's inspiration is linguistic: it provides a spoof explanation for the name of an actual village east of Oxford called Worminghall, near Thame. The Little Kingdom has similarities with The Shire, particularly the sheltered and homely life of Ham. Farmer Giles is like a complacent Hobbit, with unexpected qualities. The humor — with its mock scholarship — is similar to that in the later collection of Hobbit verses *The Adventures of Tom Bombadil.*

Meanwhile, work continued slowly on *The Lord of the Rings.* Some of it was written and sent in installments to one of his four children, Christopher, on service in World War II with the Royal Air Force. At one point Tolkien did not touch the manuscript for a whole year. He wrote it in the evenings, for he was fully engaged in his university work and other matters. During the World War II years, and afterward, he read portions to the Inklings, the literary group of male friends to which he belonged, or simply to Lewis alone.

The Lord of the Rings, the great tale of the Third Age of Middle-earth, was written in six parts. Each of the three volumes published contains two of the parts. The volumes are *The Fellowship of the Ring* (1954), *The Two Towers* (1954), and *The Return of the King* (1955).

The Lord of the Rings is a heroic romance, telling of the quest to destroy the one ruling ring of power before it can fall into the hands of its maker, Sauron, the dark lord of the title. As a consistent, unified story it stands independently of the invented mythology and historical chronicles of Middle-earth. Events of the past provide a backdrop and haunting dimension to the story. As a work of literature, the merits and demerits of *The Lord of the Rings* have been extensively discussed by scholars. Among its admirers are Auden and Lewis. Some critics less enthusiastic than Lewis have pointed out what they regard as flaws in the work: the change of tone from the *Hobbit*-like opening to the seriousness of the quest; a lack of moral seriousness (in that the good characters do not wrestle with evil); the adolescent quality of many of the characters, who never grow up; unconvincing battle scenarios; and the distraction of having to read half a book before the tale of Frodo and Sam continues.

Considered structurally, however, the opening is not a flaw but sets the scene of homeliness, so important to Tolkien. Out of this humble context the unexpected heroes, Frodo and Sam, arise. The charge of a lack of moral seriousness does not hold once the subtlety and range of Tolkien's examination of evil is explored. On Tolkien's character portrayal, it is important to realize that this is not meant to be novelistic. *The Lord of the Rings* is a heroic romance. Characters are known according to type, and in Tolkien type can be dwarf, hobbit, ent, and elf, as well as varieties of the human. What the story requires is a critical apparatus that takes narrative qualities and story seriously, including genres such as heroic romance, fantasy, and science fiction.

One mark of the quality of *The Lord of the Rings* as literature is its linguistic basis. Tolkien makes use of his invented languages in names and also in imaginative possibility. Language is the basis of the background mythology. Another mark of its literary quality is Tolkien's success in integrating the wealth of symbolism of his work. Quest, the journey, sacrifice, healing, death, and many other symbolic elements are beautifully incarnate in the book. The landscapes through which the travelers pass are symbolic, suggesting moods which correspond to the stages of the journey and to the phase of the overall story. The terrors of Moria, the archetypal underworld, contrast for example with the refreshment to the spirit of Lorien. Always these landscapes are fully part of the movement of the book, aesthetically shaped and integrated.

Tolkien's greatest achievement is the embodiment of myth in literature. It was an amazing feat to create living myth. Tolkien shared this ability with George MacDonald. It is a further achievement to make myth incarnate in literary form successfully. Had Tolkien completed his work on *The Silmarillion,* evidence suggests that there would have been several stories in which this literary achievement of embodying myth was repeated: stories like "The Tale of Beren and Luthien the Elf-maiden."

In *The Lord of the Rings* the wizard, Gandalf, discovers that the ring found by Bilbo (as recounted in *The Hobbit*) is in fact the One Ring, controlling the Rings of Power forged in the Second Age in Eregion. Frodo, inheritor of the Ring, flees from the comfort of The Shire with his companions. On his trail are the Black Riders sent from Mordor by Sauron. With the help of the Ranger, Aragorn, they succeed in reaching the security of Rivendell. There Elrond holds a great Council where it is decided that the Ring must be destroyed and that Frodo should be the Ring-bearer. The Company of the Ring is also chosen to help him on the desperate quest. The Ring can only be destroyed in the Mountain of Fire, Mount Doom, in Mordor. The tale recounts the events leading to the Ring's successful destruction, and the redemptive aftermath.

Without the destruction of the Ring, the western alliance against Mordor would have failed. Though there was no certainty of the success of the quest of Frodo and Sam, the people of Gondor and Rohan, and the other allies, were prepared to fight to the death against the dreadful enemy. The story ends with the gradual healing of the land, preparing the way for the domination of mankind. The fading of the elves is complete as the last ships pass over the sea to the Undying Lands of the West. On them are the Ring-bearers Bilbo and Frodo. Frodo's companion Sam follows later, after a happy life in The Shire, with his beloved Rosie. Though written for adults, unlike its sequel, *The Hobbit,* children as young as nine have enjoyed reading the book, and many more have experienced it through having the story read to them.

From the early to mid 1930s the Inklings had played an increasingly important part in Tolkien's life, and particularly the writing of *The Lord of the Rings.* The group did not have any consistent documentation such as the careful minuting of the fictional Notion Club, Tolkien's unfinished portrait of an Inklings-type group of friends, set in the future. Tolkien points out in a letter that "The Inklings had no recorder and C. S. Lewis no Boswell." Humphrey Carpenter's study, *The Inklings* (1978) draws on the key sources: the diaries of Maj. Warren Lewis; C. S. Lewis's letters to his brother in the early months of World War II; Tolkien's long letters to his son Christopher while in South Africa

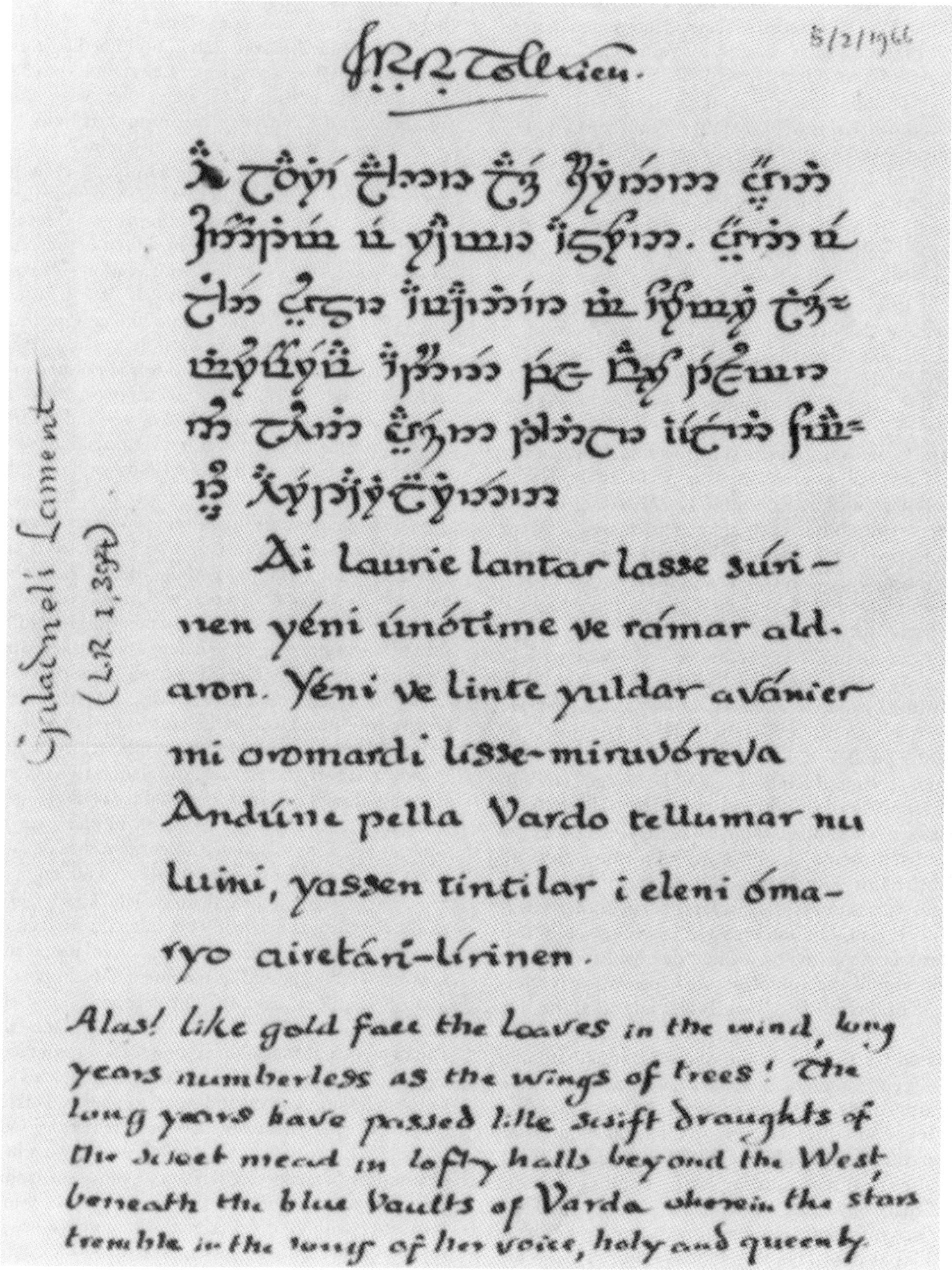
J.R.R. Tolkien.

5/2/1966

Galadriel's Lament (L.R. I, 394)

Ai laurie lantar lasse súri-
nen yéni únótime ve rámar ald-
aron. Yéni ve linte yuldar avánier
mi oromardi lisse-miruvóreva
Andúne pella Vardo tellumar nu
luini, yassen tintilar i eleni óma-
ryo airetári-lírinen.

Alas! like gold fall the leaves in the wind, long
years numberless as the wings of trees! The
long years have passed like swift draughts of
the sweet mead in lofty halls beyond the West,
beneath the blue vaults of Varda wherein the stars
tremble in the song of her voice, holy and queenly.

Page from the manuscript for The Fellowship of the Rings *(Melissa and Mark Hime,* The Hobbitiana *catalogue, 1980)* with the Royal Air Force; Lewis's introduction to *Essays Presented to Charles Williams,* and reminiscences by Inklings such as John Wain, Comdr. Jim Dundas-Grant, Christopher Tolkien, and others.

Tolkien was a central figure in the literary group of friends held together by the zest and enthusiasm of Lewis. Tolkien described it in a letter as an "undetermined and unelected circle of friends who gathered around C. S. L[ewis]., and met in his rooms in Magdalen. . . . Our habit was to read aloud compositions of various kinds (and lengths!)."

Lewis gives an insight into the Inklings almost incidentally in his preface to *Essays Presented to Charles Williams,* to which Tolkien contributed. Lewis points out that three of the essays in the collection are on literature, and, specifically, one aspect of literature, the "narrative art." That, Lewis says, is natural enough. Williams's *"All Hallows Eve* and my own *Perelandra* (as well as Professor Tolkien's unfinished sequel to *The Hobbit*) had all been read aloud, each chapter as it was written. They owe a good deal to the hard-hitting criticism of the circle. The problems of narrative as such – seldom heard of in modern critical writings – were constantly before our minds."

In his book Carpenter lists the various Inklings in a long list – but Lewis, in a letter to Bede Griffiths from December 1941, has a short list. He is explaining his dedication to the Inklings in his recently published *The Problem of Pain.* He lists Williams, Dyson of Reading (H. V. D. "Hugo" Dyson), Warren Lewis, Tolkien, and Dr. "Humphrey" Havard. He explains Tolkien and Dyson as the "immediate human causes of my own conversion" to Christianity. Remarkably, the name of Owen Barfield does not appear. In fact, Barfield rarely was able to visit. On one occasion Lewis grumbles that Barfield is visiting on a Thursday, which means he will attend the Inklings and Lewis will have less time to himself with him. It was later that the Inklings swelled further to include Colin Hardie, Lord David Cecil, John Wain, and others. Christopher Tolkien attended as soon as he was back from South Africa, and he became a significant member. It was upon this larger group that Tolkien drew inspiration for the Notion Club Papers, and it is likely that he read it all to them. Warren Lewis records in his diary of 22 August 1946 about "Tollers" reading "a magnificent myth which is to knit up and concludes his Papers of the Notions Club." This would have been "The Drowning of Anadune" (published with the Notion Club Papers in *Sauron Defeated* (1992).

A further complexity of the Inklings is that there were two patterns of meetings: Tuesday mornings in the Bird and Baby pub (The Eagle and Child, St. Giles) – except when Lewis took the chair in Cambridge, when Monday mornings were more suitable – and Thursday evenings, usually in Lewis's rooms in Magdalen but often in Tolkien's rooms in Merton College. The Thursday evenings were of more literary interest, as here members would read to each other work in progress, receiving criticism and encouragement. Much of the "new Hobbit," *The Lord of the Rings,* was read in this way, sometimes by Christopher instead of his father. After 1951 the term *the Inklings* no longer appears in Warren Lewis's diaries, and it is probable that sometime around 1950 the Thursday meetings ended, though the Tuesday meetings (or Monday ones) continued until 1962. The key years of the Inklings, in terms of their literary significance, were probably from around the mid 1930s until near the end of 1949.

The death of Williams in 1945 was a great blow to the group, particularly Lewis, and the 1950s marked a gradual cooling of the friendship between Lewis and Tolkien, which was the heart around which the Inklings formed and grew. The situation was not helped by Hugo Dyson exercising a veto against Tolkien reading from the unfinished *Lord of the Rings* at Inklings meetings. A further complexity was introduced by Lewis's at first only intellectual friendship with Joy Davidman. It is valuable to look at Lewis and Barfield in relation to Tolkien. Not all of Lewis's friends appealed to Tolkien, or at least not to the same extent, as in the case of Charles Williams. Tolkien influenced Lewis deeply, and Lewis was of great importance to Tolkien.

There was first the influence of Tolkien's Christianity. Lewis was originally an atheist, and Tolkien helped him to come to faith. The pattern of his persuasion is vividly captured in the poem "Mythopoeia," published in *Tree and Leaf.* The second, related element of Tolkien's influence was his view of the relation of myth and fact. The view can be seen as a theology of story. Tolkien had worked out a complex view of the relation of story and myth to reality. Tolkien saw the Gospel narratives – a story created by God himself in the real events of history – as having broken into the "seamless web of story." Story – whether preceding or subsequent to the Gospel events – is joyfully alive with God's presence. The importance of story became central to Lewis, expressed for example in his *An Experiment in Criticism* (1961).

The third element, also related, is Tolkien's distinctive doctrine of subcreation, the view that the highest function of art is the creation of convincing secondary or other worlds. Without the impact of Tolkien's view of subcreation on Lewis we may not have had Malacandra, Perelandra, or Glome, particularly Perelandra, one of his most successful creations, or even Narnia.

Turning the other way, what was Lewis's importance to Tolkien? Lewis clearly did not influence Tolkien's writing in the way Tolkien influenced his. In Lewis, rather, Tolkien found a ready listener and appreciator. This listening was institutionalized in the Inklings' Thursday night gatherings, where much of *The Lord of the Rings* was read. In fact, Tolkien confesses that without Lewis's encouragement it is unlikely that he would have finished *The Lord of the Rings!* We might speculate that if the Thursday meetings had continued, with the associated dynamic of Tolkien and Lewis's friendship, there would exist today tellings of the tales of Beren and Luthien, and perhaps also of Turin Turambar, and other key stories of the First Age, nearer the scale of *The Lord of the Rings.*

The two friends had a great number of shared beliefs that transcended what Tolkien had in common with other Inklings friends, such as Barfield and Williams. These convictions derived from shared tastes, and particularly from their common faith, which, though orthodox, had an original cast. They saw the imagination as the organ of meaning rather than of truth (which made their romanticism distinctive). Imaginative invention was justifiable in its own right – it did not have to serve in a didactic medium and did not have the burden of carrying conceptual truths. Though Lewis was more allegorical and explicit than Tolkien, both writers valued a symbolic perception of reality. A further central preoccupation of Lewis and Tolkien was imaginative invention (most obviously expressed in Tolkien's concept of subcreation). This was related to their view of the function of imagination as the organ of meaning rather than of truth. Products of the imagination were a form of knowledge, but knowledge discovered by making, essentially not accessible in any other way.

They also shared a sense of the value of otherness – or otherworldliness. Great stories take us outside the prison of our own selves and our presuppositions about reality. Insofar as stories reflect the divine maker, they help us face the ultimate Other – God himself, distinct as creator from all else, including ourselves. The well of fantasy and imaginative invention is every person's direct knowledge of the Other. In *Of This and Other Worlds* (1982) Lewis writes that "To construct plausible and moving 'other worlds' you must draw on the only real 'other world' we know, that of the spirit." For both men this all-pervasive sense of the other was focused in a quality of the numinous. Both successfully embodied this quality in their fiction.

Both Tolkien and Lewis were preoccupied with pre-Christian paganism, particularly what might be called enlightened paganism. Most of Tolkien's fiction is set in a pre-Christian world, as was his great model, *Beowulf,* according to his own interpretation of that poem. Even while an atheist, Lewis was attracted by pagan myths of the north and the idea of a dying god. In one of his Latin Letters, Lewis speculates that some modern people may need to be brought to pre-Christian pagan insights in preparation for more adequately receiving the Christian Gospel. Tolkien undoubtedly shared this view of preevangelism. To point out these shared concerns is not to downplay important differences, often of emphasis, between Tolkien and Lewis. Their differences gave a dynamic to their friendship.

Tolkien was also influenced by Owen Barfield, who is considered one of the core Inklings, even though he rarely attended meetings. Barfield's distinction between allegory and myth rings true of Tolkien's perception, leading to his dislike of allegory and his concern, for example, about Lewis's fondness for allegory. We can also find Tolkien-like concepts in Barfield's view of prehistoric human consciousness, which he saw as unitary, not fragmented into subject and object. It was, as Barfield notes in *Poetic Diction* (1952), "a kind of thinking which is at the same time perceiving – a picture-thinking, a figurative, or imaginative, consciousness, which we can only grasp today by true analogy with the imagery of our poets, and, to some extent, with our own dreams." Such an attention to dreams, and in shifts in consciousness with developments in language, is typical also of Tolkien, highlighted in his unfinished Notion Club Papers.

In 1945 Tolkien was appointed to a new chair at Oxford, Merton Professor of English Language and Literature, reflecting his wider interests. He was not now so cool to the idea of teaching literature at the university as he had been previously. Tolkien retained the chair until his retirement in 1959. The scholarly storyteller's retirement years were spent revising *The Lord of the Rings,* brushing up and publishing some shorter pieces of story and poetry, and intermittently working on various drafts of *The Silmarillion.* Tolkien also spent much time dodging reporters and youthful Americans, as the 1960s marked the exploding popularity of his fantasies, when his readership went in numbers from thousands to millions.

Out of this unshapely period, however, came *Smith of Wootton Major* (1967), a profound story which is written simply enough for a child to enjoy. This short story was Tolkien's last finished work and complements his essay "On Fairy Stories" in tracing the relationship between the world of Faerie and the Primary World. The story seems deceptively simple at first, and though children can enjoy it, it is not a children's story. Tolkien described it as "an old man's book, already weighted with the presage of 'bereavement.' " It was as if, like Smith in the story with his elfen star, Tolkien expected his imagination to come to an end. In a review Tolkien's friend and one of the Inklings, Roger Lancelyn Green, wrote of the book: "To seek for the meaning is to cut open the ball in search of its bounce." Like *Farmer Giles of Ham,* the story has an undefined medieval setting. The villages of Wootten Major and Minor could have come out of The Shire. As in Middle-earth, it is possible to walk in and out of the world of Faerie (the realm of elves). The story contains an elfen king in disguise, Alf, apprentice to the bungling cake maker Nokes. Nokes has no concept of the reality of Faerie, but his sugary cake for the village children, with its crude Fairy Queen doll, can stir the imagination of the humble. A magic elfen star in the cake is swallowed by Smith, giving him access to Faerie. In the village it is the children who can be susceptible to the "other," the numinous, where their elders are only concerned with eating and drinking. As in "Leaf by Niggle," glimpses of other worlds transform art and craft in human life. The humble work of the village smith is transformed into the sacramental.

The writing of the story was inspired by a growing dislike of some of the fantasy of George MacDonald, particularly his short story "The Golden Key" (1867). That story, however, is one of MacDonald's great achievements, as *Smith of Wootten Major* is one of Tolkien's.

Tolkien's great achievement is the invention, or subcreation, of Middle-earth. Strictly speaking, Middle-earth is only part of the world, or Ea. It is an old name for the world, taken from northern mythology and occurring in Old English literature. Much of Tolkien's invention concerns the history, annals, languages and chronology, and geography of Middle-earth. He was concerned to make an inwardly consistent subcreation. *The History of Middle-earth* (1983–1994) is the title of a series of eleven volumes of unfinished or preliminary material edited and published after Tolkien's death by his son, Christopher, who also provided a detailed commentary. The volumes are *The Book of Lost Tales,* parts 1 and 2 (1983–1984); *The Lays of Beleriand* (1985); *The Shaping of Middle-earth* (1986); *The Lost Road and Other Writings* (1987); *The Return of the Shadow* (1988); *The Treason of Isengard* (1989); *The War of the Ring* (1990); *Sauron Defeated* (1992); *Morgoth's Ring* (1993); and *The War of the Jewels* (1994). A further volume is in preparation.

Although much of Tolkien's writing was intended for an adult audience, there is much that can be enjoyed by children. Children frequently read *The Lord of the Rings* or have the tale successfully read to them. *The Hobbit* was written specifically as a children's book, and his short stories such as *Mr Bliss, Smith of Wootton Major,* and *Farmer Giles of Ham* are suitable for children's reading. Much of Tolkien's poetry scattered through the pages of *The Lord of the Rings,* as well as the collection *The Adventures of Tom Bombadil* can be enjoyed by children, and some will appreciate the allegorical story "Leaf by Niggle." The four great unfinished tales of *The Silmarillion* – "Beren and Luthien," "Turin Turambar," "Tuor and the Fall of Gondolin," and "Earendil the Mariner" – can be reread to children.

Letters:

The Letters of J. R. R. Tolkien, edited by Humphrey Carpenter, with the assistance of Christopher Tolkien (London: Allen & Unwin, 1981; Boston: Houghton Mifflin, 1981).

Interviews:

Daphne Castell, "The Realms of Tolkien," *New Worlds SF,* 50 (November 1966): 143–154;

William Cater, "Lord of the Hobbits," *Daily Express* (London), 22 November 1966, p. 10;

Richard Plotz, "J. R. R. Tolkien Talks about the Discovery of Middle-earth, the Origins of Elvish," *Seventeen* (January 1967): 92–93, 118;

Philip Norman, "The Hobbit Man," *Sunday Times Magazine* (London), 15 January 1967, pp. 34–36;

Charlotte Plimmer and Denis Plimmer, "The Man Who Understands Hobbits," *Daily Telegraph Magazine* (London), 22 March 1968, pp. 31–32, 35;

Keith Brace, "In the Footsteps of the Hobbits," *Birmingham* (England) *Post Midland Magazine* (25 May 1968): 1;

Cater, "The Lord of the Legends," *Sunday Times Magazine* (London), 2 January 1972, pp. 24–25, 27–28;

Anthony Curtis, "Remembering Tolkien and Lewis," *British Book News* (June 1977): 429–430;

Bibliography:

Wayne G. Hammond, *J. R. R. Tolkien: A Descriptive Bibliography* (Winchester: St. Paul's Bibliographies / Newcastle, Del.: Oak Knoll Books, 1993);

M. Hime, *The Hobbitania* (Century City, Cal.: Biblioctopus, 1980).

Biography:

Humphrey Carpenter, *J. R. R. Tolkien: A Biography* (London: Allen & Unwin, 1977; Boston: Houghton Mifflin, 1977).

References:

Humphrey Carpenter, *The Inklings: C. S. Lewis, J. R. R. Tolkien, Charles Williams and their Friends* (London: Allen & Unwin, 1978; Boston: Houghton Mifflin, 1979);

Colin Duriez, *The Tolkien and Middle-earth Handbook* (Tunbridge Wells: Monarch Publications, 1992); published as *The J.R.R. Tolkien Handbook: A Comprehensive Guide to His Life, Writings, and World of Middle-earth* (Grand Rapids, Mich.: Baker Book House, 1992);

Verlyn Flieger, *Splintered Light: Logos and Language in Tolkien's World* (Grand Rapids, Mich.: Eerdmans, 1983);

Robert Foster, *The Complete Guide to Middle-earth: From The Hobbit to The Silmarillion* (London: Allen & Unwin, 1978; New York: Ballantine, 1978);

J. R. R. Tolkien: Life and Legend — An Exhibition to Commemorate the Centenary of the Birth of J. R. R. Tolkien (1892–1992) (Oxford: Bodleian Library, 1992);

Clyde S. Kilby, *Tolkien and The Silmarillion* (Wheaton: Harold Shaw, 1976);

Paul H. Kocher, *Master of Middle-earth: The Fiction of J. R. R. Tolkien* (Boston: Houghton Mifflin, 1972); published as *Master of Middle-earth: The Achievement of J. R. R. Tolkien* (London: Thames & Hudson, 1972);

Roger Sale, *Modern Heroism: Essays on D. H. Lawrence, William Empson and J. R. R. Tolkien* (Berkeley: University of California Press, 1973);

Mary Salu and Robert T. Farrell, eds., *J. R. R. Tolkien, Scholar and Storyteller: Essays in Memoriam* (Ithaca, N.Y.: Cornell University Press, 1979);

T. A. Shippey, *The Road to Middle-earth* (London: Allen & Unwin, 1982; Boston: Houghton Mifflin, 1983);

John Tolkien and Priscilla Tolkien, *The Tolkien Family Album* (London: HarperCollins, 1992).

Papers:

A large collection of Tolkien manuscripts is housed at the Marquette University Library, Milwaukee, Wisconsin.

P. L. (Pamela Lyndon) Travers
(9 August 1899 –)

Patricia Demers
University of Alberta

BOOKS: *Moscow Excursion* (London: Gerald Howe, 1934);

Mary Poppins, illustrated by Mary Shepard (London: Gerald Howe, 1934; New York: Reynal & Hitchcock, 1934; revised edition, New York: Harcourt Brace Jovanovich, 1981; London: Collins, 1981);

Mary Poppins Comes Back, illustrated by Shepard (London: Lovat Dickeson & Thompson, 1935; New York: Reynal & Hitchcock, 1935);

Happy Ever After, illustrated by Shepard (New York: Reynal & Hitchcock, 1940);

Aunt Sass (New York: Reynal & Hitchcock, 1941);

I Go By Land, I Go By Sea, illustrated by Gertrude Hermes (London & New York: Harper, 1941);

Ah Wong (New York: High Grade Press, 1943);

Mary Poppins Opens the Door, illustrated by Shepard and Agnes Sim (New York: Harcourt, Brace, 1943);

Johnny Delaney (New York: High Grade Press, 1944);

Mary Poppins in the Park, illustrated by Shepard (London: Collins, 1952; New York: Harcourt, Brace, 1952);

Mary Poppins from A to Z, illustrated by Shepard (London: Collins, 1962; New York: Harcourt, Brace & World, 1962);

The Fox at the Manger, with wood engravings by Thomas Bewick (New York: Norton, 1962; London: Collins, 1963);

Maria Poppina ab A ad Z, illustrated by Shepard, translated into Latin by G. M. Lyne (New York: Harcourt, Brace & World, 1968);

A Mary Poppins Story for Coloring, illustrated by Shepard (London: Collins, 1969; New York: Harcourt, Brace & World, 1969);

Friend Monkey, illustrated by Charles Keeping (New York: Harcourt Brace Jovanovich, 1971; London: Collins, 1972);

George Ivanovitch Gurdjieff (Toronto: Traditional Studies Press, 1973);

P. L. Travers

Mary Poppins in the Kitchen: A Cookery Book with a Story, illustrated by Shepard (London: Collins, 1975; New York: Harcourt Brace Jovanovich, 1975);

About the Sleeping Beauty, illustrated by Keeping (New York: McGraw-Hill, 1975; London: Collins, 1977);

Two Pairs of Shoes, illustrated by Leo and Diane Dillon (New York: Viking, 1980);

Mary Poppins in Cherry Tree Lane, illustrated by Shepard (London: Collins, 1982; New York: Dell, 1983);

Mary Poppins and the House Next Door, illustrated by Shepard (London: Collins, 1988; New York: Delacorte, 1989);

What the Bee Knows; Reflections on Myth, Symbol, and Story (Wellingborough: Aquarian Press, 1989).

OTHER: "Only Connect," in *Readings on Children's Literature,* edited by S. Egoff, G. T. Stubbs, and L. F. Ashley (Toronto: Oxford University Press, 1969);

"The Death of AE: Irish Hero and Mystic," in *The Celtic Consciousness,* edited by Robert O'Driscoll (New York: Braziller, 1982).

SELECTED PERIODICAL PUBLICATIONS –
UNCOLLECTED: "The Heroes of Childhood; A Note on Nannies," *Horn Book,* 11 (May–June 1935): 147–155;

"My Childhood Bends Beside Me," *New Statesman and Nation,* 29 November 1952, p. 639;

"Where Did She Come From? Why Did She Go?," *Saturday Evening Post,* 7 November 1964, pp. 76–77;

"A Radical Innocence," *New York Times Book Review,* 9 May 1965, pp. 1, 38–39;

"The Black Sheep," *New York Times Book Review,* 7 November 1965, pp. 1, 61;

"In Search of the Hero; The Continuing Relevance of Myth and Fairy Tale," *Scripps College Bulletin,* 44 (March 1970);

"On Not Writing for Children," *Children's Literature,* 4 (1975): 15–22;

"A Letter from the Author," *Children's Literature,* 10 (1982): 214–217.

The author of ten books featuring the character Mary Poppins, P. L. Travers still prefers to use initials instead of her chosen name of Pamela Lyndon. Born Helen Lyndon Goff, she adopted this nom de plume to bring herself as close as possible to her father. She is equally reserved about the details of her life. She has given few direct glimpses of her Australian childhood, her Irish father and Scots-Irish mother, or her early addiction to writing and acting. She described herself in a 1966 interview with Richard Lingeman as "a very private person" and "rather shy of publicity." Travers has been just as forthright yet inscrutable with other interviewers. For her interview of the same year with Joseph Roddy she held forth on one of her favorite topics: "I don't write for children at all. I turn my back on them." Her answer to repeated questions about the origin of Mary Poppins is both candid and oblique: "the idea of Mary Poppins has been blowing in and out of me, like a curtain at a window, all my life" (*Saturday Evening Post,* 7 November 1964). She confided to Jerry Griswold (*Paris Review,* 1982) that the

process of creation is "dark" and "entirely spontaneous, . . . not thought out," while during Jonathan Cott's interview, which he included in *Pipers at the Gates of Dawn; The Wisdom of Children's Literature* (1983), she doubted "that biographies are of any use at all." This is not coyness on Travers's part, but the result of a fervently held belief in the wholeness and ultimate inscrutability of the human personality: as she put it to Neil Philip in 1982, 11 June 1982), "the ideas I had then move about in me now." Still an active writer in her mid nineties, Travers espouses a "radical innocence" (*New York Times Book Review,* 9 May 1956), a term borrowed from William Butler Yeats to convey an adult's linking "by some thin spider thread" to her youth.

The eldest of three children, Travers grew up in a home drenched in the Celtic twilight. Her father, Robert Travers Goff, was a lyrical and melancholy man, amiable and opinionated, who worked as a sugar planter in Australia after he had left Ireland to plant tea in Ceylon. Margaret Travers Goff, her Australian-born mother, contributed to the family's consciousness of things Irish by hiring a succession of Irish nannies. In "A Radical Innocence" (1965) Travers's recollections of her childhood are fond and discerning, evoking "an atmosphere in which tradition was still part of life, laws few, fixed and simple, and children taken for granted." Her memories of chewing ripe sugar cane, of nesting like a bird in the tall grasses and weeds, and of spending afternoons rambling amid the vines and jacaranda trees inform her early poems, dreams, and playacting. Growing up in the country, she delighted in making and populating miniature city parks – a pastime comparable to Jane Banks's designing of the idyllic Park for Poor People in *Mary Poppins in the Park* (1952).

Many parallels exist between Travers's childhood and the Poppins books. Her parents offered explanations for nothing. Margaret Goff actually purchased and consulted the book that Mary Poppins used and cherished, *Everything a Lady Should Know.* Travers's essay "The Heroes of Childhood; A Note on Nannies" (1935) reveals that among the memorable nannies assigned to the children was the stern Katie Nanna, who was remembered by her "layers of crackling aprons and always smelling of oatmeal." Another nanny, Bella or Bertha, had a parrot-headed umbrella which she wrapped ceremoniously in tissue paper upon her return from outings. Moreover, real-life equivalents existed for many of the animals, humans, and objects in the Poppins books.

Though she describes herself in "Only Connect" (1969) as "a passionately lazy child," Travers admits she "ate" her way, "like a bookworm," through the family library. Like the children's toys, the books were few and predictable: authors included Sir Walter Scott, Charles Dickens, William Shakespeare, Alfred Tennyson, Yeats, and other Irish poets. The children's books were even fewer: works by Beatrix Potter, E. Nesbit, Ethel Turner, Lewis Carroll, Charles Kingsley, George Farrow, and an assortment of raggedy penny books.

Her life changed dramatically in 1913 with the death of her father and the family's move to live with Christina Saraset ("Aunt Sass"), Travers's maternal great-aunt, in New South Wales. The scraps of information about her teenage life in Australia suggest that saddening responsibilities were placed on her as the widow's eldest child. Rather than accept a scholarship to the University of Sydney, she worked as a cashier for the Australian Gas and Light Company, as a dressmaker, and as a dancer in an army show. At eighteen she left Australia for England.

Travers worked as a reporter, had poetry published in the *Irish Statesman,* and was befriended by its editor, AE (George Russell). AE, as she recalls in "The Death of AE: Irish Hero and Mystic" (1982), saw her as "daughter, acolyte, apprentice, or as all three." She also met Yeats and established a reputation as a drama critic and travel essayist in the London-based *New English Weekly* before the first Poppins book appeared in 1934. During her recuperation from a serious but undisclosed illness, Travers began relating some of the escapades of Mary Poppins to two children. At the time she was living in the thatched Sussex cottage mentioned in *The Domesday Book* as "The Pound House." The combination of ancient surroundings and a youthful audience instigated storytelling reminiscent of the sort with which she had regaled her siblings in the old-young land of Australia.

Throughout her remarkably productive career Travers has continued to enunciate largely unchanging views about the omnipresence of myth and fairy tale in life; the possibilities to unify past and present, vision and actuality; and the needs of the child who is hidden in each of us. "On Not Writing for Children" (1975) clarifies why she disagrees so strenuously with the label "literature for children," maintaining that it is "hard both on children and on literature." She delights in having "no idea where childhood ends and maturity begins" and prefers to see the author as a "necessary lunatic who remains attentive and in readiness, unselfconscious, unconcerned, all disbelief suspended – even when frogs turn into princes and

nursemaids, against all gravity, slide up the bannisters."

Travers's poems in the *Irish Statesman* have an elfin charm: they are rich in potent, at times vertiginous metaphors foreshadowing many of the themes she has explored in a lifetime of writing. They maneuver ironic curves or keen with a cosmic grief at love gone wrong. She is absorbed with the professional, writerly pursuits of invention and theme-finding. In "Christopher" (4 April 1925) she is the proud culprit, or "song's thief," who has stolen "the sylvan note / Searing and nigh / Out of the linnet's throat / Where songs of poets float." One of the remarkable features of Travers's early poems is the way she gradually introduces erotic elements into the pastoral world. Her sonnet "Ghost of Two Sad Lovers" (9 October 1926) feelingly traces the steps of emotional grief:

> Never again shall sudden crimson birds
> Light on our cheeks; nor laughter's little doves
> Nest in our mouths; no longer shall we pass
> Imprinting warm foot-shapes upon crisp grass,
> And the sweet broken story of our loves
> Is lost beneath a wind of living words.

Clear-sightedness usually emerges from periods of disillusionment and dejection; in "The Plane Tree" (23 April 1927) she compares the lush foliage of summer and the bare trees of winter to the blandishments and exposed deceits of a philandering lover. Less pensive and more playful, "Prayer in a Field" (25 February 1928) is not merely a plea to the patron saint of lost objects but a celebration of the lovemaking of the poet and "Michael," which her lost cow used to observe. Travers's poems in the *New English Weekly* concern both childhood and sexuality. "A Memory of Childhood" (23 December 1937) grapples with the mysteries of Christmas and Easter as perceived by children. Set "in the sugar fields so green-o" of Travers's Australian past, the opening scene is festive and carefree, with its string of hyphenated and elongated words suggesting the gay, tambourine-punctuated rhythms of a linked dance:

> The father wore a silken coat
>   With an ear-ring in his ear-o,
> And silk of crimson about his throat
> And a wide-brimmed, straw-brimmed, grass-trimmed hat
>   Like a Spanish bandolero.

She captures the children's sense of awe and obeisance at the arrival of the "strange man," whom they consider "the King of Heaven," in the final stanza that, in emulating the earlier tone, and with a significant lowering of the last syllable, serves as a meditative coda:

> They knelt to the lord, the holy child,
>   That was in Bethlehem-o,
> And climbed the heavy hill and died
> With a wicked robber on either side
>   And died for each of them.
>   Oh!

For the *New English Weekly* Travers reviewed theater, films, and books from 1933 until the periodical's demise in 1949. She wrote about scores of Shakespeare performances – from those at the Old Vic to others in parks and barns – with the overriding idea that the playwright was both the timeless artist and the approachable contemporary: in a 30 September 1948 review she described Shakespeare as "a common-or-garden compact of blood and lymph and bone that one might bump up against any day walking around in time." Travers usually insists on overacting and promises that Shakespeare will triumph over the meanest surroundings. As illustration she offers this charming childhood memory (30 September 1948):

> I remember seeing "Hamlet" played in the school hall of a mining town in Australia. The show began at ten instead of the scheduled eight o'clock because the company, travelling by lorry from town to town, did not notice that the Hamlet of the evening had inadvertently fallen off as they rounded a bend. He had walked the last ten miles carrying the suitcase he had been clutching at the time of the accident, and, spurred by unkind fate and the furious catcalls of the waiting audience, he and the rest of the company gave the best performance of "Hamlet" I have ever seen. The echo still resounds.

Her criticism can be acerbic as well as nostalgic. Taking aim at two Disney cartoons for 1938, Travers objects to anthropomorphic tendencies and denounces unctuous sanctimony. She lectures the creators of "Mickey Mouse" that in place of the animation of "semi-human emotions" the audience deserves a fairy-tale spectacle that builds on "moment-to-moment absurdity" (3 February 1938). Because children are "natural moralists," she reminds them, the *truly* melodramatic character in "Snow White" remains the midnight hag. At the heart of Disney's "enlargement of the animal world," Travers discovers "a corresponding deflation of all human values" and "a profound cynicism at the root" (21 April 1938). For exactly opposite reasons, she lavishes praise on T. S. Eliot's *Old Possum's Book of Practical Cats* (1939) and Beatrix Potter's tales. She delights

Illustration by Mary Shepard in Mary Poppins from A to Z *(1962)*

in the fiction that Eliot's ditties, masterpieces of erudition, are the results of "arduous research" in feline ways (14 December 1939) and applauds Potter's brief, chastened style, its "underlying irony and non-nonsense quality that does not shrink from terrible happenings" (10 April 1947). In her review of Margaret Lane's 1946 biography of Potter, Travers, writing as "Milo Reve," posits some definitive principles governing the writing of stories for children: the book must please the author, must be told to the "hidden child" within the author, and in its combination of "ignorance and innocence" must be a "primer of magic and wisdom."

The character who incarnates such primacy – for Travers and for generations of readers – is Mary Poppins. For all her propriety and tidiness, Mary Poppins is the quintessential shape-shifter. As efficiently as she orders the nursery world at 17 Cherry Tree Lane, this extraordinary nanny celebrates, with an insider's élan, a series of gay, dithyrambic events. These unpredictable episodes, skewing the conventions of time and space, and happily suspending the disbelief of her young charges, show not just one side but several differing facets of the unique and talented heroine. At home in both a domestic reality and mythic universe, this enigma outwits all attempts to pin her down.

To appreciate her sparkling graces means to accept incongruities and mysteries. With her wooden-doll features, contemptuous sniffs, and tart rebuffs, she is the controlling, yet ultimately inexplicable, force in the Banks household. Every member of the community is subjected to her smugness; she flummoxes Mrs. Banks, reduces Jane and Michael to instant penitence or fearful silence, and leaves ordinarily gregarious shopkeepers stammering and diffident. But the children cling to her hard, bony body more often out of veneration than for protection. This curt and censorious figure is also, on occasion, an enchanting storyteller. Her voice, which can be icicle sharp, communicates with animals (wild and domestic), babies, toys, constellations, mystical characters, the Sun, and the Moon. Her eyes not only catch the pleasing reflection of her own new hats, gloves, and handbags but also penetrate the depths of the children's thoughts. The welcoming smell of newly made toast hangs about Mary Poppins, but her fixity and sense of purpose also make her an imposing pillar of starch. Proud of never wasting time with officious bumpkins like the Park Keeper, she has relatives who float in the air, turn Catherine wheels, whirl atop music boxes, and emerge from plasticine blobs. After each extraordinary escapade, like rolling and bobbing airborne during afternoon tea, waltzing with the Sun, or conversing with a unicorn, she flatly denies any connection with the fantastic. But her sympathies are easily engaged – for the poor Match-man who cannot afford an outing, the scantily clad star on a Christmas shopping spree, the transplanted court jester who appears to be an indolent man-of-no-work, and the marble statue longing for some human companionship. Although Mary Poppins defies understanding or explanation, the victims of her quick tongue label her with such tags as the Misfit, Caliban, or wolf in sheep's clothing. The more discerning characterizations come from those who revel in her remarkable metamorphosing powers; for them and for millions of fans – in twenty-five languages – she lives as the Great Exception, the Marvellous Wonder, the Mind Reader, and as what *Mary Poppins in the Park* (1952) calls the "glow-worm shining to show . . . the right way home."

Travers's sextet of Mary Poppins books, with the appended quartet of bibelots, stretches across a period of fifty-four years of Travers's life and is the home and core of her writing. In this canon of Poppins books certain stages of development are observable – even though Travers maintains that Mary Poppins has not changed at all. The first four, from *Mary Poppins* (1934) to *Mary Poppins in the Park* form a solid unit. Chapters decrease in number, and increase in size proportionally, from twelve to ten to eight to six. Characters reappear and the list of Mary Poppins's eccentric relatives grows. The often playful and ironic interrelationship of chapters in *Mary Poppins, Mary Poppins Comes Back* (1935), *Mary Poppins Opens the Door* (1943), and *Mary Poppins in the Park* is clear, with such titles as "Miss Lark's Andrew" and "Miss Andrew's Lark" and "Bad Tuesday," "Bad Wednesday," and "Lucky Thursday." Scenes of wild, cosmic celebration, where rings and chains of dance climax the festivities, are common elements, too, in "Full Moon," "The Evening Out," and "Hallowe'en." Similar formulas for whirling in and out of situations and, at times in "Balloons *and* Balloons" and "Peppermint Horses," above situations unite this quartet of books. Also recurring are Mary Poppins's formulaic denials of unseemly behavior, invariably followed by some sort of emblematic proof, a vestige of the fantastic episode visible in the domestic world. The schemes of shrews, like Miss Persimmon, Mrs. Clump, and Mrs. Mo, who harass Mary Poppins's blithe male relatives, usually backfire, but occasionally, as with Miss Tartlet, love overcomes peevishness. A concern for bringing Mary Poppins in and out of the picture plays a big role in the first three books, while the fourth is a series of discrete events that may have occurred at any time during her three visits.

The next four books, *Mary Poppins from A to Z* (1962), *Maria Poppina ab A ad Z* (1968), *A Mary Poppins Story for Coloring* (1969), and *Mary Poppins in the Kitchen: A Cookery Book with a Story* (1975), are primarily diversions recalling earlier events and previously introduced characters. Travers's most recent work, including *Mary Poppins in Cherry Tree Lane* (1982) and *Mary Poppins and the House Next Door* (1988), is anything but a tiresome rehash. Incorporating many of the insights gleaned from Travers's continuing exploration of myth and fairy tale, these full-length stories, each consisting of a single chapter, examine harmony and restitution while upholding the importance of the unresolved, unclosed narrative.

Part of the reason for the popularity of Mary Poppins is that, in the field of children's literature, she is a unique and an unparalleled nanny. Until her advent, governesses or tutors whose duty was the moral development of their charges were tedious, stock characters. Mary Poppins closes the gap between adult mentor and pliable child student. Here is a nanny whom children rush to obey. She enters the child's pastoral world and, rather than shattering illusions, joyously extends and encourages awareness. Neither a factotum nor a pious exemplar, she is not obsessed with moral dictates; nor is she above indulging in vanity. She uses entertainment and storytelling as ways of accepting and perhaps understanding those difficult concepts of unity, paradox, and continuity – concepts which, for her, precede and transcend morality.

Jonathan Cott's label of "cosmic" for Mary Poppins applies for several reasons. Her quickness to diagnose, assess, and measure the behavior of the Banks children, as she does in opening segments of the first three books by administering medicine, thrusting a thermometer into their mouths, and stretching a tape measure along their heights, betokens a certain righteousness on her part. Hers is an Old Testament righteousness that fills the measure and meets a standard (Deut. 25:15; Lev. 19:36). Her participation in the Hamadryad's Grand Chain ("Full Moon," *Mary Poppins*); the greeting she receives in the constellations' golden ring, "a swaying . . . mass of horns and hooves and manes and tails" ("The Evening Out," *Mary Poppins Comes Back*); her recognition at the Terrapin's party ("High Tide," *Mary Poppins Opens the Door*); and her birthday-eve celebration with shadows ("Hallowe'en," *Mary Poppins In the Park*) indicate that the powers of this nanny surpass all ordinary conventions and chronology. These celebrations are, strictly speaking, liturgical, which makes all the more sense when one traces the Hamadryad's observation "that to eat and be eaten are the same thing," to "The Hymn of Christ" in the Apocryphal *Acts of John*.

Mary Poppins seems to come from another world and time and yet to be also a futuristic model of understanding. Her syncretistic belief in unity, imagination, and wisdom inspires many like-minded friends. The Hamadryad insists that "bird and beast and stone and star – we are all one, all one." In *Mary Poppins Comes Back* when the children query the Sun about the difference between "what is real and what is not," his answer is a poetic one, "that to think a thing is to make it true." The Terrapin in *Mary Poppins Opens the Door* reminds them of the sea's importance as originator and model of their world: "the land came out of the sea . . . [and] each thing on the earth has a brother here." In *Mary Poppins in the Park* the Bird Woman lets them see the transporting value of the shadow, "the other part of you, the outside of your inside," as a way to wisdom, which goes "through things, through and out the other side." Although Mary Poppins has phenomenal abilities, such as ushering in spring over-

night, and exceptional friends, she also exemplifies and extols trusted human virtues like loyalty and compassion. The offer of her handkerchief as a cushion for the sleeping Robertson Ay and her story of the Tramp-Angel's awareness of everyone's illusions (*Mary Poppins in the Park*) are moving instances of this storyteller's desire to embrace and possibly heal all.

This singular heroine also raises some questions. It is curious that this talented figure must pass through so many entrances and exits to the various episodes, as well as blow into a whirl out of the Banks family home three times. Is such narrative coming and going a reminder from Travers that this mythic creature, with a foot in reality, must also submit to the logical interrogatives of how, when, and where? Mary Poppins's peremptory refusals to answer questions and her outright denials of involvement in fantastic events raise the issue of deliberately jeopardized credibility. Is this reverse psychology? Does Mary Poppins deny so vociferously to incite readers to believe in, affirm, and acclaim her with added enthusiasm? Despite the discernment of her gimlet eyes, she proves amazingly susceptible to Michael's transparent flattery. Is this Poppins peccadillo meant to corroborate her essential childlikeness? Travers offers no answers, admitting to Jonathan Cott that "anything I write is all question."

Travers served as consultant for the Disney film of *Mary Poppins* (1963). Although she hoped, as she disclosed to Roy Newquist in 1967, "that its effect [would] be to bring more people to the book," she confesses to being "disturbed at seeing it so externalized, so oversimplified, so generalized." Far from the subtlety, suggestiveness, and mythical allusions of the books, the film is designed to highlight the singing, dancing, and comedic skills of Julie Andrews, Dick Van Dyke, and an acrobatic ensemble, along with the talents of the animators employed by Disney Studios. The Edwardian setting, which Travers apparently suggested to Disney in order to retain the tale's "freshness," and the frothiness of Glynis Johns as Mrs. Banks, in a trivializing suffragette getup, are not the most saddening or unfaithful aspects of this adaptation. What is most jarring, and what probably argues against making such a book into a film, is the use of cartoon figures to translate and invariably reduce the fantasy. Ironies abound in the Disney version: the addition of "numbers" about the importance of bank accounts, moneymaking, and steady employment, mundanities that seem totally removed from the heightened reality of the books; and the decision to remake the slender, al-

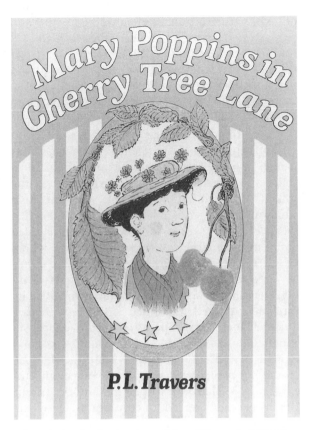

Dust jacket for the American edition of Travers's 1982 Mary Poppins tale

most androgynous, figure of Mary Poppins – presented in Mary Shepard's line drawings as a tailored and trim, poised and sensible woman, with her dark hair scraped away from the face and bound in a knot at the back of her head – into a fussy, petticoat-flipping coquette of a musical comedy star.

The six books in the Poppins canon (*Mary Poppins, Mary Poppins Comes Back, Mary Poppins Opens the Door, Mary Poppins in the Park, Mary Poppins in Cherry Tree Lane, Mary Poppins and the House Next Door*) are closely related. They share such features as energetic transformations, reconciled opposites, and heightened awareness of reality through dreams and memory of the past. There is also a distinct and developing sense of narrative art linking the episodes of the first four books with the stories of the last two. As the series proceeds, the individuation of the Banks children is more precise, and the psychological realism of their characters more detailed. In addition, as the references to books themselves increase in *Mary Poppins Opens the Door* and *Mary Poppins in the Park,* Travers's own fabulation becomes more noticeably self-conscious. Her return to the

Poppins vein more than a quarter of a century later, in *Mary Poppins in Cherry Tree Lane* and *Mary Poppins and the House Next Door,* or, as she would prefer to put it, the surprising return visit of Mary Poppins to her consciousness, shows a desire to reexamine the same issues, without episodic fragmentation but by blending all the old themes into discrete, full-length stories. This recent work aims to incorporate outsiders into community. *Mary Poppins in Cherry Tree Lane* links the Park Keeper to a moonstruck celebration, and *Mary Poppins and the House Next Door* finds an extended family for the caustic Miss Andrew.

Critical comment on Travers's accomplishment has not stayed at an even keel. While Anne Carroll Moore welcomed the first book as "a Pleasure of the first water" and Jane Yolen lionized Travers as a believer in myth who presents "strong, beautiful, alternate worlds for young people," John Rowe Townsend wondered if the American popularity might not propagate "illusions about English domestic life." Perry Nodelman concluded that, despite Travers's insistent advertising, neither Poppins nor her fantasy is engaging. Although Kenneth J. Reckford claimed all the Poppins stories as Dionysian fairy tales, Humphrey Carpenter found the recent additions to the canon slight and skimpy. The issue for Albert V. Schwartz and Robert B. Moore was racism in the "Bad Tuesday" chapter of *Mary Poppins.* Schwartz charged that it is "a racist nightmare," teaching "children to identify their fears with Third World people." Travers made no changes when the copyright was renewed in 1962, but she revised the chapter for the 1972 paperback reprint by altering most of the "pikaninny" language to standard English. The revised version of *Mary Poppins* (1981), which replaces the racial stereotypes with Polar Bear, Macaw, Dolphin, and Panda, is now the only one for sale in most bookstores.

A less-known and less-commented-on period of Travers's career involves the stories composed and published during her wartime evacuation to the United States. They are all attempts at reintegration, harmony, and peace. Though separated by both time and geography, she devoted three of her four Christmas and New Year's gift books to reminiscences of her Australian childhood. *Ah Wong* (1943) recalls the family's Chinese cook and *Johnny Delaney* (1944), their Irish handyman. The maternal great-aunt, Christina Saraset, left an indelible impression on Travers even before the family came to live with her. "Stern and tender, secret and proud, anonymous and loving," Aunt Sass, a spinster and, in some ways, a holy terror, was planted firmly as a figure of importance and authority in Travers's family, "like the central shaft of a merry-go-round." The other gift book, *Happy Ever After* (1940), which is the first draft of a chapter of *Mary Poppins Opens the Door,* charmingly permits a benign and extended glance at the few seconds when "all things are at one." Two additional books from this period employ the voice of the child, as diarist or questioner, to comment on the fractures or fresh starts effected by the war. An eleven-year-old diarist is the storyteller in *I Go By Land, I Go By Sea* (1941). With her acute ear for speech patterns of a 1940s British adolescent and sympathetic affiliation with the sensitive, artistic older child, Travers allows Sabrina Lind to recount her own experiences and feelings in crossing the Atlantic and living in America for the remainder of the war. Though published in 1962, *The Fox at the Manger,* Travers's narrative of her afternoon adventure with three little boys whom she takes to the first postwar Christmas Eve carol service at St. Paul's, is clearly set in the London of 1945. The symmetry of gifts given and ungiven unites the halves of the story; the London section climaxes with the "melodious outcry" of the Christmas bells in which Travers hears "*concord, harmony, unison, peace!,*" while the stable scene closes quietly with her vision of "barnyard beasts lying down with the fox." Since "everything must be whole," Travers underscores the hopes and insights she nursed throughout the wartime period.

In articulating her lifelong views about myth and fairy tale, Travers's most recent writing serves as a checklist for the articles of her creed. Her long brooding on the monkey lord Hanuman, of Hindu myth, resulted in the full-length story *Friend Monkey* (1971). Monkey's peregrinations, along with his more illuminating than bungling helpfulness, are some indications of the multifacetedness of the hero and the omnipresence of myth, both absorbing topics for Travers. She has pinned up her colors in many essays and talks. As an ever-inquiring devotee, she distinguishes the reverential serendipity of her approach from that of folklorists, anthropologists, and psychoanalysts. In "Only Connect," she sees fairy tales as "minuscule reaffirmations of myth . . . fallen into time and locality." Her Clark Lecture at Scripps College in Claremont, California, "In Search of the Hero" (1970), reiterates this position, maintaining that "we live in myth and fairy tale as the egg yolk lives in its albumen" and that the hero, in each form, seeks to discover his or her self-identity. In the afterword to her retelling of the story of Sleeping Beauty, Travers hints at many of the conditions that make this discovery possible. An "un-

differentiated" world, without separation between self and milieu, is crucial to the fairy tale and "common to all children." The infinitude of this world, when "the time is always now and endless," when nothing is explained, and when narrated events make their own links in our lives, is appropriate to her oft-repeated axiom that thinking is linking, which she defines as "the essence of fairy tale."

The desire to explore complex yet timeless ideas about the fairy tale lies behind *About the Sleeping Beauty* (1975). The book is not an entirely successful undertaking. Too often Travers overloads passages, forcing this fairy tale to lecture on its own importance. As the hundred years pass, the story of the princess becomes, for the local folk, a fairy tale, "something forever true but far." Not content with this label, Travers waxes in a Jungian mode: "Men came to think of the Princess, not as a person anymore, but as a secret within themselves – a thing they would dearly wish to discover if they could but make the effort." The motif of self-discovery is pronounced in this retelling, to the point of being cumbersomely underlined. As the prince gazes on the princess for the first time, Travers observes, "He knew himself to be at the centre of the world and that, in him, all men stood there, gazing at their hearts' desire – or perhaps their inmost selves." Their kiss, which causes cosmic reverberations, results in another series of over-dramatic events, as "together they plumbed all height, all depth, and rose up strongly to the surface, back to the shores of time."

Her essays, anecdotes, retellings, and occasional poetry in *Parabola* reiterate many similar arguments about myth and fairy tale. They are, in general, more successful because they are more contained. From its inception in 1976, this New York-based, illustrated quarterly "Magazine of Myth and Tradition" has been aimed at a general, educated readership. A consulting editor from the beginning, Travers has contributed short essays and reviews to almost every theme-oriented issue. *What the Bee Knows; Reflections on Myth, Symbol, and Story* (1989) is a selection of these essays and stories.

Travers continues to search in her own vale of soul-making. That is, she still strives to unite past and present, to respond to conditions that surround her today through a sympathetic, humane, and unglamorized reentry to the mythic past.

References:

Edwina Burness and Jerry Griswold, "The Art of Fiction LXXIII: P. L. Travers," *Paris Review,* 86 (1982): 210–229;

Humphrey Carpenter, "Mary Poppins, Force of Nature," *New York Times Book Review,* 27 August 1989, p. 29;

Jonathan Cott, *Pipers at the Gates of Dawn; The Wisdom of Children's Literature* (New York: Random House, 1983);

Patricia Demers, *P. L. Travers* (Boston: Twayne, 1991);

Richard Lingeman, "Visit with Mary Poppins and P. L. Travers," *New York Times Magazine,* 25 December 1966, pp. 12–13, 27–29;

Anne Carroll Moore, "Mary Poppins," *Horn Book,* 11 (January–February 1935): 6–7;

Robert B. Moore, "A Letter from a Critic," *Children's Literature,* 10 (1982): 211–213;

Roy Newquist, *Conversations* (Chicago: Rand, McNally, 1967);

Perry Nodelman, "Introduction," in *Touchstones: Reflections on the Best in Children's Literature,* volume 3, edited by Nodelman (West Lafayette, Ind.: Purdue University Children's Literature Association, 1989);

Neil Philip, "The Writer and the Nanny Who Never Explain," *Times Educational Supplement,* 11 June 1982, p. 42;

Kenneth J. Reckford, *Aristophanes' Old-and-New Comedy* (Chapel Hill: University of North Carolina Press, 1987);

Joseph Roddy, "A Visit with the Real Mary Poppins," *Look* (13 December 1966): 84–86;

Albert V. Schwartz, "*Mary Poppins* Revised: An Interview with P. L. Travers," *Interracial Books for Children Bulletin,* 5, no. 3 (1974): 1–5;

John Rowe Townsend, *Written for Children; An Outline of English-language Children's Literature* (London: Garnet Miller, 1965);

Jane Yolen, "Makers of Modern Myths," *Horn Book,* 51 (1975): 496–497.

Henry Treece

(1911 – 10 June 1966)

Caroline C. Hunt
College of Charleston

BOOKS: *38 Poems* (London: Fortune, 1940);

Towards a Personal Armageddon (Prairie City, Ill.: Decker, 1941);

Invitation and Warning (London: Faber & Faber, 1942);

The Black Seasons (London: Faber & Faber, 1945);

Collected Poems (New York: Knopf, 1946);

How I See Apocalypse (London: Drummond, 1946);

I Cannot Go Hunting Tomorrow (London: Grey Walls Press, 1946);

The Haunted Garden (London: Faber & Faber, 1947);

Dylan Thomas: "Dog Among the Fairies" (London: Drummond, 1949; New York: De Graff, 1949; revised edition, London: Benn, 1956; New York: De Graff, 1956);

The Exiles (London: Faber & Faber, 1952);

The Dark Island (London: Gollancz, 1952; New York: Random House, 1952); republished as *The Savage Warriors* (New York: Avon, 1952);

The Rebels (London: Gollancz, 1953);

Desperate Journey, illustrated by Richard Kennedy (London: Faber & Faber, 1954);

Legions of the Eagle, illustrated by Christine Price (London: Bodley Head, 1954; Winchester, Mass.: Allen & Unwin, 1954);

The Eagles Have Flown, illustrated by Price (London: Bodley Head, 1954; New York: Criterion, 1954);

Hounds of the King, illustrated by Price (London: Bodley Head, 1955; New York: Criterion, 1955);

Ask for King Billy, illustrated by Kennedy (London: Faber & Faber, 1955);

The Carnival King (London: Faber & Faber, 1955);

Viking's Dawn, illustrated by Price (London: Bodley Head, 1955; New York: Criterion, 1957);

The Golden Strangers (London: Bodley Head, 1956; New York: Random House, 1957); republished as *The Invaders* (New York: Avon, 1956);

The Great Captains (London: Bodley Head, 1956; New York: Random House, 1956);

Henry Treece

The Road to Miklagard, illustrated by Price (London: Bodley Head, 1957; New York: Criterion, 1957);

Men of the Hills, illustrated by Price (London: Bodley Head, 1957; New York: Criterion, 1958);

Hunter Hunted, illustrated by Kennedy (London: Faber & Faber, 1957);

The Children's Crusade, illustrated by Price (London: Bodley Head, 1958); republished as *Perilous Pilgrimage* (New York: Criterion, 1959);

Red Queen, White Queen (London: Bodley Head, 1958; New York: Random House, 1958); republished as *The Pagan Queen* (New York: Avon, 1958);

Don't Expect Any Mercy (London: Faber & Faber, 1958);

The Return of Robinson Crusoe, illustrated by Will Nickless (London: Hulton Press, 1958); republished as *The Further Adventures of Robinson Crusoe* (New York: Criterion, 1958);

The Master of Badger's Hall (New York: Random House, 1959); republished as *A Fighting Man* (London: Bodley Head, 1960);

Wickham and the Armada, illustrated by Hookway Cowles (London: Hulton Press, 1959);

The Bombard, illustrated by Price (London: Bodley Head, 1959); republished as *Ride into Danger* (New York: Criterion, 1959);

Castles and Kings, illustrated by Walter Hodges (London: Batsford, 1959; New York: Criterion, 1959);

Red Settlement (London: Bodley Head, 1960);

The True Book About Castles, illustrated by G. H. Channing (London: Muller, 1960);

Viking's Sunset, illustrated by Price (London: Bodley Head, 1960; New York: Criterion, 1961);

The Golden One, illustrated by William Stobbs (London: Bodley Head, 1961; New York: Criterion, 1961);

Jason (London: Bodley Head, 1961; New York: Random House, 1961);

The Jet Beads, illustrated by W. A. Sillince (London: Brockhampton, 1961);

Man with a Sword, illustrated by Stobbs (London: Bodley Head, 1962; New York: Pantheon, 1964);

War Dog, illustrated by Roger Payne (London: Brockhampton, 1962; New York: Criterion, 1963);

The Crusades (London: Bodley Head, 1962; New York: Random House, 1962); revised as *Know About the Crusades* (London: Blackie, 1963);

Horned Helmet, illustrated by Charles Keeping (London: Brockhampton, 1963; New York: Criterion, 1963);

Electra (London: Bodley Head, 1963); republished as *The Amber Princess* (New York: Random House, 1963);

Fighting Men: How Men Have Fought Through the Ages, with R. E. Oakeshott (London: Brockhampton, 1963; New York: Putnam, 1965);

The Burning of Njal, illustrated by Bernard Blatch (London: Brockhampton, 1964; New York: Criterion, 1964);

The Last of the Vikings, illustrated by Keeping (London: Brockhampton, 1964); republished as *The Last Viking* (New York: Pantheon, 1966);

Oedipus (London: Bodley Head, 1964); republished as *The Eagle King* (New York: Random House, 1965);

Splintered Sword, illustrated by Keeping (London: Brockhampton, 1965; New York: Duell, Sloan & Pearce, 1965);

Killer in Dark Glasses (London: Faber & Faber, 1965);

Bang, You're Dead! (London: Faber & Faber, 1965);

Hounds of the King, with Two Radio Plays, illustrated by Stuart Tresilian (London: Longmans, 1965);

The Bronze Sword, illustrated by Mary Russon (London: Hamish Hamilton, 1965); revised as *The Centurion* (New York: Meredith, 1967);

The Queen's Brooch (London: Hamish Hamilton, 1966; New York: Putnam, 1967);

The Green Man (London: Bodley Head, 1966; New York: Putnam, 1966);

Vinland the Good, illustrated by Stobbs (London: Bodley Head, 1967); republished as *Westward to Vinland* (New York: Phillips, 1967);

Swords from the North (London: Faber & Faber, 1967; New York: Pantheon, 1967);

The Windswept City, illustrated by Faith Jaques (London: Hamish Hamilton, 1967; New York: Meredith, 1968);

The Dream-Time, illustrated by Keeping (London: Brockhampton, 1967; New York: Meredith, 1968);

The Invaders: Three Stories, illustrated by Keeping (London: Brockhampton, 1972; New York: Crowell, 1972);

The Viking Saga [reprint of trilogy comprising *Viking's Dawn, The Road to Miklagard,* and *Viking's Sunset*] (Harmondsworth: Puffin, 1985);

The Magic Wood: A Poem, illustrated by Barry Moser (New York: HarperCollins, 1992).

OTHER: *The New Apocalypse,* edited by Treece and J. F. Hendry (London: Fortune, 1939);

The White Horseman: Prose and Verse of the New Apocalypse, edited by Treece and Hendry (London: Routledge, 1941);

The Crown and the Sickle, edited by Treece and Hendry (London: Staples, 1943);

Wartime Harvest, edited by Treece and Stefan Schimanski (London: Bale & Staples, 1943);

Transformation, edited by Treece and Schimanski (London: Gollancz, 1943);

Transformation Two, edited by Treece and Schimanski (London: Drummond, 1944);

Air Force Poetry, edited by Treece and John Pudney (London: Bodley Head, 1944);

Herbert Read: An Introduction to His Work by Various Hands, edited by Treece (London: Faber &

Faber, 1944; Port Washington, N.Y.: Kennikat Press, 1969);

A Map of Hearts: A Collection of Short Stories, edited by Treece and Schimanski (London: Drummond, 1944);

Transformation Three, edited by Treece and Schimanski (London: Drummond, 1947);

Leaves in the Storm: A Book of Diaries, edited by Treece and Schimanski (London: Drummond, 1947);

Selected Poems from Swinburne, edited by Treece (London: Grey Walls Press, 1948; New York: Crown Classics, 1948);

A New Romantic Anthology, edited by Treece and Schimanski (London: Grey Walls Press, 1949); republished as *A New Romantic Anthology* (Norwalk, Conn.: New Directions, 1949).

Throughout the 1950s and early 1960s in postwar Britain, Henry Treece wrote of the turning points of British and Scandinavian history – or, as he liked to call them, "crossroads." Treece's career as a writer for children spanned barely a dozen years, but in this short period he produced more than thirty novels for young readers as well as several works of nonfiction. During the same years Treece also published a dozen books for adult readers and many scripts, for radio and live performance, that have never been published. His output is especially impressive considering the fact that, until the last seven years of his life, Treece was a full-time schoolmaster. Like his fellow historical novelists Rosemary Sutcliff and Geoffrey Trease, he sought to replace a merely sentimental, simplistic view of empire with a rendition of history in which good and bad were intertwined; like them, he fought against the false language in which historical fiction had often been written, especially for children. Unlike Sutcliff and Trease, though, Treece had an ambivalent attitude toward war and violence. Unlike them, also, he had already made his reputation as a poet, critic, and editor before turning to books for children.

Treece was born in Wednesbury, Staffordshire, in 1911 (the exact date is uncertain), the child of Richard and Mary Mason Treece. His father's family had been in this area, the Black Country near Nottingham, since at least the sixteenth century, and Treece grew up with an extensive background of family history and stories. His mother's family had come originally from Wales, and Treece sometimes referred to himself as Welsh (adding, in one letter, "with little love for the English"). From an early age he was given historical books to read, often with striking illustrations – an influence that

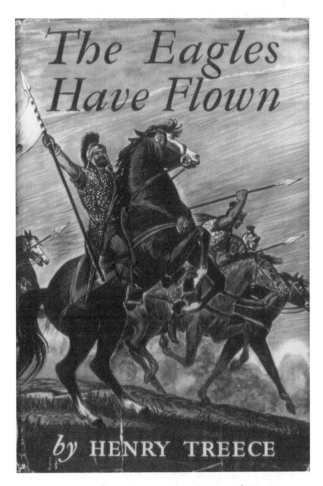

Dust jacket for Treece's 1954 Arthurian novel (Lilly Library, Indiana University)

led him, both in his teaching methods and in his books, to present history in terms of character in action and to emphasize the pictorial. He chose literature, not history, as his special subject at Wednesbury High School for Boys, where he also developed what became a lifelong interest in drawing and sketching. Awarded a scholarship to Birmingham, he read English, history, and Spanish and received his degree in 1933, followed by a diploma from the University of Santander (also in 1933) and a diploma in education from Birmingham in 1934. At university Treece was active in the literary magazine and the drama society; perhaps more surprising, he served as captain of the university boxing team.

From 1934 until coronary thrombosis made it impossible for him to pursue two careers at once, Treece was a full-time teacher: first at a school for delinquents at Shustoke, Leicestershire; then at The College, Cleobury Mortimer (which soon closed); then at Tynemouth School in Northumberland; and finally at the grammar school at Barton-upon-Humber, Lincolnshire, where he remained from 1938 until retirement in 1959. In 1939 Treece married Mary Woodman, who had taught with him at Cleobury Mortimer. When World War II began, Treece served with the Volunteer Reserve of the Royal Air Force, reaching the rank of flight lieutenant. His eyesight was too poor to allow him to fly, and Treece spent most of his war years as an intelligence officer, returning afterward to Barton-upon-Humber as senior English master. The Treeces had three children, David (who died in infancy), Jennifer Elizabeth, and Gareth Richard. Treece was active in the Barton Drama Club and the Barton Cricket Club; a more private avocation was music, particularly the piano – which he played well – and the Flamenco guitar.

Long before turning to children's books, Treece was a poet and one of the cofounders, with J. F. Hendry, of the New Apocalypse movement. Beginning with a manifesto late in 1938, the New Apocalypse opposed the Machine Age, mechanistic thinking, and totalitarianism; the movement promoted individual freedom and the importance of myth. From 1938 to 1950 Treece edited thirteen anthologies (many with Stefan Schimanski) and published seven volumes of his own poems, while also producing a considerable amount of criticism. Treece knew many of the writers he published in his anthologies, including Dylan Thomas, Herbert Read, and Stephen Spender. Through the efforts of T. S. Eliot, Treece's own poems were published by Faber and Faber. Treece's last collaboration with Schimanski, *A New Romantic Anthology* (1949), marked the end of Neo-Romanticism and the crest of the critical reaction against it. One of the prime examples of this was Robert Conquest's *New Lines: An Anthology* (1956), which included a strongly anti-Apocalyptic introduction by the editor. During 1950–1951 Treece lectured frequently on British radio and also spoke in the United States.

Gradually, as the Apocalyptic movement dissolved, Treece ceased to write poetry. He had begun writing short stories and now began to explore dramatic forms: a play that mixed verse with prose, "Footsteps in the Sea," was performed in Nottingham in 1955 but never published. Treece's more straightforward historical play about Edward II, *The Carnival King,* was performed in Nottingham in 1954 and published by Faber and Faber the following year. During the early to mid 1950s Treece wrote numerous historical scripts for use in schools and on the radio. He had written one novel for adults, *The Dark Island* (1952), when a school col-

league, in conjunction with Treece's agent and a discerning editor at Bodley Head, encouraged him to consider writing for children. From 1954 until Treece's death in 1966, the largest part of his output was for the juvenile market.

Treece's juvenile titles fall naturally into several subgroups: novels about the Celtic/Roman past, novels about the Vikings, other historical novels, and nonhistorical novels. In many cases a juvenile title has links to others on the same subject, and often to a parallel adult title as well. Like his poetry Treece's juvenile fiction had a mixed reception for many years. Most critics praised his accuracy, but some disliked his repetitive motifs and his portrayal of violence and brutality. Treece's insistence upon describing how historical characters behaved (rather than casting them as heroes) caused some reviewers to complain that his books contained few characters whom young readers could admire or emulate.

The earliest of Treece's historical novels for children concerns the conflict between Celts and Romans during the Roman occupation of Britain. *Legions of the Eagle* (1954) mirrors the tensions he had explored earlier in *The Dark Island* and, before that, in an unpublished BBC radio script, a narrative poem, and a short story: the tale of Caractacus. Gwydion, the thirteen-year-old hero, is Belgic by birth; Treece assigned him a Roman friend and a Silurian slave, thus making possible many conversations about differing customs and ways of life. *Legions of the Eagle* revolves around an essentially private quest (Caractacus himself scarcely appears) but conveys two powerful messages: the importance of tolerance and the uselessness of war. In his second juvenile title, *The Eagles Have Flown* (1954), Treece moves forward to the late fifth century A.D. for an Arthurian story about a half-Roman, half-Celtic youngster, Festus, who witnesses much of the career of Artos the Bear (Arthur). In what became a consistent pattern, Treece was also working on an adult Arthur book, which became *The Great Captains* (1956). Though neither *Legions of the Eagle* nor *The Eagles Have Flown* received much critical attention (compared to his poetry), in both books Treece developed themes that he would repeat many times: the search for a father, growth through voyaging, and the meeting of two cultures.

Treece returned to the subject of Roman Britain a decade later, but first he branched out into the period of Viking exploration; he also wrote a series of contemporary thrillers for children, as well as radio scripts. The first of the thrillers, *Desperate Journey,* came out in the same year as *Legions of the*

Eagle and *The Eagles Have Flown;* in this John Buchan–like adventure, John Ferguson (an adult protagonist, as in all the thrillers) journeys to remote parts of Britain in order to save a secret formula. The same journey motif informs the four thrillers about private investigator Gordon Stewart: *Ask for King Billy* (1955), *Don't Expect Any Mercy* (1958), *Killer in Dark Glasses* (1965), and *Bang, You're Dead!* (1965). One thriller, *Hunter Hunted* (1957), introduced the appealing amateur boxer Bill Frankland. Though Treece continued producing them throughout his career, these books never attracted much critical attention and did not appear in the United States.

The area that Treece had made peculiarly his own was the Scandinavian backdrop to British history. Treece's dozen books about Scandinavia bracket the Viking age from beginning to end and include both retellings of ancient saga and original works. As in his books about Roman Britain, Treece identified with the older way of life that was to be inevitably replaced by a more modern one. As in the thrillers, he created a fast-paced plot for each book: one that matched the spare, action-oriented style of the Norse sagas.

A connected group of Scandinavian stories, centered on the figure of Harald Sigurdson, concerns the earliest Viking voyages, about 780 A.D. In *Viking's Dawn* (1955) Harald serves his apprenticeship on a voyage with Thorkell Fairhair – a voyage from which only Harald returns alive. Appropriately, the young manhood of Harald coincides with the beginning of the Viking age of voyaging. *Viking's Dawn* is the most straightforward of Treece's Viking books, showing how a boy grows into a Viking. The loosely picaresque plot of the book, on which reviewers commented, serves merely to display the Viking values: restlessness, courage, stoicism, and a splendidly ironic habit of understatement. There is much fighting and death, to which Harald gradually becomes accustomed; endurance, whether in battle or at sea, is a key virtue. *The Road to Miklagard* (1957) continues Harald's story, taking him five years later to Ireland, Moorish Spain, and Constantinople (Miklagard), where he and his shipmates become involved in the power struggle between Irene and her weak and petulant teenage son, Constantine. Here Treece picks up a theme to which he would return in later books: the unspoiled valor and worth of the Vikings, as seen against an ancient and corrupt Byzantine world. The recognition of the Vikings' quality by many of their fellow Imperial guardsmen, especially Kristion, the Captain of the Guard, offers the satisfaction of worth rewarded but also has an elegiac quality as the dying civilization recognizes a newer and stronger rival. *The Road to Miklagard* introduces a constant comparison of different cultures – not only the Byzantine but the Irish, Moorish, and Russian. The characters, too, are more varied in this book than in its predecessor: Abu Mazur and his daughter, Marriba, in Jebel Tarik, Irene, Constantine and Kristion at Miklagard, the King of the Marshland, and the Celtic giant Drummoch, who joins Harald in his travels.

In *Viking's Sunset* (1960) the story of Harald Sigurdson comes full circle as the Viking civilization, now representing the Old (European) World, meets its match in Vinland (the new land), where American Indians decimate Harald's band and kill Harald. This was Treece's first Viking story after he stopped teaching in 1959, ordered by his doctor to choose between his two careers for the sake of his heart condition. It is possible that the more conjectural side of the book, based loosely on theories of early Viking penetration of the American mainland, has something to do with Treece's departure from teaching. As in many of his later Viking books, Treece emphasizes the air of doom about the entire Viking enterprise: a doom that encompasses both the individual and his civilization. Though critics, particularly in the *Times Literary Supplement* of 20 May 1960, agreed about the power of *Viking's Sunset,* they objected to Treece's liberties with historical fact. These included anticipating the discovery of Iceland, which actually occurred somewhat later; treating Viking settlements in America as proven fact rather than conjecture; and failing to distinguish between Eskimos and American Indians as well as attributing to the Eskimos a more advanced kind of civilization than was likely.

Beginning in the late 1950s, Treece also wrote single books about turning points in European history. *The Children's Crusade* (1958), published in the United States as *Perilous Pilgrimage* (1959), traces the journey of a brother and sister from the Auvergne through a French countryside, to slavery on the coast of Africa, and on to Cairo. The hardships and brutality of sickness, starvation, treachery, and internal dissension make this a grim story, and the rather contrived happy ending which releases the young prisoners seems out of place (as reviewers, even those who otherwise liked the books, noted). With *Wickham and the Armada* (1959) Treece returns to the English scene in a straightforward account of Elizabethan sea power, and in *Red Settlement* (1960) he describes seventeenth-century English colonists in Pennsylvania. *The Bombard* (1959), published in

Dust jacket for Treece's 1957 novel about Viking explorations in Ireland, Spain, and Constantinople (Lilly Library, Indiana University)

future life; like the young Treece, Bill is already something of a writer and is interested in Viking swords. Though successful as a character study, *The Jet Beads* lacks the strong narrative that characterizes Treece's other fiction.

From 1962 until his death in 1966, Treece produced an astonishing number of books that revisited and enlarged two of his earliest themes: the clash of Britain and Roman, and the Viking way of life. *War Dog* (1962) traces the fortunes of a Celtic warhound during the Roman campaign of 43 A.D. and again centers on activities of Caratacus (the spelling preferred by Treece). *The Bronze Sword* (1965) shows the conflict between Roman and Celtic values in an encounter between Drucus, a retired centurion of the Ninth Legion, and Boudicca, Queen of the Iceni. Treece wrote *The Bronze Sword* for the Antelope series of juveniles, published by Hamish Hamilton and strictly limited in length to eight thousand words. Here, as in his radio scripts and the many articles he contributed to both British and American periodicals, Treece showed a professional's ability to write to order when necessary. Later, he revised and expanded this short tale for his American publisher as *The Centurion* (1967), a more extended exploration of differing loyalties, intended for slightly older readers. *The Queen's Brooch* (1966) presents another young hero with conflicting values, a Roman raised in Britain. Marcus, appointed a tribune while still in his teens, later becomes a chieftain of Boadicea (*sic* – Treece used both spellings), then ends up on the Roman side once more at the final battle in which the Queen and her followers perish. In addition to its portrait of the complex and fascinating Boadicea – a portrait delineated earlier in the adult novel *Red Queen, White Queen* (1958) – the book is notable for its disillusionment with war. Marcus, sickened by the last battle, determines to leave the Ninth Legion. Several critics objected to the brutality of this book as unsuitable for children, and it is sometimes listed (erroneously) as an adult title. The fact that it is intended for older children is confirmed by its lack of illustrations.

The Golden One (1961) presents another journey of brother and sister, like *The Children's Crusade,* but this time the journey takes place almost entirely in the Middle East during the time of Constantine and Theodora. Critics justly praised its rich landscapes, varied characters, and understated theme of tolerance. Treece returned once more to British scenes in *Man with a Sword* (1962), a character study of Hereward the Wake. Meanwhile, he was producing nonfictional works about the Crusades and about warfare and castles through the ages. *Castles*

the United States as *Ride into Danger,* concerns David Marlais, a young man of mixed English-Welsh heritage (like Treece himself) and the conflicts of the Welsh marches in the time of the Black Prince. David's adventure at Crécy and elsewhere show more open criticism of war than usual. The use of cannon, both in France and at home, brings out much of Treece's discomfort with the brutality of war: discomfort that is kept at bay in the Viking stories where the fighting is man-to-man. (Fighting in Treece's stories of Roman Britain is also man-to-man, although, as Treece was aware, the Romans used various machines of war with great skill.)

Treece's only attempt at a contemporary realistic story came in 1961 with *The Jet Beads,* an account of a short period in the life of Bill Neasden as he studies for the pivotal Eleven Plus examination and takes stock of his life. Like Treece, Bill loves to draw but is uncertain how this talent will fit into his *and Kings* (1959), a book for all ages, has as its juvenile counterpart *The True Book About Castles* (1960). The adult title *The Crusades* (1962) became, in much simplified form, *Know About the Crusades* (1963). *Fighting Men: How Men Have Fought Through the Ages* (1963), written with R. E. Oakeshott, describes the minutiae of warfare without sentimentality.

In the last four years of his life Treece produced a final group of Viking books, a retelling of the Trojan War, and an enigmatic story of prehistoric people. *Horned Helmet* (1963), set in Iceland, begins grimly as Beorn, whose father jumped off a cliff rather than fight the huge, ill-natured Glam, becomes Glam's property. Fleeing from Glam, Beorn is rescued by a band of sea rovers who tie Glam and leave him to drown in a tidal pool. The tone of this book, more explicit than earlier ones, can be seen in Beorn's reaction ("I do not like anyone to be hurt, Jomsviking") and the response of one of his rescuers ("then you should have been born into another world than this. Everyone gets hurt, as you should know by now"). Starkad, Beorn's new father figure, turns out to be a baresark – a figure that fascinated Treece. The Harald Sigurdson stories had contained men, like Thorkel and Ragnar, who fought with the cold fury of the baresark, but no explanation was offered in the narrative. *Horned Helmet* makes the idea explicit. "When the froth comes on his mouth . . . he is already at the first stage," explains a comrade. "The next stage is when he rips off his war-shirt. . . . The third stage is when he begins to roll his eyes round and bite at things. And the last state is when he screams out and runs at whoever gets in the way. That is a baresark." *Horned Helmet,* set in the early eleventh century, marks the passing of the great seafaring days for bands of Vikings. Beorn, grown and prosperous, throws his treasured helmet and his sword into the sea before returning to settle in with his adopted parents on a small farm. The novel, with its moving depiction of father-son bonding, incorporates passages from Old Norse and Old English verse at strategic points.

The sense of a doomed way of life also characterizes Treece's adaptation from the sagas, *The Burning of Njal* (1964). Episodic and rich in minor characters (like its source), the Njal story focuses on a dowry feud, a central section in which Njal's family becomes enmeshed in the feud and eventually is burned alive, and a concluding section about the aftermath. Gone are the genealogies and courtroom narratives of the original. Critics complimented Treece's evocation of the laconic humor and grim understatement of his original and complained less than usual about the violence.

Splintered Sword (1965), like *Horned Helmet,* concerns a young boy who leaves a life of thralldom for a wanderer's lot. The story begins at Orkney in 1098, when fifteen-year-old Runolf, a mistreated foster child, befriends a hungry baresark. After two further encounters with the baresark, Runolf inherits his treasured sword, runs away, and discovers that he is himself a baresark. After many adventures Runolf swears allegiance to the Norman Earl of Chester, who tells him that the time for baresarks is past: "Has no one told you that those days are over? All that is finished, these three generations past. Only cracked-brained old dreamers in the northern isles still think of such antics without a smile." Reviewers were divided, some admiring the inventiveness of the tale and others complaining of its purposelessness.

Treece's finest Viking book, *The Last of the Vikings* (1964), eulogizes Harald Hardrada, King of Norway. Introduced as a minor but scene-stealing character in *Hounds of the King* (1965) and *Man with a Sword,* Hardrada appears here on center stage. The material is adapted from the *Heimskringla;* however, instead of including Snorri Sturluson's many details of Hardrada's battles and intrigues, Treece focuses on two battles and on a formative period in the hero's youth. The book begins at Stamfordbridge, the battle in Yorkshire in which Hardrada died, and ends there with the conquering English king eulogizing him and putting pennies on his eyes. The entire midsection of the book is a flashback, beginning with the battle of Stiklestad in which Hardrada's brother Olaf died and continuing with his travels to Miklagard and throughout Russia. One of Treece's great characters, the mysterious Arsleif Summerbird, serves as Hardrada's foster father and eventually gives himself up to the enemy to save him. *The Last of the Vikings* is one of the few books for which Treece did not write an introduction or afterword; none was needed. It is the story of a great hero's life, lived in the increasing knowledge that everything he stands for is becoming obsolete. It is the only book Treece wrote that begins and ends within a twenty-four-hour period. Treece revived Hardrada in *Swords from the North* (1967). Based again on the *Heimskringla,* the novel recounts Hardrada's ten years in Miklagard as captain of the imperial guard. As in *The Road to Miklagard* a decade earlier, Treece focuses on the meeting of two cultures; however, Harald Hardrada dominates this story far more than Harald Sigurdson did the earlier one.

The Windswept City (1967), written to order for Hamish Hamilton, shows the Trojan War through the eyes of a twelve-year-old slave. Though it contains some memorable scenes – Asterius the slave boy meeting by chance with Agamemnon, for example, or the entrance of the horse, here an ingenious siege machine – the book assumes some prior knowledge of the story. Treece's favorite device, the release of the protagonist at the end, again seems contrived.

Posthumously published, *The Dream-Time* (1967) is Treece's most ambitious book for children, and the only one to contain drawings by him. It is also the only one not located firmly in a historical period. Treece had explored British prehistory many years earlier in *Men of the Hills* (1957), a story of the confrontation between the dark Celts and groups of blond Continental invaders (a tale told for adult readers a year earlier in *The Golden Strangers*). *The Dream-Time,* however, mixes various prehistoric eras deliberately to tell the story of Crookleg, exiled from his tribe because he is an artist. Joined by Blackbird, a girl of another tribe similarly exiled because of her dancing, he eventually finds acceptance among the Red Men and their painted caves. The book marks Treece's most outspoken statement against human aggression, a subject which had always fascinated him but about which he had previously been much more ambivalent. It is also his most experimental book in terms of language, as he tries to render the thoughts of preliterate people in modern verbal equivalents.

In some lecture notes written on 20 May 1966, not long before his death, Treece observed that "for the past fifteen years or so the two principal themes in my writing had been the Father seeking the Son (or the son the Father) *and* the theme of the Distracted Woman, the woman drawn away from gen-

tleness and mercy into other, perhaps more sinister paths; the Maenad, the Bacchante." Here lies the difference between his adult titles and those for children: the Distracted Woman, with the possible exception of Boudicca and Irene, is missing in the latter. Treece's are, like many other adventure stories, books primarily for boys. The ideal relationship between the sexes is brother and sister, and several books feature a brother-sister pair, either actual or metaphorical (like Crookleg and Blackbird).

At the time of his death Treece was regarded as one of Britain's major writers for the young, as attested by many glowing obituaries. In the next decade some influential critics in his own country raised doubts (notably John Rowe Townsend, Frank Eyre, and Marcus Crouch, in their histories of children's books). Critics in the United States, who had been generally enthusiastic about his juvenile books, no longer mentioned Treece; there have been British reprints but few American ones, except for the picture book *The Magic Wood: A Poem* (1992). However, libraries on both sides of the Atlantic have retained Treece's books in large numbers, and circulation records show that children are still reading them.

References:

[Pauline Clarke], "Henry Treece: Lament for a Maker," in *TLS 5: Essays and Reviews from The Times Literary Supplement 1966* (London: Times Publishing, 1966), pp. 128–135;

Margery Fisher, "Henry Treece," in *Three Bodley Head Monographs* (London: Bodley Head, 1969), pp. 7–104;

Arthur Edward Salmon, *Poets of the Apocalypse,* Twayne's English Authors Series, 360 (Boston: Twayne, 1983).

Alison Uttley

(17 December 1884 – 7 May 1976)

Barbara Carman Garner
Carleton University

BOOKS: *The Squirrel, the Hare and the Little Grey Rabbit* (London: Heinemann, 1929);

How Little Grey Rabbit Got Back Her Tail (London: Heinemann, 1930);

The Great Adventure of Hare (London: Heinemann, 1931);

The Country Child (London: Faber & Faber, 1931; New York: Macmillan, 1931);

Moonshine and Magic (London: Faber & Faber, 1932);

The Story of Fuzzypeg the Hedgehog (London: Heinemann, 1932);

Squirrel Goes Skating (London: Collins, 1934);

Wise Owl's Story (London: Collins, 1935);

The Adventures of Peter and Judy in Bunnyland (London: Collins, 1935);

Candlelight Tales (London: Faber & Faber, 1936);

Little Grey Rabbit's Party (London: Collins, 1936);

The Knot Squirrel Tied (London: Collins, 1937);

The Adventures of No Ordinary Rabbit (London: Faber & Faber, 1937);

Ambush of Young Days (London: Faber & Faber, 1937);

Mustard, Pepper, and Salt (London: Faber & Faber, 1938);

Fuzzypeg Goes to School (London: Collins, 1938);

High Meadows (London: Faber & Faber, 1938);

A Traveller in Time (London: Faber & Faber, 1939; New York: Putnam, 1940);

Tales of the Four Pigs and Brock the Badger (London: Faber & Faber, 1939);

Little Grey Rabbit's Christmas (London: Collins, 1939);

Moldy Warp, the Mole (London: Collins, 1940);

The Adventures of Sam Pig (London: Faber & Faber, 1940);

Sam Pig Goes to Market (London: Faber & Faber, 1941);

Six Tales of Brock the Badger (London: Faber & Faber, 1941);

Six Tales of Sam Pig (London: Faber & Faber, 1941);

Six Tales of the Four Pigs (London: Faber & Faber, 1941);

Alison Uttley

Ten Tales of Tim Rabbit (London: Faber & Faber, 1941);

The Farm on the Hill (London: Faber & Faber, 1941);

Hare Joins the Home Guard (London: Collins, 1942);

Little Grey Rabbit's Washing-Day (London: Collins, 1942);

Nine Starlight Tales (London: Faber & Faber, 1942);

Sam Pig and Sally (London: Faber & Faber, 1942);

Country Hoard (London: Faber & Faber, 1943);

Cuckoo Cherry-Tree (London: Faber & Faber, 1943);

Sam Pig at the Circus (London: Faber & Faber, 1943);

Water-Rat's Picnic (London: Collins, 1943);

Little Grey Rabbit's Birthday (London: Collins, 1944);

Mrs. Nimble and Mr. Bumble, with *This Duck and That Duck* by Herbert McKay (London: James, 1944);

The Spice Woman's Basket and Other Tales (London: Faber & Faber, 1944);

When All Is Done (London: Faber & Faber, 1945);

The Adventures of Tim Rabbit (London: Faber & Faber, 1945);

The Weather Cock, and Other Stories (London: Faber & Faber, 1945);

Some Moonshine Tales (London: Faber & Faber, 1945);

The Speckledy Hen (London: Collins, 1946);

Little Grey Rabbit to the Rescue: A Play (London: Collins, 1946);

Country Things (London: Faber & Faber, 1946);

The Washerwoman's Child: A Play on the Life and Stories of Hans Christian Andersen (London: Faber & Faber, 1946);

Little Grey Rabbit and the Weasels (London: Collins, 1947);

Grey Rabbit and the Wandering Hedgehog (London: Collins, 1948);

John Barleycorn: Twelve Tales of Fairy and Magic (London: Faber & Faber, 1948);

Sam Pig in Trouble (London: Faber & Faber, 1948);

Carts and Candlesticks (London: Faber & Faber, 1948);

The Cobbler's Shop, and Other Tales (London: Faber & Faber, 1950);

MacDuff (London: Faber & Faber, 1950);

Little Grey Rabbit Makes Lace (London: Collins, 1950);

Snug and Serena Meet a Queen (London: Heinemann, 1950);

Snug and Serena Pick Cowslips (London: Heinemann, 1950);

Buckinghamshire (London: Hale, 1950);

The Little Brown Mouse Books, 12 volumes (London: Heinemann, 1950–1957);

Yours Ever, Sam Pig (London: Faber & Faber, 1951; Harmondsworth: Puffin, 1977);

Hare and the Easter Eggs (London: Collins, 1952);

Plowmen's Clocks (London: Faber & Faber, 1952);

Little Grey Rabbit's Valentine (London: Collins, 1953);

The Stuff of Dreams (London: Faber & Faber, 1953);

Little Grey Rabbit Goes to Sea (London: Collins, 1954);

Little Red Fox and the Wicked Uncle (London: Heinemann, 1954; Indianapolis: Bobbs-Merrill, 1962);

Sam Pig and the Singing Gate (London: Faber & Faber, 1955);

Here's a New Day (London: Faber & Faber, 1956);

Hare and Guy Fawkes (London: Collins, 1956);

Little Grey Rabbit and Cinderella (London: Heinemann, 1956);

A Year in the Country (London: Faber & Faber, 1957);

Magic in My Pocket: A Selection of Tales (London: Penguin, 1957);

Little Grey Rabbit's Paint-Box (London: Collins, 1958);

Little Grey Rabbit and the Magic Moon (London: Heinemann, 1958);

Snug and Serena Count Twelve (London: Heinemann, 1959; Indianapolis: Bobbs-Merrill, 1962);

Tim Rabbit and Company (London: Faber & Faber, 1959);

The Swans Fly Over (London: Faber & Faber, 1959);

Something for Nothing (London: Faber & Faber, 1960);

Sam Pig Goes to the Seaside: Sixteen Stories (London: Faber & Faber, 1960; Harmondsworth: Puffin, 1978);

Grey Rabbit Finds a Shoe (London: Collins, 1960);

John at the Old Farm (London: Heinemann, 1960);

Grey Rabbit and the Circus (London: Collins, 1961);

Snug and Serena Go to Town (London: Heinemann, 1961; Indianapolis: Bobbs-Merrill, 1963);

Three Little Grey Rabbit Plays (London: Heinemann, 1961);

Wild Honey (London: Faber & Faber, 1962);

Little Red Fox and the Unicorn (London: Heinemann, 1962);

The Little Knife Who Did All the Work: Twelve Tales of Magic (London: Faber & Faber, 1962);

Grey Rabbit's May Day (London: Collins, 1963);

Tim Rabbit's Dozen (London: Faber & Faber, 1964);

Cuckoo in June (London: Faber & Faber, 1964);

Hare Goes Shopping (London: Collins, 1965);

The Sam Pig Storybook (London: Faber & Faber, 1965);

The Mouse, the Rabbit, and the Little White Hen (London: Heinemann, 1966);

Enchantment (London: Heinemann, 1966);

A Peck of Gold (London: Faber & Faber, 1966);

Recipes from an Old Farmhouse (London: Faber & Faber, 1966);

Little Grey Rabbit's Pancake Day (London: Collins, 1967);

Little Red Fox (Harmondsworth: Puffin, 1967);

Little Red Fox and the Big Big Tree (London: Heinemann, 1968);

The Button Box, and Other Essays (London: Faber & Faber, 1968);

Little Grey Rabbit Goes to the North Pole (London: Collins, 1970);

Lavender Shoes: Eight Tales of Enchantment (London: Faber & Faber, 1970);

A Ten O'Clock Scholar, and Other Essays (London: Faber & Faber, 1970);

The Brown Mouse Book: Magical Tales of Two Little Mice (London: Heinemann, 1971);

Fuzzypeg's Brother (London: Collins, 1971);

Secret Places, and Other Essays (London: Faber & Faber, 1972);

Little Grey Rabbit's Spring Cleaning Party (London: Collins, 1972);

Little Grey Rabbit and the Snow-Baby (London: Collins, 1973);

Fairy Tales, edited by Kathleen Lines (London: Faber & Faber, 1975);

Hare and the Rainbow (London: Collins, 1975);

Stories for Christmas, edited by Lines (London: Faber & Faber, 1977);

Little Grey Rabbit's Storybook (London: Collins, 1977);

From Spring to Spring: Stories of the Four Seasons, edited by Lines (London: Faber & Faber, 1978); republished as *Rainbow Tales* (London: Pan, 1988);

Tales of Little Grey Rabbit (London: Heinemann, 1980);

Little Grey Rabbit's Second Storybook (London: Collins, 1981);

Tales of Grey Rabbit (London: Heinemann, 1984);

Tales of Little Brown Mouse (London: Heinemann, 1984);

Our Village: Alison Uttley's Cromford, edited by Jacqueline Mitchell (Cromford: Scarthin, 1984);

Foxglove Tales, edited by Lucy Meredith (London: Faber & Faber, 1984);

Little Grey Rabbit's Alphabet Book (London: Collins, 1985).

OTHER: *In Praise of Country Life: An Anthology,* edited by Uttley (London: Muller, 1949);

Country World: Memories of Childhood, edited by Lucy Meredith (London: Faber & Faber, 1984).

Alison Uttley's contributions to literature for children younger than ten make her well deserving of a place in this volume. While much of her work was published after 1960, her first animal story appeared in 1929, and she is a contemporary of Enid Blyton. Uttley's anthropomorphic animals were compared, she felt to her disadvantage, with those of Beatrix Potter and Kenneth Grahame. During the war years her books were published on government-regulation paper, and many a child clutched one of the Grey Rabbit or Sam Pig books as he went down into the air-raid shelters. One of her characters, Hare in the Little Grey Rabbit series, even

joined the Home Guard. The Grey Rabbit books gave Uttley international fame, and her cult following grew as a result of her regular additions to her series of animal stories and of her publishers' attempts to offer a new book each year for the Christmas market. Uttley was also fortunate in her illustrator for the Grey Rabbit series, Margaret Tempest, though at first there was a disagreement over whether the author or the illustrator should receive more pay for a book. The issue of awarding Tempest five pounds more for the first book was resolved by allotting equal pay to writer and illustrator thereafter. Although Tempest and Uttley tolerated one another, in later years Uttley sought her own illustrators for many of her works, and her publishers Faber and Faber, Collins, and Heinemann engaged them to do the illustrations.

Alison Uttley was the daughter of Henry Taylor and Hannah Dickens, Henry Taylor's second wife, who was eleven years younger than he. Her parents married in 1884 when Hannah was thirty, and Alice Jane (Alison) was born just over nine months later on 17 December 1884. Alison had a brother George who was a close playfriend in childhood, but they grew apart after Alison went away to school and pursued an academic career. Uttley's childhood home, Castle Top Farm, had been the home of the Taylor family for more than two hundred years, and, like his ancestors, Henry Taylor was a kind and hardworking tenant farmer. Uttley's father was not a literate man, but he knew the ways of animals and of men, loved music, was religious (although he never went to church), and was a respected member of the community. He had his own strange system of account keeping, which included mysterious marks made on the barn doors, and his "strange, grim stories" inherited from his ancestors were fondly remembered by his daughter. In an essay entitled "The Ladder to Writing" in *Wild Honey* (1962), Uttley acknowledged her father's storytelling ability while commenting on Thomas Hardy's novels: "I found the life depicted in the books very similar to tales told by my father of his childhood, in our farmhouse, with shepherds and ploughmen, guisers and fairs."

While Alison's father provided ample demonstrations of how to tell a tale, her mother, a devout Christian, insisted that Alison attend the Anglican church twice on Sunday. A lover of literature and the arts, Hannah Taylor sang and recited poetry to her young daughter and read aloud to her husband books including Mrs. Craik's *John Halifax, Gentleman* (1856) and George Eliot's *Adam Bede* (1859) and *The Mill on the Floss* (1860). During the long winter evenings family and servants would listen to her read many novels of Charles Dickens and such favorites as Daniel Defoe's *Robinson Crusoe* (1719), Robert Louis Stevenson's *Treasure Island* (1883), and Johann David Wyss's *The Swiss Family Robinson* (1814). Playacting parts of *Robinson Crusoe* also occupied young Alison many a day at Castle Top Farm.

The family always had to work hard to make ends meet. To improve finances the Uttleys boarded select visitors during the summer, as did other farms: "we took one or two families, of professional people, and clergy, of people whom we liked, who came again and again, every year, until the children were adult, they came with a nanny, books and high spirits." Alison was treated well by these visitors and profited from the summer arrangement; she loved to read the marvelous books that these families brought with them and was even given French lessons by one governess. When the guests were enjoying an excursion, Alison would sneak into the parlor and play the music or read the books which they had brought. She was given piano lessons and used every opportunity to acquire pieces of music. She avidly read whatever the visitors left lying in the parlor, even the occasional book of history and philosophy belonging to some professor on vacation. She never felt jealous of these visitors' children, who had many advantages, but considered it a privilege to associate with them during the summer. Uttley retells many of these childhood reminiscences as well as her early school experiences in *The Country Child* (1931) and *The Farm on the Hill* (1941), whose main character Susan Garland is really Uttley herself. Although these books are not generally classed among her works for children, they are well suited for young readers and capture what growing up in rural England was like in the last two decades of the nineteenth century.

Uttley was both a sensitive and imaginative child. She had a Wordsworthian appreciation of nature and was able to give life even to the objects like rocks and stones that she encountered in her daily activities. Her first experiences at Lea Board School when she was seven were mixed. Like her character Susan Garland, she was frightened of going through the woods, which she believed to be haunted, and was certain that some rocks were friendly and could be tramped on while others were dark and sinister and must never be touched: "Some stones must be trodden upon always, they demanded human companionship, and the touch of hand or foot. Others were inimical, sinister, sharp-tongued, and cruel. Susan avoided these at all costs, even when she pursued her backward way." She used to cajole other

Dust jacket for Uttley's 1934 book about an animal skating party (Lilly Library, Indiana University)

students into walking partway home with her by telling them stories, but it was still a long walk for a little girl to make on her own in all weather conditions. Years later she was upset when she took her husband through these same woods and he, stepping almost lightheartedly on good and bad stones alike, seemed oblivious to the specters of her childhood.

Though she had some attendance problems at Lea Board, Uttley managed to garner a scholarship to the Lady Manners School, which she attended via the milk train each day. There she grew to love her studies, particularly science and mathematics, although she was also good in English literature. At the end of her courses she received a scholarship to attend Manchester University in 1903, and three years later she was the second female to graduate with an honors degree in physics from there. She then completed a one-year course in the Theory and Practice of Teaching at The Ladies' Training College in Cambridge. She met her husband James through his sister while she was studying at Manchester University. They were married in 1911, whereupon she quit her teaching job in London. They had one son, John.

Alison Uttley dedicated her life to making the countryside of her childhood, with its flora and fauna, live on in the minds of both young and old readers. Her Little Grey Rabbit and Sam Pig books, her collections of short stories and essays, her autobiographical writings – *The Country Child, Ambush of Young Days* (1937), and *The Farm on the Hill* – all attest her desire to make known the country ways of her childhood and to echo speech patterns of an earlier time, whether through the language of the common country peasant, of fairy tale and nursery rhyme, or of Shakespeare and the Elizabethans so dear to her own heart. Intermingled with the literary echoes in her work are the folklore and stories of her native Darbyshire. Her interest in science gives added dimension to her stories for children, but the magical and the fanciful predominate and take readers into that realm where dreams come true as they explore with Uttley's characters the possibilities of the great "What if?" Her most artistically and successfully fashioned work, *A Traveller in Time* (1939), sometimes appears on adult reading lists and is often unfamiliar to devotees of Uttley's Sam Pig and Grey Rabbit series.

A Traveller in Time was published independently in both Canada (Ryerson) and the United States (Putnam) in 1940. *A Traveller in Time* transports readers to the peculiar world of Penelope Taverner, a young girl from Chelsea who is sent along with her siblings, Ian and Alison, to the country home of their aunt and uncle, Cicily and Barnabus Taverner, to recuperate from illness. Penelope has always been a dreamer, and her sister Alison calls her fey. Soon after she arrives at Thackers, Penelope is carried back in visions to the house as it was when it belonged to the Babington family in Elizabethan times. She is later mysteriously drawn into the past – partly by her own longing to be there and partly by Sir Anthony's younger brother Francis. Francis is the one person in the past who is able to understand that Penelope is from another time, although Jude, an idiot boy who carves a little Elizabethan man for her in the past, partially understands her presence in his world.

Surviving the centuries, the carved Elizabethan man is given to Penelope by her Aunt Tissie (a nickname for Cicily) in the present, when the girl finds it being used as a bobbin boy among her aunt's embroidery silks and is attracted to it. The bobbin boy becomes a kind of talisman that helps Jude rescue Penelope from death in the past and allows her to return safely to the present near the end of the novel. Penelope shares with her Aunt Tissie's ancestor and the Babington family the tense period

of the 1580s when Sir Anthony Babington was trying to free Mary, Queen of Scots, to whom he had pledged his allegiance. Sir Anthony confides in Penelope and enjoys her witchlike powers and knowledge of the future. He tells her of his aspirations and once calls her to find his miniature of the queen, a jewel that he considered his good luck charm. Penelope finds the locket in the present but is unable to give it back to Anthony in the past. In this novel Uttley cleverly uses many techniques and devices that have become standard practice in timeslip fantasies, yet her novel preceded these fantasies of "enchanted realism" by more than thirty years – perhaps one reason why many critics have felt that this is Uttley's best literary work.

The Elizabethan setting and the three-hundred-year-old story of *The Traveller in Time* are more real than the present-day farmhouse and its occupants. As always, natural surroundings and local color seem to have been prominent in Uttley's mind as she weaves her tale. The flowers and herbs of the country garden and hedgerow are here in abundance, as are local remedies and customs – and, as in all her books, the sense of the English countryside that surrounded her as she was growing up at Castle Top Farm is kept alive. As many have noted, Penelope Taverner bears a striking resemblance to Uttley herself, striving to discover the roots of her ancestors and to understand some of the shadowy figures enfolded in the pages of history. Penelope's experiences are similar to ones Uttley herself had concerning Thackers, the Babington country estate. It seems fitting that she gave her own home in Buckinghamshire the name Thackers. She could identify with Penelope's longing to become part of the life of the house in time past. In fact, she often spoke of the mysterious powers that the house at Castle Top had on all who came there.

Uttley glorified her own childhood and tried to recapture it in many of her books, whether they were about animals or her own past. As her authorized biographer Denis Judd notes, she did not always tell the truth in various accounts of her own childhood in her autobiographical works. With access to her forty volumes of journals, which cover the period from January 1932 to the end of 1971, he offers new insights into the woman behind the cozy exterior she presented to the world for more than fifty years. Elizabeth Saintsbury's biography of Uttley has rightly been pronounced limited by Judd, for Saintsbury had access solely to Uttley's own published accounts of her life and "a few interviews." Saintsbury records of Uttley: "It was not until she began to invent stories for her small son that she committed anything to paper. She transformed her childhood experiences into those of small animals in animal community for his benefit and for her own satisfaction, and the world of Grey Rabbit and Company was born." Yet it seems that not even Uttley suggested that her writing career commenced in just this fashion. Saintsbury is also mistaken about the publication dates of Uttley's books, thinking that the Sam Pig series did not appear until the 1950s. She does make, however, one telling observation about the difference between the animal stories of Beatrix Potter and those of Alison Uttley: "She did not write to escape the environment of her youth, as Beatrix Potter had done, but to enter more deeply into it and give it immortality."

Professor Samuel Alexander, the Manchester University philosophy professor whom Uttley had admired from afar while studying at the university, was responsible for her initial attempts at writing, though his influence was accidental. He had confused her with another student who had the same surname, and asked her at an Altrincham exhibition they both attended whether she was still writing poetry. This gave her the incentive she needed, and, sitting at her childhood desk in an attic gable at Downs House, she secretly commenced writing the story of her early years at Castle Top Farm. Her vivid powers of recollection sometimes convinced her that she was reliving moments of her childhood. *The Country Child* was her first-written, although not first-published, book. When Uttley showed the work to her husband James, he called it rubbish and threw it across the room. Uttley put the manuscript away in a drawer. Even though her friend Lily Meagher, to whom she had shown it earlier, encouraged her to continue, James's negative remarks prevailed. Uttley's own account of how she first wrote tales for children, recorded in *The Button Box, and Other Essays* (1968), seems as accurate as one can come to explaining how Uttley became a published writer. She recounts, "Every day in our walks, in England, Wales and France, I told stories of hares and Weasels, wolves and foxes, each one different and new. I was compelled by a strong urge to write down a tale and send it to him [John, her son, who had just left for boarding school]. This was my first little book, *The Squirrel, the Hare and the Little Grey Rabbit*" (1929). The series grew to more than thirty titles by the end of her writing career.

The first of the Little Grey Rabbit books is less tightly constructed than many of the others, but it employs an animal-story pattern that Uttley continued using until the end of her career. Her tiny animals establish families in the communities in which they live and are aware of the social niche into which they should fit. Some critics think that Grey Rabbit is modeled on Uttley's mother; others say she has the character of Uttley herself. At any rate, Grey Rabbit possesses wisdom, foresight, and courage and is keen to help others by sharing her skills and possessions with them. She provides for and rescues her animal family comprised of Squirrel and Hare. The household cannot run smoothly without her, yet she too is sometimes called away on an adventure or acts foolhardily and needs diplomacy and the help of friends to overcome difficulties.

Such is the case when she gives her tail to Wise Owl in exchange for knowledge of how to make carrots grow, so that she will not have to risk her life by venturing into the farmer's vegetable garden to obtain them. She is also naive, thinking that yellow canaries will spring from the canary seed to which she helps herself in the store when, while the storekeeper is dozing, she picks up carrot, lettuce, radish, parsley, cabbage, poppy, and mignonette seeds. She is clever in deceiving the weasel, who has absconded with her family while she was at the store, and, in a sequence of events recalling those of "The Three Little Pigs" and "Hansel and Gretel," she succeeds in rescuing her friends and pushing the weasel into the oven, where he had hoped to cook Squirrel and Hare. They are thankful and apologize for ever being rude and proud in her presence. Little Grey Rabbit does not want the life of luxury they promise her for saving their lives, and she prefers work to leisure, although she admits that it would be nice to sit in the rocking chair sometimes and to have a party. At the end of *How Little Grey Rabbit Got Back Her Tail* (1930), Uttley tells how "the little company," the close-knit group of animals loyal to Grey Rabbit, retrieved her tail. They give Moldy Warp, the mole, a bottle of primrose wine for making a bell, which so pleases Wise Owl that he returns Grey Rabbit's tail — which he has been using as a door knocker.

Sometimes party preparations go awry for Uttley's animals. Such is the case when Rat invades the animals' party site while they are all having a skating party in *Squirrel Goes Skating* (1934). He devours the feast laid out for the family upon their return, and in events similar to those of "Snow White" or "Goldilocks and the Three Bears," Rat is discovered asleep and snoring in Squirrel's bed. The animals pool their resources to teach him a lesson, and, with Grey Rabbit as leader, they decide that Rat "ought to be punished. . . . We ought to make him remember his wickedness." Squirrel ties a large

Illustration by Margaret Tempest from Uttley's Little Grey Rabbit and the Weasels *(1947)*

knot in Rat's tail. Later that evening Water Rat and Moldy Warp arrive with two hampers of goodies that make up for the feast the Rat had devoured, but the shame and difficulty that the knot tied in Rat's tail causes him are the subjects of another story, *The Knot Squirrel Tied* (1937). No one can untie the knot, but as Rat reforms and starts modifying his behavior by being kind when he could be mean, or by stopping himself from preying on other animals, the knot gradually unties itself.

By October 1936 Collins reported that sales of Uttley's Little Grey Rabbit books were around a thousand a month, and in 1937 more than eleven thousand were sold in the six months prior to Christmas. The games and humor included in the tales enhanced their appeal. In the successful *Little Grey Rabbit's Party* (1936), Hare takes the animals to see a children's party, and they wish to have one too. Little Grey Rabbit consults Wise Owl, and he gives her a book titled *How to Give a Party*. They

learn how to play "Turn the Trencher," "Blind Man's Bluff," and "Hide the Thimble." These and similar games like "Musical Chairs" in *Little Grey Rabbit's Christmas* (1939) and "Puss-in-the-Corner" in *Little Grey Rabbit's Spring Cleaning Party* (1972) become popular in the Grey Rabbit books. Grey Rabbit's naiveté adds humor that the young child appreciates. "R.S.V.P.," she explains, means "Rat shan't visit party," and the "Iced Cake" has "cold snow and ice" on top, for the cake is "covered with icing which Hare had brought from the top of the pond." Owl is invited to the party, even though the tiny animals are terrified of him, and Rat, the dreaded foe, is given a mince tart to eat outside. Grey Rabbit explains Wise Owl's invitation to the party by saying, "A party is a Truce." Late in her writing career, in *A Ten O'Clock Scholar, and Other Essays* (1970), Uttley comments on the animal kingdom as follows: "Animals are mysterious, a race apart. . . . They are too noble to be humanised in story and fable, they are too great for our small civilizations, and yet only by a humanisation shall we know them and learn to love them." She also believes that animals are wiser than humans, waging no wars and using no poisons as they struggle to survive.

Little Grey Rabbit's Christmas continues to examine the relationships between the animal and the human worlds but also insists on allowing the animals to remain true to their animal natures and their understanding of how the world should be. Moldy Warp decorates a tree in the forest with lighted candles and treats for all the birds and animals. Rat finds the sleigh, Grey Rabbit's present to the family – a present that Hare had lost the night before – and brings it to Moldy Warp's party along with three gifts for Grey Rabbit. The animals give Rat three cheers and now address him as "kind Rat." The decorating of Grey Rabbit's house for Christmas recalls the decorating of Castle Top Farm described in so many of Uttley's autobiographical reminiscences about Christmas.

Christmas, as Judd and others have pointed out, held a fascination for Uttley. She herself was a Snow-baby, and Judd even suggests that she thought she created the season. She loved the kissing bunch, which predated the Christmas tree in her part of England by more than a hundred years. This is perhaps why Grey Rabbit, who has made a kissing bunch for her family and who sees Moldy Warp's Christmas tree, asks, "Is it a Fairy Tree?" Uttley gives explicit instructions for the construction of a "Kissing-Bunch" in the story by that name included in Kathleen Lines's edition of Uttley's *Stories for Christmas* (1977).

Uttley's social conscience and her country instinct that one should try to understand individuals before condemning them for their different ways inform much of her writing for children. She explores this message in *Grey Rabbit and the Wandering Hedgehog* (1948). Hare confronts Hedgehog, the milkman, with "There's a relation of yours down the lane without a coat to his back. What are you going to do about it?" Grey Rabbit and Hare collect scraps of material from members of the animal community, and Hare gets a book from Wise Owl that tells how to make a patchwork coat. Wandering Hedgehog is pleased with his "coat of twenty colours," and vows he has never seen such a coat except one worn by the emperor of China. The animals have been generous to this wanderer whom they first addressed in such derogatory terms as a "beggarly old hedgehog" and "dirty old ragamuffin." After Grey Rabbit joins this hedgehog for a meal, she wisely

disregards those who tell her that she will become "a raggle-taggle gipsy" if she continues to associate with him. There are many lessons to be learned from Uttley's books, but they are never preachy. Uttley understands how a child's mind works and stretches it without being patronizing or frivolous. She subtly proffers the proverbial wisdom of "live and let live" in all her animal stories.

The young child will identify with Fuzzypeg the hedgehog, who makes the common childish mistake of taking idiomatic sayings literally. In *Little Grey Rabbit's Christmas* his mother tells him, "You mustn't let the cat out of the bag," and he replies, "There wasn't a cat in the bag, Mother. There wasn't." He gets lost and becomes frightened as a young child would. The child who knows his alphabet will laugh at Hare's lesson on the A-B-Cs in *Fuzzypeg Goes to School* (1938): *A* is for Hay, *B* for Bee, and *C* for Sea. When Fuzzypeg tells his father what he has learned, he dreamily says that he learned "Straw, Wasps and Ponds." He then remembers correctly, but his father replies, "You've not Larned much . . . and they say 'A little larning is a dangerous thing.'" Old Jonathan, their teacher, is better; he teaches them the Mother Goose counting rhyme, "One, two, buckle my shoe, / Three, four, knock at the door," and to perform the actions as they sing. Even little hedgehogs are told fairy tales at school. Grey Rabbit visits the class and tells them the story of Red Riding Hood.

This intermingling of nursery rhyme and fairy tale in Uttley's text forms a pattern in her animal books. *Little Red Fox and Cinderella* (1956) is one of two such works. Swan tells Billy and Bonny Badger and the little fox "the ancient story of Cinderella," and Cinderella is a rabbit with little glass slippers in her version of the tale. In "The Fox and the Little White Hen" and "The Little White Hen and the Three Fox-cubs" from *Lavender Shoes: Eight Tales of Enchantment* (1970), Uttley's last collection of short stories, The Little White Hen also has a repertoire of fairy tales that she tells the little red foxes, tales recognizably drawn from those such as "Sleeping Beauty," "Puss-in-Boots," and "Red Riding Hood." In White Hen's version of Cinderella, White Hen becomes the fairy godmother, and two little foxes become the horses for Cinderella's carriage.

Nursery rhymes, songs, phrases that imitate birds' songs, and proverbial sayings are interspersed throughout Uttley's books. In *Nine Starlight Tales* (1942, a selection from the *Candlelight Tales*, first published in 1936), Uttley constructs a story around many nursery rhymes to explain how they came to be written. These tales are clever and delightful to the imaginative child who may often have wondered how those four and twenty blackbirds got baked in a pie, or why the cow jumped over the moon. The early reviews were favorable and suggested that mothers and nurses would delight in these tales. Uttley also effectively integrates songs as well as rhymes into her tales. Little Grey Rabbit sings "Mowing the Barley," "Strawberry Fair," "There was a Jolly Miller," and "Rule Britannia." Tim Rabbit has a pipe given to him by the scarecrow – a pipe that plays "Lady Greensleeves," "Mowing the Barley," "Who Killed Cock Robin," and "Oats and Beans and Barley Grows." These and such time-honored songs as "I Had a Little Nut Tree" keep appearing in Uttley's stories; Sam Pig knows many songs and rhymes. Uttley was so concerned about keeping alive the songs and rhymes of her childhood that she included a dozen of them together with the music in her book *Carts and Candlesticks* (1948).

Uttley's Fuzzypeg, the little red foxes, and Sam Pig are really like young children – exploring, learning, paying attention to parental figures, venturing out on their own, and running away from home when they feel ill-treated. The tales of their day-to-day living take young readers on one series of adventures after another. Often these stories follow the cumulative pattern of old tales in which ultimately all join what was originally a one-person excursion. A. A. Milne follows a similar pattern in his Winnie the Pooh stories.

Uttley's fictional worlds are intentionally happy and pleasant. She explains her plan as one to "take the children, or anyone who reads the books, into a land without real fear – although there are small fears which are surmounted." There is danger in the animals' world, even though Uttley stated that she keeps it to a minimum. The stoats, Weasels, and rats, like Grahame's wild-wooders, pose threats to the little animal company Uttley created. The foxes are cunning, but even a little animal like Fuzzypeg can become a hero – as he does in *The Speckledy Hen* (1946) when he, as the only one who can read, distracts the Fox with Aesop's fable "The Fox and the Grapes" so that the speckledy hen can lead ten chicks back to the safety of the barnyard.

Sometimes magic and sometimes perseverance allay the predators and protect innocent characters. In *Grey Rabbit and the Circus* (1961), the Black Hare, a magician, protects the little animals from their enemy: the Fox has heard a sound, "but when he came towards the circle of animals there was an invisible barrier which no savage creature could get through. It had been made by the Black Hare who

had spilled fern seed all around to protect the circus." The threat is greater in *Little Grey Rabbit and the Weasels* (1947), when Grey Rabbit is captured to be the housekeeping slave of the weasels and is rescued by Wise Owl. Even in captivity Grey Rabbit bravely bargains with the weasels. She makes them promise not to hurt her friends or continue to steal from them, as they have been doing, before she will sing a note for them. White Hen uses magic to escape from the fox in "The Fox and the Little White Hen." A garland of cowslips put around her neck makes her invisible.

Sometimes magic occurs simply for the enjoyment it provides. The boyish characters Sam Pig, Fuzzypeg, Tim Rabbit, and the little foxes encounter magical figures similar to the old gypsy woman who gives Mrs. Trout and her daughter Susanna a saucepan that always supplies food in "The Saucepan," from *The Little Knife Who Did All the Work: Twelve Tales of Magic* (1962). The wind gives Sam Pig a magic whistle, and either in dream or reality he visits the other side of the moon and goes with Santa Claus and his reindeer on Christmas Eve to deliver parcels to all the animals.

The Adventures of No Ordinary Rabbit (1937) includes eighteen tales of the "boyish adventures" of Tim Rabbit who, as Denis Judd notes, has a lot in common with Sam Pig. Tim is wont to tell people he meets that he is no ordinary rabbit. He is the only one of his family who can speak and be understood by humans, but sometimes he hides this ability – as he does when he is captured by a man who thinks he will make a good pet for his son Billy. Tim Rabbit becomes a favorite of an old man who rescues him by paying five pounds for him. This is one of the few relationships that develops between animals and humans in Uttley's animal stories; another develops when Sam Pig falls in love with Betsy Bywater, a little girl with golden curls in "Sam Pig on the Register" from *Sam Pig and the Singing Gate* (1955). Sam Pig is like Tim Rabbit in that he is the only one of the pigs who can speak "man's language."

The Sam Pig series commenced with *Tales of the Four Pigs and Brock the Badger* (1939) and grew to thirteen collections of Sam Pig stories. Peter de Sautoy comments, "Sam Pig was the one the children loved.... Sam Pig is like a little boy really, rather mischievous and getting up to all sorts of adventures and so on. I used to think that he was in a way her son ... John, fictionalised." Guardian to the boyish Sam Pig and his sister is Brock the Badger. Like Badger in Kenneth Grahame's *The Wind in the Willows* (1908), Brock is an authority figure who lives underground. He has unearthed the treasures of a Roman city, and Uttley builds a story around his generosity with the treasure he is guarding. Moldy Warp accidentally discovers this treasure and thinks it is in Aladdin's Cave in *Moldy Warp, the Mole* (1940), part of the Grey Rabbit series; one can see how even different series of Uttley's animal stories share the same characters.

In *Six Tales of the Four Pigs* (1941) Sam reveals his knowledge of fairy tales in "The Wolf." As he sets off on an excursion to Badger's castle, he tells his sister Ann, "I'll take a bag of pebbles and drop them. Hop-o'-my thumb did that. Then I can find my way back if I don't get to Badger's castle." Sam is a musical pig who plays the fiddle and even earns money so that all the family can have a good time at the fair. Humans throw "pence and sixpences and even shillings to the little fiddler." In this same story, Badger helps the pelicans to escape from captivity, and this too is typical of the efforts the animals make to keep their kindred free. Sam Pig helps Farmer Greensleeves in order to earn money to buy Brock the badger a birthday present. Sam Pig does some things well, but he can be foolish, as when he breaks all the eggs because he does not think that Mrs. Greensleeves will want the shells, or when he paints the farmer's cart blue and yellow rather than just cleaning it, as he had been asked to do. He becomes a plumber's apprentice in "The Plumber's Mate" and ends up in a Christmas pudding in "Sam Pig Visits the Big House." He is mistaken for the notorious title-character, in "Guy Fawkes' Day," by children celebrating the fifth of November, and, after escaping, he persuades Brock to let them have fireworks to celebrate. Thirty-five Sam Pig stories are published in *The Sam Pig Story Book* (1965).

Uttley's other animal series, the Little Brown Mouse stories, have not been as popular with children; in fact, they bored even Uttley herself. The same activities that occur in the Grey Rabbit series — spring cleaning, parties, going to the fair, the invasion of the home by weasels and stoats, and riddles and games — also figure in this series.

Uttley's collections of short stories merit special attention. The first, *Moonshine and Magic* (1932), consists of twenty-eight stories and has remained one of her most popular collections. Many have been reprinted in other collections throughout the years. *Some Moonshine Tales* (1945) includes seven from that collection; *The Weather Cock, and Other Stories* (1945) includes nine, and *The Spice Woman's Basket and Other Tales* (1944) includes another six. In turn, the Penguin collection of stories, *Magic in My Pocket: a Selection of Tales* (1957), reprints three tales from *The Spice Woman's Basket*, one of which appeared in the earlier *Moonshine and Magic*. As this brief publishing history of some of Uttley's stories illustrates, it is difficult to treat her fourteen collections in chronological sequence. The Kerlan collection's vertical file on Alison Uttley includes copies of five of her earliest stories published by *My Magazine* in its section "The Storyteller."

Uttley indicated that these were her first published stories. The first, "The Dark Chamber," reappears with minor variations in a chapter of *John at the Old Farm* (1960), the book Uttley wrote commemorating "her son's long visit to the house of her childhood." Retooled as part of her young son's experiences at Castle Top Farm, this early story was obviously etched indelibly in Uttley's mind. She frequently recycled material and once published, as Judd notes, the same story about the Little White Hen under a different title. This is not surprising in a writing career that spanned fifty years. Certain thematic patterns became staples of her craft and were used time and again.

Uttley's books of country lore are usually classed with her works for adults. Her fairy tales and the play she wrote about Hans Christian Andersen, however, definitely belongs with her works for children. *The Washerwoman's Child* (1946), a dramatization of seven of Andersen's fairy tales, reveals that Uttley was indebted to Andersen for many of her own storytelling features, especially those of giving common household objects like knives and spoons a life of their own, as well as her presentations of human longings and desires. Andersen's influence can be seen particularly in the stories included in *The Little Knife that Did All the Work: Twelve Tales of Magic*.

Alison Uttley's life story as well as her philosophy have much in common with those of the Canadian author Lucy Maud Montgomery, and it seems ironic, as one looks at the public and private lives of these female writers, that Uttley was asked by her publishers in 1937 to try to write a book like Montgomery's *Anne of Green Gables* (1908). The authors are more or less contemporaries; both were married in 1911. The depressions Uttley suffered, her despair over her husband James's melancholia, her strong and sometimes domineering personality, her inability to get along with many of her relatives and keep servants for any length of time, her worries over financial matters, her two or three close female friends kept throughout her life, her deep and possessive love for her son, and her passionate and almost irrational hidden self are all qualities shared in part by Montgomery. Like Montgomery, who had two male correspondents in whom she could confide, Uttley had two male friends who stood by her after her husband's suicide. Professor Samuel Alexander, and later Walter de la Mare, became close friends and advisers. Professor Alexander even helped with her son John's education. Uttley, like Montgomery, put much stock in dreams and recorded hers faithfully in her diary, and she later wrote a book entitled *The Stuff of Dreams* (1953).

After the publication of *The Country Child,* in which Uttley's own childhood is presented as that of Susan Garland, Uttley was also compared to Laura Ingalls Wilder. Montgomery, Wilder, and Uttley were all interested in the same essential qualities that enrich life, and each wanted to record her own childhood experiences in her fiction for others to share. In 1937, in response to her publisher's demands for a book like *Anne of Green Gables,* Uttley gave them *Ambush of Young Days,* the only one of her autobiographical stories told in the first person. This book differs from the later *The Farm on the Hill,* which continues the story of Susan Garland's childhood and school days and is much better integrated than the earlier and even more episodic *The Country Child. Ambush of Young Days* is a rather flat narrative and not as successful as the retelling of early childhood experiences through the character of Susan Garland. In this rendition of her life, Uttley exposes the bittersweet cast of the events of her early years. As with Montgomery, Uttley's personal journals shed light on the woman behind the mask and re-

veal the fusion of fiction and reality in the autobiographical writings as well as in the purely fictional works.

Uttley's writing, in addition to all the enjoyment it has given generations of children, deserves to be remembered as a testimony to a way of life in England that might have entirely disappeared had she not so faithfully recorded it in her various literary endeavors. As a Saturday's child, she knew from the old rhyme that she would have to work hard for her living. Judd mistakenly believes that the old rhyme states that Saturday's child has far to go. Uttley may have appropriated this identity of the Thursday's child for herself, but she never slipped up on an old rhyme and quotes the Mother Goose version correctly in her "Thursday's Child," one of the Sam Pig stories. Alison Uttley's works deserve to be remembered as an accurate repository of fairy and folk wisdom, and she as an author who achieved variety as well as excellence in her contributions to literature for children.

Biographies:

Elizabeth Saintsbury, *The World of Alison Uttley Biography: The Life and Times of One of the Best Loved Country Writers of Our Century* (London: Howard Baker, 1980);

Denis Judd, *The Life of a Country Child (1884–1976): The Authorized Biography* (London: M. Joseph, 1986).

Elfrida Vipont
(Elfrida Vipont Foulds, Charles Vipont)
(3 July 1902 – 14 March 1992)

Margaret Stickney Bienert

BOOKS: *Quakerism: An International Way of Life,* as Elfrida Vipont Foulds (Manchester: 1930 Committee, 1930);

Good Adventure: The Quest of Music in England, illustrated by Estella Canziani (Manchester: Heywood, 1931);

Colin Writes to Friends House, illustrated by Elisabeth Brockbank (London: Friends Book Centre, 1934; revised edition, London: Bannisdale Press, 1946);

Blow the Man Down, as Charles Vipont, illustrated by Norman Hepple (London: Oxford University Press, 1939; Philadelphia: Lippincott, 1952);

Lift Up Your Lamps: The Pageant of a Friends' Meeting, as Elfrida Vipont Foulds (Manchester: 1930 Committee, 1939);

The Lark in the Morn, illustrated by Terrence Reginald Freeman (London: Oxford University Press, 1948; Indianapolis: Bobbs-Merrill, 1951; revised edition, London: Oxford University Press, 1970; New York: Holt, Rinehart & Winston, 1970);

The Lark on the Wing, illustrated by Freeman (London: Oxford University Press, 1950; Indianapolis: Bobbs-Merrill, 1951; revised edition, London: Oxford University Press, 1970; New York: Holt, Rinehart & Winston, 1970);

A Lily among Thorns: Some Passages in the Life of Margaret Fell of Swarthmoor Hall (London: Friends Home Service Committee, 1950);

Sparks among the Stubble, illustrated by Patricia Lambe (London: Oxford University Press, 1950);

The Birthplace of Quakerism: A Handbook for the 1652 Country, as Elfrida Vipont Foulds (London: Friends Home Service Committee, 1952; revised, 1968; revised again, 1973; revised again, 1987);

Let Your Lives Speak: A Key to Quaker Experience, as Elfrida Vipont Foulds (Wallingford, Pa.: Pen-

Elfrida Vipont

dle Hill, 1953; London: Friends Home Service Committee, 1954);

The Story of Quakerism 1652–1952 (London: Bannisdale Press, 1954); revised as *The Story of Quakerism Through Three Centuries* (London: Bannisdale Press, 1960; revised edition, Richmond, Ind.: Friends United Press, 1977);

Arnold Rowntree: A Life (London: Bannisdale Press, 1955);

The Family at Dowbiggins, illustrated by Freeman (London: Lutterworth, 1955; Indianapolis: Bobbs-Merrill, 1955);

The Heir of Craigs, as Charles Vipont, illustrated by Tessa Theobald (London: Oxford University Press, 1955);

Living in the Kingdom, as Elfrida Vipont Foulds (Philadelphia: Young Friends Movement, 1955);

The Quaker Witness: Yesterday and Today, as Elfrida Vipont Foulds (Richmond, Ind.: Friends United Press, 1955);

Five More (Oxford: Blackwell, 1957);

The Secret of Orra, illustrated by D. J. Watkins-Pitchford (Oxford: Blackwell, 1957);

The Spring of the Year, illustrated by Freeman (London: Oxford University Press, 1957);

More about Dowbiggins, illustrated by Freeman (London: Lutterworth, 1958); republished as *A Win for Henry Conyers* (London: Hamish Hamilton, 1968);

Ackworth School, From Its Foundation in 1779 to the Introduction of Co-Education in 1946 (London: Lutterworth, 1959);

Henry Purcell and His Times, illustrated by L. J. Broderick (London: Lutterworth, 1959);

Changes at Dowbiggins, illustrated by Freeman (London: Lutterworth, 1960); republished as *Boggarts and Dreams* (London: Hamish Hamilton, 1969);

Flowering Spring, illustrated by Shirley Hughes (London: Oxford University Press, 1960);

The Story of Christianity in Britain, illustrated by Gaynor Chapman (London: M. Joseph, 1961);

What about Religion?, illustrated by Peter Roberson (London: Museum Press, 1961);

A Faith to Live By (Philadelphia: Friends General Conference, 1962); republished as *Quakerism: A Faith to Live By* (London: Bannisdale Press, 1966);

Search for a Song, illustrated by Peter Edwards (London: Oxford University Press, 1962);

Some Christian Festivals (London: M. Joseph, 1963; New York: Roy, 1964);

Larry Lopkins, illustrated by Pat Merritt (London: Hamish Hamilton, 1965);

The Offcomers, illustrated by Janet Duchesne (London: Hamish Hamilton, 1965; New York: McGraw-Hill, 1967);

Rescue for Mittens, illustrated by Jane Paton (London: Hamish Hamilton, 1965);

Stevie, illustrated by Raymond Briggs (London: Hamish Hamilton, 1965);

Terror by Night: A Book of Strange Stories (London: Hamish Hamilton, 1966); republished as *Ghosts' High Noon* (New York: Walck, 1967);

Weaver of Dreams: The Girlhood of Charlotte Brontë (London: Hamish Hamilton, 1966; New York: Walck, 1966);

A Child of the Chapel Royal, illustrated by John Lawrence (London: Oxford University Press, 1967);

The China Dog, illustrated by Constance Marshall (London: Hamish Hamilton, 1967);

People of the Past (London: Oxford University Press, 1967);

The Secret Passage, illustrated by Ian Ribbons (London: Hamish Hamilton, 1967);

Children of the Mayflower, illustrated by Evadne Rowan (London: Heinemann, 1969; New York: Watts, 1970);

The Elephant and the Bad Baby, illustrated by Briggs (London: Hamish Hamilton, 1969; New York: Coward-McCann, 1969);

Michael and the Dogs, illustrated by Pat Merritt (London: Hamish Hamilton, 1969);

The Pavilion, illustrated by Prudence Seward (London: Oxford University Press, 1969; New York: Holt, Rinehart & Winston, 1970);

Towards a High Attic: The Early Life of George Eliot (London: Hamish Hamilton, 1970; New York: Holt, Rinehart & Winston, 1971);

My England (London: Heinemann, 1973);

Bed in Hell (London: Hamish Hamilton, 1974; New York: St. Martin's Press, 1975);

George Fox and the Valiant Sixty (London: Hamish Hamilton, 1975);

A Little Bit of Ivory: A Life of Jane Austen (London: Hamish Hamilton, 1977);

Swarthmore Hall, as Elfrida Vipont Foulds (London: Quaker Home Service, 1979);

The Candle of the Lord, as Elfrida Vipont Foulds (Wallingford, Pa.: Pendle Hill, 1983).

RADIO: *A True Tale,* 1952;
John Crook, Quaker, 1954;
Kitty Wilkinson, 1956;
Dr. Dinsdale in Russia, 1956.

OTHER: *The High Way: An Anthology,* edited by Vipont (London: Oxford University Press, 1957);

Bless This Day: A Book of Prayer, edited by Vipont, illustrated by Harold Jones (London: Collins, 1958; New York: Harcourt, Brace, 1958);

The Bridge: An Anthology, edited by Vipont, illustrated by Trevor Brierley Lofthouse (London: Oxford University Press, 1962);

Leonard S. Kenworthy, *Nine Contemporary Quaker Women Speak,* includes excerpts from Vipont's writing (Kennett Square, Pa.: Quaker Publications, 1989).

SELECTED PERIODICAL PUBLICATIONS –
UNCOLLECTED: "Writer's Debt to Children," *Junior Bookshelf,* 15 (July 1951): 98–103;

"Catching Them Alive," *Junior Bookshelf,* 19 (July 1955): 117–125;

"Books and the Countryman," as Elfrida Vipont Foulds, *Library Association* ([Harrogate Conference Proccedings] 1957): 65–69;

"Old Stories Never Die," *Junior Bookshelf,* 22 (November 1958): 245–255.

Elfrida Vipont Foulds is perhaps best known for her books for young adults, *The Lark in the Morn* (1948) and the Carnegie Award–winning *The Lark on the Wing* (1950). These two books, which chronicle Kit Haverard's development as a professional singer, were followed by *The Spring of the Year* (1957) and *Flowering Spring* (1960), which also revolve around the Haverard family. Still popular in the 1990s is her 1969 book for primary readers, *The Elephant and the Bad Baby,* which won the Book World's Spring Festival Book Prize in 1970.

Vipont considered her primary task to be the writing of fiction for children and young people, and she wrote more than twenty juvenile fiction books during a period of forty years. Vipont also wrote notable biographies for adolescent readers and wrote and edited several general religious books for youth. Her many books for adults on Quaker history, biography, and spirituality include the comprehensive volume *The Story of Quakerism 1652–1952* (1954), which is frequently cited as a scholarly work in its field. Her adult historical novel, *Bed in Hell* (1974), provides an intriguing character portrayal of the malevolent narrator and displays Vipont at her best as a writer of fiction.

Elfrida Vipont was born in 1902 in Manchester, England, the daughter of Edward Vipont, a physician, and Dorothy Crowley Brown, both devout Quakers. She attended Mount School and went on to study as a professional singer in London, Paris, and Leipzig. In 1926 Vipont married Robinson Percy Foulds, a research chemist, who died in 1954. They had four daughters. During World War II Vipont was headmistress of the Quaker Evacuation School at Yeland Manor. Curi-

ously, the war was never a subject of her fiction, although she is reported to have started a young adult novel set in World War II.

Vipont made her home in the heart of "1652 Country" where Quakerism was born in a seventeenth-century home, "Green Garth," in Yealand Conyers, Lancashire. Her imagination was captured by the historical and spiritual significance of the landscape of the Lancashire region. Most of her fiction is set here. When she was not writing, Vipont was heavily involved in the Society of Friends, conducting tour guides of the region and serving for twenty years as chairman of the Friends Historical Society. Throughout her career she traveled abroad extensively, lecturing for schools, colleges, children's libraries, and Quaker groups, and forming lasting friendships on the way. Vipont was a member of the P.E.N. society and in 1984 received her Honorary Doctorate in Humane Letters from Earlham College.

The name most often used by the author for her works of fiction was "Elfrida Vipont." The Charles Vipont pseudonym was used for her two relatively early "boys" stories, and the first in the Dowbiggins series. For her writing on the Quaker faith and tradition, the author most often used her full married name, Elfrida Vipont Foulds.

Although as a young girl Vipont felt drawn toward a career in music, her strong imagination and natural talent as raconteur were also evident. In childhood she often used the Friends' Meeting time for "making up stories," just as Kit Haverard in the Lark stories used Quaker meeting time for inventing "pretending games."

Vipont's writing career began with a few early children's stories concerning Quakerism, including *Good Adventure: The Quest of Music in England* (1931), *Colin Writes to Friends House* (1934), and a pamphlet on music in England. With *Blow the Man Down* (1939), Vipont, using the pseudonym Charles Vipont, made her debut as a strong writer of historical fiction.

Blow the Man Down is a seventeenth-century adventure intended for twelve- to sixteen-year-old children, and is told in the first person by Richard Croly, a cabin boy on an English frigate at the battle of Santa Cruz. Richard goes on to further adventures in the pirate-infested waters of Algiers. He struggles throughout for recognition of his legitimacy by his father. This is readable, exciting fiction that includes factual events from the life of the Quaker, Thomas Lurting (Richard's hero). An early review praised this novel for the intriguing external and internal drama, saying that this just misses being an exceptional book because the two lines of plot (Richard's search for legitimacy and the Thomas Lurting story) are never satisfactorily unified. This problem recurs in some of Vipont's subsequent novels, such as *The Pavilion* (1969).

The Lark in the Morn, The Lark on the Wing, The Spring of the Year, and *The Flowering Spring* are "career stories" featuring the Haverard family. In *The Lark in the Morn,* Kit Haverard struggles toward a recognition of her true vocation as a singer, despite the lack of understanding of her cousin Laura, who has cared for her since birth. Kit experiences the inner struggle between the traditional Quaker ideals of self-sacrifice in the service of truth and full artistic expression. Kit's foil in finding her vocation is her lonely and eccentric Great-Aunt Henrietta, whose unhappiness stems from the fact that her strict parents stifled her ambitions as a musician, believing art was the work of the devil. Kit Haverard, like Vipont, belongs to a new generation of women and of Quakerism.

The inner freedom and independence championed in *The Lark in the Morn* are interwoven with a fine story of Kit's boarding-school days and friend and family interactions. The autobiographical elements in this story are strong: family closeness; the Quaker inner life; conflicts between artistic expression and religious convention; a strong woman finding her career; a deep love of singing; and the pleasure derived from the "pretending" world of the creative imagination.

In the second of the Haverard stories, *The Lark on the Wing,* the stronger plot and vivid evocation of the aesthetic beauty of German lieder and oratorios make this one of Vipont's most noteworthy novels for young people. In the portrayal of the pleasure derived from a disciplined striving after artistic endeavors, the novel is intended to inspire the reader toward similar wholehearted involvement in a vocational pursuit. This educational element escapes being didactic, for it has an authentic base in Vipont's own experience. The romantic interest between Kit Haverard and Terry Chauntesinger provides a satisfying resolution to the story, complementing Kit's successful debut as a singer, where "the lark has mounted up in the air." The Quaker theme of living sacramentally is closely interwoven with the story line, as it applies to Kit putting her life into her music, or to anyone being able to put their lives into everything he or she does.

Despite the success of the first two Haverard novels, reviewers have noted several literary weaknesses: Kit Haverard's naiveté in not realizing that four men were in love with her stretches credibility.

The books have been accused of being a little sentimental and of "cultural snobbery" and "exclusiveness" by those unsympathetic to the Quaker belief. However, even if compared with major modern works whose writers would express their moral convictions in a more sophisticated fashion, the merits of the Lark books far outweigh any minor flaws.

Many of Vipont's novels —including the Lark and Spring stories, the Dowbiggins stories, and *The Pavilion* — center around a world close to Vipont's own experience: a close extended family; a rambling Lancashire home; a profusion of animals and houseguests; folk characters; music; and quiet Quaker wisdom. In these family stories Vipont expresses a spirituality of immanence, of God being very much in the here and now.

Vipont is more successful in some of these novels than others in creating enduring fiction. The Dowbiggins stories of the five Conyer children and their Lancashire home received mixed reviews. For example, a review of one of the books in the Dowbiggins series, *More About Dowbiggins* (1958), found it a "scrappy chronicle" of "minor doings in a north country village." One of Vipont's personal attributes was her ability to accept criticism of her work without being daunted and to continue in spite of criticism. She had the endearing ability of being able to laugh at herself, often parodying her own novels for delighted houseguests. She has said of her work, "I found out by experience that hard work and discipline were essential to my craft. I soon learned that the ability to take criticism and learn from it was another necessary ingredient, as well as the courage to recognize failure and pick myself up and begin again. There was, however, another type of criticism which must be resisted at all costs, the criticism which strikes at what your book has to say about life, which – take it or leave it – is what you were born to say." In her steady outpouring of work for many ages and genres through mixed literary success, Vipont's certainty of what she was born to say guides her course.

In *The Heir of Craigs* (1955), Vipont, again writing as Charles Vipont, provides a strong historical novel set during the reign of William and Mary. When young Nigel is taken at night from his mother's people to live with his paternal grandfather at Craigs in Lancashire, he suffers six years under the cruelty of a jealous uncle. A visiting cousin, Nicholas, takes Nigel away on a political visit to the Americas. Their ship is wrecked, and there are terrifying attacks by Indians and meetings with English slaves sold after Monmouth's rebellion. Nigel and Nicholas return to Lancashire,

Illustration by Evadne Rowan from Vipont's Children of the
Mayflower *(1969)*

where Nicholas is killed in a duel with the jealous
uncle. Interwoven with the exciting story is a theme
of utter dependence upon God and the strength of
the Quaker witness.

This novel was well received as a "moving
piece of work" and a "work of the creative imagination." Vipont's fascination with Lancashire history
and her ability as a storyteller is at play. An earlier
reviewer acknowledged that there was too much
sadness for children in this novel, although adolescents could enjoy the story and the theme.

In Vipont's anthologies of devotional writing
and her books of religious instruction for young
people, we find the spiritual depth and scholarship
that belong to enduring religious classics. Her anthologies *The High Way* (1957), *Bless This Day: A
Book of Prayer* (1958), and *The Bridge* (1962) appeared after a difficult period in her life in the early
1950s. In the space of two years Vipont lost her husband, her father, and a son-in-law. She writes in one
of her Pendle Hill pamphlets, *The Candle of the Lord*
(1983), of entering a local chapel in a downcast state
of mind and being struck by the biblical phrase,
"who going through the vale of misery use it for a

well." From this well of personal suffering and her
extensive reading in the tradition of her faith, Vipont draws richly for the compilation of three noteworthy devotional books.

In *The High Way,* a devotional anthology for
adolescents, selections are chosen from Rufus M.
Jones, Thomas Merton, Brother Lawrence, Meister
Eckhardt, T. S. Eliot, Thomas R. Kelly, and many
others. *Bless This Day,* for primary and junior ages,
includes prayers organized around themes such as
praise and thanksgiving, waking, and sleeping.
Prayers are from ancient church liturgies, the Bible,
modern poets, and spiritual writers (including Vipont) and are vividly complemented by warm, colorful illustrations. The child's approach to God is
conveyed in its simplicity and joy.

The Bridge, a sequel anthology to *The High
Way,* is illustrated with striking wood engravings by
Trevor Brierly Lofthouse. The author chooses passages on the theme of love based on Saint Paul's
first letter to the Corinthians, chapter 13. While *The
High Way* and *The Bridge* are designed for young
people, they can be equally savored by adults.

Vipont's instructional books on faith for
young people, including *The Story of Christianity in
Britain* (1961) and *What About Religion?* (1961), have
lost little in relevancy in the more than thirty years
since they were written. In *The Story of Christianity in
Britain* Vipont's skill as a writer of history complements her ecumenical vision of cooperation and
love among the various branches of the Christian
churches. Her metaphor is of the Dream Cathedral
(an interesting metaphor for a Quaker) in which all
branches of the Christian church have a part. In
What About Religion?, Vipont deals with topics such
as faith, prayer, the Sacraments, life after death, and
jargon in a forthright, approachable manner. Her
humility, humor, and earnestness combine to create
an invaluable book for any young person questioning the tenets of Christianity.

Terror by Night: A Book of Strange Stories (1966),
later published as *Ghosts' High Noon* (1967), is a collection of strange tales taken from the Lancashire
countryside, historical writings, and experiences of
the author's friends. Vipont's belief in the dark side
of the supernatural is consistent with her firsthand
experience of childhood nightmares recounted in
this volume (a story was also fictionalized in *The
Lark in the Morn*). In a Pendle Hill pamphlet on
Quaker spirituality, *Let Your Lives Speak: A Key to
Quaker Experience* (1953), Vipont speaks of "the thick
darkness that can be felt." The vivid descriptions of
the supernatural in this volume of ghost stories
allow us to believe that Elfrida Vipont was familiar

with the nature of the darkness of which she spoke. What distinguishes *Terror By Night* from other collections of ghost stories for young people is the strong presence of the counterbalancing theme of divine light and protection. While for the most part supernatural events do not enter Elfrida Vipont's fiction, in the contrast between supernatural good and evil in *Terror By Night* she may be compared to the Christian writers Madeleine L'Engle and Charles Williams. Primarily, however, *Terror By Night* shows Vipont at her best as a magnificent storyteller. In the adult novel, *Bed in Hell,* Vipont again allows herself freedom to explore the dark side of human experience.

Where Vipont's general fiction may have gone out of fashion for some young readers, her historical fiction and biographies provide lasting scholarly and imaginative treatments of their subjects. In each of her biographies for young people, treating Margaret Fox, Henry Purcell, Charlotte Brontë, George Eliot, and Jane Austen, Vipont provides a rendering of her subject that is sympathetic and objective. Her biography on George Fox was written for both young people and adults.

In *Weaver of Dreams* (1966) Vipont's identification with Charlotte Brontë, who inhabited a world of the imagination both in her childhood play and in her subsequent writing, is evident. Vipont's view is that Charlotte Brontë, unlike her siblings, was able to achieve a balance between her creative inner world and the outer world of career and social obligations. Between the lines the book reveals Vipont's parallel struggles and success. *Weaver of Dreams* is a particularly sensitive and moving biography. The boardinghouse experience, the eccentric isolation of Haworth Parsonage, the wildness of the moors, and interrelationships between the Brontë siblings provide fascinating reading and valuable background to the Brontë novels. Vipont's sensitivity as a biographer is conveyed in her recounting, without psychological interpretation or qualification, of the boarding-school abuse and deaths of Charlotte's older sisters, as well as in her leaving Emily to herself.

Between the writing of *Weaver of Dreams* and her next literary biography, Vipont produced a work of historical fiction for junior readers, a picture book for young children, several works of general fiction for children, and a novel for adolescents concerning the next generation of the Haverard family.

Children of the Mayflower (1969) is Vipont's contribution to the series Long Ago Children's Books, for seven- to nine-year-olds featuring boys and girls

in authentic historical settings. In exemplary historical fiction writing, the author describes how Daniel, Seth, and their little sister, Mercy, endure the tedious and difficult journey of the Mayflower and the hardships of a new life in an unknown country. The adventures of the Puritans, their friendship with the Indians, and their sowing the seed of liberty along with the seed of corn, are depicted in a story line and dialogue accessible to the junior reader. Lively illustrations enhance this text and continue to make this a worthwhile book for young readers.

The Elephant and the Bad Baby is a picture book illustrated by Raymond Briggs, who also illustrated Vipont's earlier children's novel *Stevie* (1965). This award-winning story tells of an elephant and bad baby who go "rumpeta, rumpeta, rumpeta, all down the road," stealing from shop owners, creating havoc, and leaving a trail of angry adults behind them. This book frequently receives a great deal of praise for Briggs's illustrations, while Vipont takes second mention. However, the endearing story of a bad baby has a wonderfully satisfying resolution in a pancake supper and bedtime. Children derive a wonderful happy comfort in knowing that all is well, although all kinds of naughty things have happened. Vipont's sense of humor, so often subtly at work in her writing, finds a natural place in this popular story for the very young.

The Pavilion builds upon the Lark and Spring stories with the story of how Kit Haverard's nieces and nephews try to save a historic music pavilion, along with "The Corders," a decrepit but historic five-hundred-year-old section of town, from destruction by unscrupulous developers. The pavilion becomes a metaphor for an inner sanctuary and "all the beauty and the loving in the world" (a term Vipont borrows from John Galsworthy's *The Forsyte Saga* [1922]), which the children (the defenders of the faith) must strive to preserve. While the plot could be tighter, the subtle thematic developments are of interest to the more serious adolescent reader. However, because it lacks in excitement, this novel, while pleasurable reading, falls short of being memorable. With *The Pavilion* Vipont is self-consciously attempting to write a later-twentieth-century novel. Martin, the teenage protagonist, ponders his Aunt Kit (Haverard's) struggle for freedom in her life and career: "Everything was different now, of course. . . . there did not seem to be any need to fight for one's freedom any more. One had it, only one did not know what to do with it." The problems of the new generation of Haverard children are of a different nature than those of their elders.

In *Towards a High Attic: The Early Life of George Eliot* (1970), a biography of George Eliot, Vipont brings to bear her own struggles with conventionality, her creative struggles as a writer, and her travel to Europe to convey Eliot's breaking away from a harsher interpretation of Christianity, her period of seeking "a very high attic" in Geneva, and her achievement of what Lascelles Abercrombie called a "significant world." Vipont allows herself both distance from and sensitivity to Eliot's religious doubts and rebellion and conveys the very real inner pain and turmoil of a sensitive spirit who was an enigma to herself.

When she began writing serious fiction in her forties, Vipont was still dealing with conventions of girls' school stories, as found in the work of Angela Brazil, where writing for young people did not venture very deeply into the subtler waters of human relationships or the emotional development of the protagonists. Vipont's emergence from these conventions is deliberate, if uneven. While her plots and characters could be more fully developed at times, she has been compared with Louisa May Alcott for her Lark series. By the time of her writing of biographies for adolescents, and her adult novel, *Bed in Hell,* in later life her literary abilities were well refined.

Some readers of Vipont have found the Quakerism that pervades her writing to be exclusive. While there may be some truth to this, even more noteworthy is the broad human understanding and affirmation of life and the individual that lie at the heart of Vipont's writing. The Quaker tradition of the light within, as well as the tradition of constant struggle against the world of darkness, lies behind even her carefree novels of childhood Lancashire life. Vipont's protagonists achieve joy and fulfillment despite the negative counterworld of self-absorption and fear and the forces that threaten to stifle the God-given creative impulse.

In Vipont's metaphor of a sanctuary or pavilion, we may attain insight into her own contribution as a writer. Her own "significant world" of creative endeavor first took shape in the Quaker meeting house where she made up stories for her own amusement. From these meetings also emerged a quiet faith and humility which characterize her life and her approach to her work.

The flaws that may be found in her fiction do not obscure her larger success. Vipont once said that "life is the essential thing." Without preaching or condescension Vipont's fiction calls the young reader to adherence to the Quaker ideal of a "sacramental life," which is in tune with what Galsworthy termed the "beauty and loving in the world."

Reference:

Mary S. Milligan and Edward H. Milligan, "Elfrida Vipont Foulds (1902–1992)," *Friend* (15 May 1992): 621–622.

Papers:

Collections of Vipont's manuscripts are contained in the Kerlan Collection, University of Minnesota, Minneapolis, and the Lancaster Library, Lancashire.

T. H. White

(29 May 1906 – 17 January 1964)

Hugh T. Keenan
Georgia State University

BOOKS: *Loved Helen and Other Poems* (London: Chatto & Windus, 1929; New York: Viking, 1929);

The Green Bay Tree; or, Wicked Man Touches Wood, Songs for Six-pence, No. 3 (Cambridge: Heffer, 1929);

Dead Mr. Nixon, by White and R. McNair Scott (London: Cassell, 1931);

Darkness at Pemberley, illustrated by White (London: Gollancz, 1932; New York: Putnam, 1933);

They Winter Abroad, as James Aston (New York: Viking, 1932; London: Chatto & Windus, 1932);

First Lesson, as James Aston (London: Chatto & Windus, 1932; New York: Knopf, 1933);

Farewell Victoria (London: Collins, 1933; New York: Smith & Haas, 1934);

Earth Stopped (London: Collins, 1934);

Gone To Ground (London: Collins, 1935);

England Have My Bones, illustrated by White (New York: Macmillan, 1936; London: Collins, 1936);

Burke's Steerage (London: Collins, 1938);

The Sword in the Stone, illustrated by White, with endpapers by Robert Lawson (London: Collins, 1938; New York: Putnam, 1939);

The Witch in the Wood, illustrated by White (New York: Putnam, 1939; London: Collins, 1940); revised edition published as *The Queen of Air and Darkness* in *The Once and Future King*;

The Ill-Made Knight, illustrated by White (New York: Putnam, 1940; London: Collins, 1941);

Mistress Masham's Repose, illustrated by Fritz Eichenberg (New York: Putnam, 1946; London: Cape, 1947);

The Elephant and the Kangaroo, illustrated by White (New York: Putnam, 1947; London: Cape, 1948);

The Age of Scandal (New York: Putnam, 1950; London: Cape, 1950);

The Goshawk, illustrated by White (London: Cape, 1951; New York: Putnam, 1952);

T. H. White

The Scandalmonger (New York: Putnam, 1952; London: Cape, 1952);

The Master: An Adventure Story (New York: Putnam, 1957; London: Cape, 1957);

The Once and Future King [a tetralogy composed of *The Sword in the Stone, The Queen of Air and Darkness, The Ill-Made Knight,* and *The Candle in the Wind* (previously unpublished)] (London: Collins, 1958; New York: Putnam, 1958);

The Godstone and the Blackymor, illustrated by Edward Ardizzone (London: Cape, 1959); republished as *A Western Wind* (New York: Putnam, 1959);

Verses (Alderney, U.K.: Privately printed, 1962); re-
     published as *A Joy Proposed,* introduction,
     afterword, and notes by Kurth Sprague (Lon-
     don: Bertram Rota, 1980; Athens: University
     of Georgia Press, 1983);
America at Last, edited, with an introduction, by
     David Garnett (New York: Putnam, 1965);
*The Book of Merlyn: The Unpublished Conclusion to The
     Once and Future King,* introduction by Sylvia
     Townsend Warner, illustrated by Trevor
     Stubley (Austin: University of Texas Press,
     1977);
The Maharajah & Other Stories, selected, with an intro-
     duction, by Sprague (New York: Putnam,
     1981; London: Macdonald, 1981).

OTHER: *The Book of Beasts: Being a Translation from a
     Latin Bestiary of the Twelfth Century Made and Ed-
     ited by T. H. White* (London: Cape, 1954; New
     York: Putnam, 1955).

Like British scholars C. S. Lewis and J. R. R.
Tolkien, Terence Hanbury White turned his concern for the events leading to World War II into the
unexpected – a highly original children's book, *The
Sword in the Stone* (1938). Unlike them White wrote
his first Arthurian novel in the isolation of a
gamekeeper's cottage at Stowe Ridings after resign-
ing as the popular head of the English department
of the Stowe School. At Stowe Ridings he deliberately lived a reclusive life, removing himself from
the temptation of his strong pederastic feelings, de-
voting all of his energy to the voracious reading of
books and the arduous accomplishment of ordinary
skills such as milking and plowing, and exotic ones
such as falconry. He reserved his affection solely
for Brownie, his red setter. Vehemently opposed to
war, he waffled between active participation and escape to Ireland.

White's children's novel about Arthur's youth
and Merlyn's education of the boy who would become King Arthur was greatly revised in *The Once
and Future King* (1958), which in turn became the
basis for the musical *Camelot* (1960) and the subsequent film (1965), cultural icons of the 1960s. By
that stage White's children's story of Wart had
been lost in the famous adult romance of the
Arthur-Guinevere-Lancelot triangle.

His early interest in Sir Thomas Malory's
Morte d'Arthur (1485) and experience as a tutor and
teacher led White to invent the comic and didactic
details of Wart's education and to give Merlyn a
more active role. As a tutor he had earned his way
through Queen's College, Cambridge; he was

briefly a teacher at Saint David's preparatory school
in southern England (1930–1932) and finally the demanding but charismatic head of the English department (1932–1936) at Stowe School on that famous English estate. Royalties from *The Once and
Future King* made White a wealthy man, able to indulge his whims and vagaries and to break his self-
imposed isolation. He befriended celebrities such as
Julie Andrews and her husband Tony Walton and
played host to groups of deaf and blind persons during the summer at his home on the Channel Island
of Alderney.

The Sword in the Stone will probably remain his
best-known story, partially through retellings by
others. He wrote three other children's books: *Mistress Masham's Repose* (1946), *The Goshawk* (1951),
and *The Master: An Adventure Story* (1957). Some critics of children's literature would include all of the
Arthurian novels that White wrote. But the other
Arthurian works are unsuitable either by their tone
or subject matter, especially the revised versions of
the 1958 tetralogy. Humphrey Carpenter – who in
Twentieth-Century Writers for Children (1989) adds *The
Witch in the Wood* (1939), *The Ill-Made Knight* (1940),
The Once and Future King (1958), and *The Book of
Merlyn* (1977) to the list – concedes that "Many of
T. H. White's books have been read by children,
but his claim to be a children's writer rests chiefly
on *The Sword in the Stone* and *Mistress Masham's Repose.*"

In a letter of 14 January 1938 to his former
Cambridge tutor L. J. Potts, White called *The Sword
in the Stone* a "warm-hearted" story "mainly about
bird and beasts" and "more or less a kind [of] wish
fulfillment of the kind of things I should like to have
happened to me when I was a boy." But *The Witch in
the Wood,* written during his self-exile in Ireland
(1939–1945), is a dark novel of what his early education and family life were really like, a tale of an
abusive childhood and a sadistic military-college education at Cheltenham College (1920–1924). His
hatred for a mother who first smothered and then
rejected him is reflected in the novel's Queen
Morgause. It poisoned the whole work, as he, his
friends, and the critics recognized. Queen Morgause
manipulates and psychologically distorts her four
teenaged sons – Gawaine, Gareth, Gaheris, and
Agravaine – leading them to kill sadistically the unicorn for her sake. Her incest with Arthur produces
Mordred. *The Ill-Made Knight* concerns the dilemma
of an ugly Lancelot who wants to remain a virgin to
achieve the Quest of the Grail but who capitulates
to his lust for Queen Guinevere. *The Candle in the
Wind* (1958) gives the traditional story of betrayals

within the family, the leadership, and the nation that lead to the fall of the Round Table and its ideals. Hailed in prepublication *The Book of Merlyn* proved a disappointing diatribe by Merlyn about war, nations, and honor to a disillusioned, mature, and defeated King Arthur. In retrospect the publishers, Collins, were right to reject it in 1941. When the four novels were revised to become *The Once and Future King,* White scrapped most of the fifth book, adding Arthur's experiences in the anthill and with the flocks of geese to the first book of the tetralogy.

The early life of T. H. White did little to foster a varied and skilled writer. At age thirty his mother, Constance, the daughter of a Indian judge, married Garrick White, a district superintendent of police, only to spite her parents. After his birth the marriage turned highly acrimonious and she refused further sexual relations. Her husband became a violent alcoholic. His parents brought White ill with parathroid to live with her family at Saint Leonard's in England, and his father returned to India. Constance rejoined him in 1914 but returned to England, again in 1915. In 1920 White was sent to a military school, Cheltenham College, where the masters enthusiastically caned the students. Loving grandparents raised him, while his parents tried another fruitless reconciliation in India. In 1923 his parents were divorced and his mother became a pig farmer on a small scale. White remained alienated from his father until Garrick White's death in 1946. According to François Gallix, White credited his mother with both a love of storytelling and an attraction to violence and cruelty. Certainly he worked to control his sadistic impulses, which took psychological, not physical, forms.

As a result White said his affections were so distorted that he could not find a normal relationship with a woman, and he refused to practice the homosexuality of his strong inclinations. Throughout the years he formed crushes on several unavailable or unsuitable women, such as the nurse who cared for him during his appendectomy, a barmaid, a thirteen-year-old girl, and an eighteen-year-old debutante. Late in his life, after abstaining from expressing his homosexual feelings for twenty years, he fell in love with Zed, the teenage son of friends, but resisted and was desolated when the boy's parents called an end to their friendship. Through most of his adult life he transferred his affection to a mixture of animals including badgers, owls, goshawks, grass snakes, and particularly red setters, especially one named Brownie. When Brownie died in 1944, White wrote that she "was mother, child and mistress to me for fourteen years."

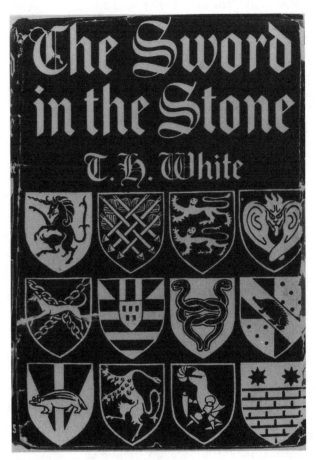

Dust jacket for White's children's book based on the Arthurian legend

His books of conventional poetry – *Loved Helen and Other Poems* (1929) and *The Green Bay Tree; or, Wicked Man Touches Wood* (1929) – the two detective novels – *Dead Mr. Nixon* (1931) and *Darkness at Pemberley* (1932) – and the two academic novels – *They Winter Abroad* (1932) and *First Lesson* (1932) – resemble those of many other bright Cambridge graduates. Yet in minor ways they contribute to his children's books. As a dashing teacher at two schools, he played the role of young man of the world, driving an old Bentley, pursuing field sports, and fishing while working on five books. At the same time he wrote ironically in 1931 to his tutor L. J. Potts that snobbery is "one of the best parlour games known to me – for persons not among the gentry." Role-playing, and making fun of it, became a large part of his complex character.

He reached a crisis in 1935–1936: a car accident in March 1935 left him temporarily blind. But the modest financial success of *England Have My Bones* (1936), a series of detailed essays on the pleasures of ordinary country life, allowed him to resign from Stowe School in 1936 and to move into a primitive gamekeeper's cottage on the grounds and take up a different impoverished, independent life. Writing about subjects of real interest to him had proved to have a market. He also began hormonal treatments for his homosexuality as well as periodic drinking bouts that would continue throughout his life.

From this point on, his life was filled with various writing projects, the learning of skills as various as plowing, flying, operating a boat, oil painting, and training goshawks, and always with omnivorous reading. His books for children reflect his wide reading, his intimate knowledge and empathy with animals, and his championing of independence.

The Sword in the Stone begins with a famous parody of medieval education reduced to a public-school week: "On Mondays, Wednesdays and Fridays it was Court Hand and Summulae Logicales, while the rest of the week it was the Organon, Repetition and Astrology." Perspectives in the book shift constantly between medieval and contemporary life, a matter expedited by Merlyn, who is a twentieth-century person living backward into the fifteenth. Several themes hold the book together. The first is the search for a proper tutor after the sexual hysteria of the governess becomes evident. Another is Wart's discovery of his identity and fate, and a general one is the pleasures of country life. White's double perspective allows him to fill the book with accurate details of medieval farming, haymaking, and hunting and to counterpose these to the detailed and foolish aspects of King Pellinore for the Questing Beast. After Wart finds Merlyn in the forest, the book follows Jean-Jacques Rousseau's familiar model for children's literature in which a wise teacher waits for the student to ask questions and then provides the learning experiences.

The novel is full of autobiographical details. Merlyn's study, like White's, is messily full of books, animals, and insects. An owl named Archimedes sits on Merlyn's head just as it did on White's. Proclaiming that "Education is experience," he turns Wart into a fish, a hawk, a grass snake, an owl, and a badger to learn the limitations of Might as Right and military life; the insanity of those who live to fight; and some alternative myths and fables. On his own in the ordinary world, Wart learns responsibility by retrieving his goshawk; courage from rescuing Dog Boy, Wat, and Friar Tuck from Morgan the Fay; the need for the rules in the fall hunt; loyalty to one's home from the conversation with the badger; and finally humility and

honesty in offering the sword from the stone to Kay.

In addition to explicit details about medieval life and its continuity with country life, the book also parodies medieval themes and situations. The Questing Beast nearly dies of a broken heart when King Pellinore ceases to chase it. White's Merlyn, often inept as a magician, says a spell incorrectly and gets a series of wrong hats and has to be corrected by the owl Archimedes. There are various inside jokes, some as obvious as the double entendre about the governess's muddle with her astrolabe and others more recondite, such as Little John's insistence that Robin Hood's real name is Robin Wood, probably White's allusion to *Robin des Bois,* the original title of Carl Maria von Weber's *Der Freischutz* and its famous hunting-horn overture.

There are allusions to classic children's literature. Kay and Wart are invited to dine and are trapped by Madame Mim in her cottage in the forest, an episode which recalls Hansel and Gretel. The later description of the temptations of sweets at the castle of Queen Morgan both recalls the edible cottage of this story and burlesques the excessive food imagery of some children's books. As in many children's tales, friendly animals aid the child-hero to achieve a quest. At the end of the novel Wart calls upon their spirits to give him strength to pull the sword out.

The book delights in the incongruous, such as the neon movie sign over Morgan's door – "THE QUEEN OF AIR AND DARKNESS, NOW SHOWING" – and her description as "a very beautiful lady, wearing beach pajamas and smoked glasses." Quotations from classics such as William Shakespeare's lyric poems and the Latin refrain from William Dunbar's *Lament for the Makaris* (circa 1507), as well as silly rhymes and parodies of popular tunes, fill the pages.

The realistic hunting scenes and the fantastic battle against the mythological griffins and wyverns are lively. Wart and Kay talk and act like young teenaged boys. But the adults are mostly comic stereotypes. Throughout, the author's simple but skilled line drawings for head- and tailpieces suit a children's book. The reviewers of *The Sword and the Stone* gave unanimous praise. It was made a Book-of-the-Month Club selection. Walt Disney bought the rights to make the film, finally produced in 1963.

When White drastically revised this novel to become part of *The Once and Future King,* he decided that the Arthurian story was really about the futility of war, rather than a domestic tragedy of incest. As a result the revised version is more somber and lacks much of the playfulness and extravagance of the original as well as White's clever drawings. The later version, designed for a general reading audience, displaced this masterpiece for children.

During White's years in Ireland he completed *The Once and Future King.* In his farewell he turned his experiences of six years as the lodger of Mr. and Mrs. McDonagh in Doolistown into the satiric novel *The Elephant and the Kangaroo* (1947), which owes much to Chaucer's *Miller's Tale* and ended his friendship with the McDonaghs. He returned to England in 1945 to stay for a year with his new dogs Quince and Killie in Duke Mary's, a Yorkshire cottage of his longtime friend David Garnett. While there he became enamored of a thirteen-year-old farm girl and was inspired to write *Mistress Masham's Repose,* a comic children's novel whose complex plot owes something to his earlier detective novels but much more to his experiences at Stowe and his enthusiasm for Jonathan Swift's *Gulliver's Travels* (1726), especially the visit to the Lilliputians.

Dedicated to Amaryllis Virginia Garnett, his friend's daughter, this book proves that White could write well about women, if they were young enough. The book's orphaned heroine, ten-year-old Maria, is a studious bespectacled yet impulsive and adventurous sort with dark hair, pigtails, and brown eyes. She is good at games and afraid both of cows and her mean governess Miss Brown. She enjoys music and plays the piano but hates the fifth of November (Guy Fawkes' Day) because of the noise.

She lives in Malplaquet, a ruined eighteenth-century Northamptonshire mansion four times longer than Buckingham Palace and modeled on the Stowe Mansion and estate. It has fifty-two state bedrooms and twelve company rooms. Only the two bedrooms that she and her governess use do not leak. Mrs. Noakes, the cook and only servant, lives in the basement kitchen and has to pedal a bicycle through the corridor to wait on the two of them. Six of the 365 windows are unbroken. Stripped of most of its furnishings, the house is "surrounded by Vistas, Obelisks, Pyramids, Columns, Temples, Rotundas, and Palladian Bridges, which had been built in honor of General Wolfe, Admiral Byng, the Princess Amelia, and others of the Same Kidney." This setting allows White to crowd in all sorts of allusions to persons, literature, events, and gossip of the eighteenth and nineteenth centuries, the sorts of things that fill his eighteenth-century social histories, *The Age of Scandal* (1950) and *The Scandalmonger* (1952), and his novel of the Victorian age, *Farewell Victoria* (1933). His horse-obsessed Lord Lieutenant

Self-portrait by White, 1942

recalls hunting details of *Earth Stopped* (1934) and the satire of such sports in *Burke's Steerage* (1938).

Maria's friends are the Cook, whose illiterate speech and writing recall Mrs. Malaprop, and an old professor, who lives in a gamekeeper's cottage on the grounds and devotes his existence to scholarship and an eclectic menagerie. Maria's nemeses are Miss Brown, who uses flowerly speech and spreads "as a toad on one's hand" when she sits, and the local vicar and her guardian Mr. Hater, who as a schoolmaster is fond of caning boys. He drives a Rolls Royce bought with the money embezzled from Maria's estate. While playing pirate and invading an island in the midst of an ornamental lake, Maria discovers that Mistress Masham's Repose, a classical summer pavilion, is home to five hundred descendants of Swift's Lilliputians.

The plot has two parts. One concerns Maria's relationship to the Lilliputians. She kidnaps a woman and her baby until she learns that "people must not tyrannize, nor try to be great because they are little." Then she tries patronizing them by giving gifts and playing with them like pets until she almost gets one killed in a model airplane and loses the whalelike pike that the ship's crew is trying to land. When Miss Brown and Mr. Hater learn of the Lilliputians and try to capture them to sell them to the circus or the movies, Maria and the Professor join forces to prevent this.

The other plot concerns the discovery of a document that will restore Maria's inheritance to her. The two plots come together when Maria, the Professor, and some of the Lilliputians are locked in a dungeon. The novel allows White to fill in the history of the Lilliputians up to the twentieth century, to give minute details of their farming and hunting, and to imitate their eighteenth-century British speech through high-flown, capitalized nouns and verbs.

Like Merlyn in *The Sword in the Stone,* the Professor acts as the Rousseau-like instructor of Maria. He is also an absent-minded, scholarly pacifist, difficult to tear away from his scholarly researches and somewhat inept in practical matters. White satirizes himself as an improvident medieval scholar of "Isidore, Physiologus, Pliny, and similar people," the sort of research that resulted in *The Book of Beasts* (1954), a translation of a twelfth-century bestiary first proposed to him by medievalist Sir Sydney Cockerell in 1938. Puzzled and frustrated by not knowing the meaning of *Tripharium,* he hatches far-fetched schemes to get a copy of Du Cange's dictionary of medieval Latin, asking even the Cook for help though her only book is Mrs. Beeton's famous Victorian cookbook. The gloss to this word appears in the notes to his *Book of Beasts.*

The novel is filled with incongruous scenes, such as the Professor chopping wood with a six-penny hatchet from Woolworth's beneath a marble monument to the theater dedicated "to Congreve, or to somebody of that sort." Other topographical jokes are erudite: the estate Malplaquet, named for one of Marlborough's minor battles; the monument to Admiral Byng, court-martialed for cowardice; Mrs. Masham's Repose, named for a bitter political enemy of Sarah Churchill; the pyramid, dedicated to John Burgoyne, who surrendered at Saratoga to the American army.

The novel has obvious debts to Swift's *Gulliver's Travels* and Lewis Carroll's *Alice's Adventures in Wonderland* (1865). But unlike Swift's Lilliputians, White's are kind, generous, and noble. There are echoes of other books. The Lilliputian scout and trapper Gradgnag is compared to Allan Quatermaine, the hero of H. Rider Haggard's *King Solomon's Mines* (1885). A few faults make the book just miss being the classic that David Garnett thought revision could have made it. Miss Brown's and Mr. Hater's plot to murder Maria does not ring

true. The last chapter shifts in tone and perspective, first describing a Christmas party for Maria and then asking Amaryllis to imagine the appearance of the restored house as a stately home on tour and with 365.2564 servants (one for each day of a real year). Too often some of the language and allusions in the novel recall White's research notes on the eighteenth century.

This is children's literature only for the very bright. But its message of the difference between love and possession and how to become a true friend is clear. With excellent illustrations by Fritz Eichenberg, the novel proved a popular Book-of-the-Month Club selection. To avoid income taxes, White moved to the Channel Island of Alderney. Having sold too cheaply to Disney the film rights for *The Sword in the Stone,* he refused to sell the film rights to *Mistress Masham's Repose.*

Wren Howard, of his new publishers Jonathan Cape, visited him at Alderney in March 1949 and discovered under a cushion the typescript of *The Goshawk* (1951), written during 1936–1939. Howard read it and insisted that it be published. White added a postscript to the three sections. It has become a nature story for children, at least in England, according to François Gallix in *T. H. White: An Annotated Bibliography* (1986). Many of the details and even the names of White's goshawks Gos and Cully as well as their characterizations as insane and lunatic had been used in *The Sword in the Stone.* Its Attic style makes it easy reading. Its detailed explanation of the quixotic, arduous task that White set himself – to become an astringer or trainer of hawks using seventeenth-century handbooks on falconry – soon becomes a narrative of the contest of wills and the love/hate relationship between the man and the bird. The man discovers his flaws of character, especially those of impatience and pettiness. After six weeks of arduous training, the first goshawk, Gos, escapes through White's own folly, and he experiences great personal loss and yet joy because the bird has its freedom. The shorter second section details his fruitless attempt to recapture Gos. The brief third one deals with his training of Cully, a replacement, and the merlin Balan, who also appear in *The Sword in the Stone.* The postscript reveals that modern methods would have made all of this arduous labor unnecessary and that the sight of Gos free in the wild was a fictional invention. Probably the bird died, caught by its jesses in a tree. Like his other books for children, this one is filled with exacting falconry details about jesses, swivels, and creasance but also with a message about the harm in trying to own even an animal.

This book has some of the same concerns as his children's books: the contrast between past and present, the inferiority of the present to the past, the evils of possession, the destruction of war, and the folly of mankind. It has been broadcast over the BBC "Children's House," was made into a BBC film in 1969, and sold widely abroad where it has won film awards in the United States and Australia.

White's last children's story, *The Master: An Adventure Story* (1957), which continues some of the themes of his earlier books, is a curious failure. Dedicated to Robert Louis Stevenson, because of White's respect for *Treasure Island* (1883), and bearing a quotation from Shakespeare's *Tempest,* this formula adventure novel set on the sterile island of Rockall, halfway between Russia and America, marks White's farewell to children's books. The story and its main character, originally called Alpha, show White's concerns about Adolf Hitler and World War II. White abandoned this story in 1944 and took it up again in 1955. But situations and character types that have depth and humor in other books are here flat, stereotyped, and dull. As the action begins, twelve-year-old twins Nicky and Judy, kidnapped on barren Rockall Island and believed drowned, are abandoned by their wealthy parents. With their dog Jokey they are held prisoner in the caverns of Rockall by the megalomaniac Master, a grotesque scientist 157 years old, and his small staff of associates: drunken Dr. Jones, also called Totty and Dr. McTurk; Squadron Leader Frinton, a demobbed and handsome but weak World War II airman; Pinkie, the tongueless black cook; Mr. Blenkinsop, a cultivated but villainous Chinaman; and a couple of anonymous mechanics. As the plot develops, Nicky is being educated by the Master so he can eventually rule the world. The Master plans to conquer the world in order to save it from the atomic bomb. The Master plans to use first mass hypnotism and extrasensory perception and later a super vibrator in the caverns to destroy all technology worldwide.

The novel is full of topical references to the Cold War, President Dwight D. Eisenhower, Prime Minister Sir Anthony Eden, and Premier Nikita Khrushchev. The characters' discussions of Might-is-Right and Might-for-Right, vital in the Arthurian novels, sound only academic and petulant here. The Master, a perversion of White's voluble teacher figures such as Merlyn and the Professor, speaks only Latin and English proverbs, and those only after drinking whiskey. As he represents mainly intellectual abstraction and not action, he is offstage through much of the book and intervenes

White, 1962

only to drive his cohorts to suicide when they attempt rebellion.

Just when the Master has total control and has switched on the ray machine, killing all of the birds on the island and causing a plane to crash thirty miles away, he goes for a walk and trips over the dog Jokey, breaking his hip. The Master then hurls himself from the cliff as Tchaikovsky's Fifth Symphony plays on the stereo. At the end of the book Judy, Nicky, and Mr. Frinton are back at Gaunt Godstone, the family country estate, preparing to give tours to tourists. Judy finds their adventure pointless; only Jokey seems pleased, eating his Wednesday kipper.

As Sylvia Townsend Warner writes in *T. H. White* (1967), *The Master,* though White considered this the kind of book he would have liked to have read as a boy and something like *Treasure Island,* could not be less like that classic: "*The Master* was written for a highly-strung introvert, ill-read, insecure, much more of a Shorter Catechist than the Scotch boy, and combating his fears by inventing terrors." After the revision of his four earlier Arthurian novels to make *The Once and Future King,* White's best writing was over. *The Master* may have been a deliberate farewell, as well as an attempt to capitalize on his name by writing a formula adventure book for children.

The Godstone and the Blackymor (1959), a miscellany, also draws upon much earlier materials from his experiences fishing and hunting in Ireland, and on his investigation of a fertility Godstone at Inniskea and his encounter with a black salesman of patent medicines. He enjoyed the success, publicity, and money attendant on the American musical *Camelot* (1960). Supposedly he saw the play seventy times. He became friends with the cast. Julie Andrews and Tony Walton were his guests at Alderney. From November 1962 to February 1963 he traveled in Italy. He had one hundred copies of his *Verses* (1962) privately printed at Alderney for friends. From September 1963 through December 1963, with Carol Walton (the young sister of Tony Walton) as his secretary, he made a successful lecture tour of various colleges and universities. As usual he kept a detailed diary of his experiences and observations about American life and culture. Edited by David Garnett this diary was published posthumously as *America at Last* (1965). On 17 January 1964, while White was aboard the S. S. *Exeter* accompanied by Vito Mariconi, an Italian college student acting as his secretary, and on his way to vacation in Egypt, Lebanon, and Greece, he died from a heart attack. He was buried in the Protestant Cemetery in Athens.

His grave marker reads "T. H. WHITE / 1906–1964 / AUTHOR / WHO / FROM A TROUBLED HEART / DELIGHTED OTHERS / LOVING AND PRAISING / THIS LIFE." For the readers who know White's *The Sword in the Stone* and *Mistress Masham's Repose,* this delight in life and learning appears on every page. But often the reputation of his books is better known than the books. A recent two-volume collection of scholarly essays, *King Arthur through the Ages* (1990), mentions White's Arthurian novels only in passing, even though one essayist claims he is "the most enduringly popular of modern British Arthurian novelists." An essay on "Children's Reading and the Arthurian Tales" in this same volume does not mention White at all. His bibliographer Gallix, noting the few critical essays on White, blames his failure to fit into literary classifications. Though several theses and dissertations on his work have appeared and a large collection of research materials and unfinished manuscripts exists, as well as three published collections of witty and detailed letters to three close friends, John K. Crane calls White "a writer whom nearly everyone admires but whom scholars continue to neglect." Because his works for children are so few, so learned, and unique in their points of view, White's work will probably remain sui generis in the history of children's literature.

Letters:

The Best of Friends: Further Letters to Sydney Carlyle Cockerell, edited by Viola Meynell (London: Hart-Davis, 1956);

The White/Garnett Letters, edited by David Garnett (New York: Viking, 1968);

Letters to a Friend: The Correspondence between T. H. White and L. J. Potts, edited by François Gallix (New York: Putnam, 1982; Gloucester: Alan Sutton, 1984).

Bibliography:

François Gallix, *T. H. White: An Annotated Bibliography* (New York: Garland, 1986).

Biography:

Sylvia Townsend Warner, *T. H. White* (New York: Viking, 1967).

References:

John K. Crane, *T. H. White* (New York: Twayne, 1974);

Cynthia A. Eby, "White's *Mistress Masham's Repose,*" *Explicator,* 40 (1982): 53;

Martin Kellman, *T. H. White and The Matter of Britain: A Literary Overview* (Lewiston, N.Y.: Edwin Mellen, 1988);

Valerie M. Lagorio and Mildred Leake Day, eds., *King Arthur through the Ages,* 2 volumes (New York: Garland, 1990).

Papers:

White's papers are contained in the T. H. White Collection of the Harry Ransom Humanities Research Center, University of Texas at Austin.

Ursula Moray Williams

(19 April 1911 –)

Joanne Lewis Sears
California State University, Fullerton

BOOKS: *Jean-Pierre* (London: A. & C. Black, 1931);

For Brownies: Stories and Games for the Pack and Everybody Else (London: Harrap, 1932);

The Autumn Sweepers and Other Plays for Children (London: A. &. C. Black, 1933);

Grandfather (London: Allen & Unwin, 1933);

The Pettabomination (London: Search, 1933);

More for Brownies (London: Harrap, 1934);

Kelpie, the Gipsies' Pony (London: Harrap, 1934; New York: Lippincott, 1935);

Anders and Marta (London: Harrap, 1935);

Adventures of Anne (London: Harrap, 1935);

Sandy on the Shore (London: Harrap, 1936);

The Twins and Their Ponies (London: Harrap, 1936);

Elaine of La Signe (London: Harrap, 1937); published as *Elaine of the Mountains* (New York: Lippincott, 1939);

Adventures of Boss and Dingbatt, with Peter John (London: Harrap, 1937);

Tales for the Sixes and Sevens (London: Harrap, 1937);

Dumpling: The Story of a Pony (London: Harrap, 1937);

Adventures of the Little Wooden Horse (London: Harrap, 1938; New York: Lippincott, 1939);

Adventures of Puffin (London: Harrap, 1939);

Peter and the Wanderlust (London: Harrap, 1939; New York: Lippincott, 1940; revised edition, London: Hamish Hamilton, 1963);

Pretenders' Island (London: Harrap, 1940; New York: Knopf, 1942);

A Castle for John Peter (London: Harrap, 1941);

Gobbolino, the Witch's Cat (London: Harrap, 1942);

The Good Little Christmas Tree (London: Harrap, 1942);

The House of Happiness (London: Harrap, 1946);

The Three Toymakers (London: Harrap, 1946; Nashville, Tenn.: Thomas Nelson, 1971);

Malkin's Mountain (London: Harrap, 1948; Nashville, Tenn.: Thomas Nelson, 1972);

The Story of Laughing Dandino (London: Harrap, 1948);

Jockin the Jester (London: Chatto & Windus, 1951; Nashville, Tenn.: Thomas Nelson, 1973);

The Binklebys at Home (London: Harrap, 1951);

The Pettabomination: A Play in One Act (London: Samuel French, 1951);

The Binklebys on the Farm (London: Harrap, 1955);

Secrets of the Wood (London: Harrap, 1955);

Grumpa (Bath: Brockhampton Press, 1955);

Goodbody's Puppet Show (London: Hamish Hamilton, 1956);

The Golden Horse with a Silver Tail (London: Hamish Hamilton, 1957);

Hobbie (Bath: Brockhampton Press, 1958);

The Moonball (London: Hamish Hamilton, 1958; New York: Morrow, 1960);

The Noble Hawks (London: Hamish Hamilton, 1959); published as *The Earl's Falconer* (New York: Morrow, 1961);

The Nine Lives of Island MacKenzie (London: Chatto & Windus, 1959); published as *Island MacKenzie* (New York: Morrow, 1960);

Beware of This Animal (London: Hamish Hamilton, 1964; New York: Dial, 1965);

Johnny Tigerskin (London: Harrap, 1964; New York: Duell, Sloane & Pierce, 1966);

O For a Mouseless House! (London: Chatto & Windus, 1964);

High Adventure (Nashville, Tenn.: Thomas Nelson, 1965);

The Cruise of the Happy-Go-Gay (London: Hamish Hamilton, 1967; New York: Meredith Press, 1968);

A Crown for a Queen (New York: Meredith Press, 1968);

The Toymaker's Daughter (London: Hamish Hamilton, 1968; New York: Meredith Press, 1969);

Mog (London: Allen & Unwin, 1969);

Boy in a Barn (London: Allen & Unwin, 1970; Camden, N.J.: Thomas Nelson, 1970);

Johnny Golightly and His Crocodile (London: Chatto, Boyd & Oliver, 1970; New York: Harvey House, 1971);

Ursula Moray Williams

Hurricanes (London: Chatto & Windus, 1971);

Castle Merlin (Camden, N.J.: Thomas Nelson, 1972);

A Picnic with the Aunts (London: Chatto & Windus, 1972);

The Kidnapping of My Grandmother (London: Heinemann, 1972);

Children's Parties and Games for a Rainy Day (London: Corgi Books, 1972);

Tiger-Nanny (Bath: Brockhampton Press, 1973; Camden, N.J.: Thomas Nelson, 1988);

The Line (London: Puffin, 1974);

Grandpapa's Folly and the Woodworm-Bookworm (London: Chatto & Windus, 1974);

No Ponies for Miss Pobjoy (Camden, N.J.: Thomas Nelson, 1975);

Bogwoppit (Camden, N.J.: Thomas Nelson, 1978);

Jeffy, the Burglar's Cat (London: Andersen Press, 1981);

Bellabelinda and the No-Good Angel (London: Chatto & Windus, 1982);

The Further Adventures of Gobbolino and the Little Wooden Horse (London: Puffin, 1984);

Spid (London: Andersen Press, 1986);

Grandma and the Ghowlies (London: Andersen Press, 1986);

Paddy on the Island (London: Andersen Press, 1987).

Author of seventy novels, Ursula Moray Williams has given children readable, absorbing tales, both fanciful and realistic, for more than half a century. Her books have been widely translated: *Adventures of the Little Wooden Horse* (1938), for instance, exists even in Japanese and Romansh. The majority of Williams's stories employ fantasy rooted in everyday reality, but she writes in so many modes, and to such varied age levels, that her work occupies no fixed niche in the history of children's literature. Imaginative narratives untrammeled by consistent logic and sets of lively characters untroubled by psychological complexity give her work broad appeal.

Ursula Moray Williams was born 19 April 1911 in Petersfield, Hampshire, to classics tutor A. Moray Williams and teacher Mabel Unwin. The

Williamses rejoiced at the birth of twin daughters — Ursula and her sister Barbara — on what would have been the second birthday of an earlier child lost in infancy. The Williams children were educated at home in Petersfield by their Froebel-trained mother. Reared in rural isolation, the twins read widely and entertained one another with their own stories, tales they later wrote down and illustrated as gifts.

In a 1988 essay Williams describes her childhood as a happy one in spite of World War I. After the war the family moved to Eastleigh, now part of Southampton, where their father tutored classics in a nearby school. The eccentricities of the large Victorian palazzo ("The Folly") in which the family lived inspired *Grandpapa's Folly and the Woodworm-Bookworm* (1974) and provided the setting for *A Castle for John Peter* (1941). The twins succumbed to what Williams describes as "horse madness," a passion for ponies that she celebrates in several books, including *The Twins and Their Ponies* (1936) and *No Ponies for Miss Pobjoy* (1975).

The girls continued their home education with a governess until at seventeen they went to a girls' school on Lake Annecy in the French Alps. Though Williams claims they "loathed" studies at the lycée, she fixed the alpine setting in memory, and it later provided the background for several of her novels, notably *The Three Toymakers* (1946), *Malkin's Mountain* (1948), *The Toymaker's Daughter* (1968), and *Boy in a Barn* (1970).

After their year in France, the sisters returned to the Winchester College of Art, where, after some months of study, the two began to move in different career directions. Barbara continued in art; Ursula committed herself to writing children's stories. "My parents very generously allowed me to stay at home and write," she says. Her uncle, publisher Sir Stanley Unwin, helped her place early books and find a good agent.

In 1935 Williams married Peter John, great-grandson to Robert Southey, former Poet-Laureate of England (1813–1843). Barbara moved to Iceland with her husband, an Icelandic sculptor, and continued her career as wood engraver and artist. She illustrated a few of Ursula's books until geographical distance made continued collaboration difficult. Ursula Williams and her husband, Peter, moved to Hampstead, where she combined writing children's books with homemaking.

Her thirty-nine-year marriage produced four sons, most of them born during World War II. During 1940 she lived in Claygate, southwest of London, but when Peter's war work took him to Beck-

ford, Gloucestershire, the family went too. There they shared a Beckford house with a mother and two little girls seeking safety from London bombings. Shared nannies took charge of the children every afternoon, and this, Williams reported, allowed her writing to prosper. These years produced some of her most popular books, such as *Gobbolino, the Witch's Cat* (1942) and *The Good Little Christmas Tree* (1943).

Ursula Moray Williams's first major success, *Adventures of the Little Wooden Horse,* typifies her most satisfying work. An unassuming protagonist tumbles unintentionally into wild, picaresque adventures in which events occur rapidly and often without clear causal links. The protagonist survives by a combination of luck and wit. The Little Wooden Horse's adventures subject him to harsh employers, unexpected sea voyages, and work in a coal mine, as a circus horse, and as a seaside children's donkey. Steadfast loyalty, courage, and unselfishness sustain the reluctant hero, who craves security and affection more than adventure.

The four novels constituting the Toymaker Tetralogy — unified by Marta, the morally ambiguous mechanical doll — represent Williams's most complex and thematically interesting work. Not published in narrative sequence, these books stirred Williams's imagination for years — beginning with *Anders and Marta* (1935). Ageless and beautiful, Marta vacillates between being a passive toy and a morally awakened human child. In *The Three Toymakers* Rudi, an alpine wood-carver, competes for a prize with other toymakers including Marta's creator, the evil Malkin, who has taught her seductive, mischievous, and controlling ways. Rudi's young brother, Anders, befriends Marta and awakens human compassion and generosity in her. Anders, a well-intentioned but flawed human, nearly brings about disaster through his own naughtiness, curiosity, and misplaced enthusiasm. Though Malkin loses the toy competition because of Marta's bad behavior, he remains unregenerate, exiled with Marta to the other side of the mountain.

Malkin's Mountain finds Rudi married and the father of twin sons. The twins and their Uncle Anders rescue Rudi, held captive by Malkin inside the mountain, while Malkin's army of wooden soldiers threatens to destroy the good people of Rudi's village. Marta, now Malkin's doll-queen, taunts Rudi, captures his twins, and tries to seduce good characters with offers of power. Anders's faith and diligence provide Rudi with materials for the golden key needed to break Malkin's power. Rudi's inventiveness and persistence prevail, and Malkin is foiled. Marta, selfish and perverse as ever, inadvertently frustrates Malkin's evil plan and thus allows good to triumph.

The redoubtable Marta reappears a generation later in *The Toymaker's Daughter*. Dropped by an eagle at the feet of Anders's daughter Niclo, Marta is just a vulnerable wind-up doll. Claiming she wants to learn to be a real person by living with Anders's family, she confesses the secret of her key to Niclo and promises to learn humility and generosity. But her efforts to eliminate the half-mad, self-destructive behavior she has learned from Malkin fail. Malkin tempts her with power as queen of his household, where she can have things just as she likes. In the end she chooses Malkin and the other side of the mountain. To Williams's credit, the tetralogy engages problems of absolute evil through an unself-conscious, absorbing narrative — one that retains shades of moral complexity without damaging the pace of the plot.

The opening sentence of *The Nine Lives of Island Mackenzie* (1959) demonstrates Williams's mastery of audience-baiting storytelling: "One August afternoon a little shipwrecked cat called Mackenzie was swimming for his life toward a desert island, pursued by eight hungry sharks." Mad adventures befall Mackenzie and Miss Pettifer, a maiden lady who rivals Mackenzie in the affections of Captain Foster. The plot has the spontaneous air of an ad-libbed bedtime story: shipwrecks, fires, cannibals, and storms precede a happy if improbable ending. Edward Ardizzone's illustrations share Williams's daring mixture of madcap phantasm with the banal quotidian.

Williams, widowed since 1974, lives at Court Farm in Gloucestershire. She served as magistrate on the Evesham bench into her seventies, and she says that she has "probably stopped writing books at the moment" in favor of tending to her acre of garden and her family. "What fun it was!" she says of her story-making capacity, a gift for which she is grateful. Of her creative resources she once said, "When winter comes I dive into my imaginary bag and pull out the outline of a plot. . . . So I begin. . . . " Sometimes inconsistent, even incoherent, her plots never fail to engage. Her prose is graceful, lively, surefooted. Her simple, forthright values and amusingly unrepentant protagonists please children far removed from the sunshine world she once shared with her twin sister, Barbara.

Appendix

Omnibus Essay on Pony Stories

Gwyneth Evans
Malaspina University College, British Columbia

Below are listed representative examples of the work of leading pony-story writers between 1929 and 1960, including some of their nonfiction books about horses; this list also includes some later examples of pony books referred to in the text of this article.

Judith M. Berrisford, *Ten Ponies and Jackie* (Leicester: Brockhampton Press, 1959);

M. E. Buckingham, *Phari: The Adventures of a Tibetan Pony,* illustrated by K. F. Barker (London: Country Life, 1933);

Joanna Cannan, *A Pony for Jean,* illustrated by Anne Bullen (London: John Lane, 1936; New York: Scribners, 1937);

Cannan, *Another Pony for Jean,* illustrated by Bullen (London: Collins, 1938);

Cannan, *More Ponies for Jean,* illustrated by Bullen (London: Collins, 1943);

Cannan, *They Bought Her a Pony,* illustrated by Rosemary Robertson (London: Collins, 1944);

Cannan, *Hamish: the Story of a Shetland Pony,* illustrated by Bullen (London: Penguin, 1944);

Cannan, *I Wrote a Pony Book* (London: Collins, 1950);

Moyra Charlton, *Tally Ho, the Story of an Irish Hunter,* illustrated by Lionel Edwards (New York: Putnam, 1930);

Primrose Cumming, *Doney,* illustrated by Allen Seaby (London: Country Life, 1934);

Cumming, *Silver Snaffles,* illustrated by Stanley Lloyd (London: Blackie, 1937; New York: Mill, 1937);

Cumming, *The Silver Eagle Riding School,* illustrated by Cecil Trew (London: A. & C. Black, 1938);

Cumming, *Rachel of Romney,* illustrated by Nina Scott Langley (London: Country Life, 1939; New York: Scribners, 1940);

Cumming, *The Wednesday Pony,* illustrated by Lloyd (London: Blackie, 1939; New York: Mill, 1939);

Cumming, *Ben: The Story of a Cart-Horse,* illustrated with photographs by Harold Burdekin (London: Dent, 1939; New York: Dutton, 1940);

Cumming, *The Chestnut Filly* (London: Blackie, 1940; New York: Mill, 1940);

Cumming, *Silver Eagle Carries On,* illustrated by Trew (London: A. & C. Black, 1942);

Cumming, *The Great Horses,* illustrated by Edwards (London: Dent, 1946);

Cumming, *Four Rode Home,* illustrated by Maurice Tulloch (London: Dent, 1951);

Cumming, *Rivals to Silver Eagle,* illustrated by Eve Gosset (London: A. & C. Black, 1954);

Cumming, *No Place for Ponies,* illustrated by Tulloch (London: Dent, 1954); republished as *The Mystery Pony* (New York: Criterion, 1957);

Cumming, *The Deep-Sea Horse,* illustrated by Mary Shillabeer (London: Dent, 1956);

Cumming, *Flying Horseman,* illustrated by Sheila Rose (London: Dent, 1959);

Monica Edwards, *Wish for a Pony,* illustrated by Bullen (London: Collins, 1947);

Edwards, *No Mistaking Corker,* illustrated by Bullen (London: Collins, 1947);

Edwards, *The Summer of the Great Secret,* illustrated by Bullen (London: Collins, 1948);

Edwards, *The Midnight Horse,* illustrated by Bullen (London: Collins, 1949; New York: Vanguard, 1950);

Edwards, *The White Riders,* illustrated by Geoffrey Whittam (London: Collins, 1950);

Edwards, *Black Hunting Whip,* illustrated by Whittam (London: Collins, 1950);

Edwards, *Punchbowl Midnight,* illustrated by Charles Tunnicliffe (London: Collins, 1951);

Edwards, *Cargo of Horses,* illustrated by Whittam (London: Collins, 1951);

Edwards, *Spirit of Punchbowl Farm,* illustrated by Joan Wanklyn (London: Collins, 1952);

Edwards, *No Entry,* illustrated by Whittam (London: Collins, 1954);

Edwards, *Punchbowl Harvest,* illustrated by Wanklyn (London: Collins, 1955);

Edwards, *Rennie Goes Riding* (London: John Lane, 1956);

Edwards, *Strangers to the Marsh,* illustrated by Whittam (London: Collins, 1957);

Edwards, *Fire in the Punchbowl,* illustrated by Whittam (London: Collins, 1965);

Ruby Ferguson, *Jill's Gymkhana,* illustrated by Bonar Dunlop (London: Hodder & Stoughton, 1949);

Ferguson, *A Stable for Jill,* illustrated by Dunlop (London: Hodder & Stoughton, 1951);

Ferguson, *Jill Has Two Ponies,* illustrated by Dunlop (London: Hodder & Stoughton, 1952);

Ferguson, *Jill Enjoys Her Ponies,* illustrated by Caney (London: Hodder & Stoughton, 1954); republished as *Jill and the Runaway* (London: Knight Books, 1972);

Ferguson, *Jill's Riding Club,* illustrated by Caney (London: Hodder & Stoughton, 1956);

Ferguson, *Rosettes for Jill* (London: Hodder & Stoughton, 1957);

Ferguson, *Jill and the Perfect Pony,* illustrated by Caney (London: Hodder & Stoughton, 1959);

Ferguson, *Pony Jobs for Jill* (London: Hodder & Stoughton, 1960);

Ferguson, *Jill's Pony Trek,* illustrated by Caney (London: Hodder & Stoughton, 1962);

Mary Gervaise, *Ponies and Mysteries,* illustrated by Bowe (London: Lutterworth Press, 1953);

Gervaise, *Pony from the Farm,* illustrated by Bowe (London: Lutterworth Press, 1954);

Gervaise, *The Pony Clue,* illustrated by Bowe (London: Lutterworth Press, 1955);

"Golden Gorse," *The Young Rider* (London: Country Life, 1928);

"Golden Gorse," *Moorland Mousie,* illustrated by Edwards (London: Country Life, 1929);

"Golden Gorse," *Older Mousie,* illustrated by Edwards (London: Country Life, 1932);

Esme Hamilton, *Speedy* (London: Bodley Head, 1940);

Katherine Hull and Pamela Whitlock, *The Far Distant Oxus,* illustrated by Whitlock (London: Cape, 1937; New York: Macmillan, 1938);

Hull and Whitlock, *Escape to Persia* (London: Cape, 1938; New York: Macmillan, 1939);

Hull and Whitlock, *Oxus in Summer* (London: Cape, 1939; New York: Macmillan, 1940);

K. M. Peyton, *Flambards* (London: Oxford, 1967; Cleveland: World, 1968);

Peyton, *Fly by Night* (London: Oxford, 1968; Cleveland: World, 1969);

Peyton, *The Edge of the Cloud* (London: Oxford, 1969; Cleveland: World, 1970);

Peyton, *Flambards in Summer* (London: Oxford, 1969; Cleveland: World, 1970);

Peyton, *The Team* (London: Oxford, 1975);

Peyton, *Prove Yourself a Hero* (London: Oxford, 1977);

Peyton, *Flambards Divided* (London & New York: Oxford, 1981);

Peyton, *Free Rein* (New York: Philomel, 1983); republished as *The Last Ditch* (London: Oxford, 1984);

Peyton, *Who, Sir? Me, Sir?* (London: Oxford, 1983);

Christine Pullein-Thompson, *It Began with Picotee,* with Diana and Josephine Pullein-Thompson, illustrated by Rosemary Robertson (London: A. & C. Black, 1946);

Pullein-Thompson, *We Rode to the Sea,* illustrated by Mil Brown (London: Collins, 1948);

Pullein-Thompson, *We Hunted Hounds,* illustrated by Marcia Lane Foster (London: Collins, 1949);

Pullein-Thompson, *I Carried the Horn,* illustrated by Charlotte Hough (London: Collins, 1951);

Pullein-Thompson, *Goodbye to Hounds,* illustrated by Hough (London: Collins, 1952);

Pullein-Thompson, *Riders from Afar,* illustrated by Hough (London: Collins, 1954);

Pullein-Thompson, *Phantom Horse,* illustrated by Rose (London: Collins, 1955);

Pullein-Thompson, *A Day to Go Hunting,* illustrated by Rose (London: Collins, 1956);

Pullein-Thompson, *The First Rosette,* illustrated by Rose (London: Burke, 1956);

Pullein-Thompson, *Stolen Ponies,* illustrated by Rose (London: Collins, 1957);

Pullein-Thompson, *The Second Mount,* illustrated by Rose (London: Burke, 1957);

Pullein-Thompson, *Three to Ride,* illustrated by Rose (London: Burke, 1958);

Pullein-Thompson, *The Lost Pony,* illustrated by Rose (London: Burke, 1959);

Pullein-Thompson, *Ride by Night,* illustrated by Rose (London: Burke, 1960);

Pullein-Thompson, *The Horse Sale,* illustrated by Rose (London: Burke, 1960); (and many other titles through the 1960s, 1970s, and 1980s);

Diana Pullein-Thompson, *I Wanted a Pony,* illustrated by Bullen (London: Collins, 1946);

Pullein-Thompson, *Three Ponies and Shannan,* illustrated by Bullen (London: Collins, 1947);

Pullein-Thompson, *A Pony to School,* illustrated by Bullen (London: Collins, 1950);

Pullein-Thompson, *Janet Must Ride,* illustrated by Mary Gernat (London: Collins, 1953);

Pullein-Thompson, *Horses at Home, and Friends Must Part,* illustrated by Bullen (London: Collins, 1954);

Pullein-Thompson, *Riding with the Lyntons,* illustrated by Bullen (London: Collins, 1956);

Pullein-Thompson, *Riding for Children* (London: Foyle, 1957);

Josephine Pullein-Thompson, *Six Ponies,* illustrated by Bullen (London: Collins, 1946);

Pullein-Thompson, *I Had Two Ponies,* illustrated by Bullen (London: Collins, 1947);

Pullein-Thompson, *Plenty of Ponies,* illustrated by Bullen (London: Collins, 1949);

Pullein-Thompson, *Pony Club Team,* illustrated by Bullen (London: Collins, 1950);

Pullein-Thompson, *The Radney Riding Club,* illustrated by Rose (London: Collins, 1951);

Pullein-Thompson, *Prince Among Ponies,* illustrated by Hough (London: Collins, 1952);

Pullein-Thompson, *One Day Event,* illustrated by Rose (London: Collins, 1954);

Pullein-Thompson, *Show Jumping Secret,* illustrated by Rose (London: Collins, 1955);

Pullein-Thompson, *Patrick's Pony,* illustrated by Whittam (Leicester: Brockhampton Press, 1957);

Pullein-Thompson, *Pony Club Camp,* illustrated by Rose (London: Collins, 1957);

Pullein-Thompson, *The Trick Jumpers,* illustrated by Rose (London: Collins, 1958);

Pullein-Thompson, *How Horses are Trained* (London: Routledge, 1961);

Pat Smythe, *Jacqueline Rides for a Fall,* illustrated by J. E. McConnell (London: Cassell, 1955);

Smythe, *Three Jays Against the Clock,* illustrated by McConnell (London: Cassell, 1957);

Smythe, *Three Jays on Holiday,* illustrated by McConnell (London: Cassell, 1958);

Mary Treadgold, *We Couldn't Leave Dinah,* illustrated by Stuart Tresilian (London: Cape, 1941); republished as *Left til Called For* (New York: Doubleday, 1941);

Treadgold, *No Ponies,* illustrated by Ruth Gervais (London: Cape, 1946);

Treadgold, *The Heron Ride,* illustrated by Victor Ambrus (London: Cape, 1962);

Treadgold, *Return to the Heron,* illustrated by Ambrus (London: Cape, 1963);

Treadgold, *The Rum Day of the Vanishing Pony* (Leicester: Brockhampton Press, 1970).

The pony story is a uniquely British phenomenon: while novels and stories about horses have appeared in many countries, the particular ethos that informs the pony-story genre is rooted in British social organization and topography and closely tied to the development of the Pony Club itself. Its essence is the description of the relationship between a child and a pony, set in the context of the riding clubs, gymkhanas, and horse shows of the British countryside in the middle decades of the twentieth century. In the period of its flowering, from the 1930s through the early 1960s, the Pony Story underwent many changes at the hands of its different practitioners, from the animal autobiographies of "Golden Gorse" and Esme Hamilton to tales of mystery and adventure, or of social and athletic competition wherein the ponies themselves become little more than decorative adjuncts to the human protagonists. While the genre has permitted individual writers to slip into formula-writing and encouraged young readers to look to it for the reassurance of a predictable story pattern and happy outcome, the relationship of child and animal upon which it is based has such inherent appeal that writers of quality such as Mary Treadgold from the 1940s, Monica Edwards from the 1950s, and K. M. Peyton from the 1960s and 1970s have continued to explore and remake the pony story for new generations of readers.

One element of the appeal of the pony books lies in the idea of a pony as something small, lovable, and manageable by a child (though the last quality is something of a misconception since ponies, as the pony books often show, can be stubborn and as difficult as larger horses). While horses have traditionally been associated with wealth and power, ponies — many of them, such as the New Forest, Exmoor, and Welsh Mountain ponies, native to wild areas of the British Isles — were used for centuries as pack animals, for pulling carriages and carts, and for laboring underground in mines. By the time of the great popularity of the pony books, motor transport had supplanted them for most practical labor, but they were becoming increasingly popular for pleasure riding by children. The Pony Club was founded in Britain in 1929 to encourage young people to ride for pleasure and to provide competent instruction in riding and horse care; it is surely more than coincidental that the first pony book, *Moorland Mousie,* appeared in that same year. The rapidly increasing membership of the Pony Clubs, which quickly spread across Britain and into other Commonwealth countries and exceeded twenty thousand members throughout the 1950s, indicates the passionate enthusiasm felt by large numbers of children in the pre- and postwar years for spending their leisure time with horses. For every child who had the opportunity to ride, of course, there were others who could only long to do so, and the pony books undoubtedly provided compensation and satisfaction for those who fantasized about riding, as well as fictionalized instruction for those who actually had ponies.

The pony's past history of hard work under often harsh conditions sometimes contributes to the pathos and affection evoked by his small stature and the possibility of the pony's decline from beloved pet and mount to a working drudge or — worse — horseflesh for the knacker is a common plot device in the pony stories. From such a fall the pony is often rescued by someone who recognizes him from his former life: Moorland Mousie is rescued from the thoughtless greengrocer by his former owner; Phari, in *Phari: The Adventures of a Tibetan Pony* (1933), disguised by a horse thief in India, is purchased by an English officer who remembers his prowess on the polo field; Olga's Crusoe is bought by Edwin in Christine Pullein-Thompson's *The Horse Sale* (1960); and Toadhill Flax in Peyton's *The Team* (1975) and Orlando in Josephine Pullein-Thompson's *Ride to the Rescue* (1979) are purchased by Ruth and Frances just in time to save them from being auctioned off for horse meat. The pony's name, often an affectionate diminutive ending in *y* or *ie,* suggests the protective attitude taken toward him by the fond owner of such animals as Mousie, Speedy, Phari, Titbit, and Ruth's "Toad" and "Fly" (*Fly By Night,* 1968). Mousie's name, in the first of the true pony books, sets the tone, emphasizing the pony's nature as soft, small, appealing, and vulnerable. On the other hand, some pony owners choose to rename the pony to suit their sense of romance and beauty: Jean renames her pony "Cavalier" in *A Pony for Jean* (1936) and Tamzin renames hers "Fallada" (*Wish for a Pony,* 1947).

An ability to see beyond superficial physical defects, especially those caused by hunger and harsh treatment, enables the protagonist in many pony stories to acquire an animal that responds to kind handling and proper feeding and proves a beauty, or a great jumper, and a treasure after all. The basic pattern of a great many pony stories is thus one of rescue, followed by a series of small setbacks and triumphs, culminating in some grand event in which the salvaged pony is revealed to be admirable and worthy, while the merit of its owner's patience, affection, and hard work is also revealed and rewarded. This pattern perhaps has its origins in the late-Victorian moral tale, with its abandoned or poverty-stricken child rescued and set on the road to social and spiritual redemption by

the kind intervention of a more privileged person. Anna Sewell's *Black Beauty* (1877) is the prototype, linking the moral tale with the naturalistic animal story through its autobiographical account, in the horse's voice, of his sufferings at the hands of cruel or thoughtless owners and his eventual rescue and rehabilitation. When the pattern was taken up by British children's authors in the 1930s, however, the change in perspective from the horse's view of his owners to the owner's view of the horse meant a significant change from the perspective of the victim to that of the rescuer and trainer, from directly narrated suffering to a focus on the process of rehabilitation.

Not all pony stories, of course, use this pattern of rescue and rehabilitation, but most of the later stories do; unlike *Black Beauty,* they focus on the experience of the child rather than the feelings of the horse. The pony book invariably concludes with some sort of triumph, usually of a physical and often of a competitive nature, whereby the inherent value of the animal is confirmed or revealed and the child owner or rider is vindicated in his or her choice of the animal, ability to ride or train it, or some other choice or decision that the child has made. Pony and child are usually in the struggle together, while the antagonists may be hostile or doubting adults or other children — often more privileged with money and resources to stable and train their animals. Where the pony story proper is grafted onto a mystery or adventure tale, the struggle is to put the clues together and to outwit the villains, and the ponies in most cases are a means to an end — carrying the riders on midnight rescue missions or bucking off ill-doers who attempt to escape on them, rather than providing in themselves the central motive for the action. Where the novel is concerned with a group of children, rather than a single protagonist and her pony, the focus tends to be on action and adventure and on relationships among the children rather than between child and horse, but some books such as Josephine Pullein-Thompson's *Six Ponies* (1946) and Peyton's *The Team* use the contrasting personalities of several young riders and their mounts to explore the different ways in which people and animals in similar circumstances may react to each other. Such stories generally show gentleness and persistence rewarded at the end, in the traditional triumph of the poor girl over the wealthy; in Peyton's novel, however, the well-off families have just as much trouble as the poorer ones, but all the young people are vindicated in their defiance of attempted adult interference in their relationships with their horses.

The close physical connection between pony and rider is undoubtedly a strong aspect of the appeal of riding, and the pony books often evoke the child's delight in the physical presence of the pony as well as the exhilaration of being mounted on a lively animal. Joanna Cannan's *A Pony for Jean* provides an example of the physical attraction of rider to animal: "Now that I know his dear face so well and have groomed every hair on his body, it is difficult to remember him as he was then, but I shall never forget the long soft look he gave me." The physical stimulation provided by the motion of horseback riding is, as far as the pony books are concerned, purely athletic; the exhilaration of a gallop across the moors or a successful round in the jumping ring remains just that, and any Freudian or metaphysical undertones that there might be in the experience are left unexplored. How one can best ride a pony and care for it are subjects considered in some detail by the various books, but why one might yearn to ride, and whether or not man has any natural right to exert this sort of mastery over another species, are not issues on which most pony books encourage speculation. A cautionary tale in *Moorland Mousie* warns that ponies may be irritated by too much petting and hugging: "they patted me to please themselves because I felt warm and silky and alive. I do not call that kindness. . . . What I want is justice and not slobber." Sentimentality about animals, especially if it is not accompanied by good sense in caring for them, is frequently ridiculed in the pony books, and vegetarians and – in more-recent books – people who protest against fox hunting generally appear as rather ridiculous and lacking in proper understanding of country life.

While many of the pony books describe the schooling of the ponies, virtually every book in the genre is more deeply concerned with the schooling of human beings, in the sense that the story is concerned with right and wrong behavior and with appropriate and inappropriate reactions to situations that arise through owning and riding the ponies. Many of them contain lessons in proper riding, based on an appreciation of the pony's needs and character, so that children who ride with too short a rein – causing the pony to pull and toss his head to relieve the pressure on his mouth – or who fail to let the pony cool down properly after hunting, or who punish a pony when he is frightened and instead needs reassurance have the errors of their ways pointed out. Putting the comfort and interest of her pony before her own is the one universal characteristic of the attractive human characters in the pony books: virtue in the pony books consists in such responsible and unselfish behavior, and it is always rewarded.

While in some pony books, particularly those about a group of young riders, the pony appears primarily as an enjoyable means of transportation from one adventure to another, in others the pony is valued as a companion for a solitary child. Children who view their ponies as status symbols are generally satirized, although Andrea in Monica Edwards's *Black Hunting Whip* (1950) is more closely seen than are most pony snobs:

> Moonstone was Andrea's favorite. She had loved her because she was elegant and proud and breedy, because of the row of her rosettes in the tack room and because of her milky-white coat. She and Lindsey would quarrel often and fiercely about the two ponies. Lindsey thought Sula was worth ten of Moonstone because she had so much character. But with Andrea the breeding counted most. . . . Andrea was not hard hearted, as she so often seemed to other people. But whereas horses, to Lindsey, were like people and loved accordingly, to Andrea they were mostly horses and valued for their quality.

Andrea does have a slight change of heart during the novel and chooses to buy a less than handsome black pony because he is such "a good ride." But characters like her who focus on appearance, and who speak of their ponies as possessions rather than living individuals, do not generally fare well in the pony books. Jean in *A Pony for Jean* responds with sincere if comical indignation to her cousin Camilla's scornful comment that it would have been kinder to have had her pony destroyed, wishing that Camilla would choke on a cobweb and die, "and then you wouldn't be so keen on having other people destroyed." To the lonely Jean, as to hundreds of other lonely girls (and the occasional boy) in the pony books, her pony is truly a "person," and a better companion than she has found elsewhere. In many ways he seems like an extension of her own emotional life: he learns to jump by Jean's jumping on foot beside him, is anxious and nervous when she feels that way, and excels when she herself "throws her heart" over the jumps.

Black Beauty provided a prototype for the pony story as early as 1877, when Sewell used the horse himself to narrate the history of his happy early life, the suffering inflicted on him by thoughtless and cruel owners, and his eventual return to an enlightened and kindly home. The pony story as a genre really begins, however, with the publication of *Moorland Mousie* in 1929; within a few years, Mousie was followed by a great many other literary ponies in children's books that imitated or developed the pattern of a tale about the relationship between pony and its owner or succession of owners. Since comments on proper riding practices are often prominent in the pony books, it is interesting to note that Country Life, the publisher of *Moorland Mousie,* had in the previous year put out a riding manual by the same author, "Golden Gorse." Many of the principles of caring well for a horse that are expounded in *The Young Rider* (1928) reappear, in almost the same words but in a narrative context, in *Moorland Mousie.* After having cautioned the Young Rider to learn the difference between good hay and bad hay, and to have the pony's feet reshod so that he doesn't outgrow his shoes, Golden Gorse in her next book shows what happens to poor Mousie when a foolish owner purchases bad hay and leaves Mousie's shoes on too long. As a story, attached to a personality the reader has come to care about, generally has much more impact and is more memorable than direct instructions, Golden Gorse made doubly certain of reaching young readers through employing fiction to impress the most important principles of her riding manual.

Moorland Mousie is not, however, simply an instruction book in disguise. Narrating his own story, Mousie is an engaging character whose eager and affectionate nature predisposes the reader to sympathy with his confusion when he and his companion are captured from the wild herd on Exmoor and brought to live among humans; like Black Beauty, Mousie is movingly patient and uncomprehending of the mistreatment that undeservedly falls to him. Much less of *Moorland Mousie* than *Black Beauty* is devoted to the pony's misfortunes, and the author's messages are conveyed through the positive examples of wise handling as well as by the cautionary ones. Mousie's autobiography, however, is supplemented by stories told by several other ponies he encounters, all of whom have had experiences with thoughtless young owners who bring them needless grief. While the events of the story are realistic, Mousie's narration does strain credibility somewhat, particularly in the early descriptions of his life on Exmoor where the rather sophisticated vocabulary and frame of reference, including many quoted passages of English poetry, seem charming but unlikely elements of a pony's consciousness. After Mousie's capture, he is taken with his friend Tinker Bell to live at the country house of Colonel Cope, where gentle handling by Cope's aptly named daughter Patience makes the ponies into tractable mounts. Mousie, the handsomer of the two ponies, wins first prize at a show, but pride and exuberance

lead him to bolt one day and Patience has a serious fall. While the docile Tinker Bell remains in their happy home, the contrite Mousie is sold as unsuitable for riding; he is fortunate in his first owner, a butcher who teaches him to pull a cart, but later falls into the hands of a careless and ignorant greengrocer who feeds him badly and makes him pull too heavy a wagon. In desperately poor condition, Mousie is discovered by Patience, who buys him back, tends him lovingly, and trains him to be a safe and willing mount for her nervous younger brother.

Mousie's story is continued in *Older Mousie* (1932), the only other work of fiction by Golden Gorse, whose real identity is not known. Like a great many of the pony books that were to follow, the two Mousie books were generously illustrated, in this instance by charcoal drawings by Lionel Edwards, an accomplished animal artist whose work was highly valued by *Country Life* readers. The drawings for the Mousie books — scenes of the ponies and wild stags on Exmoor, riders at the hunt — are more generic than specific to the incidents of the story in most cases but certainly enhance the appeal of the books and effectively convey the atmosphere of their setting. While some artists like Edwards, K. F. Barker, and Stanley Lloyd paid most attention to the horses, in backgrounds of rural landscape, many illustrators of the pony books came to concentrate upon the human figures involved, with the horses themselves becoming the decorative background rather than the central figures.

The pattern of tracing a pony's life from his birth in the wild countryside through his experiences, good and bad, with a succession of owners and riders, was quickly picked up by other writers, among them M. E. Buckingham with *Phari: The Adventures of a Tibetan Pony,* illustrated with expressive drawings of the animals and the exotic locale by Barker. Phari's life in various parts of the Indian subcontinent, playing polo and going on a military campaign, is rather more exciting than that of most of the English ponies, but its basic pattern of training by a good master, loss, ill treatment, and eventual rescue is similar. Phari's tale is told in the third person rather than the first person, but other writers of pony biographies favored letting the pony tell his own story. Esme Hamilton's Connemara pony, in *Speedy* (1940), does so with a flavor of Irish dialect: her story also makes considerable use of local color, of the Irish tinkers, tradesmen, and hunting stables. Speedy puts her emphasis, however, on explaining why good riding practices please her and make it easy for her to obey, while bad ones injure and confuse her. An amusing section of the book describes her efforts to teach a novice to ride, rewarding his correct moves with obedience and bucking him off when he makes too many mistakes.

While Speedy is sometimes the teacher in this novel, few of the pony books give the horse's point of view of riding instruction in quite this way (although C. S. Lewis does so in *The Horse and His Boy* of 1954, when his Narnian talking horse, Bree, teaches Shasta to ride): for the most part, the development of the pony books sees emphasis increasingly placed on the child rider rather than the pony, and the perspective of the story becomes almost exclusively that of the child. *A Pony for Jean* was most influential in the development of the child-centered pony book. Again told in the first person, *A Pony for Jean* is narrated not by the pony but by Jean — and the title is significant in its emphasis on ownership. Jean is a London-raised child, with an engaging naiveté and a willingness to admit to her mistakes and ignorance, whose family moves to the country when her father loses his job (many of the early pony books, like this one, have the economic problems of the Depression and war years as part of the background). Given a starved and scruffy pony with the descriptive name of The Toastrack, Jean renames him Cavalier and sets out with the help of a riding manual to teach herself to ride. "Mummy used to come out with the book, which had pictures of good riders and bad ones, and she used to tell me which I was looking like." The elements of the later pony books are virtually all present in *A Pony for Jean,* as Jean succeeds through diligence and determination in getting her pony to look more like a cavalier than a toastrack, learning to ride, and showing up her snobbish cousin by beating her in several classes at the local gymkhana and going on to win the silver cup for jumping. The subtext of the story, however, has less to do with gymkhana ribbons than with the gradual growth in maturity and confidence made by Jean as she learns to become a responsible countrywoman.

This increasing maturity is evident also in the sequel, *Another Pony for Jean* (1938), when both at boarding school and at home Jean's self-reliance and conscientiousness win her friends and success: she is given her second pony by a local nobleman in gratitude for her having applied a tourniquet to his horse's injured leg on the hunting field, thus saving its life. Fortunately, Jean is also modest and has a good dry sense of humor, which keeps the account of her adventures appealing, but this second volume already shows the signs of how easy it will be for the pony books to fall into predictable patterns. Camilla, the snobbish cousin, is the foil to Jean and, despite her much more privileged life, consistently

fails where Jean succeeds. Guy, an older cousin, is a kindly mentor, but the other characters of the books are shadowy, with the exception of Jean's lively young mother, who has cheerfully given up her London socialite life for the country and manages riding injuries, burglars, and difficult relatives with great aplomb. The character of the pony is of some interest in the first of Cannan's books, and his efforts to understand and oblige the novice Jean are sympathetically evoked; in the sequel, however, the ponies are more simply functional.

In her *Doney* (1934) and *The Wednesday Pony* (1939), Primrose Cumming puts the emphasis back on the pony, although the stories are still told very much from the point of view of the human characters. *The Wednesday Pony* is again about being educated by one's pony: Martin and Tabby, whose father is a butcher, are permitted to ride only on Wednesday afternoons when early closing liberates the hackney pony who pulls the shop's delivery cart. While they love the lively and reliable Jingo, his docked tail and bouncy gait mark him as a working pony, and they long to own a real riding pony. They fantasize about a dream pony that will come galloping to them out of the mist of the Sussex Downs, where they live. Meanwhile, they enter Jingo in the local horse show, where he excels in some classes, but Tabby is mortified when the false tail she has attached in hopes of making him more suitable for a riding-pony class falls off in the show ring. Highly amused by Tabby's stratagem and its failure, one of the judges offers to lend the children a pony; elegant and well-trained, this new pony nevertheless makes the children appreciate Jingo somewhat more, as she is far less trustworthy and tolerant. One day the children get lost on the Downs in a heavy mist; Jingo is knocked down a steep bank by the nervous new pony, and the children fear both for his safety and that they will have to spend a cold night in the open. Suddenly Jingo appears through the mist, trotting back to find them and lead them safely home; Martin and Tabby realize that "he had been the dream pony all along." *The Wednesday Pony* is one of the best of the pony books. It is humorous and realistic in its treatment of both the animals and the human characters and free of the social snobbery that leads many writers of pony books to caricature people outside the Pony Club set; its themes are conveyed by the whole story rather than by creeping in as lessons; and the gallant personality of Jingo is memorably evoked, without recourse to the awkwardness of having him as a narrator describing things well beyond the scope of a pony's awareness.

Cummings's Silver Eagle books, although written for somewhat older readers, are more conventional in their approach and in their social attitudes: three sisters decide to turn their family stables into the Silver Eagle Riding School, and succeed – to everyone's surprise and after much hard work. When one of them, Josephine, leaves to pursue a career in show jumping, they are joined by a self-possessed, sardonic girl who had been working as a sign painter but turns out to be titled and wealthy. In *Silver Eagle Carries On* (1942), the outbreak of World War II brings Josephine back to the stables, and the girls learn to harness and drive some of the horses, to help with wartime fuel shortages. A hostile horse dealer who has a commission to requisition horses for the army nearly succeeds in making off with their beloved horses and thus their livelihood, but he is foiled by their resourcefulness and an appeal to a higher authority. The interactions among the four girls, usually united in their aims but different in personality, and between them and their rather motley collection of pupils, provide the chief interest of the novels; the horses are named and described but never become real characters in these novels as Jingo did in *The Wednesday Pony*.

A remarkable novel by two schoolgirls, *The Far Distant Oxus* (1937), published with a complimentary preface by Arthur Ransome, was one of the first books to link the pony story with the story of summer adventure in the Ransome mode. Its authors, Katherine Hull and Pamela Whitlock, were fifteen and sixteen, respectively, when they wrote the story, and its virtues of energetic action, direct observation, and delight in the processes of making a holiday life outdoors have helped to keep it appealing to children for more than fifty years. Like Ransome's children, the children in Hull and Whitlock's books have been given complete freedom to roam and explore, and they gallop their ponies about Exmoor much as the Swallows and Amazons sailed their dinghies around the Lakes: ponies are as good as sailboats in providing interesting means of transportation and a challenging way to develop new skills. The children in the Oxus books have more imagination than do the children in many other pony stories, whose horizons seem limited to the stables and ambitions to galloping around the show ring with a blue rosette. These children instead re-create the Devonshire landscape as Persia and name themselves and their surroundings from Matthew Arnold's *Sohrab and Rustum: An Episode* (1853). Their adventures thus are largely of their own making and imagining, as are those in

Ransome's books: they sneak out of the farmhouse at night and build a shelter, rescue a foal from the roundup of wild ponies, and make a week-long journey with their ponies and a raft down their river, Oxus, to the sea. The ponies are individually named and appreciated, but the children's adventures with them are more imaginative and less structured than in most of the pony books, in which Pony Club meetings and adult-regulated competitions are the focus of the children's activities. The Oxus children dispense with adults as far as possible, although they are glad enough of a kindly farmer's assistance when they arrive triumphantly at the river's mouth only to realize that they have no means of getting their raft back home against the current.

Romance is provided in the Oxus books not only by the Arnold poem with its richly evocative place-names – Siestan, Cabool, Peran-Wisa, and Elbruz – but also by the mysterious character of Maurice, a dark boy with a black pony and Labrador dog, who seems to be living on the moors with no home or means of support and who is the leading spirit in the children's adventures. The sequels *Escape to Persia* (1938) and *Oxus in Summer* (1939) reveal a little more about the origins of Maurice and again evoke the delightful freedom of action and imagination which makes these novels a vision of the ideal summer holiday, spent harmoniously among like-minded companions and entirely untroubled by the anxieties that would prevent children later in the century being given such freedom. It is perhaps not coincidental that the last of the Oxus books was published in 1939, at the outbreak of World War II; the social changes that accompanied and followed the war in Britain were inevitably reflected in the pony books, even in those that turned away from postwar realities to seek security in the traditions and hierarchies of show ring and hunting field.

In Mary Treadgold's fiction, the horizons of the pony story are dramatically expanded, in both a geographical and a social sense as they are set outside England and deal with problems arising from war and its aftermath. The children in her novels are still from a privileged upper middle class, but they are touched by experience of the outside world in ways that are not to be found in the pony story again until the mature work of K. M. Peyton. Treadgold, who had worked as a children's book editor for Heinemann and not been too impressed with the material submitted, began work on her first novel in an air-raid shelter in her garden during the Blitz, and the anxiety and displacement created by World War II give a sober though never morbid background to her writing. *We Couldn't Leave Dinah* (1941), the first and most enduringly popular of her books, is not only one of the most exciting of the pony/adventure stories, it is also one of the best children's books produced in Britain during the war and was awarded the Carnegie Medal for 1941. The Pony Club on the (fictitious) Channel Island of Clerinel has more serious problems than gymkhanas or even horse thieves to contend with: when Clerinel is invaded and occupied by the Nazis, the English residents flee, but thirteen-year-old Caroline and her slightly older brother, Mick, are accidentally left behind, and they find themselves using their secret Pony Club headquarters in a cave not to play but to survive in, and help to thwart a Nazi invasion of England.

The novel opens with a powerful sense of contrast between the shadow of rumored invasion and the golden late summer days of the children, spent galloping on the beach and running the island Pony Club along independent, child-directed lines unimagined by the English organizers of that institution. The invasion happens in an eerie scene, observed but only partly understood by Caroline, as the Nazis infiltrate a Pony Club masquerade party; eventually realizing that the invaders were assisted by their friend Peter Beaumarchais' father, they suffer feelings of betrayal as well as abandonment. M. Beaumarchais turns out to be a double agent, however, and the children join in a plot to obtain information about a planned invasion of England. The children are characterized distinctly, and the novel goes beyond the simple adventure story in presenting the problems of conflicting loyalties, betrayal, and trust, and a recognition of humanity within the ranks of the enemy — issues of great relevance during wartime but not generally raised in the jingoistic fiction produced while war is being waged.

Each of the three ponies belonging to Caroline's family has an important and distinct role to play in the action: surefooted and reliable Punch carries Caroline along the cliff in the fog; lively Dinah bears her swiftly for help; and little Bellman, the former lawn-mower pony, bucks off the Nazi commandant's imperious granddaughter Nannerl, thus giving Mick a pretext to enter the commandant's study and find the needed information. As in all pony stories, there is the obligatory scene where the novice rider — here Nannerl — is reproved for jerking the pony's mouth, and there is enough emphasis on the children's feeling for the ponies for the novel to qualify as a pony story. The world of *We Couldn't Leave Dinah* is, however, a much larger

world than that of most pony books, and while the children initially are most concerned about leaving their ponies behind, they rapidly become aware of other concerns more urgent and more significant even than ponies.

Subject matter arising out of the war is found in almost all of Treadgold's fiction, although ponies are not: Mick and Caroline are ponyless as they continue their adventures and their discoveries about the complexity of human nature, in *The "Polly Harris"* (1949). In *No Ponies* (1946) another family of children has an exciting adventure involving ponies, this time in the south of France; again, however, issues of human behavior in response to the stresses of war make this more than simply an adventure story, and the children learn much more about troubling ethical issues than about how to put on a bridle. Treadgold's last pair of pony stories, *The Heron Ride* (1962) and *Return to the Heron* (1963), are set in the English countryside and begin with the now-standard situation of a young girl who longs to ride but lacks the means to own a pony. Sandra and her brother become involved with a group of children staying on holiday at a local riding school and are dissatisfied with the way the school is being run by its new owner. A refugee from Central Europe who works with displaced children arrives for a short vacation and turns out to have once worked at the famous Riding School in Vienna; an unassuming little man with a comical accent, he helps the children catch some horse thieves, saves the local riding school by agreeing to teach there, and is the means of Sandra's getting to learn to ride after all. Once again not far in the background of the horsey adventures is an awareness of the human tragedies created by the war, giving a valuable perspective and sense of proportion to the concerns of the rest of the story.

Monica Edwards is another writer who locates her pony stories within the context of a world of nonequestrian interests and concerns. Although she began writing shortly after World War II, her concerns are more local than those of Treadgold: a countrywoman who also wrote for adults about nature and rural life, she fills her books with a sense of the life of a particular place, whether it be the Sussex fishing village of her childhood or the Surrey farm where she raised her own children. Her pony-loving child characters are thus continually dealing with other characters who have no particular feeling for horses but are allowed to be interesting people nonetheless. Tamzin's remark to Rissa at the end of *The Summer of the Great Secret* (1948) has a cautionary tone perhaps directed at the reader:

Speaking as someone who has had a pony for nearly a year, I think a person should have other interests in her life than just ponies and riding. No one could love their pony more than I love Cascade, but I don't want to grow up a long-faced horsy woman with no other string to her bow. I want time for swimming and boats and tennis and all sorts of things like those, as well as riding.

Edwards makes sure that there is room in her pony stories for "swimming and boats . . . and all sorts of other things," especially spending time with adults who have done various and interesting things with their lives. While Edwards's villains are stock characters merely there to help out the plot, her other numerous adult characters are strikingly quirky and likable; the amount of significant interaction between the children and adults in her books is unusual for adventure stories of this period, when the dominant influence of the Ransome books had made adults seem a necessary nuisance, to be dispensed with as quickly as possible.

The spirit of place that is so strongly conveyed in Edwards's books includes not only the natural environment of landscape and wild flowers but the country people as well, with their rich dialect, practical perspectives, and connections to the past. Old Jim the ferryman (and erstwhile smuggler) of the Romney Marsh series and ancient Joshua Pyecraft of the Punchbowl Farm series who gives Lindsey a sleigh bell in *Black Hunting Whip* are living links between the children's modern England and the centuries-old traditions and ways of life of which urban children may be hardly aware. While the novels, which are generally episodic in structure, do include some horse shows and prize-winning, their focus seems to be more on events that connect the children with nature, farm life, and the human past of the place where they are living. Some local efforts at smuggling, an outbreak of hoof and mouth disease, and the rescue of horses from a ship taking them to the Continent for slaughter as meat provide plot lines for the Romney Marsh books about Tamzin and Rissa and, in the later books, their friends Roger and Meryon. While the title of Edwards's first book, *Wish for a Pony,* suggests the conventional story line whereby an eager and worthy young girl eventually achieves the pony of her dreams, this basic story is subsumed into the larger story of the life of the fishing village: Tamzin finds her badly needed jodhpurs when she is coerced into helping at a rummage sale and eventually gets her pony through the intervention of a man rescued from a sinking cargo ship by the local lifeboat volunteers. A Sussex clergyman's daughter herself, Edwards makes her Tamzin the daughter of the vicar,

a man learned in local history and as deeply involved as his daughter becomes in the life of the whole community, not just the horsey set.

Edwards's second series, which begins with *No Mistaking Corker* (1947), emphasizes family more than community, but as the Thorntons establish themselves (as the Edwards family had) in their picturesque but drastically neglected Punchbowl Farm, their dedication to their seventy acres and their ruined Tudor farmhouse soon begins to connect them both with the life of the neighboring farmers and with those who have lived at Punchbowl Farm in the generations before them. *Black Hunting Whip,* the novel in which they purchase the farm, is largely about daily life there – parents and four children working with the various animals they buy, including a Jersey cow that calves and two new ponies (about which, once they have been selected and brought home, surprisingly little is said). These parts of the story are rich in personality, humor, and felt life; they convey a real sense of the interaction between humans and animals, through the seasons, and also to some extent develop interesting family relationships.

The story of *Black Hunting Whip* has another dimension, unusual in the pony book, which is that of time-slip fantasy. In a cellar under a former wing of the house, Dion finds a boy's journal from a century earlier, in which an ill-treated boy records his longing to ride his black pony to victory in an agricultural show, carrying the black hunting whip that his father had bequeathed him. Through most of the novel the Thornton children are searching to uncover traces of the past, either in the physical foundations of the building or through documents like the diary, the Parish register, and an old map that gives them the location of a former barn. During a horse show at the climax of the book a boy on a black pony mysteriously appears as a late entry in the jumping class, borrows the whip from Dion and rides to victory. This supernatural element provides a focus for the plot and for the children's researches but doesn't fit particularly well with the realistic evocation of everyday farm life that otherwise distinguishes this novel.

Ruby Ferguson, in her 1950s series of books about Jill Crewe, focuses her plots entirely upon the world of horses, as experiences by one young girl who moves from novice to skilled horse trainer and teacher. The first in the series, *Jill's Gymkhana* (1949), bears a strong resemblance to Cannan's *A Pony for Jean.* Both are narrated in the first person and address the reader directly, describing the eagerness and anxiety of a young girl who gets a pony and learns to look after and ride it. Like Jean's, Jill's family has no money to spare for a pony, and she has to improvise and economize to manage to keep him. Jill is lucky, however, in finding an ideal private riding teacher, a Royal Air Force pilot injured in the war who offers to help her and, of course, prepares her so well that she triumphs over her snobbish, wealthy rival in the final gymkhana. Through Jill, Ferguson writes as one schoolgirl to another (boys have little place in this world), about rivalries and resentments, gymkhana fever, and the longing to do well. The special tutoring she has received from Martin, however, does rather undercut Jill's assurances to the reader that any determined girl could do as well as she; Martin's lessons provide the opportunity for Ferguson to make some points about proper horse care and riding but would seem to put Jill at rather more of an advantage than she acknowledges.

Having established herself, by the end of the second volume of the series, as a skilled rider, Jill goes on in later volumes to help other children learn to ride. Plot complications are provided by awkward and difficult pupils, a greedy farmer who is secretly selling old horses for meat and a friend lost on the moors during a pony trek, but a happy resolution is always accomplished, with Jill often learning to appreciate the merits of someone she had previously disliked and raking in the ribbons at the final horse show. Jill is a modest and cheerful character, who lives only for horses and tends to be impatient with those who do not and is engagingly capable of losing her temper and behaving selfishly or otherwise badly upon occasion. Despite her impressive abilities as a rider, Jill is a character with whom the reader can readily identify: she is chronically short of money and frank about her feelings of inadequacy and discouragement. Humor in the Jill books is more direct than that of Cannan or Cummings, whose work they resemble in other ways; a recurring joke is the maudlin writing for children done by Jill's otherwise sensible mother, whose books, much to Jill's embarrassment, bear titles like *The Little House of Smiles* and *Winnie Wish-Too-Much*. Though never maudlin or overtly didactic, Ferguson's own Jill books do have something in common with Jill's mother's in that they clearly set out to provide the reader with reassurance and a satisfying fantasy of obstacles overcome and worthiness triumphant. Their titles linked by the name of their central character, they are more uniform in structure, length, and outlook than the work of other pony-book authors discussed thus far, and their popularity has influenced the development of other pony-book series.

The name with which the pony book is most often associated is Pullein-Thompson, and the novels of the three Pullein-Thompson sisters have much in common. Josephine and her twin sisters Diana and Christine are the daughters of Joanna Cannan, whose *A Pony for Jean* established the pattern of the pony book that focuses on the young girl longing and learning to ride. Working from that pattern, the Pullein-Thompson sisters have written a great many lively, popular pony books that describe the adventures of one child or a group of horse-minded children in the stables and the fields. Raised in an environment that mingled literary interests and horsey ones, the sisters began writing early and collaborated on a pony novel that was published while the twins were still only sixteen. In the same year, 1946, Josephine published her first individual novel, *Six Ponies*, which describes the selection of six children each to be given the opportunity to train an unbroken New Forest pony. While the reader's sympathy is particularly directed toward the eager but unconfident Noel, whose father cannot afford to buy her a pony, and some of the affluent, snobbish children are caricatured, the novel gives a realistic and perceptive view of the various kinds of children who are attracted to horses and the vicissitudes as well as the delights of the training process. Characters from this first novel reappear in later accounts of this pony club and its doings, and Josephine Pullein-Thompson shows a particular gift for effective depiction of groups of children working, playing, and competing together. Although some of her later novels such as *Race Horse Holiday* (1971) and *Fear Treks the Moor* (1979) have rather melodramatic adventure plots, her early books concentrate on the schooling of horse and rider. She creates believable and interesting child characters and takes the opportunity to develop at least some of them in subsequent volumes; through their anxieties, misadventures, and successes she is able to hold the reader's interest in detailed accounts of how to acquire a good seat and hunting manners in books like *Plenty of Ponies* (1949) and *Pony Club Team* (1950). In *Show Jumping Secret* (1955) the customary learning-to-ride tale is varied in an account of the therapeutic riding undertaken by a polio victim who learns to become a successful jumper.

All three of the Pullein-Thompson sisters have written instructional nonfiction books about riding, and the twins Diana and Christine directed a riding school for many years, during the time that they wrote their early pony books. The lively and realistic dialogue of their child characters suggests how attentive were the ears of the Pullein-Thompsons to the conversation of their pupils. While the subject matter of their pony books helps to account for some of their popularity with children, the ability of all three sisters to sketch in recognizable characters and situations that hold the attention of the reader have made that popularity remarkably long-lasting, and the books are frequently reprinted despite the fact that some of their many details about pocket money (how it is to be spent on pony supplies is a constant preoccupation of the pony books) and clothing have obviously become dated. Diana and Josephine have also written for adults, and Christine has published many children's books that are not about ponies, as well as the great many that are.

Christine is the most prolific of a prolific literary family, having written well over thirty pony stories as well as riding manuals and anthologies. The stories can generally be classed as pony/adventure novels, with a lot of fast-paced action and less emphasis on riding instruction. Intended to provide a quick and enjoyable read, they do not devote much attention to elegance of literary style or to detailed development of character; they do, however, effectively convey the atmosphere and ethos of the hunting field, stable, and gymkhana ring, where the author's vivid sense of humor helps to put triumphs and disasters into perspective.

An early series by Christine Pullein-Thompson describes the efforts of a group of children from two contrasting families to start a pack of foxhounds. Written in the lean postwar years, the series makes an interesting struggle out of the children's efforts to fund and put together their hunt; overcoming economic adversities is actually made as exciting in these novels as are the rigors of leaping the five-barred gate and catching up with the pack of hounds. In *We Hunted Hounds* (1949) a great deal of foxhunting lore is conveyed unobtrusively through the account of the conception and early days of the children's hunt. As in many of her sisters' books, a group of children rather than an individual is the focus, and relatively little attention is given to the ponies themselves. Characterization of the children themselves is brief and direct but often vivid: "Felicity and Prudence were nice, but in rather a quiet way. I couldn't help thinking that they had probably been washed too often all their lives and I decided that they had a nanny, who called them 'Precious,' and no brothers." Lawrence threatens his bossy sister, the first-person narrator of the series, that "If you're not careful you'll grown into a hard-faced horsy woman in a hair net," but that fate does not seem to alarm her. Toughness is admired, and sentiment is allowed no place on the hunting field, but an underlying kindliness is present in the children's relationships, and scrupulous care for the horses is of course an absolute value.

While most of the pony books have not been highly regarded by reviewers and critics, the frequency with which many of the earlier books have been reprinted through the 1960s, 1970s, and 1980s, and new series begun during those years, marks the vitality of the genre with children. In the 1950s other writers explored the format of the pony/adventure series, such as the Three Jays books by the well-known show jumper Pat Smythe, Mary Gervaise's stories of the adventures of Susan and Georgie in which the Devonshire background plays an important role, and Judith M. Berrisford's series about Jackie, published from the 1950s to the 1970s. Despite their names, Georgie and Jackie are girls, and while the books depicting a group of children usually have an equal number of girl and boy characters, relatively few have a boy as the single central character; the pony story has tended to be the work of female authors and read chiefly by girls. In this the British pony books differ from the horse-story genre in the United States, which often has a male focus, as in the popular Black Stallion series, and which is also more inclined than the British stories to bring in romantic relationships with the opposite sex.

The pony story, like the infatuation with horses that strikes so many adolescent girls, has often appeared to be an alternative to infatuation with boys and provides a cheerful, "right-minded" narrative in which the darker aspects of adolescent angst rarely surface. The occasional pony book such as Christine Pullein-Thompson's *The Horse Sale* and K. M. Peyton's *The Wild Boy and Gypsy Moon* (1994) does touch on male-female attraction among its older characters, but for the most part conflict in the pony books arises from concerns about acquiring or maintaining one's pony, doing well in competition, or having the sort of adventures that is exciting but does not trouble the soul. Pony books thus have a kind of innocence about the world: goodness is recognized and rewarded, while genuinely evil characters are remote – cardboard villains readily defeated by resourceful children, and the worst kind of behavior exhibited by the children themselves is conceit and bad sportsmanship. Strong emotions certainly are felt by many of the characters, but they are contained within the bounds of a story pattern that give the young reader the assurance and security that all will be well in the end. Although families may be short of money, codes of good manners, correct riding attire, and a general sense of what is and isn't done are treated as important in all the pony books; except for a few of the summer-adventure stories like those of Hull and Whitlock in which the children create their own worlds, the pony stories are set within a structured social world that provides clear-cut expectations and rewards and whose basic principles are never challenged.

The credibility and scope of the pony story in Britain has been extended in recent years by the work of K. M. Peyton, who began her own writing career with pony books and whose romantic Flambards series for older readers draws upon some elements of the pony stories. Some of her later books, however, such as *Fly By Night, The Team, Free Rein* (1983), *Who, Sir? Me, Sir?* (1983), and *The Wild Boy and Gypsy Moon* are true pony stories in that a relationship between a child and a horse is at the center of the story, yet they have some marked differences from the traditional pony-story genre. Peyton's books have strong male characters, are free of the class snobbery that is so marked in many of the older pony books, and locate their conflicts within the realities of late-twentieth-century life rather than evoking a pastoral ideal of the English village life and countryside. While retaining many of its attractive qualities, Peyton has thus been able to lead the pony story away from conservative nostalgia into fresh new pastures.

School Stories, 1914–1960

Donnalee Kathryn Smith
Scarborough Public Library, Ontario, Canada

BOOKS: Mabel Esther Allan, *The Glen Castle Mystery* (London: Warne, 1948);

Allan, *The Adventurous Summer,* illustrated by Isabel Veevers (London: Museum Press, 1948);

Allan, *The Wyndhams Went to Wales,* illustrated by Beryl Thornborough (London: Sylvan Press, 1948);

Allan, *Mullion,* illustrated by R. Walter Hall (London: Hutchinson, 1949);

Allan, *Cilia of Chiltern's Edge,* illustrated by Betty Ladler (London: Museum Press, 1949);

Allan, *Trouble at Melville Manor,* illustrated by Veevers (London: Museum Press, 1949);

Allan, *Holidays at Arnriggs* (London: Warne, 1949);

Allan, *Jimmy John's Journey* (London: Dean, 1949);

Allan, *Chiltern Adventure,* illustrated by T. R. Freeman (London: Blackie, 1950);

Allan, *Over the Sea to School,* illustrated by W. Mackinlay (London: Blackie, 1950);

Allan, *School Under Snowdon* (London: Hutchinson, 1950);

Allan, *Everyday Island* (London: Museum Press, 1950);

Allan, *Seven in Switzerland,* illustrated by Veevers (London: Blackie, 1950);

Allan, *The Exciting River,* illustrated by Helen Jacobs (London: Nelson, 1951);

Allan, *Clues to Connemara,* illustrated by Philip (London: Blackie, 1952);

Allan, *The MacIains of Glen Gillian* (London: Hutchinson, 1952);

Allan, *Return to Derrykereen* (London: Ward Lock, 1952);

Allan, *A School in Danger,* illustrated by Eric Winter (London: Blackie, 1952);

Allan, *The School on Cloud Ridge* (London: Hutchinson, 1952);

Allan, *The School on North Barrule* (London: Museum Press, 1952);

Allan, *The Secret Valley,* illustrated by C. Instrell (Leeds: Arnold, 1953);

Allan, *Room for the Cuckoo: The Story of a Farming Year* (London: Dent, 1953);

Allan, *Three Go to Switzerland,* illustrated by Veevers (London: Blackie, 1953);

Allan, *Lucia Comes to School* (London: Hutchinson, 1953);

Allan, *Strangers at Brongwerne* (London: Museum Press, 1953);

Allan, *Meric's Secret Cottage* (London: Blackie, 1954);

Allan, *Adventure Royal,* illustrated by C. W. Bacon (London: Blackie, 1954);

Allan, *Here We Go Round: A Career Story for Girls* (London: Heinemann, 1954);

Allan, *Margaret Finds a Future* (London: Hutchinson, 1954);

Allan, *New Schools for Old* (London: Hutchinson, 1954);

Allan, *The Summer at Town's End,* illustrated by Iris Weller (London: Harrap, 1954);

Allan, *Adventures in Switzerland* (London: Pickering & Inglis, 1955);

Allan, *The Mystery of Derrydane,* illustrated by Vera Chadwick (Huddersfield, Yorkshire: Schofield & Sims, 1955);

Allan, *Changes for the Challoners* (London: Ward Lock, 1955);

Allan, *Glenvara* (London: Hutchinson, 1955); republished as *Summer of Decision* (New York: Abelard Schuman, 1957);

Allan, *Judith Teaches* (London: Bodley Head, 1955);

Allan, *Adventure in Mayo* (London: Ward Lock, 1956);

Allan, *Balconies and Blue Nets: The Story of a Holiday in Brittany,* illustrated by Peggy Beetles (London: Harrap, 1956);

Allan, *Lost Lorrenden,* illustrated by Shirley Hughes (London: Blackie, 1956);

Allan, *Strangers in Skye* (London: Heinemann, 1956);

Allan, *Two in the Western Isles* (London: Hutchinson, 1956);

Allan, *The Vine-Clad Hill,* illustrated by Freeman (London: Lane, 1956); republished as *Swiss Holiday* (New York: Vanguard Press, 1957);

Allan, *Flora at Kilroinn* (London: Blackie, 1956);

Allan, *The Amber House* (London: Hutchinson, 1956);

Allan, *Ann's Alpine Adventure* (London: Hutchinson, 1956);

Allan, *At School in Skye,* illustrated by Constance Marshall (London: Blackie, 1957);

Allan, *Black Forest Summer* (London: Bodley Head, 1957);

Allan, *Sara Goes to Germany* (London: Hutchinson, 1957);

Allan, *Murder at the Flood* (London: Stanley Paul, 1957);

Allan, *Ballet for Drina,* as Jean Estoril; illustrated by Eve Guthrie and M. P. Steedman Davies (London: Hodder & Stoughton, 1957);

Allan, *Blue Dragon Days* (London: Heinemann, 1958); republished as *Romance in Italy* (New York: Vanguard Press, 1962);

Allan, *Drina's Dancing Year,* as Estoril (London: Hodder & Stoughton, 1958);

Allan, *The Conch Shell,* illustrated by Freeman (London: Blackie, 1958);

Allan, *The House by the Marsh,* illustrated by Sheila Rose (London: Dent, 1958);

Allan, *Rachel Tandy* (London: Hutchinson, 1958);

Allan, *Amanda Goes to Italy* (London: Hutchinson, 1959);

Allan, *Catrin in Wales* (London: Bodley Head, 1959);

Allan, *A Play to the Festival* (London: Heinemann, 1959); republished as *On Stage, Flory* (New York: Watts, 1961);

Allan, *Drina Dances in Exile,* as Estoril (London: Hodder & Stoughton, 1959);

Allan, *Drina Dances in Italy,* as Estoril; illustrated by Guthrie and Davies (London: Hodder & Stoughton, 1959);

Allan, *Shadow Over the Alps* (London: Hutchinson, 1960);

Allan, *A Summer in Brittany* (London: Dent, 1960); republished as *Hilary's Summer on Her Own* (New York: Watts, 1961);

Allan, *Drina Dances Again,* as Estoril (London: Hodder & Stoughton, 1960);

Allan, *Tansy of Tring Street,* illustrated by Sally Holiday (London: Heinemann, 1960);

Allan, *Holiday of Endurance* (London: Dent, 1961);

Allan, *The First Time I Saw Paris,* as Anne Pilgrim (New York & London: Abelard Schuman, 1961);

Allan, *Drina Dances in New York,* as Estoril (London: Hodder & Stoughton, 1961);

Allan, *Bluegate Girl* (London: Hutchinson, 1961);

Allan, *Pendron under the Water,* illustrated by Freeman (London: Harrap, 1961);

Allan, *Home to the Island,* illustrated by Geoffrey Whittam (London: Dent, 1962);

Allan, *Drina Dances in Paris,* as Estoril (London: Hodder & Stoughton, 1962);

Allan, *Clare Goes to Holland,* as Pilgrim (New York & London: Abelard Schuman, 1962);

Allan, *Signpost to Switzerland* (London: Heinemann, 1962);

Allan, *The Ballet Family,* illustrated by A. R. Whitear (London: Methuen, 1963);

Harold Avery, *The School's Honour and Other Stories* (London: Sunday School Union, 1894);

Avery, *The Orderly Officer* (London: S. P. C. K., 1894);

Avery, *An Old Boy's Yarns* (London: Cassell, 1894);

Avery, *A Boy All Over,* illustrated by Walter Buckley (London: Sampson Low, 1896);

Avery, *Frank's First Term; or, Making a Man of Him* (London: Nelson, 1896);

Avery, *Soldiers of the Queen; or, Jack Fenleigh's Luck* (London: Nelson, 1897);

Avery, *The Dormitory Flag* (London: Nelson, 1898);

Avery, *Stolen or Strayed* (London: Nelson, 1898);

Avery, *The Triple Alliance* (London: Nelson, 1898);

Avery, *Heads or Tails* (London: Nelson, 1900);

Avery, *A Toast-Fag and Other Stories* (London: Nelson, 1900);

Avery, *All Play and No Work,* illustrated by Harold Copping (London: Partridge, 1901);

Avery, *With Wellington to Waterloo,* illustrated by J. Finnemore (London: Wells Gardner, 1901);

Avery, *Sale's Sharpshooters* (London: Nelson, 1902);

Avery, *"Wrinkles" for Young Writers* (London: Chilver, 1902);

Avery, *An Armchair Adventurer* (London: Simpkin Marshall, 1903);

Avery, *The House on the Moor* (London: Nelson, 1903);

Avery, *Manor Pool Island* (London: Collins, 1903);

Avery, *Highway Pirates* (London: Nelson, 1904);

Avery, *Out of the Running* (London: Collins, 1904);

Avery, *Under Padlock and Seal* (London: Nelson, 1905);

Avery, *Firelock and Seal* (London: Nelson, 1906);

Avery, *The Magic Beads* (London: Nelson, 1906);

Avery, *Play the Games!* (London: Nelson, 1906);

Avery, *Captain Swing* (London: Nelson, 1907);

Avery, *Through the Wood,* illustrated by John Hassall (London: Nelson, 1907);

Avery, *True to His Nickname* (London: Nelson, 1907);

Avery, *The Enchanted Egg* (London: Nelson, 1908);

Avery, *The Wizard's Wand* (London: Nelson, 1908);

Avery, *In the Days of Danger* (London: Nelson, 1909);

Avery, *Off the Wicket* (London: Nelson, 1910);

Avery, *A Week at the Sea* (London: Stanley Paul, 1910);

Avery, *Not Cricket!* (London: Partridge, 1911);

Avery, *The Forbidden Room* (London: Nelson, 1911);

Avery, *Every Dog His Day* (London: Stanley Paul, 1911);

Avery, *Head of the School* (London: Partridge, 1912);

Avery, *Talford's Last Term* (London: Partridge, 1912);

Avery, *The Chartered Company* (London: Nelson, 1915);

Avery, *Line Up!* (London: Collins, 1918);

Avery, *Caught Out* (London: Collins, 1919);

Avery, *Jack and the Redskins* (London: Nelson, 1920);

Avery, *The Runaways,* illustrated by Gordon Browne (London: Collins, 1920);

Avery, *Schoolboy Pluck* (London: Nisbet, 1921);

Avery, *A Choice of Chums* (London: Nelson, 1922);

Avery, *The Prefects' Patrol* (London: Nisbet, 1922);

Avery, *Between Two Schools* (London: Nelson, 1923);

Avery, *A Fifth Form Mystery* (London: Boy's Own Paper, 1923);

Avery, *The Spoil Sport, and Double Dummy* (London: Nelson, 1923);

Avery, *The Adventures of Woodeny and Other Stories,* with Ethel Talbot and Ada Holman (London: Nelson, 1923);

Avery, *Thumbs Up* (London: Nisbet, 1925);

Avery, *Pocket Thunder and Other Stories,* with others (London: Nelson, 1926);

Avery, *A Sixth Form Feud* (London: Ward Lock, 1926);

Avery, *Who Goes There?,* illustrated by Roy (London: Nelson, 1927);

Avery, *Won for the School,* illustrated by Archibald Webb (London: Collins, 1927);

Avery, *Any Port in a Storm and Other Stories,* with others (London: Nelson, 1928);

Avery, *Day Boy Colours,* illustrated by J. Phillips Paterson (London: Nelson, 1928);

Avery, *Cock-House of Claverhill* (London: Collins, 1929);

Avery, *A Term on Trial* (London: Partridge, 1930);

Avery, *The Cock-House Cup* (London: Nelson, 1933);

Avery, *A Close Finish and Other School Stories* (London: Partridge, 1934);

Avery, *The Marlcot Mystery* (London: Ward Lock, 1935);

Avery, *Chums at Charlhurst* (London: Nelson, 1936);

Avery, *Through Thick and Thin,* illustrated by Paterson (London: Nelson, 1938);

Avery, *The Side Line* (London: Ward Lock, 1939);

Avery, *The Girl at the Helm* (London: Nelson, 1941);

Angela Brazill, *The Mischievous Brownie* (Edinburgh: Patterson, 1899);

Brazill, *The Fairy Gifts* (Edinburgh: Patterson, 1901);

Brazill, *Four Recitations* (Edinburgh: Patterson, 1903);

Brazill, *The Enchanted Fiddle* (Edinburgh: Patterson, 1903);

Brazill, *The Wishing Princess* (Edinburgh: Patterson, 1904).

Brazill, *A Terrible Tomboy,* illustrated by Angela and Amy Brazil (London: Gay & Bird, 1904);

Brazill, *The Fortunes of Philippa* (N.p., 1906);

Brazill, *The Third Class at Miss Kaye's* (London: Blackie, 1908);

Brazill, *The Nicest Girl in the School* (London: Blackie, 1909; Boston: Caldwell, 1911);

Brazill, *Bosom Friends: A Seaside Story* (London: Nelson, 1910);

Brazill, *The Manor House School,* illustrated by F. Moorsom (London: Blackie, 1910; Boston: Caldwell, 1911);

Brazill, *The New Girl at St. Chad's* (London: Blackie, 1911);

Brazill, *A Fourth Form Friendship* (London: Blackie, 1912);

Brazill, *A Pair of Schoolgirls* (London: Blackie, 1912);

Brazill, *The Leader of the Lower School* (London: Blackie, 1913);

Brazill, *The Girls of St. Cyprian's* (London: Blackie, 1914);

Brazill, *The School By the Sea* (London: Blackie, 1914);

Brazill, *The Youngest Girl in the Fifth* (London: Blackie, 1914);

Brazill, *The Jolliest Term on Record* (London: Blackie, 1915);

Brazill, *For the Sake of the School* (London: Blackie, 1915);

Brazill, *The Luckiest Girl in the School,* illustrated by Balliol Salmon (London: Blackie, 1916; New York: Stokes, 1916);

Brazill, *The Madcap of the School,* illustrated by Salmon (London: Blackie, 1917; New York: Stokes, 1922);

Brazill, *The Slap-Bang Boys* (London: Nelson, 1917);

Brazill, *A Patriotic Schoolgirl,* illustrated by Salmon (London: Blackie, 1918);

Brazill, *For the School Colours,* illustrated by Salmon (London: Blackie, 1918);

Brazill, *A Harum-Scarum Schoolgirl,* illustrated by John Campbell (London: Blackie, 1919; New York: Stokes, 1920);

Brazill, *The Head Girl at the Gables,* illustrated by Salmon (London: Blackie, 1919; New York: Stokes, 1920);

Brazill, *Two Little Scamps and a Puppy,* illustrated by E. Blampied (London: Nelson, 1919);

Brazill, *A Gift from the Sea* (London: Nelson, 1920);

Brazill, *A Popular Schoolgirl,* illustrated by Salmon (London: Blackie, 1920; New York: Stokes, 1921);

Brazill, *The Princess of the School,* illustrated by Frank Wiles (London: Blackie, 1920; New York: Stokes, 1921);

Brazill, *Loyal to the School,* illustrated by Treyer Evans (London: Blackie, 1921);

Brazill, *A Fortunate Term,* illustrated by Evans (London: Blackie, 1921); republished as *Marjorie's Best Year* (New York: Stokes, 1923);

Brazill, *Monitress Merle,* illustrated by Evans (London: Blackie, 1922);

Brazill, *The School in the South,* illustrated by W. Smithson Broadhead (London: Blackie, 1922); republished as *The Jolliest School of All* (New York: Stokes, 1923);

Brazill, *The Khaki Boys and Other Stories* (London: Nelson, 1923);

Brazill, *Schoolgirl Kitty,* illustrated by W. E. Wightman (London: Blackie, 1923; New York: Stokes, 1924);

Brazill, *Captain Peggy,* illustrated by Wightman (London: Blackie, 1924; New York: Stokes, 1924);

Brazill, *My Own Schooldays* (London: Blackie, 1925);

Brazill, *Joan's Best Chum,* illustrated by Wightman (London: Blackie, 1926; New York: Stokes, 1927);

Brazill, *Queen of the Dormitory and Other Stories,* illustrated by P. B. Hickling (London: Cassell, 1926);

Brazill, *Ruth of St. Roman's,* illustrated by F. Oldham (London: Blackie, 1927);

Brazill, *At School with Rachel,* illustrated by Wightman (London: Blackie, 1928);

Brazill, *St. Catherine's College,* illustrated by Wiles (London: Blackie, 1929);

Brazill, *The Little Green School,* illustrated by Wiles (London: Blackie, 1931);

Brazill, *Nesta's New School,* illustrated by J. Dewar Mills (London: Blackie, 1932);

Brazill, *Jean's Golden Term* (London: Blackie, 1934);

Brazill, *The School at the Turrets* (London: Blackie, 1935);

Brazill, *An Exciting Term* (London: Blackie, 1936);

Brazill, *Jill's Jolliest School* (London: Blackie, 1937);

Brazill, *The School on the Cliff,* illustrated by F. E. Hiley (London: Blackie, 1938);

Brazill, *The School on the Moor,* illustrated by Henry Coller (London: Blackie, 1939);

Brazill, *The New School at Scawdale,* illustrated by M. Mackinlay (London: Blackie, 1940);

Brazill, *Five Jolly Schoolgirls* (London: Blackie, 1941);

Brazill, *The Mystery of the Moated Grange* (London: Blackie, 1942);

Brazill, *The Secret of the Border Castle,* illustrated by Charles Willis (London: Blackie, 1943);

Brazill, *The School in the Forest,* illustrated by Mills (London: Blackie, 1944);

Brazill, *Three Terms at Uplands,* illustrated by D. L. Mays (London: Blackie, 1945);

Brazill, *The School on the Loch,* illustrated by W. Lindsay Cable (London: Blackie, 1946);

Elinor M. Brent-Dyer, *Gerry Goes to School,* illustrated by Gordon Broe (Edinburgh: Chambers, 1922; Philadelphia: Lippincott, 1923);

Brent-Dyer, *A Head Girl's Difficulties,* illustrated by Nina K. Brisley (Edinburgh: Chambers, 1923);

Brent-Dyer, *The Maids of La Rochelle,* illustrated by Brisley (Edinburgh: Chambers, 1924);

Brent-Dyer, *The School at the Chalet,* illustrated by Brisley (Edinburgh: Chambers, 1925);

Brent-Dyer, *Jo of the Chalet School,* illustrated by Brisley (Edinburgh: Chambers, 1926);

Brent-Dyer, *A Thrilling Term at Janeways,* illustrated by F. M. Anderson (London: Nelson, 1927);

Brent-Dyer, *Seven Scamps Who Are Not All Boys,* illustrated by Percy Tarrant (Edinburgh: Chambers, 1927);

Brent-Dyer, *The Princess of the Chalet School,* illustrated by Brisley (Edinburgh: Chambers, 1927);

Brent-Dyer, *The Head Girl of the Chalet School,* illustrated by Brisley (Edinburgh: Chambers, 1928);

Brent-Dyer, *Judy the Guide,* illustrated by L. A. Govey (London: Nelson, 1928);

Brent-Dyer, *The New House Mistress* (London: Nelson, 1928);

Brent-Dyer, *Heather Leaves School,* illustrated by Tarrant (Edinburgh: Chambers, 1928);

Brent-Dyer, *Rivals of the Chalet School,* illustrated by Brisley (Edinburgh: Chambers, 1929);

Brent-Dyer, *Eustacia Goes to the Chalet School* (Edinburgh: Chambers, 1930);

Brent-Dyer, *The School by the River* (London: Burns Oates, 1930);

Brent-Dyer, *The Chalet School and Jo,* illustrated by Brisley (Edinburgh: Chambers, 1931);

Brent-Dyer, *The Feud in the Fifth Remove* (London: Religious Tract Society, 1931);

Brent-Dyer, *Janie of La Rochelle* (Edinburgh: Chambers, 1932);

Brent-Dyer, *The Little Marie-José* (London: Burns Oates, 1932);

Brent-Dyer, *The Chalet Girls in Camp* (Edinburgh: Chambers, 1932);

Brent-Dyer, *The Exploits of the Chalet Girls,* illustrated by Brisley (Edinburgh: Chambers, 1933);

Brent-Dyer, *The Chalet School and the Lintons,* illustrated by Brisley (Edinburgh: Chambers, 1934);

Brent-Dyer, *Carnation of the Upper Fourth* (London: Religious Tract Society, 1934);

Brent-Dyer, *The New House at the Chalet School* (Edinburgh: Chambers, 1935);

Brent-Dyer, *Jo Returns to the Chalet School,* illustrated by Brisley (Edinburgh: Chambers, 1936);

Brent-Dyer, *Monica Turns Up Trumps* (London: Religious Tract Society, 1936);

Brent-Dyer, *Caroline the Second* (London: Religious Tract Society, 1937);

Brent-Dyer, *The New Chalet School,* illustrated by Brisley (Edinburgh: Chambers, 1938);

Brent-Dyer, *They Both Liked Dogs* (London: Religious Tract Society, 1938);

Brent-Dyer, *The Chalet School in Exile* (Edinburgh: Chambers, 1940);

Brent-Dyer, *The Chalet School Goes to It,* illustrated by Brisley (Edinburgh: Chambers, 1941);

Brent-Dyer, *The Highland Twins at the Chalet School* (Edinburgh: Chambers, 1942);

Brent-Dyer, *The Little Missus* (Edinburgh: Chambers, 1942);

Brent-Dyer, *Lavender Laughs in the Chalet School* (Edinburgh: Chambers, 1943);

Brent-Dyer, *Gay From China at the Chalet School* (Edinburgh: Chambers, 1944);

Brent-Dyer, *Jo to the Rescue* (Edinburgh: Chambers, 1945);

Brent-Dyer, *The Lost Staircase* (Edinburgh: Chambers, 1946);

Brent-Dyer, *Lorna at Wynyards* (London: Lutterworth, 1947);

Brent-Dyer, *Stepsisters for Lorna,* illustrated by John Bruce (London: Temple, 1948);

Brent-Dyer, *Three Go to the Chalet School* (Edinburgh: Chambers, 1949);

Brent-Dyer, *Peggy of the Chalet School* (Edinburgh: Chambers, 1950);

Brent-Dyer, *The Chalet School and the Island* (Edinburgh: Chambers, 1950);

Brent-Dyer, *Fardingdales* (London: Latimer, 1950);

Brent-Dyer, *The Chalet School and Rosalie* (Edinburgh: Chambers, 1951);

Brent-Dyer, *Carola Storms the Chalet School* (Edinburgh: Chambers, 1951);

Brent-Dyer, *Schoolgirls Abroad [Verena Visits New Zealand, Bess on Her Own in Canada, A Quintette in Queensland, Sharlie's Kenya Diary],* 4 volumes (Edinburgh: Chambers, 1951);

Brent-Dyer, *The Chalet School in the Oberland* (Edinburgh: Chambers, 1952);

Brent-Dyer, *The Wrong Chalet School* (Edinburgh: Chambers, 1952);

Brent-Dyer, *Shocks for the Chalet School* (Edinburgh: Chambers, 1952);

Brent-Dyer, *Bride Leads the Chalet School* (Edinburgh: Chambers, 1953);

Brent-Dyer, *Changes for the Chalet School* (Edinburgh: Chambers, 1953);

Brent-Dyer, *Janie Steps In* (Edinburgh: Chambers, 1953);

Brent-Dyer, *The Susannah Adventure* (Edinburgh: Chambers, 1953);

Brent-Dyer, *Nesta Steps Out* (London: Oliphants, 1954);

Brent-Dyer, *Kennelmaid Nan* (London: Lutterworth, 1954);

Brent-Dyer, *Joey Goes to the Oberland* (Edinburgh: Chambers, 1954);

Brent-Dyer, *Chudleigh Hold* (Edinburgh: Chambers, 1954);

Brent-Dyer, *The Condor Crags Adventure* (Edinburgh: Chambers, 1954);

Brent-Dyer, *The Chalet School and Barbara* (Edinburgh: Chambers, 1954);

Brent-Dyer, *Beechy of the Harbour School* (London: Oliphants, 1955);

Brent-Dyer, *A Chalet Girl from Kenya* (Edinburgh: Chambers, 1955);

Brent-Dyer, *The Chalet School Does It Again* (Edinburgh: Chambers, 1955);

Brent-Dyer, *Tom Tackles the Chalet School* (Edinburgh: Chambers, 1955);

Brent-Dyer, *Top Secret* (Edinburgh: Chambers, 1955);

Brent-Dyer, *A Problem for the Chalet School* (Edinburgh: Chambers, 1956);

Brent-Dyer, *Leader in Spite of Herself* (London: Oliphants, 1956);

Brent-Dyer, *Mary-Lou of the Chalet School* (Edinburgh: Chambers, 1956);

Brent-Dyer, *A Genius at the Chalet School* (Edinburgh: Chambers, 1956; revised edition, London: Collins, 1969);

Brent-Dyer, *Excitements at the Chalet School* (Edinburgh: Chambers, 1957);

Brent-Dyer, *The New Mistress at the Chalet School* (Edinburgh: Chambers, 1957);

Brent-Dyer, *The Chalet School and Richenda* (Edinburgh: Chambers, 1958);

Brent-Dyer, *The Coming-of-Age of the Chalet School* (Edinburgh: Chambers, 1958);

Brent-Dyer, *Theodora and the Chalet School* (Edinburgh: Chambers, 1959);

Brent-Dyer, *Trials for the Chalet School* (Edinburgh: Chambers, 1959);

Brent-Dyer, *Joey & Co. in Tirol* (Edinburgh: Chambers, 1960);

Brent-Dyer, *Ruey Richardson – Chaletian* (Edinburgh: Chambers, 1960);

Brent-Dyer, *A Leader in the Chalet School* (Edinburgh: Chambers, 1961);

Brent-Dyer, *The Chalet School Wins the Trick* (Edinburgh: Chambers, 1961);

Brent-Dyer, *The Feud in the Chalet School* (Edinburgh: Chambers, 1962);

Brent-Dyer, *A Future Chalet School Girl* (Edinburgh: Chambers, 1962);

Brent-Dyer, *The School at Skelton Hall* (London: Parrish, 1962);

Brent-Dyer, *The Chalet School Reunion* (Edinburgh: Chambers, 1963);

Brent-Dyer, *The Chalet School Triplets* (Edinburgh: Chambers, 1963);

Brent-Dyer, *Trouble at Skelton Hall* (London: Parrish, 1963);

Brent-Dyer, *Jane and the Chalet School* (Edinburgh: Chambers, 1964);

Brent-Dyer, *Redheads at the Chalet School* (Edinburgh: Chambers, 1964);

Brent-Dyer, *Summer Term at the Chalet School* (Edinburgh: Chambers, 1965);

Brent-Dyer, *Adrienne and the Chalet School* (Edinburgh: Chambers, 1965);

Brent-Dyer, *Challenge for the Chalet School* (Edinburgh: Chambers, 1966);

Brent-Dyer, *Two Sams at the Chalet School* (Edinburgh: Chambers, 1967);

Brent-Dyer, *Althea Joins the Chalet School* (Edinburgh: Chambers, 1969);

Brent-Dyer, *Prefects at the Chalet School* (London: Chambers, 1970);

Dorita Fairlie Bruce, *The Senior Prefect,* illustrated by Wal Paget (London: Oxford University Press, 1920); republished as *Dimsie Goes to School* (N.p., 1933);

Bruce, *Dimsie Moves Up,* illustrated by Paget (London: Oxford University Press, 1921);

Bruce, *Dimsie Moves Up Again,* illustrated by Gertrude D. Hammond (London: Oxford University Press, 1922);

Bruce, *Dimsie Among the Prefects,* illustrated by Hammond (London: Oxford University Press, 1923);

Bruce, *The Girls of St. Bride's,* illustrated by Coller (London: Oxford University Press, 1923);

Bruce, *Dimsie Grows Up,* illustrated by Coller (London: Oxford University Press, 1924);

Bruce, *Dimsie, Head-Girl,* illustrated by M. S. Reeve (London: Oxford University Press, 1925);

Bruce, *That Boarding-School Girl,* illustrated by Roy (London: Oxford University Press, 1925);

Bruce, *The New Girl and Nancy* (London: Oxford University Press, 1926);

Bruce, *Nancy to the Rescue* (London: Oxford University Press, 1927);

Bruce, *Dimsie Goes Back,* illustrated by Reeve (London: Oxford University Press, 1927);

Bruce, *The New House-Captain,* illustrated by Reeve (London: Oxford University Press, 1928);

Bruce, *The King's Curate* (London: John Murray, 1930);

Bruce, *The Best House in the School,* illustrated by Reeve (London: Oxford University Press, 1930);

Bruce, *The Best Bat in the School* (London: Oxford University Press, 1931);

Bruce, *The School on the Moor,* illustrated by Reeve (London: Oxford University Press, 1931);

Bruce, *Captain of Springdale,* illustrated by Coller (London: Oxford University Press, 1932);

Bruce, *Mistress-Mariner* (London: John Murray, 1932);

Bruce, *Nancy at St. Bride's,* illustrated by Johnston (London: Oxford University Press, 1933);

Bruce, *The New House at Springdale,* illustrated by Johnston (London: Oxford University Press, 1934);

Bruce, *Nancy in the Sixth* (London: Oxford University Press, 1935);

Bruce, *Dimsie Intervenes,* illustrated by Johnston (London: Oxford University Press, 1937);

Bruce, *Prefects at Springdale* (London: Oxford University Press, 1938);

Bruce, *Nancy Returns to St. Bride's,* illustrated by Johnston (London: Oxford University Press, 1938);

Bruce, *Captain Anne,* illustrated by Johnston (London: Oxford University Press, 1939);

Bruce, *The School in the Woods,* illustrated by G. M. Anson (London: Oxford University Press, 1940);

Bruce, *Dimsie Carries On,* illustrated by W. Bryce Hamilton (London: Oxford University Press, 1942);

Bruce, *Toby at Tibbs Cross,* illustrated by Margaret Horder (London: Oxford University Press, 1943);

Bruce, *Nancy Calls the Tune,* illustrated by Horder (London: Oxford University Press, 1944);

Bruce, *A Laverock Lilting,* illustrated by Horder (London: Oxford University Press, 1945);

Bruce, *Wild Goose Quest* (London: Lutterworth, 1945);

Bruce, *The Serendipity Shop,* illustrated by Horder (London: Oxford University Press, 1947);

Bruce, *Triffeny,* illustrated by Horder (London: Oxford University Press, 1950);

Bruce, *The Bees on Drumwhinnie,* illustrated by Horder (London: Oxford University Press, 1952);

Bruce, *The Debatable Mound,* illustrated by Patricia M. Lambe (London: Oxford University Press, 1953);

Bruce, *The Bartle Bequest,* illustrated by Sylvia Green (London: Oxford University Press, 1955);

Bruce, *Sally Scatterbrain,* illustrated by Betty Ladler (London: Blackie, 1956);

Bruce, *Sally Again,* illustrated by Ladler (London: Blackie, 1959);

Bruce, *Sally's Summer Term,* illustrated by Joan Thompson (London: Blackie, 1961);

Bruce, *Dimsie Takes Charge,* (Aylesbury, Buckinghamshire: Goodchild, 1985);

Hylton Cleaver, *The Tempting Thought* (London: Mills & Boon, 1917);

Cleaver, *Brother o' Mine: A School Story* (London: Oxford University Press, 1920);

Cleaver, *The Sporting Spirit and Other Stories* (London: Newnes, 1920);

Cleaver, *The Harley First XI* (London: Oxford University Press, 1920);

Cleaver, *Roscoe Makes Good: A Story of Harley* (London: Oxford University Press, 1920);

Cleaver, *Captains of Harley: A School Story* (London: Oxford University Press, 1921);

Cleaver, *On with the Motley* (London: Mills & Boon, 1922);

Cleaver, *The Old Order: A Public School Story* (London: Oxford University Press, 1922);

Cleaver, *The Harley First XV* (London: Oxford University Press, 1922);

Cleaver, *Second Innings* (London: Oxford University Press, 1924);

Cleaver, *One Man's Job* (London: Collins, 1926);

Cleaver, *Rugger! The Greatest Game* (London: Christophers, 1927);

Cleaver, *The Greyminster Mystery* (London: Collins, 1927);

Cleaver, *The Short Term at Greyminster* (London: Collins, 1928);

Cleaver, *Foxbound: A Novel* (London: Hutchinson, 1928);

Cleaver, *Captains of Greyminster* (London: Collins, 1929);

Cleaver, *A House Divided* (London: Collins, 1930);

Cleaver, *The Term of Thrills* (London: Warne, 1931);

Cleaver, *The Secret Service of Greyminster* (London: Collins, 1932);

Cleaver, *The New Boy at Greyminster* (London: Collins, 1932);

Cleaver, *Captains of Duke's* (London: Warne, 1933);

Cleaver, *Buttle Butts In: A Story of Duke's* (London: Warne, 1933);

Cleaver, *The Ghost of Greyminster* (London: Collins, 1933);

Cleaver, *The Forbidden Study* (London: Collins, 1934);

Cleaver, *Boxing for Schools: How to Learn It and How to Teach It* (London: Methuen, 1934);

Cleaver, *The Phantom Pen: A Story of Duke's School* (London: Warne, 1934);

Cleaver, *They Were Not Amused* (London: Methuen, 1934);

Cleaver, *The Haunted Holiday* (London: Warne, 1934);

Cleaver, *The Happy Company* (Dublin: Mellifont Press, 1934);

Cleaver, *The Test Case* (London: Collins, 1934);

Cleaver, *Gay Charade* (London: Methuen, 1934);

Cleaver, *The Hidden Captain* (London: Warne, 1935);

Cleaver, *The Further Adventures of the Happy Company* (Dublin: Mellifont Press, 1935);

Cleaver, *The School That Couldn't Sleep* (London: Warne, 1936);

Cleaver, *Double Room* (London: Methuen, 1936);

Cleaver, *The Pilot Perfect* (London: Warne, 1937);

Cleaver, *Leave It to Craddock* (London: Warne, 1937);

Cleaver, *Sports Problems: One Hundred and Fifty Intricate Sports Questions And Authoritative Rulings* (London: Warne, 1937);

Cleaver, *The Blaze at Baron's Royal* (London: Warne, 1938);

Cleaver, *The Forgotten Term* (London: Warne, 1939);

Cleaver, *The Knight of the Knuckles* (London: Warne, 1940);

Cleaver, *Dawnay Leaves School* (London: Warne, 1947);

Cleaver, *The Deputy Detective* (London: Bruce Publishing, 1947);

Cleaver, *St. Benedict's Goes Back* (London: Warne, 1948);

Cleaver, *Dead Man's Tale: A Detective Story* (London: Warne, 1949);

Cleaver, *No Rest for Rusty* (London: Warne, 1949);

Cleaver, *Lawson for Lord's* (London: Warne, 1950);

Cleaver, *Lucky Break* (London: Warne, 1950);

Cleaver, *Captain of Two Schools* (London: Warne, 1950);

Cleaver, *Sporting Rhapsody* (London: Hutchinson, 1951);

Cleaver, *Danger at the Ringside* (London: Hutchinson, 1952);

Cleaver, *Dusty Ribbon* (London: Warne, 1952);

Cleaver, *The Vengeance of Jeremy* (London: Warne, 1953);

Cleaver, *Nizefela Makes a Name* (London: Museum Press, 1955);

Cleaver, *They've Won Their Spurs* (London: R. Hale, 1956);

Cleaver, *A History of Rowing* (London: H. Jenkins, 1959);

Cleaver, *Their Greatest Ride* (London: R. Hale, 1959);

Cleaver, *Before I Forget* (London: R. Hale, 1961);

Gunby Hadath, *The Feats of Foozle,* illustrated by W. F. Thomas and T. M. R. Whitwell (London: A. & C. Black, 1913);

Hadath, *Paying the Price: A Public School Story* (London: Partridge, 1913);

Hadath, *Schoolboy Grit: A Public School Story,* illustrated by Arthur Twiddle (London: Nisbet, 1913);

Hadath, *The Last of His Line: A Public School Story* (London: Partridge, 1914);

Hadath, *The Outlaws of St. Martyn's; or, The School on the Downs* (London: Partridge, 1915);

Hadath, *Sheepy Wilson: A Public School Story* (London: Nisbet, 1915);

Hadath, *Fall In!: A Public School Story* (London: Partridge, 1916);

Hadath, *Never Say Die!: A Public School Story* (London: Partridge, 1916);

Hadath, *Won By a Try* (London: Cassell, 1922);

Hadath, *The New House at Oldborough* (London: Hodder & Stoughton, 1923);

Hadath, *According to Brown Minor* (London: Hodder & Stoughton, 1924);

Hadath, *Against the Clock: A Public School Story* (London: Hodder & Stoughton, 1924);

Hadath, *His Highness: A Public School Story* (London: Nelson, 1924);

Hadath, *Pulling His Weight: A Public School Story* (London: Hodder & Stoughton, 1924);

Hadath, *Sparrow in Search of Expulsion* (London: Hodder & Stoughton, 1924);

Hadath, *The Fattest Head in the Fifth* (London: Hodder & Stoughton, 1925);

Hadath, *Go-Bang Garry: A Public School Story* (London: Hodder & Stoughton, 1926);

Hadath, *The Secret of the Code* (London: Hodder & Stoughton, 1926);

Hadath, *Carey of Cobhouse* (London: Humphrey Milford, 1928);

Hadath, *The Lost Legion* (London: Hodder & Stoughton, 1928);

Hadath, *Wonder Island* (London: Cassell, 1928);

Hadath, *Young Hendry* (London: Hodder & Stoughton, 1929);

Hadath, *Sparrow Gets Going* (London: Hodder & Stoughton, 1929);

Hadath, *The New School at Shropp* (London: Oxford University Press, 1930);

Hadath, *St. Palfry's Cross: A Story of Adventure in the Alps* (London: Cassell, 1930);

Hadath, *Brent of Gatehouse: A Public School Story* (London: Oxford University Press, 1931);

Hadath, *The Mystery Cross,* illustrated by Margaret Freeman (New York: Stokes, 1931);

Hadath, *The Big Five!: A Public School Story* (London: Oxford University Press, 1932);

Hadath, *The Mystery of the Seventh Sword* (London: Cassell, 1932);

Hadath, *Mystery at Black Pearl Island,* illustrated by George H. Mabie (New York: Stokes, 1933);

Hadath, *The Mystery at Ridings: A Public School Story* (London: Oxford University Press, 1933);

Hadath, *Twenty Good Ships: A Tale* (London: Cassell, 1933);

Hadath, *Revolt at Fallas: A Public School Story,* illustrated by Reginald Mills (London: Oxford University Press, 1934);

Hadath, *Grim Work at Bodlands: A Public School Story,* illustrated by Mills (London: Oxford University Press, 1935);

Hadath, *The Hand and the Glove: A Public School Story* (London: Newnes, 1935);

Hadath, *Mystery at Three Chimneys,* illustrated by Charles E. Pont (New York: Stokes, 1935); republished as *The Mystery of the Three Chimneys* (London: Nelson, 1936);

Hadath, *Sparrow in Search of Fame* (London: Hutchinson, 1935);

Hadath, *Happy-Go-Lucky: A Public School Story* (London: Collins, 1935);

Hadath, *The House That Disappeared* (London: Newnes, 1936);

Hadath, *Living Up to It: A Public School Story* (London: Collins, 1938);

Hadath, *Major and Minor: A Public School Story* (London: Oxford University Press, 1938);

Hadath, *From Pillar to Post* (London: Collins, 1940);

Hadath, *Blue Berets* (London: Lutterworth, 1941);

Hadath, *Grim and Gay: The Story of a School Which Stayed Put* (London: Lutterworth, 1942);

Hadath, *The Swinger: A Story of School Life in Wartime* (London: Faber & Faber, 1942);

Hadath, *Fight It Out* (London: Lutterworth, 1943);

Hadath, *All Clear!: A Public School Story* (London: Oxford University Press, 1944);

Hadath, *The Bridgehead* (London: Oxford University Press, 1945);

Hadath, *What's in a Name?* (London: Lutterworth, 1945);

Hadath, *The March of Time: A Story of School Life in Wartime* (London: Faber & Faber, 1946);

Men of the Maquis (London: Lutterworth, 1947);

The Fifth Feversham (London: Lutterworth, 1948);

Fortune Lane (London: Faber & Faber, 1948);

The Atom, illustrated by Norman Howard (London: Oxford University Press, 1949);

The Shepherd's Guide, illustrated by John Drever (London: Temple, 1949);

No Robbery (London: Lutterworth, 1950);

Playing the Game (London: Latimer House, 1950);

Honours Easy, illustrated by Drake Brookshaw (London: Nelson, 1953);

Elsie J. Oxenham, *Goblin Island,* illustrated by T. Heath Robinson (London: Collins, 1907);

Oxenham, *A Princess in Tatters* (London: Collins, 1908);

Oxenham, *The Conquest of Christina,* illustrated by G. B. Foyster (London: Collins, 1909);

Oxenham, *The Girl Who Wouldn't Make Friends* (London: Nelson, 1909);

Oxenham, *Mistress Nanciebel,* illustrated by James Durden (London: Hodder & Stoughton, 1909);

Oxenham, *A Holiday Queen,* illustrated by E. J. Overnell (London: Collins, 1910);

Oxenham, *Rosaly's New School,* illustrated by Overnell (Edinburgh: Chambers, 1913);

Oxenham, *The Girls of the Hamlet Club* (London: Collins, 1914);

Oxenham, *Schoolgirls and Scouts,* illustrated by A. A. Dixon (London: Collins, 1914);

Oxenham, *At School with the Roundheads,* illustrated by H. C. Earnshaw (Edinburgh: Chambers, 1915);

Oxenham, *Finding Her Family* (London: S. P. C. K., 1915);

Oxenham, *The Tuck-Shop Girl* (Edinburgh: Chambers, 1916);

Oxenham, *A School Camp Fire* (Edinburgh: Chambers, 1917);

Oxenham, *The School of Ups and Downs,* illustrated by Earnshaw (Edinburgh: Chambers, 1918);

Oxenham, *Expelled from School,* illustrated by Victor Prout (London: Collins, 1919);

Oxenham, *The Abbey Girls,* illustrated by Dixon (London: Collins, 1920);

Oxenham, *A Go-Ahead Schoolgirl,* illustrated by Earnshaw (Edinburgh: Chambers, 1920);

Oxenham, *The School Torment,* illustrated by Earnshaw (Edinburgh: Chambers, 1920);

Oxenham, *The Twins of Castle Charming* (London: Swarthmore Press, 1920);

Oxenham, *The Girls of the Abbey School,* illustrated by Elsie Wood (London: Collins, 1921);

Oxenham, *The Two Form-Captains,* illustrated by Tarrant (Edinburgh: Chambers, 1921);

Oxenham, *The Abbey Girls Go Back to School,* illustrated by Wood (London: Collins, 1922);

Oxenham, *The Captain of the Fifth,* illustrated by Tarrant (Edinburgh: Chambers, 1922);

Oxenham, *Patience Joan, Outsider* (London: Cassell, 1922);

Oxenham, *The Junior Captain* (Edinburgh: Chambers, 1923);

Oxenham, *The New Abbey Girls,* illustrated by Wood (London: Collins, 1923);

Oxenham, *The Abbey Girls Again* (London: Collins, 1924);

Oxenham, *The Girls of Gwynfa* (London & New York: Warne, 1924);

Oxenham, *The School Without a Name,* illustrated by Brisley (Edinburgh: Chambers, 1924);

Oxenham, *"Tickles"; or, the School That Was Different* (London: Partridge, 1924);

Oxenham, *The Testing of the Torment,* illustrated by Hickling (London: Cassell, 1925);

Oxenham, *Ven at Gregory's,* illustrated by Brisley (Edinburgh: Chambers, 1925);

Oxenham, *The Abbey Girls in Town,* illustrated by Rosa Petherick (London: Collins, 1926);

Oxenham, *The Camp Fire Torment,* illustrated by Nina Browne (Edinburgh: Chambers, 1926);

Oxenham, *Queen of the Abbey Girls,* illustrated by E. J. Kealey (London: Collins, 1926);

Oxenham, *The Troubles of Tazy,* illustrated by Tarrant (Edinburgh: Chambers, 1926);

Oxenham, *Jen of the Abbey School,* illustrated by F. Meyerheim (London: Collins, 1927);

Oxenham, *Patience and Her Problems,* illustrated by Molly Benatar (Edinburgh: Chambers, 1927);

Oxenham, *Peggy Makes Good!,* illustrated by H. L. Bacon (London: Partridge, 1927);

Oxenham, *The Abbey Girls Win Through* (London: Collins, 1928);

Oxenham, *The Abbey School* (London: Collins, 1928);

Oxenham, *The Crisis in Camp Keema,* illustrated by Tarrant (Edinburgh: Chambers, 1928);

Oxenham, *Deb at School,* illustrated by Brisley (Edinburgh: Chambers, 1929);

Oxenham, *The Girls of Rocklands School* (London: Collins, 1929);

Oxenham, *The Abbey Girls at Home* (London: Collins, 1929);

Oxenham, *The Abbey Girls Play Up* (London: Collins, 1930);

Oxenham, *Dorothy's Dilemma,* illustrated by Brisley (Edinburgh: Chambers, 1930);

Oxenham, *The Second Term at Rocklands* (London: Collins, 1930);

Oxenham, *The Abbey Girls on Trial* (London: Collins, 1931);

Oxenham, *Deb of Sea House,* illustrated by Brisley (Edinburgh: Chambers, 1931);

Oxenham, *The Third Term at Rocklands* (London: Collins, 1931);

Oxenham, *Biddy's Secret* (Edinburgh: Chambers, 1932);

Oxenham, *The Camp Mystery* (London: Collins, 1932);

Oxenham, *The Girls of Squirrel House* (London: Collins, 1932);

Oxenham, *The Reformation of Jinty* (Edinburgh: Chambers, 1933);

Oxenham, *Rosamund's Victory* (London: Harrap, 1933);

Oxenham, *The Call of the Abbey School* (London: Collins, 1934);

Oxenham, *Jinty's Patrol* (London: Newnes, 1934);

Oxenham, *Maidlin to the Rescue,* illustrated by R. Cloke (Edinburgh: Chambers, 1934);

Oxenham, *Joy's New Adventure* (Edinburgh: Chambers, 1935);

Oxenham, *Peggy and the Brotherhood* (London: Religious Tract Society, 1936);

Oxenham, *Rosamund's Tuck Shop* (London: Religious Tract Society, 1937);

Oxenham, *Sylvia of Sarn* (London & New York: Warne, 1937);

Oxenham, *Damaris at Dorothy's* (London: Sheldon Press, 1937);

Oxenham, *Maidlin Bears the Torch* (London: Religious Tract Society, 1937);

Oxenham, *Schooldays at the Abbey* (London: Collins, 1938);

Oxenham, *Rosamund's Castle* (London: Religious Tract Society, 1938);

Oxenham, *Secrets of the Abbey,* illustrated by Heade (London: Collins, 1939);

Oxenham, *Stowaways in the Abbey* (London: Collins, 1940);

Oxenham, *Damaris Dances* (London: Oxford University Press, 1940);

Oxenham, *Patch and a Pawn* (London & New York: Warne, 1940);

Oxenham, *Adventure for Two,* illustrated by Horder (London: Oxford University Press, 1941);

Oxenham, *Jandy Mac Comes Back* (London: Collins, 1941);

Oxenham, *Pernel Wins,* illustrated by Horder (London: Muller, 1942);

Oxenham, *Maid of the Abbey,* illustrated by Heade (London: Collins, 1943);

Oxenham, *Elsa Puts Things Right,* illustrated by Horder (London: Muller, 1944);

Oxenham, *Two Joans at the Abbey,* illustrated by Horder (London: Collins, 1945);

Oxenham, *Daring Doranne* (London: Muller, 1945);

Oxenham, *An Abbey Champion,* illustrated by Horder (London: Muller, 1946);

Oxenham, *Robins in the Abbey* (London: Collins, 1947);

Oxenham, *The Secrets of Vairy,* illustrated by Horder (London: Muller, 1947);

Oxenham, *Margery Meets the Roses* (London: Lutterworth, 1947);

Oxenham, *A Fiddler for the Abbey,* illustrated by Horder (London: Muller, 1948);

Oxenham, *Guardians of the Abbey,* illustrated by Horder (London: Muller, 1950);

Oxenham, *Schoolgirl Jen at the Abbey* (London: Collins, 1950);

Oxenham, *Selma at the Abbey* (London: Collins, 1952);

Oxenham, *Rachel in the Abbey,* illustrated by M. D. Neilson (London: Muller, 1952);

Oxenham, *A Dancer from the Abbey* (London: Collins, 1953);

Oxenham, *The Song of the Abbey* (London: Collins, 1954);

Oxenham, *The Girls at Wood End* (London: Blackie, 1957);

Oxenham, *Tomboys at the Abbey* (London: Collins, 1957);

Oxenham, *Two Queens at the Abbey* (London: Collins, 1959);

Oxenham, *Strangers at the Abbey* (London: Collins, 1963);

A. Stephen Tring, *The Old Gang,* illustrated by John Camp (London: Oxford University Press, 1947);

Tring, *The Cave By the Sea,* illustrated by T. R. Freeman (London: Oxford University Press, 1950);

Tring, *Barry's Exciting Year,* illustrated by C. Hough (London: Oxford University Press, 1951);

Tring, *Barry Gets His Wish,* illustrated by Hough (London: Oxford University Press, 1952);

Tring, *Young Master Carver: A Boy in the Reign of Edward III,* illustrated by Alan Jessett (London: Phoenix House, 1952);

Tring, *Penny Penitent,* illustrated by Freeman (London: Oxford University Press, 1953);

Tring, *Penny Dreadful,* illustrated by Freeman (London: Oxford University Press, 1953);

Tring, *Penny Triumphant,* illustrated by Freeman (London: Oxford University Press, 1953);

Tring, *Barry's Great Day,* illustrated by Hough (London: Oxford University Press, 1954);

Tring, *The Kite Man* (London: Blackwell, 1955);

Tring, *Penny Puzzled,* illustrated by Freeman (London: Oxford University Press, 1956);

Tring, *Frankie and the Green Umbrella,* illustrated by Richard Kennedy (London: Hamish Hamilton, 1957);

Tring, *Penny in Italy,* illustrated by Freeman (London: Oxford University Press, 1957);

Tring, *Pictures for Sale,* illustrated by Christopher Brookes (London: Hamish Hamilton, 1958);

Tring, *Peter's Busy Day,* illustrated by Raymond Briggs (London: Hamish Hamilton, 1959);

Tring, *Penny and the Pageant,* illustrated by Kathleen Gell (London: Oxford University Press, 1959);

Tring, *Ted's Lucky Ball,* illustrations by J. Russell (London: Hamish Hamilton, 1961);

Tring, *Penny Says Goodbye,* illustrated by Gell (London: Oxford University Press, 1961);

Tring, *The Man With the Sack,* illustrated by Peter Booth (London: Hamish Hamilton, 1963);

Tring, *Chad,* illustrated by Joseph Acheson (London: Hamish Hamilton, 1966).

School stories are generally believed to have begun with the publication of Thomas Hughes's *Tom Brown's Schooldays* (1857). Indeed, the genre flourished between this date and the middle of the twentieth century. After World War II, however, the carefree lifestyle represented in these books changed, and the genre dissipated.

While boys and a few girls were sent away to schools in the beginning of the nineteenth century, in the latter part of the nineteenth century boys were sent to school in large numbers; in the beginning of the twentieth century girls were sent to school in large numbers. Britain was one of the leading countries in the world; the industrial revolution was booming, and the middle class began sending their sons, and later, their daughters, away to schools to learn how to become proper gentlemen and ladies. When World War II demolished Britain's economy, the empire broke up and the class consciousness that had pervaded the boarding school system was no longer viewed favorably.

For many individuals the concept of sending one's own children or of being sent to a large boarding school far from one's home and family at a young age seems unnatural or even bizarre, but Victorians and Edwardians did not think this way. To be sent away to school was accepted as normal. Children of rich families went to boarding schools, and less-wealthy families sent their children to school in an attempt to make an important social statement in a world dominated by a social hierarchy. The more prestigious the school, the better it looked on one's social résumé. Schools were viewed as places to make important social connections, not just as places to learn math or Latin. Each school had its own reputation and emphasized different criteria, and choosing a school was something parents did carefully. Fees could differ greatly from school to school, but families would often opt to pay for a school with high fees in the belief that they were doing their best for their children.

Young children often went to a local day school until they were either young teens or pre-teens. If there was a suitable local high school available, children could attend there, but if none was available, it was customary to send the children to boarding schools. There were boarding schools for children as young as seven or eight, but it was common to wait until a child was ten or twelve before sending him or her away – still a young age for a child to be separated from his or her family.

In most school stories the children love the school once they settle in, even if they have been reluctant to go in the beginning. It becomes the one constant that dominates their lives, and their family's importance consequently fades into the background. In *Jill's Jolliest School* (1937) by Angela Brazil, she explains that "If girls liked to talk about their homes they could do so, but nobody showed any particular curiosity about them, school topics being of vastly more interest and importance."

School stories tend to concentrate on the teenagers in the fourth, fifth, and sixth forms, particularly the fourth. Students in the younger forms were of little importance in the school hierarchy, while sixth-form students usually provided the prefects or monitors. Therefore they were too responsible to engage in the necessary mischief required of the middles by most school-story authors.

School stories are a product of their time. Early school stories reek of Victorian attitudes and ideals and often focus on morals, good character, and relationships between individuals. Religion often plays a large part in these early school stories. Over time, however, school stories increasingly began to strive for cheap thrills and excitements. Events like near-drownings, kidnappings, lost treasures, fires, secret passageways, and elaborate pranks became commonplace. Boys' school stories in particular began to capitalize on thrills and excitement, and Gillian Avery suggests in her book *Childhood's Pattern* that since it was deemed an accomplishment to get boys to read at all, dramatic adventure stories were used to entice them to read. By the time the genre declined after World War II, school stories were becoming simple, formulaic adventure stories in a school setting peopled with stock characters. War and adventure stories dominated the period of World War I, and the mystery story began to appear in large numbers in the 1920s. Boys found these more entertaining genres than the comparatively tamer school stories, and the popularity of boys' school stories began to wane. War, adventure, and mystery stories also appeared for girls, but without damaging the popularity of girls' school stories. Girls seemed to have a greater capacity for enjoying a variety of genres.

If one examines some critical works on nineteenth-century school stories, it would seem that only boys went to school and the only significant school stories are boys' school stories. Girls did not attend boarding schools in the numbers that boys did, but to ignore them is inexcusable. The education of girls was under revision, while the pattern of boys' education was more established. Girls did not really start attending boarding schools in any numbers until after 1880, and that is when girls' school stories began appearing. By the beginning of the twentieth century girls were being sent away to schools by the dozens, and this resulted in a huge wave of girls' school stories being written in the first half of the twentieth century. On a simple level, then, the nineteenth-century school story is the boys' school story and the twentieth-century school story is the girls' school story, but there are plenty of exceptions to these loose rules. Although most early school stories were written by men for boys, girls certainly read them as well.

Tom Brown's Schooldays is devoted to the cult of sports, and whether this was established before the publication of this book or whether it became established following its publication is an ongoing debate. Either way, this book places little emphasis on scholarly events or achievements, and much time is taken up with games and matches. This is a pattern repeated throughout the history of the traditional school story – particularly the boys' school stories but also girls' stories of the twentieth century, especially those of Angela Brazil.

Two different styles of school story were explored in the two earliest examples of the genre: Hughes' *Tom Brown's Schooldays* and Frederick William Farrar's *Eric; or, Little By Little* (1858). The mood and theme laid down by Hughes, however, came to dominate the genre, and these were further entrenched in Talbot Baines Reed's *The Fifth Form at St. Dominic's* (1881), which also became one of the early classics of the genre. Most later boys' school stories show the influences of Hughes and Reed. The ideal schoolboy was to be a manly boy: he was to follow a rigid code of honor that included not snitching on other boys, never backing down from a fight, and never giving in to his feelings or emotions. The ideal boy was brave, tough, and full of pluck.

This ideal is the one presented in *Tom Brown's Schooldays. Eric* presented a much different picture of school life and was a well-read school story for the first few years after its publication, but it soon faded in popularity and importance. *Eric* is a much more emotional boy than Tom Brown and often gives way to his feelings. Morals and a sense of self are much more important in *Eric* than in the happier and more boisterous *Tom Brown's Schooldays*. The musings and morals of *Eric* soon lost place to the more interesting and exciting romps found in the school stories of later authors, and *Eric* has long passed from living literature to literary history.

The first serious writer of girls' school stories was L. T. Meade (1854–1914). Meade's *A World of Girls* (1886) was a great success, and she continued to write many more girls' school stories, but Meade was a prolific writer who wrote children's stories in several other genres as well. Her early books tend to be almost evangelical stories using the street-Arab motif, and she also wrote many adventure and romance stories. Her school stories, however, brought Meade her fame, stories filled with some adventure and excitement as well as intense schoolgirl passions and friendships. Girls who were still confined to their homes longed for the comparative freedom of a school and eagerly latched onto this new genre. Meade's school stories really set the pattern for girls' school stories in general – a pattern that Angela Brazil would later establish and dominate. Brazil's characters experience passionate friendships, but school activities dominate her pages. In some of Meade's stories, such as *The Hill-Top Girl* (1896), being sent to school was viewed as a punishment, not a pleasure, but this attitude soon vanished from the genre after Brazil established the jolliness of schools.

Meade's schoolgirls do not take up the cult of sports but are more interested in cultivating manners and social graces. Sports did not become important until the works of Angela Brazil. By then, in subscribing to this mania for athletics, schoolgirls also endorse the cult of manliness that accompanies it. They also have codes of honor that include not snitching, being brave about injuries, and taking punishments with equanimity. They call each other good "fellows" and look down on tears and emotional outbursts as a feminine weakness. In some stories a type of fagging is even carried out, in which a younger girl is attached to an older girl to fetch and carry and do errands for her.

Angela Brazil (1869–1947), perhaps the most famous author of girls' school stories, was born in Preston, Lancashire. She attended Manchester High School, Ellerslie College, Manchester and Heatherley Studio, London. Her autobiography, *My Own Schooldays* (1925), is usually dismissed as a somewhat fanciful version of her early days, more of what she would have liked her life to have been rather than what it really was. She is also the subject of a biography by Gillian Freeman, *The Schoolgirl Ethic: The Life and Work of Angela Brazil* (1976). Brazil is credited with establishing that fixture of girls' school stories, the jolly schoolgirl who lived a privileged life full of hockey, dramatics, and special societies. Brazil even used the word *jolly* in several of her titles – *The Jolliest Term on Record* (1915), *Jill's Jolliest School,* and *Five Jolly Schoolgirls* (1941).

Brazil's first school story, *The Fortunes of Philippa* (1906), is about an English girl who is raised in South America and sent to England for her education, and about the friendship she makes with Cathy Winstanley and the jolly Winstanley family. At school Philippa actually suffers a nervous breakdown because of pressure put on her by a harsh schoolmistress. It is a more serious work than Brazil's later school stories, which become quite formulaic. *The Fortunes of Philippa,* Brazil's only story written in the first person, is often quite contemplative, but also contains such a stock figure as the unfriendly rival who resents the new girl and tries to make trouble for her, this rival rejoicing in the name Ernestine Salt.

A more typical story is *The Luckiest Girl in the School* (1916), the story of Winona, who mistakenly receives a prestigious scholarship at Seaton High School, which she reluctantly attends. When her grades fail to meet the expected standard, Winona is then offered a second chance to prove herself, and she of course makes good – brings her grades up to standard through hard work, makes many friends, and becomes the school games captain, as Brazil provides many sporting details throughout.

Brazil's earliest school stories are her best, with the more interesting characters and relationships; her later stories are her most formulaic, such as *Jill's Jolliest School.* Jill is reluctant to attend Linwood Grange and has great trouble fitting in at first. After being erroneously accused of being a thief, she manages to run away through a long-hidden secret passage. But she is given another chance to prove herself, and she does. She becomes popular and responsible and grows to love Linwood Grange. She also becomes a heroine at the end by saving Linwood Grange's playing field from a developer by finding the clue to an old deed.

Many of Brazil's books written during the war have interesting wartime details, and in some cases the war formed the basis of important subplots, particularly those of *A Patriotic Schoolgirl* (1918). Brazil became notorious for the use of schoolgirl slang in her books, and this prompted some headmistresses to speak out against her works; the slang adds much color and humor, though perhaps not intentionally. Her books still provide entertaining, pleasant reading, but the outdated slang and the many war and other period details certainly make them dated.

Three other writers of girls' school stories, although they are not as influential as Angela Brazil, are still well known as authors of popular school-story series: Elinor Brent-Dyer, Dorita Bruce Fairlie and Elsie J. Oxenham.

Elinor M. Brent-Dyer was the professional name used by Gladys Eleanor May Dyer. She was born in South Shields, Durham, and attended St. Nicholas's School in South Shields, the City of Leeds Training College, and the Newcastle Conservatoire of Music. Brent-Dyer worked as a teacher at Baring Street and other schools (1912–1915), taught at Western House School (1922–1923), worked as a governess (1933–1938), and was founding headmistress of the Margaret Roper School, Hereford (1938–1948). She also wrote almost one hundred books for girls, most of them school stories. Brent-Dyer was the focus of a book by Helen McClelland, *Behind the Chalet School* (1981).

Brent-Dyer is the author of the Chalet School series, which is still in print. Between the first Chalet School book, *The School at the Chalet* (1925), and the last, *Prefects at the Chalet School* (1970), almost sixty titles appeared in the series. This school is founded by a young Englishwoman, Madge Bettany, who is responsible for looking after a delicate younger sister, Joey. Madge locates her school in the Austrian mountains, which she believes will be a healthy environment. From a few English pupils and a few local European ones, the school soon grows to become an established institution with an international reputation. The presence of many foreign students adds glamour and spice to the series, and the colorful setting in the mountains lends itself easily to such natural events as storms, avalanches, near-drownings, and lost, stranded schoolgirls – situations that occur on a regular basis. Slang is limited in this series, since the Chalet Girls must pay a fine for using slang, but the foreign words and phrases peppered throughout the book add some zip.

Although Madge soon takes a back seat in the series, many nieces and cousins and daughters maintain a thread of continuity throughout the stories. Regular characters move up through the forms and eventually graduate in these books, and this adds a pleasing sense of progression to these books. The tendency of graduated Chalet School girls to maintain their devotion to the Chalet School and to continue to hang around in the series is a bit annoying. Many of the students in the later books are the daughters of former students. In an apparent attempt to find endless youth, Joey herself has eleven children.

The stories are lively though repetitive. A typical story is *The Chalet School and the Lintons* (1934), a story of two sisters. Gillian, the elder, fits into the school well and in later books becomes a monitor and, eventually, a teacher at the Chalet School; Joyce, her rebellious younger sister who initially causes many problems at the school through such behavior as passing forbidden notes, using slang, and initiating midnight feasts, eventually reforms and becomes a proper Chalet girl. The school is forced to move because of the war and because of such problems as drains, and is relocated first in the Channel Islands, then in Wales, and then the Oberland. These relocations also provide added drama and interest. It is arguably the most successful school series ever written, especially since it is still in print. Much of the early success was because of the character of its protagonist, Joey Bettany, which is why Brent-Dyer insisted on keeping Joey around long after she graduated.

Another successful girls' school series is the Abbey Girls series by Elsie J. Oxenham. This was the professional name used by Elsie Jeanette Dunkerley, whose father, William Arthur Dunkerley, was a writer who used the name John Oxenham. She was born in Southport, Lancashire, and is the author of ninety books for girls. Not all of her books are school stories, for she wrote many stories about Girl Guiding and the Camp Fire movement, books for which she was also well known.

The Abbey Girls series, with about forty titles, is Oxenham's most significant contribution to the genre, but even many of these books are not really school stories. The best in the series are the early ones, when the main characters – Joan, Joy, Jen, and, later, Rosamund and Maidlin – are still schoolgirls. The name Abbey Girls comes from the ruined Abbey actually owned by Joan. The Abbey, and Joy and Joan's great house beside it, Abinger Hall, serve as an interesting and unusual setting. For example, in *The Girls of the Abbey School* (1921), the character Jen is introduced, the school itself is temporarily relocated to Joy and Joan's home because of an epidemic, a secret tunnel from the Hall to the Abbey is found, and a buried treasure is found in the Abbey. A subplot concerns two difficult younger children who refuse to fit in with the other students and cause mischief.

Later Abbey Girl books have little or no elements of school stories at all. For example, *Robins in the Abbey* (1947) would be better described as a love story. Most of the Abbey Girls get married, although their husbands are significant only in that they make it possible for the Abbey Girls to have children. Later books in the series seem to concentrate on the rivalry between the Abbey Girls to have the most children. Husbands come and go with few or no lines, but children pop out like rabbits. Many of the Abbey Girls start having twins, and some even have multiple sets. While Brent-Dyer's Chalet girls also have a multitude of offspring, the proliferation of children in Oxenham's Abbey Girls series becomes ridiculous.

A sense of continuity and originality is provided by the country dancing in the series. The Hamlet Club, originally a school club dedicated to country dancing, remains a focus for all of the Abbey Girls long after they finish school. Each year a queen of the Hamlet Club is chosen, and the different main characters each have turns as queen. The details about the dancing are quite entertaining, and this continued interest in the club serves to link the characters and the series together.

The frequent moralizing in the series, however, unfortunately slows the pace of the books and makes them too dated and ponderous. This moralizing can seem shockingly harsh and old-fashioned, such as in *The Abbey Girls Win Through* (1928), a volume devoted to personal crises and turmoil. For example, when Jen suddenly learns that her mother has unexpectedly died, she is understandably shocked and upset, but instead of being allowed to cry and mourn, she is instantly rebuked for her selfishness by another character and told to be "glad" that her mother and father are together again. Jen instantly agrees that she has been being selfish, and she explains that the news "knocked her silly for a moment" and thanks the other character for this comfort. The language in this series is frequently stilted and old-fashioned, but the rigid attitudes and insensitivity of the characters make them seem particularly unnatural to modern readers.

Dorita Fairlie Bruce (1885–1970) was the author of several popular smaller school series. Her best-known series is the Dimsie series, but her Nancy and Springdale series were also popular. While her plots may be similar to those of Brazil, Bruce is unlike Brazil in that Bruce wrote series books, with a heroine who gradually ages during the series. Her books concentrate on schoolgirl relationships, games, and the routine of schoolgirl life. Bruce tries to avoid excessive sentimentalism among the schoolgirls, and Dimsie and her friends actually form an Anti-Soppist League to counteract excessive "mushiness." Her books presenting her heroines as young schoolgirls are more successful than the later volumes portraying them as adults.

Bruce herself was Scottish and used Scotland as an effective setting in many of her books.

Many other writers of girls' school stories never achieved the renown these authors enjoyed. While others may have been successful, they did not establish a character or series with the same appeal. Ethel Talbot, Nancy Breary, Doris A. Pocock, Dorothea Moor, and Christine Chaundler are all now largely forgotten, yet they had successful careers as prolific school-story authors.

In contrast to the girls' stories, boys' school stories declined between 1914 and 1960. It is not enough, however, simply to say that it was a defective genre. Boys as a group did not then, nor do they now, read as much fiction as girls. Books in this genre had become predictable and cliché-ridden, and no new, exciting author of boy's school stories had come along to rejuvenate the genre. Boys' school stories were still being written, bought, and read – not in the numbers they had been – but their novelty had worn off, and the focus had changed from exploring relationships to presenting after-hours hijinks and thrills. Four twentieth-century authors who valiantly attempted to keep the boys'-school story a viable genre are Harold Avery, Gunby Hadath, Hylton Cleaver and A. Stephen Tring.

Harold Avery was born in Redditch, Worcestershire. He attended Dunheved College in Launceton, Midland Collegiate School in Birmingham, and New College in Eastbourne and served in World War I. Avery began publishing boys' school stories before World War I, when the market for these stories was still at its peak. After the war, when demand severely declined, he continued producing them. His stories are extremely pro-British, and his schoolboys are training to become honorable, brave British men. His characters are stereotypical, his plots derivative, and his morals simplistic. Yet his writing style was fairly energetic, and he enjoyed popularity in his own time. Now his books appear to be obsolete representations of the British past – when the future was bright, the sun never set on the British Empire, and to be a British schoolboy full of pluck and potential was the ideal state.

Hylton Cleaver (1891–1961) was born and died in London and educated at St. Paul's. In addition to his many school stories for boys, he wrote many sports books and had a career as a journalist. At school Cleaver was particularly unathletic and suffered from asthma and a very severe stammer. This made social success at school difficult for him, and his school stories, focusing on school matches and games, are perhaps an attempt to relive that time in his life. By joining the army and getting involved in athletics and the outdoors, however, Cleaver did succeed in becoming more athletic, and he became involved in sports and writing about sports for the rest of his life. None of his school stories are particularly remarkable, but he was a thriving writer in his own time.

Gunby Hadath (1880–1954) was the opposite of Hylton Cleaver in that he was a tremendous success at school, where he was a school captain and excelled in rugby, soccer, and cricket. He attended St. Edmund's School in Canterbury and Peterhouse College, Cambridge. He served in World War I and was a schoolmaster himself. In addition to his many schoolboy stories, he also wrote many songs and contributed to boys' magazines. He created a popular series of books about an ingenious schoolboy named Sparrow who inevitably came out on top against great odds. Hadath's books were fast-paced and often humorous. In addition to his own name, Hadath wrote under such pseudonyms as John Mowbray, Felix O'Grady, and James Duncan.

A. Stephen Tring (1889–1980) is the pseudonym used by Laurence Meynell for his boys' school stories. Meynell was a prolific writer of mysteries under his own name and also used the names Valerie Baxter, Robert Eton, and Geoffrey Ludlow. He was born in Wolverhampton, the son of Herbert and Agnes Meynell, and his first wife, Shirley Darbyshire, was also a novelist. He attended private schools in Britain, served in both world wars, and maintained careers also as a schoolmaster and estate agent.

As A. Stephen Tring, Meynell wrote his many boys' school stories. His post–World War II stories give a new vitality to a tired genre: their sense of realism and intelligence restored what had disappeared from the genre and had been replaced with stereotypes and formulas. Tring's books are fast-paced and full of action, humor, and lively dialogue. His trilogy about schoolboy Barry Briggs also has mystery to it, and it has unusually well-rounded characters for a school story. His Penny series for girls is not quite as convincing as the boys' series. Tring's books do show, however, that as late as the 1950s the school story was still a viable genre that could present a realistic and entertaining story while using traditional settings and devices.

Many magazines that featured school stories remained popular well into the twentieth century. While the preference for boys' school story novels waned, the popularity of school stories in boys' magazines such as the *Magnet* and *Gem* remained constant. Billy Bunter remained popular from his creation in 1908 until the 1960s, and he was so popular that a cousin named Bessie Bunter was created to entertain girls. Bessie was a lot like Billy in that she was overweight and unattractive and was used as the butt of jokes. Bessie appeared in the *School Friend*, a magazine for girls featuring an ongoing school-story series. Other popular girls magazines included *Schoolgirls' Own* and *Schoolgirls' Weekly*. A novel about Bessie titled *Bessie Bunter of Cliff House School* appeared as late as 1949. The school stories featured in magazines were perhaps the most formulaic of them all, peopled with stock characters and endless unlikely adventures. Novelist, essayist, and social critic George Orwell expressed surprise in 1940 that this type of publication still existed. The paper restrictions caused by World War II marked the end of many of these publications.

Although school stories as a large, viable genre did die off after World War II, it was not because it was an inferior or mediocre genre, but because the way of life intertwined with the genre ended. Britain has changed drastically since World War II. During a time when Britain has experienced a poor economy and high unemployment with no change in sight, many British children have grown up discouraged, troubled, and pessimistic about what the future holds for them. Consequently, novels about privileged children who have seemingly auspicious futures and enjoy great fun and games at safe, private schools just no longer have the same appeal.

School stories, however, still exist in many forms. School, after all, is an enormously important and influential place for a child, and books are still published with schools as significant settings. But they are more likely to be modern schools, not old-fashioned, exclusive boarding schools — although new stories set in boarding schools still do appear. And some of the older school stories are still in print, such as Elinor Brent-Dyer's Chalet School books and Enid Blyton's Malory Towers and St. Clare's stories. Modern school stories still feature intense friendships, near-drownings, and buried treasure, but often include issues like divorce, the environment, and abuse.

As long as children are attending schools, there will be school stories, but the schools featured will never again be the safe, controlled settings of the past. Many of the schools in the traditional school stories had walls around the school boundaries, and the students were prohibited from crossing the line. Reality seldom crossed the line inside these fictitious schools. Now, with the proliferation of information children are exposed to through television and other media, it is almost impossible to contain children in a safe, insulated world for long. Modern school stories reflect this new reality. The old school stories have now become quaint collectibles, but children of the past had needed this type of story, and the many writers who provided these stories had the satisfaction of giving hours of pleasure to thousands of these children.

References:

Mary Cadogan and Patricia Craig, *You're a Brick, Angela!: A New Look at Girls' Fiction from 1939 to 1975* (London: Gollancz, 1976);

Gillian Freeman, *The Schoolgirl Ethic: The Life and Work of Angela Brazil* (London: Allen Lane, 1976);

W. O. G. Lofts and D. J. Adley, *The Men Behind Boys' Fiction* (London: Baker, 1970);

P. W. Musgrave, *From Brown to Bunter: The Life and Death of the School Story* (London: Routledge, 1985);

Isabel Quigly, *The Heirs of Tom Brown: The English School Story* (London: Oxford University Press, 1984).

Checklist for Further Readings

Avery, Gillian. *Childhood's Pattern: A Study of the Heroes and Heroines of Children's Fiction, 1770–1950.* London: Hodder & Stoughton, 1975.

Cadogan, Mary, and Patricia Craig. *You're a Brick, Angela! A New Look at Girls' Fiction from 1839–1975.* London: Gollancz, 1976.

Carpenter, Humphrey. *Secret Gardens: The Golden Age of Children's Literature.* Boston: Houghton Mifflin, 1985.

Cott, Jonathan. *Pipers at the Gates of Dawn.* New York: Random House, 1983.

Crouch, Marcus. *The Nesbit Tradition: The Children's Novel, 1945–1970.* Totowa, N.J.: Rowman & Littlefield, 1972.

Crouch. *Treasure Seekers and Borrowers: Children's Books in Britain, 1900–1960.* London: Library Association, 1962.

Darton, F. J. Harvey. *Children's Books in England: Five Centuries of Social Life,* second edition. Cambridge: Cambridge University Press, 1958.

Eyre, Frank. *British Children's Books in the Twentieth Century,* revised edition. London: Longman, 1971.

Fisher, Margery. *Intent Upon Reading: A Critical Appraisal of Modern Fiction for Children.* New York: Watts, 1961.

Green, Roger Lancelyn. *Tellers of Tales.* London: Kaye & Ward, 1947.

Hildick, Edmund Wallace. *Children and Fiction: A Critical Study in Depth of the Artistic and Psychological Factors Involved in Writing Fiction for and about Children.* London: Evans Brothers, 1970.

Hurlimann, Bettina. *Three Centuries of Children's Books in Europe.* Oxford: Oxford University Press, 1967.

Kensinger, Faye Riter. *Children of the Series and How They Grew.* Bowling Green, Ohio: Bowling Green University Popular Press, 1987.

Lochhead, Marion. *Renaissance of Wonder.* New York: Harper & Row, 1980.

Lofts, W. O. G., and D. J. Adley. *Old Boys' Books: A Complete Catalogue.* London, 1967.

Meek, Margaret, Aidan Warlow, and Griselda Barton. *The Cool Web.* New York: Atheneum, 1978.

Muir, Percival Horace. *English Children's Books, 1600–1900.* London: Batsford, 1954.

Townsend, John Rowe. *Written for Children.* New York: Harper, 1965.

Trease, Geoffrey. *Tales Out of School.* London: Heinemann, 1950.

Contributors

David Barratt .... *Chester College*
Margaret Stickney Bienert .... *Hamilton, Ontario, Canada*
Patricia J. Cianciolo .... *Michigan State University*
M. Margaret Dahlberg.. *University of North Dakota*
Patricia Demers... *University of Alberta*
Rosanne Donahue .... *University of Massachusetts – Boston*
Colin Duriez.. *Inter-Varsity Press*
Harry E. Eiss..*Eastern Michigan University*
Gwyneth Evans....................................*Malaspina University College, British Columbia*
Susan R. Gannon..*Pace University*
Barbara Carman Garner .... *Carleton University*
Wayne G. Hammond ....*Chapin Library, Williams College*
G. G. Harper ....*Calvin College*
Donald R. Hettinga.. *Calvin College*
Caroline C. Hunt .... *College of Charleston*
Peter Hunt .... *University of Wales*
Nancy Huse ....*Augustana College*
Judith Gero John .... *Southwest Missouri State University*
Hugh T. Keenan... *Georgia State University*
Carol Y. Long .... *University of North Dakota*
Catherine M. Lynch .... *Penn State, McKeesport Campus*
Margaret J. Masson.. *St. John's College, Durham*
Alice Mills .... *University of Ballarat*
Francis J. Molson.. *Central Michigan University*
Charlotte F. Otten..*Calvin College*
David L. Russell .... *Ferris State University*
Gary D. Schmidt..*Calvin College*
Joanne Lewis Sears... *California State University, Fullerton*
Donnalee Kathryn Smith ....*Scarborough Public Library, Ontario, Canada*
Jon C. Stott ....*University of Alberta*
Ruth Waterhouse ....*Macquarie University*
Ian Wojcik-Andrews .... *Eastern Michigan University*
Lisa A. Wroble .... *Plymouth, Michigan*

Cumulative Index

Dictionary of Literary Biography, Volumes 1-160
Dictionary of Literary Biography Yearbook, 1980-1994
Dictionary of Literary Biography Documentary Series, Volumes 1-12

Cumulative Index

DLB before number: *Dictionary of Literary Biography,* Volumes 1-160
Y before number: *Dictionary of Literary Biography Yearbook,* 1980-1994
DS before number: *Dictionary of Literary Biography Documentary Series,* Volumes 1-12

A

Abbey Press DLB-49

The Abbey Theatre and Irish Drama,
  1900-1945 ....DLB-10

Abbot, Willis J. 1863-1934 ....DLB-29

Abbott, Jacob 1803-1879 ....DLB-1

Abbott, Lee K. 1947- DLB-130

Abbott, Lyman 1835-1922 ....DLB-79

Abbott, Robert S. 1868-1940 ....DLB-29, 91

Abelard, Peter circa 1079-1142 .....DLB-115

Abelard-Schuman DLB-46

Abell, Arunah S. 1806-1888 ....DLB-43

Abercrombie, Lascelles 1881-1938 ...DLB-19

Aberdeen University Press
  Limited.....................DLB-106

Abish, Walter 1931- DLB-130

Ablesimov, Aleksandr Onisimovich
  1742-1783 ....DLB-150

Abrahams, Peter 1919- DLB-117

Abrams, M. H. 1912- DLB-67

Abrogans circa 790-800 ....DLB-148

Abse, Dannie 1923- DLB-27

Academy Chicago Publishers DLB-46

Accrocca, Elio Filippo 1923- DLB-128

Ace Books DLB-46

Achebe, Chinua 1930- DLB-117

Achtenberg, Herbert 1938- DLB-124

Ackerman, Diane 1948- DLB-120

Ackroyd, Peter 1949- DLB-155

Acorn, Milton 1923-1986 ....DLB-53

Acosta, Oscar Zeta 1935?- DLB-82

Actors Theatre of Louisville DLB-7

Adair, James 1709?-1783? DLB-30

Adam, Graeme Mercer 1839-1912 ...DLB-99

Adame, Leonard 1947- DLB-82

Adamic, Louis 1898-1951 ....DLB-9

Adams, Alice 1926- Y-86

Adams, Brooks 1848-1927 ....DLB-47

Adams, Charles Francis, Jr.
  1835-1915 ....DLB-47

Adams, Douglas 1952- Y-83

Adams, Franklin P. 1881-1960 ......DLB-29

Adams, Henry 1838-1918 ....DLB-12, 47

Adams, Herbert Baxter 1850-1901 ...DLB-47

Adams, J. S. and C.
  [publishing house] DLB-49

Adams, James Truslow 1878-1949 ...DLB-17

Adams, John 1735-1826 ....DLB-31

Adams, John Quincy 1767-1848 .....DLB-37

Adams, Léonie 1899-1988 ....DLB-48

Adams, Levi 1802-1832 ....DLB-99

Adams, Samuel 1722-1803 ......DLB-31, 43

Adams, Thomas
  1582 or 1583-1652 ....DLB-151

Adams, William Taylor 1822-1897 .. DLB-42

Adamson, Sir John 1867-1950 ......DLB-98

Adcock, Arthur St. John
  1864-1930 ....DLB-135

Adcock, Betty 1938- DLB-105

Adcock, Betty, Certain Gifts DLB-105

Adcock, Fleur 1934- DLB-40

Addison, Joseph 1672-1719 ....DLB-101

Ade, George 1866-1944 ....DLB-11, 25

Adeler, Max (see Clark, Charles Heber)

Adonias Filho 1915-1990 ....DLB-145

Advance Publishing Company DLB-49

AE 1867-1935 ....DLB-19

Ælfric circa 955-circa 1010 ....DLB-146

Aesthetic Poetry (1873), by
  Walter Pater DLB-35

After Dinner Opera Company Y-92

Afro-American Literary Critics:
  An Introduction DLB-33

Agassiz, Jean Louis Rodolphe
  1807-1873 ....DLB-1

Agee, James 1909-1955 ......DLB-2, 26, 152

The Agee Legacy: A Conference at
  the University of Tennessee
  at Knoxville.....................Y-89

Aguilera Malta, Demetrio
  1909-1981 ....DLB-145

Ai 1947- DLB-120

Aichinger, Ilse 1921- DLB-85

Aidoo, Ama Ata 1942- DLB-117

Aiken, Conrad 1889-1973 ....DLB-9, 45, 102

Aikin, Lucy 1781-1864 ....DLB-144

Ainsworth, William Harrison
  1805-1882 ....DLB-21

Aitken, George A. 1860-1917 ......DLB-149

Aitken, Robert [publishing house] ...DLB-49

Akenside, Mark 1721-1770 ....DLB-109

Akins, Zoë 1886-1958 ....DLB-26

Alabaster, William 1568-1640 ......DLB-132

Alain-Fournier 1886-1914 ....DLB-65

Alarcón, Francisco X. 1954- DLB-122

Alba, Nanina 1915-1968 ....DLB-41

Albee, Edward 1928- DLB-7

Albert the Great circa 1200-1280 ...DLB-115

Alberti, Rafael 1902- DLB-108

Alcott, Amos Bronson 1799-1888 .....DLB-1

Alcott, Louisa May
  1832-1888 ....DLB-1, 42, 79

Alcott, William Andrus 1798-1859 ....DLB-1

Alcuin circa 732-804 ....DLB-148

Alden, Henry Mills 1836-1919 ......DLB-79

Alden, Isabella 1841-1930 ....DLB-42

Alden, John B. [publishing house] DLB-49

Alden, Beardsley and Company DLB-49

Aldington, Richard
  1892-1962 ....DLB-20, 36, 100, 149

Aldis, Dorothy 1896-1966 ....DLB-22

B

G

I

J

N

O

Q

R

Documentary Series